COUNTERTRANSFERENCE

AND
RELATED SUBJECTS

COUNTERTRANSFERENCE

AND
RELATED SUBJECTS

Selected Papers

by
HAROLD F. SEARLES, M.D.

INTERNATIONAL UNIVERSITIES PRESS, INC.

New York

Library of Congress Cataloging in Publication Data

Searles, Harold F
    Countertransference and related subjects.

    Bibliography: p.
    Includes index.
    1. Countertransference (Psychology)—Addresses, essays, lectures. 2. Schizophrenia—Addresses, essays, lectures. I. Title. [DNLM: 1. Counter-transference (Psychology)—Collected works. WM62 S439c]
RC506.S4   616.8′982′06   77-92186
ISBN 0-8236-1085-3

Third Printing, 1981

Manufactured in the United States of America

To
David and Sandy
Sandra and Peter
Don and Valerie

Contents

Acknowledgments

I could not have written these papers nor seen to bringing them together in this book without the loving support, throughout, of my wife, Sylvia Manninen Searles. Martin V. Azarian, President of International Universities Press, has been gracious and helpful with this book project since its inception. Mrs. Irene Guttman, who was Editor at the time this project got under way, was unfailingly helpful and accommodating to me. Ms. Sue Heinemann, Editor (as well as Production Coordinator) at I.U.P. throughout this project since the end of its opening phase, has been remarkably helpful, tactful, and highly effective in her work with me. I have accepted readily a very high percentage of her suggestions for revision, since it has been obvious to me that these changes have made for greater clarity and brevity in the presentation of my findings. I feel deeply indebted to her, and hope to have the opportunity to work again with her in the future.

Norman A. Senior, Attorney at Law, was a model of helpfulness in the work on my end of the book contract. In retrospect, I probably could readily have dispensed with any legal counsel in my negotiations with the so-cooperative Mr. Azarian; but I must say that Mr. Senior is an attorney whom I would wish to have at my side should I ever encounter formidable difficulties in negotiating a book contract.

As regards secretarial assistance, it has been my good fortune to find a series, over the years, of exceptionally competent persons who have done much to lighten my load of work in the initial publishing of these various papers. Ms. Joan B. Cook, more than any other secretary, typed numerous ones among these papers; I am lastingly grateful to her. Ms. Nan T. Ackerman, Ms. Edyth H.

Baish, Ms. Joyce Burke, Ms. Sheila Campbell, and Ms. Norma S. Player all have done superlative jobs of typing one or more of the papers included here.

I am grateful to the following publishing houses, or journals, for their permission to include the various papers, enumerated here, which (as shown in the respective sourcenotes) they published originally: Jason Aronson, Inc. (for Chapters 14, 15, 18, 19, and 22); *Psychiatry-Journal for the Study of Interpersonal Processes* (Chapters 1 and 2); International Universities Press (Chapters 10, 17, and 20); *The Psychoanalytic Review* (Chapters 4 and 13), through the courtesy of the Editors and the Publisher, National Psychological Association for Psychoanalysis, New York, N.Y.; J. B. Lippincott Company (Chapter 5); Little, Brown and Company (Chapter 6, copyright 1968); *The International Journal of Psycho-Analysis* (Chapters 3 and 7); *Contemporary Psychoanalysis,* journal of the William Alanson White Institute and the William Alanson White Psychoanalytic Society, N.Y. (Chapters 9, 23, and 24); *Contemporary Psychology,* copyright 1970 by the American Psychological Association (Chapter 11); Holt, Rinehart & Winston (Chapter 8), also Bernard Landis and Edward S. Tauber, Editors of the volume in which this Chapter 8 appeared; *The British Journal of Medical Psychology,* by permission of Cambridge University Press, copyright 1972 (for Chapter 12); Human Sciences Press, 72 Fifth Avenue, New York (Chapter 16), copyright 1977; Grune & Stratton, Inc. (Chapter 21). For permission to reprint Chapter 10, I am indebted also to *The Annual of Psychoanalysis.*

Chapter 24 is based, in part, on a presentation at the Ninth Annual Conference of the Adelphi University Program in Psychotherapy, "The Psychoanalytic Therapy of Non-Hospitalized Schizophrenic Patients," May 24, 1973, at Adelphi University, Garden City, New York. George D. Goldman and Donald S. Milman, Editors of the prospective book comprised of the papers given at that Conference, have kindly permitted me to publish my paper earlier, and I appreciate their generosity.

The black and white reproduction of Uccello's painting, *St. George and the Dragon,* is with the kind permission of The National Gallery (London).

To a number of authors or publishers, or both, I am grateful for their permission to include, here, relatively long quotations from these authors' writings; the References contain the source information in full detail. J. B. Lippincott Company permits me to quote from "The Ego Defect in Schizophrenia," by Robert W. Gibson. The quotes from Phyllis Greenacre's article, "Certain Relationships Between Fetishism and Faulty Development of the Body Image," are with the generous permission of the author herself, as well as that of *The Psychoanalytic Study of the Child* and that of International Universities Press. International Universities Press has given me permission, also, to include the quotes from *Schizophrenia and the Need-Fear Dilemma,* by Donald L. Burnham, Arthur I. Gladstone, and Robert W. Gibson; and those from Edith Jacobson's *The Self and the Object World.* The passages from Marjorie McDonald's "Transitional Tunes and Musical Development" are quoted with the permission of the author as well as with that of *The Psychoanalytic Study of the Child* and that of International Universities Press. Marion Milner, as well as International Universities Press, have kindly permitted me to quote from her volume, *The Hands of the Living God.* The quotes from Arnold H. Modell's "The Transitional Object and the Creative Act" are with the permission of *The Psychoanalytic Quarterly.*

The quotes from the volume, *Roles and Paradigms in Psychotherapy,* edited by Marie Coleman Nelson et al., are by permission of Ms. Nelson and of Grune & Stratton. The passages from Erwin Singer's "The Patient Aids the Analyst: Some Clinical and Theoretical Considerations" are quoted with permission from Bernard Landis and Edward S. Tauber, Editors of the book in which this paper originally appeared. Permission to quote from John S. Kafka's "The Body as Transitional Object: A Psychoanalytic Study of a Self-Mutilating Patient" was kindly given by Cambridge University Press, publishers of *The British Journal of Medical Psychology.*

Introduction

My introduction to my 1965 book of collected papers was sufficiently detailed and relevant for this present book that I can be relatively brief here. The major themes which run throughout these
various papers are so clearly recurrent as not to need the kind of
summarizing I presented in that earlier introduction. Throughout
these papers, surely, is the predominant title-theme, the exploration
of the countertransference.

Near the beginning of 1964 I left the staff of Chestnut Lodge,
after nearly 15 years of "full-time" work there in psychoanalytic
therapy with chronically schizophrenic, and comparably ill, patients.
Chapter 5 details some of my experiences and emotions during my
final year there. All the papers contained in this book were written
after I left there and entered the full-time office practice of
psychoanalysis and psychotherapy.

Throughout my years at Chestnut Lodge I had conducted (as
had my colleagues there generally) a part-time psychoanalytic practice. Nonetheless, this change in my career has been a very major
one for me. I shall mention but one facet of it, by way of example.
Since 1958 I had been a Supervising and Training Analyst in the
Washington Psychoanalytic Institute, and the proportion of my
work-week devoted to this activity increased sharply with my entry
into full-time private practice. In contrast, therefore, to my having
felt relatively free to discuss with other colleagues at Chestnut
Lodge our various countertransference and technical difficulties in
working with the patients there, I have had to adapt to the fact of
my spending much of my work-week in analyzing persons about
whom one must maintain the highest degree of confidentiality—

and about whom it is essentially impossible, for reasons of this same confidentiality, to write in one's papers.

My patients collectively, during these now nearly 15 years in full-time private practice, have been an ostensibly incongruous mixture of occasional schizophrenic patients plus many candidates in the analytic institute, as well as many psychiatrists and members of allied professions who have sought analysis for personal (non-psychoanalytic-institute) reasons. There have been a fair number of patients who have not belonged to any of the foregoing three categories.

I have done a good deal of presenting of papers, and interviewing of patients in teaching situations, as an authority in psychoanalytic therapy of schizophrenic patients, despite a nagging doubt as to whether my predominant work activities during these years since the beginning of 1964 entitle me to such a role. But the teaching activity itself has been so abundant, and so clinical in nature, as to provide me, in itself, much continuing experience in that role. I have interviewed more than 1,500 patients, most of them schizophrenic, in the 20 years (1956-60 and 1962-78) I served as a Consultant in Psychiatry at the National Institute of Mental Health in Bethesda, Maryland; the seven years (1963-70) I was a Consultant in Psychotherapy at the Sheppard and Enoch Pratt Hospital in Towson, Maryland; the nine years (1964-73) I was a Lecturer in Psychiatry at the National Naval Medical Center in Bethesda; and the nine years (1964-73) I was a Lecturer in Psychiatry at the New York State Psychiatric Institute (Columbia University College of Physicians and Surgeons, New York City). Since 1964 I have been a Clinical Professor in Psychiatry at Georgetown University School of Medicine in Washington, D.C. and, until a couple of years ago, did a teaching patient-interview at each of my monthly visits there.

Nonetheless, it is inescapably true that I have been working during by far the major portion of my time, these past 15 years, with patients who have been far less ill than were those to whom most of my efforts were devoted during the preceding 15 years, at Chestnut Lodge. It has been enormously interesting to me to find that, just as the work with the more severely ill patients helps one to understand the deepest conflicts of the less ill individuals, so does the work with the less ill persons help one to understand one's far more ill, and therefore in many instances much less articulate, patients. Various of these papers attempt to highlight such cross-relevancy. Pertinent here is Harry Stack Sullivan's (1940) oft-quoted but ever-wise observation that "... we are all much more simply human than otherwise ...." One finds this confirmed, day after day, in one's work with patients who vary widely in the kinds and degrees of emotional illness from which they suffer; and one finds this confirmed, most essentially, in the exploration of the counter-transference feelings one finds within one's own self in working, throughout, with one after another of these various persons.

These papers were written without the benefit of any research grants. They were written, mostly on Sunday mornings, with such energy as I had left over from a very heavy schedule of working with patients. I hope you will like them and will find them useful to you.

1

The Schizophrenic Individual's Experience of His World

Each time I write a paper, after having collected all the separate theoretical points I want to include, all the illustrative clinical vignettes, and all the relevant items from the literature, I then become immersed for days or weeks in very considerable confusion, despair, and anxiety. When I began work on this presentation, I felt threatened with overwhelming panic at the unorganized vastness and complexity of the subject; I had not too little, but too much—far too much—clinical data, and these data seemed so entirely unorganized. I felt at a loss for any coherent, organizing principles to grasp and communicate the essence of a large number of clinical experiences which have been, to me, fascinating and, often, deeply moving. Then I realized that the anxiety, confusion, and despair which I always feel in the course of preparing a paper were in this instance specifically relevant to the topic—akin, that is, to the panic that chronically grips the schizophrenic individual who is so greatly

This paper was presented as the Tenth Annual Frieda Fromm-Reichmann Memorial Lecture, under the auspices of the Washington School of Psychiatry, at the Clinical Center, National Institutes of Health, Bethesda, Md., on November 18, 1966. It was first published in *Psychiatry*, 30:119-131 (1967).

I am indebted to Milton G. Hendlich, M.D., of Chestnut Lodge, and William E. Abramson, M.D., of the Sheppard and Enoch Pratt Hospital, for their kind permission to use two of the clinical illustrations.

at a loss for reliable organizing principles to render meaningful and manageable the chaotic perceptions which assail him. He has no reliable way of knowing whether what he is perceiving is part of an inner, fantasy world, or part of an outer, real world; whether it is something that exists in present or past or future time; whether it is alive or unalive, human or nonhuman; and so on. He can neither differentiate among essentially different kinds of psychological experience, nor integrate what are for the healthy adult essentially coherent patterns of perceptions.

The healthy parent functions as a guide and interpreter in the child's perceiving, and in the understanding of what the child perceives—leaving him increasing freedom to see, hear, feel, and interpret on his own. But in the upbringing of the to-become-schizophrenic child, all this is submerged in the parent's and child's conflicts concerning individuation. Both parent and child struggle ceaselessly to achieve individuation and to be, toward one another, whole and separate-but-related individuals; but neither is strong enough to bear the loss of the fantasied omnipotence which attends their symbiotic mode of relating to one another, and to settle for the real but clearly limited strength of a truly human individual.

The ambiguous, and unpredictably shifting, family roles make it impossible for the child to build up reliable and consistent pictures of the world around him. The emotional responses of the other family members are so enigmatic and inaccessible, or if clear-cut so extremely changeable, as to render his potentially outer reality either inscrutable or kaleidoscopic, or both.

In these families, even the most primitive kind of differentiation, that between alive and unalive, is not clearly established; hence all subsequent, more sophisticated differentiations must be precarious and easily lost. One little girl, for example, found it hopeless to compete with two baby boys, born before her, who had died in infancy; they were of much more lively emotional significance in her mother's memory than she herself could become in her mother's awareness. A pretty, young schizophrenic woman had long ago concluded, "An attractive person is considered a mechanical thing." At another point, this woman said, hopelessly, "Nobody responds emotionally to me." Another young woman felt herself to be a "lapel ornament" for her narcissistic father.

The father of the former young woman, a highly intelligent but complex and emotionally remote person, contributed to the childhood confusion of his eventually hebephrenic daughter by frequently expressing himself in double entendres, of which one of the simpler examples is: "You can tell a lady by the way she picks her teeth." During adolescence, the young woman's painful awkwardness at the few parties she attended was heightened by her attempts to repeat various cynical witticisms which her father had coached her to say but which she did not begin to understand. Also, when she tried of her own volition to identify with him by closing a letter to him from boarding school with a witticism in vogue there, "Yours for Life or any other ten-cent magazine," he was hurt and offended.

It was extraordinarily difficult for me to discern, during an initial history-taking interview with him, the feelings of this reportedly devoted father on the day that he brought his daughter to Chestnut Lodge. I had to conclude, with amazement, that he seemed more amused than anything else. A year or so later, as he was leaving my office one day, he said philosophically, "*Es gibt viele Krankheiten, aber nur eine Gesundheit,*" evidently assuming that I could switch to German without breaking stride. I felt both bewildered and embarrassed to have to ask him to repeat this. When he did, I was able to understand it as meaning, "There are many illnesses; but there is only one health." About three years after his daughter's admission, at the end of still another interview, he said feelingly but obscurely, "I don't have to tell you what I think of you." Although I felt this remark was intended as an expression of heartfelt gratitude on his part for my devotion to the treatment of his very ill daughter, it was quite unclear whether there was not something steely and menacing in it, and I replied uneasily that I'd feel surer about what he thought of me if his daughter were only well enough, by now, to be living off a locked ward.

Ego differentiation in the child vis-à-vis such a parent is, of course, difficult or impossible; my glimpses into his daughter's autistic world were scarcely harder to come by than were my divinings of what this father was feeling.

By contrast, parental behavior that is more explicit but paradoxical and unpredictably changeable makes for ego fragmentation, or failure of ego integration, in the child. Often, the husband and wife seem so ill-matched as to make for a comparable unrelatedness between the child's identifications with the father and his identifications with the mother. Further, the parents tend to be full of contradictions, such that their faces or their vocal tones say precisely the opposite of what their word content is emphasizing. The parental prejudices, derived from their parents in turn, are experienced as more real than any potential perceptions of immediate reality, dominating the efforts at individuation of both parent and child.

A borderline schizophrenic young man conceptualized such superego injunctions or prejudices as being huge solid blocks hovering menacingly in the air overhead. A hebephrenic woman evidently felt in similar awe of the whole realm of words; she once said to me, "There are a lot of words in the room," giving me the feeling that, for her, the whole room was crowded with jumbled, solid words. Another deeply regressed woman spoke in a similarly awed tone of "15 giant thoughts, standing outside," alive and far too vast to be in anyone's head. With more than one chronically schizophrenic person, I have come to feel after several years of work that his whole illness is entirely understandable in terms of hopelessly conflictual, family-derived values which seem utterly immutable and which cancel out, for him, any possibility of human living. One hebephrenic man, for example, after years of being essentially silent in treatment, revealed that he had long been paralyzed by various sets of contradictory values, such as the view that (1) energy was precious and must be carefully conserved, over against the view that (2) the world was permeated by the most intense, jungle-warfare type of competitiveness, in which he could not afford to give a moment's thought to the conservation of energy, lest he be overwhelmed by his innumerable and deadly foes.

Partly as a refuge from parental hostility, but more importantly as an unconscious defense against the deeply ambivalent feelings which the poorly integrated, unpredictably changeable parent tends to engender in him, the child identifies with the parent in a primitive, automatic, indiscriminate fashion. Moreover, it should be seen that the parent is thus being introjected not as a single entity. Rather, innumerable part-aspects of the parent are taken in, variously, as if each part were a person in itself. The parent's varying, paradoxically conflictual superego injunctions or prejudices form the hard cores of many of these primitive identifications. The resultant introjects, which abound in and encroach upon the child's developing ego, largely dominate ego functioning, and hence dominate what is perceived. Thus the child perceives relatively little with his own eyes and ears, so to speak; rather, he sees now with mother's eyes, and now through the very different eyes of father (to describe this in a highly oversimplified way). One hebephrenic young woman said to me, concerning a colleague of mine at the Lodge to whom she had formed an intense father-transference, "Dr. L—— sees the world through me." She was projecting upon him the symbiotic dependency she had had upon her father: she had seen the world through her father, until her overwhelming disillusionment with him had shattered their symbiotic relationship and precipitated her overt schizophrenia.

The child's experience of himself and of his surrounding family world is rendered chaotic and ambiguous by, more than any other circumstance, his having no well-established, developing identity in the family, no single predominant and consistent family role *from which to view* himself and the outer world. He does not feel that his parents and siblings perceive *him* realistically and consistently, in such a way as to allow him increasingly to feel that his own inner reality is that of a single, living, human entity. The mother may suddenly shift, for example, from reacting to the child as being a little boy, to his being a monster, or the mother's own mother, or God, and so on, often imposing two or more of these essentially incompatible roles upon him simultaneously.

One woman was treated by her mother as being, variously, a boy, a terrifying thunderstorm, an embodiment of Teutonic domination (traceable to the father's Germanic background), "a reincarnation," and so on. In contrast, the father seems to have treated her more realistically, to the extent that he was aware of her existence, as a beloved daughter. But overall, her perceptions were meaninglessly chaotic, since she had no reliable frame of reference, based on a well-defined and consistent family role, with which to focus her perceptions. Similarly, a little boy may not know how to hear his father's words, because he is given to feel variously that now he is to hear them as a son, now as a father, now as a brother, now as a mother or a wife or a mistress, now as an alter ego for father, and so on. But it is the nonhuman roles that predominate, more than any of these human ones, in the life of the child who eventually develops schizophrenia.

It is said that a hierarchy is, to those at the top, a lowerarchy. Such a child's world is, depending upon the unpredictably changing and paradoxical ways in which mother or father relates to him, now a hierarchy, now a lowerarchy, and now both at once—to employ an analogy which is the grossest oversimplification of the state of affairs I am trying to convey here. A nurse's report of a shopping trip with a chronically schizophrenic woman who had had such a childhood conveys the same principle:

> As a whole, she talked very sensibly to clerks. . . . She kept asking me if it was summer or winter or what. She says if she doesn't get a home soon she'll go out of her mind—that *everybody needs a focal point, even in thinking* [italics mine].

The child cannot build up realistic perceptions except insofar as there is a reliable, mutually trusting emotional climate in which he knows where he stands with each of his parents—knows who he is to them, and knows that he is loved and accepted by them. In these families there is so little of trustful, leisurely sharing of one another's thinking as to leave little time and emotional security for the weighing of perceptions before meanings must be imposed upon them. Instead, a perception has barely been made before it must be reacted to, by both parent and child, as confirming one or another emotional prejudice, one or another rigid superego standard, derived from parental indoctrination. The child is led to feel that not to *know*—to exist in a state of uncertainty and of searching for a meaning—means to be *crazy*, to be something beyond the human pale. He comes to feel, essentially, that the only alternative to oneness with the parent is total isolation, craziness. All too often, he finds himself in a position where he must choose between his parent and his own perceptual equipment. He feels required to accept the parent's world-view and ignore the contradictory data, which come to him through his own eyes, ears, nose, and tactile-kinesthetic sensory organs. He is not strong enough to rely on his own sensory equipment and go it alone; he cannot brave the parental threat of being considered crazy if he accepts the evidence of his own eyes and ears and so forth. Accurate perceptions both foster, and require, individuation, and the family's heaviest taboo is reserved for this. I recall here a man in his thirties, married and the father of several children, who, only after a number of years of treatment, was able for the first time to really look at his mother during one of her visits to his home.

The child identifies with the parent in, among other regards, the registering of perceptions. Thus, since his parental models massively deny unconsciously, or are otherwise unable to cope meaningfully with, innumerable significant perceptions, he develops built-in impediments to perceiving his own world realistically and in detail.

But his family role as regards perception is deeply *conflictual*. On the one hand, the other family members, themselves striving to become whole, integrated individuals, implicitly react to him as the *spokesman for* their own dissociated personality aspects, and hence unwittingly encourage him to be aware of personality traits and interpersonal processes in the family, which they are dissociating. But, on the other hand, they react to him as being crazy to the extent that he functions as an individual who *is* aware of these aspects of the reality of the family world around him.

One woman recalled that as a child she had been harshly told by her mother that she was crazy when she expressed the realization that she, the child, was a mother, and, similarly, when she ventured to reveal her experience of herself as a princess. There was much figurative truth in both these realizations—she was in many ways a mother to her several younger siblings, and she was a princess in her father's eyes. But the mother, instead of helping her to differentiate between metaphorical and literal aspects of reality, called her crazy for reacting to the figurative aspects. The daughter felt, literally, that she was walking on quicksand, and when she confided this to her mother and older siblings, they "would jump down my throat and tell me I was crazy," without, again, helping her to see that she was experiencing concretistically the anxiety of her being metaphorically not on solid ground in the family. She experienced the family neither as a family nor as individual persons with consistent identities. Unable to trust her own senses, she relied upon her dog to tell her whether this or that person in the family was her friend or her enemy. At one point she told me with intensity, "I spent my entire youth under a piano with a dog, because I'd rather be with a dog than with people who lied to me and slapped my face and told me *I* was evil because *they* were!"

As a result of such family experiences as I have been describing, the patient shows innumerable perceptual distortions in terms of both nondifferentiation and fragmentation of his experiential world.

Nondifferentiation, for example, appears in this complaint of one man to his therapist: "I don't know, when I talk to you, whether I'm having a hallucination, or a fantasy about a memory, or a memory about a fantasy." He was unable to distinguish at all clearly and reliably between inner and outer worlds. A symbiotic mode of relatedness may hold sway over such a patient to the degree that he cannot maintain himself at a sufficient distance from persons and things around him to be able to perceive them at all objectively; one cannot truly perceive that in which one is immersed. Such a patient seems to feel either meaninglessly unrelated to the ingredients of the world around him or so fused with, blended with those ingredients that, again, perception and meaning are not achieved. The outer world may be so little differentiated from himself that he may speak, as one hebephrenic man spoke, of its "insubstantiality." A hebephrenic woman experienced the world as one gigantic movie set; presumably her low emotional investment in the "real" world caused her to experience it as artificial, not fully real, hence man-made. She would say, with absolute conviction, "Everything is *made!*"

In general, and to a high degree, schizophrenic patients experience inner emotions not as such but rather as distorted perceptions of the outside world. All of outer reality becomes kaleidoscopically changed because of the impact upon it of the patient's unconscious feelings. That is, what are essentially inner emotional changes are experienced as perceptual changes in the surrounding world. A hebephrenic young woman, unable to experience as such the full intensity of her anger at a nurse, instead perceived the nurse's face as being "bashed in." Similarly, when she was threatened with intense upwelling feelings of disillusionment and contempt toward other persons, she instead distortedly perceived these persons as having become midgets. At the end of a session in which, for the first time, she began to express feelings of disillusionment with a long-idolized boyfriend, Eddie, she said, "I used to think he was taller . . . Eddie shrank." One recurrently psychotic young man, who spent many weeks continuously in a seclusion room, experienced not inner emotional turmoil and change in himself over the weeks, but change in the room. As he explained to his therapist, "When I am in the seclusion room, it is like being in three different rooms. The first room is dark and completely silent; the second room is full of turmoil and is very stormy; the third room is bright with light. I feel I am somewhere between the first and second rooms and will get to the third room."

As an example of the fragmentation—or, more accurately, nonintegration—characteristic of schizophrenic experience, I recall a woman whose deceased mother was described by the patient's older brother as having been a remarkably changeable person. For instance, on Sunday mornings she would return from the Baptist church in a beatific mood of religious exaltation, and in the next few moments would be furiously throwing a kitchen pot at one of her several children. The patient herself, in a treatment session with me, protested, "When you use the word 'mother,' I see a picture of a parade of women, each one representing a different point of view." For several years, she tenaciously disavowed ever having had a mother. Her current life experience was comparably nonintegrated. For example, one day a male aide, Mr. Bennett, escorted her to a football game in Washington. In her next therapy session, she made clear to me that in the course of the outing Mr. Bennett had been replaced eight or nine times, each time without warning, by as many different Mr. Bennetts in succession. A gentlemanly Mr. Bennett had been replaced by a boorish Mr. Bennett, and once a Mr. Bennett whose face was flushed with anger had appeared. She said, disappointedly, that at no time during the whole trip had her favorite Mr. Bennett appeared. When I suggested to her the possibility that actually there had been one aide throughout, but that her *feelings toward* him had undergone various changes such that he had appeared differently to her, she most emphatically asserted that an adult person, which she of course considered herself to be, never has such experiences. She asserted scornfully that if one's feelings toward another person underwent changes as a result of things the other person said and did, the perceiving individual in question would be a "will-o'-the-wisp." I have no doubt, incidentally, that this is an instance of a family-ingrained superego standard such as I was discussing earlier, despite the fact that the mother was in actuality so extremely changeable.

This woman, year after year, felt her own existence as highly discontinuous, could recall only "splashes of memory," dissociated—both at the time and in retrospect—much that she did, and had the delusion that she had many "doubles" who were doing, and had done, many of the things which people attributed to her. In her work with me, she perceived me not as being the same person, session after session, but rather as being a series of distinctly different and unrelated persons, from one session to the next, and, often, as being replaced several times during a session by a series of strange men, women, children, and, frequently, nonhuman creatures, whom or which she had never seen before. She could not recognize that I was the same person but in a different mood, a different combination of feelings, than she had ever seen me in before, or the same person but one toward whom she was experiencing a new combination of feelings. Instead, I would suddenly and unexpectedly become, to her, a different person—or, very often, a different combination of persons. Much of the time she experienced me as multiple beings simultaneously, whom she had never seen before and who, she was equally sure, had never before set eyes upon her. To a nurse she once protested, "One day he's a nun; the next day he's a priest; the next day he's a lawyer; the next day he's a doctor. . . ."

Another similarly unintegrated woman patient had long idolized her father but now oriented her life around a father-image which was more delusional than real. The ingredients of this image came from all areas of her interpersonal experience over the years. She spent months in the hospital penciling innumerable letters to him, beseeching his help. The envelopes would be addressed to "Father, Daddy, Dad, Sugar Daddy . . ."—often running to 20 or 30 titles on each envelope. These were attempts on her part, apparently, to collect together, and integrate into one being, all the different part-aspects of him (the stern Father, the fond Daddy, the reliable Dad, the sexually interested, indulgent Sugar Daddy, and so on), part-aspects which she experienced not as such, but as a collection of different but related whole persons.

In this connection, the paranoid individual's delusions concerning a pervasive, all-embracing plot by the Communists, the Mafia, or whatnot, can be seen as efforts to arrange a chaotic perceptual experience in some sort of order, a kind of artificially imposed, delusional order, for lack of the healthy kind of order and meaning that emerge in the perceptions and experiences of the adult person whose feeling-capacities are readily available to awareness.

The paranoid individual's experiencing the plot, further, as *centering upon himself* is in part a reaction to his being most deeply threatened lest he be as insignificant, as outside of everyone else's awareness, as other persons tend to be in his awareness, as he himself, with his severe repression of his own dependent feelings, tends to regard other individuals as being. One chronically schizophrenic man who had had several prolonged episodes of overt paranoid schizophrenia responded, after I had inquired whether he had perhaps reacted thus and so to something I had just done, with his customary furiously controlled scorn, as though trying for the millionth time to communicate with an earthworm: "I don't have any reactions to you, any more than I would have reactions to that little spot on the wall over there." He was a single man, without siblings or friends. His mother was dead and his father rarely showed any interest in him except when obtaining a "loan" from the patient's maternal inheritance. He was shielded in his psychosis from deeplying feelings of being totally insignificant in the eyes of his fellow human beings by the delusion that the ancient lineage of Irish kings was destined to be re-established in a position of power through his elevation to the restored Irish throne.

Now I want to highlight the point, already touched upon, that all these schizophrenic phenomena function as unconscious defenses against intolerable emotional conflicts. I indicated earlier that the child's introjection of part-aspects of the parents—occurring as an unconscious and automatic defense against the intolerably conflictual, ambivalent feelings which would have to be faced and integrated were he able to perceive the parent as a separate object—is a process that takes precedence over any developing capacity in himself to perceive himself and the world about him in a relatively conflict-free and realistic fashion. So it is with all schizophrenic experience: it is defensive against various intense emotions, and combinations of emotions. The relatively healthy person can experience such emotions in awareness, without resort to such unconscious defenses as ego fragmentation and ego dedifferentiation through regression to fully symbiotic relatedness. But the schizophrenic individual has far more intense, and intensely conflictual, feelings outside his awareness than the healthy person, whose upbringing has been less threatened, ever has to reckon with, and at the same time he has far less capacity to face and integrate such feelings.

Thus the schizophrenic person does not experience the grief and nostalgia mature persons feel, but, misidentifying other persons in current life, bewilderedly sees the beloved people from his past unaccountably about him. In general, rather than experiencing such relatively complex emotions as disillusionment and hurt and jealousy, he feels himself either an observer at, or wholly immersed in, eerie, terrifying, bizarre, fascinating, and bewildering events. One hebephrenic woman was unable to feel as such her murderous jealousy of various male doctors, aides, and patients, because of their status in the eyes of the nurses and other women patients whom she hungrily needed as mother-figures; instead of experiencing jealousy, she perceived the eyes of these males, and her own eyes, as being at times triangular. For example, while sitting on one man's lap, she talked about his pupils' looking triangular; on another occasion, she gigglingly reported to the nurse that she herself had been "making three-cornered eyes at Dr. Wilson."

To another woman, whom I have already mentioned, it was inconceivable, for the first several years of her treatment, that a person has complex feelings which are continually changing. Instead, in her inflexible view, if the other person's demeanor changed from angry to kind, she felt he had been replaced by a "double" who was kind; this distorted perception spared her from feeling guilt at exchanging hostile words with a person basically capable of forgiveness and kindness. She once said to a nurse, "You must have a double, because sometimes you are so nice to me, then other times you are rude just like you are now." This perception tended to protect her against feeling hurt: the kind nurse was not being rough with her, but must have an ungentle, rude double. She reacted similarly with a person she transitorily idolized; in her experience, the idol had not done something disillusioning, but rather he had been replaced by a double who was contemptible. She avoided experiencing the fullness of her envy of another woman patient whose legs were prettier than her own with the delusion that "they" had cut off the other woman's legs and put them on herself. She once hurled at me the chilling accusation, "To think you would cut off the hands of someone I know, and attach them to yourself and use them to try to eat into my memory!" She later made clear that the hands she had seen on me were what I would call her mother's; but she was genuinely unable to remember ever having had a mother. It came across to me clearly that the hands were terribly, painfully dear to her and that, rather than experience this as such, she seemed ready to murder me and everyone else if necessary to avoid such overwhelming grief. She asserted, at one point in this session, that I should be shot, and for many months at this phase of our work I had little doubt that had she possessed a gun she would have shot me on my way to her room for the sessions to which she was invariably ragingly opposed. For a full ten years she refused ever to set foot in my office.

She once said to a nurse, "Even your voice can be changed by wiring to sound like the voice of a person that I know." It seemed that the weirdness she felt in response to this strange phenomenon obscured any sense of loss of the person from her past. She herself was the mother of several children, whom she had not seen for many years, and whom she could not remember as such; a not unusual daily nurse's report contained the following item: ". . . thinks the trees outside are her children." One summer she became fond of a college student, young enough to be her son, who devoted much time to her. One day I found her looking even more acutely unhappy than usual, and suggested that perhaps she was missing Mr. Hamilton, who had left only a day or two previously to return to college. She immediately dismissed my suggestion by reminding me that "there are 13 Hamiltons" who were still all about the Lodge; so how could she possibly be grieving about any one of them?

For years, one of her delusions was that if she were to write to someone at home, this would "constitute a call"—that is, the person to whom she wrote would, as she had found from experience, be brought into the Lodge, or—as she actually experienced it, into one of the 53,000 Chestnut Lodges among which she was continually being moved—and be incarcerated like herself. This delusion was evidently based upon her misidentification of current figures as being the persons to whom she had written pleas for rescue, misidentification which defended her against her feelings of missing them and also against her feelings of envying and hating them for being free while she was committed to this mental hospital as being insane. For a very long time, I found it impossible to avoid being drawn into long arguments with her about her innumerable delusions that tended seriously to undermine my own sense of reality. Eventually I saw that her arguing was not oriented toward any genuine resolution of her delusional thinking, but was her *transference way of relating* to me as being her mother, now long dead, with whom she had loved to argue, and toward whom she still possessed so much hatred, fear, guilt, and envy that she was not yet able to work through her grief.

The most awesomely grief-filled human being I have ever seen was a hebephrenic woman, initially young, with whom I worked for 13 years, four hours per week. Her experience was flooded with hallucinated persons from the past, and was comparably distorted in numerous other respects. In one session after three and a half years, for example, when I went to her seclusion room she said, in a harsh tone, "I wouldn't come in here if I were you," and later complained that I had come in without introducing myself. Much later in the session, after much other talk, she said, "I can't introduce you fast enough." She said this in an apologetic tone, clearly under intense pressure, while her glance kept flickering to one side. I suggested that there were so many people coming onto the scene so rapidly that she couldn't introduce them all to me, and she confirmed this. I began to realize that she really did need to have me introduce myself each time I came in, whereas I had long been offended because her behaving as though she had never met me seemed immensely contemptuous. Still later in the session she said in a perfectly natural, interested, friendly tone, "You look like Ralph Ellsworth [apparently one of the numerous young men she had known] this morning." I told her this was a memorable moment for me, saying that for a long time she would only have been able to experience me as *being* Ralph Ellsworth. Nearly a year later my notes read that it was evident how much her earlier, complete misidentification of me had changed:

> Today she made clear to me that when I say certain things, or make certain gestures, these *remind* her *of* other persons she's known. For example, when she indicated she wanted to know how old I am, I told her 37, and she replied, "That's Ross."

When I lit her cigarette at one point, she addressed me as "Albert." On one or two other occasions, she commented about "Bruce," in response to something I'd said or done. The most memorable thing was the *feeling* I got during today's hour, for the first time, that she was reacting to me as a kind of conglomeration of guys, but with some continuity now—that I didn't totally shift, in her perception of me, from one person to another, but rather that I vividly reminded her of now one guy, now another. When I talked to her in this vein about this, she repeatedly seemed to corroborate the point. At one juncture she asked, "Did they change your name?" and seemed to be trying to warn me to be careful about what I said and did, lest "they" change my name.

On another occasion she let me know that when I walked across the room, I reminded her of a whole stream of persons from her past. In a predominantly friendly session during the sixth year of our work, she walked past me, came to a stop, and said, "You *know* you don't see the same person when I move," as if to say, "Come on and admit that you experience this same perceptual phenomenon that *I* do." For years she would say with intensity, in her daily life on the ward, "I can't stand people who *move*," and at times would grab a passing nurse or fellow patient by the hair to make her stop and be still.

My notes on a session during the fifth year read:

> During today's hour I got a new bit of insight into how a psychotic person's world may look to her.
>
> For about the first two-thirds of the hour I was sitting near Dorothy's bed, on which she was sitting, with my chair near the window. As time went on I got rather cold and, explaining, "I'm cold; I'm going to move my chair over to the other side of the room," I did so, placing the chair about the same distance from the bed as I had been before and in very much the same position in relation to her.
>
> She looked down toward me, now sitting on her left side, and said, in a surprised tone, "Huh!" After a couple of moments she said, "Now I'll have to start all over." She then went on and in the next very few moments said something about "two men and a girl," and about a minute later still she said, "I am not with Dr. Snow"—this being her usual name for me.

It dawned on me that she had experienced me, now, as being a different person, and I realized more clearly than before why she has objected for years to people's "moving." I now realize not only that she often misidentifies a person when the person moves—something I had realized before—but also that she experiences the room as being filled with an *increasing number* of people. That is, the Dr. Snow who had been sitting on the former side of the room did not disappear from her experience; but a new doctor was added to the situation, so that there were now two men and a girl. [She had often made clear, in earlier years, that she experienced as many as "200 guys" in the room during our sessions.].

I formulated this to her rather briefly in much these same terms, and she said sneeringly, "I'm very impressed with you." [This woman, whose deameanor manifested her tragic need for help from me but whose penis envy and competitiveness with father-figures was immense, usually reacted with sneering contempt and resentment on the relatively infrequent occasions when I was able to grasp what was happening and to make some intended contribution to her. To summarize this incident, it emerged that she had perceived me not as being one person who had moved from one place to another, but more like the separate and coexisting stills from a motion picture film.]

It became abundantly clear that her inability to integrate feelings of grief was a major factor in the perpetuation of such distorted perceptions. At a staff conference, for instance, her administrator movingly reported, "She hallucinates her parents quite frequently. After their recent visit, she saw them under every bush and tree for several days." Years later, after her father had died following a surgical operation and her widowed mother had married a kindly, helpful man to whom the patient soon became fondly attached, I went to her room for a session with her the day following a visit from her mother and stepfather, Mr. McKenzie. When I unknowingly sat down in the chair in which the stepfather had sat the day before, she exclaimed in horrified concern, "You're sitting on Mr. McKenzie!" To her, he was still there.

It is, of course, through our seeing all schizophrenic experience in its defensive functioning—in its serving, that is, to keep under repression all sorts of feelings in the patient, including not only grief and love but also hatred and envy and other "negative" feelings—that we therapists make contact with the patient's own tenacious clinging to his illness. He clings to it in order to defend himself unconsciously against a too-painful and too-disillusioning awareness of his own emotions, and in order to act out unconsciously, through his schizophrenic behavior, his hatred and rejectingness toward the outer world. Schizophrenia cannot be understood simply in terms of traumata and deprivation, no matter how grievous, inflicted by the outer world upon the helpless child. The patient himself, no matter how unwittingly, has an active part in the development and tenacious maintenance of the illness, and only by making contact with this essentially assertive energy in him can one help him to become well. This paper is not an attempt to comprehend schizophrenia in its entirety. It is an attempt to focus upon the patient's own subjective experience of himself and his world. It therefore necessarily makes the role of external trauma seem to loom large in the etiology of the illness and the role of the patient's own projected hatred, for example, seem small, simply because, in the patient's own view of things, he is so largely unaware of his own murderous feelings, for instance, and thus distortedly perceives the surrounding world as disproportionately malevolent.

In the course of the patient's treatment any ease and security we therapists have found in comfortably and self-righteously blaming the parents for his illness must be relinquished, as we find that he arouses in *us* fully as much hate toward him as the supposedly malevolent mother expressed toward her supposedly innocent child. He arouses in us, too, discoordinate and poorly differentiated feelings that fully deserve comparison with the kind of paradoxical inconsistency and inscrutable ambiguity of emotional expression I described earlier as characterizing the patient's childhood family. Often, our feelings become so disturbing to us, or so obscurely unknown to us, in response to what the patient is saying and doing, that we need the help of an analyst or supervisor to help us to cope with them or to discover what they are. It is thus that we come humbly to feel forgiving and accepting of the patient's parents, and to feel impressed with his own power—power not merely for the maintenance of his illness through the unconscious transference re-creation about him of the ambiguous and chaotic interpersonal world of his childhood, but also for, increasingly, healthy change and growth.

I shall conclude with a number of suggestions concerning psychotherapeutic technique.

First, one must realize that the patient has arrived at his perceptual world over years of employing the best judgment of which he is capable. It is a world deserving of our respect; we cannot ask him to relinquish it at all readily and to embrace gratefully the view of "reality" we offer him. Invariably, the better I come to know him, and his life, and myself in relation to him, the more I am impressed at how much accuracy, often powerfully incisive accuracy, there is in his perceptions of me.

Second, I have found it advisable, particularly early in therapy, to endeavor to share the patient's *feelings about* the world as he perceived it, rather than to challenge the accuracy of his perceptual world itself. For example, rather than arguing with him that I am not a homicidal maniac, nor a machine bent on killing him, I try largely to put aside my own view of reality, to put myself in the patient's place and to think how terrified I would be to find myself closeted with a therapist whom I perceived thus. This enables me to appreciate the patient's terror and suspicion. To that degree, he now has a therapist with whom he can genuinely share such feelings, rather than one who tells him, in effect, that he is crazy for holding the world-view he holds.

Third, the patient's perceptual experience is dominated by his immediate interpersonal environment far more than he realizes, and more than the therapist realizes until he examines the perception and the environment in detail. For example, I noted that a schizophrenic young man standing in the hallway of a disturbed ward, shoutingly immersed in his hallucinatory experience of a submarine-combat world, was actually responding to small cues from his immediate ward environment; but these were so delusionally distorted by him that the interconnections were not apparent to a superficial observer. In the therapeutic relationship, above all, we find that the most subtle and unconscious communications by the therapist are tremendously influencing the patient. The latter loftily assumes that his perceptual world has no connection to the therapist; he must arrogantly dismiss the therapist's significance to him, because in actuality it is that of a God the Creator, analogous to the importance of the mother in the infant's or young child's developing relation to reality.

Fourth, it follows that the patient's moment-by-moment, changing perceptions of the therapist, in the course of the therapeutic session, form a crucial, ongoing theme for both participants to explore together. It is important here that the therapist candidly acknowledge and confirm, in some fashion or other, the increments of reality in the patient's distorted views of him—no matter how embarrassing or painful these may be. In this process the patient comes to remember his long-forgotten, never well-differentiated and well-integrated past by discovering, in the therapist, not only the persons and part-persons important to him in earlier years, but also the important nonhuman ingredients of his past—the scenes, the pets, the buildings, and so on.

Fifth, and in the same vein, the perceptions that the therapist comes to have of the patient, feeling-laden, unusual, and at times highly contradictory, are of great therapeutic significance. In a sense, the patient's own repressed self-images, his many highly contradictory, unrelated, unintegrated self-images, derived in large part from conflictual family roles, become integrated into a single, coherent, three-dimensional whole indirectly, in the therapist's developing image of him, an image which is enriched, step by step, through the therapist's seeing and responding to a succession of different persons, so to speak, in the patient. Following along this indirect avenue, the patient becomes subjectively, increment by increment, a whole and integrated human being, partially through identification with the feeling-image the therapist is developing, facet by facet, of him.

Sixth, the therapeutic process requires that we alternatively, and in varying doses, look with the patient at *his* world—that is, share his view of the world—and give him glimpses of *our* view of the world. Thus, in nicely timed sharings and confrontings, analogous to a mother's nursing her infant, we help him to realize that there is both an inner and an outer world. By helping him to see, and at times insisting upon, the differences between *his* world and *ours*, we help him to realize that he is a human being among fellow human beings, each of whom has his own individual world-view, and that all these collective world-views can coexist and be meaningfully interrelated.

During this process, the therapist finds that the whole realm of the patient's view of himself and his world, with all its bleakness and its color, all its monotony and its chaotic changeability and complexity, is but an instrument—although a most powerful one—in the service of his unconscious, and deeply ambivalent, desires on the one hand to preserve his autistic or symbiotic modes of existence, and on the other hand to achieve a more mature kind of relatedness with the therapist and, eventually, a healthy individuation vis-à-vis the latter.

Hence we find, clinically, that the patient will entice us with fascinating glimpses into his world, a world at once incredibly different from our own and poignantly reminiscent of the half-remembered, and never fully to be recaptured, world of our own early childhood. But when we get too close to him, we find him confronting us with aspects of his perceptual world which in effect close the door between him and us. He is too afraid, as yet, that to really come into relation with another human being is to be devoured, or to open the Pandora's box of his own supposed world-destructiveness.

The therapist finds himself involved so deeply in the same conflict concerning individuation, in the treatment relationship, that the individuation which eventually results can truly be called a mutual one. Only gradually do patient and therapist become unafraid, each of his own world and of the other person's world. Only over the course of many moments and hours of very real fear, in each, that successively deep revelations of one's own world will impel oneself or the other to suicide or incurable insanity, do both participants develop the trustful realization that their two worlds can be fully looked at and freely shared. These are aspects of what I have described in earlier papers as the phase of therapeutic symbiosis. The mutual individuation which follows, again by dint of many ambivalent weaning struggles by both patient and therapist, leaves each deeply changed. The patient will never again, presumably, be so vulnerable to psychosis. But neither will the therapist ever again need to repress so fully his own more primitive processes, processes which include the kind of nonintegration and nondifferentiation of experience that have comprised the defenses of the formerly psychotic patient.

Schizophrenia is, in a sense, the shadow cast by the emotional deficiencies of our culture. Thus the study of what the schizophrenic individual experiences is of value not merely in being poignantly evocative of our irretrievable childhood, but also in a prospectively constructive way. By the light we thus acquire on the hypocrisies and previously unquestioned, implicit assumptions in our own "normal" existence, we are better equipped to achieve a healthier culture and to live more fully, freely, and knowingly.

It is not that the schizophrenic individual is a supernormal, hyperenlightened variety of human being; he is indeed ill. But because he perforce—not by choice—has been living on the sidelines of humanity, he is in a position to tell us some important things which we have been too immersed in "normal" living to see. His usefulness, here, is analogous to that of the analyst who may be working with an analysand more intelligent and creative and even in important respects more emotionally healthy than himself, but who is potentially of use to the analysand precisely because he, the analyst, has not lived the analysand's life—has lived in some basic ways differently, and is able therefore to help the analysand look at his life from a new vantage point.

To the schizophrenic individual, for example, the question has been not *how* but *whether* to relate to his fellow man and, through becoming familiar with his views, we realize that in us, too, this has been, all along, a meaningful and alive and continuing conflict, heretofore hidden from ourselves. He helps us to realize, further, that silence between persons is not necessarily a gulf, a void, but may be a tangibly richer communion than any words could constitute. Above all, through working with him, the therapist is compelled to question, one by one, each of the tenets about human existence, individually and collectively, of which he has felt most unthinkingly sure. In this process we come eventually to realize that nothing about human beings and human behavior can be assumed, can be taken for granted. This has been, for me, one of the endlessly rewarding, exciting aspects of this work.

2

Feelings of Guilt
in the Psychoanalyst

First, before looking at the sources of what might be called the occupational guilt inherent in doing analysis, we need to consider the possibility that our very choice of analysis as a profession has been, to a significant degree, a guilt-based choice. Thus, it may not be so much that our doing of analysis tends to promote guilt in us, but rather that we originally entered this profession in an unconscious effort to assuage our guilt, and that the practice of analysis fails to relieve our underlying guilt. For example, we may have chosen this profession on the basis of unconscious guilt over having failed to cure our parents. Or we may still be stubbornly clinging to forbidden, guilt-laden oedipal aspirations, which over and over find a tailor-made refuge in this profession, wherein "forbidden" erotic aspirations naturally, and to a degree necessarily, tend to develop between patient and doctor.

Second, we can see that we do our daily work, as analysts, burdened or constricted by various traditions that are conducive to guilt. The traditions of our general culture do not value highly those achievements that are intangible and of a mental-emotional

This paper was presented as the author's contribution to a panel discussion on this subject at a meeting of the Washington Psychoanalytic Society, Washington, D.C., on September 24, 1965. It was first published in *Psychiatry*, 29:319-323 (1966).

28

sort; we live instead in a culture that values a tangible job well done. But we do work that is neither tangible nor, in the usual sense of the term, completable.

Further, the medical tradition in which we have been trained holds that, as physicians, we should not have any notable feeling-reactions to our patients except such feelings as active and compassionate dedication; as physicians, we are never to experience toward our patients such emotions as hatred, envy, rejection, and so forth. In my work with psychiatric residents at a number of hospitals, I have come to believe that nothing hampers these young psychiatrists' efforts to work with schizophrenic patients more than their feeling so constricted by their identity as physicians, a role that tends to render them helpless in the face of the patients' sadistic misuse of their conscientious dedication (Searles, 1967b).

Our training, after medical school, in the classical analytic tradition tends to restrict still further the emotions we can feel, without attendant guilt, toward our patients. That is, much of the classical literature and teaching leads us to believe that any reaction to the patient, beyond one of neutral attentiveness, is quite taboo. Further, while we urge or encourage or exhort the patient to say whatever comes to his mind—while, that is, he "confesses all"—we are secretive about our own thoughts and feelings—another built-in aspect of analysis, in particular of classical analysis, which is guilt-provoking.

Third, let us now look at the analyst's guilt in terms of its defensive functions and its denial functions. Let us see what unconscious feelings it serves to maintain under repression in the analyst, and what are the aspects of his patient to which it tends to blind him.

The various traditional constrictions, which I have mentioned, upon our own emotional role tend to foster our projection, upon our patient, of our critical, condemnatory, reproachful, blaming feelings, with the result that we tend chronically to feel guilty in the face of his presumed—in addition to his real—blaming. We need clearly to realize that our invitation to the patient to say whatever comes to his mind need *not* carry with it a guarantee of a neutral

response on our part. For far too long we have failed to see that
the analyst, not only for the sake of his own mental hygiene but
also in order to work effectively as an analyst, must be free to think
and feel critically, judgmentally, and, not at all seldom, condemningly.

Some 17 years ago, while working in a chronically blame-ridden
way with one of my first patients, I found myself having a difficult
time trying to desist from compulsive note-taking. I had noticed
that various of my patients in that era would uneasily express wonderment at my noting down everything they said, no matter how
trivial it seemed. With this particular patient, I finally deliberately
put aside my notebook, determined to stop this compulsive note-
taking. Within seconds, then, as he continued his usual verbalized
ruminating, I was immediately struck with the thought, "What *shit!*"
In more recent years, from time to time I have had the ironic
thought that instead of healing souls, I am half-consoling heels.
Likewise, whereas I used to feel highly vulnerable to blame by the
parents of hospitalized patients with whom I was working, I found
this spectre to vanish upon my experiencing an upsurge of blaming
feelings on my *own* part toward the parents—blaming them for the
fact of the patient's pathology. I do not mean to say that this is a
rational and balanced view of the patient's illness. But the recognition of my own previously unconscious and projected feelings of
blame toward the parents greatly relieved me from the dread I
used to feel lest I be blamed and condemned by them upon their
forthcoming visits.

Our guilt is likely to contain not only unconscious condemnatory feelings, but also sadism toward the patient. In our guilty,
overly conscientious way of working, we tend to make him feel uneasy, to feel himself a burden to us, to feel that we do not enjoy
seeing him and working with him.

Further, our guilt implies unconscious contempt on our part,
for it implies that we view the patient as being so weak and fragile
that we fear we have irreparably damaged him by some past word
or act, or we fear that we would do so, if we were to say to him
what we are tempted to say.

The guilt-ridden analyst tries to "keep the patient in" treatment, consciously, in face of the patient's outrageous demands upon him, while unconsciously trying to frighten the patient out of treatment through an indulgent, cozening, pursuing, devouring attitude (a reaction formation against anger and rejectingness), which arouses the patient's paranoid fears. Here, increased freedom to feel rejecting toward the patient is the specific remedy.

I want to note, further, that guilt involves an unconscious clinging to the past—the past as represented by the past incident or situation about which we remain immersed in guilt—and is thus a defense against feelings of loss on our part.

I used to feel guilt at finding myself powerless to help patients to experience and express grief, and then gradually came to realize that in situations in which the patient is beginning to deal with grief, nothing is required of me, except not to interfere. This is an example of how, in our guilt, we become overactive and intrusive, and interfere with the analytic-growth process. Hence our guilt is apt to cloak our unconscious wish to cling to the patient. This is not a "bad" desire; only the fact that we repress it—in part because of our medical tradition—is bad.

As for those aspects of the patient to which our immersion in guilt tends to blind us, I want here to mention, in particular, the patient's sadism. As I indicated about the psychiatric residents, we tend repeatedly to lose sight of the extent to which our patient is sadistically thwarting our efforts to help him, and sadistically enjoying watching us beat our dedicated heads and hearts against the cliff of his resistance.

Time after time in supervision, I have heard on recordings the sadistic quality of the schizophrenic patient's confusing verbalizations, and the frustration of the therapist as, quite unaware of the sadism, he struggles on in his dedicated effort to untangle and decipher what the patient is saying. Similarly, in my own work with a schizophrenic woman years ago, she would repeatedly express the most intense physical anguish, and I, feeling anguishedly helpless to relieve her symptoms, would keep trying desperately to explore them and to think of things to say. Then, as I became more aware

of the sadism in her reproachful expressions of physical anguish, I
left off trying to rescue her. Following this, she would hobble into
the session, wracked with pain, vent her *fury* upon me for an hour,
and walk out a physically rejuvenated and robust person.

Fourth, I want to suggest that our most troublesome guilt reactions are a function of our having regressed, in our relationship
with the patient, under the impact of, and as a defense against, the
helplessly ambivalent feelings that our work with him tends to in-
spire in us, to a defensively symbiotic relationship with him, in
which our view of ourself and of the world is an omnipotent view.
In this state of subjective omnipotence, we are totally responsible
for all that transpires in the analysis, for there is no world outside
us; there is no real, flesh-and-blood other person. Hence all our
erotic and angry responses to the patient are felt by us as crazy, for
we fail to see their interpersonal origin; they are felt instead as
being exclusively crazy and frightening upwellings from within us,
threatening irreparably to damage or destroy the patient, who
seems so insubstantial and fragile. Since we do not experience any
clear and firm ego boundaries between ourself and the patient, his
acts are, in their guilt-producing capacity, our own acts; we feel as
guilty about his sexual or aggressive or other kinds of acting out as
if we ourself had committed and were committing those acts.

We fear to say the angry word to our patient, lest he be destroyed by it. So we suppress our anger, and it grows, and we hate
the patient for our unfreedom, and we feel guilty about our hate.
Being unfree, essentially, to relate to the patient, we relate more
and more to our own superego, our superego based upon the for-
bidding and punitive and constricting figures from our own past.
Also, we cannot say the angry word for fear that the patient's
image of us—and worst of all, our own image of ourself—as being
omnipotently and unambivalently loving will be irretrievably lost.

Omnipotence-based guilt is really, then, a relating to one's
self—to, that is, warded-off aspects of one's self—rather than a
genuine interpersonal relationship. It shuts out the patient; it represents a clinging to our own past; it underestimates the impact of
the patient upon us. And to *feel* blamed by a blaming patient, for

what he feels to be early injustices on our part in the treatment, is a form of disguised nostalgia, on our own part, for that earlier phase in the treatment.

In our guilt about not having made the "right" response, we fail to see the depth of the patient's ambivalence—the impossibility of their being *any* "right" response that will somehow satisfy, simultaneously, both sides of his conflictual needs. The fact that the patient's desires are deeply ambivalent desires makes it inevitable that he will make us feel, over and over again, that we are failing him, that we are unsatisfactory, that we are not giving him what he wants and needs. Hence, instead of remaining immersed in *our guilt*, we should be pointing out to him the presence of *his conflict*. Here, our guilt reveals our own clinging to the omnipotent fantasy that life can be wholly gratifying and conflict-free.

In our omnipotence-based guilt, we try not to see that, while consciously we struggle to help the patient to mature and become well, unconsciously we have been struggling to make him become increasingly regressed, and thus to lend us a godlike status, and vicariously to fulfill, through his acting out, the various warded-off aspects of our self. I want to emphasize that we all do this, in my opinion, in our work with all our patients, in varying degrees.

Increasing freedom from neurotic guilt requires us to become increasingly ready to forgive our parents and others whom we tend to blame for their falling short of meeting our demands upon them. Such persons notably include our patients; occupational guilt probably has as one of its most important roots the fact that we are unconsciously focusing on our patients the demands our parents failed to satiate, and the ungratifiability of which we refuse to accept.

What else comprises the "way out of" guilt? First, let us not feel guilty *because* we feel guilty—that is only another facet of omnipotence. In line with Mabel Blake Cohen's (1952) concept about the inevitability of our responding in terms of the patient's transference, we shall often feel guilt, for the parents with their problems of unconscious omnipotence were such deeply guilt-ridden persons. To give an example of how guilty I used to feel because I felt guilty, at one time I was working with a very competitive, critical, compulsive young man who came into the office one morning and saw me trying to greet him with my usual careful friendliness, while hampered by a stiff neck. His immediate, hawklike reaction was, "Ah!—feeling guilty about something, eh?" to which I could give only a wry, sickly grin.

In marked contrast, since I have been doing more consultation work, I have learned that a particular kind of guilt-providing effect is one of the most reliable criteria of schizophrenia. In general, in most consultation and teaching interviews done before a one-way mirror, for example, I tend to feel callous, brutal, bullying, and to feel that I have grievously and inexcusably let down the so-eager and so-needful patient. It is to the extent that I can cope with such guilt feelings, and look upon them in the light of what they may be saying about the patient, that I am able to do this work. When I am left with such feelings in particular intensity, feelings that I am unworthy to be called a human being, I find this a reliable diagnostic criterion of schizophrenia in the patient.

Repeatedly, in this discussion, I have found myself starting to use the phrase "unresolved omnipotence." It has dawned on me, however, that omnipotence is never "resolved," and that it is pernicious to speak of such a fantasy as "unresolved omnipotence." Rather, we need to become more freely *aware of* our omnipotent strivings, which are never "resolved" throughout life and which remain, indeed, our most priceless wellsprings of energy.

It has occurred to me that perhaps a new set of moral standards needs to evolve for any one relationship, perhaps even for any one analytic session or any one moment. At any rate, the essential thing is relatedness to immediate, ever-changing *reality*. To relinquish neurotic guilt, which serves as a kind of restraint, one must be able to find a better restraint: *reality*. Neurotic guilt, as I have already indicated, bespeaks poor relatedness with immediate reality.

A random point, now: I have become determined to give as good as I get, hour by hour with my patients. In this way, resentment does not build up in me, nor guilt about such resentment.

The question of what are the realizable goals of psychoanalysis is highly relevant to this question of what is "the way out of" guilt. One needs to come to reject, for example, the goal of enduring freedom from envy, or guilt, or whatnot, on the part of either patient or analyst. One does not become free from feelings in the course of maturation or in the course of becoming well during psychoanalysis; one becomes, instead, increasingly free to experience feelings of all sorts.

How many of us can really accept, without guilt, a patient with whom we are no longer working (and whom we chance to meet subsequently)? I cannot, and I feel that my guilt contains not-too-readily-conscious resentment at him for failing to fulfill all my expectations. But again, I surmise that wholehearted acceptance of the patient is another unrealizably omnipotent goal. We could unambivalently love and approve of and accept our patient only if he were somehow able to personify our own ego ideal—and in that impossible eventuality, we would of course feel murderously envious of him anyway.

3

Identity Development in Edith Jacobson's The Self and the Object World

Edith Jacobson's *The Self and the Object World* (1964) portrays the development of identity, as formulated in terms of psychoanalytic genetic psychology, beginning with the earliest phases of ego development through latency, adolescence, and adulthood. Dr. Jacobson writes as one who has no superiors, and few if any peers, in her grasp of psychoanalytic theory, and the depth of clinical experience which is crystallized in this small book is manifested in the numerous points at which her concepts illuminate one's own experiences with patients. The book is, in fact, so masterfully and authoritatively written that the project of doing a more than merely laudatory review of it seems at first almost awesomely formidable.

Among the book's many other virtues, we find in it valuable—though at times offensively condescending—critiques of the work of Klein, Erikson, Lichtenstein, and others, and more appreciative acknowledgment of contributions to this subject by Freud, Greenacre, Benedek, and a considerable number of others.

First published in *International Journal of Psycho-Analysis*, 46:529-532 (1965).

As regards Jacobson's own contribution here, what I value most is her highlighting the essentially healthy nature of aggression, and the identity-building value of the separations which are necessitated by one's seeking adequate means for venting the aggression manifest in increasingly powerful and complexly differentiated ego capacities. All this I find a valuable counterbalance to my own emphasis, like that of Lichtenstein and others, upon the role of symbiosis in identity formation and maintenance. A few quotes will point up her orientation in this regard:

> ... [Lichtenstein] regards the symbiotic mother-child relationship as the beginning of human identity formation. I find this view acceptable, even though the child's separation from the mother and the resulting process of individuation seem at least as essential ... [p. 30].

> ... experiences of likeness are bound to arise from the child's close intimacy with his mother and, as Greenacre stresses, will be favored by the mutual affective identifications between mother and child. ... But what about the experiences of differences, which are a prerequisite for the development of identity feelings? [p. 60].

> ... the child, already at the age of about eight months, sometimes even earlier, begins to distinguish different objects: his mother from his father, from the nurse, from strangers, etc. The distinction between objects can probably proceed more rapidly and consistently than the distinction between self and objects, because perception of the external world is easier than self perception and, besides, because the child normally has less instinctual motivation for a fusion between different objects than for a re-merging with his mother. In fact, the child's insatiable instinctual appetites stimulate his ability to discriminate between persons who may offer him supplementary gratifications and those who bar his way to need fulfillment [p. 60].

> Passing through many frustrations, disappointments, failures, and corresponding hostile experiences of envy, rivalry and competition, the child eventually learns the difference between wishful and more or less realistic self and object images. Thus, not only the loving but also the hostile components of the infantile self- and object-directed strivings furnish the fuel that enables the child to develop his feeling of identity and the

testing of external and inner reality, and on this basis to build up his identifications and object relations [p. 61].

Expressive of this personal taste for separation, for cleavage, for differentiation, there is in her conceptual edifice, similarly, a heavy emphasis upon the making of *distinctions* between various theoretical constructs: between ego, self, and self-representations; between body-image and image of the mental self; between wishful self-images and realistic self-representations; between shame and inferiority feelings on the one hand and guilt feelings on the other hand; and, always, between objective identity formation and the corresponding subjective experience of it. This critique is typical:

> . . . Melanie Klein fails to distinguish the constitution of self and object representations, and of object relations and ego identifications, from superego formation [p. 94].

Although—as we can see—these differentiations become at times cumbersome, for the most part they greatly further conceptual clarity, and in aggregate form one of the book's strongest features.

Jacobson's superb portrayal of the formation and functioning of the superego would, even if taken alone, ensure this book's destiny as a classic. Particularly illuminating are her description of superego formation as comprising an achievement of the ego, her description of how the superego helps to regulate and maintain self-esteem, and—as indicated in the following passage—her emphasis upon the liberating effect of the establishment of the superego:

> . . . Toward the end of this phase [i.e., the oedipal period, there is established] . . . a new functional system, the superego, which gives all developmental processes an enormous impetus. Large amounts of psychic energy can now be liberated and utilized for aim-inhibited pursuits. From then on, the development of (nonsexual) physical activities, of social, intellectual, and cultural interests can make rapid progress [p. 89].

Among the many other strong features of her book are a beautiful description of the role of identifications in identity formation, an equally beautiful description of the role of bowel training and reaction formation in early personality development, and a highly original exposition of the self-critical ego functions. The last quarter of the book, devoted to puberty and adolescence, is so perceptively sympathetic in its portrayal of the typical conflicts of this phase of life that even lay readers can find much of value in it, for help in their relations with teenage children (I myself have two). In fact, I found this portion of the book helpful in a fuller understanding of the conflicts of my own adolescence. The following passage is typical of the powerful, trenchant, nontechnical style of much of this final section of the book:

> . . . the adolescent . . . feels himself in the grip of overwhelming instinctual impulses, which he must soon learn to master, since before long he will have to make the most important decisions of his life: vocational choice, which will determine his work and his future economic and social situation, and the choice of a love object—ultimately of a marital partner [p. 162].

But here I must veer over to my more critical comments about this book, for the above passage stands in such refreshing contrast, in its writing style, to the great bulk of the book. My first-formulated dissatisfaction with this work had to do with the extent to which Jacobson's many creative insights are expressed through a Procrustean bed of technical jargon, of which the following passage is a fair sample:

> . . . During adolescence these [early identity] conflicts are apt to become remobilized and greatly intensified. They will then disturb the restructuring of ego and superego, and prevent the final reconciliation between the opposing trends of the superego and the id. Subsequently this will interfere not only with the final establishment of a mature ego ideal, of stable ego goals, and of autonomous ego and superego functions, but also with the adult's further development of sound selective personal and group relations and identifications [pp. 204-205].

Secondly, it gradually grows upon the reader that there seems to be nothing which leaves the author mystified, as though her theories encompassed everything, accounted for everything, and left no matters for contention, for debate, and, above all, for further investigation. For example, I wonder how she can say that there is "no doubt" concerning so inherently unprovable an assumption as this:

> ... there is no doubt that long before the infant becomes aware of the mother as a person and of his own self, engrams are laid down of experiences which reflect his responses to maternal care in the realm of his entire mental and body self [pp. 34-35].

And when she says with absolute finality that:

> ... sexual renunciation concerning the incestuous love object is enforced with absolute finality which by far surpasses the restrictions imposed on the child's pregenital drive components [p. 120].

I fail to suppress a small but nagging question, "*Is* it, really?" I recall a hebephrenic woman with whom I worked for more than 11 years, who was able to express genital interest toward me, as a father-figure in the transference relationship, some several years before she was able to express her more deeply repressed pregenital (breast-oriented) interest in me as a mother-figure.

Thus I came to feel that Jacobson's views are not only too technically structured, but are also expressed with too much finality, too much "authority," and to this extent the reader is left with a kind of sterile-finality feeling of there being nothing left to say.

But wait. Not all has been packaged; the final nail has not yet been driven through the coffin-lid; mystery still beckons. I wish to note, now, some of the major respects in which this book falls short.

It does not at all adequately convey how ceaselessly conflictual, how ambivalent, human beings are concerning the development of an identity—and concerning, as well, the development of object relations: in short, concerning the development of any psychological structures and the exercise of psychological processes which are dependent upon structures. The subjective psychological disadvantages inherent in the acquisition and maintenance of an identity are scarcely weighed at all in the balance by Jacobson, who presents

identity as something inherently desirable and, by implication, to be
striven for unambivalently:

> I ... understand by identity formation a process that builds
> up the ability to preserve the whole psychic organization—
> despite its growing structuralization, differentiation, and
> complexity—as a highly individualized but coherent entity
> which has direction and continuity at any stage of human de-
> velopment [p. 27].

How could anyone in his right mind not strive wholeheartedly
for something so worthy? But many of our patients are not in their
right minds and, if we look more closely into this matter, we see
that the price one pays for identity formation and maintenance is
such as to give anyone continual food for thought. Jacobson underestimates, above all, man's valuing of symbiotic relatedness. It is as
though she is determined not to look back, almost as though she
dare not look back, but fixes her view firmly on "further structuralization and differentiation," as in the following typical passage:

> ... While thus propelling the ego toward further struc-
> turalization and differentiation, the set of standards offered by
> the superego, if uniform and consistent, concomitantly stimu-
> lates the process of organization to which I pointed previously
> [p. 139].

*I see
it as an
impinging
stimulus
for different.*

She greatly underestimates the role of symbiosis, ceaselessly returned to more or less overtly, and ever-present at a subterranean
level in human relatedness. Similarly, instead of her seeing identity
to possess many and constantly changing faces, and identity formation to be going on throughout life, she describes all these as
though in some developmental era they were finally achieved, with
a relatively static structure existing thereafter:

*implications
of 'neurotic'
functioning.*

> ... human beings achieve full physical and mental maturity,
> ego and superego autonomy, instinctual and emotional mastery
> and freedom only after adolescence [p. 31].

> ... the last phase in the solution of the oedipal conflicts
> must also bring about a final liberation from the symbiotic
> bonds with the family [p. 171].

It seems to me that in the final six and a half pages of her book, beginning with the statement, "I shall conclude my comments with a few brief examples which demonstrate such psychotic pathology," the author herself unconsciously reveals her own rebellion against all the so-precise, imposed structure which her book has been delineating, for here, in her descriptions of psychotic cases in which the identity foundations have been blown into chaos, she shares the reader's relish in these as a kind of dessert which steals the show.

Probably the greatest reason why we tend to rebel against our developing individual identity is because we feel it to have come between, and to be coming increasingly between, ourself and the mother with whom we once shared a world-embracing oneness. I believe that the more successfully the infant and young child internalizes, as the foundation of his personal identity, a symbiotic relationship with a predominantly loving mother, the more accessible is his symbiotic level of existence, in all its infinite richness, to the more structured aspects of his identity that develop—develop not primarily as imposed restraints upon him, but as structures that facilitate the release of his energies and capacities in creative relatedness with the outer world.

But I find evidence in Jacobson's book that she has a predominantly frightened view of symbiotic relatedness, and I think perhaps I see why she has such a view. In a discussion during which she has been emphasizing the valuable role of aggression in man's relations to his *Umwelt* and in the process of identity formation, she goes on to speak of

> ... the struggle for survival, for which man and animal must be equipped. In fact, living organisms not only need, feed, and gratify each other; they may also fight each other to the point of extinction of the species. This double-faced ... *Umwelt* cannot be compared to the relationship of an organ to a whole organism *or to the truly symbiotic mother-infant relationship, which normally do not involve a destructive struggle* [p. 31; italics mine].

I feel that even a "truly" symbiotic mother-infant relationship contains at least the seeds of the "destructiveness" which—I fully agree with Jacobson—is so necessary in one's assertive behavior toward the outer world. I would share her apparent fear of symbiosis, too, if I saw it to be at heart devoid of such seeds of "destructiveness," for without these there could indeed be no liberation from exclusively symbiotic functioning.

I see her essentially fearful attitude toward symbiosis in this passage, too:

> In general, maternal attitudes will impose themselves more easily and drastically on the total ego during the first childhood years. The more prolonged the child's dependency situation, and the deeper and more powerful the imprint of the mother's attitudes on the preoedipal forerunners of superego and ego ideal, the more will the parental influences, instead of gradually and selectively modifying the ego, interfere with, arrest, or even smother its autonomous development. They will invade, spread out, and pervade the whole personality and fixate it on a preoedipal level [p. 212].

This view, however commendably dramatic, showing the mother in the role of a mortician filling the helplessly dependent child with a kind of embalming fluid, does justice neither to the child's active part in perpetuating this pathological, but to him undoubtedly gratifying, symbiotic relationship; nor to the mother's essential insecurity, and her essentially unmalevolent clinging to a child whom she genuinely finds indispensable to her; nor, therefore, to the lovingly devoted sacrifice of individuality which the child's active part in all this is expressing. It is, I believe, a natural consequence of Jacobson's putting firmly behind her—as evidenced in her above-described theoretical orientation—any urge toward symbiotic relatedness, that her monograph grossly underestimates the *mutuality*, between parent and child, of dependency and of identificational strivings. That is, she scarcely mentions the power, and essentially healthy nature, of the parent's dependency upon the child, and of the child's contribution to the parent's identity formation.

The realm of the nonhuman—whether objectively nonhuman or, no less importantly, subjectively nonhuman—in ego development is given by Jacobson only the scanty acknowledgment which is found, if at all, in the usual exposition of psychoanalytic ego psychology. This is the only attention she pays to it, in her whole book:

> As the child enters his second year of life, changes in the nature of his relations to the object world set in, which . . . presuppose the ability to distinguish single physical and mental features of the love objects, to compare and perceive differences between objects—*animate and inanimate*—as well as between the objects and the self [p. 49; italics mine].

By contrast, I have found that the theme that expresses the deepest and most comprehensive meaning of any human being's identity struggle—of, in fact, his whole psychological life—consists in his effort to demarcate himself as a single, living, human entity over against an outer world which is, in by far its vastest part, objectively nonhuman; to free himself from internal components which are subjectively nonhuman and sensed, further, as hostile to the self which is struggling to become established as warmly human; to maintain, and further develop, meaningful relatedness with those also-vast areas of the objectively nonhuman world which can contribute affirmatively to his own internal human world—can "help" him, through his identifying with these (and here I have in mind such nonhuman "things" as a beautiful tree, a majestic landscape or seascape or starscape, a puppy), to find consolation, strength, absorption-in-life, and above all a meaning in existence through the knowing that he is at once uniquely individual and indissolubly part of the universe.

Is this the same symbiotic wish further projected onto nonhuman wld.

or ?

4

Concerning the Development
of an Identity

In the course of doing a review (Searles, 1965b) of Jacobson's (1964) monograph concerning identity development I have had occasion to formulate the theoretical considerations and bring together the clinical data to be presented here. My review, while taking note of much that I found masterfully instructive in her monograph, pointed out her undervaluing of the role of symbiosis in identity development and maintenance, her failure to see the significance for man's identity formation of his relationship with his nonhuman environment, and her underestimation of the mutuality of parent-child dependency—dependency in regard to, among other matters, the formation of their respective identities. I shall take the opportunity here to flesh out those briefly made points and to describe other aspects of identity not touched upon by Jacobson—in particular, to discuss the relationship between murderousness and identity formation and to describe the functioning of a healthy sense of identity as comprising one's most reliable organ for perceiving the world.

First published in *Psychoanalytic Review*, 53:507-530 (Winter 1966-1967).

45

AMBIVALENCE CONCERNING IDENTITY; THE ROLE OF THE
NONHUMAN ENVIRONMENT IN IDENTITY FORMATION; HEALTHY
IDENTITY SEEN AS BASED IN AND EXPRESSIVE OF INTERNALIZED
MOTHER-INFANT SYMBIOSIS

As I stated in my review, Jacobson's monograph does not portray "how ceaselessly conflictual, how ambivalent, human beings are
concerning the development of an identity—and concerning, as
well, the development of object relations; in short, concerning the
development of any psychological structures and the exercise of
psychological processes which are dependent upon structures." In
this regard her emphasis is like that of Erikson (1950, 1958, 1959),
whose illuminating and influential writings have highlighted the
young person's anxious struggle against identity diffusion.

But we should not forget Fromm's similarly valuable stressing,
in his *Escape from Freedom* (1941) and other writings, of our universal urge to yield up our individual identity and flee into, for example, totalitarian political ways of relating ourselves to our fellow
men, because we find so heavy the demands inherent in individual
freedom. In my monograph on the nonhuman environment (1960),
I pointed out that we all struggle against deep urges to yield up
our identities as individual human beings and to regress to oneness
with our nonhuman environment as a means of escaping from such
universal ingredients of human living as anxiety concerning death,
sexual conflicts, loneliness, helplessness, feelings of the instability of
our identities, and superego pressures which torment us, toward
the ever-receding goal of omnipotence. As I indicated in my review
(1965b), the theme that, in my personal and clinical experience,

> . . . expresses the deepest and most comprehensive meaning
> of any human being's identity struggle—of, in fact, his whole
> psychological life—consists in his effort to demarcate himself as
> a single, living, human entity over against an outer world which
> is, in by far its vastest part, objectively nonhuman; to free him-
> self from internal components which are subjectively nonhu-
> man and sensed, further, as hostile to the self which is struggling
> to become established as warmly human; to maintain, and fur-
> ther develop, meaningful relatedness with those also-vast areas

gaining ident. destroys symbiosis – Infant needs to feel his 'leaving' isn't cause of retaliation or worse (ie. death)

of the objectively nonhuman world which can contribute affirmatively to his own internal human world—can "help" him, through his identifying with these (and here I have in mind such nonhuman "things" as a beautiful tree, a majestic landscape or seascape or starscape, a puppy), to find consolation, strength, absorption-in-life and, above all, a meaning in existence through the knowing that he is at once uniquely individual and indissolubly part of the universe.

In another paper (1963a), I described the psychotic patient's use of the mirror as expressive not merely of his attempt to cling to his identity, as suggested by Elkisch (1957) in her paper concerning such phenomena, but as expressive, rather, of ambivalent desires both to cling to *and to lose* (through externalization upon the mirror) his identity.

yes — AS essence of pre - differentiation ie. volcan

In my experience, identity crystallization is reacted to by patients, whether psychotic or neurotic, as being as great a threat as the identity diffusion so valuably described and emphasized by Erikson. One hebephrenic woman, who in our first session expressed her intense scorn for words, came to say despairingly much later on, "We gotta find words for the wind." This statement gave me a sense of how hopeless it was, from her view, to express herself—an immensely powerful self, as I came well to know during nearly 12 years of work with her—through so constrictingly structured a medium as words. We need to realize that just because a person's identity is largely founded, as was hers, upon identifications with nonverbal, nonhuman things (such as the wind, trees, horses, fields of grain, and so on) does not mean that such an identity is weak. Some of the strongest persons I have known have been chronically schizophrenic patients whose identity was changeable, elusive, and *seemingly* poignantly evanescent. So frequently that which we term a precarious identity is actually a strong one which tenaciously refuses to be captured.

new ☆ my paper on neurosis

☆ Ident. + Struct. & differed Entities

Such patients are convinced that in analysis one is endeavoring primarily to congeal their identity within some stereotyped mold. One deeply and chronically confused woman, who for years was convinced that I was trying to rob her of her individuality, came to confide to me that "I hang you on a cross whenever you try to straighten me out." This I understood to mean that she would crucify me on a cross—she herself very often suffered crucifixion in her delusional experience—consisting of the intense ambivalence she engendered in me whenever I endeavored to help her to resolve her incredibly severe identify diffusion. On another occasion she explained that to be "straightened out"—which she thought my goal for her—meant to be locked in a vault and stripped of all that she valued in herself.

I have seen hebephrenic patients who evidently were filled with a sea of grief so massive, by contrast to their tenuous sense of identity, that they could not afford the luxury of grieving, lest it wash away all vestige of any subjective identity structure. Looked at another way, this highlights one "disadvantage" of having any identity, and sooner or later the grief, refusing to be contained any longer, bursts this identity shell, exploding sometimes in the form of tears and often in the form of assaultive behavior, a distorted expression of the fierce grief which has been so long pent up.

As I stated in my review (1965b), "Probably the greatest reason why we tend to rebel against our developing individual identity is because we feel it to have come between, and to be coming increasingly between, ourself and the mother with whom we once shared a world-embracing oneness." One of my most deeply ill hebephrenic patients gave me to sense, through data too long to reproduce here, that probably the very young child is so reluctant to advance at all beyond the symbiotic state because there is so very little of any external world—any world external to the symbiosis with the mother—*there* to relate to, at first. For this particular patient, it was as though the relinquishment of the symbiosis with me meant her having to cling to, as a substitute, no longer a solid symbiotic world but only something as insubstantial as, say, the minute amounts of matter in interstellar space. It would seem that the mother of this patient must have been unable, during the girl's childhood, to offer her a sufficiency of genuine individuality, on the mother's own part, with which to identify. My observations of this mother during several interviews over the years of my work with her daughter strongly support such a surmise. Later in this paper I shall discuss briefly the crucial role in identity formation of the child's identifying with the parent's courage to be an individual.

In many patients it is apparent that the achievement and acceptance of an individual identity are reacted to as tantamount to ego fragmentation and decimation, equivalent to a change from a symbiotic identification with mother to a far more constrictive identification with one of her introjects. By taking into account the ego-fragmented internal state of such mothers, one can better understand the resistance of such patients to accepting, for example, any one career identity, resistance I used to think representative simply of a reluctance to relinquish their infantile omnipotence. One patient, struggling to find a career, expressed repeatedly his determination to keep "the big picture" in view. The relationships, or in the more pathological instances the lack of relationships, among the mother's various ego fragments (i.e., introjects) are highly relevant. The child may well be deeply ambivalent about identity structuralization if the advancement beyond a symbiotic identity with the mother means identifying with one of her introjects which either possesses no discernible and reliable relationship to the remainder of her overall ego constellation, or is in deadly conflict with various of the other introjects in that constellation.

On the other hand, one sees patients who, to keep from being swallowed up in a chaotic symbiotic relatedness with the less differentiated, larger area of the parent's personality, cling compulsively to a defensive ego identity founded upon identification with some part-aspect of either mother or father. But if this person is to achieve in the course of analysis a much deeper and larger identity, the maelstrom which comprises both the vast bulk of the mother's "insides" and his own true potential self must, despite his fear of the "craziness" of regressive ego disorganization, be braved and explored.

The very fact of one's preoccupation with the uniqueness of one's own identity is likely to be serving as a defense against one's unconscious fear of recognizing that human existence is lived largely at a symbiotic level of relatedness. One so preoccupied with preserving his so-precious identity possesses, in truth, a fragile one, fragile primarily because of his unconscious wish to be free of it. Such a person might well be ambivalent about the possession of an identity which is alien to, rather than firmly grounded in and expressive of, symbiotic relatedness; for such a fragile and essentially defensive identity stands between him and his potentially limitless, symbiosis-based self.

The healthy individual, by contrast, subjectively functions in terms of his unique identity only a relatively small proportion of the time, or at least only to a relatively small degree. It is as if his total identity were an iceberg (as in Breuer's [1893-1895] metaphor to illustrate the relative power of conscious versus unconscious realms) in which by far the greater, symbiotic portion is under the surface, subliminal, in terms of awareness of identity. It may well be that the predominance of personality functioning, even in healthy adult persons, is subjectively undifferentiated, at an unconscious level at least, from the great inanimate realm of the environment—that only in comparatively minor part do we function as subjectively animate beings; that we function in even smaller degree as animate *human* beings; and that we function to a still lesser degree—or, perhaps, still less frequently—as predominantly *uniquely* living human beings. Probably, in waking life we function all the time on all levels simultaneously, in varying degrees; but it is comparatively seldom that the healthy adult person, who is unafraid of simply *existing* in a predominantly symbiotic relatedness with the totality of the "outside world," need be highly conscious of himself as a uniquely human being.

THE MUTUALITY OF PARENT-CHILD DEPENDENCY (OR, IN THE TRANSFERENCE, ANALYST-PATIENT DEPENDENCY) IN IDENTITY FORMATION

It is, I believe, a natural consequence of Jacobson's unawareness, as described in my previously published review (1965b), of the power of the adult's unconscious urge toward symbiotic relatedness, that her monograph "grossly underestimates the mutuality, between parent and child, of dependency and of identificational strivings. That is, she scarcely mentions the power and essentially healthy nature of the parent's dependency upon the child and of the child's contribution to the parent's identity formation."

In another paper (1959c), I pointed out that the schizophrenic patient's advancing identity formation, from an initial ego fragmentation (and attendant identity diffusion) to an increasingly integrated, coherent, single, and continuous identity, is a process that involves a very real sense of loss not only for the patient but also for the analyst who is so deeply involved in the treatment relationship with him. A few months ago I felt this loss with poignant intensity following a mere half-hour teaching interview with an acutely schizophrenic 19-year-old girl whom I had never seen before. To me, the most striking aspect of the interview was the great extent—unprecedented in my memory—to which I felt free to let my own fantasies roam and be verbally expressed to her. She seemed to have a great deal of grief in her and a great deal of cold hatred also; but particularly notable was her reporting, in a playful fashion, hallucinatory material about things coming out of her ears, about animals and spiders in the room, and so on. I felt most unusually free to join in with her and to describe my own upwelling fantasies to her. After the interview was over I was filled with a feeling I could not name.

My first thought was that perhaps I was reacting simply to the tragedy of this young person's being so grievously ill, so deeply psychotic. But that did not serve to "explain" the feeling, nor did my next thought—that perhaps I was filled with shame at having proved so contemptibly incapable of restoring her to the world of reality. But then I felt that what I was suffering from more than anything else was my own loss of her—for I assumed that, in the nature of the situation, I would never see her again. And at a still deeper level what I felt was that, for all practical purposes, in losing her I had lost a part of myself: I felt that never again—since it had happened but this once in all the remembered years—would I have an opportunity to function, with another human being, with such unfettered access to my own fantasy life.

the reality of its ever present existence
new phantasies → reality / new realizations
perceptions / thinking etc →

And I felt, still further, that it is most essential for us as analysts not to endeavor to hide from our patient such feelings of personal loss. My belief is that any human being, whether healthy young child or adult patient, can progress from one developmental phase to the next only if he finds that the sense of loss that this change, this step in maturational "progress," entails is shared by the parent or analyst. Thus I think of an analyst as not simply helping a patient to progress through various developmental stages, but as going through himself, in a very real sense, these developmental stages with the patient, sharing with the latter the feelings not only of fulfillment but of loss which have to be faced and integrated in order for the next stage of maturation and of interpersonal relatedness to be established. In a paper concerning schizophrenic communication (1961b), I described, for example, the sense of loss felt by both patient and analyst when, after many months of predominantly nonverbal relatedness, they become able to communicate with one another, increasingly reliably, in words—leaving behind their mutually cherished, more predominantly symbiotic, nonverbal relatedness. I recommend highly the writings of Lichtenstein (1961, 1963, 1964), who does so much more justice than does Jacobson to the role of symbiosis in identity formation.

Parental dependency is dismissed by Jacobson (1964) in this startlingly naïve, folksy comment:

> ...the initial symbiosis between mother and infant...is a situation which yields only gradually to a position of autonomy and mutual independence, and which is during or after adolescence rather reluctantly relinquished by both parents and child! [p. 32].

And she adds the following footnote: "Frequently parents, especially mothers, develop depressive states when all their children have left the home."

The essentially threatened, cautious nature of her scanty acknowledgment of the existence of parental identifications with the child is well shown in this passage:

> ...The parental identifications with the child are of a different order. Born of memories of the infantile past, they are

limited to passing and changing fantasy and feeling identifications only, which serve the empathic understanding of the child and must be kept in bounds so as not to undermine the parental position [p. 57].

My own writings have repeatedly emphasized the essentially healthy, "permissible" aspect of the parent's (= analyst's) dependency upon the child (= patient), and the mutuality of growth in their respective identities over the course of childhood or of treatment. For instance, I pointed out that we identify with our patients not only in terms of the so-often-emphasized transitory identifications which arise from an empathic sensing of the patient's conflicts and which are of essentially communicative value only in furtherance of the patient's treatment, but also "we identify with the healthier elements in our patients, in a fashion which entails enduring, constructive additions to our own personality" (Searles, 1958a).

I continue to be impressed with the intensity of the felt taboo, for me at least, upon the analyst's identifying deeply with his patient in this fashion. For some years I have been aware that one or another of my patients, when immersed in a phase of healthily identifying with me, will watch my face with absorbed wonderment and adoration, and only more recently have I realized that on occasion I watch the patient's face with no less deep and pleasureful and enriching an identificational immersion. One tends to shy away from such experiences as evidence of a forbidden and frightening "being in love with" the patient. By the same token, we tend to label a father's identificational need of this sort, turned toward a growing son who has become in some important regards more mature than himself, as indicative basically of homosexual interest on the father's part. While such parental hunger-to-identify may represent an unconscious defense in the parent against the child's frighteningly devouring efforts to identify with him, we need to realize that the genuine identificational need may be, not infrequently, greater in the parent (or analyst) than in the child (or patient).

Lichtenstein (1961) describes the foundation of identity development as consisting in the mother's imprinting an identity upon the infant and young child. But particularly in those instances in which the parent's identity is not well integrated, it may be a moot question as to who is going to imprint an identity upon whom, and their relatedness may persist in a predominantly symbiotic form overlong, pending the resolution of this issue. In retrospect, what I have described as a mutual parent-child struggle to drive one another crazy, manifested in the evolution of the schizophrenic patient's transference relationship with the analyst (Searles, 1959a), may well involve the issue of who is going to imprint his identity upon the other, with—from the viewpoint of each participant— one's own identity sensed as sanity and the other's identity sensed as craziness. Stierlin's (1959) paper, "The Adaptation to the 'Stronger' Person's Reality," is of interest in this connection.

It must be deeply significant to the child's developing self-esteem as to what effect, if any, he feels he has upon the identity of each of his parents during the course of his growing up. This particular aspect of the whole matter of identity tends to strike one as a new thought, and a far from entirely comfortable one. One wonders, for example, how much one contributed, out of some unconscious malevolence, to an obviously increasing masculinization in one's mother and a steadily worsening invalidism in one's father, who became ridden with a series of psychosomatic illnesses over the years of one's childhood, adolescence, and young manhood. It must be hard for many children not to think—if they permit such thoughts to occur to them—that they are having a predominantly negative effect upon their parents' identity development, particularly in those frequent instances in which the parents blame the children for the very fact of the parents' own aging: "You'll be the death of me yet," in the words of the reproachful aging mother or father.

On the other hand, I have seen many patients, at the healthier end of the scale, who clearly had had a largely supportive, growth-fostering effect upon their parents' identities, though I think it comparatively rare for parents to acknowledge at all openly that the child is making, or even is interested in—let alone wholeheartedly

Development of an Identity

3

devoted to—making, such a contribution. And I have seen some patients who initially appeared essentially schizophrenic but who proved, on the basis of criteria which I cannot take space to detail here, to be persons of relatively intact ego structure. Their "schizophrenia" was what might be termed an identification schizophrenia, traceable to the impact of years of coping with the heavy identificational needs of, say, a much more deeply schizophrenic father whom the child was unable to cure, but in whose deeply distorted identity the child was able himself to avoid becoming hopelessly enmeshed.

One probably cannot clearly distinguish between pathological instances of a markedly ill parent's striving to identify with a child who is not really perceived as a separate person but is reacted to, rather, as the embodiment of the parent's hopelessly unattainable ego ideal and, on the other hand, healthy instances of a relatively mature parent's identifying with the realistic strengths of a child who is truly perceived and accepted as a flesh-and-blood young human being with both strengths and weaknesses. In supervisory relationships, by way of analogy, I sometimes find that I try to get the supervisee to live up to my own ego-ideal aspirations, in the hope that if I can help one after another supervisee to practice what I preach, then these supervisees will be tangible persons with whom I can identify, so that, hopefully, I may some day have the courage and skill, myself, to do with patients what (so I tell them from my vast experience) they "obviously" should set about doing. My point is that sometimes all this works successfully for both the supervisee and me as well as for the patient, and sometimes it does not; there is a continuum between clearly pathological and clearly healthy processes here.

I find that my views about the mutuality of child-parent dependency are in all respects coincident with, or elaborative upon, the beautifully expressed insights of Benedek (1959), who says, for example:

> . . . In the mother, through introjection of good-thriving-infant = good-mother-self, the mother achieves a new integration in her personality [p. 393].

...not only corresponding with and as a result of the physiologic symbiosis of pregnancy and the oral phase of development, but in each "critical period" the child revives in the parent his related developmental conflicts. This brings about either pathologic manifestations in the parent, or by resolution of the conflict it achieves a new level of integration in the parent [p. 397].

But I do feel that where Benedek tends to stop with seeing the child as confirming the parent *as parent* and with seeing the parent as finding his or her own outgrown-*child*-self again in the child, I tend more literally to see the child as often serving as parent to the parent—in terms of the parent's not only reacting to the daughter, for instance, as being a transference-mother, but also in reality finding in the daughter personality traits and areas more mature than the parent's own, in relation to which, by identification, the parent realistically can develop an increasingly mature own identity. Moreover, I am not aware that Benedek has attempted to spell out, as my clinical experience has required me to do, the implications of these concepts for the understanding of the psychoanalytic relationship.

For several years I have been working with a man whose ego functioning and sense of identity are deeply fragmented. Early in his treatment it became evident that his mother, who died several years prior to my becoming his therapist, had been a person whose sense of identity was comparably chaotic, and that he had felt, throughout his upbringing from about age eight onward, that he was the parent and she the child. In his transference relationship he has reacted to me predominantly as being his crazy child-mother, whose own sense of identity is chaotic and almost constantly shifting and who is deeply but deniedly dependent upon him for the development of a reliable and continuous sense of identity. In the earlier years of his treatment I had been aware that unconscious guilt about his having been unable to cure his mother was one of the main sources of psychopathology which needed to come into his awareness and to be worked through. Such guilt is an important factor in the work with any patient, psychotic or neurotic, whose parents have suffered from grievous and unresolved emotional illness, and seems to be, by the way, one of the important factors motivating persons to become psychiatrists.

But the work with this man has shown me that successful treatment must involve, in this regard, not simply his becoming free from irrational and unconscious guilt about having *failed to cure* his mother. It must involve our actually *curing* her, in a sense—in the sense of his achieving, with my help and through the medium of his transference relationship to me as being his mother, an internalized *image of* her as being, however many-sided in her identity, essentially whole and a fit keystone, therefore, for his own sense of identity. It is not too much to say that in the work with such a patient the whole treatment consists in an attempt to help the (internalized) parent to achieve a whole, integrated identity.

This effort is for both participants a deeply conflictual one. My patient, for example, let me know on one recent occasion, during one of our more difficult sessions, that with the immensely confusing and emotionally upsetting torrent of his communications he was trying to—as he phrased it—"turn" my "cerebral" cortex into "pulled-apart wood pulp" and to "disperse" my "ego." My assumption is that as a child he had tried ambivalently to help his mother to become a whole and separate individual, but also recurrently to drive her crazy again—to disperse again her precariously established ego—in order to keep her available for the still-so-necessary symbiotic relatedness.

For my part I have developed a variety of largely unconscious techniques, comparable to his own in their diabolical nature, for attempting to ensure that he will not become integrated too rapidly—more rapidly, that is, than I can bear the loss of him. My employment of some of these individuation-delaying techniques has been discovered, retrospectively, on my own; others have been pointed out to me by colleagues with whom I have discussed this treatment and still others have been revealed by playbacks of recordings of the treatment sessions. On rare occasions the patient, for all his confusion, has been able to confront me with the treatment-undoing nature of a response I have just made. These techniques, in sum, are essentially those detailed in my paper, "The Effort to Drive the Other Person Crazy—An Element in the Aetiology and Psychotherapy of Schizophrenia" (1959a).

THE CHILD'S ACCEPTING AND IDENTIFYING WITH THE PARENT'S INDIVIDUALITY

To Jacobson's portrayal of the processes involved in the establishment of identity I would add the processes of the developing child's identification with the parent's individuality—or perhaps better described, his identification with the parent's courage to be an individual—and at the same time his acceptance of the fact that each of the parents has an individuality, an identity, which he cannot otherwise possess (except through identification).

Jacobson writes illuminatingly of "special identifications, the superego identifications" (p. 111), which, as the phrase implies, consist in identifications with the parental superegos. I suggest that analogously the core of the individual identity that develops in the child who is emerging from the mother-infant symbiosis consists in his identification with the mother-as-an-individual.

As regards clinical experiences, I found it significant when a borderline schizophrenic woman, whose individual identity is now emerging after several years of treatment, recently expressed, in the same session, both admiration for her mother's "different" quality—her special love for and appreciation of music and other artistic things—and keen pleasure in having come to care for her home in her *own* special way, to tell bedtime stories to her young son in her *own* way, and so on.

But it should be seen that one of the major resistances to identity development consists in one's unwillingness to let the mother have her own special identity. Time after time I have seen how ragefully unwilling patients are to let me have my own separate and unmanageable aliveness. Typically, the patient who is convinced that the analyst is trying to force him into an individuality-less mold is projecting upon the analyst his (the patient's) own unconscious determination to require the mother-figure analyst to function, as one of my patients put it, as a kind of Coke machine exclusively and automatically dedicated to the gratification of the patient's needs. To become an individual himself, the child must accept the fact of the mother's unpossessable individuality; but his recognition that each of them is an individual puts him subjectively at the furthest remove from the symbiotic oneness with her that both of them so poignantly long to recapture. Jacobson's nearest approximation to what I am saying here is found in the following passage which, however stimulating, points up neither the significance of the parent's uniquely individual identity, nor the child's resistance to "granting" him or her that identity:

> ... probably the most incisive and difficult step is the gradual establishment of enduring new identifications with the parents as sexually active persons, who will ultimately grant him, too, the right to engage in sexual and other adult activities [p. 175].

In this regard I find in the resolution of the oedipal conflicts a significance for identity formation which Jacobson does not describe: the acceptance of the parents-in-intercourse marks an unprecedentedly deep integration of the young person's identifications with his father on the one hand and with his mother on the other hand. This landmark in identity development is seen in projected form, in the context of the developing transference relationship in analysis, in those rare but deeply significant instances when the patient reacts to the analyst as being both parents simultaneously, engaged in sexual intercourse with one another.

To go back a bit, now, to the matter of the child's identifying with the parent's individuality, we see how difficult it is for the child in the so-frequent instance when the parents' own individualities (individual identities) are poorly established. A few nights ago I was awakened by a neighboring couple who were arguing. As I lay there listening to them shouting at one another—each angry, adamant, tenacious—for a very long time, it dawned on me that they were struggling to demarcate the boundaries between one another, boundaries largely breached by symbiotic processes. It then occurred to me that one reason why the child feels torn apart in hearing his parents' arguing is that neither of the parents is functioning as a separate and well-defined entity. Thus the child may be affected even more deeply than if he were feeling torn apart by divergent loyalties to two well-defined individual parents: he feels unwhole through identification with the revealed incompleteness of each of his arguing parents. These parents, the internalized images of whom have formed the foundation of his own sense of identity, are revealed as unwhole, incomplete; the very building blocks of his own identity are revealed as fragmentary. His need for each of his parents to become whole—a need that springs from undifferentiated "selfish" and "altruistic" motives—now places him under pressure to somehow fill, himself, the incompleteness in their respective identities.

THE RELATIONSHIP BETWEEN MURDEROUSNESS AND IDENTITY FORMATION

The most devastating harm to identity formation is traceable to the intrusion of unmasterably intense murderousness into the mother-infant relationship before the infant has become able to distinguish between (a) himself and his mother as flesh-and-blood persons, and (b) internal *images* of each, as distinct from the actual persons. Jacobson only hints at this; for instance, in speaking of the era prior to the establishment of the superego, she says that ". . . at this early stage, love and identification can scarcely be differentiated" (p. 95).

In healthy development the mother and infant become aware of murderous feelings in manageable increments and the child's murderous feelings become one of his most powerful assets in the struggle for fashioning an identity, a weapon wielded in a workmanlike—ruthless, when necessary—way to psychologically dissect each parent, carve from him or her that which is valuable and make it his own and discard the rest, with recognition on both their parts, however unformulated, that this process is not actually destroying the parent as a person in outer reality.

But in many instances, most typically in schizophrenic patients, the reverse happens: identification processes and identity formation become the tools of murderousness (become modes for the acted-out expression of murderousness).[1]

Recently, during a teaching-demonstration interview with a hospitalized schizophrenic man who suffered from a loss of personal identity many times a day, I repeatedly felt that a sense of emotional communion became established between us, only to be destroyed by the acting out of murderous feelings on his part. For example, in the midst of a comment from me he suddenly looked away in an "erasing" fashion over at the one-way viewing mirror. I distinctly felt this to be correlated with the vicissitudes, which he verbalized, of his own now-present, now-gone sense of personal identity. It seemed that during our moments of emotional communion or symbiosis, so long as he could maintain an internal feeling-image of me, he could experience his usual sense of identity, but that his massive murderousness (other evidences of which I cannot detail here) would repeatedly supervene, wash away his internal image of me and with it his own sense of any identity.

I surmise that in the early development of such a patient the mother's murderousness toward the child is primarily due to the fact that his *structure*, his existence as a potentially developing individual structure, apart from her, threatens her identity—an identity as world-embracing, a defensively symbiotic identity. My surmise is, further, that she does not merely react (unconsciously) as though it automatically *happens* that his developing individuality will destroy her omnipotent, pathologically symbiotic identity, but rather as though he were bent upon becoming an individual basically for this malevolent purpose: *in order to* destroy her world-self. This latter surmise accords with my finding, in the treatment of one paranoid patient after another, that the paranoid person tends to feel not

---

[1] I surmise that the question of whether mother and infant can successfully integrate their murderous feelings toward one another—or, more adequately expressed, their ambivalent feelings toward one another—will hinge largely upon the question of whether the mother's identity is *divorced from and defensive against* symbiotic relatedness, or is instead firmly *based in* a healthy symbiotic relatedness with her own mother.

loss, but a sense of having been robbed. I postulate that the mother in question has such a paranoid orientation toward the child's individuation.

Looking at matters in this way has helped me to understand why one of my schizophrenic patients, a mother of three children, reacts to the so-innocent baby as being malevolent. The baby qualifies as the supreme threat to the mother's omnipotent identity because unlike other persons round about, he was once indeed part of her; therefore his significance cannot be so easily dismissed or ignored as that of other people in the world. *No, she part of her mother.*

Further thought suggests—and supportive transference data from my work with schizophrenic patients tend to confirm—that the mother reacts *ambivalently* to the individuality-acquiring infant: she does not merely react to him as posing a malevolent threat to her cherished omnipotent identity; she also reacts to him as failing to *save her from* the omnipotence-based world-identity in which she is drowning. One reason why he fails her is that she feels it so impermissible—as does, evidently, Jacobson—for a mother seriously and deeply to identify with a growing child. Another reason why he fails her is that from his view she so fiercely opposes his developing individuality that he fails to see her unconscious, unacknowledged need to join him in this individuation process—*her* need to grow up, too. *— only to 'symbiose' (ie. Louise & her kids & her guilt-ki her mom?)*

The fragility of these mothers, in face of any indication of murderous feelings on the part of the child, is worthy of note. A healthy mother, who has not had to repress intensely conflictual feelings within herself, can cope with the intense interpersonal conflict that is an inevitable part of any child's upbringing. But the mother who has had to defend herself against the awareness of internal conflict through the maintenance of a defensively symbiotic, omnipotent identity is intensely threatened by any evidence of conflict between herself and the child who is felt to be so much at one with her. In any single instance, the sheer fact that her child feels inimical to her threatens to rob the mother of her symbiotic (i.e., "conflict-free") identity. It is as if God would no longer be God, were the hand of a single man to be raised against Him. In still other terms, her child's murderousness is equivalent, for her (because the boundaries between her and him are so incomplete), to her own long-repressed murderousness, so terrifying to her.

One begins to sense, here, how secondary the whole matter of fear of murderousness is, among schizophrenic patients, to the matter of identity formation and maintenance. In an earlier paper (1962a), I described my sense of momentous discovery at the analogous realization that the communications of a certain patient of mine could now be best understood, not in the frame of reference of increasingly intense homicidal violence, but in terms of a struggle to become liberated from concretistic thought.

The young child who, for whatever reason, lives in an atmosphere permeated by a high degree of separation anxiety, tends to feel that his identifying with the now-here, now-gone parent has killed the latter. In such instances the parent typically experiences the child's striving-to-identify, to merge with or enter into the parent, as expressive of an intention actually to devour, erase, or—so some mothers and fathers evidently sense it—to rape the parent. The parent then suddenly withdraws, psychologically—tantamount, for the child as yet unable to distinguish between image and actual object, to the physical disappearance of the parent. Further, the parent is of course similarly frightened of her or his own unfulfilled, repressed identificatory needs, sensing these as horrifying desires to devour or otherwise do physical violence to the child. On the other hand, and equally threatening, individuation from one another is sensed by both parent and child as equivalent to annihilation through loss of large and vital parts of the physical self.

These difficulties are seen as truly formidable when one realizes that the parent is indeed acting out her or his own repressed murderousness, specifically by mutilating, dismembering, starving, and otherwise harming the child's tentatively developing identity. In transference relationships we find many instances where, analogously, the analyst acts out his repressed murderousness by unwittingly cutting off the patient's efforts to identify with him, while bitterly resenting at a conscious level the fact of the patient's continuing refusal to do so; and the patient is expressing his own murderousness by indeed refusing, in the main, to become well—to identify with the healthy aspects of the analyst-mother. Sometimes these difficulties arise from what one is tempted to call genuine misunderstandings: the patient whose parent has shied anxiously away from his strivings-to-identify has grown to assume that these are essentially hostile. Thus he expresses his identificatory needs toward the analyst in a heavily disguised, rather than openly needful, way—for example, in a derisive, taunting, depreciatory fashion. This tends to humiliate the analyst and render him self-conscious about possessing the very trait the patient disguisedly admires. Affronted, the analyst then psychologically withdraws from or attacks the patient, thus severing the identificatory bridge the latter is trying to construct across the gulf between them.

One borderline schizophrenic man revealed through dreams and free associations that at an unconscious level he was reacting in a paranoid way to his former selves, perceiving these as hostile persecutors. Much evidence indicated that he was unconsciously defending himself against a grief-laden realization that the experiences these personified were precious and were now irretrievably gone. An overtly and chronically paranoid woman experienced consciously not only her own former selves, but also the former selves of fellow patients who had since changed (progressed, in psychoanalytic terms), as being actual persons who were now unaccountably no longer here, and for whose destruction she would—so she anxiously and uneasily felt—be held responsible.

In my work with this paranoid woman, it came to me as a recurrently memorable realization when I saw, time and again, that what I had been regarding as basically murderous feelings in her (expressed by her repeatedly, forcefully, and diversely misidentifying me in a way I found deeply disturbing to my own identity) represented, instead, a healthy striving on her part to help me—perceived by her as a chaotically psychotic mother in the transference—to find an identity, and through identification with me to establish her own identity in the same process. So convinced was she that this individuation process consisted in nothing but destructiveness on her own part that it was all the more difficult for me to recognize it as being, instead, basically healthy. Even in restrospect I am still convinced that during the earlier years of our work the whole arena of identity formation had been indeed given over to the acting out by her of her murderous feelings, very intense and evident to me and to everyone else engaged in her hospital treatment, but for several years steadfastly unrecognized by her and projected upon her environment. So I believe it meant that a real change had occurred in her when I could now see the striving-for-identity emerging through the long-pathological murderousness. Significantly, she had now become able to be aware of her own murderous feelings as such.

In attempting to formulate such a clinical evolution in general theoretical terms, one can say that the analyst mistakenly feels that the so-murderous-appearing patient is basically and consciously bent upon murder, and fails to see that she is basically and consciously trying to fashion an identity. The patient, for her part, fails to see that in her conscious attempt to fashion an identity she is unconsciously trying to murder the mother-analyst. Her biological mother failed to distinguish between the child's murderous feelings and identificational strivings; hence both patient and analyst must go through a prolonged and difficult struggle before this distinction becomes evident, at a feeling level, to each of them. The murderousness is real, but it needs to be distinguished from and placed in the service of the individuality strivings.

In any event—to return to the data from this particular woman's treatment—what I had earlier felt to be instances of a murderously hostile misidentifying of me by her, now came to feel like a genuine effort to discover her own past, and with this her self, in me. During one of these later sessions she was looking at my face in fascination as I was making some comment, and said, "When you're talking about different people, your eyes become the eyes of whomever you're talking about. It's like a kaleidoscope. I've never seen anything like it before; it's fascinating."

For years I had been hearing such comments from her as: "The sicker one of your eyes is . . ." and "You're still a committee" (i.e., rather than an individual person—she would indicate this while peering at me closely), and "Is that the head [referring to my head] Tom Matthews lost in Oneida Lake that time?" and—still more upsetting—in the earliest years of the work she had reacted to me as being predominantly a conglomeration, or unending series, of such essentially nonhuman things as machines, corpses, rocks, and so on. But now, even her perceptions of me as nonhuman felt less and less intentionally dehumanizing and had more and more the quality of remembrance of her long-forgotten past by discovering, in me, not only the persons important to her in the past but also the important nonhuman ingredients of her past: scenes, pets, buildings, and so on.

At times this process involved a startling perceptiveness on her part of my "own" psychic contents and as this therapeutic symbiosis came more and more to the fore I no longer found it threateningly imperative to maintain a bulwark between her previously frighteningly crazy psychic contents and my own. As a matter of fact, I had been quite afraid of the potential impact upon her of some of my own psychic contents; it was with great relief that I found, over and over again, that just as nothing in her was literally destructive to me, so nothing in me proved actually destructive to her. Specifically, we each came to see with great relief that we could survive one another's most hostile and most tender communications without being instantly destroyed or driven to suicide.

The Sense of Identity as a Perceptual Organ[2]

In light of the foregoing concepts, one's sense of identity emerges as being, in a tangible and thoroughly dynamic sense, one's most valuable organ for perceiving the world. When this essential function of the sense of identity is grasped it becomes understandable why the fashioning of an identity seems to us so endlessly fascinating and significant. The struggle for identity is no

---

[2] This section was embodied in my paper, "The Sense of Identity as a Perceptual Organ" (1965c).

mere narcissistic interest but is, rather—among its other fundamental significances—a struggle to fashion and ceaselessly perfect one's potentially most sensitive and reliable instrument for psychologically grasping the outer world.

Man's identity enables him to perceive the world not merely by mirroring it, but, at a symbiotic level of relatedness, by literally sampling it through processes of introjection and projection.

For years, a deeply and chronically schizophrenic woman, whose identity (including her body-image) was chaotically disturbed, endeavored to construct in miscellaneous ways, including knitting, a "body" for herself, out of all sorts of materials. For hours on end she would knit various things which she described as being one or another body part. One day I found her knitting a large saucerlike structure with an aperture in the center. She explained that she was knitting an eye, and said tiredly that she had made 40 of them before this. It occurred to me that "eye" might also mean "I," and I said, "I wonder if making eyes has something to do with making identities?" She nodded confirmation, explaining, "That's the way you see out." I said, "By having an identity?" She agreed, "Yeah," and went on, "I could see out [gesturing toward her right eye] until yesterday, when Mr. Bennett [an aide] came along and wanted me to teach him about eyes," at which point, she described, she had shown him on the blackboard in this room (a small room used for teaching of personnel as well as for analytic sessions) how eyes work, or are made. Later in this session she drew on the blackboard a map of the world as she perceived it: three large mountain peaks in the center, the head of an Indian prince on the left, and a submarine on the right; she "explained" these in her usual extremely confused way. In essence, she conveyed to me how crazy is the world-view of one who has no reliable "I" with which to see.

When this woman was a child growing up in a home where denial was very pronounced in her interpersonal environment, she felt that she was walking on quicksand, and relied upon her dog to tell her whether this or that person was her friend or her enemy. She was unable to rely upon her own eyes and ears, for the persons about her, notably her parents, were so prone to deny the evidence *overstim (under?)*

of these sensory organs of hers. For such a child there may well be an overloading of the function of the developing identity as an organ for perceiving the world, so that, like a weather vane whirling about crazily in the wind, the child's identity becomes the creature of the forces it is trying to measure, and through its lack of developing continuity and stability becomes useless either for reliably perceiving the world or for furnishing the inner direction we customarily regard the sense of identity as providing.

Somewhere midway through my own analysis, after I had undergone much change, I visualized the core of myself as being, nonetheless, like a steel ball bearing, with varicolored sectors on its surface. At least, I told myself, this would not change. I have long since lost any such image of the core of my identity; it became dissolved in grief, and my sense of identity now possesses something of the fluidity of tears. But for a number of years anything that threatened that so-rigid view of the core of myself was experienced as terrifying craziness. "Countertransference" reactions in my work with patients were a paramount source of such threats. In a succession of papers I have described the process whereby my sense of identity has become sufficiently alive to change, open to symbiotic relatedness, aware of change through change in itself, so that it is now my most reliable source of data as to what is transpiring between the patient and myself, and within the patient. I have described, in effect, the "use" of such fluctuations in one's sense of identity as being a prime source of discovering, in work with a patient, not only countertransference processes but also transference processes, newly developing facets of the patient's own self-image, and so on; and, in supervision, of discovering processes at work not only between the supervisee and oneself, but also between the supervisee and the patient (Searles, 1965a).

But only within the past few years, really, have I come to conceptualize it, and in interviews experience it, in specifically the way I describe here. Previously I experienced these clinical phenomena in terms of noticing various unusual and significant *feelings* in myself, whereas now I experience these phenomena and find it more meaningful to conceptualize them in terms of fluctuations in my sense of identity.

Michelle in her house as mother in my house as ?

During the past two years I have had occasion to do single interviews for teaching and consultative purposes with a relatively large number of hospitalized patients. In this work I have encountered the well-known problem of how best to cope with massive amounts of data which need to be assimilated quickly—what criterion, what point of orientation to employ in order to find coherence and meaning in all that transpires. I have found that the most reliable data are gained in these necessarily brief contacts from my noticing—and, increasingly, sharing such information with the patient—the vicissitudes in my own sense of identity during the session. It is thus, I have found, that I can best discern what are the patient's most centrally important transference distortions in his reactions to me, and what are the aspects of his own identity he is repressing and projecting upon me. I find equally significant, of course, any changes in my experience of myself during the aftermath of the interview.

As a matter of fact, it was such an aftermath experience that first alerted me, several years ago, to the usefulness of such data. Following a single consultative interview with a schizophrenic man—one who had been making a thoroughgoing ass of himself with certain hebephrenic symptoms—I experienced myself, as I drove away from the hospital, as being an incredibly gifted and perceptive consultant. But then I caught myself and wondered what this was saying about the patient's dynamics. I was immediately struck with the likelihood that he tended to project onto other persons, including me, his own best ego capacities. This man, who had done such wonders, transitorily, for my self-esteem while abasing himself, committed suicide about two months later. We never know why these things happen; but among the likely causes is the possibility that he came to find insupportable the burden others placed upon him in their unconsciously exploiting him for the enhancement of their own subjective identities. In any case I have learned to view primarily as informational data about the patient, rather than primarily as food for personal jubilation or despair, any post-interview experiencing of myself as being, for instance, either a jewel of an analyst beyond compare, or—at least equally often—a totally worthless, less-than-human creature.

As I stated in my review (1965b) of Jacobson's book, "I believe that the more successfully the infant and young child internalizes, as the foundation of his personal identity, a symbiotic relationship with a predominantly loving mother, the more accessible is his symbiotic level of existence, in all its infinite richness, to the more structured aspects of identity which develop—which develop not primarily as imposed restraints upon him, but as structures that facilitate the release of his energies and capacities in creative relatedness with the outer world." Such a symbiosis-based identity serves as one's most sensitive and reliable organ for perceiving the world, not merely by mirroring a world set at some distance, but through processes of introjection and projection, literally sampling, literally mingling with—in manageable increments—the world through which, moment by changing moment, one moves.

We come to see, now, that the two seemingly contradictory uses of the word "identity"—as meaning on the one hand unique set-apartness, and on the other hand sameness, unity—are not really contradictory; for identity embraces, at once, one's unique self and the world with which that self is at one.

'movement' in + out ability.

way of moving 'in' (psychotic core : symbiosis – autism ?) +
move out again : reality of external space

is internal space – feeling?

5

The "Dedicated Physician" in the Field of Psychotherapy and Psychoanalysis

Psychiatric patients, above all schizophrenic patients, cause one to doubt one's capacity to love, and to feel that one's devotion is meaningless or, worse, malevolent. For example, when I used to see a hebephrenic woman, with whom I had been working for ten years, walking about on the hospital grounds, appearing vague, disheveled, bleakly unloved, I felt her to be a kind of living, ambulatory monument to my cruelty and neglect. Even though I had not forgotten that I had been subjected to something like 2,000 hours of her reviling me, ignoring me, sexually tantalizing me, making heart rendingly unanswerable appeals to me either mutely or in largely undecipherable words, and so on, I still winced at the sight of her. It was as though the Methodist hell of my boyhood yawned widely for my thus-proven un-Christlike soul.

A year or two previously, on one of the rare days when she had her wits sufficiently about her to be considered able to come with me to my office, about 100 feet away, she stood in confused helplessness while an ostensibly kind, loving, gentle female aide,

First published in *Crosscurrents in Psychiatry and Psychoanalysis*, edited by Robert W. Gibson (Philadelphia and Toronto: J. B. Lippincott, 1967), pp. 128-143.

who (as I later came to realize) busily infantilized all the patients, put shoes on this woman's feet. I felt remorse because I did not feel at all like doing so—because I was feeling, at that moment, nothing toward the patient except hatred, impatience, and contempt.

My papers have chronicled my findings, to my mingled relief and self-deflation, how able schizophrenic patients are not merely to endure, but to turn to therapeutic benefit, one's expressions of deepeningly intense feelings of all kinds. But the events of my final year at Chestnut Lodge showed that I had, nonetheless, underestimated to the last these patients' strengths. I gave notice, one year in advance, of my intention to leave the Lodge; such notice was required by my contract which in turn, of course, was based on clinical and staffing necessities. As I regarded it feasible to go on working with no more than two of my six patients after I left there, I was now faced with the immensely difficult matter of which two, among six patients, each of whom I had been working with intensively for years, I would go on seeing. With one of these patients I had worked for nearly six years; with four, between ten and eleven years each; and with one, for thirteen and a half.

My ambivalence toward each of these individuals, like his or her own toward me, of course, knew no bounds. I wanted utterly to be rid of the whole lot of them, yet felt almost unbearably anguished at the prospect of losing any one of them. A passage from my last staff presentation at the Lodge, just before I left, expresses something of what I had come to learn of the strength each of these persons possessed:

> The one biggest lesson . . . I have learned in working with schizophrenic patients in my last year here has been to see how very tough they are. . . . I can say that I have, in this last year, burdened or battered, or whatever, each of these six patients with all the sarcasm, harshness, contempt, and just general resentment and reviling that I'm capable of and they've all survived it fine, see, just fine, and I have felt that I have just barely been operating in their league—just barely been qualifying to be in the major leagues. When I start this with Edna she is soon on the offensive again; she can take all I've got and she can go on more.

Another way that I conceptualize it is, the work is so goddamned difficult that we cannot do it if we deny ourselves certain parts of our armamentarium. We can't do it with one hand tied behind our back. So this has been something memorable to me; this I'm going to keep using with patients. I am.

My experiences with colleagues over all these same years, as a supervisor or a consultant in their work with their schizophrenic patients, have shown me, similarly, with what toughness, tenacity, and sadistic virtuosity their patients tend to coerce these therapists into the ever-alluring role of the dedicated physician treating the supposedly weaker patient. Typically, to the extent that one feels bound by the traditional physician's role, one feels wholly responsible for the course of the patient's illness, and feels it impermissible to experience any feelings toward the patient except for kindly, attentive, long-suffering, and helpful dedication. The psychiatric resident, in particular, relatively fresh from the dedicated-physician atmosphere of the medical school and general internship, is often genuinely unaware of feeling any hatred or even anger toward the patient who is daily ignoring or intimidating or castigating him, and unaware of how his very dedication, above all, makes him the prey of the patient's sadism. It has been many years since a young schizophrenic man revealed to me how much sadistic pleasure he derived from seeing a succession of dedicated therapists battering their heads bloody against the wall of his indifference, and I have never forgotten that.

In general, if the patient's illness is causing more suffering to the therapist than to the patient, something is wrong. But it is not at all easy, technically, to become more comfortable than the patient. With many schizophrenic patients, one tends to feel like a butterfly, pinned squirmingly in their live-butterfly collection, without any reliable way of drawing blood from the invulnerable patient. It is our omnipotent self-expectations that, more than anything else, pinion us and tend, as well, to stalemate or sever the therapeutic relationship. The obnoxiously behaving paranoid patient cannot help but wonder what ulterior motives make us so concerned to *keep him in therapy*; instead of our becoming aware of our angrily wanting to be rid of him, we act out our repressed desires to reject him, by manifesting an omnipotence-based, devouring, vampirelike devotion which understandably frightens him away from treatment. And the suicidal patient, who finds us so unable to be aware of the murderous feelings he fosters in us through his guilt- and anxiety-producing threats of suicide, feels increasingly constricted, perhaps indeed to the point of suicide, by the therapist who, in reaction formation against his intensifying, unconscious wishes to kill the patient, hovers increasingly "protectively" about the latter, for whom he feels an omnipotence-based physicianly concern. Hence it is, paradoxically, the very physician most anxiously concerned to *keep the patient alive* who tends most vigorously, at an unconscious level, to drive him to what has come to seem the only autonomous act left to him—namely, suicide.

The therapist's functioning in the spirit of dedication, which is the norm among physicians in other branches of medicine, represents here, in the practice of psychotherapy and psychoanalysis, an unconscious defense against his seeing clearly many crucial aspects of both the patient and himself.

Among the aspects of the patient to which such dedication tends to blind him is the already-mentioned sadism. He does not see how much sadistic gratification the patient is deriving from his therapist's anguished, tormented, futile dedication. He does not realize that, as I overheard one chronically schizophrenic man confide to his therapist, "The pleasure I get in torturing you is the main reason I go on staying in this hospital." I had heard this therapist describe how, for many months, he had never known, when he went into this man's room on the disturbed ward, whether to expect a blow or a kiss from the patient.

Further, the dedicated therapist does not see how much ambivalence the patient has about change, even change for the "better." He does not see that the patient has reached his present equilibrium only after years of thought and effort and the exercise of the best judgment of which he is capable. To the patient, change tends to mean a return to an intolerable pre-equilibrium state, and the imposition upon him of the therapist's values, the therapist's per-

sonality, with no autonomy, no individuality, for him. He resents
the therapist's presumption in assuming that the patient is pitiably
eager to be rescued, and in assuming, equally humiliatingly, that
the intended help is all unidirectional, from therapist to patient.

A dozen years ago I reached the conviction that it is folly to set
out to rescue the patient from the dragon of schizophrenia: the patient is both the maiden in the dragon's grip, and the dragon itself.
The dragon is the patient's resistance to becoming "sane"—
resistance which shows itself as a tenacious and savage hostility to
the therapist's efforts.

The heart of this resistance springs from the fact that the patient's own raison d'être, since early childhood, has been as a
therapist, originally to the parent whose unwhole integration he,
the child, was called upon to complement, in a pathological and
unnaturally prolonged symbiosis. He was given over to this
therapeutic dedication, as a small child, for the most altruistic of
reasons—he lived in order to make mother (or father) whole—as
well as for reasons of his own self-interest, so that he would have a
whole parent with whom to identify, for the sake of his own maturation. But he failed in this therapeutic dedication and, more
hurtfully still, the fact of this dedication was not even recognized by
the parent, who incessantly hurt, disparaged, and rejected him.
Thus now, as an adult schizophrenic patient in treatment, he takes
vengeance upon this rival, "official" therapist of his, and causes his
therapist to feel as anguished, futile, and worthless or malevolent
an intended healer as he, the patient, had been given to feel by his
mother or father. Only insofar as the therapist becomes able to see,
and respond to, the patient's genuinely therapeutic striving toward
him, and earlier toward the parents, will the patient be himself receptive to therapy. Among my feelings during my final year at
Chestnut Lodge was, prominently, grief at various of my patients'
having refused to identify sufficiently with my healthier aspects
and, by the same token, grief at my own having failed to help them
do so. I surmise that such grief is of a piece with the patient's own
repressed grief, stemming from early childhood, at being unable to
save the sick parent through encouraging the latter to identify with

the healthier aspects of the patient as a growing child.

We therapists tend to feel frightened away from seeing how concerned our patients are to help us, partly for the reason that the transference distortions, in which this therapeutic striving of theirs is couched, are very great. That is, our patient tends to see us as being not merely somewhat depressed today, but as being his deeply, suicidally despondent father; or he perceives us as being not merely somewhat scatterbrained today, but as being his insane, hopelessly fragmented mother.

Patients' specific therapeutic aims, and their individual techniques in pursuing those aims, are manifold. Various patients of mine, for example, have rescued me from periods of withdrawal and depression by presenting themselves as being in such urgent need of rescue that I have felt it necessary to bestir myself, come out of myself, and thus cast off the chains of my depression in order to save them. Others, by presenting themselves as being infuriatingly, outrageously undisciplined, have eventually "made a man of" me—have made me, through impelling me into being a stern disciplinarian, into the kind of man they had been unable to make their wishy-washy father into.

Their therapeutic techniques are outwardly so brutal that the therapeutic intent is seen only in the result. One apathetic, dilapidated hebephrenic patient of mine received considerable therapeutic benefit from a fellow patient, newly come to the ward but, like him, a veteran of several years in mental hospitals. This fellow patient repeatedly, throughout the day, gave my patient a vigorous and unexpected kick in the behind. From what I could see, this was the first time in years another patient had shown any real interest in him, and my patient emerged appreciably from his state of apathy and hopelessness as a result.

As for the many crucial aspects of himself, in relation to the patient, against which the therapist is unconsciously defending himself with his physicianly dedication, I have already touched upon some of these. He is unaware of how much he is enjoying his tormenting the patient with this dedication, of which the patient, who feels himself to be so hateful and incapable of giving anything worthwhile to anyone, feels so unworthy. He is unaware, similarly, of how much scorn his own "dedication" is expressing. I asked a female colleague, who was describing her work, a very actively dedicated and ostensibly maternally loving work, with a deeply regressed woman, how much ego she felt the patient to have. The therapist replied, as though this were obvious, "None." Such unconscious scorn for the patient—for the patient's own strength and for his ability to reach out, himself, for help from the therapist, without the therapist's having constantly to keep pushing the help at him—seems to me to betray much self-contempt on the part of the therapist. If the therapist is convinced that he himself is a worthwhile person, with something useful to give—with something, that is, which this fellow human being, the patient, can be relied upon to discern and to admire and want—he will not need to try, anxiously and incessantly, to persuade the patient to accept his help.

Further, the "dedicated" therapist, who feels under such intense pressure to cure the patient, goes on oblivious of his placing, in his dedication, equally great pressure upon the patient. Here I can offer a vignette from my own work. A paranoid schizophrenic woman whom I have been treating for years has come, in recent months, to spend many sessions wet-eyed, describing in verbose detail her life experience, current and past, in terms implying that there is an ocean of grief in her, but never with any frank outpouring of tears. Finally, at the end of one such session, I confided to her, with mixed feelings of guilt and exasperation, that at the end of such an hour as this, as had happened so many times before, "You always make me feel remiss in not having said or done something that would enable you to weep." To my surprise, she instantly responded with something which had evidently been on her mind, similarly, for many sessions—"and *you* always make *me* feel remiss for not weeping."

The supervision of other therapists gives one a chance to see these things more objectively and, of course, with less harsh narcissistic injury to oneself. Specifically, one can clearly feel how sadistic are the demands upon himself, week after week, of the so-

dedicated therapist who is so agonizedly eager to cure his patient.
One such therapist, chronically depressed and long-suffering about
the work with his patient but chronically "dedicated" to the latter,
would tell me, week after week, of his patient's asking him, "What
do I do? What's the right thing to do?" The therapist himself was
passing along to me much this same kind of draining and unanswerable demand, by implicitly asking me, throughout each supervisory session, "Doc, what do I do to relieve my suffering at the
hands of this patient who is crucifying me?"

Our "dedicated-physician" way of relating to the patient serves
not only to act out our sadism toward him, but also to express our
unconscious determination to maintain the status quo—to preserve
the patient's present, immature level of ego functioning in order to
ensure the inflow of deniedly cherished supplies from him. Thus,
the loosening of the stalemate requires that the therapist become
aware not only of his sadism and other negative feelings toward the
patient, but also of his cherishing what the latter has been providing him.

In other words, an intensely pressuring, dedicated therapeutic
zeal denotes an unconscious determination, on the part of the
therapist, to protect and preserve, for reasons of his own psychic
economy, the patient's present level of psychotic or neurotic ego
functioning. This determination arises from the various narcissistic
and infantile gratifications the therapist is receiving from the patient, who represents at one level a transference-mother who is
feeding him, as well as from the fact that the patient's illness serves
to shield the therapist from seeing clearly his own illness.

So, unconsciously, the therapist is bent upon maintaining the
patient in an infantilized state, and is opposing that very individuation and maturation to which, at a conscious level, he is genuinely
dedicated. As I have already indicated, I, for one, tend dedicatedly
to remain immersed in a rescue effort toward the "fragile" patient,
in order to avoid seeing him or her as being stronger, or potentially
stronger, than myself. For example, one hebephrenic woman, from
whose incredibly low levels of ego functioning I derived much fascinating data about the schizophrenic patient's subjectively "prehu-

man" identity (data included in my monograph on the nonhuman environment [1960]), finally told me, in vigorous protest, "I can't stay down forever!" This woman would evidence, from time to time over the years of our work, remarkable forward surges in her ego functioning, and unfailingly I would find that my rejoicing in this development was outweighed by an upsurge of my feeling inadequate. I had been feeling despair at how grievously ill she was; but now I would find her manifesting an appearance of blooming physical health which made me feel old and jaded. I would be reminded, ruefully, too, that she was physically taller than I. In the same process, she would reveal a kind of effortless savoir faire, in matters both interpersonal and cultural, traceable to an upbringing far richer in social and cultural "advantages" than my own. In short, I would feel her to be an all-around hopelessly larger person than myself. Then, as if quickly detecting that I still couldn't take it, she would soon be, again, her deeply fragmented, "hopelessly ill" hebephrenic self, and I was once more in my comfortable role of the long-suffering Christ trying to heal the wounded bird.

Even more embarrassingly, I found my feelings toward another long-schizophrenic woman oscillating, often session by session for months on end, from my viewing her as a hopelessly confused mental patient who, clearly incurably ill, would undoubtedly be spending the rest of her life in psychiatric hospitals, to my viewing her as a predominantly well, wonderfully warm, intelligent, and witty woman for whom I felt greatly tempted to give up everyone and everything else in my life, but who, I had anguishedly to realize, recurrently, could never practicably be mine. At this point, incidentally, it should be abundantly clear that, among the needs for which the "dedicated" therapist is obtaining gratification are his masochistic needs.

If one examines more deeply the psychodynamics of the dedicated-physician therapist who is unconsciously devoted to preserving the status quo, one finds that he holds, at an unconscious level, split images—one an idealized image and the other a diabolized image—of himself and of the patient as well. One also finds that he is dedicated, unconsciously but tenaciously, to preserving these split images and preventing their coalescence, with the leaven of reality, into realistic images of himself and of the patient as two fellow human beings, each possessing both strengths and limitations upon his strengths, each capable of both hating and loving.

As a function of his unconscious effort to preserve these split images, the therapist represses the ingredients of his diabolized self-image—his hatred, his rejectingness, his subjectively nonhuman unfeelingness, and so on—and projects these upon the patient. At the same time that he is placing intense, though unwitting demands upon the patient to emerge in such a healthy way as will enable the therapist to realize his idealized self-image as an all-loving, omnipotent healer, he is unconsciously holding at a safe distance, or driving progressively deeper into autism, this patient who personifies the diabolized, unacceptable, and therefore vigorously projected aspects of his own self-image. Thus the therapist's dedication becomes, as seen from this vantage point, an anxious, deeply ambivalent effort to both make contact with and keep safely at a distance the projected components of his *self*.

To describe this a bit further, we see how well it serves the therapist's unconscious rejectingness for the patient to become progressively withdrawn. Consciously, he is dedicated to making contact with the patient and helping him to join him in the "real world"; but unconsciously he wants to be rid of the disappointing, frightening, and otherwise unsatisfactory patient—the patient who by any standards is so, and all the more by reason of the therapist's unconscious image of him as presently diabolical, no matter how much the therapist clings also to the unconscious hope that the patient may one day fit an ideal image. In still other terms, the therapist is trying consciously to help the withdrawn patient to materialize, while unconsciously he wants to make the latter disappear. In proportion as the patient becomes able to evidence love, the therapist's projected image of himself as diabolical comes home to roost, and he tends to perceive himself as subhumanly bad, malevolently obstructing the full liberation of the patient's supposedly suprahumanly good self. What makes this so formidable a difficulty in therapy is not so much that the therapist is unadulteratedly neurotic, but rather that the chronically schizophrenic patient contributes, to the maintenance of these processes of splitting, a degree of intensity and tenacity of which the therapist's own stake in the matter is a relatively small sample. But it is the therapist's own dawning recognition of his "countertransference"—his own contribution to these stalemating processes—that provides the best handle for his effecting a change in the therapeutic relationship; that is why I dwell here upon the therapist's contribution to the difficulties.

We tend, thus, to make the patient feel both idealized and diabolized by us, with a hopelessly unbridgeable gulf between these two so-different creatures we are calling upon him to be, toward us. At the same time that we are unwittingly calling upon him to fulfill our diabolized image of him, we are unconsciously looking to him to provide our life with its central meaning, to give us a raison d'être, to make real our idealized self-image. I want to emphasize that it is no pernicious thing *consciously* to regard the patient as supremely important and meaningful to oneself. For us consciously so to relate to him cannot but enhance his self-esteem and help him to become whole. The pernicious thing is that we repress both our idealized image and our diabolized image of him, hide both from ourself, and at the same time act out both these toward him by inappropriately employing, in psychotherapy and psychoanalysis, the traditional dedicated-physician-treating-his-patient approach which, however conventionally accepted in the practice of medicine generally, congeals and reinforces the wall between patient and doctor when we employ it in this field.

Paradoxically, the withdrawn patient is likely to be identifying with the very therapist who is consciously devoted to a diligent and even desperate attempt to help him emerge from the withdrawal, but much of whose feelings are in actuality withdrawn from his conscious attitudes toward the patient. That is, the patient, in seeking the isolation of the seclusion room, may well be identifying with those increments of the therapist which are secluded off from access to the therapist's conscious ways of viewing, and relating to, the patient. This is one variety of what I have termed, in an earlier paper (Scarles, 1963b), the patient's delusional identification with his therapist; in general, these are instances in which the most tenacious, treatment-resistant aspects of the patient's craziness are found to be based upon his exaggerated and distorted identifications with real but unconscious aspects of the therapist's own personality and ways of functioning in the treatment relationship.

In discussing, now, the phenomena marking the resolution of these dedicated-physician stalemates—phenomena of which I have already given some hint—I have in mind the form this resolution takes in one's work with the schizophrenic patient on the one hand, and with the depressed patient on the other hand; but there are many patients, of course, who show prominently both these varieties of psychopathology.

In any case, as the therapist becomes aware of the whole gamut of his feelings toward the patient, he comes to see that the latter is a real and separate person, afflicted with an illness which is also a part of genuinely outer reality for the .therapist, rather than its being the product of the therapist's heretofore-repressed, subjectively omnipotent hatred and infantile demands.

As we become free from our previous, compulsive "dedication" and able now to view the patient and our relationship with him with this new objectivity, we no longer assume a wholehearted, dedicated interest on our part as a *given* in the situation, and can notice fluctuations in our interest toward him, fluctuations often fostered by him and of much transference significance. For example, I have seen that, with various patients of mine, just as we get to working closely and most constructively together, the patient will do something (such as making a last-minute, inconsiderate and impersonal cancellation of a session) which cools my interest in him. This action reveals to me his fear of closeness with me, his fear of my strong and sustained and deepening interest in him, which I would not have detected had I gone on holding myself totally responsible for maintaining an unflagging interest in helping him—had I gone on feeling guilty whenever I found myself disinterested in him and not caring whether or not he might elect to continue with our work. This is but an example of how, in analytic terms, a therapist's physicianly, compulsive "dedication" interferes with the kind of free-floating objectivity which is so necessary an ingredient of the analyst's effective functioning.

As our previous, compulsive dedication loosens its grip upon us, we become aware, lo and behold, of a keen aesthetic appreciation of that very illness, in the patient, which heretofore we have felt so desperately and guiltily responsible for curing. Several years ago, I found myself having to face the fact that I seemed to find the schizophrenic aspects much more fascinating than the more conventional and healthier aspects of my patients' functioning. At first, I felt deeply troubled at this discovery, for I felt it must mean that I am dedicated more to the causation and preservation of severe and exotic illness than to the fostering of health in my patients. But then I began to see that this preference, on my part, was not so unnatural after all. Keeping in mind the point I made earlier, that the schizophrenic patient is not only the maiden in the dragon's grip but the dragon also, let me ask you which of these you find more fascinating—the relatively pallid and conventional lady, or the exotic and colorful dragon?[1]

I have been deeply reassured to find, as time has gone on, that this very aesthetic appreciation is a form of scientific interest which, in contrast to my earlier, so anguished therapeutic dedication, enables me to be of maximal real use to the patient. For example, I used to feel, for years, desperately and urgently concerned to relieve the indescribably severe confusion of one of my chronically schizophrenic patients, and it was with guilt bordering on self-loathing that I began to realize that I was actually fascinated by the vivid, intricate, so-unconventional nature of her confusion itself. At

[1]A mere second, or even first, glance at Uccello's painting (p. 84), will show that, in this particular artist's rendition of the myth of Saint George and the dragon, there is a tongue-in-cheek quality, for the dragon is the lady's pet on a leash. I use the painting here despite, rather than because of, this aspect of it. I by no means regard schizophrenia as being, in any overall sense, within the patient's conscious control like a pet on a leash. Vivid paintings portraying Saint George and the dragon and the lady are less easy to find than I had assumed.

PAOLO UCCELLO. *St. George and the Dragon.*

first my interest in this felt unclean, perverse, unworthy of any physician; but gradually I came to feel that I was facing a genuine work of creative art which was after all, as I now clearly see, the product of the highest forms of the patient's intelligence and creative originality. As for her, she showed every evidence of finding much more useful my appreciative, unanxious, and unguilty studying of her confused verbalizations than she had found my desperate attempts to somehow shut them off.

Along with such aesthetic-scientific interest one comes to feel, as one becomes freer from omnipotent guilt about the patient and his illness, companion gratifications in the realm of humor and playfulness—all necessary ingredients of the phase of the mutually enjoyable therapeutic symbiosis I have described in a number of papers. Time after time I have found that the patient benefits most from our sharing of humorous, playful moments together. When I can leave off my deadly serious dedication, and be amused at the patient's craziness, he can come to laugh with warm and loving amusement at the delightfully crazy foibles of his mother, whom he had been desperately dedicated, heretofore, to curing, at an introjected level, in his own so-tragic craziness. When one is working in this new spirit with the patient, one is very close to him, openly showing how much one likes and enjoys being with him. His formerly maddening symptoms are now only part of the background music in an atmosphere of contentment.

As the therapist becomes aware of how much gratification the illness is providing to himself as well as to the patient, he becomes free of his infantile-omnipotence-based, guilty feeling of *having to cure* the patient. The patient genuinely is faced now, not simply at one crucial juncture but ongoingly, session after session, with the choice as to whether he himself wishes to cling to the gratifications of remaining ill, or whether he wishes to accept the therapist's *also*-offered assistance in becoming a healthy adult. He now becomes able to feel, as one patient told his therapist:

> It's like I see a more distinct me inside of me, and I can see a great future, and that I have promise. . . . It used to be like my mother and father and I were all lumped together, and it

was sick. If they want to stay sick and screwed up, it's their business and their choice; but it's not mine. I feel like I can get away from their sickness, and I damned well don't have to stay in it.

In concluding, I want to mention briefly three points. First, it seems to be impossible—and perhaps it would be untherapeutic, were it possible—for a therapist to have, at the beginning of his work with any one patient, and to maintain throughout the treatment, a realistic as opposed to an omnipotence-based feeling of dedication. It would be unclinical to postulate that there is some one most therapeutic attitude, as regards dedication, which the therapist should have at the beginning of the therapy, and maintain throughout it, beyond his dedicating himself as fully as possible to becoming aware of whatever thoughts and feelings are being called forth in the treatment process, in himself as well as in the patient. It seems inescapable that we shall go through torments of feeling omnipotently responsible for each of our patients, that we shall repress our sadism and project it upon the patient, shall come to develop split images of ourself and of the patient, and so on as I have been detailing, and it may well be that our becoming thus enmeshed, for a time, in the patient's illness is necessary to the therapeutic process. But I suggest that the considerations discussed here will facilitate our going through this evolution and emerging to a more realistic experience of ourself in relation to the patient. I suggest, in other words, that these considerations will help us to avert, or at least to shorten, such covertly sadomasochistic stalemates as are familiar clinical experiences to all of us.

Second, we see that the kind of therapist devotion characteristic of such stalemated situations is a genuinely "selfless" devotion, but selfless in a sense that is, in the long run, precisely antitherapeutic. That is, so many of the therapist's own unconscious ingredients are being projected onto the patient that he is in a real sense selflessly submerged in the patient's narcissism. In this sense, the therapist is deriving the unconscious gratification of functioning without the responsibility for having a self and thus, paradoxically, in his "selflessly dedicated" functioning, is burdening the patient with a total responsibility for the whole relationship. Such "devotion," which temporarily supports the patient's narcissistic world-self, inevitably must be revealed, one day, as a lie. This disillusioning discovery, now, that the therapist after all is a separate person with a self of his own and self-interest of his own, after the patient has been led for so long to assume otherwise, will repeat, for the patient, his bitter childhood experience that, as one schizophrenic woman put it, "People are only interested in themselves." And, as a borderline schizophrenic man phrased it, "Kidding your children for 20 years that you love them and want them—this is what I'm bitter about, I guess; mother has *pretended* that she put me first, and it's just been her little game. It's not been true—she's more interested in herself, in her neurosis."

The paranoid individual is especially prone to assuming that if the therapist proves not to be wholeheartedly devoted to his (the patient's) welfare, then the therapist must be bent upon sabotaging and destroying him. This seems referable to the patient's experiences as a child, in which the parents maintained a "wholeheartedly devoted" demeanor toward him, in a reaction formation against their largely unconscious, more sinister feelings toward him—their hostility toward him, their wishes to be free of him. Hence he will remain suspicious, and with good reason, if we endeavor to submerge, from the beginning of his treatment, our self-interest in his "welfare."

Third, in earlier papers (Searles, 1965a) I have described the therapeutic symbiosis, which implies a degree of selflessness on the part of therapist as well as patient, as marking the most essential aspect of the treatment. But this stands in the most direct contrast to the kind of "dedicated-physician selflessness" this paper is calling into question. Where the latter is a defense against hatred and other "negative" emotions, this former kind of merging between patient and therapist can occur only after all emotions, of whatever variety, in either participant, have become sufficiently unthreatening so that these need no longer be defended against by the maintenance of a "self," a structure which, in light of the processes at work in this stage of the treatment evolution, could serve only as a hindrance to the therapeutic processes, which are streaming toward new and deeper patterns of individuation for both patient and therapist, patterns at this point unpredictable and therefore all the more exciting and fulfilling.

6

Paranoid Processes among Members of the Therapeutic Team

THE SUBJECTIVELY EXPERIENCED MILIEU

In the study of the schizophrenic quadruplets at the National Institute of Mental Health (NIMH) a few years ago I had a relatively small role, serving as supervisor throughout the individual therapy of one of the so-called Genain quads, and intermittently in the same capacity with a second member of the foursome. Tangential though my role was as a consultant with these limited functions, I shall never forget the awe with which this fantastically complex project was regarded, not only by myself but also by, as far as I could see, everyone else connected with it. The project seemed not so much to be composed of, but to be chronically devouring, four individual therapists and their several supervisors over the years, several administrators, innumerable social workers, nurses, and aides, and a galaxy of diverse scientists such as psychologists, sociologists, geneticists, and so on. At the nucleus of this chaotic mass, which was not divided into any such neat categories as I have enumerated

This paper, as presented in the McLean Hospital symposium, was originally titled "Individual Psychotherapy and the Therapeutic Milieu." It was first published in *Psychotherapy in the Designed Therapeutic Milieu*, edited by Stanley H. Eldred and Maurice Vanderpol (Boston: Little, Brown, 1968), pp. 95-113.

but which seemed to swirl maelstromlike, was the family itself, with the tangibly awesome quadruplet evidence of the schizophrenogenic power of that family. One felt that this whole unembraceably vast vortex was less a team, or even a collection, of separate human individuals than a giant unicellular organism which threatened to engulf any individual who came into contact with it.

This essentially paranoid view of a certain therapeutic milieu may be taken, notwithstanding the obvious uniqueness of that study at NIMH, as a paradigm of the deeply threatened views which, whether latent or ragingly predominant, give rise to the most formidable labor for all those concerned with either individual therapy or the therapeutic milieu. I speak primarily as a psychotherapist of chronically schizophrenic patients, one who has had some limited and relatively uncreative experience of doing ward administration, but who has had much experience of collaborating with some dozens of ward administrators of widely varying personal styles and theoretical orientations.

The word "milieu" tends to evoke in us a feeling of something nonindividual, nonhuman, structureless, and all-pervasive, a feeling genetically traceable to our earliest stages of ego development, before we had come to experience ourselves as a human individual in a world comprising at least one other individual for each of us, the mother. Instead, with this word "milieu" we tend to feel plunged into the largely unknown, and inherently indescribable, psychology of matrices rather than of separate and truly human individuals. The therapist, for example, tends to feel his aloneness pitted against a suprahuman milieu composed of many persons en masse—all the more so in those instances when the administrative psychiatrist is so forceful and dynamic that the ward staff function predominantly not as persons in their own right, but as extensions or facets of him. In this instance, the whole milieu tends to be felt by all concerned as a manifestation of this one individual's personality.

Because it is so largely unknown what, realistically speaking, are the things that are therapeutic for a patient, either in the designed milieu or in the individual therapy, it is easy for everyone concerned to regress to magical-omnipotent modes of experience. The therapist feels all his medical school and later specialized training pale into insignificance in contrast to the therapeutic efficacy of a kindly, large-bosomed aide, while she in turn attributes omniscience to the highly trained therapist or administrator who is working with the so-mystifying patient.

THE THERAPIST'S RESPONSE TO THE REGRESSED PATIENT

The most formidable pressure toward such subjectively omnipotent modes of experience springs, of course, from the deeply regressed patients who have so largely lost the ability to experience themselves and their surrounding world in a mature, highly differentiated fashion.

One chronically paranoid woman would assert, with deeply delusional conviction, "I'm closer to God than anybody else in this world!" and, for a number of years in my work with her, asserted that she actually was God. Only after many years of treatment and much talk about "God-rot" (presumably the decay of subjectively omnipotent introjects) was she able to realize that "I used to be God; now I'm a woman." Meanwhile, over the years, she had progressed through viewing me as omnipotently malevolent, the evil master planner (bad mother) who had held her throughout her whole life in my evil grip, controlling all her tortured and terrified experience, causing all her disturbing mental associations and bizarre physical symptoms, ordering her nightmarish dreams, and so on. Later, she had come to perceive me as benevolently godlike, and had been able to endure the separations from me, between therapeutic sessions, only by seeing me everywhere, in everyone about her. She would perceive others among the personnel as omnipotent—would beg, for example, a female aide to "say the magic word" which would transform the world into goodness, security, and beauty.

Similarly, another chronically paranoid woman attributed omnipotence to my thoughts, incessantly pleading with me that if only

I would think "nice thoughts" about her, and "want me well," she would be well. She was inclined to assume that it was the air conditioner in my office that made the huge trees, out on the hospital grounds, move in the wind, and that it was I personally who had put up the Christmas decorations over the streets of the nearby city of Bethesda. Whenever, during a therapy session, an extraneous noise occurred, from no matter how far off in the building or from outside it, she would instantly ask, "What's that, Dr. Searles?"—as though my eyes and ears extended everywhere.

Such a patient is almost entirely unable to differentiate between therapist and administrator as two separate individuals with important but limited functions in his life. A schizophrenic man, hospitalized for many years, angrily demanded that his therapist[1] restore to him a dilapidated pair of shoes which the aides had recently replaced with a new pair. The therapist finally replied in exasperation, "I have nothing to do with your shoes!," whereupon the patient demanded, "If you are not the chief of all these bastards, who the hell is directing them, anyway?"

A hebephrenic young woman frantically demanded, "What created the world? What happened to the power that created the world?" and seemed frightened lest this power reside in her. For many months she felt her existence to be totally dominated by a "watcher machine" which she found not eerie and terrifying, as I at first assumed, but rather her only reliable source of security in a chaotic and terrifying world. Parenthetically, it required about two years of treatment for her to come to mention to me the name of any other patient on her ward. Analogously, when in the sixth year of our work she described how a hospital "is run"—but by implication, how it ideally should be run—I found her concepts shockingly harsh. These concepts included an absolutely remorseless, automatic blotting-out of existence of whoever or whatever failed to conform to the rules. She (who had spent much time in seclusion rooms) stated that if a room were to be locked, this room would

---

[1] Dr. Jaime Buenaventura, of the Chestnut Lodge staff, has kindly permitted me to include this clinical illustration.

automatically cease to be part of the place. For many months she lived in chronic terror lest she be raped, and actually provoked physical attack by fellow patients on several occasions; prominent among her "rules" for the hospital was that "No raping is permitted," no attacking. I came to see that, shockingly concentration-camp-like though she conceived the hospital to be, she needed to perceive it so for the sake of her own security in the face of her projected impulses. Further, in her upbringing she had felt helpless to deal with her father's and mother's precisely opposed, authoritarian injunctions concerning, for example, social behavior. Once she made me feel how helpless she had felt in the face of conflicting rules from as many as six different authority figures in her childhood. Her monolithic ideal hospital was uncomplicated by any such diverse and clashing authorities.

She came to burden me with brutalized and brutalizing descriptions of how her administrator kept her to himself while starving her for affection; but much evidence accumulated that she delighted in so interpreting her relationship with him—she liked to feel possessively loved by a ruthlessly omnipotent figure. Of another therapist on the staff toward whom she maintained an intense transference, as a father, for more than two years she said, "He sees the world through me." In actuality, she had seen the world through the eyes of her father until her disillusionment with him had become irrepressible, shattering their symbiotic relationship and precipitating her schizophrenia. In the seventh year of our work, she was able to recall more of the events which had led to her first hospitalization, 14 years previously. She remembered how suicidal she had felt, saying, "Everything else in the world had fallen to pieces, except Steve H.," a young man toward whom she had maintained desperately an omnipotent-father transference for a number of months before this, too, had disintegrated.

During the first several months after her admission to Chestnut Lodge, when in the words of her administrator she was chronically "crawling with terror," she tried to see her terror as being evoked by an omnipotent and basically therapeutic agency. She had received 190 insulin comas and an uncounted number of electroshock

treatments at previous hospitals, and now construed that the purpose of her being at the Lodge "is to be scared," which she considered some incomprehensible "part of growing up, I guess." Of her
being assaulted frequently by other patients she said that one
needed this sort of thing in order to stimulate one's brain into activity.

A young man suffering from chronic paranoid schizophrenia
had slit his throat with a razor shortly after a previous admission to
Chestnut Lodge, and would have bled to death but for the unpredictably prompt appearance of the doctor on call. Some several
months thereafter, in a long letter to a friend, the patient described, in meticulous detail, his deliberate and careful cutting of
his throat, and went on to make clear his then current experience
of what we would call the therapeutic milieu of the Lodge:

> I believe I may have mentioned something about my photo-
> static mind. Indeed it seems to me that the treatment I have
> had here would astonish a layman, particularly this mind busi-
> ness. I have got thoroughly used to it, but it is really startling.
> It is a fact that everyone on this floor can understand every-
> thing I think. It may sound surprising, but it's true. Also, my
> thoughts can be understood a distance of several hundred
> yards from the sanitarium. People answer my thoughts from
> that distance. When I go downtown the people on the street
> understand what I think. The way I think is by saying words to
> myself, without uttering a sound. How it is done I don't know.
> I can't understand the thoughts of any of the other patients. It
> does put one at a disadvantage to be, so to speak, mentally pub-
> lic. Yet, I believe that it has helped a great deal to cure me, be-
> cause it has prevented brooding and hindered introspection.
> However, I hope that it will end soon. This is the absolute
> truth. If you were here, you, like anyone else, would under-
> stand every thought I had. No one will admit to me that they
> understand my thoughts; yet, they do.
> Less remarkable are the electric shocks, which have been a
> psychiatric practice for some time. In fact, Forel mentions
> them. These consist of slight electrical shocks being felt at times
> all over the body, at times in most personal places, or should I
> say place. Perhaps, you get what I mean. To be blunt, I refer to
> electrical erection. Also, my feet or legs can be so electrified

that I can hardly walk; I can be given a headache; my heart can be touched; my teeth, ears, etc. can be made to hurt. . . . The scars on my throat are often electrified particularly when shaving. My eyes can be hurt electrically, etc. In fact, it is quite unusual, but not so surprising as the "wired brain," as I call it.

The treatment here has really been very successful. As I said, I did not think that I could get well when I came here. I had never dreamed of such a contrivance as a readable brain nor scarcely imagined the "electrical shocks." The electricity also follows me downtown, incidentally. It is all quite astounding.

Psychiatry is really remarkable. . . .

THE MILIEU EFFECTS OF REGRESSIVE DIFFERENTIATION

Severe schizophrenia includes a regressive dedifferentiation, in the patient's perceptual experience, so profound that animate and inanimate, human and nonhuman ingredients of his world become no longer clearly distinguished as such. He may experience himself essentially as a mechanical thing, run by nonhuman forces; he may feel himself to be a living but nonhuman creature—and, for that matter, may be reacted to, by the therapist and other personnel members, as being essentially nonhuman; he may feel the very building to be alive; he may perceive the therapist as a machine sent to kill him, or essentially as a beloved pet dog from his past.

One woman, for example, delusionally distorted the meaning of three surgical operations she had undergone in girlhood. She now saw a mastoidectomy as having been a matter of "their" having made a hole in her skull through which "they" were now running her brain; the drainage of a breast abscess she now saw as "their" having placed a still-present chain upon her heart; and an exploratory laparotomy had involved, she was convinced, "their" installing machinery in her abdomen. Over the years of my work with her, she would storm about "this goddamned machine, and say, "They who exploited me didn't know I was a machine." With a facial expression of stony desolation, she once said, "I'm a machine. I have no control over myself," and spoke of her being "filled with radioactive material." She demanded once, "What is this building? My sister Edith? I want my own home—that is, I want my own body." She experienced the walls of the building as teeming with the persons from her past and once, when the walls evidently felt not so to her, asked a nurse what she should do to make a wall of the building come alive. Herself the mother of three children, she often heard children in the walls screaming in terror all night long and, when a noisy new patient came to occupy a room overhead, asked the nurse who the patient was "on the ceiling."

Another woman, who for years lived so stereotyped an existence as to function more as a robot than as a living person, would say, "This place is so crazy!" and "This place acts like a nitwit!" and would refer to a fellow patient as "that thing."

Still another patient lay for many months largely mute and motionless in her bed, and on one occasion, after moving a bit, said, "I was afraid you might think I was part of the bed." There were many times when she seemed to react to me, as I sat for long periods motionless next to her bed, as being part of the chair. Later on, during sessions in my office, she gave evidence of coming to feel so much at one with the office that, upon leaving it at the end of each session, she was threatened with loss of her self. She clearly identified more with various inanimate objects, and with animals, than with human beings. The tenuousness of her felt relatedness to other persons is indicated, for instance, in such statements as, "I used to live in a home, with my family, and now all I have is worry," and "I'm crazy. I'm not a person anymore."

In the case of a hebephrenic woman, for a number of years the inanimate walls and furnishings of her room on the disturbed ward were not perceived as such, but were imbued with the hallucinated members of her parental family, as well as innumerable other figures who provided companionship and guidance to her, but who much of the time kept her confused and terrified with commands. One time she nodded toward the radiator and confided, fondly and intimately, "That's Daddy's place." On another occasion, she stood in awe in the center of the room, looking down at the floor and feeling it fearfully with her foot, and explained, "My father is down there." For many months she experienced neither herself nor me as human. She felt herself, for instance, to be embedded in glass, and was afraid of being touched by me. One time when I was smoking, she looked at me as at an uncanny mechanical apparition, and said aloud to herself, in awe and incredulity, "What does the smoking?"

THE MILIEU EFFECTS OF INTENSE AMBIVALENCE

Such "nonhuman" subjective experience is, like other schizophrenic symptoms, a defense against the unmasterably intense ambivalence which the struggle to live as a person among other persons has involved for these patients. Since that ambivalence causes so much splitting between therapist and ward milieu, it deserves a brief discussion. The sheer intensity of the patient's feelings (both hateful and loving feelings), their conflictual or discoordinate nature, and their bewildering changeability are all formidable aspects of the ambivalence. This ambivalence, through its evoking of comparably intense ambivalent feelings in the therapist by way of response, is one of the major factors impelling the therapist toward the position of being the isolated, crazy one who sees the designed therapeutic milieu in such distorted terms as I have described. More than once I have felt close to psychosis in trying to cope with intense and simultaneous feelings of rage, hurt, sexual desire, grief, and so on, which a deeply psychotic patient was arousing in me. All this is evoked in a context of the patient's powerful and tenacious transference to the therapist as being the crazy—whether openly or covertly—mother or father of the patient's childhood.

One woman, for example, reacted to me as being her odd recluse of a mother. Whenever I would try to communicate with her in comparative or figurative terms, she would reassert her deeply threatened conviction that I was crazy. When I would endeavor to call her attention to the many evidences of erotic feeling on her part, she reacted to me as being a dangerous sex fiend. Only after several years of increasingly collaborative work, by which time her psychosis had narrowed to sporadically evidenced ambulatory schizophrenia, did her diagnosis of me modify to an infrequent "You have a streak of insanity in you, Dr. Searles."

Another woman, whose mother and father were both highly schizoid persons with serious depressive tendencies, for years reacted to me as being essentially unreachable and then, as we achieved more contact with one another, treated me as being dangerously, even suicidally, depressed.

Still another woman, whose mother had evidently been ambulatorily psychotic throughout the girl's upbringing, treated me for years as being openly crazy. She revealed helpless longings to give me her head for my poor, sick one, and consciously identified herself as the doctor and me as the patient seeking state hospitalization. In innumerable ways she thus functioned as the doctor-daughter whose life was devoted to the overwhelming task of giving support to her desperately psychotic patient-mother.

THE ISOLATION OF THE THERAPIST IN THE MILIEU

Such phenomena are usually due in large part to the patient's unconscious reprojection, upon the therapist, of pathological introjects derived from the parents. In the course of the patient's becoming well, the therapist must serve for a time as the bearer of these introjects. Hill (1955) has stated that the illness is left with the doctor—in my opinion not a definitive state for which we must settle, but indeed an inescapable way station. The therapist tends, so long as this phase continues, to feel himself the repository of the patient's old, sick identity, and to be so treated by the ward staff, until the patient becomes able not merely to project, but to rework, and to assume responsibility for, his formerly predominant psychotic aspects.

Because of this inability of the patient to undergo broad-scale change on all fronts simultaneously, his early evidences of improvement in treatment may be detectable only in the individual therapy setting, while the ward staff still have to cope with a patient whom they find maddeningly, discouragingly, and seemingly unrelentingly ill. Thus, for these months, the therapist feels himself to be alone in seeing and appreciating changes which neither the patient nor the ward staff sees or appreciates.

When the individual therapy must still take place largely or wholly on the ward, there are times when the therapist is in effect shut out by a too-confused and too-noisy ward atmosphere, in which his patient remains submerged along with the other patients and an often undermanned or predominantly hostile ward staff. In this situation the therapist feels alone and unable to make a dent in the patient's usual ward life, unable to create even a tiny island of individual-therapy milieu in the midst of the confusion.

A few months ago I had occasion to go to the ward for an hour with a chronically psychotic woman who generally comes to my office for her sessions. With this woman I have labored mightily, for years, to help her to realize that her real name is Edna Bennett (a pseudonym) and not, as she ragingly insists, variously Martha Ramsey or Sarah Norton or Celia or Beryl, and so on. There has been no more significant issue, no more important focal point, in her treatment. When I went to the building where she lives, she was in a bathroom. A motherly aide who has long been very important to the patient went to the bathroom door, knocked and said, in a pleading, intimidated voice, "Martha, your doctor is here." At this point I felt that all my therapeutic efforts had been occurring in a vacuum as contrasted with the patient's ward-life "reality."

The therapist may receive, from the patient, so little acknowledgment of himself as he experiences himself that he may feel, in the individual therapy situation itself, almost unbearably isolated. The only schizophrenic patient whose session I ever had to leave, because he made me so uncomfortable, was a little middle-aged man who for years was unable to differentiate at all well between me and any of the other persons, or even at times various of the inanimate things about him (such as furniture and the building itself). The first session from which I walked out early was one in which, in the midst of his unending complaints, he walked over to his dresser, seized some clothes newly returned from the hospital laundry but not impeccably done, thrust them before me and demanded, "Is this any way to do laundry?"—fully as though I were the hospital laundress who had done them. I was so furious and upset that I walked out. It was, I think, not so much the social derogation (to which I was long accustomed) that upset me, but rather the total lack of acknowledgment of my identity as a therapist. Unconsciously, the role of laundress must have been tempting to me, for in that role I would have been relieved of the task of the therapy itself. But no; it should not be forgotten that, to him, these roles were not separate; he saw me as omnipotent, with my laundress function inseparable from my therapist function. At times when he was reacting to me as being administrator rather than therapist, this was in part due to my dabbling some at being the administrator, as an escape from my helplessness as his therapist.

The therapist's feeling of anxious isolation is heightened in relation to those designed therapeutic milieu situations where there is an emphasis on "total push." He comes to feel that if he is not digested into this milieu (which is often run by some particularly dynamic administrator) there will be no room for him at all. One administrator began making this explicit by reaching the conclusion that the fostering of a ward-group therapeutic milieu required that the several individual therapists of patients on his ward schedule their sessions in the afternoons, leaving the mornings fully devoted to the therapeutic milieu activities. His opinion of his colleagues' talents for individual therapy was so outspokenly low as to make it clear that, if he were left unbridled, he would soon find it imperative to set aside the afternoons also, and then the individual therapists would be squeezed completely out of his unit.

Incidentally, such a "total-push" emphasis also makes it inordinately guilt-provoking for the therapist to be aware of his dependent feelings toward the patient, which are so essential a part of the patient's making contact with his own inner strengths and capacities for loving and for essentially therapeutic relatedness. We do not want to settle for the patient's letting a kind of essentially ego-alien "healthy activity" be temporarily imposed upon him. Some patients are able to emerge into aliveness only on the ward, while for months they need to be largely silent and motionless in their sessions, so that their inner self and their outwardly manifested self can remain in contact and grow hand in hand. In these patients there has been, since early childhood, an increasing lag between their inner, feeling-invested, ego-identity development and the outwardly manifested, environmentally demanded, but largely uninvested-with-feeling "social self." A patient who spends the bulk of his time in the total-push environment of the ward, and who is therefore being pressured to manifest behavior he does not deeply feel as genuinely his, needs to find in the psychotherapy situation an atmosphere which fosters his being in, at an emotional level, what he is doing, and which enables him to know that he is deeply meaningful to the therapist in being and doing what he is being and doing—namely, just existing, and growing as a plant grows or as a fetus grows.

In some of these instances of what I have termed, in a number of papers (Searles, 1965a), *therapeutic symbiosis*, outward signs of aliveness in the psychotherapeutic sessions are largely absent and, particularly when the milieu is deeming it all-important for patients to be active, the therapist tends to feel left behind and stuck not only in isolation but in inanition. Of the therapy he can only report, to the administrator, the nurses, and the aides, a striking lack of activity and of words, and is deeply ashamed to let even himself know how much he cherishes this very relatedness with the patient and how greatly he dreads losing it.

Just as the long-hospitalized patient has long since been largely replaced, in the parental or marital family, by other family members, so the therapist may come to feel threatened with total replacement in his relationships with the personnel of the therapeutic milieu by, ironically but not coincidentally, the patient himself, in the phase of treatment in which the patient is functioning in a much more healthy fashion, and in which the therapist is transitionally being the repository of the patient's former, more psychotic identity components. The therapist now feels as isolated, when he comes on the ward, as the patient's former behavior indicated him to be, and the ward personnel now embrace the patient in their fold as they once at least sporadically embraced the therapist. Needless to say, the patient does much to promote and to perpetuate his being the accepted one on the ward, and his therapist the outcast there.

For long periods of time the therapist feels that the only role available to him, for relatedness with the patient, is that of a subjectively omnipotent parent. For literally years, in a number of instances, I have found myself shying away from being viewed by the patient as being, essentially, everyone and everything in the patient's life. One of the unacceptable aspects of this role is that it is essentially that of the seemingly omnipotent, but inwardly helpless, much-hated, much-despised, and much-blamed "schizophrenogenic" parent.

In the same vein, the therapist fears, often with encouragement from the ward staff, that he is seen not as benevolently, but as malevolently omnipotent. For example, one day when I went down to the Lodge dining room for a badly needed respite at lunch, I happened to sit next to a young male aide who had been working for about two years with a woman, now in her early thirties, whom I had been treating for about ten years. He told me, in simple, forthright, and passionately felt terms, that he felt I had robbed her of ten of the best years of her life by not using tranquilizing drugs in her treatment.

Similarly in incidents of a patient's acting out with, as the therapist senses, a clear relationship to the events of the individual therapy, he feels genuinely guilty in face of the ward personnel's holding him omnipotently responsible. One of my patients threw a heavy fire extinguisher downstairs, without concern whether it might kill someone, the day after I had told her I had to cut down her hours from four to three per week. Another patient repeatedly set fires on the disturbed ward and I, who am admittedly not completely comfortable about my own pyromaniac tendencies, was held fully and personally responsible for these events by the nurse in charge, just as though I had set the fires with my own hand.

A hebephrenic man was for about two years largely silent in our sessions, except for his variously belching, passing flatus, and launching into vitriolic cursing at me. He would evidently hallucinate my saying insulting things to him, and without warning would show every evidence of being at the point of hurling himself upon me. He became more and more convinced that I was there to sexually molest or murder him, or both. I made sure to uncross my knees, throughout each of the extremely tense sessions, sufficiently often to keep the circulation in my legs in excellent condition, and spent much time thinking, "Now, if he comes over the bed at me, I'll go over there," and so on. Meanwhile, the ward personnel continued fondly to see Eddie, as they called him, as being a cheerful and thoroughly innocuous, albeit manifestly homosexual and hebephrenic fellow, and the charge nurse told me that, if Eddie should become assaultive, as I repeatedly warned her he seemed to me on the verge of becoming, he would simply be "acting out *your* assaultiveness." The day came when all concerned with Eddie found reason to know that he had been repressing an abundance of aggression of his own; but for some months, in the interim, I felt very much alone and intensely threatened in relation to the patient and that "therapeutic milieu."

Obviously, one reason why the therapist cannot accept the omnipotent role, which the patient (and the charge nurse in the aforementioned instance) perceives him to occupy, is because it contrasts so utterly to the helplessness he is feeling in himself so much of the time. The patient's transference is to him as an *ostensibly* all-powerful, but inwardly and in actuality helplessly inadequate parent. One hebephrenic woman once commented about her father, long viewed by her as omnipotent, "Mr. Adams is a very important thing." In such a vein she long reacted to me, as being very important, and at the same time a thing, not a person. She would occasionally, though not frequently, report dreams, and it was not until eight and a half years after the beginning of our work that her first reported dream about me occurred.

In the fourth year of my work with another hebephrenic woman, there occurred one of the most productive hours I had spent thus far with her. When, after knocking, I went into her room on the disturbed ward, I found her entirely nude and suggested she get some clothes on. She quickly started showing an active interest in doing this herself; with the help of the charge nurse she got into an attractive dress. One of a number of meaningful exchanges ensued when, standing a few feet behind and to one side of me, she said, "I can't get him," with a kind of exasperated longing in her tone. I felt this referred to me, and asked, "You can't capture him—you can't understand him?"—not feeling sure, as so very often was the case, what her word "get" meant. She made no reply, but a bit later talked about someone's putting something into a hole, and I said, "If you're wondering how long it'll be before you get me to put my penis in you, that is not going to happen." She replied, in a tone of genuine wonder and puzzlement, "How will you tell where I am?" I said, with some surprise, "You feel that's the only way I can tell where you are?" There was no answer; then, within a few seconds, suddenly feeling I now saw why she had been trying for years to get me to have intercourse with her, I said, "Perhaps you feel that would be the only way *you* could tell where you are." She made no immediate response, but after a few seconds she asked calmly, rather flatly, with just a faint trace of dryness and sardonic quality, "What do you think of the crops this year? Do you think they'll come up without your putting your penis into them?" This conjured up in me a fantasy of broad fields of grain, a vast and majestic picture of growth, in relation to which my penis was so incomparably puny as to be beneath scorn. I felt this to be her way of conveying that her growth-drive was presently far too powerful to wait for my penis.

Daily nursing reports are another effective medium for helping the therapist to feel isolated. When, for example, a charge nurse dutifully reported, concerning a psychotic physician-patient, Dr. Ryan, " 'Searles is a shit,' observed Dr. Ryan calmly," I clearly heard the message from both of them.

A student nurse wrote, concerning another of my patients:

She kept wondering what they did to her chest. "You can't

trust these doctors. They keep breaking my bones and letting them knit just to prove that they would knit. . . ." Seemed delighted to give me one of the lollipops that she bought.

Six months later, on the day before my return from vacation, another student nurse reported, concerning the same patient:

> Mrs. Smith sounded upset and I went up to her. I rubbed her back for awhile and she talked to me. She said she wanted me to kill her doctor and I told her I could not do that. She said it would be justifiable homicide and to tell everyone that she had told me to do it. I told her that it would not be the thing to do, but she couldn't understand why. She was almost asleep when I left the room.

Over a period of some three years this woman, the mother of three children whom she had disowned for several years, would function in her sessions with me in a manner which often evoked savagely condemnatory responses from me. Meanwhile the daily reports from a female aide, who herself was also a middle-aged mother, showed the aide to be deeply touched and moved by the patient's yearning to give and receive mothering. For instance, the aide was moved at the patient's deeply felt conviction that a fly on the ceiling was the patient's child; and on another occasion reported: "She pointed to a tree and said it was her child. . . . Wants to go to Georgetown Hospital to have a huge lump removed from her throat."

On another occasion, during a friendly talk, the patient told the same aide, "You're in the iron curtain now." A few months later, the aide reported: ". . . said she would love to go home and stay in bed a whole month and let them carry her sugar and good sweet things to eat."

Only two days later, by way of contrast, another aide reported concerning this patient: "On the way back from town she was ranting about how all the doctors, especially 'the Searles,' should be pulverized and ground up into hamburger. . . . 'Who the hell does he think he is? He's not my mother and father.' "

On another typical occasion, her favorite aide reported her saying, "I talked to that Dr. Searles about my childhood and it is like having a knife in my heart." It was a red-letter day for me when after some three years this aide, an earthy farm woman of little schooling, in a special note to me said, "I think you are the right analyst for her and you've helped her a lot."

No less isolating for the therapist is the transference position of the totally good parent to whom the patient incessantly turns for protection from the supposedly malevolent ward milieu. Since I have become better able to deal with this kind of positive transference I have almost never found occasion, for something like a decade now, to intrude into whatever particular type of therapeutic milieu this or that one among a long succession of administrators has fostered for various of the patients I have been seeing. Two considerations have helped me to deal with this transference: (1) seeing clearly the acted-out sadism on the patient's part toward me, in his making me the helpless, victimized, captive audience for endlessly detailed recitals of the brutality and neglect he suffers on the ward; and (2) seeing, and helping the patient to see, the subtle clues, during the session itself, indicating that the brutal administrator, or frighteningly murderous fellow patient, of whom the patient complains, is a disguised representation of the therapist himself. Only as such previously unconscious transference distortions on the patient's part (in his experience of the overall hospital setting) become resolved does the therapeutic milieu become really available to him as such. One comes to see, now, that one has been receiving from the patient a jaundiced view of his ward life, partly because he has unconsciously greatly feared the therapist's envy and jealousy of him in relation to its more gratifying aspects, and partly because he has been unconsciously involved in a conflict of loyalties between his relationship with the therapist and his relationships with the other persons in the ward milieu. The threatened-paranoid view of this milieu, on the part of either patient or therapist, is now seen in retrospect as having been a defense against his longing to give himself up wholly to a cherished milieu which can never be wholly his, and which he must someday completely lose.

ISOLATION OF THE THERAPIST: ITS THERAPEUTIC VALUE

The individual therapist needs to become free of having to campaign, in his work, for the goals the ward milieu sets up as laudable; he must be free to focus with the patient on what is emerging here and now in the individual session. If he does this, he best fosters the patient's developing autonomy and, through discerning and helping to resolve the transference distortions (as I have mentioned), he best fulfills his particular role in the overall milieu. For example, a series of administrators have striven to help one of my patients move out of the hospital into a long-ready apartment, and I, too, have long felt this to be a desirable goal. But I find that the unconscious meanings which this apartment has for her can emerge, in the psychotherapy, only insofar as I am not bound by a conscious duty of somehow getting her to move into the apartment as being a laudable goal in reality. Similarly, a therapist who becomes too greatly reality-bound will be unable to discern all-important symbolic meanings in what the patient, the typically concretistic patient, is saying. The administrative context lends itself to masking what are essentially intrapsychic problems. It is all too easy for the therapist to become caught up in the patient's conscious demands to move out of the seclusion room or the hospital, and fail to see that his task is to help the patient to move out of his unconscious psychological state of interpersonal isolation and impoverishment of emotional life.

I shall close with the thought that there is a dynamic equilibrium between, or opposition between, the ward personnel's consciously striven-for therapeutic milieu for the patients, and the patients' more subtle, but to the personnel unconsciously gratifying and cherished, therapeutic milieu. The patients are largely invested in relating to the therapeutic milieu as an incomplete mother whom they are dedicated to complementing, and it is difficult for all of us to acknowledge how deeply we cherish the dilapidated hobo patient who supplies to the milieu a kind of warm humanity by meandering about, uttering earthy obscenities; or the princess patient who makes us feel somehow knighted at the privilege of bringing her a glass of juice; or the colorfully acting-out patient whose dramatic escapades gives vicarious excitement to our humdrum workaday lives; or the cramped and crippled-looking woman, one of Leo Kanner's original autistic children decades ago who, pushing a hated broom and grunting curses, beautifully personifies just how inspired and effective we, in our contributions to the glorious over-all therapeutic milieu, often privately feel ourselves to be.

7

A Case of Borderline Thought Disorder

Mr. Bennett,[1] a mathematician in his early thirties, who was working as a computer programmer for IBM, stated in his initial interview that he had come for analysis in dissatisfaction with himself for "not wanting to face the reality of things—wanting to postpone things, not face up to them. I keep myself busy so as not to face up to them." This rather small, slight, erect, and precise person seemed confident and outgoing—seemed a comfortable man of action. But I felt him to be, behind this appearance, a markedly passive-dependent person, who sat silent much of the time waiting for me to initiate conversation.

His wife, who unlike him had already had some years of analysis and who suffered from a variety of psychosomatic ailments, had called me some several weeks previously, wanting analysis and tearfully indicating that she despaired of being able to endure her husband much longer. I referred her to a colleague. This added to

First published in *International Journal of Psycho-Analysis*, 50:655-664 (1969).

[1] The name given here is, of course, fictitious, as are various other potentially identifying details, such as the patient's specific profession and the names of his colleagues. If the details presented here happen to coincide with a description of any actual person, this is unintentional.

an early impression of mine that Mr. Bennett had felt coerced by her into seeking analysis, an impression he soon confirmed. I privately noted the broad, sadistic smile with which he spoke of his wife's ulcer symptoms, and of the fact that while they had been living in Chicago he had made 31 business trips, totaling 19 weeks, in one year—after his having made clear to me that such trips always caused her much distress. At the end of the initial interview, one of the notes I made said: "Inquiry as to what he was experiencing during the silences suggests that he may have considerable difficulty with his thinking processes."

I confess that during the early months of my work with this man I felt a degree of embarrassment at the thought of my colleagues', in neighboring offices, seeing him come to my office. To one used to a stream of either intellectually and culturally well-honed training analysands, or wealthy, urban-reared chronically schizophrenic patients coming to his office, I found myself, to my shame, feeling snobbish toward this gray, expressionless man, who would come in looking like a farmer uncomfortable in his first suit of clothes, and even faintly reminiscent of an immigrant still more ill at ease in the apparel and environment of this, to him, new and foreign land. He always wore a white shirt, a dark, uncolorful tie, a black or near-black suit, and black shoes.

He lay stiffly on his back on the couch, feet crossed at the ankles. His torso and the lower half of his body rarely if ever shifted position throughout the hour. When his eyes were not closed, he was staring straight up at the ceiling. Often, for long periods, his right hand was holding the top of his left shoulder, and his left forearm was crossed over the right one, with the heel of the left hand pressed motionlessly upon the middle of his forehead, as though he were concentrating intensely in an effort to make contact with the Infinite. This often reminded me, ironically, of the magazine advertisements of the Rosicrucian Order. His whole demeanor was one of agonized concentration, and I soon came to see, and repeatedly point out to him, that he was endeavoring to think his way through psychoanalysis.

This man grew up as the youngest among seven children of an

Alabama farmer and part-time carpenter, in a family which eked out a bare subsistence in a generally poor area of the country. All the patient's three brothers were now several inches taller than he, and all, as well as more than one of his sisters, had been valedictorians in the local high school before him. He grew up heavily burdened by the feeling that in the eyes of both his parents he could not possibly match the achievements, physical or intellectual, of his siblings. His father, the only other physically small male in the family, while widely respected as the best carpenter in the area and included as an equal among the cracker-barrel philosophers and amateur politicians of the nearby village, was generally held in the family to be a lazy and weak man. The home was run by the patient's mother, a physically large and loud-voiced woman. An event of dramatic and pervasive import upon the patient's upbringing was the death, caused by lightning, of the family's oldest child, a girl, on Good Friday, one month before her graduation from high school. The same bolt of lightning had killed a black hired hand and knocked unconscious, for some few hours, both the patient's mother and another sister. This had occurred when the patient was six or seven months old.

Among the earliest apparent determinants of the patient's thought disorder were *tantalizing, sadistic* motives. He dwelt much upon his having dreamed during the previous night, having remembered the dream upon awakening, but having gone back to sleep and having found that, by now, he remembered nothing of it. For example (month 7), "I know that the dreams gave me feelings of insecurity—or—it's not really insecurity—something unpleasant or—it was an uneasy sort of position or feeling that I had—I *try* to remember these things and I lose *all traces* of it." He indicated, lying there in his usual agonized posture on the couch, that he was finding all this to be tantalizing. But there was sufficient apology in his demeanor so that, coupled with my memory of his sadistic smiles on various previous occasions, it left me in no doubt that he was deriving sadistic gratification from the presumed tantalizing effect of all this upon me. Still more directly and with more telling effect—for I had long been used to much more silent and communicatively tantalizing patients than he—he would express amazement that, day after day as the date for bringing in his monthly check came and went, he would have had it in mind just before leaving the house, and would then remember on the way to my office that he had forgotten to bring it along.

In month 8, he mentioned, "—sadist— . . . I had a mental block on this word—I had the damnedest time thinking of this word." I took this as a sign of his guilty and fearful unreadiness to explore his own sadistic feelings. But it was early evident, too, that fear lest he be sadistically teased and derided comprised another determinant of the thought disorder in this man who evidently had had more than his share of such treatment from his many older siblings.

> [month 6] . . . there was always somebody in the family who was kidding me about some insignificant thing that could have a double meaning— . . . I was conditioned to try to be perfect—to avoid any vulnerability on any kind of issue. The reward for not making slips of the tongue was to not be kidded or teased about something. [He went on to say that, when he was about five or six, he had seen at church a little girl his age whom he knew, whose mother had her all dressed up.] And I made a comment to somebody about what a pretty bonnet she had, and for a good six or eight years after, I was kidded about this girl—Ruth Ann Jones—bein' my girlfriend . . . and as a result I halfway hated the girl, shied away from her—she was in my class—I was afraid to have anything to do with her for fear the wrath of the whole family would fall on me.

As the analysis went on, it appeared that his lack of freedom in thinking and feeling was due in part, further, to his *feeling unloved, unwanted, his consequent fear of his family's death wishes, and his fear of revealing aliveness*. In month 4, he remembered "one time when the subject came up, of whether Edgar [his next older sibling] and I had been wanted. I seem to recall my mother saying that she thought Edgar was a change-of-life baby—that when he was born he was just skin and bones, and that she had no idea that he would live—and I'm thinking that if she thought Edgar was a change-of-life baby, that if [N.B. "if"] two and a half years later I was born, I must've been a hell of a surprise!"

In the previous month (month 3), he had reminisced that one time he had made a cigarette out of coffee (which may well have been expressive of an effort to integrate his identifications with father and with mother, as I shall subsequently discuss). He mentioned, "and I got a pretty good [N.B. "good"] beating for that— . . . most of the time, when I got a whippin', my mother would make me go out and get a limb off a tree, or off of a bush, and then would use that to whip me with— . . . it's double punishment to me." I commented, "They sometimes seemed like limbs off a tree?" to which he replied, "Right, and I'm sure many of the whippin's I got did feel that way. It seems to me I have been sent back a few times because the one I brought wasn't satisfactory—I must've learned pretty early that it would only prolong the agony to bring back a limb that was smaller than her specifications, let's say." All this was said in a tone that conveyed to me how much despair and fear and helpless hatred he must have felt. "I can remember, too, times when I was told that I'd been bad and the only thing I could expect from Santy Claus was a stocking full of switches." That comment still makes me feel like weeping as I read it. "I don't recall all of [i.e., any of] the beatings I got—I have a feeling I just wiped 'em right out of my mind," he added, in a comment particularly relevant to the blockage of his thought processes.

Four months later (month 7), he reflected, "It seems that I grew up with a negative attitude toward life in general—it seemed that there were no rewards; there was only punishment— . . . I was good because I was told that I would get the livin' hell beat out of me if I was bad [startling violence in tone]." Later in the same session, he made a significant slip of the tongue: an intended statement, "Let me recall," came out as "Let me crawl"—a clue to his transference to me as a brutally domineering mother whose beatings he evidently felt ambivalently as both evidence that she did not love him, and yet as acts of love.

During the next session (month 7), he said, "Another problem I have [is] in expressing emotions—for some reason I have great difficulty in expressing emotions—one thought I have is that I wasn't allowed to express emotions—when I was punished by my mother, I wasn't allowed to cry or make too much noise, or else I'd be punished more, or perhaps sent out of earshot." All this was said matter-of-factly, with only a kind of gentle interest in his tone.

Two further among the relatively easily discernible determinants of his thought disorder were his *competitiveness* and his at times lightninglike *impatience*. For example, in month 6 he said, "I've noticed that my thoughts occur much faster than I can express 'em—I have thoughts and then I stop to express 'em and then my thoughts are off on some other— . . . they're fragments, I guess— . . . I'm impatient at the pace I move—in other words, I don't wanta be slowed down to the talkin' pace when I can think ten times faster, or whatever it is—I think this has to do with not sayin' everything that I think— . . ." Later in this session, during which there were many silences of a few minutes' length, he said, "I'm anxious to progress as fast as I can—maybe without realizing it, I'm trying subconsciously to analyze my own thoughts to determine what is significant— . . . the more significant the things are I say, the faster we can move."

Two months later (month 9), he mentioned that one can "dump memory" in a computer and "desk check" the printed-out results of such dumping, and said he guessed that one doesn't have access to the human memory the way one does to the memory of a computer. This last was said with undertones of not only exasperation and disappointment, but also of competitive triumph over me—with the implication that he could cause a computer to work so much more easily and efficiently than I was proving able to cause him to work. Later in this same month (9), he commented, "My thinking processes are clearer now than they were a few months ago—I think I learn more now from experience than I did—I know that two people can go through the—can start off equal, and have the same experience for a period of time and at the end of that time one has benefited from that experience more than the other— . . . I think now that I'm more aware of the significance of events that I experience than I was before I started analysis." I asked, "Who would the other person be?" to which he replied, "I think I was thinking of Wilson [another man at IBM] for instance." I felt this to be a hint of his competitive transference toward me, most probably as a representative of his next older sibling, Edgar, like himself a mathematician and the only other college-educated member of the family.

Concerning impatience, he said further:

[month 6] . . . there is a relationship between a child and waiting in my thoughts—it was an accepted custom or procedure for children to wait in my family— . . . [to wait, for example, their turn to eat when older family members and guests filled the table, or to wait to play dominoes after the more expert, older family members had had their fill of playing].

[month 7—This item touches upon his identification with his mother, a subject to be discussed later.] My mother was extremely impatient with my father and it seems to me she was also impatient with the rest of us—with me and my brothers and sisters—"When are you gonna get this job done?"—I get a picture of her yellin' at somebody because a job wasn't done, or because it wasn't done right—"right" meaning the way she thought it should be done—

[month 9] . . . I suffer from impatience—and when I say I suffer, I think I use the word correctly.

During the last month (month 17) of our work, I experienced at first hand what he may have meant by such "suffering": in one session I suddenly felt, with panicky anxiety, that I was going crazy from impatience—that I could not stand this working as an analyst. This was a feeling of a type, and an intensity, that I had experienced only a very few times in the preceding 15 years of such work.

Early in the analysis, data began emerging which indicated that his thought disorder was due, in major part, to *conflictual identifications with his father on the one hand and with his mother on the other hand.* In his tenth session (month 2), he said that for two years now, he has often blocked and been unable to think of a word. Later in the same session, he mentioned that two years ago his father showed much grief over the death of a friend. "He'd start to talk to you, and all of a sudden he'd start to cry. . . . He was incoherent quite a bit in his speech—all of a sudden would start talking about an entirely different subject, or would mumble inaudibly," and for some weeks the father felt that he, too, was near death. Such an outpouring of incoherent thoughts evidently represented a marked change in the patient's image of his father, and his own unconscious guilt about his father's actually long-standing depression evidently had much to do with the emergence of his own thought disorder.

In month 7, after describing, as he often had by now, his mother's ordering him and the other family members about, he said, ". . . occurs to me that maybe I *hated* her being this way. Somehow, because of this I have inherited habits from my father that I never ever wanted . . . like not talking to my wife, for instance . . . the inactivity and losin' myself in television programs rather than family participation— . . . I was the youngest of seven children—the pattern that all my brothers and sisters followed was the same: they were always loyal and loving and devoted to my mother, and a little estranged or removed from my father . . . so it seems to me such a set pattern preceded me that I had no choice—that's what I had to be; I had to follow the pattern of my brothers and sisters, my predecessors." His unconscious defiance of his mother's, and his siblings', pressure to follow that pattern evidently had accentuated, as had his unconscious guilt, his identifications with consciously disapproved-of aspects of his father.

[month 3] My mother always had a lotta things to rake my father over the coals about, and as I recall he *never* had anything to say—he wouldn't say yes, no—wouldn't even seem to hear— . . . pretty well took it and tried to ignore what she said.

In month 9, he expressed his conviction that some of the other employees at IBM were "out to get" a certain one of their number whom the patient felt to be unaware of this intention, and whom he considered innocent. He went on, "There's something in me that says, 'Ya can't stand by and see a guy crucified when he's done nothing wrong.' " Being reminded of his typically agonized, immobile posture on the couch, I felt that this remark was of transference significance: it was as if he were the silent, crucified father lying there, a reproach to the son who was failing to rescue him from his suffering and his isolation. In month 3, he had said, "I surmise that my hesitance in talking comes from the fact that my father didn't talk very much . . . and it's confusing that my [talkative] son hasn't followed the same pattern as I did." It seemed to me that the patient, during his own upbringing, had been sufficiently more vocal than his father (being regarded in the family as always ready to argue, even with a signpost), that he may have felt guilty for following so relatively little the father's pattern—may have felt responsible for the father's confusion, confusion because the son had not followed more closely the pattern of his father.

The patient's own deprivation, as regarded any sense of contact with his father's thoughts and feelings, presumably was an important factor in his presently being so out of touch with his own thoughts and emotions, and clearly had fostered a sadistic attitude toward his father:

[month 6] I don't think my father was ever very much concerned about anything—I get a blank impression of his reactions to just about everything.

[month 7] . . . my father always controlled his feelings so well that I guess it was difficult to know what his feelings really were—I've told you that my mother could yell at him loudly enough [example from month 3: "Alvin, get off your ass and go cut some wood!"] to shake the foundations of a stone building, and he'd give the appearance of not even hearing her . . . I know my father used to complain of having a weak ear. [But he said that at seemingly unrelated times the father, regarded in the family as not only lazy but a hypochondriacal cry-baby, would cry out.] It was a groaning, sorta weird feeling I got from it. I think [said with vindictive relish] that was one of his better attempts to express himself. He was pretty good at blocking out the things my mother used to say; but he wasn't so good at blocking out the pain.

[month 10] Bruce [his son] is eight years old today [said with great fondness and pleasure; then, after a brief silence]—the thing that I think about most, the thing that concerns me most, is my lack of communication, or lack of expression, of my feelings to my wife and children—I think I have adopted a distant attitude, an attitude of "don't get too close"—I don't know why—I don't think my father was very close to any of us children, and I know he wasn't close to my mother . . . [and he went on, later in the session, to reminisce about how] as a boy, I used to wear bought ovcralls and home-made shirts and home-made underclothes, and during the summer I went barefoot all summer—my mother used to clip my hair . . . and sometimes shave my head—we didn't spend any money on haircuts—we had a nice garden and cattle and hogs and chickens [the care of which was all, he had made clear in earlier hours, under his mother's dominion]—we always had plenty of meat to eat—I guess there were months when our grocery bill was as much as eight or ten dollars—that seemed like an awful lot to be spending—we didn't buy much from the grocery store— . . . I'll say this about the depression years, though: I wasn't aware that there was a depression at that time.

He evidently had been unaware of the fact of his much vilified and scorned father's depression throughout that era; but his own deep-lying compassion and concern and guilt about this apparently had fostered his introjection of the depressed father. Two months later (month 12) he began bringing out, with much feeling of love and grief, treasured memories, from an earlier era of his childhood, of walking with his father on Sundays over to a farm some distance away, where the father's mother and sister were living. Father and son had walked together in intimate silence and pleasureful contentment on these occasions.

In a session during the penultimate month (month 16) of our work together, there emerged the following material which expressed not only his oft-voiced concern at finding in himself qualities he had disliked in his father, but a new and poignant concern to maintain some sense of identification with his father in the face of his mother's "brainwashing":

> And this silence is something else that reminds me of my father's habit pattern—the—uh—what I would classify emotional problem, or inability to express full affection for my children and wife, is another characteristic, I believe, of—that reminds me a great deal of my father—the thing that's extremely confusing is that I—I can recall—uh—disliking these—uh—characteristics of my father—and I'm certain that there was a conscious effort and desire on my part to avoid following this pattern, yet somehow through evolution I have found that I have adopted the same habits, same characteristics—I find that

I ask myself the question, "What else—what else about me is like my father?—uh—Is the only thing about me that's like my father things that displease me? [tone of concern]"—I think I ask myself this question because it occurs to me that there was a desire to somehow identify with my father, or somehow recognize the fact that he was [N.B.] my father.

(I'm struck right there with your use of the past tense [since his father was still living].)[2] Yeah, I guess—uh—the thought strikes me and I guess pretty much in the same vein—there was a helluva lotta brainwashing going on, and the remarks my mother would make about my father were derogatory, and an attitude like this has a cumulative effect, and it seems to me there was an effort, whether it was conscious or otherwise, on the part of my mother to—I'm lost for expression—to somehow discredit—I don't know if "discredit" is the word I'm looking for—in—other words to—uh—wash out the words of my father—if this went far enough it would be as if I had no father whatsoever—in other words, you know, "A father doesn't do things like this" and "A father shouldn't do things like this"—eventually ya begin to doubt whether this man is your father— ... an effort to discredit, or completely wash out the recollections of my father really being a father—the thought occurred to me that—uh—that through spite or—or otherwise, I might have—uh—adopted some of the habits of my father, just to perhaps convince myself or others that I recognize that he was my father I accepted him as bein' my father seems to me kinda a ridiculous thing to do to adopt habits I dislike; but I have to face that possibility.

A month earlier (month 15), after having described his father's appearing absolutely unmoved by the mother's yelling demands, he had said, "I felt that men were the unemotional types who just stayed silent." As I shall elaborate more fully later, it was apparent that the new-found freedom to feel and to express emotion, which developed as the analysis proceeded, undermined the patient's sense of masculinity—masculinity as defined in the just-mentioned idiosyncratic terms—and I clearly felt, although I could not help him to see, that his fear of "homosexuality" was one of the major

---

[2] The analyst's comments, in excerpts from the material of the sessions, are shown in parentheses.

motives in his finding it expedient to move away from further analysis.

The role of repressed *defiance* in his thought disorder—defiance of the domineering mother-figure (i.e., mother, wife, analyst, and so on) became quite clear early in my work with him.

> [month 2—It suddenly occurred to him that] Maybe I resent it when a new thought comes into my mind—maybe I feel pushed by a new thought—maybe I suffer from the same thing in my mental processes as I do in everyday routine test aspects.

> [month 4] I'm confident that as a child I received a great many whippings [from mother]; but I can't remember any of those whippings and I can't remember what I got any of them for.

> [month 11—This excerpt occurred late in an hour in which a reported dream, and his associations to it, indicated that his father's elusive emotionality was being portrayed by fish in a lake in his home area.] It seems strange to me [voice now strained for the first time in the session]; but I don't recall ever going hunting or fishing with any of these people [i.e., various home-town persons he had been mentioning] . . . I remember people used to throw dynamite in the water to get the fish, and they also poisoned the water with buckeye—to explain buckeye: it's a kind of fruit with a nut and this nut is poisonous—I don't know if it's deadly poisonous; but it would make the fish come to the top for air and when they'd come to the top they'd catch 'em [silence of several minutes]. I was trying to think of some situation now or in the past where I felt I was being pushed into something or forced into something—my wife exerted a lot of pressure for me to go into analysis, is one thing that comes to mind [silence of several minutes]. I was thinking of playing golf again [silence]. (I notice you don't say what you were thinking about playing golf; but I also notice I don't feel like asking you for fear you'll feel pushed.) [He then went on to speak of a tournament in which he had participated on the preceding Saturday.]

Through such silences, and the reporting of only tantalizing glimpses of what was going on in his mind, he put intense pressure upon me to resort to some form of dynamite or buckeye, as his mother evidently had done incessantly with his inscrutable father.

For several years I have become increasingly impressed with the evidence, in one patient after another—whether neurotic, border-line like this man, or frankly psychotic—that unconscious denial can be best understood as a part of the individual's *autonomy struggle*. Considerable data in this man's treatment, for example, suggested that both thought and emotion were subjected to massive denial, or repression, as in his experience both were felt to be primarily the manifestations of enslavement imposed from without. Such data are of a piece with his defiance discussed earlier. Almost incessantly, with his inscrutability and his conveying of subtle or only fleetingly glimpsed areas of feeling, he would invite me to try to coerce him to express thoughts and feeling. From the very beginning, I rarely succumbed to this pressure; from time to time, I endeavored to help him to see that he was inviting me to try to coerce him. Generally, my verbal responses were of a neutral, noncommittal sort; and the vast proportion of the time, I said nothing.

Frequently, in the early months of our work, in saying anything he would emphasize, in introducing it, that, "The thought occurs to *me* that . . ."

> [month 15—speaking of his father] . . . takin' care of his family was always secondary to takin' care of his mother—I was always aware of that— . . . this partiklar thing was a source of irritation to me—I don't know if it was a source of irritation to me because I felt my father should pay more attention to me, or because I heard my mother and brothers and sisters talk about the deficiencies and inadequacies of my father—I don't know if it was something I felt myself or something I was brainwashed with—I have a feeling that part of my struggle is to separate my own thoughts from what I was brainwashed with—I have a feeling that some of what I was brainwashed with is still present, but I don't know what the hell it is.

At this juncture I was reminded of his having expressed earlier in the analysis his feelings of exasperation, in his struggle to rid himself of psychological difficulties, by saying that it was as if there were a spring of clear water into which muddy water was recurrently flowing—that one might get the spring cleaned out, only to have it dirtied again with the influx of muddy water. I commented,

"Sounds like that analogy between clear and muddy water." He replied:

Yeah—two springs, one which puts out water that, say, is colored, and the other puts out water that's clear, and the mixture of these two sources gets something that isn't any strong, vibrant color, but that certainly isn't clear—the brainwashing that entered into my partiklar philosophy is, I'm sure, deepseated, and when I have independent or individual thoughts, or develop some partiklar philosophy on something, goes back and conflicts with this stored philosophy; I'm sure there's a great deal of internal struggle to decide which of these internal philosophies to follow, and as a result I probably don't follow either one of 'em . . . but perhaps something in between, and perhaps not— . . . there's a—I suspect—feeling on my part that letting the emotions play too great a part in directing thought processes will cause me to make mistakes, following the direction of emotions rather than the directions of logic, for instance—I guess there's a fear of letting the emotions play too great a part in—uh—in—my—uh—thought processes.

It was in the following hour that, in a similar state of confusion, he said, "I don't know what my attitudes were, separated from the brainwashings that I received."

The above passages not only reflect this man's intense struggle for individuality, but show his deep confusion as to where his own true self lies. Is it to be considered the clear spring, and is the "brainwashing" that muddy water which contaminates it? But this other spring, which was once seen as consisting of muddy water, is now seen as being water of a vibrant color—strongly suggestive of emotion. Is, then, this vibrantly colored spring to be considered the wellspring of his individuality—of his own true self? On the other hand, so he seems to feel, emotions are contaminants, imposed upon him from the outside and not a part of his essential self, contaminants which cause flaws in the purity of his thought processes. What he evidently does not realize, at this juncture, is that conflict is inescapable, and that an individual self can be born only out of such conflict.

This man's thought disorder, at perhaps its deepest level, included a *lack of qualitative differentiation between inner and outer reality*—between mental images and verbal thoughts on the one hand, and the corresponding objects in outer reality. This reification of his thoughts greatly complicated his ability to think freely, for he feared the tangible power of thoughts to do harm either to him or—since, as I shall shortly describe, he greatly feared his own hostility—to others.

I have already quoted his speculation that "maybe I feel pushed by new thoughts," much as though these were equivalent to the persons whose pushing he rebelled against. I have also noted his reacting as though the destruction of his father-identification, by the mother's brainwashing, would be equivalent to the destruction of the father in outer reality. In one session (month 7), he came in looking at his most gray and cheerless, and after a brief silence began:

> There've been a lotta thoughts running through my mind—I see a fragment—of one thought—and then I see another—the first thought I've been able to hold together is that I just live from one day to the next without purpose, really—without enjoying the day.

The word "fragment" was said with a startling concreteness, as if it were a rock fragment. I was reminded of his having begun a session earlier in the same month with:

> Did you ever see anyone tease an animal . . . till it became frustrated?—I have a feeling that as a kid, my brothers and sisters older than me did this to me—and then when I could stand it no longer, I have an image of pickin' up a rock and throwin' it at one of 'em—if I did somethin' like this I would be punished—I should think somethin' like this would affect the control of emotions— . . . I get the feeling that I was boiling, so to speak, all the time; I was being annoyed or teased, or whatever it might be called.

He reacted much of the time, indeed, as though the free experiencing and expression of thoughts were potentially as destructive as would be his throwing rocks at me. In a session two months later (month 9), after speaking sympathetically to a black man at work whom he felt to be discriminated against by the other employees, and after mentioning recent news reports of rock-throwing at black students in the South, he said that he knows his father is a member of the Ku Klux Klan, "because one time I found an old sheet with the eyes cut out in the trunk." He added, "I could get a picture of him out there throwing rocks at these colored people."

One could find, in the manifestations of this man's thought disorder, evidence of its representing a struggle against identification with various aspects of both the father, as is hinted at in the above material, and the mother, whose domineering verbosity he had so greatly resented during his upbringing. There was much evidence that, during his upbringing, words—and hence at a deeper level the thoughts that gave rise to the words—were used as weapons to inflict hurt.

From the very beginning of the analysis, there were many indications that this man was afraid that his *rage* might get out of control, and there were times, during his rigid silences, when I felt a nagging uneasiness lest he suddenly get up and hit me. These fantasies on my part gained substance from such material as the following:

> [month 3—speaking of his wife's childhood] . . . when she was a kill—when she was a kid, her parents yelled at her a great deal . . . I know that my wife had an extremely rough time as a kid . . . [Then, in response to my suggestion that he see what his slip of the tongue, "when she was a kill" brought to mind] When I was 14-15 years old I hit my father for some reason— glasses—around one eye a spot bleeding—some blood on his glasses—I don't know why I can't recall what caused this—it was in the house—it was in his bedroom—I don't remember who else was there; but I remember his reaction: he didn't say anything or do anything—he just got busy with something else and seemed to ignore the fact that anything had happened . . . I know there was some strong talk, heated talk, before we had this conflict—I don't remember what the argument was about . . . I told him I wouldn't stand for his touchin' me, or somethin' [a hint of the unconscious fear of homosexuality which contributed greatly to his eventual flight from the analysis]—I don't remember what the conversation was about—but I do remember takin' a poke at him, and I still remember there was some bleedin' around one of his eye—that

was the only time I can think of when I might been so mad that I coulda killed him. . . . (One gets the impression, from your description, that if you had gone on, he would not have defended himself.) I think that's true [calmly]—I think the sight of blood shocked me back into the reality of what was happening.

Another major theme which ran through this man's analysis and contributed greatly to his thought disorder was his *striving to rid himself of his so-conflict-ridden human status by becoming an omnipotent and immortal machine.* This striving evidenced itself very early in our work; within the first two months I gained the ironic impression that prior to the analysis he had nearly succeeded in becoming an IBM machine, and had come grudgingly to the analysis primarily in an effort to divest himself of his few remaining contaminants of human emotion.

[month 2—This session began with 10 to 15 minutes of silence.] If I could control my thought processes so that I could control my thoughts when I'm angry, I'd be very happy.

[month 2] I have a feeling that when your emotions start takin' effect in a discussion, that's when it changes from a discussion to an argument. . . . This is what I would like to be able to control.

[month 3] . . . the communications problem I have with my wife. . . .

[month 3] . . . I have a feeling that I should be keen mentally all the time.

[month 4] When I have a memory block, it's as if something inside me says, "I'm afraid you're going to mess up."

[month 4—He mentioned that, for over a year now, he has been working with a special type of IBM machine of which only a few have been built, specifically for the particular government department which is renting them.] . . . without a doubt, I know more than anybody else about this equipment. Yesterday I was away for just one and a half hours, and while I was away, three of the six machines broke down. Sanderson made the remark that every time I leave there, the place crumbles. I have a feeling that I withhold some of the knowledge and keep it to myself so that I'll be needed more.

His despising of himself for his human limitations was at times
shocking in its intensity:

[month 3] When I was a kid I was small, underdeveloped, or
weak . . . [He went on to say that he had had a great deal of
trouble with muscle cramps in his calves, but that this had not
alarmed him] because I would have expected it to go along with
a general sickly condition . . . I know that I was a sickly individual [tone of hissing scorn] and I guess I expected to be ill
and have pain—these sort of things.

[month 4] To realize I made a mistake kinda shatters
me . . . I get the impression I've had lots of fights with my conscience . . . [He says that after an exchange with a customer, he
used to think to himself] "That wasn't right. You're not a
salesman. If you were a salesman you wouldn't have done
this!"—I don't tell myself what I would have done . . . [and he
went on with a rather staggering account of how typically critical he is toward himself]. My confidence is shattered when I
criticize myself for doing something wrong . . . I seem to remember, as a kid growing up, feeling *extremely* limited in my
activities—the boundaries of activities for me were extremely
limited by evil—I had extremely strong images of what was
right and wrong—I don't feel I have that strong images of what
is right and wrong [i.e., anymore] . . . I'm afraid that I've got
the categories of superior, good, average . . . mixed up with
good and evil—as far as judging myself is concerned, I think of
myself as evil if I don't achieve what I could achieve.

All this was really quite shaking in its latent intensity, and reminded me how uncomfortable it is for the analyst to occupy the
role of such a superego; I understood better, now, why I had been
uncharacteristically lenient toward him about a late check recently.

[month 7—He described a premarital affair with a girl in
Mexico.] There's a feeling of *guilt*. I don't even recognize it; but
I'm sure there's a feeling of guilt, [and he added that the feeling of guilt] probably contributes to my emotional block. [He
then went into detail about his having been taught, by his
mother, that many things are bad.] As a kid I was taught
saintlike behavior [said with a deliberateness born of suppressed
fury] . . . I didn't dance as a kid—this was one of the things that
was considered bad—I didn't drink wine or any alcoholic
beverage— . . . But it concerns me that there's perhaps still

something within me that tells me these things are bad— . . . I wonder if it's become a permanent standard— . . . It—the standards would be mad at me [N.B.] for . . . [He associated the premarital affair with his going upstairs at night as a kid and stealing a nickel or dime from his father's pocket.]

[month 8] There's still a great deal of me that's child, I guess—and I suspect that there's a desire to hide this phase of me. . . . Bruce, instead of saying, "When I get old enough" to do something, will say, "When I get young enough to get a BB rifle and go out in the woods and hunt."

[month 15—He referred to his childhood situation as regards his mother's yelling and his father's silence, as] choosing between those two evils [N.B.], those two extremes . . . [in such a tone as forcibly to convey with what godlike superiority and condemnation something in him had reacted to both his parents].

He often likened himself to a machine, at times consciously and figuratively, but often unconsciously and with a startling concreteness:

[month 6—He expressed the feeling that, at work, in their present methods of logging production by the IBM machines] They're being unfair to the machine. . . . I told Sanderson we were logging the performance of a machine, not of an operator [conveying a feeling of closer kinship with the machine than with his human co-workers].

[month 7] I was running this rewards and punishments thought through my mind at various ages, the various stages of my life, and nothing comes . . . [for all the world as if he were speaking of running cards through an IBM machine].

In a session in month 12, while speaking of a current work project, he described it in what he called "our language," namely "machine language." I found it striking how congenial he seemed to regard "machine language" as applied to himself.

Early in the treatment there appeared evidence that one of his deepest conflicts was that between *his striving, on the one hand, to become fully an omnipotent machine and, on the other hand, to retain an image of himself as being a mentally and physically retarded child who had been beloved and pitied as such by his mother.* In month 3, he mentioned that until he went into the Army, at 17:

> . . . my mother used to call me "Baby"—maybe she'd still be calling me that; but I haven't been around much since I was 17—When I was a kid, I was the Charles Atlas when he was a 97-pound weaklin'.

He said that until age 11 or 12 he had been "very sickly," with tonsillitis, adenoids, hayfever, and nosebleeds, but added that he had been ill only a couple of times since age 13 or 14. He described a scene which had occurred frequently in his boyhood, when his mother and sister would be working together out on the lawn, doing the washing, while the patient lay on a "pallet" under a nearby tree. It was evident to me that these experiences had been among the most peaceful, contented times in his life. But it was not until month 8 that he said, ". . . question arises in my mind whether I miss bein' ill myself. . . ." It was becoming evident now how greatly he was threatened lest his own omnipotent strivings be fulfilled and thus disqualify him from sharing human love.

That is, presumably one of the determinants of his thought disorder consisted in his experience-based conviction that, if only he showed me what an agonizingly difficult time he had in trying to think, then I would give him motherly solicitude and protection. But his own conflict-born sense of helplessness and futility was very real. In month 3, for example, he said, "It occurs to me that I got the impression somewhere along the way, as a kid, that I was retarded both mentally and physically . . . mentally, especially as far as maturity is concerned. The forces I feel are 'You're retarded in this area' and 'I want to be mature.'" Each of these forces was expressed by him with great intensity. I asked, "Where are *you* in all that?" to which he replied with one of the most moving communications from a conflict-ridden self that I have ever heard: "Where *I* am is the battleground."

In these closing months of my work with him, it became evident that what the analysis was exploring (with specific regard to his thought disorder) was not his thinking per se, but his thinking as expressed in vocalization. With the considerable derepression of his oral desires during these months—expressed in dreams about touching a girl's breast, about drinking a Coke, and so on—I saw in retrospect something of how greatly the *repression of his sucking and biting impulses* had been hindering the free flow of his speech and, since thought and speech are so much wedded, presumably had been hindering the differentiation and free exercise of his thought processes as a still deeper consequence. During these final months, an impressive liberation of thought and speech went hand in hand with the emergence from repression of his oral desires. As part of this liberative process he became more freely able to experience an intuitive, "one grand swoop" (as he called it) kind of thinking, formerly reacted against as womanly, for it was characteristic of an incisively quick-witted aspect of his mother. (Her letters, so it now became revealed, were full of playfully darting innuendoes aimed at his wife.) This mode of thinking was unlike that of his relatively inarticulate father.

During the last several months there emerged many nostalgic, grief-laden memories of his boyhood, with considerable working through of *feelings of loss* in relation to each parent, and, in month 12, a dream provided a clue to the heavy childhood burden he had borne in trying to cope with his father's depression·

> My Uncle Luther had died and it was a sudden and unexpected death . . . some very small kids, four- or five-year-olds, were acting as pallbearers. Seemed like the casket was too heavy for them and some men around them raised the casket and put it up [for the funeral service]. . . . Aunt Cora, Uncle Luther's wife, most significant thing about her was her expression: she seemed very calm and solemn but not crying. I remember saying to somebody that she must still be in shock.

Upon hearing this I was reminded of the patient's characteristic demeanor and I sensed, in retrospect, to what an extent such shocking and overwhelming loss (the casket too heavy for the children), at a level more deeply unconscious than his previously revealed sadism and defiance and other negative feelings, had been contributing to his thought disorder.

A dream reported during this same month (12) reflected his

newly liberated identification with his mother's liveliness, and his ability to cope more freely with grief:

My brother Edgar and our cousin John and I were cleaning out a pool which was divided into little sections. . . . In the area where we hadn't specifically worked, Edgar told me there wouldn't be any fish in those sections. I didn't believe this, and went and got a pole, to catch a fish and show him. I remember seein' a fish, a little bitty one, and saying to him there *was* fish there. At this point the water was clear—kind of a school of fish like porpoise that were leaping in and out of the water, going all over the pool [slightly awed tone]—all sections of the pool. . . . As I was thinking about the dream this morning, it seemed to me the pool and the contents of the pool might represent me. . . . To me it was significant when Edgar said there won't be any fish in that part of the pool, and then seeing a fish—of course it was a little bitty one; but it represented a school of fish, then seeing this school of porpoise swimming through all the sections of the pool [rising tide of energy in his tone] represents to me that all sections of the pool were filled as far as schools of fish are concerned. This comment of Edgar, that there won't be any fish in that section of the pool, represents the environment we grew up in, which was a negative environment [covered with prohibitions].

His whole tone in describing the dream was expressive of the growth and liberation the dream content portrayed.

The final hour (month 17) was one marked by both grief and relief for both of us—for him, grief at losing me, admixed with relief at his becoming free of an analyst who was still viewed, to a significant degree, as his domineering, brainwashing, and infantilizing early mother; and for me, grief at losing a person with whom I had been through a great deal and with whom much had been accomplished together, but relief, too, that I would not have to come to grips with his most deeply paranoid proclivities, which were still menacing in their intensity.

Conclusion

In a paper concerning the thought disorder in schizophrenia (1962a), I reviewed the relevant literature in this field. During the subsequent years I have not encountered additional writings which seem necessary to mention in this brief paper. In this sketchy account of one among the main themes of a highly incomplete psychoanalysis I have endeavored to show something of how multidetermined, and how essentially reversible, this man's thought disorder proved to be.

8

Pathologic Symbiosis and Autism

In my experience, I have found the concepts of *autism, symbiosis,* and *individuation* to be reliably helpful in understanding not only the bewildering and awesome phenomena of schizophrenia, but also the psychodynamics of therapeutic change in one's analytic work with any patient, whether neurotic or psychotic.

This paper is the first of a series reporting what I have learned of these processes in recent years. It flows mainly from the following sources: (1) psychoanalytic work with nonpsychotic patients for 22 years, (2) intensive psychotherapy with 18 chronically schizophrenic patients at Chestnut Lodge and subsequently, in some instances for nearly 18 years, and (3) single consultation-and-teaching interviews at a variety of institutions with some 1300 patients, the vast majority of them suffering from schizophrenia of widely varying acuteness, type, and severity (interviews held mainly during the six years since my departure from the staff of Chestnut Lodge).

These papers are not intended to replace my earlier ones, most of which were written from a vantage point of my immersion in my work at Chestnut Lodge with relatively few chronically schizo-

First published in *In the Name of Life—Essays in Honor of Erich Fromm*, edited by Bernard Landis and Edward S. Tauber (New York: Holt, Rinehart and Winston, 1971), pp. 69-83.

phrenic patients, and among colleagues similarly engaged. That is a vantage point I cannot recapture, and I feel a kind of respect for what I then found valid, such that I wish here to put these more recent findings alongside those earlier ones, rather than suggesting that my present views invalidate my earlier ones. Since 1958 I have been a supervising and training analyst in the Washington Psychoanalytic Institute, and for the past six years I have been mainly that, but meanwhile I have continued to work with two long-term, chronically schizophrenic patients and have accumulated, through my consultation-and-teaching interviews, far greater experience with a multitude of schizophrenic individuals, including many acute cases, than I ever had occasion to encounter at Chestnut Lodge.

The categories that I shall describe of pathologic symbiosis, autism, therapeutic symbiosis, and individuation depict what I regard as successive phases of ego development in therapy. Whether any one patient needs to run that whole course will depend upon the level of ego development he has already attained at the beginning. He may already have achieved, for example, a strong capacity for a therapeutically symbiotic relatedness, in which case the first two phases of ego development would be relatively little in evidence in one's work with him.

In writing this paper I have had, more often than not, great difficulty in deciding what particular phase of the evolving process of illness resolution is being manifested in any one of the clinical vignettes presented here. It is often difficult, for example, to evaluate whether some striking and indubitably significant incident of patient-therapist interaction signifies a transition, on the part of the patient, from autistic relatedness toward symbiotic relatedness, or whether it is giving a glimpse, instead, of his transition from a predominantly therapeutically symbiotic type of relatedness toward individuation, which would imply that the work is much nearer to completion. Even what one experiences with the most chronic, slowly changing patient does not lend itself to an effortless conceptualizing of the work in terms of the stages of ego formation; but it is particularly the relatively well patient—the borderline schizophrenic patient or the neurotic patient—who is much involved in the therapy, whose ego functioning is so flexible, so elusive, so subtle, quite simply so alive, as powerfully to resist one's efforts to characterize his development through such theoretic crystallizations as are depicted here.

Despite the high degree of felt artificiality in this effort to categorize these part-aspects of living processes, the effort is, nonetheless, surely worth making. I have more than once felt, when assaulted by a psychotic patient's ways of responding to me, that both to protect one's own sanity and to help the patient regain his, one must develop a weapon and an instrument exceeding in power his psychotic thought processes—namely, that represented by a strong, accurate, and well-thought-out armamentarium of theory concerning these psychotic processes.

PATHOLOGIC SYMBIOSIS

The individual who, at the beginning of therapy, gives us to understand that his characteristic mode of relating to other persons is dominated by the ego defense of pathologically symbiotic relatedness, forms with us a relationship in which he is a part of a whole person, and we (the therapist) are the other, complementary part. This is in contrast to the autistic patient, who functions as though he himself, or contrariwise the therapist, were the whole—the single conceivable and perceivable and palpable—world. Pathologically symbiotic relatedness also contrasts with therapeutically symbiotic relatedness in many regards. Whereas in pathologic symbiosis the patient and therapist form two relatively fixed, complementary parts of a whole system, in therapeutic symbiosis both persons function in thoroughgoing and rapidly changing flux and interchangeability, with all parts of potentially whole and separate persons and, far beyond that, whole and separate worlds, flowing from and into and between, and encompassing, both of them. Also, the affective tone of therapeutic symbiosis is one of liveliness or contentment or fulfillment, while that of pathologic symbiosis is one of constriction, incompleteness, unfulfillment, or inner disturbance to the point of threatened insanity.

Typically, the pathologically symbiotic patient either coercively puts parts of himself into the therapist, or coercively evokes the therapist's attempt to complete his (the patient's) self, manifested as poignantly needful and incomplete.

On numerous occasions, for example at the Sheppard and Enoch Pratt Hospital in Baltimore, I have had teaching interviews during the course of a day with two or three schizophrenic patients, each of whom tended powerfully to deny, unconsciously, the presence of the crazy, sadistic introjects within him, to attribute these instead to me—to, quite literally, experience them as residing within me—and to leave at the end of the interview with its having been formidably established, not only in his mind but in the minds of the onlooking staff and in my own mind, that he is the human being deserving of compassionate rescue from the inhuman, unfeeling monster of schizophrenia personified by myself. Then, at the end of the day, during the hour and a half of high-speed and hazardous rush-hour beltway driving to my office in Washington to see training analysands in the evening, I would feel one or more of those patients as disturbingly present within myself.

These are the patients who, barred from access to an initial human identification in infancy and early childhood with a healthy mother, but presented instead with a chronically depressed or schizoidally remote mother or an openly psychotic mother who disturbingly and unpredictably invaded them with her own inner contents, now in a sense identify with the therapist; but they do so coercively, vengefully, and invasively in the manner described by Bion (1959).

These are the patients who have little healthy ego of their own but are, instead, a constellation of vengeful identifications with other persons, present and past. These identifications, because of the hatred and guilt and unworked-through grief which have attended their installation in the patient's personality, are indigestible by his ego; hence his unconscious effort to rid himself of them, to expel them into the therapist. Consequently, the therapist may find his sleep troubled by the patient who has invaded, and now disturbingly pervades, his whole life.

To the extent that the analyst-in-training manifests such ego defenses as do these schizophrenic patients, and to the degree that the training analyst's own ego functioning relies much upon introjecting the experiences of others, the training analyst may feel that the collective problems—the uncured components—of all the patients of his training analysands are being attributed to or funneled into him as, variously, a satanic source from whom all malevolence radiates, an omniscient oracle and healer, or, more mundanely, an omnipotently responsible grandparent. Similarly, the schizophrenic person whose ego functioning depends (as is true for all these pathologically symbiotic patients) upon complementing the ego incompleteness of those about him will come to one's office from his daily life on a ward surrounded by schizophrenic patients, and in a palpable sense bring with him all the most urgently disturbed among his fellow patients—his own patients, in a sense—in the ambivalent and secret hope that this rival therapist will convey the cure for all of them, in what happens between the two participants here in the office.

A patient's therapeutic striving is no less valid and real than one's own. The differences are mainly that (1) the patient's ego identity is *predominantly* as a therapist whose own hope for ego wholeness resides in his effort to complement the incompleteness of the other person's ego; (2) his effort is largely unformulated as such by himself, and is unshared in collaboration with acknowledged colleagues; and (3) his effort goes largely unsung by those about him, including his therapist—a hated rival who enjoys the distinction of being acknowledged as a therapist in title if not, so the patient is largely determined, in actual functional effectiveness.

The pathologically symbiotic patient whose poignant incompleteness tends to evoke our functioning so as to complete his wholeness—or who, instead, reacts to us as being poignantly incomplete and needing him to make us whole—differs much in his style of relating from the more clearly sadistically attacking patient who rapes us with his introjects. But these so-different styles of relating bespeak, so far as I can discern, a similar level of incomplete ego development, and surely any one patient may manifest, at one time or another, either style of relating (as, of course, at one time or another, may the therapist himself).

The sense of threat that often pervades one's sessions with these patients has basically to do, I believe, with the patient's paranoid sense (however unformulated it may be) that if this effort of patient and therapist to complement one another and achieve a single wholeness is successful, his only known identity, as a part of a person, will be lost.

The most dangerously paranoid patients, in my experience, are those most formidably able to involve one in intensely ambivalent conflict over this issue: namely, that the patient and oneself can exist psychologically only by achieving and maintaining complementarity to one another; but just as failure to complement the other will mean the loss of existence through nonengagement, so a too-successful complementing of him will mean a loss, beyond recapture, of one's individuality as a part-person.

As to the kinds of part-person I have found various pathologically symbiotic patients to be toward me, I want to mention, as examples, the silent and immobile patient who is my own subjective deadness—safely externalized and apart from, and yet complementing, the parts of me more readily acceptable to my own sense of ego identity; the easily labeled crazy patient who personifies my own subjective, repressed craziness; the patient who has the quality of an eternal child, who personifies my lost-child self or, more probably, the child I never was but never gave up hoping to be; the patient who personifies the unconsciously fantasied ideal woman I could have been, had I been born female, or even—in one recent instance, so the evidence went—the child of my fantasied woman-self; the patient who holds within himself, if only I can "cure" him, the key to the realization of my omnipotent strivings; the patient who represents one or another of the nonhuman ingredients of my past, whether a pet dog, or beloved trees, or diabolically frightening things, or whatever; the patient whose changelessness is my immortality; and so on.

In both my own analytic (i.e., therapeutic) work and in doing supervision, I have encountered many instances of the patient's functioning as though he were the only link between the analyst and a real world where there are real people who are living, who are involved in doing things and experiencing feelings. In short, the patient functions as though he were the analyst's aliveness, as though the analyst could gain access to living only vicariously, through the patient's own living outside the office.

To some degree this is a realistic reaction on the part of the patient to the sedentary aspects, the recluse aspects of the analyst's living as the patient can only limitedly know it. But it is more significantly a transference reaction to the analyst as personifying the more schizoid, detached, preoccupied components of one or another figure from the patient's early life, and as personifying, by the same token, the patient's own detachment from living. That is, the schizoid part of the patient himself, the part that participates little in his own daily living, he projects upon the analyst.

Thus the patient, in his recounting of various daily-life incidents, communicates these in a fashion which tends to make the analyst feel a recluse in this garret, secretly jealous of all the living the patient is doing; or secretly guilty because he cannot be filled, as he feels he should be filled, with altruistic joy on behalf of the actually narcissistic patient immersed in this recounting; or secretly grateful to the patient for speaking in a fashion which enables him to share the "reliving" of the incident. Neither the subtly schizoid patient nor the analyst may realize that the former was not at all fully living the original incident now being "relived"—that he is only now really living it for the first time, in this setting of "reliving" it in connection with the analyst who symbiotically personifies his own unconscious and projected schizoid self.

In one session with a deeply oral-dependent man, I felt considerably under pressure from him to share his radiant happiness about his imminent vacation, until the thought struck me, "Why should *I* be so happy?—It is *his* vacation, not *mine*." He, in his narcissism, had been making me feel that his happiness should be the center of my happiness, too, and of course at the same time he had been leaving it to me to feel the separation-anxiety-born inertness he was having to repress and project upon me.

In a supervisory session, the supervisee reported a recent session in which his schizoid patient had been describing a recent evening of bowling so vividly and amusingly and absorbingly that the supervisee had felt himself to be there at the very bowling alley, sharing the experience with fully as much pleasure as the patient purportedly had enjoyed in the original experience. In supervision, it is often the supervisor who, finding himself left wooden by a supervisee's delighted recounting of such data (as I felt left in this instance), senses the warded-off schizoid aspect of the patient's psychopathology.

Much more often, the analyst wonders what is wrong with himself if he fails unambivalently to rejoice in the patient's reporting of an incident, since the previous session, which indicates newly achieved growth on the patient's part. The analyst uneasily wonders, for the millionth time, if deep down he is basically opposed to health; the possibility does not occur to him that the patient's transference to him is symbiotic in nature, a transference in which the analyst personifies the patient's "older"—more accustomed—self which tends to feel left behind by, and jealous of, the new growth in the patient.

AUTISM

The patient who functions autistically in the transference functions, as I mentioned before, as though he himself were the whole world or, contrastingly, as though the therapist were the whole world. At other times, patient and therapist function as separate and unrelated worlds.

Parenthetically, it seems to me that the pathologically symbiotic patient needs to come, gradually and slowly, to have the experience in analysis of what one might call "healthy autism," an experience fostered by the analyst's functioning in a fashion impervious to the patient's efforts to coerce him into dovetailing with the patient's

customary pathologically symbiotic relatedness. Now, confronted by
this wall, the patient is thrown back into himself; and out of the
consequent changes within him, a capacity emerges for healthy
symbiotic relatedness with the analyst.

But here I wish to discuss those patients who come to us either
with autism manifestly permeating their whole daily-life functioning, as is true of the most severely and chronically ill among
schizophrenic patients,[1] or with autism present far more subtly at
the core of the ego functioning, as is true of the much less ill,
schizoid or pseudoneurotically schizophrenic patient. The "as-if"
patient described by Helene Deutsch (1942), Greenson (1958), and
others should be placed, for the purposes of this discussion, with
the latter patients, whose ego functioning is flawed at its foundation
by autism which, masked in their relatively capable daily living,
emerges with clarity in the evolution of their transference.

Many patients who seem to be leading lives filled with relatively
active and well-differentiated interpersonal relationships prove, on
closer scrutiny, to be living predominantly autistically. What seem
to be genuinely interpersonal relationships in their lives are not so
but are, instead, unconsciously fostered re-enactments of early-life
relationships, with the aim of achieving a solid sense of identification with a parent from long ago. This earliest human identification
was never sufficiently achieved for the patient to be said, yet, to
have a basically human identity and to be capable of genuinely interpersonal relationships. (These are patients to whom we give one
or another of various diagnostic labels, including schizoid personality, borderline schizophrenia, "as-if" character structure, and hysteria.)

Some 20 years ago I began seeing evidence that the child identifies, unconsciously and pathogenically, not merely with the aggressor in the parent but with, in particular, the detached, out-of-
touch aspects of the parent. It is as if the forming of this primitive

---

[1] In an earlier paper (1961e), I described such patients in discussing what I then
preferred to call the "out-of-contact" phase in the course of psychotherapy with the
schizophrenic patient.

identification is the child's unconscious way of grasping the parent in circumstances when the parent is being especially remote and inaccessible.

I first observed this in a borderline psychotic young woman who evidently had copied unconsciously, in detail, the behavior of her father at those times when he was being at his most psychologically remote, having secluded himself in the fortress of his library. He provided her at other times with her earliest human model for identification, for her more schizoid mother was much less utilizable for this purpose; hence it was desperately important to her to maintain an internal image of him, as the foundation for her own developing self.

Incidentally, I believe that much "as-if" behavior, which strikes us as repellently and contemptibly "phony," relates to an early-life impoverishment as regards any living, human models for the behavior which the patient presently feels called upon to evidence. In his need for adequate models, he has to resort to what he has seen in others with whom he was barred from genuinely identifying, or fall back on characters he has seen only in movies, or read of in books. Viewing these patients in such a light yields a sense of compassion which one badly needs in one's work with these exasperating persons.

Since that incident of some 20 years ago, I have found many times that instances of what one might call masochistic suffering in the patient actually stem from an unconscious effort to consolidate previously unachieved bits of the necessary mother-infant symbiosis, in order to become free of a basically early-infantile-autism mode of ego functioning. I am convinced that many instances of what appears to be masochistic love of suffering are unconsciously motivated, in part, by what is basically a healthy striving for identification. For example, a man, in describing a particularly bleak and despair-filled experience of the day before, said, in a tone of notable pleasure and fulfillment, "I felt like my father yesterday ... I was thinking to myself, 'This must be how he always felt!' " A woman, describing a recent experience of much inner conflict in relation to her marital family, said, in a similarly memorable tone of pleasurable discovery and fulfillment, "I thought, 'My God, *this* must've been what my mother was up against!' " Another man, saying that his sons at times reproach him that he does not love them, added, "This is what I did to my parents, and I'm feeling how it feels to have your child tell you you don't love them."

This man, like some but by no means all the patients I am discussing, was often told by his father, "Just wait and see when *you're* a father, then *you'll* know how it feels to have your children tell you you don't love them!" I am not trying to do justice, here, to all the complex psychodynamics of such a despairful and vindictive curse from a father to a child. Surely one resultant motive in the child is the unconscious effort to prove that the vindictive but supposedly omniscient father was, indeed, right; the child, now chronologically adult, still has a deep need to maintain an image of the father as omnipotent as regards, for example, this supposed omniscience concerning the child's future destiny. Such an unconscious striving on the patient's part is a milder form of the schizophrenic patient's unconscious determination to live out his life in such a fashion as to give reality to what were in actuality delusions on the part of an ambulatorily schizophrenic mother, whose craziness the patient cannot yet see as having been there.

The point I wish to focus on is the basically healthy unconscious striving to gain a greater sense of immediately felt reality as to what was going on inside the emotionally inaccessible parent many years ago, by unconsciously contriving present-day "interpersonal" situations (no matter how grievous) to yield that discovery.

It is awesome to see to what tenacious lengths some patients will go in this effort. One hebephrenic woman, for example, with whom I worked for seven years, would say at the end of each session some variation of, "Is that all, Doctor?" To this exasperatingly repetitious question I would reply variously, in a more or less guilty and attemptedly gentle, or annoyed, or disgusted, or curt fashion, "There's plenty more; but that's all the time we have for today," or, "Of course that isn't all; but I have to go now," and so on. Surely I made dozens of different brief replies to this question of hers upon my leaving her room, where our sessions had to be held by reason of the severity of her schizophrenic symptoms. It was only after several years that I learned that she had been trying, each time, to maneuver me into saying, "That settles it," an expression frequently used by a sister of hers who had been the most healthy and therefore most available for identification among the other members of her parental family. I now understood a little better why, as I left the building where she lived, I could so often hear her raging furiously in her room: she never succeeded, in all those hundreds of hours, in impelling me to say, "That settles it," and so to foster the identification she was struggling to attain. This is only one example of the extent to which this woman's life was given over to such game-playing. She had been married for some ten years to a man who did not at all share her love of art, and she once gave me to understand what a memorable triumph it had been to her, evidently quite unbeknownst to him, when she had once succeeded in maneuvering him into bringing up something, interestedly and so far as he knew spontaneously, about art.

The child who in later years is striving unconsciously to experience, at first hand, what mother (or father) used to feel in such and such a situation is trying not only to build more firmly an own self, but is trying also to complement the mother's incomplete self. The father who had said, "Just wait . . . *you'll* know how it feels . . ." does not himself know, at a full feeling level, what it—this immediate situation—feels to him, and is in a sense asking the child to some day discover what his—the father's—inaccessible feelings are. Such a father is being toward his child as a schizophrenic woman used to be toward me. This woman, a hebephrenic patient with whom I worked nearly 15 years, clearly had enormous difficulty in experiencing feelings and being able to differentiate among them. For years she had unconsciously to deny that she had this problem. Finally, one day, in describing some daily-life situation on the ward, she said, vehemently and in a tone of protest, "How do you think *I* feel?" That cliché seemed intended to make me think she was quite aware of anger; but I felt that she was trying to gloss over, as usual, how unknown to her were her own feelings. I replied, "I guess it *is* hard for you to know how you feel, isn't it, Margaret?" to which she replied thoughtfully and, so I felt, very usefully, "Yes, I guess it is hard for me to know how I feel."

Invariably, when the patient says, "Now I know just how my
mother [or father] used to feel!" this is said in such a tone of fulfillment as to make clear that this expressed discovery is so long-
sought, so cherished, as to make worthwhile all the years of
struggle—in treatment and before—toward it.

Now I shall give a number of examples of patients' autistic
modes of experience. One young woman consciously hungered for
emotional responses from me, and repeatedly expressed feelings of
hurt, anger, dissatisfaction, disappointment, and discouragement at
my silence. Yet the nature of the material she presented, despite its
being in many regards analytically rich, did not enable me to make
transference interpretations. What gradually became apparent to
me was that the more the analysis proceeded in a spirit as though
she were the only person in it, the more she thrived, and that the
consciously desired responses from me were unconsciously warded
off by her as intrusions upon an experience of herself as an oceanic
world-self. A male patient gave a glimpse of this same unconscious
wish for the absence of any interpersonal relationship by saying,
". . . the feelings that exist between you and me." It was the tone in
which he said this seemingly unremarkable phrase which was so
striking: it made clear that he was unconsciously saying, ". . . the
unwanted barriers that exist between you and me."

The patient immersed in autism is having so complex an experience that the analyst can be sensed only as an encompassing matrix
which must not become separate and add to the already overwhelming complexity. For example, a patient who is experiencing
himself as a shifting flux of unrelated somatic sensations, thoughts,
mental images, memories, and so on, is in no condition to hear and
utilize a verbal interpretation from the analyst. But such a patient
may, at the same time, be highly attuned to any sound, any physical
movement, from the analyst as a hoped-for beacon in his mystifying world. In this regard, he functions as if the analyst were omnipotent, were the only reality, and comprised the whole world.
The patient may experience himself only as an appendage or a re-
flection of that world, a world from which all initiating of thoughts
and feelings must flow. He experiences no feelings or thoughts of

his own and mystifiedly scans that analyst-world, in the spirit that if he can discern what it is calling for, *then* he will know how to feel and what to think. All his responsibility for being is attributed to it. One chronically schizophrenic woman, seeing the huge trees outside on the sanitarium grounds waving in the wind, wondered whether my air conditioner were causing them to move; and whenever she heard a sound from any other part of the building where my office was located, or from far away outside, would immediately ask, "What's that, Dr. Searles?" as if I of course knew instantly—as though I were omniscient, as though my eyes and ears extended everywhere.

A long-hebephrenic woman said, "If people think I'm a prostitute, I'll act like a prostitute," as indeed she did. There was much more than mere spite in this; she was helpless to be anything other than what she felt the world outside her called upon her to be. At another time she said, "People think I'm crazy; so I act crazy."

This same woman once said, of a colleague of mine on the sanitarium staff, to whom she was tenaciously and mindlessly attached for years, "Dr. Edwards sees the world through me." During her upbringing she had seen the world through the eyes of her father until, in her teens, her disillusionment with him had caused her world, and her fragile ego which had been founded and structured upon that world, to fall into pieces.

In the fifth month of my work with another hebephrenic woman she said, in the midst of much of her usual scattered talk, "I feel like a china doll in pieces." She said this with a demeanor and in a tone of helplessness and despair. Then, after approximately three years of therapy, there occurred a session immediately after a visit from her long-idealized father, who visited her every few months, and toward whom she had begun to experience some of the scorn and anger which had underlain her idealization of him. She began saying something of how he had looked and behaved during the visit, then exclaimed, in a tone of amazed discovery, "Why, he is really like a little boy!" and a few minutes later she suddenly seized her forehead, saying in a tone of terror and anguish, "My whole forehead is shattered!" I felt shocked, but understood her communication to spring from a tangibly somatic experiencing, on her part, of the shattering of her idealized picture of her father—of the shattering, that is, of an introjected, idealized image of him, an image which had formed part of her own body-image. In retrospect it seemed quite possible that her having experienced herself as a "china doll in pieces" had been a product, similarly, of her struggle to cope with feelings of disillusionment with some person outside herself, by introjecting that now-shattered image into her own body-image.

Another hebephrenic woman, whose husband failed to fulfill her hopes that he would rescue her from her long hospitalization, but who, instead, after several years divorced her, came to experience tiny fragments of him as being scattered all over the grounds of the sanitarium. She made relatively casual mention of this experience of hers, which—like all her experiences—she apparently assumed to be obvious to her supposedly omniscient therapist. I found much evidence that this perception was based in part upon her still-unconscious murderousness toward him. But the predominant feeling-tone in her casual remark was memorably poignant: it gave me a momentary glimpse into how deeply unable she felt to cope with her devastating feelings of disillusionment with him and her loss of him. She had to perceive him as vast in extent, something like an invisible covering of snowflakes over everything, and here, rather than—as he actually was—a person far away and in her past.

Autistic patients tend to assume that they have essentially no effect upon the analyst and that any effect they might conceivably have would be a shattering impact upon this world-matrix-analyst. Data from the parental-family relationships show how far from fanciful are such convictions. One schizophrenic woman had lived, as the social worker described it, only as the dim shadow of her mother. For months in my work with her, of the life she had had she could only say, "I went to the corner grocery store." Almost everything she said during her sessions was expressed highly tentatively, in the form of a question directed to me. It seemed clear that any functioning on her own was equivalent to terrifying craziness. Her rigidly controlled and controlling father refused, for a long time, to let her see her mother; he was convinced that were her mother to see her "changed," this would "crush" the mother. Years later, after she had improved very markedly, he confided to me his persisting apprehension lest word of her hospitalization at Chestnut Lodge reach the midwestern university where the patient's brother held a prestigious post. "It would be shattering to Leonard," he said.

A woman in her twenties with a borderline psychotic character structure manifested an almost rocklike resistance to analysis until, after several years, we were able gradually to explore the identification with her schizoid mother which had formed the core of her own subtly autistic mode of functioning in the analysis and elsewhere. She reported now, in exasperation and with desperate intensity, "I have the sudden conviction that for me to grow, I must abolish my mother; but my mother is a thing permeating everything . . . damnable part of myself; it's like a boulder . . ." During the following day's session she reported in a similar tone, "Whenever I think of my mother I think of just tiny fragments—she's someone I must enclose somehow—she's explosive—she's menacing . . ." For years she had reacted to me in the transference as being such a mother—a dangerous force which she had to control so tightly and unwaveringly that she could scarcely afford the luxury of any emotional spontaneity on her own part, lest I explode. Her so-conflictual views of her mother as being essentially nonhuman, whether in the form of something ineradicably all-permeating, or of a maddeningly unyielding boulder, or of dangerously explosive fragments, are strikingly similar to data conveyed to me by other patients with illnesses of markedly varied degrees of severity.

In my monograph in 1960 I included much data relevant to my present topic, concerning patients' transferences to the analyst as being something nonhuman. Rosenfeld (1965) and Little (1966) are among the other writers who have reported related clinical phenomena.

As the months and years of the analyst's work with the autistic patient wear on, the analyst is given to feel unneeded, incompetent, useless, callous, and essentially *nonhuman* in relation to his so-troubled and beseeching and reproachful, but so persistently autistic patient. It is essential that the analyst be able to endure this long period—a period in which, despite perhaps abundant data from the patient, transference interpretations are rarely feasible—in order that the patient's transference regression can reach the early level of ego development at which, in the patient's infancy or very early childhood, his potentialities for a healthy mother-infant symbiosis became distorted into a defensively autistic mode of ego functioning. At that level of ego development, the infant or young child had not yet come to achieve a perceptual and experiential differentiation between himself and his mother, *nor between his mother and the surrounding nonhuman world*. When in the evolution of the transference that early level of ego functioning becomes accessible, then it is possible for therapeutically symbiotic processes to occur between patient and therapist, and be interpretable as such. In due course, this phase of therapeutic symbiosis will subsequently usher in the phase of individuation.

9

Autism and the Phase of Transition to Therapeutic Symbiosis

This is the second in a series of papers reporting my current concepts about autism, symbiosis, and individuation.[1] I am concerned, here, not only with patients suffering from schizophrenia of whatever degree of severity, but with, for example, the subtly present autism that emerges in the course of the neurotic patient's analysis.

In the first paper (1971), which dealt with pathologic symbiosis and autism, I mentioned:

> As the months and years of the analyst's work with the autistic patient wear on, the analyst is given to feel unneeded, incompetent, useless, callous, and essentially *nonhuman* in relation to his so-troubled and beseeching and reproachful, but so persistently autistic patient. It is essential that the analyst be able to endure this long period—a period in which, despite perhaps abundant data from the patient, transference interpretations

---

This paper was presented in slightly abbreviated form as the second annual Harry Stack Sullivan Lecture, under the auspices of the William Alanson White Psychoanalytic Society, at the New York Academy of Medicine, New York City, on May 20, 1970. It was first published in *Contemporary Psychoanalysis*, 7:1-20 (1970).

[1] At present (1978), I have yet to write the intended paper on individuation. But see the many items under "Individuation" in the index (p. 781) of my 1965 book of collected papers.

are rarely feasible—in order that the patient's transference regression can reach the early level of ego development at which,
in the patient's infancy or very early childhood, his potentialities for a healthy mother-infant symbiosis became distorted
into a defensively autistic mode of ego functioning. At that level
of ego development the infant or young child had not yet come
to achieve a perceptual and experiential differentiation between
himself and his mother, *nor between his mother and the surrounding
nonhuman world*. When in the evolution of the transference that
early level of ego functioning becomes accessible, then it is possible for therapeutically symbiotic processes to occur between
patient and analyst, and be interpretable as such.

Meanwhile, during the autistic phase of the treatment, the
analyst's attempts at transference interpretation meet with a
thoroughly defeating response. Either the patient essentially ig-
nores them, or responds with such devastating derision and contempt as to make one feel crazy for having uttered them, or he
finds them so deeply and destructively disturbing that it may require him the bulk of the hour to digest, as it were, this foreign
body and expel it and restore, thus, his temporarily damaged autistic world to its state prior to this rude interruption. All this makes
the analyst feel thoroughly stupid and useless; but the patient has
unconsciously thus to destroy or ignore what the analyst offers him,
in order to keep repressed his own infantile need toward the
analyst as a mother who is far more than a mere person—who is
the whole functional world for him. To hear and accept and utilize
the analyst's interpretation would mean, for the patient, the relinquishment of his only known world, in exchange for one which
feels entirely unknown to him, namely, that comprising the analyst.
Hence there is an unconscious need in the patient, almost
physicochemical in its primitiveness, to dissolve any bridging structure offered by the analyst in the form of transference interpretations. The analyst senses, in general, that it is wise for him to comment only sparingly, for the relatively dispassionate emotional tone
of his comments clearly has a dampening effect upon the slowly
developing intensity of the schizoid patient's own emotions. It is all
too easy for a calm remark from the analyst to replace a dawning

aliveness in the patient with the latter's usual deadness. One can speculate, further, that a positive value can accrue, for the patient, to our not yet making any interpretative comment upon something we can clearly see in the patient. This may tend to foster integration, however inarticulate as yet, in the patient's preverbal ego, through identification with the silent analyst who is able to experience this material in his awareness.

In this setting, in which the analyst has access to so little of human-analyst interaction with the patient, and so little opportunity to exercise his usual analytic functions, he tends to be thrown back upon his own capacities for autistic experience. If he has not had occasion to become relatively well acquainted with these areas of himself—if he has needed to maintain these largely under repression by relating compulsively to his fellow human beings—this isolation into which he is thrown, in this work with the autistic patient, is deeply anxiety-provoking. I believe, in fact, that any analyst, however well analyzed he has been, experiences considerable anxiety at least on occasion in this phase of the work. As time goes on he tends to become related less and less to the patient, and more and more to his own increasingly regressed, archaic, self-punitive superego. The patient so tenaciously requires omnipotence of him, and his own superego increasingly finds him not qualified for benevolent omnipotence, but as qualifying for the only other alternative—malevolent omnipotence.

I have been amused in retrospect—but only in retrospect—at something I would do from time to time when I would be feeling helpless in my work with one or another chronically paranoid patient who was sure I possessed the magic cure for his or her suffering, if I would only "think nice thoughts about me," or "want me well." I would have come, long since, to experience much fondness for the patient; but all my conventional analytic armamentarium had failed to help her resolve her psychotic symptoms. Now I would find myself smiling helplessly and pleadingly at the patient (who was sitting in a chair across from me), with a feeling of wanting desperately to cure her, somehow, with my love. This, of course, like everything else I had found myself doing, did not work, and the intendedly magical love would be replaced by an equally omnipotence-based hatred, such that I would glare at the patient with, for example, a fantasy of burning out the inside of her skull.

A phobia concerning heights survived my analysis which ended some 17 years ago, and I have had much occasion for self-analysis in this regard during, for example, the 150 more or less anxious trips I have made over the Triboro Bridge in New York City during the past five and a half years. I have had many different experiences of this bridge, a fair number of them mundane and comfortable enough. The most memorable were panic-stricken experiences of it as full of immensely brooding menace, awesome and terrifying in its inhuman unfeelingness; and one particularly cherished first experience of it as comparably benign and protective in its immensity. Each of these I relate to perceived aspects of my mother in early years of my childhood which were little explored in my analysis, and to comparable aspects of my identification with her, aspects which do not have nearly as free a play in my work with my own patients as that work really needs.

My second analytic patient, for example, a schizoid man who put two years of analytic work to relatively good use, recurrently projected aspects of himself into a fantasy of a gigantic stone mountain, which was experienced variously as broodingly sinister, benignly massive and strong, and so on over a great variety of aspects during those two years. In a sense, this fantasied stone mountain was the most creative aspect of his analysis; but rarely, if ever, did the transference data depict me as that mountain. My own self-awareness was too limited, and is still too limited, freely to allow such nonhuman, or in genetic terms prehuman, pictures of me freely and explicitly to emerge. If such very early transference reactions could emerge more freely and directly, rather than their needing to be displaced outside the patient-analyst milieu as a fantasy of a stone mountain, these personality components would then become more available to the patient in human-identification terms. He could then acquire, for his conscious ego functioning, the strengths and energies bound up in such repressed and projected identifications with the mother of his "prehuman" infancy.

If we analysts can become able to work relatively freely and comfortably with these primitive areas of ego functioning, there will be some hope that the majority of hospitalized psychotic patients will be treated essentially by their fellow human beings and less by the displaced transference magic of truly nonhuman tranquilizing drugs, which are presently accorded a degree of awesome power, such as even the analyzed therapist dare not experience himself as possessing. I know of no more important problem in psychotherapy today than the increasing resort to an increasing avalanche of drugs, in an unconscious effort on the part of therapists to shield themselves from crucially therapeutic feeling-experiences in their work with their patients.

To the degree to which a patient functions autistically, he or she has not achieved a clear differentiation between, and integration among, such realms of experience as thinking, feeling emotions, and feeling bodily sensations. The analyst himself experiences strange responses in working with such a patient. I worked for years with a schizophrenic woman who experienced, for instance, a harsh verbal comment from me as being literally a bullet shot into her heart. Divided emotional loyalties were experienced not as such by her, but rather as a matter of the various physical parts of her body being controlled by various outside agencies. In some of my sessions with her I, for my part, felt physically beaten by her paranoid tongue-lashings, and on more than one occasion I left her room, after an hour in which she had been brutally hurtful, with a semisomatic fantasy of trying to hold together my eviscerated belly. On one occasion, as she was bellowing even more forcefully than usual at me, I had a somatic sensation that she was pulling the air from my pulmonary alveoli—a sensation strikingly like those which evidently gave rise to her delusion that various of her bodily organs were controlled from outside herself. Later on, at a time when she had shown much improvement in her daily life on the ward, but when she was reacting to me as being a murderous bitch of a mother who had killed my husband, I reported at a staff conference:

I remember one time when John [the administrative psychiatrist in charge of the ward] came sort of half-running up to me to tell me with great enthusiasm about how really warm an exchange he and the nurses had been having with Hilda in the nurses' station. . . . I felt defensive as all hell because I felt that it was a pointing up of—there must be something wrong with me. Everybody else, currently, apparently was finding her very likable and in my mind all I could do was to stave off double pneumonia.

This woman often expressed her delusional experience of herself as being a robot, or a machine. In many sessions, while she was forcefully verbalizing, with a sweepingly operatic freedom of accompanying physical gestures, endless delusional material into which no verbal, interpretive intervention was possible, I often felt as though there were wires running through my limbs, wires which were being pulled in such a fashion as to draw the muscles taut and render the limbs cramped. Such weird experiences were interlarded with much more ordinarily human urges to choke her, strike her, kick her, or bite her—urges comparable to those to which she actually gave vent, recurrently, during the more dangerous moments of her behavior in her daily life on the ward.

On numerous occasions, during single teaching interviews with somewhat comparably ill patients, I have found to be highly relevant, and therefore valuable for diagnosis and subsequent psychotherapy, seemingly unaccountable somatic sensations as well as fantasies on my own part. For example, one may experience an urge to strangle a silent and innocuous-seeming patient, report this to him, and learn that the control of precisely such urges, or his traumatic past experiences of having given vent to such urges, is a subject he finds of the most lively interest and relevance. Typically with the more deeply schizophrenic patients, one finds oneself experiencing bizarre fantasies and physical sensations unique to one's experience, peculiar to one's relationship with this particular patient.[2] It requires much faith in one's clinical intuition to speak of

[2] Marion Milner's (1969) book concerning her 20-year-long psychoanalytic treatment of a schizophrenic woman, has a chapter entitled "Her Lost Background: The Undifferentiated Sea of Inner Body Awareness." In this she gives some hint of her

these during the interview, for the patient, heavily defended against the recognition of his own craziness, responds more often than not with labeling one as crazy and tending to make one feel a frightening degree of isolation; further, the less experienced onlookers generally share the patient's view in this. But my utilization of such weird personal experiences has proved sufficiently valuable often enough so that, year by year, I have developed an increasing reliance upon them.

I remember, here, an experience some years ago with a pathologist who was suffering from paranoid schizophrenia. At one point in my interview with this overtly well-seeming but rather noncommittal man, I felt as though he were slicing my body serially with a gigantic microtome.

A much more recent example is provided by a fantasy evoked in me during an interview, a few weeks ago, with a 24-year-old ambulatorily schizophrenic man, before an audience of some 150 personnel members in the hospital where he was living. I knew that there had been many episodes of violence in his family history, on the part of various family members including himself. Although he now appeared nonpsychotic and well controlled, I learned after the interview that those about him on the ward were pervasively afraid of his homicidal proclivities. During the interview, in speaking of the episodes of violence between his father and himself, he detailed one "all out attack" he had made upon his father at breakfast, dur-

---

own somatic experiences in dealing with the patient's feeling of not at all fully inhabiting her body; the patient, subsequent to electroshock treatment, had felt herself cut off from all perceptions coming from inside herself and was living in a narrow area at the very top of her head.

Milner writes: ". . . she was adept at producing a state of tension in me, not only by the urgency of her demands for help, but also by her total angry rejection of any idea that was not completely formulated. . . . It was only after much suffering of such battering attacks that I eventually became able to put into words for her what seemed to be happening; how she could not stand my perplexity, just as she could not stand her own. . . . Just as there was an obvious link between avoidance of premature formulations and the capacity to tolerate unclearness, so there was also a connection between this capacity and my ability to achieve full 'body-attention' when listening to her; for the point about the body-attention is that it is extremely unclear, an unstructured awareness of all that is 'behind one's eyes' " (pp. 48-49).

ing which he had thrown a bottle of syrup which had hit his father on the head and knocked him, unconscious and bleeding, to the floor, whereupon the mother and younger siblings had rushed to the father in fear that he had been killed or mortally wounded. He had not been; but the notable thing, here, is that the patient had said "all out attack" in such a manner as to conjure up in my mind the fantasy of its having been a multiple attack upon the father, that is, an attack by many people—as, for example, a company of infantry, although I did not think specifically of the latter; what I did think of specifically was an attack by many people, more than a few, less than a horde.

Near the beginning of the interview I had sought to explore his feelings about the audience, without evoking evidence of any psychotic modes of response in him in this regard. Now, many minutes later, the fantasy I experienced in reaction to his phrase "all out attack" led me to explore, in ways I no longer recall in detail, his feelings about the audience. He now revealed fear, which he apparently had been having all along, lest all the people in the audience launch a physical attack upon him. This I found memorable, for never before, in hundreds of such interviews, had a patient let me know that he was afraid the audience would physically assault him, even though, not rarely, I had felt that a patient was functioning in the interview in such a way as to ensure that the audience would verbally attack me during the discussion period after his departure. This man's expressed fear was not discernibly of a gang rape, though I do not doubt that there were such fears at an unconscious level in this handsome and stalwart young man. In response to my surprised inquiry about his fear, he explained that his father had called him "conceited" and "a prig" so many times as to have convinced him that he is so, and he feared that the audience would perceive him so, and be carried away by their antagonism toward him. He looked very threatened, indeed, in revealing these ideas.

In working with the autistic patient, one may feel, for months or even years, that to the extent that one does not go on immersing oneself completely in his world, one has at most one or two very limited roles in which to function as an individual separate from, but related to him. For example, I worked for some 11 years with a hebephrenic man who had led, prior to his hospitalization many years before, a life of promiscuous homosexuality, in which each relationship had evidently involved not only sex but physical violence. For about two years, early in our work, he was almost totally silent, clearly felt intensely threatened sexually by me, and punctuated his long silences with sudden outbursts of vitriolic cursing at me, meanwhile seeming barely able to contain himself from making an intendedly murderous attack upon me. For my part, it was only after many months of this that, in one of the sessions, it dawned upon me, to my great relief, that it had now become conceivable to me to have a relationship with this man without either murdering him or fucking him—the only two avenues for relatedness which I heretofore had felt he was presenting to me. With another autistic patient, one who was highly verbal but functioned in the sure conviction that his was the only valid thinking in the room, any experience of myself as an individual separate from him was accompanied by an intensely uncomfortable awareness of my mental ineptitude and verbal inarticulateness. With still another patient, to function explicitly as an individual separate from him meant, almost invariably, that one was singling out, and holding up for ridicule, one or another of the more pathological aspects of the patient's characterological functioning. It is small wonder that the analyst, finding only such constricted areas for his own functioning separately from the patient, areas so highly unacceptable to his own superego, would tend to abandon such individuality for himself and immerse himself defensively, instead, in a "neutrally hovering" absorption with the patient's autistic world; this is, of course, a travesty upon the intendedly neutrally attentive role of the analyst.

Just as one's immersion in the patient's autistic world can serve as an unconscious defense against one's functioning in these difficult ways separately from him, so can such kinds of separateness be revealed as unconscious defenses against a therapeutically necessary symbiosis with the autistic patient. What needs to develop is a greater freedom, in the analyst, to oscillate between separateness

and oneness, as the changing needs of the patient's ego development require.

For the analyst, there is much of secondary gratification in his
functioning in an essentially selfless manner—in, that is, his functioning in a manner coinciding with the autistic patient's transference to him as being only a shadow. He may unconsciously delay
an otherwise timely transference interpretation of this state of affairs in order to prolong this largely denied gratification on his own
part. In my work with one such patient, for example, for a number
of years any verbal intervention from me clearly caused him relatively severe and prolonged disruption of his autistic world, with
only rarely any discernibly constructive result. He was also highly
sensitive to, and intolerant of, any other sounds from me, behind
the couch. Finally in one session when he indicated that a slight
cough from me came as an outrageous intrusion into his
monologue, I retorted in ironic fury, "I'm sorry I can't exist here
without making some sign that I exist. I say almost nothing, hour
after hour; but I do need at times to breathe or to move about."
The awkward but significant thing was that, when I said, "I'm
sorry...," I heard a note of genuineness come through my intended irony. It dawned on me that I was indeed sorry, for my own
sake, that I was unable fully to relinquish my own separate existence, an existence so tormented by this sadistically controlling,
autistically "fragile" man, and to be fully at one with the world in
which he remained so single-mindedly immersed.

I mentioned in the first of these papers (1971) a chronically
schizophrenic woman who, for a long time after the beginning of
our work, expressed herself verbally only in the form of highly tentative questions, often leaving the second half of a question unsaid,
as if needing my full concurrence almost word for word, lest any
venturing forward on her own be tantamount to the craziness
which had engulfed her in her previously acute psychosis. I was interested to find, after some years of at least moderately successful
work with her, that my own verbal behavior had long since come to
assume a form not markedly different from what her own had
been at the outset. I had become trained over these years in experiences, with her and other such patients, that the patient could ac-

cept an observation of mine only if it were grounded, to a very high degree, in her already-held view of the world, with the proferred new addition to the picture being given the connotation of but one more step. I discovered, now, that my own comments in the sessions were not merely infrequent but almost invariably in the form, not of unequivocally stated impressions, but rather of tentative questions addressed to an oracle, much as though I were incapable of functioning as a decisively separate self, lest such a venture plunge me into craziness and unrelatedness with anyone. Another such patient, far more ill than this one, in my best judgment—even retrospectively—required of me an even higher degree of sharing her view of the world while holding my own view of the world (that is, of reality) in abeyance. On one occasion, in the midst of her usual outpouring of reported delusional perceptions, she expressed her assumption that I had no eyes of my own, but was totally dependent upon her eyes to see at all.

I surmise that not a few work-addicted analysts tend, as I do, unconsciously to defend themselves against an unendurably sustained experiencing of their own individual life by keeping themselves immersed in the collective lives of their patients, one after another, throughout nearly all their waking hours.

A word should be said for the surprising power of transference interpretations of the patient's reacting to one as being, for example, his shadow, his dead mother, his mind, his tongue, the pet dog of his childhood, or some other "nonhuman" transference object. Whereas previously attempted transference interpretations of a more ordinarily human sort have been utterly lost upon him, this crazy-seeming transference interpretation proves the key which unlocks at least one of the successive doors of the patient's autism, and the analytic relationship becomes more alive, more human. One patient, for instance, whose years-long stony demeanor was generally unaffected by my interpretations, began a session by saying, with considerable animation, "I was very much moved yesterday by your interpretation that I was experiencing you as a part of the furniture here."

The analyst, to keep in touch with himself while working with the autistic patient who is so little able to acknowledge the analyst's own separate and human reality, must be able unashamedly to set such limits as his individual self finds necessary, relatively little intimidated by concern as to what his colleagues deem necessary in their respective ways of working with patients. I, for example, have tolerated usefully a schizophrenic patient's temporarily rearranging, for the sessions, the chairs and the lighting in my office. This behavior of hers interested but did not disturb me, whereas the supervisor of the analysis, years ago, said he could never permit a patient to do this. But I have felt a sense of conviction, in working with one autistic woman who controlled events in the office to a high degree, that if she made a move to close the Venetian blinds, or to open the window, I would kill her before I let this happen. Likewise, I have been able to stand years of silence from one or another patient, and I am now working with one woman who for the first ten years of her four-hour-per-week treatment never set foot in my office; I always had to bring the treatment to her. But my separation anxiety takes such a form that I cannot work with a patient who finds it necessary to control the timing of both the beginning and the end of the session. I have worked, and am working, with chronically tardy patients; but such patients are not free, in their work with me, to also depart from the session on the basis of some inner timing, irrespective of whether the alloted hour has ended. In one's work with a deeply ill patient, one needs to maintain respect for one's own limitations as being expressive of one's individual self, a self which, permitted thus functionally to exist, can provide the autistic patient with the only kind of outer reality of use to him, namely, a real other individual, with whom it eventually can become possible for the patient to develop a genuinely interpersonal relationship, and with whom he can come usefully to identify in the process of developing his own individual self.

Phase of Transition between Autism and Therapeutic Symbiosis

During this phase the patient's formerly autistic, automatonlike mode of functioning begins to give way, such that one can glimpse, at first only rarely and momentarily, but increasingly often and prolongedly, underlying fluidity, ambiguity, confusion, and chameleonlike qualities. One such patient for years had functioned with so single-minded a rigidity as to drive me to despair; he had striven chronically, so I felt, to impose upon me his reality as being the only conceivable reality. Then I began to hear from him such comments as these in one of the sessions typical of this transition phase:

> I have a sensation—don't know how to express it in words—of drifting realms. . . . [Then I interrupted with some comment.] You become gigantic in size, as the disruptor of the cosmos that I'm trying to put right. . . . I'm feeling discouraged. It's as if this building were a haunted house, and I'm in it with only you for a companion, and I keep thinking: It would be better to be alone, to be completely alone with my daydreams, than to have to cope with the disappointing realities.

It is my impression that the mercurial, chaotic ingredients within such a patient's formerly autistic rigidity are traceable to early childhood experiences of multiple, nonstable maternal objects. Many such patients have had a stream of nursemaids, of most of whom they have no conscious memory; or they may remember only a hand, without any more complete memory-image which tells them to whom the hand belonged. But the major aspect of childhood etiology of this chaotic core within the adult autistic patient, which we now see emerging, is referable to an own mother who was physically there consistently enough, but psychologically so poorly integrated that she constituted, for the child, a multiple and unpredictably changing stream of mothering-figures. One schizophrenic woman, who had had such a mother, protested, "Whenever you use the word 'mother,' I see a whole parade of women, each one representing a different point of view" (Searles, 1959b). This woman, in my sessions with her, for years saw an endless stream of persons in me—in, specifically, my eyes—and seldom experienced me as being a single person; usually I was two persons to her simultaneously, and her experience of her own identity was comparably chaotic and multiple.

Concerning a 21-year-old chronically schizophrenic woman whom I once saw in a teaching interview, the history stated:

> Betty worked as a toll collector on the Golden Gate Bridge for approximately ten weeks last summer, a job she despised but "endured" in order to get money to buy a violin and embark on a career in music. One day while working in the toll booth she began to ruminate about the unreality and meaninglessness of life, and felt that it was stupid to ask people to pay money to ride across a bridge. She looked into the "souls of the drivers" who were passing her booth and felt that they were "empty." At this point she started to cry and refused to continue working. She went to the supervisor's booth and refused to talk to anyone and only sobbed occasionally. After several hours, her supervisor brought her to the —— Hospital's emergency room. . . . The patient's mother is a 58-year-old woman, raised in rural Oregon, whose own mother was described as a paranoid woman who required electroconvulsive treatment but no hospitalization. The patient indicates that her mother was the "scapegoat" of the family and was abused verbally, periodically, throughout her own childhood. She [the patient's mother] married at the age of 16 "to get out of the house" but was deserted . . . after having given birth to the child.

This history, depicting this girl's experience of working as a toll collector at the bridge, is for me a memorable example of the alienating aspects of our culture such as Fromm (1955) has highlighted in his book, *The Sane Society*. But the point I wish to make about this girl is simply to suggest that her psychotic breakdown occurred in that setting less because of its formidable sociologic impact than because it served as a repetition of her early-childhood experience of her own mother, who had comprised, I suggest, not a single and consistent and intimately familiar person with whom to identify, but rather an endless stream of impersonal, empty-souled figures.

I have described it as characteristic of this phase of transition between autism and therapeutic symbiosis that the analyst now begins to find it possible effectively to make transference interpretations. This is in contrast to the earlier, autistic phase, during which he had to adapt to long stretches of time during which he was given the feeling of being useless, neglectful, irrelevant, uncaring, incompetent, and more than anything else, essentially nonhuman, precisely for the reason that the patient needed to regress, in his experience of the analyst, to the level of the young child's experience of the mother as being something far more than merely human, as a person is seen through adult eyes. The patient needed to come to experience the analyst as being equivalent to the early mother who comprises the whole world of which the infant is inextricably a part, before he has achieved enough of an own self to be able to tolerate the feeling-experience of sensing her as separate from his own body, and the two of them as separate from the rest of the actual world. The transition phase likewise stands in contrast, as regards the timeliness of transference interpretations, to the subsequent phase of therapeutic symbiosis, in which such interpretations are almost limitlessly in order.

I have felt, in working with the autistic patient, that this so-narcissistic patient could not endow me with sufficient significance to him to attend seriously to transference interpretations of my emotional meaning to him. One chronically paranoid man, who had emerged recently from an episode of acute psychosis, retorted scornfully to a prematurely attempted transference interpretation from me, "You are of no more significance to me than that flyspeck over on the wall there." What neither he nor I at that time knew was that for me to be experienced as something both significant to and separate from him would have been tantamount to losing his self, losing his mind, losing his whole significant world. I felt convinced by his scorn of me, and was unprepared to know how awesomely important I was, in his unconscious, preindividuation dependency upon me. At an unconscious level, his dependency upon me was so total that he could permit only a speck of me to be outside him.

A narcissistically absorbed patient expressed, year after year in his analysis, chronic dissatisfaction with his career as a lawyer, and recurrent ruminations about whether to abandon his present position for different ones, in any of several other cities. The time

came when, as he was once again so ruminating, I sensed that his
ruminations were in part based upon unconscious perceptions of
me as being dissatisfied with my work; he knew that I was going to
be absent from my office during the ensuing days, and he had
never reported any conscious conjectures whether I, too, might be
casting longing eyes at possible positions elsewhere. But I did not
feel free, as yet, to make such an interpretation to him; I sensed
that it would be overestimating his ability to attribute significance to
me—that it would be depicting myself as being of greater importance to him than his narcissism would permit as yet. His reaction
to my tentative comments confirmed that such a transference interpretation would be premature. I suggested, "You perhaps assume that the next two days I'll be doing something other than private practice?" He replied, "Yeah." I suggested, "Let's see what
comes to mind." His reply was to describe, quite accurately, what in
general I would be doing in my out-of-town work; he did not go on
to speculate that my taking time off for such a trip might mean
that I was something less than fully content with my usual work at
the office.

   This same man recurrently experienced a symptom of
"empty-mindedness" during the sessions, and remained for years
autistically unaware that this phenomenon might have something to
do with what he might experience the state of my mind as being.
In one session, for example, after eight minutes during which I as
usual had said nothing, and he had spoken only briefly from time
to time, he said, after another pause of a minute or so, "Seem to be
empty again today." I felt an impulse to ask, " 'Seem to be empty
again today': *I* seem to be empty again today?—*You* seem to be
empty again today?" I had no doubt that he had meant, consciously, that *he* seemed to be empty again today. But various clues
made me feel that it was not yet time thus to make my presence
felt. In retrospect, had I spoken so, I think it would have been
most valuable, potentially, to add to my questions, "—*We* seem to
be empty today?" for this would not so sharply call upon him to
exchange one world-view for another.

   The magnitude of the shift as the patient experiences it, from his former autism to a sudden sense of blending with some aspect of the analyst, can be illustrated by an incident from a session I had with a chronically schizophrenic woman whom I had been treating for many years. During all those years she had given me to understand that she frequently experienced auditory hallucinations. At the time of her acute psychosis, a year before I became her analyst, her family, in their great reluctance to place her in a mental hospital, had called into the home, to see her, a succession of seven or eight psychiatrists, each of whom had recommended hospitalization, before they finally had acquiesced. She had almost no memory of that experience, and recurrently expressed, in her work with me, the dark suspicion that those doctors "did something to me that caused me to hear voices," which, she was persistently convinced, emanated from an electrical apparatus somewhere outside herself. She repeatedly expressed her suspicions in such a way as to imply that the "something" they had done to her had been obscurely and malevolently sexual in nature. Also, for a number of years of our work at first, she manifested significant apprehension, never explicitly stated, lest the reason that the nearly whole first year of her illness was being kept shrouded in secrecy from her was that she had killed someone. Actually, she had not; but the clouded nature of that approximately one year, felt by her as a matter of her being kept by others in the dark about it, but due in actuality largely to her own amnesia for it, made her feel that so dark a secret could only mean that something terrible had been done to her or, even more horrifying, that she had murdered someone.

During one session, I told her that, as I understood it, a series of seven or eight doctors had been called by her family to see her at her home, and that her family had been reluctant to have her hospitalized. She came into the next session and began by saying, "What you told me last time about that group [N.B.] of doctors frightened me. You know I've been worried about it [that is, since the last session], don't you?" As I recall, I made no comment to this, or only a noncommittal one; my notes do not include it. She began recounting, later in the session, the names of the "doctors" she had had at Chestnut Lodge, who she felt wished her well, wanted her to be well, wanted her to be able to live outside the sanitarium. (Actually all the names she cited were of certain ones among her long series of administrative psychiatrists.) She further pointed out that these totaled eight—apart from a number of doctors whom she did not name, "who I didn't know about" (that is, about whom she had not been able surely to judge whether they wished her well or ill). She clearly found this significant; as best I could determine, she looked upon these, in aggregate, as serving as an antidote for the "group" of seven or eight doctors who had come to see her at her home and "done something to" her.

At the end of the hour, as she was readying herself to leave, while still sitting on the couch, she looked over very warmly at my face, and looked (without shifting her glance—it was more a blendedly widened glance than a shift of glances) at my green tie, with the same glowing warmth. She said, "When I look at your tie, do you know what I think happens to me?" I replied, noninformatively but with a gentle and an interested tone, "You wonder if I know what you think happens to you." She replied, with a very warm laugh, full of warm, fond feeling, "My eyes feel green! Are they green? It's so green!" "I feel so silly," she added, still laughing warmly.

When she said, "Are they green?" she did not lean toward me to make it easier to see across the five or six feet separating us. I felt guilty that I did not feel freely comfortable to look closely into her eyes and tell her what color they were. Moreover, I felt guilty for not already knowing what color they were. They appeared hazel-colored to me; but I was not sure. I felt, in essence, guilty at not finding myself unambivalently accepting of, and rejoicing in, the very fleeting moment of intimacy suddenly offered me by this woman who had functioned most of the time in a manner very distant and detached from me.

At any rate, I felt deeply moved by this incident, which I regarded as a highly significant one. I felt that what she had experienced, in this, was the essence of what the doctors "did to" her so many years before. That is, in her acute psychosis she probably had blended, I surmised, with each one (or a part of each one) in succession. She had thus lost the remainder of her already-fragmented self in the course of that fragmenting experience, during which she had been unable to work through the rapidly successive losses imposed upon her by this series of doctors, each of whom made his impact upon her and then left shortly thereafter—taking with him a part of her self—to be followed quickly by another doctor.[3] It was apparent, also, that at a much higher level of ego functioning, that earlier experience had given rise to now-repressed fantasies of herself as a prostitute, being visited in her bed by a series of men. The incident in the session I have described was charged with libidinal interest of a degree quite unacceptable to her generally held image of herself in the treatment relationship.

She may well have tended to experience the disappearance, from the scene, of one after another of these doctors as due to her having somehow murdered them. A chronically deeply fragmented woman, mentioned before, whom I have been treating for years, experiences her own identity to change unpredictably in an endless series, and she is convinced that the loss of each former identity is due to a literal act of murder, often by me. Similarly, I increasingly find reason to believe that, in the course of her finding that I am not the person(s) I was a moment before in the session, she feels vulnerable to being accused of having somehow destroyed the now-absent person(s).

Some data from three successive hours—and I wish particularly to highlight the events of the third of these—with a chronically hebephrenic woman, during the ninth of my 13 years of work with her, will serve to indicate how poignant was her longing to be able enduringly to experience a world outside herself, how instantly and intensely she at times rejected this world, and how powerful were the feelings of both love and hate which I found engendered in me in the relationship with her. This woman, 27 years of age at the time when I became her analyst, is the most deeply ill patient with whom I have ever worked. I worked with her, throughout, at a

[3] The novelist Ray Bradbury has depicted this process beautifully in *The Martian Chronicles* (1950).

frequency of four 55-minute sessions per week—the customary schedule for my work with each of my patients at Chestnut Lodge.

Prelude to, and Events of, Hour 1 (Saturday)

During an hour with her early in the week, I had found myself having to suppress a powerful urge to tell her, "I hate your bones!"—a feeling I had never before experienced toward anyone. In the final hour of that week (the Saturday hour focused upon here), she indicated her wish to go over to my office (some 60 feet from the building where she lived) with me for the session, and I acquiesced; parenthetically, only rarely in the past had it been possible for her to see me in my office. Then after she had gotten downstairs and we were about to go out the door, she appeared to be faced with overwhelming loss at the prospect of leaving Upper Cottage, and immediately began pouring out words, of a kind I had often heard from her before, of antagonism, scorn, and impatience toward me concerning the office. I replied, viciously, "Then let's stay here," and walked back upstairs to her room, while she sat down downstairs, near a nurse. After a few more minutes I came back downstairs, burning to tell her how much I despised and hated her, and said to her sarcastically in the nurse's presence, "Look at it this way, Charlotte: You tried to come over to my office for the hour, and you didn't get as far as the door of Little Lodge [another dwelling for patients, nearby]—I mean Upper Cottage; but you've had a big day!" I then walked out, 15 or 20 minutes before the end of the allotted time (which was most unusual for me), intensely hoping I had wounded her. I was still seething with hatred of her when I went on over to the dining room for some coffee. On walking in and seeing the woman in charge of the dining room, I felt very tempted to ask her, "jokingly," "Mrs. Schaefer, how much would you charge to put cyanide in a patient's food?" Such a thought had never occurred to me before, about anyone.

Over the weekend, I looked forward with grim relish to the coming week with Charlotte, planning to make her suffer for the

Saturday session, by firmly and imperturbably making her sweat out the hot hours in her room throughout the four sessions of the week. Incidentally, I forgot that we would be having but three hours, since one of the hours fell on the 4th of July.

Hour 2 (Monday)

But to my surprise, I found that on Monday the tenor between us was clearly positive, though quietly so. In the course of the session she said to me, "Then it's all right for me to live?"—as if she had found confirmation of this from me. She had come with unusual alacrity upstairs to the hour, without having to be led by a nurse, and had gone into several minutes of silent but profuse weeping, sometimes with an affect of grief coming through, sometimes with no affect coming through, and sometimes with, I sensed, an affect of pleasure. I asked her, unemotionally, whether she noticed any feeling as she wept—whether of grief, or none, or—perhaps—pleasure. She made no reply. Such a way of responding on my part was not unprecedentedly "cold"; but I doubt that I had ever felt quite so free from doubt and guilt at so responding to her.

Hour 3 (Wednesday)

I had not seen Charlotte since Monday, because Tuesday was a holiday (the 4th of July). When I went over to Upper Cottage Wednesday morning for the hour, Mrs. Weber (an aide) told me that Charlotte was upstairs. I felt a sense of relief, of contentment that she was up there in bed, feeling that this made it easier for me than when she is up and about. Yet I felt a twinge of guilt, feeling that I wouldn't be glad that she isn't up and about; I've known for many weeks that the personnel at Upper Cottage are concerned about how much time she spends in bed, and that they try to get her up and about.

She was lying on her side in bed, facing me, sucking her thumb, when I went in and greeted her. I sat down contentedly several feet from her bed and made myself comfortable. She made a few efforts at vocalization during the first few minutes; but she didn't speak loudly enough for me to hear, and the words sounded garbled, and I didn't press her to repeat; I said nothing. Then, after a few more minutes of silence, while she was lying there sucking her thumb, looking as usual confused and broken up, I asked, in a semi-ironic tone, "How are things in your world?" She replied, "I can't see much of it." Then a few minutes later, while she was looking at one of the two tall bedposts at the foot of her bed, she asked, "Do you see anything wrong with that bedpost?" I replied, "It doesn't look like the other one to you?" She agreed. She then began asking, several times over, "Why don't you give me the key—the key to the bedpost?" I didn't know what she meant; she rejected some comment from me (which is not set down in my notes made following the hour) intended to acknowledge the bedpost and the wished-for key as symbolically phallic in quality; surely I used no such technical or abstract terminology. She then glanced at the fly of my trousers, saying, "She [note the use of the third person, which she often used] wants to see it—do you know what I mean?" I replied, "It *sounds* to me as though maybe she wants to see my penis." She rejected this impression of mine; but I still felt it valid. "She wants to see the outside world," she explained, and added with a bereft expression on her face, "Some people do."

I replied, gently, "You don't see much of the outside world, I guess, do you?—and you'd like to be able to see more of it." To this she instantly retorted harshly, antagonistically, and scornfully, "I [note her use of the first person now] don't *care* about the outside world! I care about the *inside!*" Then during the next few moments she looked rejected, and made brief comments conveying her feeling rejected. I said, kindly and firmly, "Now you get feeling rejected—you very quickly get feeling rejected, don't you?" She replied, feelingly, "It's hell, isn't it?"

Shortly afterward, while she was sitting and looking at the white shirt I was wearing, she said, with much of tearful grief in her voice, "That's a nice shirt. I like to sit and look at the shirt."

Later, she asked, "Do you know what my mother feels?" in a dubious tone, as if to say, "—whether she feels anything?" She then explained, "Do you know what she feels about sitting?" I heard it as asking whether I were feeling anything; whatever response I made led to no further clarification. At one moment in the course of the hour, she fondly called me "Mom." At the end of the hour, while she was laughing pleasurably, I came over to the bed and gave her a kiss on the temple, very much as I do with my twelve-year-old daughter. She wiped it off, very much as my four-year-old son does, but went on laughing in the same way, which reassured me in my momentary misgiving lest I had made her anxious; I had never before kissed her. We had never before had a more fond, contented hour together.

It is my impression that a major reason for the intensity of such a patient's ambivalence concerning any relatedness with the "outside" world is that this "outside" world is equivalent to the mother's own autism. That is, my experience with this patient, and with other less severely autistic patients, indicates that the first "outside" world with which the patient was presented, in infancy and very early childhood, was composed of a mother who was herself autistic to a formidable degree. Thus, to the extent that the child emerged into a relationship (via processes of projection, introjection, identification, and more mature object relatedness) with that special form of "outside" world, this meant intolerable confinement for the child's potentially developing self. One can understand that if, from the child's (unformulated, of course) point of view, the only conceivable outside world were that represented by a deeply preoccupied mother, the child might well react violently against becoming incarcerated in that "outside" world—might remain, instead, immersed in the limitless fantasies comprising his own autistic world. To identify with, or otherwise relate to, the only available "outside" world would be equivalent to committing oneself to the world of the mother's autism—that is, the mother's insanity or depression.

10

Concerning Therapeutic Symbiosis:
The Patient as Symbiotic Therapist,
the Phase of Ambivalent Symbiosis,
and the Role of Jealousy
in the Fragmented Ego

In 1958 I postulated that symbiotic relatedness constitutes a necessary phase in psychoanalysis or psychotherapy with either neurotic
or psychotic patients, and introduced the term "therapeutic symbiosis" for this mode of patient-analyst relatedness (Searles, 1959b).
In 1959 I stated that what the analyst offers the patient that is new
and therapeutic, in this regard, is not an avoidance of the development of symbiotic, reciprocal dependency with the patient, but
rather an acceptance of this (1959a). My several subsequent discussions of this subject have included mention of the role of symbiotic
relatedness in healthy, adult living (1965a, 1966-1967).

The present paper is the third in a series of reports on what I

This paper was presented as the Sixth Annual Franz Alexander Memorial Lecture, under the auspices of the Cedars-Sinai Divisions of Psychiatry and the South-
ern California Psychoanalytic Society and Institute, in Los Angeles on March 21,
1972. An earlier version had been presented to the Canadian Psychoanalytic Society,
Ontario, in Toronto on January 27, 1972. It was first published in *The Annual of
Psychoanalysis*, Volume 1 (New York: Quadrangle/The New York Times Book Co.,
1973), pp. 247-262.

have learned in recent years concerning autism, symbiosis, and individuation. In these papers I am concerned not only with patients suffering from schizophrenia of varying degrees of severity but also with, for example, the subtle autism that emerges in the course of the neurotic patient's analysis. The first two papers included these passages:

> The categories . . . of pathologic symbiosis, autism, therapeutic symbiosis, and individuation depict what I regard as successive phases of ego development in therapy. Whether any one patient needs to run that whole course will depend upon the level of ego development he has already attained at the beginning. He may already have achieved, for example, a strong capacity for a therapeutically symbiotic relatedness, in which case the first two phases of ego development would be relatively little in evidence in one's work with him [1971].

> I have described it as characteristic of this phase of transition between autism and therapeutic symbiosis that the analyst now begins to find it possible effectively to make transference interpretations. This is in contrast to the earlier, autistic phase, during which he had to adapt to long stretches of time during which he was given the feeling of being useless, neglectful, irrelevant, uncaring, incompetent, and, more than anything else, essentially nonhuman, precisely for the reason that the patient needed to regress, in his experience of the analyst, to the level of the young child's experience of the mother as being something far more than merely human, as a person is seen through adult eyes. The patient needed to come to experience the analyst as being equivalent to the early mother who comprises the whole world of which the infant is inextricably a part, before he has achieved enough of an own self to be able to tolerate the feeling-experience of sensing her as separate from his own body, and the two of them as separate from the rest of the actual world. The transition phase likewise stands in contrast, as regards the timeliness of transference interpretations, to the subsequent phase of therapeutic symbiosis, in which such interpretations are almost limitlessly in order [1970].

I shall use the term "therapeutic symbiosis" in this paper to include both ambivalent and preambivalent types of symbiosis in the patient-analyst relationship, although earlier I reserved that term

for preambivalent symbiosis—that is, a symbiosis that is felt as a
thoroughly adoring, contented oneness, and that is traceable genetically to experiences in the very early infant-mother relationship,
before significant increments of hate have come to intrude into this
oneness and transform the emotional matrix of it into one of pervasive ambivalence. Both types of symbiosis are clearly full of potential for therapeutic effect, as, indeed, is each of the other phases
of ego development mentioned in the first quotation above.
Moreover, I have come to regard it as impossible to find any clearly
defined, long-sustained instance of preambivalent symbiosis and am
more than ever mindful of a reservation I expressed in 1961:

> ... there is no sure criterion by which we can
> know ... whether we are involved in a genuinely preambivalent
> symbiosis with the patient, or rather in the predominantly
> paranoid symbiosis which is a defence against hatred ... and we
> must remain open-minded to the ever-present possibility
> that ... a basically constructive, subjectively preambivalent sym-
> biosis will be misused unconsciously from time to time, by both
> participants, to keep increments of particularly intense hostility
> out of awareness [1961e, p. 542].

The Patient as Symbiotic Therapist

An understanding of the nature of therapeutic symbiosis requires that one grasp something of the extent to which the patient
is himself devoted to functioning as a therapist in relationship to
his officially designated analyst, as well as in his relationships with
other persons in his life. Not only is the striving for an essentially
psychotherapeutic effect upon the other person a concern of those
relatively few persons who select the practice of psychoanalysis or
psychotherapy as their life work, but it is also a basic and pervasive
concern of human beings generally. But probably it is those persons whose childhoods to a large extent were devoted to functioning as therapist to other family members, and whose therapist-
functioning proved both complex and absorbing and fundamental
to their sense of personal identity, as well as frustrated in clear and

lasting and acknowledgedly successful results, for whom such activity becomes a naturally absorbing adult-life work.

Although one can usefully explore the ways in which a genuine individual—that is, a person who possesses a whole self, a person who has a relatively whole ego—thus unofficially functions as therapist to other persons who likewise have experienced psychological individuation and are thus whole individuals, I am concerned here with the "symbiotic therapist," the person who himself has not firmly achieved individuation, and whose most deeply meaningful human relationships consist in his complementing the areas of ego incompleteness in other persons. This mode of relatedness is founded upon a relationship with his mother in which his ego functioning was fixated similarly at a level of relatively infantile fragmentation and nondifferentiation, partially because the precarious family intactness required that he not become a whole person but remain instead available for complementing the ego incompleteness of the others in the family, individually and collectively.

The patient seen in this light is not merely a victim exploited by mother and family; to leave the conceptualization at that is to take into account only the potentially hostile components of what is transpiring. In these symbiotic processes, just as self and object are not clearly demarcated, neither are hate and love clearly differentiated. It is as much as anything the patient's nascent capacity for love, and for the development of mature human responsibility, that impels him to perpetuate this mode of relatedness. From the not-yet-well differentiated, "selfish" point of view, he strives, for his psychological and physical survival, to maintain the only mode of relatedness he knows, and hopefully to so enhance, so strengthen the mother as to enable her to mature further, to provide himself with a model for identification, for the sake of his own maturation. From the "altruistic" point of view, which is also not well differentiated, he goes on literally sacrificing his own potential self, for the sake of complementing the mother and thus ensuring her survival.

Just as the seeds of the most intense paranoid hate can be

found in all this, so, too, can be found here the sources of the most genuinely selfless human love. The more ill a patient is, the more deeply indispensable does he need to become, at this preindividuation level of ego functioning, to his transference-mother, the analyst. This necessary transference evolution is made all but impossible by the traditional view of the analyst as the healthy one, the one with the intact ego, who is endeavoring to give help to the ill one, the patient, seen as afflicted with an "ego defect" or "ego deficit." The latter is thus "afflicted," indeed, but to some real degree, so (like everyone else) is the analyst. Without this "affliction," in fact, he could not hope to function effectively as the analyst in the therapeutically symbiotic phase of the patient's treatment.

No one becomes so fully an individual, so fully "mature," as to have lost his previously achieved capacity for symbiotic relatedness. The so-called "ego defect" of the schizophrenic patient, seen in its dynamic function rather than as static crippledness, is really the area of his most intense, though fixedly symbiotic, aliveness. It is of the same nature as the symbiotic basis of healthy adult ego functioning—that basis which enables a healthy adult to come to feel, creatively and restoratively, at one with (or, one might say, part of) another individual, a group of his fellow human beings, mankind generally, the whole external world, a creative idea, or whatever.

In psychoanalytic treatment what is needed, more than anything else, to resolve the fixation in the patient's ego development—his having achieved, that is, only a fragment, or fragments, of an ego—is his discovery that a fellow human being, the analyst, can come to know, and to work with him in implicit acknowledgment of his indispensably important role in the analyst's own ego functioning. Only through such a process can the patient become a more whole individual. Further, the individuation which he undergoes more successfully this time, in the context of the transference relationship, is in a real sense mutual, in that the analyst too, having participated with the patient in the therapeutic symbiosis, emerges with a renewed individuality which has been enriched and deepened by this experience. Just as we need to realize that, in healthy human living, symbiotic relatedness is not confined to infancy and early childhood but forms, at largely though not entirely unconscious levels, the dynamic substrate of adult living, so, too, individuation is not a once-and-for-all, irreversible process. It is not only a deeply ill patient who can achieve, in psychoanalytic treatment, a fuller individuation than the relatively fragmentary and superficial individuation he achieved in childhood. A healthy adult, too, by definition, lives a daily and yearly life which involves, in its most essential ingredients, experiences—whether measured in moments or phases of his life—of symbiotic relatedness and reindividuation.

It is currently one of our great human tragedies that hundreds of thousands of persons are living out their lives in gigantic mental hospitals, existing largely in chemical cocoons, because behind our scornful shunning of them is our unformulated sensing that any one of them, if we were to permit him or her to do so, would become personally more a part of us than we dare to allow.

In recent years I have learned that one of the most heavily defended emotions in the schizophrenic patient in his sense of guilt at having failed to enable his fragmented mother to become a whole and successful mother to him. This sense of guilt is based partially upon subjective omnipotence and is therefore to a degree irrational; in this regard it is analogous to the guilt we would have the supposedly omnipotent "schizophrenogenic mother" bear, single-handedly, for the fact of the patient's schizophrenic illness. But it is essential for us to perceive that the patient's sense of guilt at having thus failed his mother has also a realistic aspect, for it is this realistic component that provides the key to his capacity for developing a sense of more mature responsibility in his interpersonal relationships in general. It is only as he comes to enable his analyst to function as analyst—analogous to mother—in relation to him (despite whatever intense hatred and other "negative" feelings) that the crippling effect of this heretofore unconscious guilt can be undone. We can now see, in retrospect, that the pathogenic introjects which constituted the core of his schizophrenia represented not only his unconscious means of coping with an otherwise intolerable outer reality, but also his unconscious, primitive way of trying to heal that "outer reality"—that is, those most deeply ill components of mother and subsequent mother-transference figures—by taking those components into himself and trying thus to free her (and her successors) from the burden of them.

THE PHASE OF AMBIVALENT SYMBIOSIS

As regression deepens in the analytic relationship—regression not only on the part of the heretofore autistic patient but also on the part of the analyst, who, as I described in an earlier paper (1970), has become considerably caught up, himself, in autistic processes—there are now encountered sudden and increasingly frequent bits of the ego-splitting, intense ambivalence against which, in the history of each participant, autistic processes had developed as a defense. In this stage of ambivalent symbiosis, in which ego boundaries are by definition unreliable in either participant, there is much of both projecting and introjecting, with each person feeling threatened by the other by reason of the other's personifying his own as-yet-unintegratable inner contents. For example, each projects upon the other his own murderous feelings, and feels correspondingly in fear for his life. The loss, for each, of what he has felt to be entirely his own (autistic) world—its disruption by, for example, one's patient who now feels to be chaotically permeating one's whole life—is accompanied by intense rage, fear, and the most primitive kinds of loss reactions. One's subjective experience is that one no longer has either a world, or a self, of one's own.

It is to be noted that ambivalence that is largely unconscious, rather than conscious and therefore integratable by the ego, requires symbiotic relatedness with the other person, relatedness in which the other personifies those components of the ambivalent feelings which one is having to repress at the moment. Contrariwise, when one can face and accept one's own ambivalent feelings, one can be a separate person and can react to the other as being, also, a separate person. I shall never forget the sense of achieved inner freedom which enabled me to tell a hebephrenic woman, in relation to whom I had been enmeshed in anguished symbiotic relatedness for years, that I would never allow her to visit my home—as she long had yearned to do—even if my refusal meant that she would stay in a mental hospital all her life. Where one draws the line, in such matters, is an expression of the analyst's individual self; this is where *I* draw the line. Theoretically, it is not essential, and it may be unwise, although in my experience rarely if ever disastrous, to say these things to the patient; the important thing is that one become able to feel them—to feel, in this instance, a degree of intense rejectingness which I had projected for years upon this, in truth, remarkably rejecting woman. The degree of ambivalence of which I am writing is so intense that it can be met, as I hope to show further in this paper, only if the two participants function to a high degree as one in the experiencing and acknowledging of it.

Some years ago, at a time when I had not experienced enough *pre*ambivalently symbiotic relatedness with my patients to be able to conceptualize it, and when I assumed all symbiotic relatedness to be highly ambivalent, I wrote in my notes, following a session with this same woman:

> I have referred to symbiotic relationships in two recent papers and have been wanting lately to try to describe in detail what are the characteristics of such a relationship. I have just come from an hour with Carol Fleming [a pseudonym] which has been like hundreds of similar hours with her and which is, I think, a typical one to represent the [ambivalently] symbiotic relationship.
>
> When I went up to see her she was lying in bed, silently, in her bare-walled room—lying in her steel bed—and the only other items of furniture were the two chairs. I felt a sense of deep discouragement when I went in there, and aversion to going ahead with the work. As the hour progressed, an hour in which she said little and this only in a fragmentary fashion, while looking antagonistically toward me most of the time, I noticed that what I felt was perhaps most of all a sense of helplessness in the face of my own feelings, and a nonaccep-

tance of them, whether these were feelings of antagonism, or sympathy, or tenderness, or whatnot. I felt strong urges simply to abandon the work with her and abandon her, but felt again a sense of conflict and helplessness at doing this.

I felt a sense of what one might call being at the mercy of her own playing upon my feelings, whether by making me antagonistic through hateful behavior, or by evoking tenderness and sympathy from me when she would suddenly have a friendly look on her face and make a kind of beseeching gesture. Another thing to be stressed is that my feelings were in quite a welter and were rapidly changing. At one period in the hour I got to feeling as though we were two rattlesnakes with our fangs in one another's necks, each refusing to let go because by staying in the relationship we were best expressing the boundless hatefulness we felt toward one another. Throughout the hour there was an element of dissatisfaction on my part with my own feelings.

A few months earlier I had written:

> The entire time of the small group[1] today was taken up with my presenting my work with Carol Fleming. I brought it up because I was feeling under a good deal of pressure about the forthcoming visit of the mother and father. As I was telling the others about the way it was going with Carol, I began to see more and more indications in myself of a massive submerged rage at her because of my feelings of failure in the work. I felt as though there were a large, heavy stone in me . . . it felt unmistakably like depression with a good deal of rage associated with it. The thing that came to me in the course of presenting this was that even my "positive," tender feelings toward her were a burden to me, as well as my formerly strong feelings of cruelty and sadism. These "positive" feelings were a burden, I felt, because I did not feel free to express them to her—as by, for instance, touching her head when I felt like it. I have felt all along that such expressions of tenderness were a kind of misuse of my therapist position, something which would frighten her and would simply be a kind of gratifying of my own dependency feelings, using her as a mother-figure. In the course

[1] This was one of several groups into which the overall therapist staff members were divided. We met regularly to discuss, informally and as candidly as we could, whatever were the most pressing problem situations at the moment.

of the rest of the day it came to me that the *most important thing in my life at Chestnut Lodge*[2] at present is my anger at Carol Fleming. It was a quite startling thing, indeed, to come to this realization; it occurred to me later that this may be some measure, too, of the importance of the relationship to the patient herself.

No one or two vignettes can be fully typical of the varied clinical phenomena I am conceptualizing. This patient, for instance, was still more invested in her years' long autism, still relatively little invested in explicitly discernible, ambivalently symbiotic relatedness, than have been most of the patients I have in mind as I write.

With these latter patients, most of whom, in my experience, have been borderline schizophrenic or ambulatorily schizophrenic—considerably more readily accessible, that is, than the woman just mentioned—there is the additional circumstance that both participants almost constantly react to one another, whether in a verbal, or in a tangibly nonverbal, fashion and with feelings that shift rapidly about over the whole spectrum, from fury to tenderness to scorn, and so on, often in extraordinary mixtures of emotions.

Much of my own experience with ambivalently symbiotic relatedness has occurred during my work with some hundreds of borderline or ambulatorily schizophrenic patients with whom I have had one-time interviews for consultative and/or teaching purposes. I have also encountered this form of symbiotic relatedness during the final several months of my 11 years of work with a hebephrenic man. He had achieved this way of functioning at a time when both of us knew that before long I would be leaving the hospital where he dwelt. I have wondered about the role of mutual separation anxiety in this so-active responding, under these special circumstances of approaching termination or one-time interviews. But my experi-

[2] I am chagrined to see that I had to write, and to feel, this qualification: "at Chestnut Lodge"; I could not experience this simply as the most important thing in my life. This I regard as evidence of my then-unconscious resistance to acknowledging the patient's full importance to me—my own resistance, that is, to the development of a fully felt, preambivalently symbiotic relatedness with her.

ences with various other long-range treatment cases have confirmed
my belief that the separation anxiety involved has less to do with
the imminence of physical separation than with the imminent
threat to both participants lest their lively symbiotic relatedness give
way at any moment, unpredictably and uncontrollably, to autism or
individuation (outcomes which do not seem differentiated in the
patient's grasp of the situation, nor at all well differentiated in my
own understanding in that context). Thus the imminence of either
outcome poses the same subjective threat of one's being torn asun-
der at any moment.

The symbiotic instability of ego boundaries makes it impossible
to know whether the anger or depression, for instance, which one
suddenly experiences is one's "own," or whether one is empathically
sensing a feeling of the patient's "own" against which *he* is successfully defended unconsciously (as by projection). Also, as regards the
patient's verbal communications, it is often impossible to know, and
it feels urgently important to ascertain, whence and to whom these
communications are coming.

For example, one such patient who at a nonverbal level was well
established in ambivalently symbiotic relatedness with me, but who
had not yet achieved a comparable level of verbal articulateness,
confined his verbal communications over many months to certain
stereotyped comments. In one session, he expressed each of the following stereotyped comments at least once: "Take your time."
"Abide with what ya have." "Remain happy." "Time and place f'r
everything." "No need to say." For me it was something like listening to one side of a telephone conversation. I told him that I had
no way of knowing whether each of these comments was—and here
I utilize numbers, which I did not use in communicating to him—
(1) his response to thoughts he was having, (2) his response to
voices he was hearing, (3) his conjecture as to what I was thinking,
(4) his accurate report to me of what he was hearing the voices say,
or (5) some mixture of all these. Not surprisingly, in response to so
complex a comment from me, he offered no illuminating reply. I
assumed that he was quite unable to differentiate among these var-

ious possibilities, to which I now added another: (6) Were his stereotyped comments giving behavioral expression, by processes of introjection, to what he tended unconsciously to perceive as being my own silently hallucinated state? I was not in fact subject to hallucinations, stressful though these sessions often were; but one of his most discernible transference reactions was in terms of my being his "shellshocked" father (who had died long ago), a man so ego-fragmented as to have been incapacitated from useful career activity throughout the patient's childhood, and a man who may well have suffered, therefore, from hallucinations.

Considerably earlier in the work I had become aware, more simply, that things he said could be expressive of *my* presumed feelings or attitudes, from his point of view, as well as of his own feelings and attitudes. When, for example, in the middle of a prolonged silence he would say reproachfully, "You don't ever intend to say," this seemingly could refer variously to how he viewed me, or how he viewed himself, or how he assumed I viewed him. On another occasion, when I went into the building where he lived to have the hour with him, I found him standing outside the nearby nurses' office, and he made no move to follow me down the corridor to his room. After a few minutes of my sitting in his room with the door open, waiting for him, I went out and got a newspaper near that office and brought it back to the room, ignoring him as I went by. After a relatively brief time he came into the room, saying, "Who the hell needs *you*, you slimy son-of-a-bitch?"—which could express equally well his attitude or the one I had manifested in getting the newspaper. What makes it feel so important to the analyst, at this stage of things, to try to locate the ego boundaries is that there is so much unintegrated, and therefore uncontrollable, hostility in the relationship. For example, the memory was still fresh in my mind of a time when he evidently had suddenly heard a hallucinatory voice, coming from me, saying deeply insulting things to him, and had reacted with such barely contained, explosive fury that I felt physically frightened of him and thoroughly helpless to affect what was going on in him.

The Role of Jealousy in the Fragmented Ego[3]

In my work with the above-mentioned man, as well as with another patient earlier and many subsequently, I have seen that ambivalently symbiotic relatedness often comes to have, at first weirdly, a quality of *group* relatedness, with jealousy a most important and difficult complicating factor. It is commonly assumed that jealousy is an emotion that occurs in a context of three actual persons (Farber, 1961). But in these patients—and, again, I refer not merely to grossly ego-fragmented hebephrenic patients, but to any patients in whom schizoid components come to light in the course of analysis, which in my opinion then includes patients generally— the pathogenic introjects have the subjective personal-identity value, and interpersonal impact, of persons. It is when the analyst comes to be invested, by the patient, with a personal significance approximately equivalent to that with which the introject in question is invested—when, in simpler words, the analyst comes to be as important to the patient as the latter's own "self" is to him—that the analyst now feels, and the remainder of the patient's identity (i.e., the area not comprising the introject) now feels, pitted in an intense three-(or more) way jealous competition.

The hebephrenic man mentioned above, for example, used to relate during the sessions to hallucinatory voices which made me feel, by contrast, totally insignificant to him. When I would try to interrupt his dialogue with a hallucinatory figure, he would snap in vitriolic fury, "Shut up! I got company!" But it was only as my feeling-significance to him increased that I began to feel jealous when he would turn from relating to me, to relating to a hallucinatory voice. At such times I had a distinct sense that a group relationship was going on in the room. (I have often had this feeling with a similarly ego-fragmented woman with whom I have worked for many years.) Still later, in my treatment of the hebe-

---

[3] An excellent paper by Pao (1969), "Pathological Jealousy," while not containing the concepts I am putting forward here, provides a useful psychodynamic background for them, as well as a valuable survey of the literature concerning jealousy.

phrenic man, I became so sure of my importance to him that I could know that the hallucinatory phenomena he manifested were secondary to the events transpiring between us, and I no longer felt vulnerable to such jealousy.

The patient's own jealousy of himself, springing from a part of him which feels left out from another part to "whom" the analyst is responding, constitutes an enormous resistance in the treatment. That is, when one island among those constituting the patient's collective "self" is able to work with the analyst in making a step forward in the work, another such island "who" feels left behind and intensely jealous, reacts with savage vindictiveness against what the two co-workers have accomplished together, and against the collaborative relationship between them. Such a patient's "self" is largely composed of a collection of poorly integrated introjects. I surmise that the jealousy is traceable in part to early life experiences of unmasterable jealousy at the closeness between two other actual persons—the parents, for example, or the mother and a sibling adored by her—jealousy which was not resolved in the patient but was unconsciously defended against by his introjection of the two, emotionally close, other persons. But I surmise that, more importantly, the jealousy had a counterpart *within the mother* (or other mothering ones) *herself*, such that the child had to cope with, and to try introjectively—by taking into himself, that is—to make whole a mother whose ego was fragmented and ridden with just such "intrapsychic" jealousy.

In the course of treatment, this jealousy can best be dealt with as an unconscious defense against the therapeutically necessary fusion involved in preambivalent symbiosis, a fusion at first frightening to both patient and analyst. It seems to me that the instances of the acting out of such jealousy that are most disruptive of the treatment occur before any strong preambivalent relatedness has developed in the transference. Any jealousy phenomena which occur later, after individuation has occurred, while perhaps not inconsiderable, can be dealt with by the now whole patient and the now whole analyst, as they explore the meaning to their relationship of some third whole person outside the office.

Finally, I shall give an example from my work with a schizoid patient—a patient whose degree of illness is common in an office practice. For several years I found this man infuriatingly smug. But the time came when, to my astonishment, I realized that what I was feeling now was jealousy; *he* so clearly favored his *self* over *me* that I felt deeply jealous, bitterly left out of this mutually cherishing and cozy relationship between the two "persons" comprising him. I emphasize that this did not happen until after several years of my work with him. In retrospect, I saw that I previously had not developed sufficient personal significance to him (in classically psychoanalytic terms, had not been sufficiently cathected as a separate object in his experience of me) to sense these two now relatively well-differentiated "persons" in him and to feel myself capable of and desirous of participating in the "three"-way, intensely jealousy-laden competition. It is my impression that such schizoid patients usually prove so discouragingly inaccessible to psychoanalysis that the analyst and the patient give up the attempt at psychoanalysis before they have reached this lively but disturbing (to analyst as well as patient) stratum, this stratum in which the patient's ego fragmentation becomes revealed and the nature of the transference becomes one of a murderously jealous "three"-way competitiveness.

Technique during the Phase of Transition from Autism to Therapeutic Symbiosis

The often long, seemingly static phase of autism proves in retrospect not to have been a mere marking of time before the onset of the discernibly active therapeutic processes of the symbiotic phase, but rather to have constituted the necessary establishing of the reliably strong context within which these latter changes can be allowed to occur. For me, this finding substantiates the positive emphasis which Milner (1969) places upon what I am calling autism. She writes of "the theme of premature ego development and the necessity, for healthy mental growth, for recurrent times when retreat into absent-mindedness [i.e., autism] is possible" (p. 155), and suggests that "behind the states that are talked about by analysts as auto-erotic and narcissistic [i.e., autistic] there can be an attempt to reach a beneficent kind of narcissism, a primary self-enjoyment . . . which, if properly understood, is not a rejection of the outer world but a step towards a renewed and revitalized investment in it" (p. 383). She also cites Heimann's (1962) paper on narcissistic withdrawal for creative work and the need for research into the changes that narcissism undergoes from its primitive manifestations, so that it becomes compatible with ego creativity and object relations.

The autistic phase involves the formation, in my view, of what Hartmann (1939) has termed "the average expectable environment," what Winnicott (1941) has called "the good-enough holding environment," and what Khan (1963, 1964) describes in terms of the mother's role as protective shield.

A high degree of reliability develops during the autistic phase. This reliability, whether expressed in terms of punctuality, regularity of seating arrangements, or whatever constellation of outward trappings in the treatment situation, must have to do with both participants' developing sureness as to what the situation will, and will not, permit. Sometimes extraordinary patience and what might seem to be inexcusable leniency are necessary on the analyst's part; other times demand murderously impatient firmness—whatever gives truest expression to the analyst's individual self in meeting the needs of the immediate treatment situation.

In my work with one chronically schizophrenic woman, I developed a technique which I described with some embarrassment to my Chestnut Lodge colleagues as the Chinese water-torture method, for the reason that it appeared on the surface to be so highly sadistic. In fact, this technique developed out of absolute necessity and proved to be immensely useful. It consisted simply in a maddeningly rigorous application of a technique emphasized many years ago by Rogers (1942): repeating what the patient said and simultaneously indicating a readiness to hear more, but without going a single step beyond her. The woman had an extremely

tenuous sense of identity and was terribly afraid, therefore, of venturing forward on her own; individuality was equivalent, for her, to
hopeless insanity. On the hundreds of occasions in the past when I
had ventured encouragingly a bit beyond her, she had immediately
reacted to me in totally alienated horror and condemnation, typically cutting me off from her with a shocked, awed, "You're crazy,
Dr. Searles!" I had learned the hard way that I must be *with* her at
each of her most tentative steps, repeating each of her tentative
comments—often only the first part of an intendedly full sentence,
which unaided she could not complete—but that I must not get at
all *ahead* of her.

I was amused when, in a staff presentation, one of my colleagues, who had found my presentation of one of my typical interviews with her quite disturbing, said in angry protest:

> . . . in that interview, every word practically that she said,
> you seized on it, you repeated it back to her and then you
> asked her some further data on it, as if you had to control each
> and every thing that she did. I wonder, God, this would be an
> awful rigidly structured business, and I wonder what she might
> think of the meaning of that in terms of her own aggressive
> feelings—why this has to be done. Surely when she said some-
> thing was driving her crazy, I think I would have had the same
> feeling, that if somebody was doing this to me, I'd really feel
> that I was going nuts and would feel like tearing out my hair or
> something.

I was amused at his reaction both because of what I felt to be
the accuracy of his description of what I was doing with her, and
because the nature of his emotional reaction to it was so akin to the
emotional reaction which was developing within the patient
herself—a therapeutically most welcome development. My relationship with her progressed through a subsequent phase of ambivalently symbiotic relatedness, during which there were a great many
stormy sessions in which we both participated most actively; and a
later, clearly identifiable and prolonged, phase of preambivalently
therapeutic symbiosis which was of enormous growth value for both
of us, and which enabled her to achieve a stronger degree of sub-

sequent individuation than any others among my chronically schizophrenic patients have, so far, ever achieved. These later developments could not have occurred, I am convinced, without my having functioned during that autistic phase as a kind of exoskeleton for her.

In my paper concerning neutral therapist responses (1963a), I detailed something of the clinical events which indicated that, in my work with one chronically schizophrenic patient who lay mute and motionless throughout the analytic sessions for months—months during which he evidently was hovering on the brink of death—it was my functioning meanwhile as a progressively mute and motionless inanimate object that served eventually, where more "active" measures had all failed, to help him to become genuinely alive and increasingly functional.

One way of construing all this is to see that the analyst must come to personify the patient's own autistic rigidity, in order for that rigidity to become translated into increasingly well-differentiated and consciously utilizable ego strength. This is achieved partially through the patient's identification with the analyst's timely and skillful "becoming alive" and his readiness to venture forth in various constructive ways from so-rigid and "inanimate," but for all patients at times so-necessary, a transference position. In everyday office analytic practice, the patients—and these include not only ambulatorily schizophrenic and borderline patients, but also neurotic ones—who complain most of the analyst's remoteness and changelessness are the very persons who need most, for the sake of the resolution and integration of erstwhile autistic components within themselves, to have him function thus in relation to them.

In my experience, for the resolution of the patient's autism to occur, the analyst must do more than function as a more reliable maternally protective shield for the patient than the latter's biological mother was during his infancy and early childhood, in the manner Khan (1963, 1964) has described. First the analyst must have become increasingly free in his acceptance of the *patient's* functioning as *his*—the analyst's—maternally protective shield. In my own way of conceptualizing it: to the extent that the analyst can become able comfortably and freely to immerse himself in the autistic patient as constituting his (the analyst's) world, the patient can then utilize him as a model for identification as regards the acceptance of such very primitive dependency needs, and can come increasingly to exchange his erstwhile autistic world for the world consisting of, and personified by, the analyst. This progression of events is in actuality composed not of discrete, once-and-for-all shifts forward, but rather of blended and ever-oscillating processes, so that at one moment the exoskeleton is being provided by the analyst, at the next moment by the patient, and, increasingly, by both at once and at one.

What I am describing here requires, again, an appreciation of the patient's therapist-orientation. Through the evolution of the transference the analyst, in finding the patient's autistic functioning to be serving as an increasingly important maternal shield in his own ego functioning, is reacting like the ego-fragmented mother whose own functioning has required that the patient remain fixated at the level of autism, as the foundation stone of her own precarious existence. What the analyst brings into the patient's life that is new is that he, unlike the mother earlier, has a sufficiently well-integrated ego to dare to *know* how indispensably important to him is this patient, this autistic patient who is able meaningfully to relate to him, at first, only as the maternal shield for those least well integrated components of the analyst upon which the patient's transference to him as an ego-fragmented mother is based.

In other words, the analyst must dare to know that, at this very primitive level, the patient is functioning, and has been functioning, as his mother-therapist. To the extent that he is conscious of this, he need not acknowledge it explicitly to the patient. It becomes mutually and implicitly understood that the patient has been helping him to confront areas of himself with which he had been previously largely unacquainted. As these areas become integrated into the analyst's conscious ego functioning, he becomes more and more the strong mother the patient has been needing. Since the patient has been mothering him successfully, as the patient's infant or fetus, there is now no humiliation for the patient in becoming increasingly aware of his own infant-need, now, for the analyst as mother.

In a recent paper (1972a) concerning my work, extending over many years and still continuing, with a deeply ego-fragmented and delusional woman, I described my gradual discovery of the awesome extent to which her highly delusional world was in actuality flowing from, and thus was based upon, her responding to various real but predominantly unconscious components of my personality—that is, heretofore largely unconscious ways of my functioning with her during the sessions. Notable for me in this increasingly clear realization of the extent to which I have been personifying a God-the-creator, early mother to the patient is the extent to which I previously had shied away from experiencing myself as possessing this degree of importance to her. For me personally, it has been easier to adore the patient as godlike, than to feel so adored by her.

In my recent papers (1970, 1971) concerning autism I have described how the analyst is thrown, in response to the autistic patient, back upon his own autistic processes. A development which comes eventually to contribute to the resolution of this autistic mode of relatedness is the analyst's surprised, recurrent, and deepening realization and acceptance of the fact that these two seemingly so-separate worlds, his world and that of the patient, are but separate outcroppings of the unconscious ground joining the two of them. This principle is commonly manifested in the analyst's finding, during, for example, one of the frequent periods of silence with a boringly schizoid patient, that his self-examination of his preoccupying and supposedly quite free associations, as he is managing to get through this workaday time by dint of such inner "freedom," yields, as he begins to examine these associations, new and highly informative cues to what is going on between himself and the patient, and within the patient. The analyst's own "private" or "autistic" inner world is not nearly so far apart from the patient as he, the analyst, was assuming it to be.

11

An Epic Struggle
with Schizophrenia:
A Review of Marion Milner's
The Hands of the Living God

This is an account of Marion Milner's psychoanalytic treatment of a schizophrenic woman. The analysis began in 1943, when the patient was 23 years of age, three weeks after she had received a course of electroshock therapy in a mental hospital. Her analysis continued for 20 years, during the first 15 years of which the frequency was five hours per week; during the last five years, the sessions occurred less frequently. All the sessions occurred in the analyst's office, where the patient used the analytic couch. The treatment, over all this awesome span of time, was interrupted only briefly by the analyst's vacations. D. W. Winnicott shouldered medical responsibility for the treatment carried on by the lay-analyst author, served as a consultant to her over the years, and wrote a foreword for this book.

Any analyst or therapist who is working with a schizophrenic patient, or who has ever had occasion to feel concerned at the length of time a particularly difficult patient's treatment is

First published in *Contemporary Psychology*, 15:539-540 (1970).

taking—and to whom among us does neither of these circumstances apply?—will find enormous clinical help in this priceless volume. I found in it innumerable parallels to and clarifications of my own work, current and past, with schizophrenic patients, including some with whom I have worked nearly as long as did Milner with this woman.

The main theme of the book, in my opinion, is the patient's development of a whole and human body-image. (This theme is not stated explicitly by Milner herself.) For a long time following the electroshock treatment, the patient felt herself to inhabit only a very small area at the top of her head. As the years go on she comes, step-by-step, to inhabit her body fully, to experience the range of human feelings, and to experience herself as a real person in a real world. Late in the book we find abundant evidence of the patient's becoming born into the world, out of a preceding oneness with the analyst.

The book's main theme, expressed in different terms, is a tracing of the process of differentiation, which was fostered by the analysis, in the patient's experience of herself and the world—differentiation between living and nonliving, human and nonhuman, inner and outer, male and female, and so on. The richly meaningful drawings, done by the patient in the course of her treatment, reflect to what a degree she unconsciously was feeling herself to be something nightmarish, or a flower or a bird or an animal, before she achieved a full experience of herself as a human being. All this material I find utterly authentic, fully akin to the varieties of schizophrenic experience my own patients have manifested. I know of no other work in the literature that equals Milner's volume in depicting the development of a human body-image.

After about six years of the analysis, the patient began making doodle drawings, and thereafter these drawings, to which she devoted increasing care, contributed enormously to the treatment. Most of these she drew between the sessions. In all she gave Milner 4,000 drawings, all of which the author studied, over the years and in preparing this book, at least twice over; this is but one of the indications of the degree of energy and devotion the author gave to this treatment and the reporting of it to us.

The title of the book refers to the unconscious—most specifically to the patient's unconscious, as a living god whose hands create, in the drawings, so much of meaning and beauty and interpersonal communion.

In this volume 154 drawings are reproduced, and much of the author's text consists in interpretations of them. One should not be hesitant about taking up this book by reason of some concern lest its reading require an abstruse art-therapy interest, for it does not. One quickly becomes used to studying, and enjoying, the drawings and the text together. Further, one finds that these fascinating drawings, many of them very moving indeed, do much to lighten a book which inevitably to some degree conveys the arduous nature of this very long and immensely difficult treatment. The book focuses upon particularly rich phases of the treatment. Thus, approximately the first half is devoted to the first seven years of the treatment; not much less than half of it, in fact, is taken up with the drawings made by the patient during the year 1950.

The author is a superlatively perceptive analyst in her work with the patient. Equally impressive and valuable, to me, is her faithfully tracing the course of development of her own theoretical concepts over all those years, giving us beautifully clear and succinct distillates of very complex psychodynamic matters. This book provides not only an *orientation toward* the relevant literature; in addition, careful study of it leaves one feeling that one has gained a very considerable *grasp of* this literature. Milner's 106 references include some as recent as 1967. She treats the works of her colleagues with commendable respect and generous acknowledgment for the help she has received from each in her work with this woman. She nonetheless deals with this literature with authoritative discrimination and command. Even more rare, her writing has a poetic beauty which does more than make this book a delight to read; her poetic capacity accounts for much of the book's scientific value, for, I am convinced, the ego-developmental phenomena traceable to a preverbal era of life can be conveyed only by a writer who is at home in writing poetry.

This is a richly seminal book. Not only is the author herself highly creative; the reader of her book gets many creative ideas which her book itself does not contain and which he had never been able to have before. Milner's book fosters one's own creative thinking. It is a book one treasures, and knows one will consult again and again in the future, for its solid clinical help in work with patients, and for its inspiring creativity.

12

The Function of the
Patient's Realistic Perceptions
of the Analyst
in Delusional Transference

BACKGROUND DATA AND OVERALL COURSE
OF TREATMENT THUS FAR

Mrs. Joan Douglas (a pseudonym) has conveyed much information which indicates to me that she began to suffer from schizophrenia, unrecognizedly, early in childhood. But it was not until the age of 33, soon after the death of her mother, that she became overtly psychotic. (Her mother had been a highly unstable woman who, in the words of a brother of the patient, had "loved to dominate" the daughter.) At this time, the patient was herself the mother of four young children. An intimidatingly domineering woman, as her mother had been, she managed thereby to stave off hospitalization during two years of increasingly delusional and chaotic behavior, at the end of which time her relatives, having good reason to fear that she would kill someone, placed her in a psychiatric hospital. That hospital, although prominent, specializes in "eclectic" (to some degree psychotherapeutic, but largely somatic) modes of treatment. In

First published in *British Journal of Medical Psychology*, 45:1-18 (1972).

her one year there, her paranoid delusions did not lessen despite—or because of—attempted psychotherapy, two courses of insulin-coma therapy totaling at least 70 comas, and two courses of electroshock totaling at least 42 treatments. A consultant advised that she be subjected to a lobotomy as, seemingly, the only recourse. But the family obtained a second consultant, who advised transfer to Chestnut Lodge for a last-ditch attempt at psychoanalysis.

Upon admission to Chestnut Lodge at the age of 36, she was an attractive, well-groomed, healthy-appearing but actually highly paranoid woman who poured forth, at the slightest provocation, intensely threatened and threatening expressions of remarkably distorted delusional experiences. Her first analyst at Chestnut Lodge quit in discouragement after one year of work with her because of the proliferating, rather than lessening, state of her delusions, and her adamant resistance to treatment. His doing so was highly unusual behavior for a Lodge staff member, and one testimony of the formidable nature of her illness.

A few months thereafter, in January 1953, I became her analyst and, having obtained by then several years of full-time experience in this work, felt strongly confident of my ability to help her become nonpsychotic. I am still working with her, and throughout all this more than 18 years I have seen her four hours per week (apart from brief vacations) for a total of some 3,500 hours at the time of this writing.

For several years she steadfastly refused to come to my office and by the end of about ten and a half years had been there only some three or four times, when she finally began to come there with some regularity. She still had to be accompanied to and from the sessions by a nurse or attendant and when, six months later, I left the Lodge and established my practice in Washington some ten miles away, she was still so delusional and resistive to treatment that an escort had to accompany her in a taxicab. Only some five years later, about two years ago, did she become sufficiently collaborative to come in the cab, although still very delusional, without any escort from the Lodge. Throughout at least 16 years of the work I lived

with the bitter knowledge that were I at any time to become sufficiently discouraged and defeated to quit, she would be far indeed
from feeling hurt, disappointed, and grieved; she would count it, I
knew, as simply one more triumph, and a not particularly notable
one at that.

The years have taken, and continue to take, their toll. Her husband, who from the first had visited no more than once or twice a
year and had seemed to me quite unconvinced about any worth-
whileness of the treatment, finally came to feel, after five years of
my work with her, that his own conscience had been appeased and,
liberating himself from his previously rigid ethical scruples, divorced her. From the first she had refused to acknowledge the existence of her children and had refused for prolonged intervals to
open letters or gifts from them. A visit from the husband and the
children prior to my becoming her analyst had been disastrous, and
only after nine and ten years of our work, respectively, did each of
the two older children visit. Each found her so disturbingly crazy
that neither has yet returned, years later. My own feelings of condemnation of her for her rejection of her children, and my own
hurt at her unpredictably harsh maternal rejection of me, have
been, for me, among the more difficult aspects of our work. Most
difficult of all for me has been the guilt and despair evoked in me,
in innumerable sessions, concerning my feelings of being, in effect,
a bad mother to her.

Meanwhile this once youthful and attractive woman has become,
in appearance and in actuality, a grandmother, at times coming to
express, indirectly, a poignant concern lest she become written off
as a geriatric patient. Several years ago she needed to be fitted with
an upper dental plate, and for several months it caused me a particular agony of guilt when, in the midst of a stream of paranoid
reproach or declaiming, she would suddenly take out her uncomfortable plate and become years older in her toothless appearance,
gesturing now with the dental plate as she spoke. I came subsequently to feel grateful to her that her own indomitable quality,
persisting despite these ravages, helped me to become largely free
from that guilt.

For more than six years I have tape-recorded all our sessions—with her knowledge; this is one of the manifestations of
her increasing investment in our work. I have saved all these hundreds of tapes, and occasional playbacks of various among them
have convinced me of their priceless value for research in the
psychodynamics, and in the difficult endeavor of psychoanalysis, of
schizophrenic patients.

This woman made, for several years following her admission, an
enormous impact upon the whole Chestnut Lodge community, by
reason of her powerfully coercive, delusion-motivated behavior, her
rare wit, and her caustic warmth. At times her delusional behavior
spilled over into the surrounding small city of Rockville, and at
times even into the somewhat more distant nation's capital. An expert equestrienne, during one of her several elopements prior to
my work with her (she made none thereafter), she went to
Washington, hired a horse, and rode up Pennsylvania Avenue to
the gates of the White House, demanding audience with the President. She was placed thereupon, by the police, in a government
mental hospital until it was ascertained that she had eloped from
the Lodge; she was then returned there. Her name was placed by
the F.B.I. upon the list of those persons known to be a threat to
Presidents of the United States.

She made a number of frighteningly serious, intendedly homicidal attacks upon various persons in the sanitarium, and I often felt
threatened in this regard. But her murderousness was expressed
mainly in her largely unconscious use of verbal communication as a
means of doing violence to one's sense of reality, including one's
sense of personal identity. There were times, particularly in unusually stormy sessions during the early years, when I felt so
threatened and enraged that I was seriously afraid lest I lost control of my own murderous feelings and kill her.

Over the more than 18 years of my work with her, a truly staggering multitude of staff personnel (as well as various fellow patients, in their fashions) have tried to help her become nonpsychotic, while presumably having largely to repress (as have I, myself)
their tremendous investment in her remaining psychotic. These

have included some ten psychiatric administrators of the various units (each housing about nine to twelve patients) in the sanitarium where she has dwelt. These administrative psychiatrists have served, in accordance with the routine of the sanitarium, from six months to several years—on the average, about two years. All of them have shown considerable devotion to her, and several have brought creative administrative approaches to bear in the treatment. A similar number of psychiatric social workers, a much larger number of nurses and occupational and recreational therapy personnel, and a far larger number still of attendants have contributed enormously to her treatment over the years. I wish here not merely to acknowledge their indispensable contributions, but to indicate what awesome demands the psychoanalytic treatment of a chronically schizophrenic patient can make upon the best efforts of a multitude of professionally trained persons. This long treatment effort could not have continued, of course, without the support, financial and psychological, of her relatives.

Incidentally, as regards modifications of the psychoanalytic approach used in her treatment, on the one hand she has never been given any form of drug treatment (such as the phenothiazines), with the possible exception of occasional nighttime barbiturates prescribed by one or another of the psychiatric administrators in the early years of my work with her; on the other hand, she has yet to use the analytic couch.

From the very beginning of our work, she manifested an awesome degree of ego dedifferentiation and ego fragmentation (or, to put the latter in Kleinian terms, splitting) as unconscious defenses against such emotions as guilt, grief, and love, and in an unconscious effort to realize her strivings for omnipotence. There were, she was utterly convinced, numerous "doubles" of everyone, including herself. When a male aide to whom she had been attached left the sanitarium, she did not miss him, for she knew there were 13 Mr. Mitchells, most or all of them still about, in various guises. She felt accused unfairly by all persons about her for her more destructive acts which, she was convinced, her malicious doubles had done. She once protested, "Well, there were nine hundred and ninety-seven tertiary skillion women [i.e., projected components, or "doubles," of herself] associated with Chestnut Lodge; so why should *I* be blamed for everything everybody did?" (The delusional experience here was, as usual, expressed as though it were the most obvious thing in the world.)

She misidentified herself and others repeatedly and unpredictably. There were several Dr. Searles, and when she went on a shopping trip with an aide she experienced a succession of different aides with her, rather than being aware of changing emotions in herself toward a single aide. She had only "splashes of memory" of any experiences prior to her hospitalization, asserted that she had never had a mother or father or husband or children, and once when I started to ask something about her mother, protested, "Whenever you use the word 'mother,' I see a whole parade of women, each one representing a different point of view." More often than not, she reacted to me with the utter conviction that she had never seen me before, and very often expressed the conviction that I was the such-and-such person who had done malevolent things to her in her childhood—raped her, murdered her, and so on.

She was unable to differentiate, in her experiencing and perceiving and thinking, between (a) figurative (metaphorical) and concrete modes of thought and communication, (b) animate and inanimate elements of reality, (c) human and nonhuman forms of life, (d) male and female persons, (e) adults and children, (f) fantasies (or nighttime dreams) and real events, or even (g) ideas and persons. Trees, walls of buildings, and so on were imbued with persons. Everything, in fact, had once existed in the form of a person who had been turned, by the malevolent, omnipotent, Circe-like outer forces such as myself, into a tree or a plant, or the wall of a building, or a rug, or whatever, and she strove anguishedly to find some means of liberating him or her into a human form again. She did not experience mental images of persons, from her current or past life, as such, but was convinced that the image was the flesh-and-blood person who somehow had been shrunk and imprisoned in her head.

For the first year or two of our work she continued in the delusional conviction that a number of actual surgical operations she had undergone, in earlier years, had consisted in "their" having placed a chain upon her heart, installed machinery in her abdomen, and bored a hole through her skull, through which "they" ran her brain. For many subsequent years, she often spoke chillingly of "this head" (her own) or "that head" (mine); heads were unpredictably replaced by the omnipotent "them." She did not experience, for example, a collection of thoughts newly come into her head, but rather that she clearly now had a different head, literally, from the one she had worn a moment before.

The content, although not the basic underlying themes, of her delusions has been ever-changing, throughout the years. For several years I used privately and wearily to feel that nearly every week she lived in some new, highly preoccupying main delusion, whose origin and possible links to reality were hopelessly unknown to me. At such times, it was utterly obvious to her that we—and, of course, all of her perceived reality—were comprised within "the giant frog," or "the sapphire," or "the duck," or whatever.

Only after several years did she begin to be conscious, for brief times, of feeling murderous, and with that development became, of course, an appreciably less dangerous person. She has improved vastly, in many regards. No longer is she convinced that she is being moved geographically all over the world, among 48,000 Chestnut Lodges. Now she knows that she is moved emotionally by various of her fellow human beings whom she encounters in her daily life. She knows that there is only one Chestnut Lodge, and she feels realistically bored and discouraged and often despairing about her constricted life there. Her memory span has lengthened from, say, one or two days (her remembered continuity of experience never used to extend farther back than that, for she was "blocked" incessantly) to, gradually, weeks, months, and, on occasion, years. She is much better able to remember, with me, events of our preceding sessions. In recent years she has become far more genuinely human, experiencing her body much more as her own—although far from fully and consistently, even yet—and now relatively seldom looks at me as being a total stranger. Bit by bit, we are able increasingly to face the enormous grief-work which must be accomplished if she is ever to become enduringly nonpsychotic.

THE PROBLEM OF PSYCHOANALYTIC TECHNIQUE, AND THE INCREASINGLY EVIDENT CONNECTIONS BETWEEN HER DELUSIONS AND REALISTIC COMPONENTS OF MYSELF

As the years went on, she came into a more and more terribly isolated social position in the sanitarium, as personnel members and fellow patients who briefly had found her "crazy talk" (as it came to be known among them) enchanting and her rare moments of highly trenchant "straight talk" refreshing, became thoroughly alienated by reason of their helplessness to feel at all predictably related to her in any meaningful way. Over all these years I myself have found that about 98 percent of all that she says has no functionally usable meaning to me. Whether she has been expressing her "crazy talk" in a playfully teasing fashion or in a spirit of physical or emotional anguish, or of paranoid accusation, I literally have never found her capable of setting it aside *in toto* and functioning in a different, more rational mode of experience and interpersonal communication—no matter whether upon gentle encouragement or harsh demand from me.

The most difficult aspect of the work, therefore, is the enduring of a quite terrible feeling of unrelatedness between us. A year or so ago I happened to see a portion of a science-fiction movie on TV, in which the central theme was the effort to communicate from earth with a being on a planet many millions of miles away—an endeavor both fascinating and eerie, during which the extraterrestrial being gradually became manifest on the earthmen's radar screen, as an electrical pattern of vaguely human body-outline. I was immediately struck with the realization that Joan's and my task of trying to communicate with one another, despite the fact that we both speak English and are human in appearance and are geographically close to one another, is no less difficult, no less eerie, than that.

Her own large-scale helplessness to bridge this experiential gulf
has required me to devote enormous effort to viewing the world,
including herself and myself, through her eyes, while keeping in
touch with my own view of reality. Moments of feeling related to
her, of seeing where her delusionally expressed views are linked up
with my own view of my reality, have aroused then in me a deeply
guilty sense of my being totally responsible for her plight. This subjective omnipotence-based sense of guilt seems clearly a sample of
that against which she herself has been defended, unconsciously,
over the years, by reason of her psychotic mechanisms such as projection and introjection, dedifferentiation, splitting, and denial.

During several years, it gradually became evident that she was
involved simultaneously in two all-absorbing tasks. One was the
struggle to become born—to leave her mode of existence as "an
element"—a boundless element, variously specified as light, or electricity, or air, or water—and to have a body of her own to inhabit.
Her unconscious ambivalence about this was enormous, although
not experienced in awareness as such, i.e., as a conscious conflict.
Not to have a body meant not existing in any substantial way, not
being a person among other persons; but to become born meant to
relinquish the state of boundless omnipresence and immortality.
She spent much of her time between sessions, over these years, trying literally to build a body (out of all sorts of materials such as
wood, canvas, yarn which she knit into body-parts, and so on) and
trying, godlike, to transform into living and human form dead
leaves, and other materials, which she flushed down the toilet, convinced that "the pipes" could be employed for such a magically
life-creating purpose. It was with clearly mingled feelings of fulfillment and of loss that she came to say about six years ago, after
much of the becoming born had finally been accomplished, "I used
to be God; now I'm a woman."

Her other, and related, struggle was to differentiate what is
"outside" (i.e., existing in outer reality) from what is "inside" (existing in fantasy). I can now see in retrospect that it is only as this
latter task has been gradually accomplished, over the years, that we
can now focus, in the sessions, upon her *intrapsychic* world (I, at

least, can now clearly see it as that; to her it is still very largely *the* world). It is only as we have become able to do this that I have become more freely able to see, furthermore, the main point I wish to make in this paper—namely, the awesome extent to which her experienced world, so remarkably delusional, is based upon, and emerges from, reality components of me, no matter how greatly distorted is her experiencing of these by reason of such processes as transference, dedifferentiation, ego fragmentation (splitting), projection, introjection, and denial.

Initially it was impossible for me clearly to differentiate, in my perception of her, an intrapsychic world which I could fully assume the responsibility for helping her to explore and understand, from the world comprising her physical self and the surrounding physical world. She blamed her seemingly incessant, and endlessly varied, experiences of bodily torture upon me, just as she blamed me for her imprisonment in the locked ward. Her psychosis permeated in its real effects, as I have said already, the domain of the sanitarium, often spreading into the city of Rockville and on occasion into the nation's capital. I was deeply threatened by her so formidably holding me omnipotently responsible for the world in which I could actually see her, in so many regards, to be really living. I was unable to function competently in a spirit of responsibility for a much more limited sphere, a much more limited function, of helping her with her intrapsychic problems, both because of the unconsciously gratifying lure of the omnipotence she attributed to me, and because of the fact that her intrapsychic world was not differentiated, either in her own experience of it or sufficiently much in my own appraisal of it, from the physical world of her daily life. Her capacity to share with me any responsibility for the treatment was so feeble that, as I have mentioned, she almost never came to my office for ten and a half years.

Meanwhile, during the sessions, she often paced about or, if she sat near me, had to busy herself with knitting or sewing, for example. This activity involved her keeping large knitting needles or scissors near at hand lest I rape or kill her, which she was convinced I had done innumerable times when she had been "blocked," i.e., not at all in possession of her own mind. The door of her room often had to be kept locked, lest she escape from the session.

She misidentified me constantly, with unpredictable changeability, and so forcefully that my own sense of my identity, and of outer reality, was often seriously assaulted and undermined. I felt far from being, say, on the observer's side of a psychiatric-research viewing window with a mirror on its other surface, or—to vary the analogy—behind an aperture in some movie screen upon the other surface of which some LSD movie was being shown to her. Her psychotic responses to me—to what she saw on the mirror-movie screen, as it were—had a far deeper impact upon, and within, me than such metaphors would indicate. She formidably treated all of what we would call outer reality, including myself, as plasticine to be molded constantly by her in her escape from unconscious feelings of grief, guilt, insignificance, helplessness, and so on.

I have often felt mystified as to why she speaks so very often of murder, is so utterly convinced that I have murdered her, innumerable times, and so frequently feels accused, herself, of murder. My surest impression, supported by much data, some of which is quite explicit, is that this delusional behavior arises primarily from the changeability in her experience of her own identity, and in her perception of the other person's (my, for example) identity. Whenever there is a shift in either of these, she evidently reacts with the conviction that the person she was a moment ago, or the person I (for example) was a moment ago, has been murdered. She has accused me many times of having murdered her during the previous session, or earlier in the current one, and clearly feels threatened with being held as a "psychopathic killer" because of the disappearance, from the scene of her perceivable reality, of the person I had been or she had been a moment before. Presumably the assaults I feel upon my own sense of identity are mild in comparison with the murderous devastation wrought upon hers by my responding to her as having personality components (such as cruelty) which she is having to repress from her sense of identity.

Such awareness as I possessed, before starting to work with her, of the kind of person I am, enabled me to build with her a consensus as to the *reality components* in her *psychotic transference reactions* to me, such that the analysis of the transference distortions has been increasingly successful. She has both required and enabled me to become increasingly aware of previously unconscious aspects of myself—surely one of the most significant aspects, for me, of our long work together.

For example, in a session during the fourth year I noticed that it was just after I had shifted to a conventional psychiatrist type of jargon (undoubtedly as a largely unconscious manifestation of my fleeing from what we had just been experiencing together) that she said, "When you talk like that, I feel as though we've been riding in an airplane together and I've suddenly been dropped into the bottom of the ocean." I asked, "When I talk like a psychiatrist?" and she said, "Yes." If she had not been able to put it that way, and I had had no awareness of my proclivity for taking refuge in the "healthy" conventional psychiatrist role, I might have heard, instead, only her usual paranoid reproaches that we were now suddenly at the bottom of the ocean.

In a session early in the tenth year, I said something to which she responded, "When you talk to me like that, I feel that I'm going to be led to the edge of the world and the people are going to decide whether I'll have to jump off or not." She conveyed the described scene with a kind of semidelusional vividness but, as is evident, she was reacting to the *way* in which *I* had spoken. She had helped me to achieve sufficient knowledge of the relevant aspect of myself for me to ask, "Do you mean that I sound so portentous?" and she replied, "Yes."

In about the fifteenth year a session occurred in which she was able to confirm that her still-recurrent experiences of our being at the bottom of the sea were reactions not to my frequently fishy-eyed, evasive look (as I had early suggested; I often responded so to her gaze with a feeling of guilt at my furtively private thoughts as to how terribly, impossibly crazy she is), but rather to the enormous *pressure* she felt under. I had become aware, years before, of something of the tremendous pressure I placed upon her to fulfill myriad, impossibly conflictual expectations I had of our work together. Her conviction that we were both at the bottom of the sea, during our sessions, was scarcely an exaggerated portrayal of the pressure upon both of us. I cannot overemphasize how innumerable have been the times, beginning in the early months of the treatment and still continuing, when she has rejected, utterly and decisively, such attempted translations into figurative, metaphorical language of experiences that to her are entirely, delusionally concrete. But my gradually increasing ability to realize, with her help, how very much of tangible reality there indeed is in them, has enabled me to help her to accept these translations increasingly frequently.

On relatively rare but therapeutically valuable occasions, I have been able to recognize various patterns of highly psychotic behavior on her part, maintained in each instance for months or even years, as being based in part upon an identification, however distorted and exaggerated, with some aspect of my own behavior. I have termed this process, in an earlier paper (1963b), delusional identification. I shall give three examples of this.

1. For a number of years, in something like the third to sixth years of the work, she behaved fully as though she owned the family-residence type of building, housing nine to eleven patients, where she dwelt. In the living room, for example, she would use the TV as she chose, and in innumerable other ways behaved obliviously of other persons' right to be there. It gradually dawned upon me that, from her view, I behaved no less outrageously as though I were the owner of her room. For instance, although I would regularly knock on her door at the beginning of each session, I would then ignore her invariably bellowed, "Don't come in!" and go in anyway, dragging a chair behind me, and wasting few if any words upon her during the process. She nearly always had the window wide open, even on the coldest of winter days, and I, having long since learned that it was useless to be more polite, simply would stride over to the window and close it, return to my seat and proceed with the session, in which I was cast in the position of sole proprietor. I cannot report that my seeing this connection between her behavior in the building as a whole, and my own behavior in

her room, led to a transference interpretation which led, in turn, to some almost magical change in her behavior. But I can report that I no longer viewed her behavior in the building as a symptom burdensome to me, and in general the staff found her becoming increasingly cooperative over the subsequent years.

2. As a second example of her delusional identifications with me, I shall mention a whole collection of phenomena—many dozens, very possibly hundreds, over the years—which first came to my attention in the earliest years of the treatment. These were manifestations of what I gradually became accustomed to construing, privately, as her capacity for gigantic irony, on the scale of Jonathan Swift or Rabelais, expressed in leg-pulling satires of me. Most dismaying—and there have been many such instances—she has said something which filled me with the sudden, highly uneasy suspicion that *all* her behavior, for months now or even over all these years, has consisted in a gigantic satire of one or another of my personal asininities. Rarely have I seen anyone more powerfully endowed with the capacity to make others, including myself, feel asinine, and on these occasions I feel that not only has the carpet suddenly been pulled out from under me, but also that I have been plunged suddenly into the ever-impending sense of omnipotent responsibility for all her existence—an existence which, let it be remembered, she almost incessantly has kept before me as being filled with suffering and tragedy.

For instance, she has filled me with sudden moments of suspicion—and simultaneously of being nakedly exposed—that her being immersed for years, in all her waking hours, with how to build a body for herself was a travesty upon my supposed childlike naïveté in not knowing where babies come from (i.e., as a result of sexual intercourse; this had connotations of her ribbing me for never making sexual approaches to her). Also, I have felt appalled at the thought that her many-years-longer endeavor to reach her mother (who in actuality had died some five years before our work began) is a caricaturing of my own small-child seeking to find an ideal mother in her. Her so-frequent immersion in large-scale psychotic plans is clearly based in part upon her view of me as a

man, typical for her of all men with their head-in-the-clouds, grandiose, intellectual planning, and their denial, at the same time, of
their infantile dependency upon the women round about them,
women of whom they are so oblivious.

   3. On occasion her delusional identification with me is most
explicit. In the session on March 4, 1971, for example, she repeatedly identified herself, by name, as Dr. Harold Searles, while
pouring paranoid accusations upon me, being utterly inhospitable
to my being in "my office," and complaining harshly of being
"forced to have hours." She succeeded in driving home the realization that, on all three counts, these were no more than exagger-
ations of my own so frequently accusatory, inhospitable, and en-
slaved demeanors.

   By late 1966 or early 1967 she had become able to sit with me,
during the sessions in my office, with our chairs placed conventionally only a few feet apart, and to join me in a mutual effort to understand what was transpiring in the relationship. She looked often,
without leaning forward, into my eyes, and in one of these sessions
she was looking at my face in fascination as I was making some
comment, and exclaimed, "When you're talking about different
people, your eyes become the eyes of whomever you're talking
about. It's like a kaleidoscope. I've never seen anything like it before; it's fascinating."

   Here again, whenever I was cognizant of some aspect of myself
as providing a real basis for her transference distortions, this
proved helpful. For instance, by the time of a session on December 22,
1970, I had long been aware of feeling, often, murderously sadistic
toward her in the frequent sessions during which I experienced
physical and emotional torture. This session soon proved to be one
of the most disturbed and disturbing ones in years. During it she
perceived me as changing *in toto* (not merely my eyes) three times,
such that she was convinced, decisively, that a succession of four
persons occupied my chair—a phenomenon which had been relatively commonplace years before. Innumerable times, she accused
me of having murdered her and of having perpetrated other
enormities upon her. She was looking predominantly threatened
and vulnerable to hurt.

At one point I developed the impression, from the manner in which she was looking at me, that in what she was saying she was expressing indirectly a wondering of what I was thinking, and I suggested, "God knows what I'm thinking, while you're talking?" She agreed, "Yeah." I commented, "You have no way of knowing what I'm thinking, huh?" She replied, "I think *God does*, though, 'cause God comes in at odd intervals and, uh, uh, is quite perturbed, and *why* he has to make himself look like *Tiny Tim*, and, uh, walk around with a *limp*, is beyond me. And *I* don't want him to be *hurt*, anyway. If he's hurt, there would be no sense in anyone ever going to a hospital, 'cause he is the last healthy person we have, absolutely, and all hospitals are attached to him, and it doesn't seem to faze him in the slightest. But we've got to be *very* careful of him, and he *cannot* be a *horse*, 'cause that's the way to kill the one and only doctor."

I said, "Guess that's what I'm intending?" She replied, "Yeah. So, uh—" I suggested, "Well, I have that—what?—cruel, calculating look as though I'm planning on running Tiny Tim as a racehorse?—poor little crippled child, as a racehorse?—That the way I look?" She agreed emphatically, "Yeah, that mean."

I commented, "That mean, huh?" which she again confirmed. "Yeah. Well, you look like part of that George Reynolds. . . ," who had been, as I had learned from her years before, an army officer whom she had long hated for his having impregnated, and obtained an illegal abortion for, a young woman whom she had had in her home as a nursemaid for her children, and for whom she had felt a parental responsibility. George Reynolds was clearly one of her bad-father figures.

The various examples given above provide glimpses into a phenomenon which has become more and more clear during the last several months: namely, the awesome extent to which the reality of the analyst's personality gives rise to the whole, seemingly so-delusional, world of the patient. In particular, over these months, the role of the other person's—the analyst's in the context upon which I am focusing here—intrapsychic world, his thoughts and feelings and fantasies, are of central power. She responds to me, in this regard, as the personification of an aspect of her father, perceived by her in childhood as an inscrutable, cold-blooded, malevolent, sadistic, vindictive, omnipotent planner and controller. But, as the above examples indicate, this psychotic transference to me is based upon bits, at least, of what I experience as being, indeed, my intrapsychic reality—in the light, for example, of the sadism I find aroused in me by her during the sessions.

It must be emphasized, here, that her ego functioning is still so dedifferentiated as to render her unable fully to distinguish, except rarely and fleetingly, between fantasy and reality, and between herself and me. Thus she tends not to construe what *my imagination* is—*my fantasies* are—at any one point; rather, she tends to experience it as the power of my mind to engender *her* only available *reality*, including the reality of her self. She literally experiences my presumed thoughts, for example, as having the power to transform her.

She is similarly vulnerable to others also. On September 5, 1970, for example, she said, "I am who everybody else thinks they are."

Her state of ego dedifferentiation is such as to have fostered, long ago, a state of symbiosis between us, symbiosis which is in part of delusional-transference origin but in part based upon the actual state of the relatedness between us, a relatedness which involves symbiosis participated in by both of us, and in which we function in terms of the power to create one another. I have termed this mode of relatedness "therapeutic symbiosis," in a number of earlier papers (1965a) in which I have described the crucial regards in which it differs from a *folie à deux* encompassing both analyst and patient.

In the session on October 3, 1970, it became evident for the first time that her attending to what the hallucinatory voices are saying, during the sessions, is an effort to discern what is going on in my mind. It further became evident that she does this in an effort to help me. She made clear that she assumes my usual silence to be based upon my helplessness to know what is going on in my mind. This perception of me, clearly involving much projection of her own inner state, as expressed by her, constitutes, incidentally, one of many instances in which I have felt the uneasy suspicion, described earlier, that her whole behavior represents a taunting satire upon my own way of functioning—my silence, in this instance, which is consciously not a matter of impoverishment or inaccessibility of my own thoughts (although only now, as I write this, do I begin to see that, here again, there is some degree of reality in her perceiving me thus). In this session, I might add, there were the customary phenomena of her evidently perceiving many different persons in my eyes,[1] and at one point she gave unusually explicit confirmation of her experiencing herself as multiple.

On December 10, 1970 she said, "Mr. Schultz [her long-deceased father; she evidently was misidentifying some other person at Chestnut Lodge as him—an extremely frequent type of phenomenon] is back at Chestnut Lodge now, making everybody think the way *he* thinks."

On December 24, 1970 she confirmed a hunch newly come to me—namely, that she experiences different persons appearing in, or disappearing from, my eyes upon her saying various things; I had noticed the seemingly close correlation between her glancing at my eyes and her making various comments. Thus, she indicated a conviction that she creates me, transforms me, to a degree very like that to which she feels vulnerable of being transformed by me. Her mother-introject (my phrase, not used in the analysis) told her, incidentally, that she (the patient) had talked with three men so far in the session; and she, the patient, was convinced that we had changed offices suddenly at some point, from a larger to a smaller one.

On December 26, 1970 it became evident, and was confirmed by her, that in at least several instances what she was saying (highly psychotic in content, as usual) was a reaction to the expression she saw on my face at the moment or, in some instances, an effort to bring to my face, once again, various different expressions she had

---

[1] I fell into assuming as the months went on that, from her way of speaking of such perceptions, she was seeing entire homunculi, as it were, in my eyes; but when I inquired into this in more detail on one of the later occasions she made clear that, as she had indicated earlier, what she was perceiving were the *eyes of* those persons in my eyes.

seen there. This was another significant glimpse, in essence, of her involvement in creating me.

(The data contained in the following three paragraphs are so complex and multidetermined as potentially to inflict upon the reader something of the confusion I experience so much of the time during the sessions themselves. One will find it helpful to keep in mind that I wish to emphasize particularly those data, in these paragraphs, which highlight the theme of the patient's experiencing the other's thoughts as having a godlike power to engender all of her perceivable reality.)

Midway along in the session of March 4, 1971, after she had referred to herself by a succession of different first names other than her own, I challenged her, joshingly, "What ten things are wrong with 'Joan'?" She replied, promptly and seriously, " 'Joan' means 'God.' " (Here one may recall that, years before, she had come to say, "I used to be God; now I'm a woman." I am reminded, too, that in her childhood her mother evidently had attributed a godlike malevolence to the girl, holding her responsible for all anguish, no matter whether real or psychotically created, in the mother's life.) She went on, later in the session, ". . . I figure I recall where I met you once, millions of years ago when I was Pamela of Britain. I went—uh—inside my *self*. You were then living in a—on a farm in my bosom, my right breast, and you took one look at me and you said, 'Oh, you're *sun!*' and you threw me up—I was [i.e., had been previously] a *soul*, see, and I wasn't even an *egg*." I commented, "But I *thought* you were a sun, huh?" She agreed, "You *thought* me [i.e., caused me] to be a sun, like that [snapping her fingers], and threw me up, and I was a *gigantic* sun, and you put me up—in the breast, and, well, I got the reputation through being known as *sun*-light, right from that *minute* on, and I had a terrible time—well, it—it really hurt my *soul* considerably, and it hurt my position as a doctor, in relation to my patients, and that's the only way that I can attribute—uh—feel that there was any reason for me to have had a soul that maggoted people [i.e., turned people into maggots]—uh—because you must never turn a soul into a moon *or* a sun if you can possibly help it, ya see. You could turn a *person*, a four-

and-a-half-medical-day-old [she often reckoned time in terms of 'medical' time, vastly longer than conventional time] *person*, into a sun, but not the *soul* of the person. But *you* people don't see the difference between soul and mind, eyesight, type of—uh—anatomy, human beings, or any other type of thing. Uh—"

I interrupted her by saying, "One thing I hadn't realized is that my thoughts ever had the power to—cause you to *become* different *forms*—that—that it was possible for me to *think you* into different *forms*. I didn't realize that." (Noteworthy, here, is my self-depreciation, my essentially shunning and shying away from the omnipotent-creator transference role which she needs me to occupy.)

After a pause of a few seconds she replied, "Well, my *mother* [and this was said with significant emphasis, highlighting reproachfully my having refused, once again, to be the perceivedly omnipotent good mother = good doctor = God whom she was needing]—uh—before she was a baby, I mean when she was a woman, she could think herself—*as* herself, and hold her face [i.e., the mother could create the mother's own self by thought, and maintain so the existence of her face], and look very well, and then she would give it to me and *I'd* look very well; but I was a *baby*, and she didn't teach me how to really *do* it, so, uh, it would *stay* that way, 'cause I was always in a soul—I never had a—really had a body, until—no, it's all *soul* material. But it fleshed, uh, and that's where we live, on my *soul*. Uh—and they—people, when I went back there to visit, said, 'Well, now that you aren't *God* anymore, we're enjoying living on your *soul*. Isn't it very dangerous for us to be here, and won't you surely be fire if we don't get off your property?' And I said, 'Probably,' and they said, 'When, uh—who do we go to now to see who *creates* souls?' And, uh, '—Who *is* God now?' And I said, 'Well, there are—any good *doctor* takes the place of God,' 'cause they [i.e., good doctors] know how to manufacture souls, and they can differentiate between soul, mind, intellect, eyesight, and the seven senses; but *average* people *don't*."

In the session of March 11, 1971 she said, "My mother thought us [clearly meaning "created us"] from her desk. . . . The old gentleman thinks us from his desk . . ." On March 27, 1971 she described that, over and over, she "was snatched up and went into another one of my mother's ideas, I guess."

Another patient, a schizoid woman, after several years of analysis began a session by saying, rather promptly after lying down on the couch, "I can see an autopsy room, and I have the thought that the analysis is like performing an autopsy." This was said in a slow, measured manner and, significantly, in a tone of obedience to my wishes—as if I had hypnotized her and had instructed, "Now I want you to see an autopsy room." As the session went on, she commented that her father had "not a speck" of humor in him, and never had had, within the patient's memory. In many previous sessions she had commented upon my own somberness. The process at work in this patient is, I think, essentially the same as that in the so vastly more ill woman I have been describing in this paper. Where the schizoid patient tended to experience that I (= father) was engendering with my mind a fantasy in her mind, the schizophrenic woman actually lives, to a remarkable degree, in a delusional world engendered, so she experiences it, by my (variously mother's or father's) mind.

DATA FROM SEQUENTIAL ANALYTIC SESSIONS

Now I shall give a few sample drops from the more general ocean of data, produced at sequential periods of time, in some instances to illustrate the theoretical points I have been discussing, in others to show something of the depth of her ego fragmentation and dedifferentiation, the resultant bizarreness of her transference perceptions of me, my psychoanalytic technique, the emotions I experience, and, above all, to convey some tangible feeling of our ongoing work together.

On May 7, 1965, during the second year of my seeing her at my private office some ten miles from the Lodge and with no attendant about—an era in which I often felt considerable anxiety lest she become physically unmanageable—she wondered what I would do if someone broke up into mercury droplets. In the following session she asserted that "there are hundreds of men standing around in this head." In ensuing months she experienced olfactory hallucinations arising from what she called "God-rot," which seemed to me traceable to the decay of omnipotent introjects, and it was some time during, or not far from, this era, that she said, "I used to be God; now I'm a woman," with mingled feelings of enormous relief and deflation in her tone.

On December 11, 1965 is my first note of her perceiving a changing succession of different figures in my eyes (some being real persons from her past, many being figures from world history, many being largely constructs of fantasy, a great many being nonhuman creatures, and all being given equal reality-value in her perception of them). On December 15, 1965 she prepared me, in apparently conscious solicitude, but unconsciously diabolic and highly psychotic detail, for her putting into me the multitude of people, dead people as I recall, that she experienced as being within her. In the next session, two days later, I experienced a transitory sense of craziness—a sense of confusion and of es- trangement from my surroundings during the session—of a sort I used to experience a few times a year, but have not experienced in more recent years, as she has become less overwhelmingly psycho- tic. My reaction in that particular instance, I believe, was related to her impregnating me more deeply than usual with the fragmented products of the "God-rot."

On December 24, 1965 she saw two men simultaneously in my two eyes, and when I attempted to foster her acceptance of her real identity as Joan Douglas, she bristled with startling antagonism at the name, saying, "If I were a cat, the hairs on my back would rise." It was evident that her aversion to her own real identity was as intense as had been her mother's aversion to her in childhood, and her own aversion to me for many years.

Coming to more recent sessions, on April 25, 1970 she saw in my two eyes two people, at war with one another. This perception, not uncommon for her, presumably is attributable not only to pro- jection but also to the intense state of emotional conflict, revealed in my eyes, which I often experience in these stressful sessions. But when she then exclaimed, with interest, "Now there's a referee there," I felt that, from the projectional point of view, we had a welcome indication of increase in her ego integration.

On April 29, 1970 she spoke of us as two babies, sitting contentedly in a perambulator, and expressed contented pleasure at the to her obvious fact that she and I were having "sexual intercourse" by talking with one another.

On May 2, 1970 she beautifully expressed her need for all her innumerable "islands" (of ego identity, I privately translated) to "coalesce," and described, with moving poignancy, many things and people as being "*all* my mother." I felt that not only was her intense *need* to find a good mother, everywhere, being more clearly expressed, but also that she was becoming better *able* to find a mother in all these—better able to let them be mothers to her.

But a few days later there occurred a highly typical example of antitherapeutic response on my part. She had started spinning a delusional fantasy, and I became alarmed at how much I was enjoying it, and "conscientiously" reacted against it in trying to help her to become in better touch with her real, adult identity as Joan Douglas. This had, in retrospect quite predictably, a very distancing effect upon her. This is one of hundreds of similar examples I could give of the difficulties I have had in trying to immerse myself in genuinely therapeutic relatedness with her, while trying to stave off the harsh requirements of my own superego, so much of the time violently activated by the patient's own accusations and reproaches to me during her long illness.

In the very next session, on May 9, 1970, she manifested a more than usually bizarre experience of herself as being the box of Kleenex on the floor next to my couch, and "Mrs. Bradley" (her formal name for her sister; the patient had long ago accepted the status of a servant or moronic sibling to her sister) as being the wicker basket (in which I keep napkins for the couch pillow), also on the floor. Again in retrospect, it might have been predictable that, having found herself rejected by me in her humanly identifying with me in the previous session, she had now to identify with a nonhuman thing. She also complained that she could not see out of her own eyes, which had been usurped by Erich von Stroheim (the silent-movie actor, who played German-villain roles) and Eric Sevareid (the news commentator). Following this session I felt so discouraged that I thought seriously of quitting with her— something which, despite years of terrible futility and disappointment, I rarely had thought seriously of doing.

But then a week later, in an again typical fluctuation between psychosis and health, despair and hope, she acknowledged, "There *does* seem to be a soul over here [gesturing toward her own body] who misses Mrs. Schultz [her mother] and who is Joan"—a tremendous forward step for her.

On May 20, 1970 I experienced as devastating her prolonged, searching, silent, childlike gazing at my eyes; it mobilized, so I felt, all my guilt over her long and terrible illness, my guilt at my sadistic and lustful feelings toward her, my guilt at subjectively exploiting her and her illness for research purposes, and my guilt at my wish never to lose her, for both deeply personal as well as scientific reasons, through her ever becoming durably nonpsychotic. During the session she made various verbal attacks upon and accusations of me—as when, for instance, she condemned me as a "baby-raper" and called me "Lucifer-Eternal Rest" (the latter, I felt, being both a condemnation of my genuinely diabolical qualities as well as a derisive needling of me for my never, in reality, making any sexual overtures to her, over all the years). But these verbal communications, though of considerable impact upon me, were not nearly as difficult to endure as was the silent gazing I have described.

On May 26, 1970 she looked full of tears, and termed the situation "almost uncontrollable"; bit by bit she has become able in recent years to experience healthy sadness, grief, and suicidal despair. She also made it unmistakably clear, for the ten-thousandth time, that someone in her mind was, in her experience, the flesh-and-blood person, somehow shrunken and installed there and needing liberation from that imprisonment, rather than any mental image, any memory-image or fantasy-imate, of a person who exists or once existed in an outer reality.

On the following day, May 27, 1970,' she treated me with
genuine sympathy as an orphan child who did not know who my
own parents were, telling me gently but firmly that there was no
room in her family for me. All this was a highly accurate projection
of her own experience in childhood, in which she did not feel herself accepted as really a member of her large and socially prominent parental family, a family full of persons who were in many
ways highly confident, remarkably talented, and outstandingly successful in many fields of endeavor. By my not challenging the projectional aspect of this perception I learned, as we explored it further, something new about the era of her childhood during which
her parents had hired, as I had long known, a domestic couple
named Bauer to take care of the home and the children. I learned
that although this couple had accepted "Joan's sister" (whenever
she spoke of her own real identity, as Joan, she always spoke in the
third person) as part of their own family, they had not accepted
"Joan"; thus Joan had felt herself to be an orphan in relation to
both the Schultz family and the Bauer "family."

Five days later, on June 2, 1970, I was feeling unprecedentedly
diabolical toward her for a time during the session, and was experiencing this as being in sufficient measure a glimpse into my
own inherent, basic fiendishness so that I found it quite disturbing.
I do not recall to what, if any, data from her this was related (data
retrieval from among the hundreds of tapes in my storeroom is one
of the mountainous difficulties here). I did note that she termed
my face, at one point during this session, as having been derived
from her "clitora" via a flower. My best guess is that although such
far from unique reactions to me did not consciously threaten me,
despite her obvious wish in this instance that I would feel degraded
by it, unconsciously in me such incessant refusals to acknowledge
what I experienced as my own real identity exacted more inner disturbance than I realized.

On July 11, 1970 she was visibly shocked and crushed at my referring to her harshly as "chronically psychotic"; she was beginning,
I think, to see something of the capacity of my words to hurt her
emotionally. For years she had reacted to various things I had said

to her as being literally my murdering her, shooting her or cutting her with knives, and so on—always before, that is, she evidently had experienced these verbal responses from me as a matter of my doing actual physical violence to her, without her realizing that these were essentially emotional traumata, caused by my words and the emotional tone of them.

On July 14, 1970 she made repeated references to me as being a "situation," and as being two children (simultaneously). On August 13, 1970 she experienced "this head" (hers) and "that head" (mine) as being in equally bad condition, and repeatedly saw Joan in my eyes. The former percept was the first of many to come, which opened up the important theme of her terror of being envied. Here, I felt, she was reacting as her at times psychotic mother to me as being the child Joan, and Joan had reason to feel that one reason for the taboo upon Joan's developing a sane mind of her own was that the insane mother would react with murderous envy toward her.

On August 22, 1970 I heard this woman, who so often for so many years had poured anguished and terrible reproaches and accusations upon me, say for the first time, "I enjoy living." But on September 3, 1970, I found the session so difficult to endure that I thought—and probably reported this to her—that a horrible death, even, would be an easy way out for me.

On September 10, 1970 she produced some data making unusually explicit one of the most major themes of her psychosis, if not its most major theme: her conviction that she is keeping her mother alive by her own tenaciously remaining psychotic.

On September 12, 1970 she perceived me momentarily but recurrently as being "the Van der Voort family." (I had never heard of this family; my best guess is that they were acquaintances of her parental family.) It was obvious to her, as usual, that this was who I was—that whole family, collectively and simultaneously. It was evident to me, also, that she did not like them and had never felt any appreciable kinship with them.

On September 19, 1970 she functioned in a highly cynical, disillusioned, caustic, antagonistic, competitive way throughout nearly the whole session—perhaps the most common kind of behavior on her part in all the sessions over all the years. On September 22, 1970, in a session during which she was mute most of the time and I found her even more exasperating than usual, I told her grimly—keeping in mind her bone-deep Catholicism and the reality of hell for her—that I was feeling sorry for Satan, for when she dies and goes to hell, as I am sure she will, he will have to spend even more time with her than I have spent. I do not recall what, if any, response she showed to this; but the immediately following session was a more collaborative one, with more progress achieved than usual. Such fluctuations between positive and negative transference (and "countertransference") have been the rule over all the years; she almost invariably has thrived when I have been able to vent my harshest feelings, which at best are relatively pale approximations of her own so much more freely expressed harshness toward me.

On September 26, 1970 I realized, from what she was saying, that the innumerable Herculean tasks in which I so frequently found her to be immersed over the years, tasks described by her in highly psychotic terms but which she regarded as the obvious and urgent business for everyone including me, were essentially the task of trying to make her perceivedly gigantic but fragmented mother whole, and at the same time the task of her own trying to identify with so-gigantic and so-fragmented a mother. This was clearly related to my own conscious task, over the years, of trying to help her to become whole, while feeling at the same time privately awed at her enormous powers in many regards—her power to transcend the usual human concerns (such as any concern for her children) which give both meaning and yet in a sense imprisonment to us more ordinary mortals, her power to deflate me and render me helpless, and perhaps above all her power (though indeed not a power possessed by her, for in actuality it possessed her) to pour forth psychotic contents wondrously crazy beyond, in innumerable instances, my own power to fantasy.

On October 17, 1970 she said, with a kind of sympathetic firmness, that she wished she could be my husband (here speaking as a man to me as a woman—her mother—as she has done on innumerable occasions; it is impossible to convey fully the literalness, and therefore the impact upon one's own sense of identity, of this); but she reminded me that I am already married (to, obviously, another man than herself). She also made the important revelation that "I talk to myself to remind myself that I exist." (She, in fact, had talked to herself for many years, alone in my waiting room, for instance, where it many times sounded for all the world as though there were two persons out there.)

On October 27, 1970 it was evident that she was filled with scarcely disguised grief, and the theme of suicide repeatedly appeared in what she said. In the following session, on October 29, she explained, "I'm sad because I'm attached to so many dead or departed people." The way she said "attached" clearly conveyed a sense of physical, bodily attachment, somewhat as a living Siamese twin might speak of being attached to a dead Siamese twin. In a much more recent session she spoke in a very anxious way of being physically attached, by a weird and miles-long bodily connection which she described in a very distorted way, to the cab driver who customarily brings her to and from the sessions, who was now during the session somewhere relatively far away and she knew not where, and to whom she was entirely unaware of any *emotional* attachment experienced as such.

On October 31, 1970 I felt momentarily referred to, by her, as the giant for whom 19 houses, one on top of the other, were needed to provide housing; I was becoming more emotionally receptive to her need to experience me, in the transference, as her perceivedly gigantic mother, a transference role from which I had shied away, over the years. Years ago I used often to recount to other Chestnut Lodge colleagues, to our mutual amusement, some of her more memorably deflating, castrative comments to me; but during that long era I had felt much more threatened by her occasional adoringly awed perceptions of me, perhaps in part because I feared too much the potential envy on the part of these colleagues.

On November 3, 1970 she reacted to me, at one point, as being "my brothers" (simultaneously). I felt that, despite the psychotic nature of her transference, it was a welcome and most unusual thing for her to speak so realistically of her brothers; she had never before spoken of them collectively in any fashion, but only of one or another of them singly.

On November 7, 1970 she described her "giant mother," lying in water, as being billions of miles long, composed of flesh up to the navel and of some other substance from there on up. One can see here, I hope, something of why it was not easy for me to avoid interfering with her attaching such transference projections to myself; recall her so very frequent castrativeness, which gave me every reason to know that such awesome size would only fleetingly be mine, at any rate, in her transference perceptions of me. In this session, or in one of those not long before this, I had achieved at last the simple realization that her experiencing her mother as being of such gigantic size was obviously her way of experiencing the awesome degree of emotional importance, of psychological significance, her mother held, and continued to hold, in the patient's life. She herself still could not accept such a distinction; but sufficient ego differentiation had occurred in her, by now, that it was possible for me to discern the distinction at last.

On November 10, 1970, in the following session, she said, with surprising realism, "I really don't remember anything about the past . . . I wonder where I ever got the idea I was the daughter of the Queen of Poland?"—referring here to one of her innumerable previous psychotic identities. On November 21, still more impressively, she was able to agree that she has four children, and that I am Dr. Searles.

On December 3, 1970 she was able to recall, during the session, several realistic bits of her childhood, in a context of her transference misidentification of me as being her little brother Ralph, two years younger than herself. On December 8, she gave me to understand that one reason why she so often had experienced us as being, quite literally, on a ship (or in a bus or an airplane) is that she had been trained by her mother, as a child, to know that it is permissible to converse with a stranger—even a member of the opposite sex—on shipboard, for example, whereas in other situations it is not permissible.

On December 10, 1970 she came in looking unprecedentedly sad, and continued to appear so for fully half an hour. Her gradually increasing ability to mourn is one of the most impressive gains of the past several years of work. I said to her, near the beginning of the session, "You look at me somewhat as though wondering if I feel as sad as you're feeling." She replied, *"Why* do I *feel* so sad?" I commented, "You wonder." She went on, "I just died, they [the hallucinatory voices] just said . . ." I commented, *"They* say that you just died—*you* can't think of *any* reason that you would feel so sad, huh?" She replied, "No—because I was just born to *Ed*, the gentleman everybody calls *God*." For a full two years, earlier in our work, she consistently had described her eldest brother, Ed, literally as having been her mother; I assumed that he had functioned, indeed, as her mother far more than her biological mother had done. I commented, "So one would *think* you would feel anything *but* sad." She said, in a tone of agreement, "Um."

I went on, "Ed's your mother?—that's what they imply?" "Sounds like it," she agreed, "but it doesn't sound right—unless I'm Mrs. John Lloyd Palmer's [a friend of her mother] daughter." I commented, after she had paused briefly, "You wonder if I will argue that?—or say, 'No, that's not so'?—You wonder if I'll say, 'No—you're Joan'—hm?" She replied, "No. Always been Barbara Palmer. Who do you think *you* are?" I replied, firmly but not angrily, "Harold Searles—I more than *think* I am; I *know* I am." She said, "You aren't James Slocum [a name, as occurs abundantly, which I had never before heard] anymore?" I commented, not at all challengingly, "I used to be?" She went on, "Or Mr Sloane [another such name]?" I said, "I *used* to be, huh?" She said, confirmingly, "Mm." I went on, "And I seem to have totally forgotten that I was—hm?" This, too, she confirmed, "Mm." I went on, "I don't seem to *mourn*—my—no longer being those people?" She agreed, "No."

Later in the session, she reported, ". . . and they said, 'Well, the least you could do, when it's a *cold* and *dying sheep*, is to go in and cheer it up!' So I said yes, I *would*. So here I *am*. But—uh—" She said this uncertainly, looking at my eyes. I commented, "But you look at *me* and you aren't *sure* you see any cold, dying sheep?"

"No," she agreed. "Well, you look like a young element that might have consumed too much gin or something—'cause my gin stars everybody [i.e., literally turns everybody into stars]." I commented, "And I look *sort* of starred, hm?" She replied, "Your eyes do. But then you're wearing very heavy glasses [as indeed, being highly myopic, I always do], and I guess you could take out some of the lenses and be able to see better." I commented, "They seem to be heavier glasses than usual?"—again not in any sharply challenging fashion. She replied, "Uh-huh." I commented, "Do they?" She responded, "For *you*." I said, with mild surprise, "Really?" and she said, "Uh-huh." I said mildly, "Just for comparison, I've worn them now for months—for six months or so; but they look heavier, somehow, to you?" Again, there was very little challenge in my tone, and a larger acknowledging of her view. She agreed, "Yeah," in an impressively collaborative, interested tone. After several seconds, I commented, with mild interest, "You're not wearing your glasses, hm?—for some—whatever reason?" She is moderately farsighted, wears glasses inconsistently, and often misplaces them, typically reacting then with the paranoid conviction that she has been deprived of them by some omnipotently malicious outside agency such as myself. She replied, with impressively unparanoid naturalness, "*I* thought I had them in my *pocket*, and then when I got down here I discovered I didn't have them. I don't know where they are."

I hope the foregoing excerpt gives at least a brief glimpse into the usual way I endeavor to function with her, keeping in touch with my own reality as I experience it while encouraging her exploring and elaborating upon her own experience of the situation. Since she possesses so very precarious a sense of reality, and since this tends to be destroyed so quickly when vigorously challenged by me, collaborative relatedness between us occurs best, I long ago learned, when I relatively strongly confirm that she is perceiving such-and-such, while not pretending that I am at one with her in that perception, and meanwhile putting before her, in a noncoercive way, bits of my own mode of experiencing the situation. There are several examples of consensuses established between us in that brief excerpt—a very great advance over the state of things years earlier, when a much deeper degree of fragmentation and a terrible unrelatedness prevailed.

DISCUSSION

I shall limit my discussion of theoretical matters to a brief mention of some of the relevant literature, for two reasons: this lengthy paper is intended primarily as a clinical one, and in a number of earlier papers I have dealt with various relevant theoretical issues. For me, an appreciation of the reality basis for distorted perceptions (i.e., perceptions distorted by such processes as transference and projection) begins with Freud's (1922) statement that paranoics "project outwards on to others what they do not wish to recognize in themselves . . . *but they do not project it into the blue, so to speak, where there is nothing of the sort already*" (p. 226; italics mine). My papers concerning the effects upon the schizophrenic patient of unconscious processes in the analyst (1958b), and concerning the reality basis for transference phenomena (1961e), as well as the paper by Greenson and Wexler (1969) concerning the nontransference relationship in the psychoanalytic situation, discuss various theoretical aspects of this paper's main topic.

As regards this patient's focusing upon perceived persons in my eyes, the relevant literature includes Spitz's (1965) discussion of the role of the mother's face in the infant's development of object relations during the early weeks and months of life, and my reporting (1959b, 1961e) of the central importance, in the experience of the schizophrenic patient whose ego integration and ego differentiation are healing in the process of treatment, of his changing perceptions of the analyst's face.

13

Unconscious Processes
in Relation to
the Environmental Crisis

Even beyond the threat of nuclear warfare, I think, the ecological
crisis is the greatest threat mankind collectively has ever faced. The
stream of articles and books calling our attention to various aspects
of this crisis comes from ecologists, population biologists, physicists,
chemists, agriculturists, economists, architects, engineers, city plan-
ners, statesmen, historians, and, mainly, concerned laymen, some of
whom provide valuable insights into the psychological ingredients
of the problem. But rarely, indeed, is a behavioral scientist heard
from, and to the best of my knowledge very few psychiatric articles
have appeared as yet concerning this subject. There is but one contribution from a psychoanalyst, Peter A. Martin (1970), who
touched upon it briefly and incidentally in a talk I heard him give
in April 1969.[1] This environmental crisis embraces, and with

First published in *Psychoanalytic Review*, 59:361-374 (1972).

[1] Gail L. Baker in her as yet unpublished article "Environmental Pollution and
Mental Health," which came into my hands after my first draft of this article was
written, includes a thorough review of the meager literature on this subject by behavioral scientists, including nonanalytic psychiatrists. Peter A. Martin, in his informal talk on "The End of 'Our' World," makes the following comments before turning to his main theme (one not relevant to the present paper):

> Psychiatrists are familiar with the fantasy met in the early stages of schizo-

rapidly accelerating intensity threatens, our whole planet. If so staggering a problem is to be met, the efforts of scientists of all clearly relevant disciplines will surely be required. It seems to me that we psychoanalysts, with our interest in the unconscious processes which so powerfully influence man's behavior, should provide our fellow men with some enlightenment in this common struggle.

My hypothesis is that man is hampered in his meeting of this environmental crisis by a severe and pervasive apathy which is based largely upon feelings and attitudes of which he is unconscious. The lack of analytic literature about this subject suggests to me that we analysts are in the grip of this common apathy. But a second factor, a special, felt hazard in our profession, tends to inhibit us from making the special contributions we could make: we fear that an active concern about this present subject will evoke, from our colleagues, nothing more than a diagnostic interest as to

---

phrenia that the world is coming to an end. . . . In the second half of this century, the actual presence of this destructive potential makes "psychotic" end-of-the-world fantasies not so obviously out of touch with reality.

Concern about world destruction is a common mass media subject. In such presentations we hear two popular theories of how the world will end. One is the "big bang" theory; the roar of nuclear explosions will herald the end of the world. Such forces may be considered as technological extensions into reality of the destructive impulses of the id. The second theory holds that the world will end with a whimper; predictions of overpopulation leading to famine, pollution, and an uninhabitable environment can be understood as stemming from two sources within the human being. One source might be extreme id impulses toward passivity which resist the obvious call for action to preserve the species. For those who believe in the debatable death instinct theory, such irrational inactivity could be explained in this way. The other source might be passivity or helplessness of the ego in the face of danger signals calling for preservation of the self.

The above preamble is presented to show what this paper is not about. . . .

Martin then develops the theme of his paper, namely, the apparent drawing to a close of an era of training and practice in psychiatry in which young psychiatrists are imbued with the set of professional values to which we middle-aged psychiatrists have been devoted. "In summary," he says, "the group of psychiatrists, referred to as 'our group,' is observing the end of its world."

Despite the obvious relevance to my paper of certain of his remarks which I have quoted, I have placed these in this footnote because, in the main, the nature of his paper is such as to confuse the development of my own remarks.

whether we are suffering from psychotic depression or paranoid schizophrenia.

As to the evidence for the general apathy I postulate, our federal budget for 1971 includes only about one-seventieth as much for dealing with environmental pollution as for military purposes (Cotton, 1970, p. 112). I have no wish to speak lightly of our military needs, but it does seem evident to me that a citizenry actively aroused about the state of our, and the world's, ecology would not accept so feeble an effort in this area.

Of the mass of statistics concerning the environmental crisis, here are a few of the items that I find awesome. We are dumping into the ocean as many as a half-million different pollutants, only a very few of which have been studied for possible effects upon ecologically vital processes (Ehrlich, 1968, p. 56). There is increasing concern lest in a few short decades the ocean become incapable of supporting living creatures, as are already many of our great rivers, various of our Great Lakes, and the Baltic Sea (Marx, 1967). The pesticide DDT, to mention but one pollutant, has been discovered as far afield as in the bodies of Arctic Eskimos and Antarctic penguins and seals (Ehrlich, 1968, pp. 52-53). Within less than two decades after their introduction, "The synthetic pesticides have been so thoroughly distributed throughout the animate and inanimate world that they occur virtually everywhere" (Carson, 1962, p. 24). Seventy percent or more of our planet's total oxygen production by photosynthesis occurs in the ocean and is largely produced by diatoms; recent studies have shown that DDT, which permeates all things in the ocean, impedes diatoms' production of oxygen (Ehrlich, 1968; Wurster, 1967).

As for the radioactive waste from atomic reactors, we are already heirs to some 80 million gallons, stored in tank farms. These tanks will have to be guarded for 600 to 1000 years. Several storage tanks have leaked thousands of gallons into the soil already, and a single gallon is enough to poison a city's water supply (Cotton, 1970, pp. 118-119). David Lilienthal, the first chairman of the Atomic Energy Commission, has stated, "Once a bright hope shared by all mankind, including myself, the rash proliferation of atomic power plants has become one of the ugliest clouds hanging over America" (Curtis and Hogan, 1970).

The accelerating overpopulation of the earth is a factor of transcendent importance. It is estimated that in 6000 B.C. there were five million people on earth and that it had required about one million years for the population to double from two and a half to that five million. From then on, doubling occurred about every thousand years to a total of 500 million (that is, half a billion) around 1650. Then the population doubled within only 200 years, to a billion in 1850. The next doubling took only 80 years, to two billion by 1930. The doubling time at present is about 37 years. If population growth were to continue at the present rate—which it obviously cannot—for another 900 years, there would then be about 100 persons for each square yard of the earth's surface, land and sea (Ehrlich, 1968, p. 18).

Famines, especially in the undeveloped countries with their higher growth rates, are one of the "solutions" to this clearly impossible situation. The population biologist Ehrlich (1968) notes that more than half the world is in misery now and that an estimated five million Indian children, for example, die each year of malnutrition. He is convinced that within this decade hundreds of millions of people are going to starve to death in spite of any crash programs embarked upon now.

The United States, with less than one-fifteenth of the world's population, uses well over half of all the raw materials consumed each year, and if present trends continue, in 20 years we will be much less than one-fifteenth of the population, yet we may use some 80 percent of the resources consumed (Ehrlich, 1968, p. 133). On the other hand, it has been pointed out that if the present level of American industrialization were extended to the rest of the world, the accompanying increase in environmental pollution would bring on another Ice Age, for the massive increase of smoke and dust in the air would diminish sunlight and produce a significant lowering of the earth's temperature; an even greater danger would be the depletion of the world's oxygen supply caused by the increased chemical poisoning of the ocean (Cousins, 1970, p. 18).

The world's current state of ecological deterioration is such as to evoke in us largely unconscious anxieties of different varieties that are of a piece with those characteristic of various levels of an individual's ego-developmental history. Thus the general apathy that I postulate is based upon largely unconscious ego defenses against these anxieties. I shall speak of those ego defenses having to do with (a) phallic and oedipal levels of development, (b) the earlier era coinciding with, in Kleinian terms, the depressive position, and (c) the still earlier era coinciding with the paranoid position (Klein, Heimann, and Money-Kyrle, 1955).

The Phallic and Oedipal Levels

First, it is apparent in how moralistic a spirit most communications about this subject are conveyed; the speaker or writer tells us, from a morally superior and therefore safe position, projecting his own oedipal guilt upon us, that we have raped mother earth and now we are being duly strangled or poisoned, as by a vengeful Jehovah, for our sin. Second, we are led to feel that the ecologists are calling upon us to relinquish our hard-won genital primacy, symbolized by our proudly cherished but ecologically offensive automobile, and to return to a state of childhood, when genital mastery was something longed for but not yet achieved. Our apathy includes an unconscious defiant refusal to do this.

Third, our fear, envy, and hatred of formidable oedipal rivals makes us view with large-scale apathy their becoming polluted into extinction. This defensive state is supported by the relatively imperceptible nature of atmospheric pollution; relatively undetectible immediately about oneself, it becomes horrifyingly evident from a distance, as from an ascending plane, as something attacking and enshrouding *them*—all the others with the exception of oneself and including, of course, one's oedipal rivals. Freud (1923), it seems to me, gave us to understand that the oedipal struggle, in normal development, has an innately foreclosed outcome: after much inner rage and anguish, the youth or young girl must eventually come to the realization that each parent belongs sexually to the other. I think Freud greatly underestimated how formidable an oedipal rival the son or daughter remains to both the parents and how frequently it is the youthful contestant who becomes in essence the victor in intensity of emotional attachment in the oedipal contest. Thus I think that one of the great reasons for fathers' relative apathy to conditions that threaten to extinguish their sons, whether these conditions be the war in Vietnam or the growing state of environmental pollution, is that these conditions promise to extinguish an oedipal rival one has never at all finally conquered. Our unconscious hatred of succeeding generations, of our progeny and of their progeny in turn, our vengeful determination to destroy their birthright through its neglect, in revenge for the deprivations, in whatever developmental era, we suffered at our parents' hands, includes and extends beyond the oedipal conflict.

Our envy of the more favored rival is provided vicarious satisfaction by the simple leveling effect of the universal environmental pollution. The poor man can have the grim satisfaction of knowing that this pollution, to which he contributes, is menacing not only himself but the rich man also. Similarly, the majority of the earth's peoples who live in the undeveloped countries can see that the envied technologically developed countries are bringing about the latter's own downfall as part of the general ruin.

One of the many unconscious meanings that environmental pollution has for us is, I think, its externalization and reification of sexual guilt, guilt which through these transformations is rendered more tolerable to us. The psychiatric dictionary gives only this meaning of pollution: "The discharge of semen and seminal fluid in the absence of sexual intercourse; the term is often used synonymously with nocturnal emission" (Hinsie and Campbell, 1970, p. 581). I surmise that the more archaic, Jehovah-like aspects of our superego so terrorize us as to render us unable to distinguish between the imperceptible and inexorable aging of our body on the one hand, and, on the other, the increasingly pervasive pollution of the morally pure ego ideal of our youth over the years of our adulthood and aging. This so-called moral pollution is projected, I suggest, onto the environment such that we feel that the pure air and water and so on of our childhood are now lost forever. Analogously, I have the notion that the well-known pictures of the mushrooming clouds of the first atom bombs may evoke in us a near physiological apathy that is necessary to our submitting to the mushrooming, Alice-in-Wonderland spurts in physical growth that we cannot stop as we are physically changed, with what we may feel to be explosive suddenness, from child into adult. If these surmises are valid, it is of life-and-death importance that we become aware of these differentiations. Environmental pollution is a real problem in truly outer reality about which we are by no means powerless.

THE DEPRESSIVE POSITION

Mankind is collectively reacting to the real and urgent danger from environmental pollution much as does the psychotically depressed patient bent upon suicide by self-neglect—the patient who, oblivious to any urgent physical hunger, lets himself starve to death or walks uncaring into the racing automobile traffic of a busy street. One day recently as I was driving on the Washington beltway, observing the general custom of traveling a few miles above the speed limit, it suddenly struck me that I was essentially hurrying to get off it—to get its murderously threatening, bleak, lonely, crowdedness over with. I wondered if the same were true of most of the other drivers also, perhaps without their realizing it. I wondered, is this not a fair sample of how we all feel, not only about the beltway, but about our whole current life as it is? Is not the general apathy in the face of pollution a statement that there is something so unfulfilling about the quality of human life that we react, essentially, as though our lives are not worth fighting to save?

I suggested earlier, here, that the fact of environmental pollution tends to shield one from becoming aware of the full depth of emotional depression within oneself; instead of feeling isolated within emotional depression, one feels at one with everyone else in a "realistically" doomed world. Pollution serves not only to foreclose the future upon progeny we unconsciously hate and envy, but also to obscure a past which we unconsciously resist remembering with poignant clarity. We equate the idealized world of our irretrievably lost childhood with a nonpolluted environment. We tend erroneously to assume that nothing can be done about the pollution of the present-day environment because of our deeper-lying despair at knowing that we cannot recapture the world of our childhood and at sensing, moreover, that we are retrospectively idealizing the deprived and otherwise painful aspects of it. The pollution serves to maintain an illusion in us that an unspoiled, ideal childhood is still there, still obtainable, could we but bestir ourselves and clear away what spoils and obscures its purity. In this sense, pollutants unconsciously represent remnants of the past to which we are clinging, transference distortions that permeate our present environment, shielding us from feeling the poignancy of past losses, but by the same token barring us from living in full current reality. We can feel not that we have lost the world of our childhood, but that, omnipotently, we have spoiled it and are choosing to go on increasingly to spoil it through our polluting of it.

In current urban living, there is not the close-knit fabric of interpersonal relationships, enduring over decades of time, which would enable one to face and accept the losses inherent in human living—the losses involved in the growing up and growing away of one's children, the aging and death of one's parents, the knowledge of one's spouse's and one's own inevitable aging and death. A technology-dominated, overpopulated world has brought with it so reduced a capacity in us to cope with the losses a life must bring with it to be a truly human life that we become increasingly drawn into polluting our planet sufficiently to ensure that we shall have essentially nothing to lose in our eventual dying.

THE PARANOID POSITION

In a monograph in 1960 I discussed the infant's subjective oneness with the nonhuman environment, the manifold functions this environment fulfills in various stages of normal ego development, and the distortions that one finds, in these regards, in the histories and present-day ego functioning of schizophrenic patients. Later (1961d) I described schizophrenia as serving to shield the afflicted individual from a recognition of the inevitability of death.

For several years I have spent a long day each month working as a consultant at the New York State Psychiatric Institute in New York City. One evening a year or so ago, as I was returning by cab on the Triboro Bridge, on the way to LaGuardia to catch the shuttle plane back to Washington, I was seized by an urge to leap from the cab and hurl myself off the bridge. Such urges are no stranger to me, a sufferer since childhood from a phobia of heights. But the urge this time was particularly powerful, and the determinant I was able to glimpse, this time, of this tenacious, multirooted symptom was particularly memorable, humbling, and useful to me. I felt I had to destroy myself because I simply could not face returning to my usual life in Washington, and the reason I found it intolerable to face was that I felt so shamefully and desperately unable "simply" to face the living out of my life, the growing old and dying, the commonest, most everyday thing, so my panicky thoughts went, that nearly all people do—all, that is, with the exception of those who commit suicide or take refuge in chronic psychosis.

However unique to my own individual life history must be the pattern of determinants that give rise to my particular omnipotent urge to destroy my life rather than surrender to the eventual losing of it through living and aging and dying, I insist that my urge is not entirely irrelevant to what transpires in my fellow human beings in general: I am convinced that each of us in his or her own particular way must cope with some such irrationally omnipotent reaction to inevitable loss.

I postulate that an ecologically healthy relatedness to our nonhuman environment is essential to the development and maintenance of our sense of being human and that such a relatedness has become so undermined, disrupted, and distorted, concomitant with the ecological deterioration, that it is inordinately difficult for us to integrate the feeling-experiences, including the losses, inescapable to any full-fledged human life. Over recent decades we have come from dwelling in an outer world in which the living works of nature either predominated or were near at hand, to dwelling in an environment dominated by a technology which is wondrously powerful, and yet nonetheless dead, inanimate. I suggest that in the process we have come from being subjectively differentiated from, and in meaningful kinship with, the outer world, to finding this technology-dominated world so alien, so complex, so awesome, and so overwhelming that we have been able to cope with it only by regressing, in our unconscious experience of it, largely to a degraded state of nondifferentiation from it. I suggest, that is, that this "outer" reality is psychologically as much a part of us as its poisonous waste products are part of our physical selves.

The proliferation of technology, with its marvelously complex integration and its seemingly omnipotent dominion over nature, provides us with an increasingly alluring object upon which to project our "nonhuman" unconscious strivings for omnipotence; hence we tend increasingly to identify, unconsciously, with this. Concomitantly, the more "simply human," animal-nature-based components of our selves become increasingly impoverished (by reason of such factors as the overpopulation, the impersonal, driven turmoil of living in a technology-dominated society, the emphasis upon consuming material products, and so on), less and less capable of integrating our "nonhuman" components. More comprehensively, we become increasingly unable to experience consciously, as an inner emotional conflict, the war between the "human" and the "nonhuman" (autistic, omnipotence-based) aspects of our self; hence we project this conflict upon, and thus unconsciously foster, the war in external reality between the beleaguered remnants of ecologically balanced nature and man's technology which is ravaging them.

Many aspects of the ecologically deteriorating world in which we live foster in us, at a largely unconscious level, the mode of experience seen in an openly crystallized form in paranoid schizophrenia and postulated as characterizing the most threatened moments of normal infancy before the establishment of a durable sense of individuality. The pervasively and increasingly polluted world in which we live, where as one concerned individual was hardly overstating it when he said, "Everything we breathe, eat, and drink is going to kill us," is reacted to as being our all-permeating enemy. This tends to paralyze us into terrorized inactivity, all the more so because in this deeply regressed mode of experience we are not at all well differentiated from the environment, hence we have no clearly separate self with which to wage a struggle with the "outer" threat.

At this level of primitive ego functioning, there is no differentiation between a good mother and bad mother. It is not to be assumed that, even at a conscious level, we have been accustomed to regarding nature as equivalent to a good mother, now in conflict with technology as a bad mother. Nature has often been a bad mother to man, often been rendered hospitable to man only through the workings of our good mother, technology. Now we are told that our good mother is poisoning us and that if we do not curb her and return nature toward its unfettered state, we are lost. We have worshiped technology, and our annual gross national product which epitomizes its growth, as a kind of god, and now we confusedly gather that we are supposed to starve this god in order to save ourselves.

A major aspect of this realistic "paranoid" threat resides in our ever-present suspense, however fluctuating from consciousness to unconsciousness, lest we all die, in a matter of hours or even less, from undeclared nuclear warfare. As James Reston (1970) recently put it, "The bomb and the missile gave the President a power unprecedented in the history of nations, and tipped the balance in the American Federal system away from the Congress, for the nation could be destroyed before the Congress could even meet to debate a declaration of war." The undifferentiated pervasiveness of all this menace evokes, deep in us, the frozen immobility of the child whose parent (equivalent to such godlike, vague entities as the hydrogen bomb or the awesomely powerful military-industrial complex [Lens, 1970]) chronically threatens violence.

The secrecy, the subtlety of these threats makes them thoroughly akin to those which grip the patient suffering from paranoid schizophrenia. We are told that, without our having realized it, we have been taking in all manner of poisons, many known and many presumably still unknown. The known ones include—to mention only a few—lead (of which our body already carries one-third of a lethal dose [Cotton, 1970, p. 165]), mercury, DDT, and radioactive wastes.

An enormously important factor is that at this level of ego dedifferentiation we project, as does the openly schizophrenic individual, our own murderousness—our own pervasive, poorly differentiated and poorly integrated murderousness, born of our terror and deprivation and frustration—upon the hydrogen bomb, the military-industrial complex, technology, and so forth. Also, because we tend to feel that sudden death from nuclear warfare is a threat entirely out of our control, we may prefer the slower, more controllable death that pollution offers as seemingly the only alternative. We know that pollution is a process to which we contribute daily; it is something that, in however small part, we know we actively do. On the other hand, to regard such slow strangulation as an inevitable agony is to yearn for the quick relief that nuclear warfare would bring.

At an unconscious level we powerfully identify with what we perceive as omnipotent and immortal technology, as a defense against intolerable feelings of insignificance, of deprivation, of guilt, of fear of death, and so on. It has been said that realistically, "When it comes to salvaging the environment, the individual is almost powerless" (Cotton, 1970). Since the constructive goal of saving the world can be achieved only by one's working, as but one largely anonymous individual among uncounted millions, in adult concert with other citizens, it is more alluring to give oneself over to secret fantasies of omnipotent destructiveness, in identification with the forces that threaten to destroy the world. This serves to shield one from the recognition of one's own guilt-laden murderous urges, experienced as being within oneself, to destroy one's own intrapersonal and interpersonal world. Our grandiose identification with technology is enhanced by the statistics which inform us that our autos collectively cause as much as 80 percent of the pollution of the air (Cotton, 1970, p. 159); that our production of wastes increases much faster than our population growth and will double within less than eight years (Cotton, 1970, p. 205); and that, as I mentioned earlier, we in the United States consume a vastly disproportionate amount of the earth's raw materials.

In childhood a fantasied omnipotence protected us against the full intensity of our feelings of deprivation, and now it is dangerously easy to identify with seemingly limitless technology and to fail to cope with the life-threatening scarcity of usable air, food, and water on our planet. By identifying with the rich diversity and wondrous integration of technology, we shield ourselves from feeling the full extent of the deprivation, the impoverishment, of our human lives. The Nobel bacteriologist, René Dubos, states, "Ecological systems can develop tolerance to pollutants but in the process they tend to lose their rich complexity and stability" (Cotton, 1970, p. 206). This is true, I believe, for man's psychological life as well.

For most of us, religion offers little hope of immortality to arm us against our fear of death, and we feel too ill assured that loved ones will be there to share our griefs or that we will live in the memories of our survivors; we sense too little contact with the descendants who will survive us. Our frustration at the knowledge that we are merely mortal is vastly intensified by the knowledge that we have created a technology which, seemingly omnipotent and immortal itself, has not extended our only allotted life span much beyond the biblical three-score years and ten. So we identify unconsciously with this technology which, being inanimate, cannot die. We find assurance that in its versatile devouring it has grown ever more powerful as it has leapt from feeding upon coal, the stores of which are now largely depleted, to oil, the stores of which are expected to be gone in about another 30 years (Cotton, 1970, pp. 10-11), to uranium. We find reason to hope that before the limited stores of uranium are gone, atomic or some still more magical power will have enabled immortal technology to leave this ravaged planet behind for limitless interplanetary homes, and we secretly nourish the hope that we shall be among the handful it brings with it. In this realm of omnipotent fantasy, in fact, mother earth is equivalent to all of reality, which is a drag and hindrance to our yearnings for unfettered omnipotence, and we want to be rid of it.

Omnipotence is not, however, something for which man unambivalently yearns. In a recent paper (1969) concerning my analysis of a man who showed a borderline thought disorder, I presented some examples of the data that showed not only his striving for the realization of his fantasied omnipotence, but also his fear lest this be fully realized and he be disqualified, thus, from sharing human love. It may be not at all coincidental that our world today is threatened with extinction through environmental pollution, to which we are so strikingly apathetic, just when we seem on the threshold of technologically breaking the chains that have always bound our race to this planet of our origin. While cognizant that this coincidence could be fully accounted for by the present developmental stage of technology alone, I suspect that we collectively quake lest our infantile omnipotent fantasies become fully actualized through man's becoming interplanetary and ceasing thereby to be man as we have known him, inseparable from earth. I surmise that we are powerfully drawn to suicidally polluting our planet so as to ensure our dying upon it as men, rather than existing elsewhere as—so we tend distortedly to assume—gods or robots, for example.

We project upon this ecologically deteriorating world the deepest intensities of all our potentially inner emotional conflicts—including, as I mentioned earlier, the conflict between the subjectively human and the subjectively nonhuman components of ourselves—and, since conflict is the essence of human life, we project in this same process, in large part, our aliveness. Thomas Wolfe was, I think, projecting upon the world his inner aliveness when he wrote in his notebooks of his struggle to find his place in the world: "What it may be finally I do not know but I must build up out of chaos a strong, sufficient inner life; otherwise I will be torn to pieces in the whirlpool of the world" (Wolfe, 1969). To react with apathy to our present pollution-ridden "real, outer" world is, I think, equivalent to defending oneself unconsciously against the experience of becoming an individual human self, a self which, in the very nature of human living, must contain a whirlpool of emotional conflicts, at times so chaotic as to threaten the dismemberment of one's very self.

Space does not permit me to include here the necessarily detailed data from my work with depressed or schizophrenic persons that would provide at least a measure of clinical documentation for these speculations. In my records there is relatively solid clinical evidence indicative, for example, of (a) patients' identifying with deadly smog; (b) patients' typically paranoid transference to me as the personification of their unwanted-child-self, which was treated in the parental family as the essentially nonhuman source of all the subtle and pervasive malevolence that actually polluted the idealized family atmosphere; and (c) the link between patients' subjectively nonhuman components and their parents' autism, such patients hating what to us is reality, because to live in that reality they would have to relinquish the yearning to identify fully with the supposed omnipotence of their parental autism. My previously mentioned monograph (1960) on the nonhuman environment is filled with detailed clinical data relevant to this subject.

We live today at a time when we must save the real world or we shall use it as the instrument for destroying us all. I think that the greatest danger lies neither in the hydrogen bomb itself nor in the more slowly lethal effect of pollution from our overall technology. The greatest danger lies in the fact that the world is in such a state as to evoke our very earliest anxieties and at the same time to offer the delusional "promise," the actually deadly promise, of assuaging these anxieties, effacing them, by fully externalizing and reifying our most primitive conflicts that produce those anxieties. In the pull upon us to become omnipotently free of human conflict, we are in danger of bringing about our extinction.

If you have found anything at all apropos among my various remarks in this elementary first effort, then I have made my initial point—namely, that we psychoanalysts must make some real contribution, along with our brothers in other fields of science, toward meeting the ecological crisis.

14

Intensive Psychotherapy of Chronic Schizophrenia: A Case Report

By the time I became the therapist of Mrs. Mildred Hendricks,[1] a divorced woman in her forties, she had been ill for nearly thirty years and had already been hospitalized at Chestnut Lodge for nearly seven years. Although there were other patients there more regressed than she, or more physically intimidating than she, by anyone's reckoning she would be included among the hard core of deeply and chronically and rigidly ill patients who formed the nucleus of the patient population in Chestnut Lodge, which specializes in the treatment of chronic schizophrenia. Millie, as she was universally known there, had long since earned a stereotyped view of herself, held by patients and staff generally, as the crazy woman who talked endlessly and loudly in public about her masturbation, and whose raging, lasting often for hours at a time, could be heard at least daily and often a number of times each day, by anyone within shouting distance of the disturbed ward where she dwelt. Frequently she yelled out from the upstairs window of her room to

First published in *International Journal of Psychoanalytic Psychotherapy*, 1 (2):30-51 (1972).

[1] A pseudonym, of course; other potentially identifying data have also been disguised.

passersby on the hospital grounds, generally about sex, giving one the impression of a crazy whore.

As I came to know her chronicity in the detail which psychotherapeutic interviews with her afforded, I found that she generally spent much of each hour lifting the back of her skirt, or sometimes the front of it, and wiping her perineum with paper towels, or with a bath towel, or with toilet paper, meanwhile passing gas in a way that had the quality of a semi-bowel-movement. She passed a great deal of flatus throughout the average hour. Often, too, she would hold a small hand-mirror in front of her face and poke about within her lower eyelid or on the sclera of her eye, almost as if she were to gouge out her eye; in fact, sometimes I felt more than a little anxious lest she do just that. Further, much of the time she would poke up into her nostril with a long plug of Kleenex. Also, she would often wipe at her eyes with a coarse bath towel, which had been soaked in water and wrung out. It quickly became clear that she was trying to conceal the fact of her chronic weeping by rubbing her face and eyes with damp paper towels. Very often, in order to make herself pass flatus, she pressed on a certain area on her left buttock, which the previous therapist had seen—I never had occasion to—and which he described as being a large and calloused knob. I found that she often poked her intestines in a masturbatory fashion, and a great deal of her wiping of her perineum had a distinctly masturbatory quality. Frequently she would spread her buttocks apart with both hands in order to facilitate her farting, and she often used to change her clothes during the hour, finding it necessary to completely denude herself down to the waist; she would then wipe under her arms with a bath towel or preen her breasts, meanwhile chatting about them. In general her absorption with her various bodily parts and functions was typical of that of hebephrenic patients.

The untidiness of her room was comparable with her untidy, slatternly appearance over a considerable number of years, until some time after I had begun working with her. She kept large bottles of Lavoris in her room, and not infrequently gargled during the hour in a way which I found to be one of the most infuriating among her almost innumerable chronic symptoms; she would spit out into the wastebasket after gargling, and this was in keeping with her quite animal-like crouching in a corner of her room on occasion, fingering her anal area, and farting.

Millie is the eldest of four living children of a retired Western professor of anatomy, a man of much inherited wealth, many talents, and formidable academic prestige, and of a woman who evidently felt she had married beneath her. The mother had had two boy babies in succession prior to Millie's birth. The first of these boys had been born prematurely and was dead at birth; the second boy baby was born by a breech delivery and died of an intracranial hemorrhage immediately after his birth. I found much evidence that the mother's unworked-through grief about the loss of these two boy babies had a tremendous impact upon Millie's own development. Among the living children, in addition to Millie, are sisters two and four years younger than the patient, and a brother seven years younger than her. It is fair to say that none of the four children has come anywhere near to equaling the father's achievements, and that the pressure upon Millie to do so was another major factor in her growing up.

Both parents seem always to have felt that Millie was from the first a difficult child, different from other children, always one to promote dissension among other people. She never did better than marginal work in school, barely managing to get through high school and into a junior college, but failing to complete this. She was first hospitalized for mental illness at the age of 16½. She was permitted to marry at the age of 22, after careful psychiatric scrutiny, but was hospitalized for the second time at the age of 30, again at 33, and again at 34. She had been subjected to repeated courses of electroshock therapy, had received insulin-coma therapy, and had been hospitalized steadily for nine years at the point when I started working with her.

Although her marriage lasted for nearly 20 years until her husband divorced her and remarried a few years before our work began, both partners had been unfaithful to one another. Her "carryings on" with truck drivers, high school boys, and other assorted males had been a disgrace in the small community in which she lived; and it was feared that she might hurt her children and other people during her outbursts of temper. She seems always to have been regarded as either some sort of borderline mental defective or some sort of chronically crazy and eccentric person. Although the father seems to have been more convinced that Millie is an intelligent person, whereas the mother has been much more inclined to regard her as feebleminded, both have responded as though Millie were inhabited by some kind of sex fiend from a very early age.

When I went for my first interview with Mrs. Hendricks, as I went into her room, a small room farthest from the nurses' station on the disturbed ward, I immediately noticed a strong odor of feces. She was looking tired, drawn, and grief-stricken, and to my relief talked in a very calm way. She made clear that she felt she had to keep talking throughout every hour, and had never had an experience, with a therapist, of simply being quiet in the sessions for any period of time. I mentioned the feces to her. She denied that there were any in the room; but I held fast to my expressed conviction that she was concealing some, somewhere in the room. I felt distinctly encouraged, by the end of the session, about the prospect of our being able to do useful work together, and I particularly felt that my insistence that there were feces in the room, despite her denials that this was so, helped to get the relationship started off on a basis of candor.

The one most prominent theme which developed, throughout my years of work with Mrs. Hendricks, had to do with her struggle to emerge from a subjectively nonhuman state, and to become a truly human being. This proved to be, in fact, what all of our work together was about.

Early in our work it became evident that she did not at all durably or consistently experience herself as an alive human individual, and a number of the determinants of this state of affairs gradually took shape, piece by piece. The earliest evidence had to do with the extent to which her relationship with her father had contributed to her not having achieved, as yet, a durably human identity.

In an hour at the beginning of the fourth week of our work, an hour full of her usual absent-minded chatter, she said, "I used to be crazy about my father," and I noticed that her eyes were full of tears as she said this. I replied, gently, "Maybe you're still crazy about your father." There was a pause then of several seconds, in which she was obviously blocking, and during which she several times started to say various things, but each time fell silent. It was evident how much she still adored him.

Later, in the fifth month of our work, a related bit of data emerged. After much scattered talk, she said, "I feel like a china doll in pieces." She said this in a tone, and with a demeanor, of helplessness and despair.

Then, after approximately three years of the therapy, during which she had begun to experience a fair degree of the scorn and anger which underlay her idealization of her father, she told me in one of our sessions, immediately after a visit from him, "Why, he is really like a little boy!" A few minutes later she suddenly seized her forehead and said, in a tone of terror and anguish, "My whole forehead is shattered!" I understood this to be a kind of somatic experiencing, on her part, of the shattering of her idolized picture of her father—of the shattering, that is, of an introjected, idealized image of him which heretofore had formed a part of her own body-image.

In retrospect, it seems quite possible that her having experienced herself as a "china doll in pieces" had been a product, similarly, of her struggle to cope with feelings of disillusionment with some person or persons outside herself, by introjecting that person, or those persons, into her own body-image.

In one of our sessions after two or three years of work, Mrs. Hendricks told me, in her usual indirect fashion, that her father never could see or register any of her body below the neck. She seemed to feel that she, being feminine, was that threatening to him. She talked about his working with animals, behind blinking lights of various kinds in his laboratory, and vividly conveyed to me her conviction that he hides thus because he is so scared of girls.

It rather soon became evident that she felt she possessed an omnipotent destructiveness, and early in our work we saw evidence that this self-concept was in part based upon an identification with her mother. In one hour in the sixth month[2] of the therapy, for the first time in all my experience with her thus far, she was able to be really at ease, and she indirectly let me know that when she was in her room by herself talking to herself, she was reacting to her own self as being a little child whom she was continually nagging and berating. This dawned on me when she asked me, "What do you do with a child of ——," indicating so-and-so many years of age. I realized that she did not know what to do with her own child-self except to constantly nag it. In an hour only a couple of days later I had the distinct feeling that the very nucleus of her illness was being laid out when she told me that her mother had had two boy babies, one born four years and the other born two years before herself. Each of them had lived only a few hours, and she thought at least one of them must have been premature. She said that she did not know what they died of, and when I asked her, she said only, "I guess they didn't know in those days what it was." But then she went on to make clear to me, by indirect communications—expressing these ideas in reference to other things—that the babies must have died either because (a) her mother had abandoned them, or (b) her mother had eaten them. In this same hour, in direct connection with the above, she indirectly expressed her preference for either (a) dying, or (b) spending the rest of her life insane, rather than doing anything that would make "my little girl" mother feel inferior as a mother. Also, in connection with her reference to the deaths of those boy babies, she tangentially revealed a conviction on her part that males are so extremely fragile that she could not let her son Eddie go out of her thoughts for a moment, for fear he might die.

Her deep-seated dread of herself as having an omnipotent destructiveness which threatened to destroy anything or anyone with whom she came into contact, fairly soon became referable in major part to the way in which her mother had evidently always shrunk

---

[2] In developing these various themes I have to retrace, repeatedly, the chronology of the treatment.

away from closeness with her. When I first met her mother, one year after the beginning of my work with Mrs. Hendricks, I wrote in my notes following my interview with both parents: "It became very clear that Dr. Morrison [a pseudonym] is far more inclined toward Millie's visiting home than is the mother. The mother looked distinctly filled with a sense of dread and discomfiture and squirmed uncomfortably when any talk about Millie's visiting home came up."

Throughout the first year of our work, there were many instances in which Mrs. Hendricks revealed bizarre subjective experiences of herself. She complained one time that there "is a rubber thing here in the left side of my head," which was sore, and would repeatedly say that there was food up her nose and that her nose was "stuffed with shit." On another occasion she said, "There's an animal in me," and described herself as a calf in intercourse from behind. Often she would have the demeanor of a wounded animal, looking piteously afraid of being wounded further, and she spoke in a tone of genuine anguish, mixed with exhibitionistic pleasure, of how in an insane asylum, "they take people to see the lunatic with the bone sticking out," evidently a reference to herself and the calloused knob on her left buttock. Her reference to herself as a "lunatic" fit precisely with the view her mother clearly had of her.

An hour in the seventeenth month of our work showed some aspects of her nonhuman experience of herself, and gave some hint of the determinants of this:

> In the course of this hour, Millie asked me, "I feel something on my left lower jaw. Do you suppose a piece of tooth got down in there and then went down into a gland?"—tracing this path with her finger down to her neck. She then went on, "My body is insane," in a tone which conveyed to me a feeling on her part of deep hopelessness, that even her *body* is insane. She repeated this a few moments later, saying, "My body is insane," but this time adding something about "here, and here, and here," indicating the place in her neck and I think the side of her torso and her buttock. It seemed to me, after the hour, that this had indicated that her body had felt to her separated or unintegrated.
>
> In any case, there was much hint that her body gets "in-

sane," or more insane, at times when she tends to have sexual feelings. I felt that the physical feelings she was having during this hour were of a piece with those she has many times expressed, about there being food up her nose, indicating an area up in her cheeks.

In an hour near the end of the second year, she said, "I feel like the sherry I had Wednesday night [said in the tone of making a complete statement]—no, I guess it . . . I feel like it went up to the top of my head . . ." This second statement was made in a by no means entirely anxious way, but in a tone with some pleasure in it. I was to discover, however, after a number of years of our work, that one of her most frequently distressing experiences was that of her "falling in love with," for example, pictures of beautiful things she saw in magazines. That is, she tended to blend with—to feel at one with—not only persons but inanimate things toward which she felt attracted.

In a staff presentation near the end of the third year, I mentioned:

> . . . about two weeks ago she described that there were "sleepers" in her eyes. She has often talked about "sleepers" in her eyes; but this time she described what she meant. These are bits of blue metal which have come down through blood vessels from her brain. This has a very bizarre feeling as she says it. It doesn't strike one as anything at all humorous, but very sick indeed. Up until six months or so ago, every once in a while when I would go into her room, I would find her wrapped up in a blanket like a mummy with her head all covered, silent and immobile. This gave me the chills. There was something not human and very threatening about it, like an apparition. This she doesn't do anymore, perhaps partly because I let her know that it made me very anxious; but whatever the case, this has changed.

Throughout our work together, as in her life on the ward, she showed an intense need to cling to her identity as a "crazy" patient. It became clear that she needed unconsciously to deny the greater part of her very considerable ego strength and to attribute this instead to others, while introjecting the ego weakness of those around her, not merely because of her own need to idealize other persons, but also as an expression of a genuine effort to help other persons by taking over their deficiencies, their "craziness." I have mentioned her basic preference for death or lifelong insanity over doing anything that would make her "little girl" mother feel inferior as a mother.

As one might expect, she very often spared my feelings, in the course of our hours; on occasions when she had started to make some very perceptive critical appraisal of me, she would then undo it, saying, "Oh, I'm crazy." Very early in our work, in response to her projection of her own ego strengths upon me, I found that a characterological smugness in me was in evidence much more often, and much more prominently, than I am generally aware of it with other persons. I noticed that it was very easy, indeed, for me to feel that I was the very bright, very perceptive, very emotionally spontaneous psychiatrist dealing with this emotionally constricted and functionally stupid woman. What would happen, over and over, is that she would promote my feeling perceptive, clever, and smug, and would then proceed to express hatred and defiance toward me because of my smugness, and would dedicate herself to proving me inept. In retrospect, what I was defending myself against, with this smugness, was an empathic sharing, deeply and sustainedly, of the tragedy and loss inherent in this woman's life and so profound that anyone who came to know her deeply and prolongedly tended to find it overwhelming.

In the seventh month of our work, I made the following note:

> In yesterday's hour there was a tremendous lot of grief in her saying in reference to Eddie that, "When he was in the sixth grade I was here." She said this in her usual way of trying to pass over in a matter-of-fact manner something which on this occasion, as on many other occasions, clearly came across to me as covering a tremendous lot of grief indeed. After the hour I felt almost overwhelmed at the amount of sorrow and grief in this woman's having been, for example, separated from her son throughout his entire sixth grade experience.
>
> But then today the sort of opposite side of the coin was showing: it was quite clear that she had a strong wish, whether

conscious or more likely unconscious, to give over her children to her sister, Frannie, and when she said in a playful, delighted tone that every once in a while, "my father gets it into his head to take me to a mental hospital," I felt a genuine sense of revulsion and of evilness about this kind of thing—namely, that she has found her father irresistible to her in, I think, a childlike fashion, such that she has given up her life with her husband and children for the sake of that tremendously deep and pathological attachment to her father. She herself used the word "irresistible" in reference to his effect upon her. When she spoke about his every once in a while taking her to a mental hospital, it had all the earmarks of a kind of fascinating game that she and he played with one another.

I shall now devote most of the remainder of this paper to a tracing of the path the therapy followed in helping this woman to achieve, to a very considerable degree, a durable identity as a human being—predominantly through the development of a warm, highly libidinized transference to me as being a fond and loving mother, after the resolution of her transference to me as being a predominantly rejecting and malevolent mother.

In the ninth month of our work, I wrote:

> It is . . . clear that the tyranny which she on occasion directs toward me and others—as she did on one occasion early in this hour—is closely comparable with the tyranny under which she labors almost constantly—tyranny which directs that she must not have such kinds of thoughts or feelings. Early in this hour she had told me in an infuriatingly tyrannical way that I must *never* say again, "It is because you want a bosom friend." I had never actually made any such statement. [It was becoming clear that her interest in the breast was particularly threatening to her.]
>
> At one point in the hour I was powerfully struck with what a supremely confident woman she can at times be—at one point, she was looking, in her pretty new blue pajamas, very much the way Ingrid Bergman looked in a movie with Charles Boyer which I saw years ago.
>
> Another point in today's hour: when she is compelled to *touch* her genitals, this seems to have something to do with her feeling at an unconscious level deeply touched in a way that I have often felt touched by her, and in the way which, as she

made clear in an indirect communication, she feels touched by, for example, an elderly uncle, whom she mentioned during this hour, who had been bereaved.

By this time in our work, I was beginning to see how necessary Mrs. Hendricks felt it to shield her mother from her deeply compassionate feelings toward the latter; she evidently felt it urgently important that the mother not see these—evidently felt with, I came to believe, good reason that her mother would find the daughter's compassion devastating.

I might interject at this point that one of the sequence of renowned consultants had suggested that it might be interesting if, in an attempt to relieve this woman's excruciating genital sensations, the nerves supplying her genital area were severed. In retrospect, one can see something of the psychodynamic meaning such an operation would have had for her—it would have meant being deprived of her compassion. In fact, I came to see that these physical feelings in her genitals were the one sure mode of experiencing emotion that she possessed for, evidently, many years. Thus to have been severed from such sensations would have meant essentially to be severed from all emotional capacities.

Also in the ninth month, it was becoming clear that Millie and her mother had loved to "bicker" or "squabble" with one another. On the other hand, in one of the sessions at this time she said, under her breath, "I have a horror of being like my mother," in a tone of unmistakable dread and horror. Her ambivalence about closeness with her mother was thus becoming more evident.

Near the end of the tenth month another development occurred in her becoming more freely able to express her positive feelings concerning her mother. In one session, now, after she had spoken of her mother and herself in a very pleasurably comradely tone, I commented that although she said she had a horror of being like her mother, I gathered that there was a conflicting, strong pleasure in thinking of herself and her mother as alike, as comrades—as, perhaps, sisters. She latched onto the last, agreeing, saying with herself as, perhaps, a younger sister. Parenthetically, not many sessions later she confided, with fond delight, that she liked to think of herself and her mother as witches—twin witches. I asked if her mother has younger sisters; Millie replied that her mother has two older brothers, one younger brother, and a younger sister, "Aunt Dorothy," who, interestingly, is "separated" from her husband—reminiscent to me of the patient's being divorced from her own husband. I regarded these facts as strongly indicative of a transference, on the mother's part, from that younger sister to Millie. Later I saw how precisely these data fit with material from an interview I came to have with the mother, material indicating that there indeed was such a transference on the mother's part to this daughter.

In all my work with this woman, nothing proved to be more basic than her defending herself against intense feelings of grief and loss. Concerning an hour in the eleventh month of my work with her, I noted:

> For at least two years now[3] I have been struck with how Millie will start to burst out in the most intense grief and then this will get turned into rage. In the hour today, when she was very near to tears, she started out of the room and said, with a note of pride and triumph in her voice, something about past experiences with ". . . tears. I broke them up with a temper tantrum every time." I saw clearly how she was thus keeping her ego identity broken up, for I saw how necessary it is in the development of ego integration for one to go on and be able to feel through such grief.

I came to see, within the first year of our work, that instead of her ever *missing* anyone or any experience from her past, she re-experienced the past in such vivid detail that she tended to become lost in it—immersed in the past. It became evident that her walking about on the hospital grounds followed a very complex pattern indeed; there were many areas of the grounds which she avoided, because they tended to remind her of grief-laden areas of her past, and I came to see that it was not simply that entering into those areas would cause her to experience grief, but rather that she had to avoid becoming actually lost in those areas of the past.

[3] I first noticed this, in passing, late in her work with the previous therapist.

Within the first year, my relative freedom from any need to deny my physical interest in her contributed toward the resolution of her father-transference and her coming more deeply into her mother-transference feelings. For example, very often she would change her clothes during the hour, and I would make no effort to look away from her seminude, or on rare occasions even totally nude, body. On one occasion she was lying on her bed and said to me, "Why don't you come and lie down with me?" I replied, "I'd like to do it; but I can't do it; we can't have that kind of relationship." She did a great deal of preening of her naked breasts during the hours, and admiring them in the mirror, and teasingly trying to get me to touch them, which I declined to do; but I did not deny my interest in looking at them. These were the breasts her father had apparently always had to blank out of his awareness; she had reason to know that I did not need to blot out of my awareness the fact that she has breasts.

Another thing which I feel helped, perhaps more than anything else, in her becoming subjectively human was the fact that I was able to accept a kind of nonhuman transference role with comparative comfort. Thus, for example, in the eighteenth month of our work, she looked directly into my eyes during one hour and let me know indirectly that she did not see me but rather a white-faced Hereford cow. On another occasion, she saw a deserted street in northern Los Angeles. She described this scene emphatically, "There were *no men*, Dr. Searles! Don't you understand?—There were *no men!*"—which came through to me as her telling me that she was not seeing any men at that moment.

On one evening within a few days of this same time, I heard her in a murderous rage out beyond the building where my office was located. I saw her out there alone and called over to the telephone operator to have someone sent to get her, which was done. Then, in the hour on the following day, it turned out that her experience had been that there was a snake there, at which she was throwing a large stone, which I indeed had seen her throwing. It sounded nightmarish. She also said it was a good thing that no woodchuck came up and got hit by the stone. Actually, her way of putting it was, "There wasn't any snake there, was there?" in such a way as to let me know that her experience had been that there *was* a snake. It should be emphasized that when I had looked out and seen her throwing the stone and raging in a murderous fashion, she was very much alone, with no one anywhere else around. I was coming now to realize that, in order to avoid reminders which would bring feelings of grief and loss, she had to delete from her own perceptual experiences so very many of the persons in her environment, and so many other aspects of her environment, that she was threatened with being left alone in an empty world, completely devoid of either real people or real animals, for example.

Two weeks later I had occasion to see still more clearly that in back of the patient's rages stood *terror*. During this particular hour she came to tell me, "There is a vapor over people sometimes." She added that there is sometimes one over me, as well as over other people. It is difficult to describe her tone when speaking of this "vapor," but it was one that clearly conveyed terror and weirdness. When I heard this, my whole orientation toward her rages shifted from my previous administrative kind of orientation over the year and a half that I had worked thus far with her, to one, now, of a genuinely therapeutic interest in the terror which led her to have these rages. Before, my attitude toward her rages had been one of a severe kind of disapproval and insistence that she must "get over them" in order to go home on a vacation, as she so often longed to do, or in order to be able to live out of the hospital, as she often poignantly expressed a wish to do.

As the work with her went on, she became more and more able to tell me at what point she was experiencing me as having a vapor over my head, and there were times when she let me know that instead of seeing my face she was seeing a death's head. On one occasion I got the *feeling* from the way in which she was looking at me, that my face was made up of hooded cobras. I hope that I am conveying something of how extremely uncomfortable this was for me; but I want particularly to emphasize my belief that my ability to endure such nonhuman transference roles—to endure such projections of her own subjectively nonhuman components upon me—

helped greatly in her becoming sure that she is a human being. Another way of thinking about this is that I had to become sure—on my *own* part—that my own humanness would assert itself over such subjective nonhuman components of myself. From this latter point of view, we see how in successful therapy the patient eventually confirms, at a deeper level, the therapist's own humanness.

In the twenty-first month, there occurred an hour involving more closeness and better communication between us than usual, and in which she showed me snapshots of her daughter. Near the end of the hour, she started out of her room, and then stopped and asked, "Dr. Searles, do you think I'm human?" I had a fleeting urge to reassure her, and to say, "I certainly do," but instead I said, "Why do you ask?" She replied, going out, "Sometimes I think everybody here is on to the fact that I'm not human." A couple of minutes later, the time now being up, I too went out and stopped at the bathroom (where I knew her to be) to tell her I would see her on Saturday morning. The bathroom door was half open. She called to me to wait a moment; I did. She came out, evidently having been weeping. I felt *very* much like kissing her on the cheek, but did not. She said something of inconsequential content to me, clearly in a way of prolonging the contact with me. She had by now become much more open about her tears than she had been when I began working with her. Throughout our work thus far, she had done a great deal of crying, but always had gone to great effort to hide her tears in one way or another; she was showing much less need, now, to hide them.

By this time—the twenty-first month of our work—it was rare for me to find it necessary to stand up to make sure that she did not hit me, whereas formerly this had been a commonplace. Also, for something like six months now, she had from time to time revealed her feeling of being in love with *everyone*. Her comments about her father had come now to have a much less incestuous tone, and much more of a tone of fondness and a grief-laden realization that he was now getting old. There had been considerable working through of grief about the breakup of her marriage, including evidences of mutual love between herself and her husband, expressions of hurt and grief about his infidelity, and the providing of data to suggest that he—an army officer during World War II—had returned from overseas suffering from a very real degree of battle fatigue, something I had not known before. This development, of her working through of her grief about her divorce, culminated in her spending a whole session, in the twentieth month of our work, in talking about the possibility of her marrying again. By this same time, she had become much more comfortable about her varied and conflictual feelings concerning her son—in contrast to the way she had used to center her life about him while *determinedly* expressing her love for him.

In about the eighteenth month of our work, for the very first time in all my experience with her, she was able to express a feeling of *missing* something: "I missed having an hour yesterday."

In the course of a staff presentation in the latter part of the third year, I reported:

> There are periods of many minutes now when she says nothing [a relief from pressure of speech which I regarded as a major step forward]. She will sometimes seem many miles away from me, and will look blankly at me; but I know, nonetheless, that this is a very useful stratum for us to have reached. About a week ago, in the course of one of these blank-looking silences, she burst out, "I love you."

I described on this occasion how she used to come over when I was standing up and say, "Here, stand over here," and take me as if I were an inanimate object—a dress form or something—and move me over, and I used to kid her about reacting as though I were inanimate. I do feel that my acceptance of her treating me in that fashion was a valuable phase in the development of our relationship.

In this same staff presentation, I reported:

> Well under way now is a process of translating her bizarre, concretistic, somatic symptoms into interpersonally referable, emotional experiences. For example, she used to spend a lot of time saying, "This food that goes up in my tooth here, it goes up into my head and behind my ear." After a few weeks, I said something in response to things like this, "That should be

enough to interest an anatomist father, shouldn't it?" Now, Millie lets it be known that I am getting under her skin. She hardly ever talks about the food's getting behind her tooth; but it is rather that I am getting under her skin, that I am beginning to mean something to her. . . . Instead of talking about her brain being tipped, and saying that there must be a tendon loose in her brain, as she used to say, now it usually comes out that she is madder than hell.

Whereas in the early months she said on innumerable occasions, in an intensely defiant and authoritarian tone, "I'm *never* going to do such-and-such again!" and then went into great detail about what the such-and-such was, it has gradually become clear that although the conscious tone was one of great defiance, beneath that there was a tone of desolation and grief that she would never in her life get to do these things again. The defiance has fallen off very markedly and been replaced by a much greater readiness to feel and to show grief. Similarly, she is now much better able to show feelings of missing people from the past, for instance from wards here in the hospital where she has lived in previous years. Formerly, she seemed quite honestly unaware of any feeling of missing these persons; but in the very richness of remembered detail, and in the immediacy of the detail, she powerfully conveyed how much these people meant to her.

During the first several months with her, I found that her greatest anxiety had to do with any close relationship with women. The points at which she would start beating her head on her breasts [another of her chronic symptoms] would, more often than not, have to do with her feeling that I was trying to make her "sleep" with another woman or to put her together with another woman. She often talked as if I were a kind of whorehouse madam trying to line up such relationships. Now she is much less threatened by closeness with women. She dances with them at times and is able to verbalize fondness about them. Perhaps in line with this is her bringing out, six months ago, feelings of being in love with everyone. Sitting over at the athletic field watching them play ball—all this quite indirectly described—indicated that she has feelings of love for everyone. She is still very inclined to think this bad or abnormal.

I had come to see something of the extent to which her desires for closeness had become tabooed by reason of the fact that each of her parents was so ready to find evidence that she is a sex fiend. Thus, for example, any warm comment to the mother was evidently taken by the latter as though this were some loathsomely sexual thing; the father also was tremendously prone to seeing Millie as being an oversexed person. Both parents were overly ready to see in erotized terms any closeness Millie showed with other people. Thus I had reason to know that on the many occasions when Millie behaved infuriatingly like a crazy whore, yelling obscenities out of her upstairs window at passersby, in all probability she felt terribly lonely and in need of human contact, but was sure that such needs stamped her as being a whore.

Early in the fifth year of our work there occurred a nice example of her reacting to me as being nonhuman: "You're the stupidest sanitarium in the world!" she said, looking me full in the face, fully as if I personally were the physical institution—the sanitarium. She had spoken leeringly many times of "your nurses" and "your aides" and "your student nurses," and had spoken to me as the collective "you" who ran the sanitarium; but there had not been this literally nonhuman impact.

By the end of the fifth year of our work, her mother-transference had become well established. She reacted to me as being a warmly and companionably loved kind of sisterly mother to whom she felt free to say on many occasions such things as, "Do you think with some men, that their penis tears some membrane in your vagina?" or "When your husband sticks his penis into your vagina, do you suppose it breaks some membrane in there?" I became reasonably comfortable at having such comments directed toward me, and she came to speak with a kind of companionable delight of "our lesbian relationship." She came to express not only warmly erotic interest in me but also tender feelings of the most touching sort—although usually quite indirectly, for example by showing loving tenderness toward a slender young plant which was placed on a table close beside where I sat.

I had long ago become so much at ease about my angry feelings toward her that, when she had been at the point, in the earlier years of the work, of attacking me physically, I had told her that if she did so, I would knock her right through the wall, or would knock her head clean off at the shoulders. Also in the earlier years, when she would defiantly thrust open the window on a cold winter day, after I had repeatedly told her not to do so, and would then stick her head out the window and yell like a crazy whore at passersby, I would walk over and tell her grimly that she had better watch out or she might get her head caught in the window, and slam the window firmly as I said this. I had noticed how in the first couple of years of our work she showed a severe and chronic guilt about having once caught her son's finger in a car door, and I think my freedom to express urges of a similar sort may have helped a good deal in her becoming free from guilt about such matters.

In the third year of our work, during a visit from the parents, an incident both touching and ironic occurred. By that time Millie had made enough progress in treatment so that she showed a considerable degree of self-possession both with me and with her mother and father. I stood in a corridor with her and her parents, and her mother endeavored, by trying to exchange knowing glances with me and with the father, to establish it or to re-establish it that we were the normal persons and that Millie was the crazy one. It was pathetically inappropriate now—it was so evident that at this moment Millie was a much healthier person than her mother, who was being her usual painfully uncomfortable and self-conscious and constricted self.

In the fifth year of our work, when I returned to the hospital after an absence of a couple of days, she met me at the front entrance, approaching me in a way clearly indicating that she had something important to tell me. She confided, "I like my mother." I replied warmly, "Well, maybe that's worth being in a mental hospital for ten years," having in mind how closely linked were her feelings toward her mother and toward herself. This represented a tremendous advance over her much earlier expressed "horror" of being like her mother.

Toward the end of the sixth year, I had decided for various reasons to leave Chestnut Lodge and, as required by my contract,

gave one year's notice. At this point I told Mrs. Hendricks that I
would be leaving one year hence, but emphasized that I hoped to
be able to go on with her after my departure from the full-time
staff, and added that this would be settled definitely, one way or
the other, about two months before I left. She reacted with hostility
of an intensity that surprised me, despite my having been accustomed for years to her hostility as well as her growing love feelings.

In my final staff presentation, a month before I left the Lodge,
I reported:

> I told her about two months ago, partly because she's had
> feelings for a lot of other patients here—a lot of positive feel-
> ings, including this one—I told her, in a strained manner, not
> looking at her, of the suicide of this particular woman who had
> killed herself quite some time after leaving Chestnut Lodge. I
> heard her say, "That's too bad"; but then I looked at her, and
> she had the damnedest smile I have ever seen on anybody's
> face. It reminded me of a sugar-coated corpse; I've never seen
> a sugar-coated corpse, but this was the quality of it, very
> strange, very sadistic. In connection with my leaving this joint,
> among many other feelings I've had suicidal feelings, and one
> thing that's been of value to me is to think that if I did knock
> myself off, I had a picture of my five patients getting together
> and nonverbally sharing their triumph. I'm sure Millie would
> be a ringleader in this group. This, paranoid though it sounds,
> has been a real help to me, because I've seen how schizophrenic
> patients, until their hostility is resolved, are, among other
> things—among more loving things—ceaselessly bent upon one's
> destruction, and if you're in a vulnerable phase of leaving some
> place and having a lot of grief, frustration, anxiety, and guilt,
> you're going to be more vulnerable to that hostility. This I
> found strengthened me—to look at it in that way. Last night I
> had a dream in which I was simply weeping and it was a simple
> grief situation about leaving Chestnut Lodge, and that is very
> much in our work, too. She is better able now to face grief than
> she was; but this is still one of the main things she fights
> against.

Actually, it was only in reading over the transcript of that staff
presentation, some months after my work with Mrs. Hendricks had
ceased, that I realized that, for her, the woman who had committed
suicide after leaving Chestnut Lodge was equivalent to me. The

delay in my realizing the personal significance of her sadistic reaction fit in with my surprise at the degree of her hostility upon learning, some nine months before, of my determination to leave Chestnut Lodge a year hence.

About one month after this incident—two months before my scheduled departure—I told her that I had decided not to go on with her. Among the factors which led me to this decision was her continuing hostility and defiance toward me which, for all her growing positive feelings and dependency, I felt to be too difficult to be handled by a therapist who would be having only a very limited contact with the rest of the hospital team. Our final session was held just before I left, about three months short of seven years after we had begun.

To indicate, meanwhile, how very far she had come, I want to mention a routine conference among the personnel on her unit, led by the administrative psychiatrist and, as was customary, not attended by me. These conferences were devoted to a discussion of each patient in turn, and this particular conference, held about nine months before my departure, was devoted to Mrs. Hendricks. A transcript of the conference shows the personnel to have become concerted in their enthusiasm about how remarkably this woman had improved, and how gratifyingly she was responding to the efforts of various among them. The general feeling was well expressed in the charge nurse's opinion: "She will be one who will leave the Lodge. She is definitely working toward that goal . . . I have a better feeling about Mrs. Hendricks than I have about anybody else over here."

I might mention at this juncture that Mrs. Hendricks, continuing her treatment with the therapist who replaced me, was indeed able to move to outpatient status, six months after my departure, and has been maintaining herself in that mode of living for the past four years, except for two very brief periods back in the hospital.[4]

[4] For a variety of well and recurrently considered reasons, none of the tranquilizing drugs was ever administered to her during the years when I worked with her. Incidentally, throughout my work with her she was the next most healthy among my current Lodge patients, most of the time totaling six, and none of them was on such

In an earlier staff conference, about two years before the end of my work with Mrs. Hendricks, the charge nurse of that era—a predecessor of the charge nurse whose comment in the ward-personnel meeting I quoted a moment ago—reported in enthusiastic detail her own work with the patient. I cannot give in full her moving description of her coming to make a continuing and close contact with Mrs. Hendricks, who had reacted at first with her usual stand-offishness, and who in the earlier years of my work with her had been at her most paranoid when threatened with any degree of intimacy with another woman. The nurse reported, in part:

> ... During the trips over to the [O.T.-R.T.] Center and back, I would find that I just unconsciously would reach out with my hand, and on occasion she would take hold of it and we would walk over to the Center. Of course I expected to hear the next day [the patient's usual subsequent reproaches], "I touched you at such-and-such a time yesterday afternoon going to the Center"; but I didn't hear any of this [from her, as their relationship developed]. There were times when we would walk over to the Center and I would not reach out to take her hand, and she would walk just as close to me as she could until our hands would touch. Then I would take her hand or she would take mine.

I mention at some length the report of this nurse, only one among many of the ward personnel who found occasion for deep gratification in their work with Mrs. Hendricks as she became progressively healthy, because of an incident which occurred during the last few months of my work with her. She and I were walking over from her ward to my office when this nurse approached us on her way to the ward. This nurse, who two years before had been, in my opinion, a rather stern and emotionally aloof person, now looked much more relaxed, comfortable, and feminine. Mrs. Hendricks murmured to me, as the nurse came smilingly toward

---

medication. As in the instances of my other Lodge patients, the frequency of her psychotherapeutic sessions was four hours per week; the sessions were 55 minutes in length.

us, "Look," with warm pleasure and pride in her voice. Here I distinctly felt that Mrs. Hendricks was responding to me as a fellow therapist, showing her pride in having me see how well her patient was doing. This incident is left with me as one of the most memorable of the innumerable events in my work with Mrs. Hendricks, and I feel that it expresses volumes as to why she went on staying so many years in Chestnut Lodge. I had long ago come to feel that patients who are hospitalized for many years develop a very real and therapeutic social importance to other persons in the hospital, both staff members and patients, and that one reason why they do not move out of the hospital is that it is so hard for them to find a situation where they will be anything like as genuinely useful to others about them as they are in the hospital. One of the tragic aspects of this is that what they do for other persons is so rarely acknowledged by anyone.

During a prolonged ocean cruise which had marked the beginning of Mrs. Hendricks's first psychotic episode as a girl in her teens, when the boat had docked at a port in the middle of the voyage, she had been found wandering dazedly in a pasture and had been seen to have her arm lovingly about the neck of a cow. I had always thought of this as evidence of her missing her mother, who was, as she knew, hospitalized for a hysterectomy back in the United States. In retrospect, when I was looking back through my records some several months after stopping the work with her, I realized that this incident had also been an expression of her frustrated desire to *give* mothering *to* her mother, and I was then reminded of the tenderness she had shown toward the slender young plant placed so near to me.

On the other hand, it was only similarly in retrospect that I realized how important, in the precipitation of her psychosis, had been her fear of her death wishes toward her hospitalized mother, and my belated realization of this is of a piece with my similarly belated realization of the fact that, for her, the woman patient who had committed suicide after leaving Chestnut Lodge stood for me—and her sugar-coated corpse kind of smile was expressing her intense wish that I would commit suicide after leaving Chestnut

Lodge. In short, then, although I had felt, in the course of my work with her, that I was seeing very clearly indeed how loving, and at other times how hateful, she was, in actuality both her hate and her love were more intense than I had realized. This is a point beautifully expressed by Freud (1923) when he says that man has a far greater capacity, both for good and for evil, than he thinks he has.

15

Some Aspects of Unconscious Fantasy

The vastness of this subject is at once evident. Unconscious fantasy is one of the major realms of the whole unconscious; along with unconscious memories, perceptions, affects, and somatic sensations it is what the whole effort of a psychoanalyst or dynamic psychiatrist is intended to help the patient to explore and to understand.

Much of the fascination involved in conducting a psychoanalysis, as well as much of the attendant anxiety, has to do with the glimpses one gains of the patient's unconscious fantasies, glimpses provided by his gestures and the changes in his posture, by the special intonations of his words, by odd word usage or slips of the tongue, by brief but highly significant pauses, and so on. Not uncommonly, when one is well attuned to a patient's richly creative inner life, of which he himself is largely unaware, one drinks deeply of the gratifications of a godlike subjective omniscience; but such gratifications are offset by a comparable feeling of unrelatedness to the patient's conscious self, an unrelatedness which accounts, more than anything else, for the oft-mentioned loneliness of doing analytic work.

I assume that fantasy activity is normally a largely unconscious

An abbreviated version of this paper was read at the joint meeting of the American Psychoanalytic Association and the American Psychiatric Association at Dallas, Texas, on May 1, 1972; this was the author's contribution to a panel discussion of "Unconscious Fantasy in the Therapeutic Interaction." It was first published in *International Journal of Psychoanalytic Psychotherapy*, 2 (1):37-50 (1973).

process, and concur with Arlow's (1969) statement that unconscious daydreaming is a constant feature of mental life. In this paper, nonetheless, I shall discuss the individual whose fantasy activity is *disproportionately* unconscious—the person who manifests an across-the-board repression of fantasy life. This individual may be either the patient in his daily-life ego functioning, or the analyst himself under the impact of the patient's transference to him. The processes of which I am writing are observed most readily in the treatment of persons suffering from an easily detectable degree of schizophrenia, whether the degree of severity be borderline, ambulatory schizophrenia, or frank schizophrenia. But these processes emerge also in any schizoid or neurotic person's analysis, as the analysis comes to disclose the effects of early vicissitudes of mother-infant symbiosis and individuation—vicissitudes I find to be a part of the early histories of all my patients, including those at the "normal-neurotic" end of the scale.

There are several typical determinants of such repression of fantasy life. Fantasies are unconsciously rejected as being worthless (equivalent, for example, to feces), irrelevant to reality, and leading, therefore, only to feelings of disappointment, helplessness, and humiliation. One unconsciously assumes all fantasy activity to be equivalent to craziness. At the same time, there is unconscious fear of one's fantasies as potentially possessing an omnipotent power, a frightening dominion over outer reality. There is so little differentiation, at an unconscious level, between inner and outer reality that any derepression of vivid fantasies tends to bring with it total confusion in this regard—a panic-stricken helplessness to know what is fantasy and what is outer reality, and a terrible sense of omnipotent responsibility for all this dedifferentiated world. To the extent that a patient has been chronically depressed, for example, and has had, therefore, largely to repress any vividly detailed, realistic *memories* of his past in order to avoid the feelings of grief and nostalgia with which such memories are laden, he is insufficiently grounded in the reality of his own past to dare, as it were, to permit himself to fantasy, lest his precarious sense of reality be entirely lost.

In my clinical experience, the most basic reason for a pathologically severe repression of fantasy life, a reason embracing the well-known subsidiary determinants just mentioned, consists in the unconscious maintenance of symbiotic relatedness with the other person and, by the same token, the avoidance of individuation. Such a patient unconsciously establishes with the analyst a symbiotic relationship in which one person does all, or nearly all, the conscious fantasying for the whole symbiotic unit. The patient has insufficient ego strength to cope with the feelings of anxiety and loss which would accompany individuation, and the feelings of realistic guilt which would accompany the assumption of a primary, personal responsibility for himself and his living, including his fantasy life.

In actuality, patients who function symbiotically in the transference relationship, as regards fantasying, tend to function at one or another of opposite extremes in this regard. There is the patient whom I have just mentioned, whose own fantasy life is inordinately severely repressed, while he functions in such a manner that the analyst, his partner in the pathological symbiosis, is the one who does the fantasying for both of them. Then there is the so-contrasting type of patient whose fantasy life is pathologically unrepressed. This patient functions in the transference symbiosis as a kind of fountain of largely fantasy material, material in which daytime fantasies, remembered material from nighttime dreams, and fragments of reality perceptions are all relatively undifferentiated, while the analyst is given to function, in the symbiosis, in a complementarily overly constricted, reality-bound fashion as being the *one* who possesses an identity and an ego capable of differentiation and integration. Both these at times so-contrasting patients are alike in that, for each, the whole role of fantasying (or repression of fantasying, as the case may be) in the psychic economy subserves the maintenance of defensive, pathologically symbiotic relatedness, rather than being in the service of individuality and enrichment of reality relatedness. One can find, of course, both types of patients, both extremes of symbiotic functioning, in any one patient at different phases in his treatment. In the analysis of both types of patients, for a healthier individuation to occur, each of these opposite types of pathologic symbiosis must first become transformed into a much more freely commingling kind of healthy symbiosis which I have termed therapeutic symbiosis in a series of earlier papers (1965a, 1966-1967, 1970, 1971, 1972a).

Pathologic Symbiosis Involving the Patient Who Is Inordinately "Reality"-Bound—Whose Fantasy Life Is Severely Repressed and Projected into the Analyst

The patient in this instance is heavily defended against his own fantasy life, which he tends to experience, if at all, as being an alien intrusion threatening to invade and overwhelm him with "not-me" experience. While functioning in a maddeningly reality-bound, unimaginative way himself in the sessions, he instills coercively but subtly, and of course largely unconsciously, his fantasy life into the analyst. The analyst therefore finds himself experiencing throughout the sessions an abundance of more or less foreign-seeming, crazy fantasies which are entirely his own responsibility, for the patient steadfastly denies any share in them, any contribution to them. The analyst thus feels at first hand the assault which the patient as a child tended to feel in face of a mother (or father) who placed the patient under intense pressure to be the one who vicariously bore the burden of her own fantasy life against which she was unconsciously heavily defended.

For this kind of symbiotic transference to become resolved, it is necessary that the analyst become more and more able, over the course of time, to realize his own stake in, his own contributions to this state of affairs, and thus to become sufficiently able to integrate these fantasy experiences so that the patient in turn, partly through identification with the analyst who has become able to cope with this material, can likewise become increasingly able to experience and integrate it.

The patient's initially unconscious fantasy life must be processed through the analyst, in this manner, in order to become—partially, as I say, through the patient's identifying with the analyst—the patient's *own* fantasy experience. This process is essentially the same as that through which the healthy infant and young child develops a meaningful relatedness with his nonhuman environment (Searles, 1960). That latter whole gigantic realm of his environment must first be processed through the mothering-figure, who is at first reacted to as comprising the totality of the environment, with the definitively human ingredients of it not yet differentiated from the definitively nonhuman ingredients. It is through his becoming able to identify with her ability to differentiate and integrate the human and nonhuman components that he, in turn, acquires the ego capacities to do this also.

We see in this process that the frightening power of the fantasy material basically is its power, once each participant has come to experience it as his own, to lead to the destruction of their erstwhile symbiotic relatedness. In the patient's childhood, that power was dimly sensed as the power to destroy both mother and child in reality, since their actual existence, biological as well as psychological, was felt to depend upon the maintenance of their symbiotic relatedness. Such mothers typically have regaled their offspring with accounts of how the latter's birth "almost tore me apart," such that the child senses, however unformulatedly, that he must not become born now out of this symbiotic oneness within the mother, lest she indeed die this time.

One such patient reported, throughout each session, material which in verbal content was most convention-bound and sterile, but she did so in a fashion—involving significant intonations, pauses, gestures, and so on—that fostered concomitantly in my mind an almost unending stream of fantasies. Whenever I ventured to report any of these to her as relevant data, she reacted to my attempts as so much water off a duck's back. In one of our sessions she told me with delight something that made me cringe privately in horror: she described how increasingly able her little son was becoming to content himself, hour after hour in his playroom, alone with his toy soldiers, rocketships, and so on, living in an increasingly fantasy-dominated world. It was evident that she found thus a vicarious release from her own boringly reality-bound daily life. I felt a sense of conviction that the at least incipient schizophrenia in the little boy, having thus to live out his parent's unconscious fantasy life, undifferentiated from his "own" fantasies, was the very sort of process against which she as a child had had to develop vigorous unconscious defenses, in her symbiotic relationship with her mother. Her little son's role in her daily-life ego functioning was essentially that, of course, which she fostered my occupying in the transference relationship.

Notable is the bond of gratitude one feels, toward such a patient, on the rare occasions when she does acknowledge one's fantasy, reported to her, as having some relevance, some reality, for herself—as being, that is, not merely one more manifestation of the analyst's supposed craziness. The analyst's experience here is entirely akin to that of the schizophrenic child in a family whose family symbiosis requires that the child occupy the role of the "crazy one" in the family, a role which keeps him chronically starved for validation of his perceptions of the interpersonal processes in the family, and pathetically grateful for such crumbs of validation as come his way, for these transitorily rescue him from the exile, the terrifying and humiliating exile, of his craziness.

On the other hand there is also, as I mentioned earlier, enormous gratification for the analyst, gratification of a subjectively omniscient variety, in his functioning in the absence of such validations from the patient, for pending these he can feel that only he can see and know what is "really" transpiring in the patient. He can feel that a magical intuitiveness is his alone. For the treatment to become successful, he must prove humble enough to realize to what an extent his feeling himself to be the "creative one" in the relationship, the one able for example freely to fantasy, has been due to the patient's projection of the latter's own unconscious creativity upon the analyst. The patient who at the beginning of the treatment was so heavily defended against his own creativity, unconsciously equated with frightening craziness, can be helped to gain access to his creativity partly through identification with the analyst who has been able to experience within himself both the patient's creativity and his craziness, at first undifferentiated, and has become able increasingly to differentiate, and concomitantly to help the patient to differentiate, between creativity and craziness.

Along the way, in one's work with so reality-bound a patient, one finds that one's own sense of personal identity undergoes vicissitudes, distortions, and at times most disturbingly total changes, in one's experiencing at an internal level, subjectively as one's own, the many repressed and projected self-images against which the patient's own brittle and rigid sense of personal identity is unconsciously thus defended. In a paper (1965c) entitled "The Sense of Identity as a Perceptual Organ," I suggested that the analyst's noting of such variations in his sense of personal identity provides him with his most valuable information as to what is transpiring in reality at an unconscious level in the patient, and from this extrapolated the suggestion that, for human beings generally, the person's sense of identity is potentially his most sensitive and reliable instrument for psychologically grasping the outer world. To the extent that one becomes basically aware enough of one's wish to be free of any continuing identity, and sure enough of who in reality one is, it becomes possible to regard momentary variations in one's sense of identity not as frightening signs of craziness, not as alarming indications that one's identity may have been lost irretrievably, but rather as fascinatingly informative weather-vane data as to what is transpiring, at a subtle and largely unconscious level, in the patient's mode of functioning in the transference relationship.

The initially so reality-bound patient becomes bit by bit more receptive to one's timely reporting to him of what one finds happening to one's sense of identity, such that he in turn becomes, partly through identification with the analyst, less frightenedly needful of clinging to some one facet of his identity as being his only "real" identity. The patient becomes more and more able, that is, to accept into his awareness and to integrate his formerly repressed self-images which he has been projecting upon the analyst. Such a kind of interpretive activity on my part has been of the most fundamental value in more than one clinical instance, serving where all else was failing to help a patient to avoid an actual loss of identity and frank psychosis.

PATHOLOGIC SYMBIOSIS INVOLVING THE PATIENT WHOSE
FANTASY LIFE IS INORDINATELY UNREPRESSED

Such a patient, in her unceasing outpouring of largely fantasy
material, material in which reported nighttime dreams and fragments of daytime reality are not at all well differentiated as such,
functions in terms of the analyst as being the reality-oriented one in
the transference symbiosis, the one who has an ego and an identity,
and who represents reality. But she functions in such fashion as to
make this role feel predominantly constricted and burdensome to
the analyst. He tends to feel an omnipotence-based responsibility
for the whole relationship, a sole responsibility for maintaining the
two participants in some touch with the surrounding reality of their
situation, and feels his own capacities for fantasy, for creativity, to
be increasingly impoverished, for he feels unable to afford himself
anything of such freedom to fantasy as that in which he sees the
patient to be luxuriating. He feels like a totally responsible nursemaid to an utterly carefree child; but this "child" of his, unlike
other children, is of adult size and playfully assaults him with not
only small-child demands, but also the demands of an at times most
lustful and aggressive fellow adult.

In his reality-bound constrictedness he secretly envies the patient who, so largely unhampered by any concern to maintain a
personal identity, seems to him to gambol with delicious freedom
throughout the undifferentiated realms of daytime fantasy, nighttime dreams, and reality, being now this person and now that one
and now no one—immersing herself in whatever mixture of experience affords her the greatest pleasure, and enables her to make
the most overwhelming demands upon him, at the moment. Feeling so impoverished of inner liveliness himself, he inevitably seeks
vicarious escape from his own position by identifying with her experience, her productions. Added now to his guilt about his secret
envy of her is his guilt for his—so he feels it—exploiting of her in a
coercively "encouraging, permissive" fashion, his fostering of her
being as undifferentiatedly crazy as possible, both to provide him
vicarious release for his unconscious fantasies—a kind of

entertainment—and to slake his research interests in a situation where therapeutic progress becomes such an ever-receding possibility that research results offer, in this ostensible treatment situation, the only justification acceptable to his by now much regressed and self-punitive superego.

Whereas in his work with the former type of patient a part of his task was to perceive to what an extent the crazy-seeming fantasies he found himself experiencing were flowing from the patient's unconscious, his work with this second type of patient requires that he become increasingly open to detecting his own, heretofore unconscious contributions to the outpouring of fantasy material which seems to be coming so exclusively, and therefore so crazily, from her alone. In a recent paper (1972a) concerning my work, extending over many years and still continuing, with a deeply ego-fragmented and delusional woman, I described my progressively discovering to what an awesome extent her highly delusional world was in actuality flowing from, and thus was based upon, her responding to various real but predominantly unconscious components of my personality—heretofore largely unconscious ways of my functioning with her during the sessions.

Whereas the former patient reacts to one's reported, intendedly interpretive "private" fantasies as being so much crazy, worthless shit, this patient reacts so to one's attempts to confront her with relatively well-differentiated aspects of reality, and one's gratitude in this situation is for the rare occasions when the patient functions as a fellow adult in cognizance of, and assumption of a degree of mutual responsibility for, the flood of largely fantasy material pouring from her.

In my work with one such patient, it has been interesting to me to find that, in order for a genuinely therapeutic symbiotic relatedness to replace increasingly the pathologic symbiosis which she from the first has fostered in the transference, I have had to become open to experiencing a gamut of gratifications, at first laden with much anxiety and guilt for me in each instance, traceable to a series of fixation points in her own libidinal development. Thus, I found early in the work that her outpouring of largely undifferentiated, largely fantasy material was a derivative of her desire, at that time unconscious, to function as an adult woman in providing sexual gratification to me, and—of much more significance in her psychopathology—to function "mind-fuckingly" as a man copulating, with this gigantic fantasy-material penis of hers, with me as a woman. Later her reporting of this material developed more a connotation of my exploitatively getting this "shit" out of her, and still later of my thus nursing upon her, as her own orality came increasingly to the fore. I began to sense that she was causing me recurrently to feel impoverished of, and hungry for, fantasy material, and then enabling me gratefully to feed from her once again. Incidentally, it is useful to see that a patient's functioning in such a manner as to cause impoverishment of the analyst's *fantasy* life is expressive of the patient's determination, whether conscious or more largely unconscious, to seduce or coerce him into giving up his attempt to function as analyst and taking refuge, out of his desperation, in an actual *physical* (erotic and/or aggressive) relationship with her—the only mode of interpersonal relatedness seemingly possible for him to find with her.

Most recently, as this woman thrives increasingly in the treatment, I have come to see that she at times treats me as being merely a fantasy of hers, and I find myself no longer threatened by the passive gratification this affords me. Such data as have come my way, concerning her relationships with the most ill among her several children, fit with the data from the transference evolution I have sketched here, in indicating that a maturationally timely symbiosis between herself and her mother, in the patient's infancy and early childhood, was warped by the mother's, and increasingly the patient's, guilt and anxiety in face of such lustful and aggressive components of premature object relatedness as those with which I found myself having to cope, successively, in helping her to retrace archaeologically, as it were, the warped stages in her libidinal development until her ever-alive, however deeply buried, potential for freely and healthily symbiotic functioning could be progressively unearthed.

Two such patients have made clear that any at all freely verbalized sharing of fantasies, between patient and analyst, has for them a connotation of incest, and one of these patients, a chronically schizophrenic woman whose own mother had been at least ambulatorily schizophrenic, means this with the most unmistakable literalness when she terms this "incest." For such patients any experience of patient's and analyst's at all freely identifying with one another empathically has, by the same token, this connotation of actual incest.

As regards the content and style of one's interpretations, in general one finds that the former, reality-bound type of patient's gradually loosening up is best facilitated by relative ambiguity in the analyst's comments, as has been well described by Marie Coleman Nelson and her co-workers (1968), whereas the fantasy-inundated patient's increasing contact with reality is best facilitated by more incisive and explicit interpretations of the kind well illustrated in Rosenfeld's (1965) writings.

With either type of patient, as the therapeutic symbiosis becomes well established, such that both participants become increasingly free to communicate with one another both reality perceptions and fantasy material without a fear-dominated need to keep these realms of psychological experience differentiated, the healthy integration and differentiation which now grows out of this relatively anxiety-free matrix highlights to what a degree either the patient or the analyst, or both, have been pursuing heretofore, unbeknownst to himself or to the other person, *fantasy* goals which were mistakenly thought to be *reality* goals.

For example, as I described in a paper in 1961:

One hebephrenic woman kept trying to get me to elope with her to Florida, and in various ways chided me for being so stodgy. In one session I sensed, with relief, that she was trying merely to get me to unbend and share such an experience with her in *fantasy*, whereupon I confessed, "Well, if you're thinking of this in terms of fantasy, I've already had intercourse with you several times in fantasy so far this hour!" To this she responded, with such pleasure as I had rarely seen in our often-despair-filled years of work, "Progress has been made in this room!" [1961c, pp. 440-441].

On the other hand the analyst may find, in a session with a predominantly silent patient, that the patient's starting again to speak may rudely confront him with the reality of the situation, dispelling a pleasurable fantasy on the analyst's part involving the patient and himself. More than once I have felt consternation when suddenly faced with the evidence of how greatly I have been relating, perhaps for years, more to a fantasy of who this patient is, than to the patient as he or she exists in reality. One realizes in retrospect, when both fantasy relatedness and reality relatedness become so much more available in the phase of therapeutic symbiosis, to what an extent one has been annoyedly pushing away the patient in reality, to keep him or her from intruding upon one's largely autistic relationship with the fantasied patient.

Surely an extreme instance of this is to be found in my work, lasting now nearly 20 years, with an awesomely crazy schizophrenic woman. For years I thought of this patient, between sessions, as being the locus of my raison d'être, the one person who would vindicate not only my professional ability but also my much more essential human worth. I would look forward to each session with great eagerness, vaguely sure that all manner of ill-formulated hopes would at last be realized. In the session I would find her still appallingly crazy as usual, would spend the time with her largely in a terrible feeling of futility, but would manage to terminate the session in a kind of nothing-daunted spirit, assuring her in a determinedly cheerful fashion that I would see her next time (while deafening my ears to her usual caustically cynical retorts). I would then return to my largely unscathed between-session fantasies as to who she is and who I am in relation to her. Presumably one could not endure such work without some such sustaining fantasies, and surely one needs to be able to visualize in the patient a potentially healthier person than she presently is, in order to be able to evoke her capacities for healthy maturity, just as a mother must be able, in functioning effectively as a mother, to help the child grow into the increasingly strong and large person she can see him potentially to be. But, as is by now obvious to me, the fantasy can become predominant over, and essentially inhospitable to, the real person. On a less awesome scale, the termination of one's analysis of a neurotic patient inevitably involves one's coming to terms with the unrealizability of one's various fantasies concerning the outcome of one's relationship with the patient.

Finally, as regards a few summarizing implications for psychoanalytic technique, I am wary of attempting to generalize about the ever-changing complexities, the living processes, of the patient-analyst relationship. The following factors are but a few of the crucial variables in the analytic situation at any one moment: the level of anxiety in each participant; the degree of clinical experience on the part of the analyst; the analyst's ability, varying in degree inversely with his anxiety level, to discern both transference and immediate-reality determinants for what is transpiring between himself and the patient; and his skill in the timing of interpretations and in dealing with the patient's response—whether of heightened or decreased anxiety—to his interpretations. Having said this, I shall venture these generalizations.

I began my work in psychotherapy (and a few years later, in psychoanalysis) nearly three decades ago, at a time when my functioning was severely constricted by predominantly obsessive-compulsive defenses. Over the years I have become slowly, step by step, less cautious and more spontaneously participative in my work with my patients. It is clear to me that the analyst's *inner freedom to experience* feelings, fantasies, and such patient-transference-related shifts in his personal identity as I have mentioned is unequivocally desirable and necessary. But it is equally clear that only his therapeutic intuition, grounded in his accumulating clinical experience, can best instruct him when it is timely and useful—and when, on the other hand, it is ill timed and injudicious—to *express* these inner experiences, in any notably affect-laden manner, to the patient.

Any potential danger in the analyst's reporting of a fantasy, for example, to the patient (the danger that in so doing he will cause an increase in the patient's anxiety or confusion, for instance) must be weighed against the potential danger in the analyst's remaining so emotionally inaccessible, so detached in relation to his own

psychological experiences, that he withholds from the patient data
which the latter vitally needs—needs, even, to maintain his perhaps
tenuous relatedness to reality. Outer reality for the patient during
the analytic session consists most immediately in the person of the
analyst and in what the analyst is feeling and thinking. I have seldom found that a patient reacts in any lastingly traumatized way to
my communicating to him, for example, the feelings or fantasies I
find myself experiencing in response to him. Years ago, more than
one patient quit working with me because of my tenacious professional remoteness, and in retrospect I know that they showed excellent judgment.

Whether the analyst reports his experienced fantasy (for example) in a relatively anxiety-free, personally responsible manner
makes all the difference. If he has an erotic and/or aggressive fantasy concerning the patient and is able genuinely to experience it
primarily as relevant data in the analytic work (data of much the
same order of informational value, say, as the patient's own reported memories, dreams, and perceptions of the immediate situation), the analyst can share the fantasy with the patient in a truly
collaborative fashion. He can share it at a timely juncture, perhaps
while most immediate and vivid, or a few minutes later, if more
suitable. But if severe guilt and alarm attends his fantasy, and he
tells the patient of it in a frightened and confessional manner, the
patient will of course be at least temporarily more upset. (In my
experience, however, such upset is rarely lasting; patients generally
are much stronger and more resilient in this regard than we customarily believe them to be.) It is much as if the patient, already
anxiety-beset, suddenly finds that he has in his lap an anxious baby
(the analyst) for whom he is solely responsible. The patient cannot
but feel, under those circumstances, that he alone has somehow
caused this transformation in his strong parent-analyst.

An analyst's undue constrictedness, in regard to using his own
fantasy material to further the analysis, suggests that here is one
repository of his unresolved and unconscious fantasies of omnipotence. He functions (as surely I did years ago) as if his innermost
contents were imbued with an omnipotently destructive power.

When he shares his fantasy and finds that a patient is essentially unscathed, and even benefited, the analyst is not only relieved and gratified but also deflated. He finds, for the nth time, that he is merely human.

An analyst who never dares to report any of his fantasies to the patient can scarcely expect the patient to gain free access to his own fantasy life and integrate it into increasingly strong ego functioning. On the other hand, the patient can usefully identify with an analyst who is comfortable with the fantasy dimension of his own ego functioning and who regards fantasy as a factor in the enrichment of human relationships.

SUMMARY AND CONCLUSION

Instances in which a patient's fantasy life is either unduly repressed or so insufficiently repressed as to render him consciously fantasy-ridden are traceable etiologically to an unresolved, pathologically symbiotic mode of mother-infant relatedness. Such a patient unconsciously establishes with the analyst a symbiotic relationship in which one person does the conscious fantasying, and the other remains rooted in reality, for the whole symbiotic unit. The analyst's own ego functioning during the sessions becomes, under the impact of the patient's transference, appreciably involved in this pathologic symbiosis, so that he is uncharacteristically inundated by, or impoverished of, fantasies. A relatively anxiety-free, and therefore more freely commingling, therapeutic symbiosis must evolve in the patient-analyst relationship in order for healthy integration and differentiation, and eventual individuation, to occur.

16

Discussion of
"The Concept of Psychoses
as a Result and in the Context of
the Long-Term Treatment Modalities,"
by Leopold Bellak

In his opening presentation for this conference, Dr. Bellak (1974) shows remarkable mastery of the several highly diverse areas of his topic. I personally have learned much from his informative address, and could easily limit myself to appreciative comments upon various of the ideas and bodies of data he has provided us. To cite but a few examples, I greatly admire his discussion of community psychiatry and his emphasis upon the iatrogenic, hospitalization— or otherwise disuse-based origin of many features of chronic schizophrenia and the psychoses of old age.

But because my background and major interests in this field are considerably different from his, and because I am convinced that the conference will benefit most from the frank comparing of dif-

This discussion was originally presented at the Colloquium on the Long-Term Treatment of Psychotic States, organized by the Mental Health Association of the 13th District of Paris and held in Paris, February 23-26, 1972. It was first published in *Long-Term Treatment of Psychotic States*, edited by Collette Chiland, with Paul Bequart (New York: Human Sciences Press, 1977), pp. 63-69.

ferent viewpoints, I choose mainly to take issue with him in what is for me a most fundamental matter.

My experience in this field consists in nearly 15 years on the staff at Chestnut Lodge, doing psychoanalytic psychotherapy with chronically psychotic patients who were not on psychotropic drugs; 12 years as a consultant to Wynne's research team at the National Institute of Mental Health, working as a cotherapist with him in the family therapy of schizophrenia, largely without resort to drugs; and, during the past nine years, doing single interviews at a dozen different hospitals, for teaching purposes, with many hundreds of psychotic—mostly, of course, schizophrenic—patients, a high percentage of whom have been on one or more of such drugs. I have supervised more than a hundred young therapists in their work with psychotic patients, most of whom have been on these drugs.

Dr. Bellak's paper gives one the impression that, beyond his faithfully carrying out his assigned task here, his own major interest and emphasis is in drug-and-diagnostic studies. This emphasis far overrides his welcomely moderating mention, concerning Goldstein's (1970) experimental results, "In some patients the drugs interfered with the problem solving involved in some psychotic processes. It would seem therefore extremely important not to administer psychotropic drugs indiscriminately or exclusively." His paper gives psychodynamics short shrift, indeed.

Where he leads into his title subject by a lengthy discussion of many drug-and-diagnostic studies, I approach this whole, admittedly difficult, subject in what seems to me to offer us a more essentially human orientation, basically in opposition to the relatively nonhuman orientation represented by a psychiatry which would maintain its focus primarily upon diagnosing and the dispensing of drugs in accord with diagnostic subcategories.

In my experience, the central problem in schizophrenia, which Dr. Bellak reports as making up 80 percent of functional psychoses, is the patient's having failed to achieve, or in more dynamic terms having rejected tenaciously at an unconscious level, a durable identity as an individual human being. While it clearly would be folly for us to rule out the possibility that genetic inheritance contributes significantly to this difficulty, a most formidable body of data, gained over approximately the past three decades, primarily from individual psychoanalytic psychotherapy and family studies, attests that interpersonal processes are for all practical treatment purposes the major, and quite sufficient, etiologic source of this impairment of humanization. The most solidly reliable data emerge from the unfolding, the evolution of the patient's transferences to the therapist. The therapist learns, from the reality of his own feeling-responses to the patient's unconscious transference reactions to him as being, for example, the mother or father of the patient's childhood, what really were the most warping elements in the emotional climate of the patient's crucial earliest years, years in which the healthy human infant and child ordinarily first becomes a truly human individual. All this, far from being merely impressionistic work on the part of an array of idiosyncratic therapists, is meaningfully validatable among them and is teachable to younger generations of therapists. Such data from psychoanalytic psychotherapy, steadily and firmly developing over the years, are providing a far more genuinely scientific foundation for dealing with schizophrenia than is provided by .the vastly more numerous and heavily financed drug studies. These studies, in the so-impressive trappings of our more traditional biologically oriented sciences—with, that is, large numbers of patients, control groups, much attention to possible external variables, and with therapeutic intuition regarded mainly as a contaminant—produce, year after year, dozens of ostensibly exciting new findings, findings which usually suggest some inherent, inborn qualitative difference setting schizophrenic persons unbridgeably apart from their fellow men including, of course, the investigators themselves, findings which prove ephemeral and are soon replaced by findings which in turn seem momentarily revolutionary, only to be similarly quickly invalidated.

Several years ago I put forward the hypothesis that to the extent that one is healthy, one's sense of personal identity is one's most reliable perceptual organ in dealing with the subtle data of interpersonal relations (1965c). It follows that, in our endeavor to diagnose our patients' difficulties, what we find happening to our sense of identity in reacting with the patient should not be assumed to consist in unwanted and unscientific intrusions of counter-transference phenomena but regarded, rather, as potentially price-less data, most highly scientific data, as to what is going on at an unconscious level in the patient. One of the surest criteria I have discovered, by which to know that a patient is schizophrenic, is my finding that I tend to experience myself as being nonhuman in re-lation to him—to feel, for example, that I emerge, in relation to him, as being so inhumanly callous or sadistic, or so filled with weird fantasies within myself, as to place me well outside the realm of human beings. I have not attempted to identify possible other kinds of diagnostically typical subjective experiences of one's per-sonal identity when one is interviewing patients of various diag-noses other than schizophrenia; but I suggest that research money spent on such projects would be well allocated.

The one main point I wish to make here is to caution against our taking refuge, collectively, in an orientation toward our patients which seems to me largely epitomized by Dr. Bellak's paper, an orientation in which we tend to think of psychotic patients primar-ily in terms of objectifying them for diagnostic purposes—trying to discern wherein they differ from their fellow men including, of course, ourselves—and in which we attempt to select this or that drug with the hoped-for magical power to reach the patient and af-fect his thinking and his feeling, without our own selves, our own feelings and private thinking, becoming much involved. In our ceaseless search for specifically powerful, but inescapably non-human, drugs we depart more and more widely from the possi-bility of access to the specifically therapeutic power within our human selves, the power inherent in intense and highly personal emotions—such emotions as Winnicott, for example, helped us to reach in his pioneering paper, "Hate in the Countertransference" (1947).

What I am doing here is no mere tilting at windmills, for my observations of younger therapists' work has solidly shown me that although the psychotropic drugs are at times used with discretion in a manner that fosters genuinely human relatedness between the patient and his therapist and other persons round about, all too often they are resorted to too quickly, or in too heavy dosage, or too prolongedly, primarily to provide the therapist, the nursing personnel, and so on, with a refuge from the therapeutically necessary emotional involvement with the patient, involvement which tends so powerfully to assault one's own sense of humanness. With the best of physicianly intentions, the therapist is choosing unconsciously to remain a diagnostician and dispenser of drugs, and to limit the so-called psychotherapy to a *pro forma* basis, rather than risk his partially becoming, in terms of his own experience of himself, the transference object whom the patient is needing, a transference object who would feel within himself, to some appreciable degree, the kinds of disturbances in various of the 12 ego functions Dr. Bellak and his research team have found diagnostic for various types of psychosis.

I emphatically do not mean that, in order to function effectively as a therapist for the schizophrenic person, one needs to become crazy, or partially crazy, along with him. What I mean is that, while keeping in touch with one's own individual identity, one must become able to experience within oneself, in manageable increments, the intense and discoordinate emotions the patient is having unconsciously to defend against with his craziness. This process provides the necessary therapeutic context for the patient's coming to explore and understand the meanings of his psychosis, his psychosis which is being projected upon the therapist as the transference personification of the crazinesses in the parents. It provides the foundation, also, for the patient's coming to accept and integrate his own human emotions, partially through identification with the therapist whose humanness has been able to cope with and integrate this projected schizophrenic onslaught (Searles, 1965a).

I should like fully to share Dr. Bellak's hopefulness about the future; but his own paper, with its heavy emphasis upon drug-and-diagnostic studies, highlights my main concern about the future of our profession and of our patients. If the present avalanche of drug use continues unchecked, there will inevitably result not only a congealing of our psychotic patients' struggle to become genuinely human, but also a dehumanization within our psychiatric culture itself—a loss of humanness within ourselves personally.

On our overpopulated, pollution-ridden planet where the quality of human existence becomes steadily more degraded, psychiatry is a profession that inherently tends to pioneer man's new ways of thinking about himself. Dr. Bellak and I come from a country where the overuse or misuse of various mind- and emotion-influencing drugs are among our most ravaging social ills—where, for example, there are nine million problem drinkers of alcohol, and where heroin is a leading, if not the leading, cause of death among young men in some of our largest cities. In such a nation-wide social context, I am troubled about an American psychiatry which itself is relying increasingly heavily upon psychotropic drugs, for it seems to me that such a psychiatry tends mainly to pioneer man's increasing alienation from himself. I have no quarrel with such drugs when they are used to help the patient to gain access to, and to integrate, his human emotions. But far too often, antidepressant drugs are used to dull a healthy grieving, and sedative drugs are used to lull anxiety and fear in a patient who needs desperately to become more part of a human world where such emotions are realistic indeed.

17

Violence in Schizophrenia

WITH JEAN M. BISCO, M.D.
GILLES COUTU, M.D., AND
RICHARD C. SCIBETTA, M.D.

The primary purpose of this paper is to highlight certain aspects of the etiology and the psychotherapeutic management of violence in schizophrenic patients. Its secondary purpose is to provide examples of a kind of interviewing technique I have developed which seems to have proved, in several hundreds of teaching interviews over the past several years at the Sheppard and Enoch Pratt Hospital and at a variety of other institutions, reasonably effective for teaching, for evoking diagnostic data, and, not infrequently, for catalyzing the patients' psychotherapy.

This article originally appeared in *The Psychoanalytic Forum*, Volume 5, 1973, John A. Lindon, M.D., Editor. Permission granted by the Psychiatric Research Foundation.

This paper was written by the senior author, and the theoretical formulations it contains are his; it is thus written in the first-person singular. Drs. Bisco, Coutu, and Scibetta are listed as co-authors as my way of expressing my gratitude to them for their most kind permission to include data from my teaching interviews with patients who were in therapy with them—data which make up a large part of this paper and are utterly indispensable to it.

Case 1

Mr. Raymond Delaney,[1] a 17-year-old freshman in a college near Baltimore, was admitted to the Sheppard and Enoch Pratt Hospital after his mother discovered that he had hidden an Italian revolver, with bullets carefully selected to fit it, under his mattress, in the frankly and dispassionately admitted determination to kill a male classmate who had been "bugging" him since their high school years together in the Washington area. Both parents, from past experience, firmly believed him capable of carrying out this intention. The youth revealed, during his consultation interview with the college psychiatrist, that throughout his upbringing he had felt isolated as the smallest boy in his class, repeatedly picked on by his larger classmates, recurrently drawn toward the notion of joining a gang and shooting someone to relieve his frustration, and had become increasingly convinced that he was a juvenile delinquent who belonged in prison among the tough men whom he openly admired. He made it clear that his mind was filled with violent thoughts, and he confirmed in a chillingly matter-of-fact way his determination to kill the particular classmate whom he had selected as "my target."

The female therapist who began working with him at Sheppard soon found reason, in his paranoid glares and delighted laughter while venting his preoccupation with bloodshed, to join the parents and the college psychiatric consultant in their fear of him. It was learned that when he had been seen briefly at a community clinic at age 16, he had been found to be preoccupied with homicidal fantasies, and had left that psychiatrist with the impression that there was considerable probability that he would act upon these. The psychological report following his admission to Sheppard stated:

> . . . Very strong aggression is indicated and although the aggression appears to be absorbed to a large extent in fantasy, the poor controls implied in his impulsiveness are likely to lead to acting-out behavior that might well include homicidal at-

---

[1] A pseudonym, as is each of the names of the patients described here.

tempts. . . . The patient's self-image is that of a powerful, competent individual who is prepared to demolish any opposition he may encounter. However, it is interesting to note that on the Rorschach the most frequent percept that he repeated was that of a gnat. This most insignificant insect probably represents his secret fears of his own basic feelings of inadequacy. [The patient had revealed to his therapist a long-standing fear lest he be "stomped" by a gang of fellow students.] . . . He appears to have adopted a vindictive, vengeful attitude toward the world and seems determined to act out against this threatening environment. This youth is seen as a dangerous person and the diagnostic impression is that of a schizophrenic reaction, paranoid type. If the patient does not respond to therapy in this hospital, a case might be made to have him declared a defective delinquent and transferred to the Patuxent Institution.[2]

When I went into the one-way-mirror interview room at Sheppard for a resident teaching interview with this youth, I was shaking in my boots. Significantly, my fear was, and remained throughout the interview, future-oriented rather than present-oriented. I had little if any fear that he would harm me during the interview itself, but great fear lest he kill me at some indeterminate time in the future when he would be armed and on the loose again, and bent on revenge for my having "bugged" him in some manner. A tall, slender youth, neither markedly attractive nor unattractive physically, he had the demeanor of a frightened kid. This demeanor, however, was interlarded with paranoid suspiciousness (especially of the mirror), angry glares, and recurrent verbal expressions of an arrogant murderousness that was both frightening and infuriating. Much of the (tape-recorded) interview went on in a vein of my harshly bugging him. Within the first few minutes he said:

> Mr. Delaney: . . . I wouldn't mind being out of this—hospital.
> Dr. Searles: You wouldn't?
> Mr. Delaney: Uh-uh.

---

[2] A Maryland state institution for young persons adjudged to be defective delinquents.

Dr. Searles: You mean in a prison? Or what are you—speaking of?

Mr. Delaney: Just *out*, ya know [suddenly].

Dr. Searles: That is an *absurd* thing to say, isn't it? What do you mean, out? [scornfully, exasperatedly]

Mr. Delaney: Out on the outside.

Dr. Searles: You mean *before* these murderous feelings of yours are—worked out? [incredulously]

Mr. Delaney: I won't—murder anybody [scoffingly].

Dr. Searles: That was just *talk*? [ironically]

Mr. Delaney: Yeah.

Dr. Searles: You were *lacking* something to talk about, were you? You just—it was like the latest movie, only you didn't have anything else to *talk* about? Huh?

Mr. Delaney: No—yeah, I guess so.

Dr. Searles: You *do* feel we are such *idiots*, huh?—as to turn you loose, huh?—until you—are no longer—uh—likely to kill somebody, huh? You think we are that *idiotic*? [scornfully]

Mr. Delaney: *I* have a—thought: If you want to straighten me out, this isn't the place to straighten me out [nastily].

Dr. Searles: In this room, huh?

Mr. Delaney: I mean anywhere in this hospital.

Dr. Searles: Oh. [20-second pause] Well, you feel you get your *pick*, is that the idea?

Mr. Delaney: How do you mean?

Dr. Searles: Where you get straightened out, huh?

Mr. Delaney: Well, yeah.

Dr. Searles: Ya do. [i.e., "Ya do feel so."]

Mr. Delaney: I don't think that I'm that—I am not the kind of kid that could come here and be straightened out.

Dr. Searles: You are not the kind of kid that could come here and be straightened out, huh?

Mr. Delaney: I think that this is for, you know, people with other kinds of problems. You know what I mean?

Dr. Searles: You mean more *minor* problems, or what? [ironically]

Mr. Delaney: Well, I really wouldn't call it *minor*; but, ya know, it's major problems for *them*.

Dr. Searles: "Major problems for them," huh?

Mr. Delaney: Uh-huh. [several seconds' pause] You know, like one guy talks to himself all the time. Another guy cries every 10 or 15 minutes, ya know. Stuff like that. I mean, it's—

Dr. Searles: Hard to feel any relation to people like that?

Mr. Delaney: Yeah. I think *they* should be—belong here.

Dr. Searles: Whereas you feel that somebody who's got more than his share—of *homicidal* impulses should be where? I am not clear where you feel such a person should be.

Mr. Delaney: Reform school.

Dr. Searles: Reform school. You know anybody who is in reform school?

Mr. Delaney: Plenty of them.

Dr. Searles: They all seem to like it, or what?

Mr. Delaney: Oh, no. They don't *like* it; but, you know, if I had a choice of a mental hospital or a training school, I'd take a training school.

Dr. Searles: You are quite disappointed in this place, I get the impression.

Mr. Delaney: Well, I'm not too happy in it.

Dr. Searles: It hasn't so far proved to be what you had—rather thought it would be, or what?

Mr. Delaney: Why, I didn't want to come here in the first place, when I found out it was a mental hospital. But—ya know, my parents said for me to give it a try—see how I like it.

Dr. Searles: See how you like it? [in amazement]

Mr. Delaney: Yeah.

Dr. Searles: They thought the idea was that you should *like* it? [incredulous tone] Really? *Jesus Christ*, it seems so *irrelevant!* I thought you had made clear that you were a *menace* to *society*, huh? And *any* place you could go that would help you to get over being a *menace* to *society*, there would be a *hell* of a lot of reason for *gratitude* about, huh? But *they* thought on top of *that* you were supposed to *like* it or something?

Mr. Delaney: Well, they thought it could straighten me out.

Dr. Searles: They thought it could straighten you out? Now, you have been here a month?—about a month?

Mr. Delaney: Yeah. A month last Saturday.

[A couple of minutes later in the dialogue—]

Dr. Searles: Are you curious at all why you got it in your mind to—*kill* a former classmate?

Mr. Delaney: I *know* why I'd kill him.

Dr. Searles: Why?

Mr. Delaney: 'Cause he bugged me a lot.

Dr. Searles: Bugged you?

Mr. Delaney: Him and a bunch of other kids, back in high school, bugged me a lot.

Dr. Searles: Well, so—your reasoning is—what?—that you would kill him, huh?

Mr. Delaney: That *was* my reasoning; but it's not that any more.

Dr. Searles: You've got other reasons now?

Mr. Delaney: No. I wouldn't kill him now. I wouldn't kill anybody now [unconvincingly].

[Later, in making some brief reference to his mother's reminiscing about Ireland, he looked full of grief and homesickness, which I took as a portrayal of her demeanor at such times.]

Dr. Searles: Have you ever cried? [gently] Let's see what comes to mind.

Mr. Delaney: Yeah. [pause of several seconds]

Dr. Searles: Now I've got to ask you *when*, or what? You know damned well I want you to say [exasperatedly, but not roughly].

Mr. Delaney: When I was 11 years old.

Dr. Searles: Eleven years old, huh? Let's hear what your thoughts are.

Mr. Delaney: I walked on the paint. My father just painted the door and I—walked on the—uh—the painted sill. I went downstairs and he followed me and hit me in the face a couple of times, hard.

Dr. Searles: . . . And you cried? Hmm? [pause of several seconds] Had you and he been on pretty good terms before that?

Mr. Delaney: Yeah [softly].

[Several minutes later in the dialogue—]

Dr. Searles: Would you rather *shoot* a number of people than *cry*, huh?

Mr. Delaney: I wouldn't do neither.

Dr. Searles: They're equally bad? [pause of few seconds] Are they? Where the hell did you get that idea? [persistently]

Mr. Delaney: I just picked it up.

Dr. Searles: From your *father*? [surprised tone] Did he see you cry? After he hit you and you cried, did you—did he see you cry? [gently, persistently]

Mr. Delaney: [affirmative mumble]

Dr. Searles: Did he show any reaction to that?

Mr. Delaney: He told me he was sorry he hit me.

Dr. Searles: Said he was sorry he hit you?

Mr. Delaney: Uh-huh.

Dr. Searles: He said it immediately after having hit you, when you started to cry?

Mr. Delaney: No. About five minutes later. [silence of more than half a minute]

Dr. Searles: What's going on in your mind in the silence? What—what do you find yourself thinking?

Mr. Delaney: I don't know. Looking at the walls.

Dr. Searles: What's your thought about them?

Mr. Delaney: They're pretty walls [sincere tone].

Dr. Searles: Nice and solid looking?

Mr. Delaney: Yeah. [pause of nearly 30 seconds]

Dr. Searles: You like walls, huh?

Mr. Delaney: I don't know. [pause of several seconds]

Dr. Searles: It's as bad to *cry* as to *kill* somebody?—huh? [tone of awe and disbelief]

Mr. Delaney: Sometimes. I don't know. I guess *not*. [long pause]

As the interview progressed, I inquired into his relationship with his mother and, forewarned by the therapist, felt that I was venturing into particularly explosive ground. At the end of the session I shook hands with him and said, "Good luck to you," to which he said, "Thank you." Hardly had those words fallen from my lips when I felt as though I had just wished him "happy hunting," and the persons viewing the interview from behind the mirror all agreed that this had clearly sounded so to them, also.

I thought of this as in part a clue to my own unconscious murderousness, projected onto the patient and pressing toward vicarious fulfillment through his carrying out his plan to kill his classmate; and in part due to my fear of him, and to my wanting, therefore, to keep his murderousness safely directed toward someone other than myself. But in one who works with such patients, who commit few if any actual violent acts but who keep one under an intensely threatened suspense lest they do so, there is, I believe, an even more basic mechanism operating: it becomes deeply important to one that the patient commit some violent act in reality, so that one can thereby differentiate between one's own murderous fantasies and his murderous act.

Until that violent act occurs, one becomes increasingly enmeshed in guilt about and fear of one's own subjectively omnipo-

tent murderous fantasies. The patient instills so much helpless fear
into one that one intensely hates him, but because one feels so
much in fear and at bay, the hatred is not freely accessible to
awareness; one projects it onto the patient instead. One then
reaches a state where one may be told, as I was told by a charge
nurse who was unimpressed with the potential violence of a hebephrenic man I was treating, "If Tom *should* become assaultive, he
would only be acting out *your* assaultiveness." In Mr. Delaney's case,
his therapist became increasingly concerned lest he commit violent
acts but exasperated that "he doesn't *do* anything" to give reality to
her increasing concern.

I saw the therapist in monthly, tape-recorded supervision of her
work with Mr. Delaney. In my first session with her, she said,
"Well, you remember the session when he was with you—sort of a
scared little boy. . . . But the next session [following the mirror in-
terview] was the one when I decided I couldn't see him in the office
anymore, because he came and he said he hated you. I tried to
pinpoint why. It was because of the remarks you made about his
mother." (I had commented—not disrespectfully, in actuality—
upon her having emigrated from Ireland, and had asked about
what his classmates had said to him about this.) The therapist went
on:

> Therapist: This was one of the times when I became very aware
> of what his hate was really like. I had not really seen it quite
> so clearly until this time. And he started saying that the boys
> said things about his mother. He was kind of hiding his face,
> as he said "dirty things." I said, "Do you mean sexy things,
> dirty sexy things?" and then he said, "I felt so bad in high
> school that I thought I'd die. I thought anybody who felt
> that bad just had to die. He just couldn't go on."
>
> Dr. Searles: "Felt that *bad*." Was this the connotation [i.e., bad
> = evil] that he made or—
>
> Therapist: No. No. He was just miserable. He felt so bad that
> he just had to die. And then he said that he would like to get
> a .38 and he would just like to push it in this kid's stomach
> and shoot him and just watch him squirm around on the
> ground in his blood and just scream. He said, "I want it slow.
> I don't want it fast."

When he was describing this, it was very vivid. . . . I know he
was unaware that I was in the room at all. He wasn't looking
at me and there was as if there was a kind of—if he was
away. Well, it was as if he was away. I don't know how to
describe this—as if he was in the fantasy, describing what was
happening.

Dr. Searles: Isn't there, in retrospect, an implication that this
was just how miserable he felt? [Therapist in the
background: Yes.] Was that your impression at the time?

Therapist: Well—he described the feeling of misery as vividly
as the other, and one went right into the other. Then I had
the tremendous feeling of hate. A quite sort of overwhelming, all-encompassing hate.

Dr. Searles: You had a feeling of hate. Now you see, that
doesn't make clear where the hate was located. *You* had the
feeling of tremendous hate.

Therapist: Well, I didn't have the feeling that it had a locus. It
was much more of a kind of general thing. And then I had
the feeling that he thought this of the boy.

Dr. Searles: But is it conceivable to you that you were hating
him intensely, or that the hate was something in which you
were participating?

Therapist: I can't say. Because I was, I think, more stunned because I hadn't seen this.

In the course of the therapy, the patient revealed that his parents, especially his mother, had beaten him severely when he was
younger. As the therapist described it in supervision, ". . . it was the
spoke out of the picket fence—that she beat him with this. At this
point he looked suddenly very cold and really quite frightening and
he said, 'She nearly killed me and it didn't hurt her a bit. She beat
me until I was as big as she was, and then she stopped. . . . She has
no conscience; therefore neither do I. How can she wonder why
I'm here?' " The parents explained to the therapist that it was "only
a few hits on the back of his legs with a rod"; but the mother talked
of this in some detail and went off into much laughter about her
son's description of being beaten.

The mother, a wan, shabbily dressed woman, who was described
as looking as though she had just stepped off a boatload of immi-
grants, would suddenly come alive in tirades about Americans, pour-

ing out hatred and envy of those who had more material possessions than she. Also, in an interview with the therapist, she became carried away in a psychotic kind of excited laughter in describing how omnipresent her mother-in-law used to be during visits to the marital home. "She used to follow us all over the house . . . right up to the bed. About the only place we were ever alone was in bed, and his mother used to try to get in there, too."

She had worked as an aide in another psychiatric hospital, and was quick to relegate her son to the category of nonpersons such as she considered mentally ill patients to be. When told that her son had come not to want the usual weekend visit from his parents, she immediately observed, "They are hopeless when they refuse to see their parents." At one point in giving the history to the therapist, she suddenly appeared threatened and said, "I'm not going to say any more. I already know from experience [at the sanitarium where she had worked years before] . . . that if they find out you talked about them, they really rip. They tear up the walls . . ." This latter comment, tying in with her son's comment about "the walls" during my interview with him, seemed to spring in part from her fear, and his, at an unconscious level, lest the wall between (meaning the distinction between) fantasy and reality be completely destroyed.

Also, he had said to me, in explanation of why his schoolmates' jibes about his mother had so greatly infuriated him, "No one likes anybody to make fun of a person's mother." It was as though he felt his status as a person to be at stake—a *person* rather than something less than a person, as his mother seemed so ready to conclude.

As more came to light about the mother, it appeared that his own smiling and looking happy when he fell to talking about stabbing, shooting, and other forms of bloodshed was in part due to his feeling happily immersed in identification with his mother, who so often in his upbringing would go off unreachably into her private, apparently comparably violent, fantasies.

As the treatment relationship developed, one of his persistent reactions to the therapist consisted in his perceiving her as an obstacle to his having unlimited privileges, unlimited freedom. In this regard, it appeared that he was reacting to her much as his fantasy-ridden mother had reacted to him as an unwanted child, an obstacle the reality of which recurrently prevented her being freely and continually immersed in exciting, violent fantasies. He had much reason to feel that it was his own aliveness, his own existence, that accounted for his mother's more customary demeanor of depressed deadness. It was as though any sign of his own aliveness interrupted, did violence to, her immersion in her fantasy world; this world was suddenly destroyed each time she had to attend to him. By the same token, he was evidently led to feel that, in subsequent relationships, only if he were violent or threatening violence would he be, in the view of other persons, anything more than part of the woodwork—as if only by that means could he make the supposedly oblivious others become aware of his existence.

The excerpts from my interview with him suggest a poignant severing of his efforts to identify with his father as a male. In addition, the parents described with amusement how much it had upset him when the father, at home, would teasingly walk with the hip-swinging, mincing gait of a girl. In the words of the therapist, "If Raymond tried to tell him how much it bothered him, his father would say no, it didn't really bother him." Additional data suggested that when the patient attempted to find in the father a real person with whom to relate, such as the fantasy-ridden, depressed mother could not adequately provide, he was faced with the threat of becoming the rapist of the father, as the agent of the mother's phallic strivings.

These historical data about the father linked up with my reaction upon learning one morning, on my weekly visit to Sheppard a few weeks following my interview with this patient, at a time when I was prominent among the persons whom he was hating, that he had just escaped from the hospital. I had innumerable frightened fantasies that he would come to my private office or my home and shoot me. Other data, with which I need not burden the reader, inescapably made me see that, however much basis in reality there was for this fear, my own unconscious passive homosexual longings had been aroused by my interview with him; I could triangulate, although not actually feel, the desire to be sexually "shot" by him. I shall never forget the relief I felt, late that evening on my return home, to see on the table inside the front door a note from my wife, conveying a telephone message which had come from the Director of In-Patient Services while I was driving home: "Delaney is back home safe with his mother."

The subsequent course of Delaney's treatment gave little cause for amusement, however. He was brought back promptly to the hospital by his parents and subsequently committed. But despite much skillful work by his therapist, who provided a rare combination of strength, courage, and ability to perceive and relate to his dependent needs, Delaney's violence in action became sufficiently serious so that the staff was no longer divided between those who regarded this as a real and frightening problem and those who scoffed at it as being nothing but a cloak worn by a frightened boy. For example, he made a preplanned and serious attack, from behind, on his male administrator one day when the administrator was walking down the corridor toward morning rounds. He hit the administrator hard, and it required two or three attendants to drag the patient back into the seclusion room. On another occasion, he made a similar attack upon a male patient, and four attendants were needed to get him back into the seclusion room. Incidentally, one evidence of his poor distinction between fantasy and reality was his way of raging to the therapist about the administrator. He would say to her, "*Look at Edwards* [the administrator]. . . ," just as though Dr. Edwards were a tangible presence with them in the therapist's office.

As the months went by it became necessary for the therapist to see him in a cold wet-sheet pack. After two such sessions he again ran away, was found and taken by his parents to another sanitarium, and ran away from there and joined the marines without divulging his psychiatric background. Our last bit of information about him was a telephone call to the therapist from an official at an army prison, stating that this man had stabbed a fellow marine three times, that his victim was barely surviving, and that an investigation was under way to determine whether Delaney was mentally competent to stand trial. The therapist and I agreed that he had finally committed the violent act which we both had known he eventually would. Again I want to emphasize the aspect of relief, of certainty, which this clearly afforded me and, I felt, the therapist also. It was as though the distinction between the patient's actualized murderousness and our own murderous fantasies and feelings was now clear beyond anyone's questioning it.

The experience with this patient highlights a number of psychodynamic aspects of violence in schizophrenia. His nondifferentiation between the human and nonhuman, animate and inanimate ingredients of his perceptual world, this nondifferentiation being an unconscious defense against otherwise unbearably ambivalent feelings of hatred and love, was recurrently in evidence. He expressed chillingly dispassionate murderousness toward "my target," as if his classmate were an inanimate thing, comparable with the views his mother expressed of psychiatric patients and the view she presumably had had of him in his childhood. The psychologist found in the Rorschach evidence that the patient had an unconscious self-percept as a gnat; and the therapist found that he reacted to her, in part, as an essentially nonhuman obstacle to his having unlimited privileges.

His appreciation of the useful limit-setting, differentiating function of my confrontation of his murderousness was expressed, in a displaced fashion, by his sincere appreciation of the "pretty walls" of the room. Such walls between fantasy and reality, and between herself and him, his mother evidently had feared he would destroy ("They tear up the walls").

Both the therapist and I, in relating to him, evidently had mobilized in ourselves such intensely conflicting feelings of love and of murderous hatred that a regressive dedifferentiation occurred in our respective ego functioning, such that we attributed to the patient our own murderous hatred, and unconsciously hoped that he would give vicarious expression to our own violence, so as to restore the wall between him and us. More broadly put, such a patient evokes in one such intensely conflicting feelings that, at an unconscious level, one's ego functioning undergoes a pervasive dedifferentiation: one loses the ability deeply to distinguish between one's self and the patient, and between the whole realms of fantasy and reality. Thus the patient's committing of a violent act serves not only to distinguish between one's own "fantasied" violence and his "real" violence but, more generally, serves to restore, in one, the distinction between the whole realms of fantasy and outer reality.

Case 2

Mr. Leonard Myers, a 25-year-old salesman, had been hospitalized repeatedly in a series of institutions, over the preceding eight years, for chronic paranoid schizophrenia. He had been fired from various jobs because of his belligerence. At home he had become increasingly abusive verbally, and increasingly slovenly, lying about naked. His father had threatened repeatedly to throw him out of the house, but his overprotective mother each time had intervened. She herself had required psychiatric hospitalization at one period, and both she and her son had received electroshock treatment, at different times, from the same psychiatrist.

The patient had come to spend several days and nights consecutively in pool rooms, and in his grandiose belligerence had gotten himself beaten up there. He had begun driving recklessly during the preceding year: "I closed my eyes—I was going about 80 miles per hour—I closed my eyes and counted to ten. And I opened them and was kind of surprised when nothing happened."

His first psychotic episode had occurred at age 17. Two years later he married a girl during her second pregnancy by him. (For her first pregnancy they had obtained an illegal abortion.) This pregnancy went to term and a daughter was born. While the daughter was still in infancy, he became violently angry at her and attacked her, slamming her against her pillow several times and causing serious neurological injury which subsequently required more than one brain operation and which left a permanent strabismus in the child, now six years of age. His wife meanwhile separated from him, and retained custody of the daughter.

It was evident that his parents had allowed him, figuratively, to get away with murder. He idealized his father as a great family man, a strong and good provider, in contrast to his own sorry record as a father, but said that "he gives in too much to my mother, who coddles me." He said that, for example, he had just heard from his mother that she had prevailed upon the father to buy him a new car when he left Sheppard. It was evident that the overprotective mother, whose covert malevolence the patient had particular resistance to discovering in the course of his therapy, had never permitted him to find firm limits in his father. In this family setting, which so hindered the development of firm object relations and thus the achievement of individuation on his part, it was evident that just as his parents did not exist as firm external objects for him, neither did he for them. Poignantly, he once recalled to his therapist that the only time either of his parents had ever turned to him for his opinion about some family matter was when his father consulted him as to whether the mother should receive electroshock treatment.

The report of the diagnostic conference on his admission to Sheppard states:

> ... He instantly revealed disorganized thought and speech, and during the entire interview remained rather restless, apprehensive, impulsive, aggressive, obviously trying to conceal murderous rage. His paranoid trend ... was obvious, although not systematized. Inasmuch as this interview seemed to induce great fear in the patient, it was discontinued after a few minutes.

Seven months after Mr. Myers's admission, at the staff conference in which the therapist presented his history prior to my interview with him, I felt an atmosphere of unusually electric tension; it was as if all of us present were acutely aware that this was an unusually frightening, formidably ill patient. I myself felt quite afraid of going into the one-way-mirror viewing room for my interview with him. When he came in he proved to be a burly, highly volatile-looking man who spoke in an impulsive, staccato fashion, with many liquidly restless physical movements. His eyes were narrow, shifty, and blinking rapidly; he seldom looked at me.

I had felt much ambivalence as to whether to shake hands, at the outset, with this man who had come so near to killing his infant daughter, but I did so, with little or no warmth, when he walked in. Throughout the interview I was unaware, as I realized later, of any rage, condemnation, or contempt toward him, and instead sat passively in my armchair.

Now, to present some passages beginning about one-third of the way through the interview:

> Dr. Searles: How did your parents react to this incident of your—injuring your daughter—
>
> Mr. Myers [quickly interjects]: They didn't know about it.
>
> Dr. Searles: —damned near killing your daughter?
>
> Mr. Myers [again quickly]: They didn't know about it.
>
> Dr. Searles: They didn't know about it?
>
> Mr. Myers: I told my father and he said, "It is not true. You didn't do it." He doesn't want me to think I did and I know I did.
>
> Dr. Searles: He would rather you would be crazy, huh, on that score, and not know reality?
>
> Mr. Myers: He would rather me feel that I didn't—yeah—that I didn't know reality that it happened, and I *know* it happened. I'm *sure* it happened [tone of healthy self-assertiveness].
>
> Dr. Searles: Well, but it's—what?—as though *he* can't bear to think that it happened?
>
> Mr. Myers: Maybe that's it. I am not sure. It could be that.
>
> Dr. Searles: Have you noticed that in him?
>
> Mr. Myers: This was a couple of years ago. I don't really remember. He loved my—my daughter.
>
> Dr. Searles: You are putting that in the past tense.
>
> Mr. Myers: Yes, because he said he gave her up because she is not my baby anymore.
>
> Dr. Searles: Not yours, or his?
>
> Mr. Myers: His. That's just—the way he talks. He knows it is not [embarrassed, brief laugh]. What I mean is—when the marriage broke up—uh, we used to go over there—*before* the marriage broke up we used to go over there twice a month on Sundays. He was very fond of my *daughter*. And after the marriage broke up we weren't going over there and—my father asked to see her one time, and take her out and buy her some clothes. And my daughter—and my wife said no, so he just gave up trying to see her, said, "She's not my baby anymore." . . .
>
> [Then, a minute or so later—]

Dr. Searles: Your mother—did she show any reaction to being told of it by you, or whatever? What did she say? About your daughter—

Mr. Myers: I don't think I told her. Just my father.

Dr. Searles: Why didn't you tell your mother?

Mr. Myers: I don't know. I didn't tell *any*body—I mean, it was such a serious thing. One day—I was living in my parents' house for six months without working or doing anything and I just felt guilty and I decided to tell my father what happened. He wouldn't believe it and wouldn't let me try—to make me not believe it, that it happened. But I know it did. I think my wife knows it—that it did, too.

Dr. Searles: You think she does?

Mr. Myers: I think she knows but I never told her. I think the doctor might have told her because she was beaten about the head and there were bruises. This is just an assumption; I don't know—whether she—whether she knows *I* did it or not. . . . It didn't show up in convulsions and spitting up of the milk until two months later. . . . She was about two months old when I picked her up by the neck and banged her head on the pillow.

Dr. Searles: You say it as though it *still* in a way feels kind of *good*. Do you feel you *would* like to do that with *some*body?

Mr. Myers: No—yes, *some*body.

Dr. Searles: Well, anybody come to mind?

Mr. Myers: Yes, one person. Corbin [another patient on his ward]. . . . I feel hostile towards him. . . . I have had the desire to—to—to, uh, hit him in the mouth. I never have. I can control my anger lately much better than I used to.

Dr. Searles: You haven't noticed the slightest irritated feeling toward *me* so far?

Mr. Myers: Yes, I have; a little bit.

Dr. Searles: How does it—make itself felt? What are your thoughts or feelings?

Mr. Myers: There *are* no thoughts right now. I am just trying to get as much in as we can. I don't think it is important whether I like you or dislike you. I don't even know you.

Dr. Searles: You don't? How long does it take you—

Mr. Myers [interrupting]: I'll probably never see you again.

Dr. Searles: Probably so [agreeing]—and—I must—I will be as candid as I *can* be: frankly, I *hope so*. To be quite honest with you, you kind of frighten me. . . . You strike me as an extremely impatient guy. Do you feel you are?

Mr. Myers: Yes.

[A minute or so later, after further conversation—]

Dr. Searles: You didn't feel hurt when I said frankly I hope I don't see you again?

Mr. Myers: I was a little surprised [tone of covert disapproval].

Dr. Searles: Doesn't sound like a very big person—for me to say that?

Mr. Myers: No.

Dr. Searles: Doesn't? Is either of your parents afraid of you?

Mr. Myers: I don't think so [confident tone].

Dr. Searles: The idea has never occurred to you, though, has it?

Mr. Myers: Probably has.

Dr. Searles: You sound as though it hasn't crossed your mind.

Mr. Myers: I say it probably has occurred to me. I don't think it's a big problem [offhand tone]. I'm not the kind of person who goes around hurting other people. I did it once, and uh—I think the reason was I was afraid—afraid to face responsibility. I wanted to get rid of what [N.B. as though referring to something inanimate] was making me feel obligated to work every week—to be uptight about everything. [There was much evidence, from other portions of this interview and elsewhere, that throughout the patient's life the father had been a highly compulsive worker; it appears here as though the patient found intolerable the only kind of father-identity he had known.]

[Then, after a minute or so of further dialogue—]

Mr. Myers: . . . I *am* curious why you said you hoped you would never see me again. You said you were afraid of me. I can't see why you would be afraid of me. I don't understand it.

Dr. Searles: It happened *once* that you wanted to kill your daughter. It seems like a completely isolated instance, huh?

Mr. Myers: Yes, it does. Because I haven't done anything since then—violent, physical. This was—five years ago.

Dr. Searles: . . . Well, you come in—with somewhat of a—of a bully look about you. You look in better physical shape than *I* feel; you look, uh—you are certainly younger. I think I would have a difficult time with you in a physical tussle— see? You're *impatient* as all hell. You strike—you strike me as very *volatile*—impatient and volatile. These are *some* of the things about you. Then I may be *projecting* onto you some of my *own* problems because I was very afraid I would kill [a member of my parental family] . . . so that I may be afraid of *myself* still, more than I thought, and I may be taking it out on you.

By the end of the interview, some ten minutes later, each of us had come to feel so close to the other that we mutually expressed the hope that we *would* see one another again. I found myself feeling deeply moved at the end of the interview.

In the conference-discussion period following the interview, the therapist reported that he had felt jolted by my telling Mr. Myers that I hoped I would not see him again because I was afraid of him. This set the therapist to wondering why he himself had never felt afraid to be in a room with the patient, and he went on to wonder whether he had promoted unwittingly a dependent relationship on the patient's part such as the overprotective, subtly malevolent mother had with him, as a protection against the patient's violence.

This interview proved, in retrospect, one of the most memorable teaching interviews I have ever had, in being utilized by both patient and therapist in a highly effective way during the subsequent course of their work together. Two subsequent interviews at yearly intervals, as well as occasional informal reports to me from the therapist in the interim, substantiated this. The patient is now living outside the hospital, while continuing to work with the same therapist.

The interview I have detailed seemed to have helped appreciably to undermine the therapist's unconscious denial of his fear of the patient, and thus to enable the continuing fact of the patient's violent urges, and his own fear of them, to be explored in the psychotherapy. Listening to the tape of my interview with Mr. Myers I was amused at my own uncharacteristically patient and soothing manner. I have found over and over again, in my own and in my colleagues' work with such patients, that one's fear is for a long time largely dissociated, but that this dissociated and deepening fear causes an increasing, subtle, and unrecognized constriction of one's freedom to speak and to feel. One's own unconscious murderous rage at the patient for thus throttling one's freedom becomes projected upon him. One then tends to feel only that one is afraid of him, not of one's own quite unavailable murderous rage toward him. Thus one inevitably comes to behave toward him over a prolonged period as did his subtly malevolent mother.

One can surmise that it was just such a malevolently constricting, infantilizing, and infantile mother whom the infant daughter had represented to the patient in his nearly fatal attack upon her. Further, this act, stigmatizing him as so terribly bad a father, enabled him to preserve some little portion of his own long-cherished image of his father as being, relatively at least, a good father, rather than seeing him as a father with his own problems of unconscious destructiveness. Surely it was not coincidental that this father's successful and steady work functioning had gone on in a context of either the mother's or the son's having to be hospitalized repeatedly for mental breakdowns.

Case 3

The following brief report is presented in order to highlight two psychodynamic points which I consider to be of general validity among schizophrenic patients: first, the degree to which rigid superego standards preclude subjective aliveness; and second, the function of violence in providing the patient with a subjective realization of his own aliveness, as a relief from the superego-enforced subjective deadness which customarily grips him.

Today at —— Clinic I saw an ambulatory schizophrenic young man who had had two hospitalizations, the most recent of them ending only about two months ago. He described his having been shot at, while over at —— University, and said that he had a mark on his thigh to prove it. I regard this experience as having been clearly delusional, nonetheless. He said that because his life was being threatened, he had pretended to be violently drunk in order to get placed within the refuge of a hospital. He had succeeded, as he described it, in getting himself taken to D.C. General Hospital, but upon admission there had been "jumped" by five male attendants, after they had had him take his clothes off. He evidently still has the delusion that they were bent on raping him. He knows karate, and this proved to be one of the most tense interviews I have ever had before a group of residents. There were a number of times during the interview when I felt it essential to be very casual lest he jump me, and it was evident that he was an extremely threatened person, by reason of his projection of both his murderous and homosexual feelings.

To this man violence evidently means throwing off a subjective feeling of deadness. He said of his mother, "She is *alive*," and there was momentarily a tremendous aliveness in his tone as he said that. It was clear that his view of her is in marked contrast to his own experience of himself. He is an extremely rigid person with tremendously rigid superego standards. His therapist's father died very recently,[3] and in terms of this patient's superego, he feels that any person *must* feel shock and grief at the death of his father—although it is very evident that, if anything, he himself tended to feel only vengeful satisfaction at the death of his own hated father two years ago. Secondly, according to his superego standards, a "mature man" would not reveal outwardly anything of his grief under these circumstances; thus, he expressed the conviction that when he does see his therapist next, his therapist will be feeling grief but will not be showing any of it. These are but two examples of many which pointed up the tremendous rigidity of this man's superego, which precludes any real aliveness. It was apparent that he experienced a submerged kind of excitement when talking about the various things (a mixture of reality and delusion) that have happened to him; at one level, these apparently had the quality of a lively, exciting playfulness.

He was an extremely well-dressed young man of perhaps 30 who, when I first saw him, I immediately assumed to be an obsessive-compulsive individual. Rather soon, however, it became evident that I was dealing with a schizophrenic person. The look on his face combined grief, of a locked-in sort typical of schizophrenic patients, locked in with a great deal of repressed rage, vindictive satisfaction (as, for example, over his father's death), and intense contempt toward people, whom he seemed clearly to equate with insects or germs.

As an example of his apparent absence of conscious emotion, he seemed genuinely unaware of feeling, or of having

---

[3] The patient had already been informed of this. The therapist, one of the residents, was therefore out of town at this point, and I was exploring with the patient his feeling about the death of his therapist's father, the consequent absence of the therapist now, and the prospect of his seeing the therapist upon the latter's return.

ever felt, any *fear*, except for one—he had been afraid when the police had come to his apartment to investigate his pretended drunkenness, for they were armed. But it was evident throughout the interview that he is filled with dissociated fear and, in fact, terror.[4] He stated that he had had infectious hepatitis prior to his first psychiatric hospitalization, "and the sheets were yellow," he added, as though by way of emphasizing how severe the jaundice had been. In essence, he is a man who is so convinced that to feel any fear is by definition cowardice—figuratively speaking, yellowness—that he has been unaware of any but the tiniest bit of the tremendous fear that clearly fills him, and instead, with hallucinatory exaggeration, may have perceived the sheets as being literally[5] and completely yellow.

Case 4

Mrs. Joan Glaser, a 25-year-old mother of two living children (a daughter of five and a half and a son of three years), had been admitted to the hospital five months previously after having drowned, two days before, her third child, an infant daughter, two months of age. Mrs. Glaser herself was the younger of two siblings, with a brother about three years older than herself. After the births of each of the two older children she had had a postpartum depression lasting a few months. This third child had not been wanted by either her or her husband. Immediately upon her return home following the delivery, she had started voicing such thoughts as, "It seems that I have no more energy left for that child. . . . It is too much. I am tied down." "I had forgotten how bad it was to have a baby. . . . I cannot cope." "Let's put the baby away for a while." "I love the baby but I cannot take care of her." She tried to persuade

---

[4] It appears that a schizophrenic individual may experience the *outer* world as being intensely *threatening* without feeling that he possesses *fear within* himself. As so frequently happens in schizophrenic experience, the disturbance is perceived as being entirely *outside* him.

[5] I do not doubt that there was a nucleus of literal reality in his perception of the sheets, but his tone and manner in describing them conveyed a hallucinatory exaggeration as well.

a neighbor to take the baby, explaining that she wanted to give her
away for good. Also, she would say, "I cannot raise her. I love all
children. I cannot harm her; I love her." Once in a while she would
go into the baby's room and stare at her for a long time without
moving or speaking. She was also seen staring into space at times.
Her mother-in-law, who had been called into the home by the husband to help take care of the children and the home at the time of
the delivery, remained there.

On returning from work one evening, the husband got the impression, from the way his agitated wife was behaving, that she had
smothered the baby with a pillow. She had not; but he was now
sufficiently concerned to have her hospitalized. She was then hospitalized, elsewhere; but to his surprise, he received word after only
three days that she was now all right, and she was discharged to
her home. Not long thereafter, while giving the infant a bath, the
patient "blacked out," and when she came to, the infant had
drowned in the tub.

At the time of this interview, the patient was persistently expressing to her therapist her conviction that she was now well and able
to return to her husband and her two living little children, and it
was my impression that all concerned, husband and hospital staff
alike, were more or less inclined to leave hands off and let it go at
that. I sensed in myself, and surmised to be present in my colleagues at the residents' teaching conference, the primitive fear and
awe which, I felt, are aroused in anyone by a mother who has killed
her own child; I had never interviewed such a person before.

Her diagnosis at the time of her admission was schizophrenic
reaction, schizo-affective type. I found her to be a woman of average size, not openly psychotic now but with a relatively impassive,
detached, and somewhat childlike, sheltered demeanor. I shall now
give some of the exchanges which occurred during our half-hour
recorded interview before a one-way viewing mirror:

Mrs. Glaser: . . . my father is still living. He is quite old—in fact,
he is 80 years old. He is an inspiration to me.
Dr. Searles: To live long?—an inspiration to live long?
Mrs. Glaser: Well, it's amazing how long he *has* lived and stayed
in such good health. Before the baby was born—I assume

[said as an aside, in the dispassionate tone of an autopsy report] you know I'm here partially due to the death of the infant.

Dr. Searles: Yeah—I would say *primarily*; that was my thought. Yeah. Before then, what?—before the birth of the baby—?

Mrs. Glaser: Yes, my father had a stroke and this was quite a blow to me.

Dr. Searles: He'd always been so well?

Mrs. Glaser: Yes. He'd always been well. He'd never been sick, and of course it was—I couldn't go to him because the baby was due to be born too—you know, too soon for me to go to him. I—I know the mistakes I made now. I—after the—baby was born I had the postpartum blues again, and—we learned we were going to be moved and somehow it was too much for me, I guess, and I—relied on my mother-in-law and leaned on everybody too much. I think I was—almost making them sick by being so—un—able to—control myself and my emotions.

Dr. Searles: When you said you relied on your mother-in-law I kinda got some impression that perhaps you feel she let you down?

Mrs. Glaser [quickly and protectively]: No, not at all. She helped as much as she possibly could.

Dr. Searles: Well, she didn't keep you from murdering your baby, you know [bluntly, and by way of reminder]. I don't know whether you feel she let you down in *that* sense, huh?

Mrs. Glaser: Why did you use the word "murder" my baby? [tone of surprise, but much softer, more personal, than when she had spoken of "the death of the infant"]

Dr. Searles: Because I understood this is what happened—that you drowned your infant, huh? [in tone of stating the obvious] I mean, maybe there's some more euphemistic way of putting it; but isn't this the fact?

Mrs. Glaser [subdued tone]: Yes.

Dr. Searles: Well, this is why I used it. Why do you ask why I used it? [in tone of vigorously consolidating this newly won territory]

Mrs. Glaser: The word just—

Dr. Searles: "Murder"? You prefer not to think in those terms?

Mrs. Glaser: I can never forget it [weeping].

Dr. Searles: Well, do you feel that your mother-in-law let you down in that sense, perhaps?—she didn't prevent you from doing it?

Mrs. Glaser: Well, I asked her to take the other children for a while, and I should have taken the walk with them instead.

Dr. Searles: Then *she* would have murdered the baby, or—?

Mrs. Glaser: No, no; I hardly think so.

Dr. Searles: It wouldn't be like her to do that?

Mrs. Glaser: No.

Dr. Searles: She's a very kind person.

Mrs. Glaser [quickly]: Very kind—she's a very kind person and my husband is a very kind person [tone of subdued resentment and bitterness].

Dr. Searles: Sort of infuriatingly kind, or what?

Mrs. Glaser: No.

Dr. Searles: Have you wondered, for example, why your husband hasn't killed *you*?

Mrs. Glaser: Regardless of what happened he still loves me very much [as though reciting something].

Dr. Searles: How does *that* make you feel?—have ya any idea?

Mrs. Glaser: Well, it makes me feel good to know that under the circumstances he still loves me [still as though reciting].

Dr. Searles: Does it cause any other feelings, besides feeling good?

Mrs. Glaser: Well, it—it helps to know that somebody still cares [weeping].

Dr. Searles: He seems to be the only one who still does?

Mrs. Glaser: No, my mother-in-law still cares—my two children still care.

Dr. Searles: How do you know? You say you haven't seen them?

Mrs. Glaser: I talked with them on the phone.

Dr. Searles: They are aware that you killed their—?

Mrs. Glaser: No, I'm quite sure they—don't know that—I don't know what they think.

Dr. Searles: You don't know what your husband or mother-in-law has told them? You have a daughter and son, right?—the older one is the daughter.

Mrs. Glaser: Yes.

Dr. Searles: Your son is about three and a half?

Mrs. Glaser: Yes. My oldest daughter was six Friday.

Dr. Searles: I notice this constellation—of a daughter, and then a son, and then an infant daughter you had. This infant daughter then had a brother three years older than she?

Mrs. Glaser: Yes.

Dr. Searles: And you have a brother five years older—is that right?

Mrs. Glaser: No; my brother is about three and a half years older than I am.

Dr. Searles: Three and a half? Ya see, I was wondering about the repeating of history thing—whether this infant daughter of yours represented something of yourself in terms of births: girl baby born into a home where this brother—huh?

Mrs. Glaser: No. I just didn't want to admit to myself that I was as sick as I was.

Dr. Searles: And nobody else perceived it?—nobody else perceived that you were?

Mrs. Glaser: Yes, they did, but—uh—and my husband—

Dr. Searles [interrupts with intensity]: I wonder how in *God's* name, then, they let you stay at home?

Mrs. Glaser: I don't know.

Dr. Searles: Have you ever *wondered?*—have you ever *wondered* why?

Mrs. Glaser: Well, I guess they didn't realize I was quite as sick as I was.

Dr. Searles: You think they still realize it, or that they still fail to realize it?

Mr. Glaser: I don't know if it is possible to get 100 percent well again. I feel like I'm well again [pleading but unconvincing tone].

Dr. Searles: You feel you *understand* why you killed your daughter, is that right? I mean, to *me* at least, this would be the primary thing—the test, really, of whether you're *well*, you see, and not to be "back-out-with-your-family" [as though to say just for the sake of being so, as a matter of form]. Have you thought in those terms?—have you thought that that would be a criterion of whether you are well, whether it's safe for you to be at home?

Mrs. Glaser: Yes [small, unconvincing voice].

Dr. Searles: You have thought in those terms? So, you feel you are well [ironically]. What's your explanation?—how do you account for your having killed your infant daughter? [persistently]

Mrs. Glaser: I don't know how I could have done such a thing [in a voice once again broken by weeping].

Dr. Searles: Um, you aren't *well*, isn't it?—isn't that the fact?

Mrs. Glaser: I *wasn't* at the time, no.

Dr. Searles: You don't know how you could have done such a thing.

Mrs. Glaser: I think about her *constantly*; I think about her *constantly*.

Dr. Searles: Think about her living, or dead, or—how do you think of her?

Mrs. Glaser: I think of her as—as—something that was very lovely that I couldn't see at the time [voice very broken with weeping].

Dr. Searles: "*Some thing*"—you think of her as something?

Mrs. Glaser: As a little—

Dr. Searles [interrupts]: —that was lovely.

Mrs. Glaser [weeping]: I'm sorry, Doctor [apologetically].

Dr. Searles: Do you feel it is an *offense* to a psychiatrist to *weep* in his presence about these matters, or what? Why do you say you are sorry? I don't get that [exasperatedly]. Do you want some of this stuff, huh? [holding out some Kleenex to her]

Mrs. Glaser: No; that's all right. I am very sorry.

Dr. Searles: You say "something," ya see, and I wondered if *that* has some significance: it was hard for you to grasp or to feel that she was a living person, a living creature, a living creature. Do you suppose if you felt she was a *thing*—

Mrs. Glaser [interrupts]: Oh me, I didn't mean *something*. I meant she's—she was a little doll—she was a very pretty baby.

Dr. Searles: "She was a little doll." A doll is a thing, is it not?

Mrs. Glaser: That's right.

Dr. Searles: Is there perhaps no significance in the words you use, or *is* there maybe something that you and I can both— learn, you see—from the way it comes out—"something beautiful"—"beautiful doll"?—huh? [persistently; then, turning away from this effort—] When you were a child, did you have a doll, or—?

Mrs. Glaser: Yes, I did [comfortable, unpressured tone now].

Dr. Searles: Do you have any memories of playing with your doll?

Mrs. Glaser: Yes, I do.

Dr. Searles: Could I hear—let's hear whatever comes to your mind.

Mrs. Glaser: Well, I can remember—playing with a doll like you would a real baby—and bathing the doll and—although

I usually—didn't use water; I just—used a washcloth or something like a sponge bath.

Dr. Searles: Usually didn't use water, huh? Any idea why not?

Mrs. Glaser: Well, when I was little the dolls weren't made of the same material as they are now and you couldn't really put them in water. [pause of several seconds; then, in slightly broken voice—] I guess I should feel very fortunate that I have the second chance to go back home.

Dr. Searles: Had that thought not occurred to you before? [gentle tone]

Mrs. Glaser: Well, I guess I—feel like maybe I don't *deserve* to go back [crying heartbrokenly now; this is the one point in the interview when, in playing back the tape, I felt like weeping in compassion for her; I do not recall whether I felt so during the interview itself].

[A minute or two later on in the dialogue—]

Dr. Searles: . . . Let's see, . . . you mentioned your mother died—she died in '57—do you remember *her* as being a kind person, much like your—mother-in-law?

Mrs. Glaser: Yes, she was very kind—they both were alike in some respects,—that they were—uh—very much interested in the house, it had to be just so all of the time.

Dr. Searles: "They both were"—you mean your mother and father?

Mrs. Glaser: Uh-huh. My father was a building contractor. He was very good—he was a perfectionist on how he built his homes. [A few minutes later in the interview—] You see, after she [the now-dead daughter] was born I went to—uh, I was doing fine and then—I started this postpartum blues again, and my husband had talked with my—doctor who had delivered the baby and—uh, they prescribed some medicine for me—but it was—too powerful and when it wore off I would be twice as nervous as before,—so I stopped taking the medicine—I still had bad thoughts towards the baby or myself—either one.

Dr. Searles: Still had bad thoughts"—you hadn't mentioned to me that you had found yourself having what you call "bad thoughts" toward the baby?

Mrs. Glaser: Yes.

Dr. Searles: —and toward yourself?

Mrs. Glaser: Yes.

Dr. Searles: When—uh, prior to the baby's birth—or—?

Mrs. Glaser: No. Afterwards.

Dr. Searles: "Bad thoughts"—what do you refer to?—"bad thoughts"?

Mrs. Glaser: Well, just the fact we had another baby and I found out we were going to be moving—leaving the area, and it was a question of leaving—leaving our friends behind—

Dr. Searles: Are those bad thoughts?

Mrs. Glaser: No, *that* isn't bad thoughts; but I felt life would be much simpler without the baby.

Dr. Searles: Well, was that a bad thought? [disbelievingly]

Mrs. Glaser: *Yes,* I think it *was*—a very *sick* thought [emphatically].

Dr. Searles: Realistic in a way, wasn't it?

Mrs. Glaser: My husband put me in a hospital and I—*thought* I was all right and I *left*—that was the mistake I made.

Dr. Searles: Now wait a minute—your husband—you would doubt that your *husband* would ever permit *himself* to have such a thought at that time, for instance,—how much simpler life would have been had this baby not been born?

Mrs. Glaser: No; he didn't have thoughts like that [emphatically, and clearly resenting my question].

Dr. Searles: How do you know? [persistently]

Mrs. Glaser: I know he loved her very much.

Dr. Searles: You can read his mind?

Mrs. Glaser: No; but he *told* me he did, and I *know* he did [insistently, vehemently, and pleadingly, as though I were trying to convince her that her own father did not really love her as a child].

Dr. Searles: Well, I *still* question—

Mrs. Glaser [interrupts]: He wanted to take care of her and he liked to see her.

Dr. Searles: I still question whether you *know* what is in a person's *thoughts*, from what they *say* or the way they *behave*. You see, you have been speaking to me today about what you call bad thoughts, huh? But you—feel confident your husband would never have such—such a thought, huh?

Mrs. Glaser: No [confirmatively].

Dr. Searles: Hard to imagine that he would ever have a thought about how much simpler life would be, if he didn't have you or any of the children?

Mrs. Glaser: Well, of course nobody could *prove* that [loud, argumentative tone]; but most people are able to control their thoughts and emotions.

Dr. Searles: *You* didn't accept the *thoughts*, did you?—I mean, you thought they were bad just because you had such *thoughts*, huh?

Mrs. Glaser: I should have stayed in the hospital in New Orleans longer.

[A couple of minutes later in the interview—]

Dr. Searles: You would—uh—doubt that *your* mother ever had occasion for any such feelings at *all* about *any*thing?

Mrs. Glaser: I don't know. She could have had feelings I don't know about.

Dr. Searles: Was it very hard to know *what* she was feeling or thinking?

Mrs. Glaser: She was very dedicated to the family [helplessly, as though her mother had been completely unreachable]—the same way my mother-in-law is—they do everything they can for their children and their husbands [sniffing].

[A couple of minutes later—]

Dr. Searles: Let's see, now—your growing up—your mother was very dedicated to—the family, huh?—was she aware of *individuals in* the family? Or do you think she saw the *family* as a unit?

Mrs. Glaser: I think more as a unit—I was not very close to my mother—I was much closer to my father.

Dr. Searles: You say you were not very close to your mother— would you put it among other things—you *hated* her considerably or—

Mrs. Glaser: *No, no*; I didn't [unconvincing protest].

Dr. Searles: Was there hate there?

Mrs. Glaser: No.

Dr. Searles: You feared her?

Mrs. Glaser: Fear her? Yes, fear would be a better word [as though relieved to be off the spot].

Dr. Searles: You *did* fear her; I see [accepting this]. What comes to mind there, as to what you feared in her; let's see what comes up.

Mrs. Glaser: Well, when I went to school I had to come home right away after school, and if I didn't get home right away she would ask where had I been and all this type of thing. I wasn't free to stop in for a Coke or something like that [in tone of feeling sure of father-Dr. Searles's sympathy].

Dr. Searles: I was thinking there of how your infant daughter made you so unfree also, huh?—wouldn't you guess?

Mrs. Glaser: Yes [very soft, subdued tone].

Dr. Searles: You weren't free to stop in as a child growing up—stop in for a Coke the way the other kids did? 'Cause if you did, then she would wonder where you'd been and you'd never hear the end of it—is that the idea?

Mrs. Glaser: Yes. If I just left the room she would ask where I was going [in a tone, again, of confidence in her having father-Dr. Searles's sympathy].

Dr. Searles: I'm conscious, in our session today [said in a tone as though I were her therapist, and as though we would have subsequent sessions], of *interrogating* you—uh, to a degree I interrogate everybody whom I interview here, but I'm more conscious of it with you. Now, I gather *she* used to *interrogate* you a great deal—huh? [pause of a few seconds; no audible reply from her] I'm still a *little* puzzled as to what was to be feared—it was such a maddening thing?—she'd keep interrogating endlessly, would she?

Mrs. Glaser: Well, I can remember when I was even—after I went to college, even when I was *in* college, if I left the room she would ask, "Where are you going?" I might just be going to the bathroom.

Dr. Searles: Did she seem very anxious for you to be out of her sight, for a few minutes, a few seconds?

Mrs. Glaser: It seemed—I think she was overprotective, and I don't want to be that way with my children—if I ever get the chance to be a mother to them again [sniffing].

[A couple of minutes later—]

Mrs. Glaser: . . . No matter how I—*try* I can't go back to that day and change what happened—that's what my mind wants to do. What I did was very, very wrong and very sick [crying].

Dr. Searles: Well, you put it still, there, as though you were a very naughty girl. When you were a child did—did your mother *treat* you as being a naughty girl?

Mrs. Glaser: Not exactly; I guess I've stopped thinking about my childhood. [pause of a few seconds] I guess I think this is costing an awful lot of money and can it—is it—can *I* get well do you think? [demanding tone; loud sniff]

Dr. Searles: I don't know, frankly I don't know [humbly]. But you wonder if you can, huh?

Mrs. Glaser: I *feel* that I am well again—I certainly don't have any bad thoughts again—the ang—any anger I have is all gone [unconvincing tone].

Dr. Searles: I'm very sorry to hear that. You never feel angry at anybody or anything? That to you is *well*? [incredulous tone]

Mrs. Glaser: No, possibly not. But somehow because of what happened I just don't have any anger left in me.

Dr. Searles: Well, maybe that *served* to *express* a very great deal of anger.

Mrs. Glaser: It certainly did, didn't it.

Dr. Searles: At whom—would you say—everybody, or somebody in particular, or—? [pause of several seconds] Any—anyone come to mind?

Mrs. Glaser: No. I certainly didn't *gain* anything by what I did; I *lost* everything [protesting tone].

Dr. Searles: Well, but the thought comes to mind, though; the thought comes to mind. You say you certainly didn't *gain* anything by it and yet the *idea* that possibly one might have gained something by that, that *does* seem to come to mind. You—you say no, that you didn't, but is there any thought about what one conceivably might gain from such an experience?

Mrs. Glaser [tired sigh]: Well, I think I've learned to—if nothing else, to be a lot more loving and kind towards people.

Dr. Searles: You didn't used to feel that you were a loving, kind person?

Mrs. Glaser: No, not all the time—no.

Dr. Searles: Jesus! I find that rather staggering [sigh]. You've learned now to be a loving and kind person *all the time*, huh? Doesn't seem like somewhat of a strain?

Mrs. Glaser: Yes, it is [small voice].

Dr. Searles: Well—are you—well, this the way your husband and mother-in-law are—they're loving and kind all the time, are they?

Mrs. Glaser: Not all the time, I'm sure. My mother-in-law [quavering, resentful tone] seems to be all the time.

Dr. Searles: Your voice quavers when you say that. Does she kind of frighten you?

Mrs. Glaser: No.

Dr. Searles: What do *you* guess—

Mrs. Glaser [interrupting loudly]: I'm very thankful we *have* her. But the only trouble is—

Dr. Searles [interrupting]: You wouldn't want *her* dead, huh?

Mrs. Glaser: No.

Dr. Searles: You've never thought life would be a helluva sight simpler if she would expire?

Mrs. Glaser: No.

Dr. Searles: Never did? [pause of a few seconds] You've heard of people often feeling that their mothers-in-law are intrusions?—you've heard of that.

Mrs. Glaser: I know; but I've never felt that—in fact, I wanted her to come *live* with us.

Dr. Searles: Against your husband's objections—or what?

Mrs. Glaser: No, my *husband* didn't object to it—he wanted her to, too; but she didn't want to.

Dr. Searles: Why not?—is she bashful or something?

Mrs. Glaser: She likes her home and—where she grew up. You can't ask somebody else to give up something if they don't want to. [pause of several seconds] And it shows that I needed her very much.

Dr. Searles: "It shows," huh?, about the—uh—having killed the—baby—shows that, huh?—Is that what showed?

Mrs. Glaser: Partially I think [sniffs]. I certainly don't want anything to happen to my *other* two children.

Dr. Searles: Thought wouldn't even *occur* to you [ironically].

Mrs. Glaser [quickly]: No.

The interview ended a few minutes later. During the subsequent discussion it quickly became clear that there had been a shocked reaction, among the approximately 20 staff members who had been watching the interview, at my having confronted her so directly with the fact of her having murdered her infant daughter. As the therapist himself expressed it, "I was awfully angry with you at first. . . . I was extremely moved during that interview; at first when you talked about the 'murder' I got so furious. . . . Then I realized more and more how much I hated that woman—I could not communicate with her—I was seeing her but I had to deny all those feelings. . . . Then I had the feeling how much I would like to work with her." (Incidentally, to dispel any lingering doubt in the reader's mind, I should emphasize that the therapist indicated that in the course of the psychotherapy it had become clear that Mrs. Glaser had indeed actively drowned her infant during her "blackout.")

I had occasion to serve as a supervisor to the therapist during the patient's several subsequent months in the hospital, before she returned home, and it was my impression that this interview had helped to foster a deep and useful feeling-involvement between patient and therapist, in the course of which her murderousness became more fully explored and resolved than it had been prior to the interview.

In the psychodynamics of this woman's murderous act, as suggested by what occurred during the interview, a number of elements can be discerned.

1. In murdering her daughter she not only was acting out her own largely denied hostility toward the infant, but also was acting out vicariously the also vigorously denied murderousness toward the infant on the part of her husband and mother-in-law, to whom she had telegraphed so clearly her brooding murderousness toward the little girl.

2. The current denial, by not only her husband but also the hospital staff, of the reality of her murderous action was serving to keep under repression much of their fear, awe, and murderously condemnatory feelings toward her. In this regard I noticed in myself, during the first few minutes of the interview, urges to kill her in condemnation for her having murdered her own child; but as the interview continued these intensely negative feelings became unavailable to me—not, I believe, because they had been genuinely resolved, but rather because they had become repressed as being too threatening to me in that situation.

3. She was clearly struggling to preserve idealized images of both her parents, her husband, and her mother-in-law, and to repair an idealized image of herself. It was as though she lived in a world of such images, and, in fact, their preservation had taken priority over the life of her flesh-and-blood infant.

4. There is some reason to presume, from the repeating-of-history sequence of the birth of the little girl with the brother about three years older, that the infant was unconsciously perceived by the patient as her own infant self, and that she, the mother, gave undisguised expression to the murderousness implicit in her own mother's overprotectiveness toward her in her childhood.

5. Presumably the confining infant daughter was also perceived

unconsciously by the patient as being equivalent to the patient's own confiningly overprotective and unconsciously hated mother. It is notable that the birth of this daughter had kept the patient from visiting her beloved father following his stroke; and one may assume that her mother's overprotectiveness during her own childhood had inhibited her access to the father. Recurrently throughout the interview it was clear from the quality of her tearfulness in speaking of her father that her most genuine love was for him. Her cherishing of the love he had felt for her was indirectly revealed in her vigorous defense of her husband as really loving his little daughter.

6. She evidently had not clearly discerned, at an unconscious level, her alive infant daughter as being essentially different from an inanimate doll. Presumably this phenomenon is traceable to her having projected upon the infant a repressed self-image of a doll rather than a living person. Her own mother's overprotectiveness would seem to have fostered a sheltered, doll-like concept of herself, rather than one of being robustly alive.

An overprotective mother, such as this woman had had, tends to give her child a feeling that the child's own aliveness is dangerous—is equivalent to murderousness. The patient made it clear that her mother had behaved as though it were somehow unsafe to let her function on her own. When later, in adult life, the patient murdered her infant upon being left on her own at home by the mother-in-law who had gone out of the house, it was as though the patient were thus confirming her own mother's view of her alive, autonomous self as being a murderous self.

For a number of years I served as a cotherapist with Dr. Lyman C. Wynne in the psychotherapy of a family which included a father suffering from borderline or ambulatory paranoid schizophrenia, a chronically depressed mother, a hebephrenic teenage daughter, and an eight-year-old son who spent most of the time in autistic silence. Violence of various kinds by the various family members was a way of life to them. Of interest here is the abundance of data from the family interviews indicating that the son was led—particularly by his father and his sister—to construe as inherently violent any self-initiated signs of aliveness on his own part. The father and sister would frequently goad him into various forms of violently disruptive behavior during the sessions, then ostensibly chide him while appearing privately delighted with his vicarious expression of their own urges. But at the infrequent moments when he would start to express signs of life of his own, unprompted by them, their response became entirely different. No matter how slight or how inherently sensible and healthily constructive and unviolent his signs of aliveness—his physical movements or his vocalizations—were, his father or sister, or both, would react with savage and threatened reprimands, as though his coming alive were an intolerable intrusion into their state of being. In one session, for example, they repeatedly and sharply reprimanded him whenever he tried to speak or move, and while he was quietly playing with a doll which had a detachable head, arms, and legs, the father leapt over, in a frighteningly violent and urgently threatened manner, to seize and immobilize him. It seemed little wonder that, on the rare occasions when the boy was able to verbalize at length, he revealed that he lived in a world permeated with unpredictable and unmasterable violence and entertained many fantasies of himself as innately and omnipotently violent.

Incidentally, an interesting paper by Leo Rangell (1952), entitled "The Analysis of a Doll Phobia," complements without duplicating some of my comments here. Rangell formulates the material in classical psychoanalytic terms, delineating various of the intrapsychic determinants of the patient's doll phobia, with relatively little emphasis upon the family etiology. He mentions that at the beginning of his work with the neurotic 38-year-old male patient, who had suffered from the phobia since at least the age of five:

> The more lifelike a figure was, the worse it was: and it was particularly the moment of a figure "coming to life" or simulating movement which was the most frightening. . . . To look at the doll was bad enough; to touch or be touched by it was frightening to conceive; to have it rub against his arm, even in thought, was enough to cause sweating and near-panic.

7. It is evident that Mrs. Glaser's murderousness toward her in-

fant daughter had enabled her to force her mother-in-law, who theretofore had been as inaccessibly devoted to the house as the patient's own mother had been, to turn and attend, instead, to the patient's own needs.

8. Lastly, one senses that this woman had unconsciously hated her baby because she had unconsciously feared it as the personification of her own unfulfilled infantile need for her mother—not for the relatively emotionally accessible but inescapably male father who evidently had fulfilled, and perhaps even largely usurped, the mothering role toward her, but for her own biological mother, who had been so unreachably devoted to "the house" and "the family." This basic meaning of the act is best discerned in her saying of it, "It showed I needed her," referring to the mother-figure mother-in-law. To see the patient's murderousness as having been in the service of repressing, and at the same time revealing, a legitimate emotional need with which one can empathize enables one genuinely to feel forgiving of her for her horrifying act. Just as it is necessary to become aware of one's intensely negative feelings toward such a patient in order to work with her, it is also necessary to become able to feel, at a much deeper than merely intellectual level, genuinely forgiving toward her.

Discussion

In earlier papers (1965a) I have elaborated upon various other aspects of violence in schizophrenia, such as the patient's equating individuation with murder of the mother (= therapist), and have noted that his struggle to differentiate between metaphorical and concrete thinking may appear, to both the therapist and the patient himself, as murderously violent behavior. I have described the violence that is done to the therapist's cherished image of himself as a lovingly dedicated physician (1967b), and wish to add here the recurrent impression I have had in recent years, that those patients who tend most violently to damage one's image of oneself—those patients who most successfully make one feel malevolent and subhuman—have no need to resort to physical violence toward one. As regards an additional covertly positive meaning of violent behavior, and related to the last-mentioned point above, I have seen that the urge to physical violence can express an effort to bridge a gulf of emotional unrelatedness. Thus, for example, in the course of my work with a male patient who for months made me feel threatened that he would physically assault me, I came to discover that I had been trying unconsciously to bring about this very event so that I would then have license to come to grips with him physically as—so I now came to see—a relief from the long underlying, weird, and terrible unrelatedness which revealed itself as much more disturbing than any threat of physical—and therefore tangible and relatively human—violence.

We begin to see here, I believe, how inextricably intertwined are love and hate, how intense and ceaseless is the conflict between one's strivings toward oneness with the other person and one's strivings for individuation from him, and how at one moment a violent urge may express a striving to be free and at the next a desire to relate and be at one.

Before concluding this paper I wish to place more emphasis than the above-described clinical material (mostly drawn from single consultation interviews) has provided upon the role of repressed grief as one of the major affective components against which the patient's violence has been serving as an unconscious defense. In previous papers (1965a) I described vengefulness as a defense against grief and separation anxiety, and assaultive behavior, among hebephrenic patients, as representing in part a distorted expression of the fierce grief which has been for so long pent up within them. In the latter connection, for example, when one hebephrenic woman's assaultive behavior, which she had many times manifested in our sessions together, was prevented by my finally and exasperatedly having her placed into a cold wet-sheet pack, she instantly began pouring out grief of an entirely unexpected and truly awesome intensity.

When five years ago I left Chestnut Lodge, one of the patients whom I had to leave was a 51-year-old hebephrenic man with whom I had been working, four hours per week, for 11 years. We had long since come to care for one another so violently that the sessions were often spent in an atmosphere of electric tension much like that prevailing the second before the gunfight at the O.K. Corral. Prior to his continual hospitalization, which had begun some 25 years previously, his chosen forms of sexual activity had included a highly promiscuous and sadomasochistic form of homosexuality in which he and his partner of the night would beat one another, and so sensational a display of transvestitism that he had succeeded in getting himself prohibited by the metropolitan police forces of several of the largest cities in the United States from again setting foot upon any of their respective domains.

Six months before I turned over his psychotherapy to another therapist, I told him this would occur. In those final six months of our sessions together it became evident that our nearly overmastering urges to tear each other physically to pieces were serving, for both of us, as a defense against the prospective loss of one another, which threatened to rend us helplessly into pieces, since we had long before become so much a part of one another. For example, my notes concerning an hour five weeks from the end of our sessions together read:

> Early in this hour, we were so furious at one another that it occurred to me that maybe there should be safeguards—aides, or both of us in cold wet-sheet packs—against our tearing one another to pieces in the closing weeks of our work together. For the past few months, since I told him I'll not be going on with him, I've been as verbally furious and contemptuous at him as he has been for years at me.
>
> But later in the same hour I felt clearly that it is our loss of one another which threatens to tear us to pieces in these final weeks.
>
> He has been looking very grief-stricken indeed of late . . . . He still says, angrily and contemptuously and with infuriating defiance, "I don't know you!" But it is very evident indeed that he *cares* intensely, and that he is deeply convinced that he is the only one of us who cares.
>
> I told him during this same hour, "I'll miss you terribly," and began to burst into tears as I said it, though I caught my-

self. He responded in a warmly understanding way to this—not that he said anything in particular.

[Concerning a session two days later—] His feelings about our coming separation are more explicit than ever. He said today, "I knew you'd leave me sooner or later," looking grieved and suffering. I responded, however, harshly and sarcastically, "Yeah—I've been the height of inconstancy, eh?—only worked with you for 11 years!"

... Whereas a week ago his main emphasis was on "I hate your rotten ass," now it's predominantly and explicitly grief.

In the loneliness of my largely private-analytic-practice existence since I left the Lodge, I find that I not uncommonly talk to myself between sessions with patients. And more often than not I utter at myself, with fond nostalgia, the vitriolic curses which for so many years he poured upon me. My ambivalent regard for him ranks in intensity with that for my long-deceased father, to whom violence was the hallmark of masculinity. Both these men, though long mourned, continue to live—at times disturbingly—within me.

Summary

In this paper I have attempted to highlight the concepts (1) that in schizophrenic patients the tyrannically rigid superego makes for a subjective world of idealized—or, at the opposite extreme, diabolized—objects, a world in which any basic human aliveness is reacted to as innately violent, and therefore to be kept under repression; and (2) that the violent acts which are so typically latent among schizophrenic patients, and not rarely are actually committed by them, are in part referable to the patient's poor differentiation between the living and nonliving, human and nonhuman ingredients of the world in which he lives. Thus the violent act can be thought of as made possible by the patient's failure to distinguish, for example, between a living baby and an inanimate doll, and at the same time as expressing his effort to achieve such a differentiation, as part of his undying struggle to establish more mature ego functioning and a better relationship with reality.

I have attempted here, further, to emphasize how difficult but essential it is for the therapist to spare neither the patient nor himself from his own awareness of feelings which, however uncomfortable and alien to traditional concepts of the compassionate physician, are crucial to the patient's grasping the reality of the latter's own violent urges and actions. I refer here to such feelings in the therapist as fear and murderous condemnation.

In closing, I emphasize that I regard the psychodynamics discussed here as not peculiar to schizophrenic persons, but rather in some degree characteristic of all human beings. I recommend as relevant reading a refreshing little book entitled *Human Aggression*, by a British psychoanalyst, Anthony Storr (1968). The tenor of that book is suggested by the following quotes from it:

> . . . there is so far no convincing evidence that the aggressive response is, at a physiological level, any less instinctive than the sexual response; and, provided that the term aggression is not restricted to actual fighting, aggressive expression may be as necessary a part of being a human being as sexual expression [p. 19].

> . . . if man were not aggressive, he would not be man at all [p. 26].

> . . . it is only when intense aggressiveness exists between two individuals that love can arise [p. 36].

DISCUSSION

John N. Rosen, M.D.

Dr. Searles has rendered a distinct service to the psychodynamic exploration of violence in his study of four patients who were capable of murderous acts. Murder and suicide (self-murder) are the most terrifying human acts with which we are confronted in the gamut of violent behavior, which extends from wars and genocide—where murder is rampant, universal, and even condoned —to the criminal murder that we read about constantly in the newspapers. Although we are all familiar with this kind of human behavior, the dynamics of it are as yet poorly understood. Dr. Searles has attempted to evaluate the nature of these acts through a verbatim presentation of clinical material.

The patients described, although they were unquestionably psychotic at the time of their acting out, do not seem to me to fit into the classical categories of schizophrenia. Perhaps this form of psychosis requires a separate clinical category altogether; I myself find it difficult to know where to place them on the psychotic scale. They have been designated as paranoid schizophrenic, but I do not see in them the organized and systematized delusion which would be necessary for this designation. It is my feeling that the difficulty in accurate diagnosis stems from the lack of study of these kinds of patients.

Dr. Searles's study, which includes verbatim material, seems to me to be the kind of approach necessary to the understanding of the etiology of violent disorders. Unfortunately, it is a little difficult to experience the emotional impact implicit in the material presented and in his reaction to it without having actually been present during the therapeutic dialogue, as were his students. I also think—and this has always been my position—that psychotherapy should be taught by live demonstration before students. It has been my experience in many decades of treating schizophrenics in this way that they do not object to it and as a matter of fact are very often impressed by it and benefit from it. It is a significant therapeutic gain when a patient has enough ego to ask to be treated privately.

On the subject of the therapist's reaction to the patient's expressions of violence, Dr. Searles reports experiencing murderous feelings toward these patients. I myself have found, from the several cases that I have personally treated that were or could have been murderers, that my reaction was not one of violence. I did not feel like killing them. In one instance I recall distinctly that my reaction was great fear; I refer to the patient R. Z., whom I described in one of my earliest papers. He came into my office and opened up a razor, saying that "they" told him he had to cut my throat. I did not feel that I wanted to kill him, but I did feel terrified at the prospect of his cutting my throat. Fortunately for me, I managed to talk him out of it and get possession of the razor. It has been said about my own work, as Eisenbud has pointed out, that I don't seem to become disturbed at being confronted by a patient's unconscious, but I don't think that this is so. I have found that a patient's violent behavior can be very disturbing to me.

I imagine that there are two possible ways of responding to demonstrations of violence: either according to the talionic principle that a murderer should be murdered, or with a more civilized and humane reaction. It is interesting that the Supreme Court of the United States recently decided against capital punishment, or retributive murder by the State. This humane decision by the majority of the Supreme Court would illustrate that the talionic principle of an eye for an eye is not an inevitable human response.

Let me say in closing that Dr. Searles is to be complimented not only for the dynamic material presented in this paper, but also for confronting these violent patients with the reality of their acts. I'm especially impressed that Dr. Searles is willing to deal with patients in this way, knowing that the attitude at Chestnut Lodge when Frieda Fromm-Reichmann was there was one of great concern about disturbing the exquisite sensitiveness of the schizophrenic patient. More clinical material of the kind that Dr. Searles has given us is necessary before we can come to any true understanding of the etiology of violence.

Millen Brand

The main purpose of the case interviews recorded in Dr. Searles's paper is to initiate therapy, to draw out some reality factors of the case and some of its emotional tone, and to prepare the patient for rapport with the doctor to whom he or she will be assigned. With that understood, there is no need to be critical of the interviews as therapy sessions.

In my novel *Savage Sleep* (1968), based on the work of Dr. John

N. Rosen (and written in close association with him), I showed that the psychotic patient was in many respects in an opposite condition from the neurotic and required an opposite technique of treatment, one in which passivity gave way to active and even aggressive concern, and in which transference was encouraged and there was no fear of interpretation. Dr. Searles partly follows this path by not being afraid to express his own aggression and fear and by gaining the confidence of the patient with his honesty. But the patient in each instance is in complete verbal contact and not at the hallucinatory extreme where he is unaware of the role of the doctor as doctor or where the doctor needs to enter the psychosis to try to lead his patient out.

It may be for this reason that Dr. Searles does not assume a role of omnipotence, of the powerful parent able to bring his child up all over again, this time under loving and beneficent auspices.

Dr. Thomas Szasz and others have made much of democracy, of equality in the exchanges between patient and doctor. This is acceptable, even admirable, in cases like those presented here, but it breaks down in situations where, for example, the therapist has to take the patient to the bathroom and instruct him in the elements of hygiene.

Psychosis is, in its beginnings and in its depths, an oral problem. The first hint of paranoia usually is fear of poisoning, the danger of eating or drinking. In Case 4, Mrs. Glaser reported that as a child she "wasn't free to stop in for a Coke or something like that" on her way home from school. She was therefore "unfree," unfree to eat outside the home, where it would have been safer. If you have seen a patient late at night preparing his own meals and refusing anything prepared by his mother, you have some idea of the source of paranoid fears.

But everywhere is also the desperate need for mother's milk and love, without which the patient dies. Even a five-percent love will be seen as salvation and fought for. In Case 4 the patient desperately denies that she hated her mother and, by implication, that her mother hated her. But her mother did hate her, and the hate was passed down, culminating in the patient's killing her own baby.

The patient's mother was "overprotective," meaning, "Would that you would die, my child." I myself interviewed a case at Brooklyn State Hospital where a mother had "protected" her newborn baby for about ten days by not letting anybody come near it, at which point it was discovered that the baby was starving to death. The mother then blanked out and thought she had been hospitalized "for a little alcoholism, I guess."

But it would be interesting in a paper like Dr. Searles's, even if he is not dealing with patients who are massively regressed, to trace out still more clearly the implications of the interviews for the oral phase and the first year of life, for here lie the origins of pathology and secretly or not they cry out.

Aggression in a parent may be healthy; it may have nothing to do with violence. Conversely, the overprotective parent may be quiet and seemingly loving. A baby who can scream and get red in the face may be a well baby; he may be confident that he is going to get what he wants and needs. But there remains a fine line between anger and fear, and this paper's dialogues can give therapists a useful indication of where that line should be drawn.

Arthur Malin, M.D.

Once again we have a most revealing paper from Dr. Searles. The revelation is not only in understanding the schizophrenic patient, but also in recognition of the deep inner impulses and feelings stirred up in the therapist. Dr. Searles, through his years of writing, has repeatedly described his own inner turmoil and eventual growth from the "symbiotic relatedness" that he allows the patient to achieve with him.

I believe that it is extremely difficult for most psychoanalysts to allow their feelings to be expressed in the therapeutic relationship on the level that Dr. Searles suggests is natural for him. Most analysts would find it very difficult to bring these feelings into consciousness and to consider them as valid material for the therapeutic relationship; they would tend to regard them as countertransference phenomena best handled in self-analysis, or perhaps in a supervisory situation. There are usually some transient emotional phenomena occurring in the analyst that serve as important clues to his understanding of the patient, but to incorporate these feelings directly into the therapeutic process would be very unusual.

How does the patient experience the development and expression of such strong feelings on the part of the therapist? Dr. Searles points out that this can be an extremely therapeutic experience for the patient, since the resulting symbiotic relatedness provides a means by which the patient can re-experience his inner psychic turmoil of the past for the later development of a more mature and integrated ego. In other papers Dr. Searles has talked about the development from the ambivalent to the preambivalent symbiosis that he believes is necessary in the therapy of schizophrenic patients. In our paper "Projective Identification in the Therapeutic Process" (1966), Dr. Grotstein and I suggested that it is the way in which a therapist responds to the patient's projections that allows modification of these projections to occur. The patient's introjection and identification of his previous projections, now modified by the response of the therapist, can be re-experienced for a higher level of integration and functioning. Dr. Searles evidently believes that his open response to the patient would fit in with the workings of such a concept. Perhaps another way of looking at it is that the patient recognizes that the therapist is willing to become disturbed and upset in his actions and statements and can still maintain the further identity of a relatively stable individual. The therapist is open to the resulting symbiotic relatedness and is not destroyed by it, but can contain and handle the patient's projections. This can be the modification that takes place and is reintrojected back into the schizophrenic patient.

I do not agree that Searles's particular approach to the schizophrenic patient is always very helpful. In my experience there are a number of schizophrenic patients who will become very frightened by what would appear to them as a loss of control on the part of the therapist. They would experience the therapist's expressing himself and his feelings in such a strong manner as Dr. Searles describes as terribly threatening. Such a patient might feel that if the therapist cannot maintain himself, how in the world is he going to help with such a chaotic inner life as the patient presents? The patient may also see this response as proof of his own inner destructiveness. I am suggesting that the problem of the way the therapist responds is a double-edged sword, and that Dr. Searles's approach is probably, at least in my experience, not applicable to all schizophrenic patients.

I want to re-emphasize, however, that when a therapist honestly expresses his feelings a patient can often feel, as Dr. Searles describes, a very strong sense of gratitude that the therapist is willing to be a "real" person in the relationship.

The specific question of violence in the schizophrenic is complicated by the intensity of the feelings aroused in the analyst. The paper makes the important suggestion that the therapist can actually encourage the violence on an unconscious level as a way of dealing with his own anxiety. An interesting statement is made: that it is within this strong, angry, destructive part of one's self that we also find a kernel of love and gratitude in a relationship.

The idea that the "urge to physical violence can express an effort to bridge a gulf of emotional unrelatedness" is a significant recognition of the tremendous defensive struggles going on within the schizophrenic patient.

Dr. Searles's paper also raises the question of the negative therapeutic reaction. The angry, violent attitude that is demonstrated by the violent schizophrenic patient and projected into the therapist can be a way in which the schizophrenic patient is hanging on to the only internal object situation he can handle: the relationship to the primary objects, the breast-mother. Are we perhaps dealing with the situation in which any attempt at growth and development means to the patient that this breast-mother must be relinquished, which he perceives as a fragmentation of all inner psychic contents and a disappearance of the self? The reaction of anger and violence may be the patient's way of demonstrating the futility of achieving maturity or any significant human relationship.

Better to maintain that inner relationship with the breast-mother than to give it up in favor of a never-to-be, hopelessly futile attempt at maturity. It is in the responses of the analyst that the projection of the patient can be modified. Dr. Searles describes how he uses his awareness of the strong feelings stirred up in him by the violent patient as a way of gaining understanding of the schizophrenic.

Margaret Little, M.R.C.S., L.R.C.P., M.R.C.PSYCH.

I have been struggling to put together some reasoned and coherent discussion of this prodigious paper, and have finally had to put aside the idea of anything but broadly "associating" to it.

Two contradictory strands seem to run through the paper: one, the intensity and totality of the undifferentiated state shown in the various patients described; and the other, Searles's insistence on the rigidity and vindictiveness of the superego in each case—a phenomenon which argues at least some degree of differentiation.

The paradox of this seems to me the crux of the matter. Tenderness is vitally necessary somewhere (whether in therapist, relative, or patient), yet it is simultaneously life-destroying—violence (murder) being the equally essential alternative, as vitally necessary in the therapist as it is in the patient himself.

This has to do with the problem of containing the violence. The strength of the container must be at least equal to that which is to be contained.

The patients described show this in quite markedly different degrees—Mr. Delaney's violence being to all intents and purposes uncontainable; Mrs. Glaser's being containable in the measure that it could be first repressed, or dissociated, then that the repression or dissociation could be undone. In my view, this is of both diagnostic and prognostic significance. I have come across a number of people, in treatment situations and elsewhere, where schizophrenia was masked by a defensive use of psychopathy: when the psychopath broke down under stress, a schizophrenic appeared. I would regard Mr. Delaney as an example of this, whereas Mrs. Glaser could almost be considered a "major hysteric."

Outside of psychiatry, a beautiful picture of this is shown in Ibsen's *Peer Gynt.* At the start of the play Peer is portrayed as a psychopath, consistently hostile to his mother, Åase. When she dies and he is driven out from the community, what reality sense he had is lost, and throughout the rest of his life he alternates between psychopathy and schizophrenia in response to varying external pressures.

I agree entirely with Searles that the reactions brought about in the therapist are of prime importance. The ability to allow his ego boundaries to dissolve temporarily—to let himself become merged with the patient, and to permit reality and delusional or hallucinatory experience to become indistinguishable—is the only route by which real contact, understanding, and ability to share in an experience can develop. But equally important are the ways in which the boundaries can be re-established, and the speed and progression of the resynthesis, when it is appropriate.

The method or technique described by Searles again is confirmed by my own experience, especially in terminating analyses of very sick patients which have been long and deeply felt on both sides.

Searles and his pupils have, on occasion, had recourse to wet packs or actual restraint. I have found it valuable when dealing with a paranoid patient to have some other person available, and known to the patient to be available even if not called upon, to relieve not only my own anxiety but also the patient's. I have, in fact, had very little experience of seriously threatened violence, for I have had little experience in treating schizophrenic patients.

Finally, this paper, which follows in the direct line of Searles's previous work, links up with a very great deal of which there is growing awareness generally, e.g., the "battered baby syndrome" and the widening fields of "protest" of all kinds, attended by widespread confusion, irrationality, and violence, which appear perhaps to be replacing "world wars" at the moment.

I think two papers of Winnicott's are particularly relevant here:

one on the need for confrontation in adolescent disturbance, and the other on the use of an object, in which he describes the subject's need to "destroy" the object, and yet have it survive, in order that he may come into being as a person in his own right. (This is what the patient is doing when he induces dedifferentiation in his therapist.)

This really subsumes the universality of violence (which, intellectually, we all recognize). Everything that exists in psychopathology exists also in normality, but the acceptance and acknowledgment of his own violence by the containing therapist are valid as assertion and demonstration both of his normality and of his growing freedom from superego dominance.

Gustav Bychowski, M.D.

Every new publication of Dr. Searles must arouse the greatest interest in all of us who are deeply involved in the psychoanalytic treatment of psychosis. The particular topic which he discusses in this paper commands, of course, our special attention. One is not disappointed in one's expectations. The paper offers original observations and fascinating examples of Dr. Searles's penetrating interview technique. In his incisive and sometimes strikingly intuitive interpretations, he is able time and again to get to the core of the patient's unconscious conflicts. Sometimes I feel that his interpretations are perhaps too rapid or even shocking—in this respect somewhat reminiscent of John Rosen's "active" analysis. However, in many instances the interpretation strikes one as illuminating. One might argue as to the timing, but then we have to keep in mind that some of the interviews are really first interviews and that they serve a didactic purpose.

As I go over the cases presented, my principal disagreement is with Dr. Searles's by now well-known countertransference interpretations. I must admit that in his former publications I had been struck by his most unusual identification with his psychotic patients. In the present paper he intersperses his excellent interpretations of

the patient's dynamics with his "countertransference" interpretations which, I must confess, seem to me arbitrary and farfetched.

He has, for instance, excellent insight into the dynamics and violent acting out of his first patient, even though I would consider it
a rather wild interpretation to say that Mr. Delaney "was faced with
the threat of becoming the rapist of the father, as the agent of the
mother's phallic strivings."

But I cannot accept Dr. Searles's interpretations of his own feelings. Instead of simply noticing his obvious and understandable
fear of this violent patient, he comments on his own "unconscious
passive homosexual longings" which had been aroused by his interview with him: "I could triangulate, although not actually feel, the
desire to be sexually 'shot' by him."

After the patient has assaulted a fellow marine, Dr. Searles
comments that this violent act gave him (Searles) the relief of certainty, since "it was as though the distinction between the patient's
actualized murderousness and our own murderous fantasies and
feelings was now clear beyond anyone's questioning it."

To read Dr. Searles's further exposition of his and supposedly
the other therapists' murderous impulses—apparently his entourage is also filled with all sort of violent feelings toward the
patients—is to be subjected to further shocks. One cannot help asking oneself: How can one help a patient if one identifies with him
to such an extent, and how can one recognize one's own feelings if
one is so ready to distort them by uncritical counteridentification?
And, indeed, the speculations which Dr. Searles develops in further
analyzing this situation acquire more and more the characteristics
of fantasies. No wonder then that Dr. Searles confesses that "such a
patient evokes in one such intensely conflicting feelings that, at an
unconscious level, one's ego functioning undergoes a pervasive dedifferentiation: one loses the ability deeply to distinguish between
one's self and the patient, and between the whole realms of fantasy
and reality."

Since our purpose is not just to study the patient and our own
unconscious but also to help the patient, I fail to see how any help
is possible when one is unable to distinguish between the patient's

violence and one's own. Indeed, one wonders about the usefulness of this procedure as applied to a patient so manifestly dangerous. One has to ask whether some other therapeutic method, such as conditioning or retraining, based, of course, on the dynamic insights, might not be more appropriate.

Similar reservations apply to other case histories. At times Dr. Searles admits some of his countertransference feelings (or speculations?) to the patient. I don't see anything useful in telling the patient: "Then I may be *projecting* onto you some of my *own* problems because I was very afraid I would kill [a member of my parental family] . . . so that I may be afraid of *myself* still, more than I thought, and I may be taking it out on you."

Some of the interviews presented are particularly moving, such as the one with the infanticide mother. But even here, as in many other instances, one feels that Dr. Searles makes too much of a patient's expression and interprets it according to his own theories. For example, when the infanticide mother speaks of her little drowned daughter as "something very lovely," Dr. Searles interprets it as her inability to see the child as a living creature.

There are many passages in the paper that strike me as unwarranted and too widely speculative. Dr. Searles's exaggerated ideas about the import of counteridentification lead to speculative interpretations which cannot, of course, be proved or disproved. It seems, for instance, gratuitous to assert that the infanticide mother "not only was acting out her own largely denied hostility toward the infant, but also was acting out vicariously the also vigorously denied murderousness toward the infant on the part of her husband and mother-in-law, to whom she had telegraphed to clearly her brooding murderousness toward the little girl." Dr. Searles admits that during the first few minutes of the interview with this mother he noticed in himself "urges to kill her in condemnation for her having murdered her own child."

It is not surprising that in view of his very special tendencies toward counteridentification, Dr. Searles develops most unusual relationships with his patients. One admires his ability to withstand the stresses of these relationships. However—to repeat—one won-

ders what is the value of identifying for 11 years, and even for
many years after the end of treatment, with a highly disturbed,
perverse schizophrenic. It was clear that in this extraordinary relationship the psychiatrist was taking over his patient's violent and
perverse wishes; but the reader can judge for himself. It is in this
case history that the psychiatrist admits to the patient that he will
miss him terribly and begins to burst into tears.

In conclusion, I feel that the excellent and profound insights
which Dr. Searles manifests in this as in his many other publications
are vitiated by his ill-founded speculations and the hypertrophy of
his counteridentification. It is to be regretted that he was unable to
cope, as he confesses, with his introjects. He admits himself that the
above-mentioned schizophrenic patient and his own long-deceased
and violent father continue to live within him. I must sympathize
with this situation, which I would find extremely disturbing in myself.

Milton Wexler, Ph.D.

Searles has not only written on "Violence in Schizophrenia," but
has managed to incorporate into the very structure and quality of
his presentation some of the essential elements he wishes to explain. The paper is filled with a violent honesty, an urgency to
make direct contact with the mind and feelings of the reader, and a
host of dark fears that need to be shared. From this viewpoint
alone it is a remarkable document. It confesses, pleads, speculates,
asserts, details, argues, exposes helplessness and insight, and jumps
hey-diddle-diddle from the most concrete to the most abstract,
from the most objective to the most personal.

Dr. Searles's interviews with patients deserve special mention.
He is mainly reality-oriented, blunt, and guided as much by his
inner feelings as by external facts, yet he is sensitive to the nuances
of what is expressed and unexpressed by his subjects. He makes no
pretence to special power, special understanding, or the Christian
virtues of kindness, charity, forgiveness, and love. He is what he is:

sometimes fearful, sometimes angry, always curious and open, and responsive both to the surface and to what may lie beneath it. In this psychoanalytic age it is refreshing to encounter an analyst who is not altogether dazzled by his own presumed mastery of primitive unconscious mechanisms.

Obviously no single formulation serves to explain the violence of the schizophrenic patient. The paranoid projections that lead to a sense of persecution and a violent defense against the persecutor represent one type. This is more nearly neurotic in structure, is based on inner unconscious conflict, and is resolved by an act of violence against the alleged persecutor. This paper deals with deeper, more regressive mechanisms, in which the threatened loss of the object, the "gulf of emotional unrelatedness," leads to violence as an act of reconstitution, reconstruction, restitution. While it may express some striving to be free, it may equally express an urgency to recontact the object and be at one with it. In that sense we learn once again how very close love and hate can be. I personally do not fully accept the notion of "vengefulness as a defense against grief and separation anxiety"; I prefer to think of such angry retaliation as an effort at restoration, as reparative in nature. The term "defense" is not altogether inappropriate, but might suggest, for instance, that we eat in order to defend against hunger. The use of "defense" in this sense tends to stretch its meaning beyond useful boundaries.

It is a commonplace that schizophrenics inflict pain on themselves in order to feel alive. They scratch, tear, cut, burn, or injure their flesh to achieve the smallest sense of being real within the vacuum of their psychic lives. This goes even beyond the savagery of their superego demands and expectations. What Dr. Searles's paper presents with such clarity and in such depth is a valid corollary: schizophrenics can salvage a sense of being alive, being related, being in contact by inflicting pain and suffering on others, by a violence which for a moment may resurrect a sense that the world is not devoid of objects. What they often cannot tolerate is the feeling of living in a void.

Dr. Searles knows these things both objectively and subjectively.

To his credit he has delved deeply enough in his own feelings to
know his own rage at the dead, the lost, the absent objects. Therefore, he can understand schizophrenic violence, can properly fear
it, and even, at moments, forgive it.

Herbert A. Rosenfeld, M.D.

This paper is mainly a contribution to the psychotherapeutic
management of violent and murderous patients, and also illustrates
Dr. Searles's interviewing technique, wherein he attempts in one
consultation to assess the personality structure of the patient
through his own countertransference reactions. In his summary Dr.
Searles stresses that he has highlighted various concepts relating to
the schizophrenic's superego and the poor differentiation between
the human and nonhuman ingredients in the schizophrenic's world.
These latter aspects, however important and interesting they may
be, do not come through very convincingly in the interviews, but
this is hardly surprising; the personality structure and confusions of
the schizophrenic often need very detailed psychoanalytic investigation to be properly understood.

I myself have never treated anybody who actually committed a
murder. However, several of my acutely schizophrenic patients
were violent and some of them suffered from delusions of having
committed murder. I also treated a young married woman doctor,
more than 20 years ago, who suffered from a severe syphilophobia
which at times was clearly delusional. She had violent murderous
impulses against her infant, particularly for the first three months
of the baby's life, and she came for treatment soon after her confinement because she was convinced that without treatment her
child's life was in real danger. While the severe syphilophobia related to an act of unfaithfulness to her husband several years previously, the illness as a whole had to be regarded as a postpartum
psychosis, and was related to an intense projective identification of
herself with the newborn infant, whom she misidentified as her
sick, paranoid baby-self which she had never been able to accept

and which she regarded as *not human*. Her murderous hatred against this self was also projected into the analyst, representing the mother; she constantly feared that the analyst could not stand her and wanted to get rid of her (kill her). In working through her earliest infantile anxieties in the transference, the patient gradually came to feel accepted by the analyst-parent (mainly standing for the mother) and made a good recovery. In the countertransference I never felt that I was the murderous mother, but I was aware of an intense pressure coming from the patient to change me into a punishing, frightening superego which threatened her with death and accused her of not being human. It was interesting that after the infant had survived the first three months of life, the patient gradually felt relieved and could accept the baby as more human. She made it quite clear that this happened when she began to feel that the baby had become more able to see the mother as a whole person; she had perceived the very young infant as aggressive, rejecting the mother and the breast, and completely preoccupied with the *nipple* as an exciting part-object—an experience which was gradually related to the poisonous syphilophobia which had completely dominated the patient since the birth of the child.

This patient was quite ignorant of psychoanalytic theories about early infantile experiences, but she taught me a great deal about the terrifying anxieties infants seem to go through. I would agree with Dr. Searles that the patient's murderousness toward her infant was related to an identification with or complete submission to an early archaic persecutory superego.

I have further clinical evidence that many violent schizophrenic patients are dominated by a very primitive persecuting superego, as I illustrated in my paper on the superego conflict in schizophrenia (1952a). At that time I had treated an almost mute, violent schizophrenic patient in a mental hospital. The only room available for his treatment was the anatomy theatre of this institution where, one day, the patient managed to dig out a box of bones a lower jaw of a skeleton. He held it in front of his face like a mask and then behaved threateningly toward me to illustrate his identification with his own threatening deathly superego. Occasionally he was able to express with a few words his preoccupation with death and dying, after which he would become more depressed. In his regressive persecutory experiences he obviously felt threatened by me, and at times became violent and murderous when he confused me with his superego. It was, however, important that while the patient had the greatest difficulty in using words himself, he often understood verbal interpretations. I used only my analytic understanding and verbal interpretations, and these generally succeeded in diminishing both his terror of me and his murderous violence, which was of course quite frightening.

There is no question that actively murderous and violent patients are the most difficult ones to treat and that they make enormous demands on the therapist's understanding. I am in general agreement with Dr. Searles that the countertransference of the therapist is of enormous help in understanding the nonverbal communications and projections of our psychotic patients. I think, however, that it is essential that the analyst who makes extensive use of the countertransference should be quite clear about the implications of his countertransference experience. Originally, countertransference reactions were regarded simply as a neurotic reaction of the analyst who transfers object relations and fantasies of the past onto his patients, thereby confusing the issue. The analyst's pathological, neurotic countertransference requires self-analysis, or analysis of the analyst, and Dr. Searles quite openly often does so in investigating his own neurotic transference feelings, illustrating in this paper the importance of self-analysis in dealing with this problem. But he does not seem to differentiate sufficiently the neurotic countertransference from the countertransference described by Heimann, Bion, and myself, and many others, which is based on two factors: first of all, there is the patient's unconscious nonverbal communication, in which he projects impulses, fantasies, and even parts of his self into the analyst; and second, there is the analyst's sensitivity and receptiveness to the patient's projections, which enable him, through this type of countertransference, to pick up very important information from the patient.

In violent and destructively psychotic patients, it is of course particularly important for the analyst to be able to recognize whether or not the murderous violence the patient communicates is a real desire to kill, because this immediately calls for protective measures for the safety of the potential victims rather than for analysis. On the other hand, the patient who communicates his murderousness out of fear of being overwhelmed by it is asking for the analyst's help in order to save himself and his objects. Here the analyst has to understand that the patient wants *him* to cope with fear and aggression better than he himself can. This kind of situation often responds well to analytic therapy.

Preverbal communications through projection of anxieties relating to destructive impulses have their basis in the situation where the small infant projects his destructiveness and his fear of it into his mother. It is the mother's capacity to contain both the aggression and the fear of disintegration (Bion) that gradually leads to a lessening of the sense of danger and to a strengthening of the infantile ego in coping with the aggressive impulses.

Robert C. Bak, M.D.

Many schizophrenics move on the extreme ends of the scale between passivity and aggressiveness. Passivity can be the expression of instinctual aim, but may just as well function as defense against aggression; sudden acting out of murderous fantasies is characteristic of some schizophrenics in the course of their illness. It is not easy to decide whether the murderous acts represent a breakthrough of aggression with the aim of destroying a person, or whether they appear in the course of restitution, i.e., re-establishing lost contact with the world (objects).

In my view, the withdrawal of libidinal investments from object representations leaves the schizophrenic with magic, omnipotent self-love (narcissism) and often exposes the objects outside and their intrapsychic representation to destruction. The further course of dedifferentiation is an archaic defense of the ego *against* the destruction of objects. That from this dedifferentiation, from the experiences of fusion and loss of individuality, the aggressive act may serve the purposes of reintegration is by no means a contradiction.

The lack of differentiation between animate and inanimate objects is not a cause of violence but in a way a consequence of it; I mean by this that the withdrawal of love is the prerequisite for experiencing persons as things. So much for theory.

Dr. Searles's consistent approach of analyzing countertransference, identification, and defenses in the therapist for the understanding of the patient and the therapeutic process is certainly a model to follow. However, one cannot help feeling that these subjective reactions of the therapist and supervisor are overdrawn. Instead of using them as *signals* for intellectual awareness, they may be *lived* for longer than necessary. Also, there is too much emphasis on subjective observation. Taking for granted the existence of many subjective elements, especially when one is confronted with cases that challenge the deepest prohibitions in one's own personality, there is still room for clinical judgment and prognostication, at least partly based on experience. Searles may give the impression, for example, that in judging the murderous potential of a patient we are almost entirely at the mercy of our own anxieties, identifications, and projections. However, the therapist's secondary reactions, elicited from the patient, are of the utmost importance, as Searles emphasizes throughout. He consistently follows the epigrammatic maxim of Bertram Lewin: Analysis is the analysis of countertransference. But it should be analyzed, not acted upon.

Alfred Flarsheim, M.D.

Much of what is written about the psychoanalysis of psychotic patients is extrapolated from work with borderline patients who may show psychotic mechanisms but are able to manage their lives outside of a hospital. Searles is one of the very few who have written about long-term psychoanalytic treatment of severely disturbed hospitalized schizophrenic patients.

This paper is very rich in concrete assistance for anyone working with severely disturbed patients, in or out of a hospital setting.

For example, Searles's way of handling his patient's demand to be released from the hospital is most helpful. The patient seeks freedom from environmental restraint, which can reflect internal restraint, and Searles presents a good example of the kind of inner restraint from which a patient may need release. His patient's inner restraint is derived from anxiety over infantile helplessness and from domination by an archaic maternal introject with which the patient was partially identified. In *The Ethics of Psychoanalysis*, Thomas Szasz (1965) points out that not only the paranoid patient but also society and the hospital administration regard the psychiatrist in a mental hospital as the opponent of the patient rather than his agent or advocate. Searles shows us how he handles this crucial issue. He accepts the patient's view of hospitalization as something imposed upon him by others for their own protection, while searching for an area in which he and the patient can work together toward a shared objective.

Searles has pioneered in the use of countertransference as a diagnostic and therapeutic instrument. Everyone talks and writes about the importance of self-knowledge, but Searles shows us what this can mean and how to use it.

I have had psychiatric residents misuse Searles's writings to justify burdening patients with their own emotional reactions, which are disruptive to the treatment. Interpretation of countertransference anxieties is fraught with dangers. This is particularly true when the patient feels accused of causing the therapist anxiety, and that therefore he must inhibit the expression of feelings that the therapist finds unpleasant. Carried to its extreme, inhibition of expression is suicide. As long as the countertransference can be used as a source of mutual understanding of the patient who contributes to its formation, and as long as we can communicate that we are enjoying being taught by the patient, we can safely interpret even the negative feelings the patient arouses in us.

I have asked myself what indications of potential violence are most anxiety-provoking in my own hospital practice. Many factors are of course important, such as a history of violent behavior in the past. But the patient's way of relating also has prognostic value.

Two patients come to mind. Both have frightened me, the hospital staff, and other patients. Both live largely in a subjective delusional world and both have been considered to be potentially dangerous if crossed, that is, if a collision cannot be avoided between the patient's subjective world and external reality. One patient has a well-developed capacity for playfulness and humor. This provides a softening of the boundaries between internal and external reality, a buffer zone between the two areas enabling him to avoid direct collision between his unrealistic subjective world and external reality and thereby avoid being provoked into dangerous destructive behavior. The other patient has a grim and humorless demeanor, and no capacity for playfulness, which implies a rigidity of the boundary between internal and external reality, with few links between them. The first patient evades conflict by lies, manipulation, and by being a playboy, acting out constant flight from responsibility. The second patient isolates himself in a darkened room and glares at anyone who interrupts his reveries; he lacks this buffer zone and is therefore the more dangerous of the two.

Another mechanism that I have observed in violent patients is the use of external reality as a defense against internal reality. There are limits to the patient's capacity for actual, in contrast to fantasied, destruction. The latter can be without limits, particularly in the presence of ego fragmentation which separates love and hate so that love cannot set limits to hateful destruction. Anxiety about fantasied destruction can be a helpful area to explore with some patients whose dream and fantasy life is impoverished and who act out destructively. Discussion of the fantasied consequences of a fantasied act can make the act itself unnecessary. In addition, interpretation of the meaning of a fantasied action in terms of genetic reconstruction or symbolic meaning can show the patient that the fantasies are valuable in themselves, and that violent actions are not needed to communicate meaningfully.

With outpatients we are more often concerned about possible suicide than about externally directed violence, and Searles's formulations about the therapist's fear of the patient's violence can be applied to violence directed against the self. I will devote the remainder of my comments to this topic.

In "Aggression: Adaptive and Disruptive Aspects," Peter Giovacchini (1969) classifies violent behavior along a hierarchical continuum from the diffuse temper tantrum on the one hand to aggression organized toward a specific aim and object on the other. Personality disintegration to the level of an infantile temper tantrum is a self-destructive event, and hostile aggression directed toward a separate object externalizes destructiveness, and can thus defend against suicide.

Searles points out that the therapist's fear of the patient can be a derivative of the therapist's unconscious destructive impulse. The therapist's impulse to attack the patient can be repressed or denied, leading to vicarious relief and enjoyment when the patient acts out aggressively toward the therapist or toward others, or it can be experienced and used in the service of the therapy. The therapist's unconscious destructiveness toward the patient can also take the form of an unconscious wish for the patient to commit suicide; this may first be experienced by the therapist as anxiety lest the patient commit suicide.

Experiencing something in the present reality of the transference can be the patient's way of remembering and regaining unintegrated ego segments. Stimulating the therapist to experience something in the countertransference can also be a way for the patient to deal with unintegrated ego segments, which originally may have belonged to the self, to an object, or to an archaic undifferentiated self-object. I have had a patient who *needed* to stimulate me to want her to kill herself before she could start to free herself from suicidal impulses that derived from her mother's death wishes toward her when she was a small infant. Another patient, a 14-year-old girl, compulsively starts dangerous fires. The fire-setting is "exciting" for her, and I am only just beginning to get some ideas about possible reasons for the choice of fire-setting as the preferred form of destructive activity. We have, however, found that destructiveness is directed toward a maternal imago with which she is partially identified. Not only is there a suicidal element in the fire-setting itself, but when for some reason or other she is unable to set fires, she resorts to manifestly self-destructive behavior such as slashing her abdomen. In effect, her fire-setting defends against more direct methods of suicide.

Searles stresses that violence can be an unconscious defense against repressed grief. I am reminded of two adult patients in whom compulsive head-banging was relieved only when they became able to cry.

In this and other papers Searles has described the effects of a mother's intolerance of her child's "basic human aliveness." The parent with a severe ego defect can maintain only a precarious equilibrium and cannot tolerate a relationship with a separate independent person. Any relationship such a parent can have with anyone, including the child, can only be one of rejection or of engulfing narcissistic exploitation in the service of the parent's precarious ego integration. But it is not always vitality and vivaciousness that are intolerable to parents. Indeed, a parent may exploit a child's liveliness to counteract his own depression. The "basic human aliveness" to which Searles refers here implies rather the child's individuation as a separate *autonomous* individual. A suicidal patient can be complying with a parent's need to eliminate this "aliveness," which his parent experienced as an intolerable threat.

I have read this paper five times, and have learned something new from it with each reading. The most significant comment I can make is to urge any readers who have not yet done so to immerse themselves in Dr. Searles's writing.

AUTHOR'S RESPONSE

I find on re-reading this paper, for the first time since submitting it three years ago for publication, that it is still fully consonant with my theoretical views, with one exception: it omits mention of the dimension of the patient's, and the therapist's, suicidal proclivities. If I were writing this paper over again today, I would make at least brief mention of the fact that just as suicide can be a defense against murder, so can murder be a defense against suicide; as Mrs. Glaser, for example, is quoted as saying to me, "I still had bad thoughts towards the baby or myself—either one." In a similar vein, I would suggest today that the therapist's anxiety lest the patient murder him is likely to be based not only upon his reality-based awareness of the patient's murderousness, and upon the therapist's projection (as I have mentioned) of his own unconscious murderous feelings onto the already murderous patient, but also upon some increment of an unconscious longing on the therapist's part to be murdered by the patient. At any rate, I believe the opening paragraph of my paper makes clear that I was not setting out to cover nor even to touch upon every major dimension of so broad a subject.

A word employed by Little, "prodigious," nicely describes my task in responding to the thoughtful comments of the nine discussants, all of them persons of wide experience in working with schizophrenic patients and equipped, therefore, to speak with authority about the psychodynamics and psychotherapy of such patients. My task now is similar to that which I have had each time I have faced an audience for an often critical dissection of a just-completed teaching interview. In one respect it is much harder, for I have never had an audience which contained so many comparably prestigious authorities in this field, and in another it is much simpler, for at least I have had time for contemplation.

Toward Rosen, despite some wide differences in theoretical concepts and psychotherapeutic approaches, I have a strong comradely feeling as regards teaching interviews, for he is the only colleague whom I regard as having had more experience than I with the stresses of doing such teaching interviews and then discussing them afterward, in detail, with the onlookers. I surmise that he would concur with my view that, more often than not, one's relationship with the audience proves more challenging than that with the patient himself. It seems to me probable that many experienced colleagues who eschew this priceless teaching technique, ostensibly out of concern for patients' needs for privacy or presumed fragilities of one sort or another, are in actuality unprepared to brave the stresses involved in allowing one's colleagues to witness one's therapeutic, or quasi-therapeutic, work at first hand and subject it to the kind of searching scrutiny in post-interview discussions which these nine discussants, with varying degrees of approval and disapproval, and much clarification and stimulation for me, have provided here.

Incidentally, Bychowski is indulging in a fantasy when he attributes to me a mindlessly sycophantic "entourage"; I have known little, indeed, of the dubious pleasures such a situation might provide. On balance, most of my audiences have been more critical of my interviews than these nine discussants collectively have been. My audiences usually have consisted largely of psychiatric residents and junior staff members, and persons of this degree of experience tend to be, although not infrequently impressed in various ways, also somewhat shocked, angered, and mystified by some of my responses to the patient. But any long-experienced onlookers are usually relatively understanding of and not alienated by what they see and hear me doing during the interview—are "with" me to just about the extent that most of these discussants have proved to be, and on such occasions I feel fortunate.

For me, the greatest stress involved in a teaching interview with a schizophrenic patient consists in being faced with the potentially terrifying threat of isolation from one's fellow human beings, of being perceived by them as something nonhuman. One's feeling of strain in this regard is surely in part derived from empathy with the patient, whose illness is designed, as it were, specifically to protect him from the conscious awareness of such a feeling. This component of the interview situation, specifically as regards schizophrenic patients, is so significant to me that I find I cannot work effectively, or with anything like the requisite degree of personal freedom to respond to the patient, unless I feel that at least a small minority of the onlookers will hesitate to write me off as crazy, or as someone who—as I am sure Bychowski or Bak, for example, would say—does "wild analysis," or who is sadistically victimizing a patient viewed by the onlookers as being himself devoid of sadism or other forms of hatefulness.

Now I shall respond to each of the discussants in turn, at varying length, dwelling largely of course upon their more critical comments, while privately being grateful for their more favorable responses of which, as I hope to have made clear already, I need at least some modicum from my colleagues in order to pursue this kind of teaching activity.

Rosen says, "The patients described, although they were unquestionably psychotic at the time of their acting out, do not seem to me to fit into the classical categories of schizophrenia." I think it could be said that each of the three patients whose interviews are presented at length was functioning, during the interview itself, with a no more than borderline schizophrenic degree of impairment of ego functioning (although the history in each instance shows what seems unmistakable evidence of frank psychosis on occasion), and one experienced colleague has raised a sobering question as to whether Mrs. Glaser might more accurately have been diagnosed as suffering from a psychotic depression than from schizophrenia. For this reason the paper might perhaps better have been entitled "Violence in Psychotic Conditions." Here I would add only three considerations: (1) I have used the term "schizophrenia" in this paper to include schizophrenia of whatever degree of severity, including borderline schizophrenia; (2) I wanted to include particularly clear—and frankly, for reader interest, dramatic—instances of violence on the part of patients; and (3) as I am sure Rosen well knows, interviews with frankly schizophrenic patients often consist so largely in nonverbal responses that it is impossible to provide any very meaningful typescript of them. I could not agree more with his long-held position that "psychotherapy should be taught by live demonstration." The verbal data that this paper contains, no matter how faithfully reproducing what I heard in playbacks of the sound-tapes, cannot be more than a relatively pale and dry approximation of the actual interviews.

Rosen mentions that in his own experiences of treating potentially murderous patients, his reaction was not one of violence but in one instance, at least, of great fear. I remind him that I experienced fear in response to each of the three patients described at length in this paper, and I reassert the importance of the therapist's (or interviewer's) projection upon the patient of the former's unconscious—and to me quite understandable, under the circumstances—murderous feeling. This component, no mere idiosyncrasy of mine, is one I have seen at work in many instances of colleagues' treatment of potentially dangerous patients, as described in supervisory sessions concerning patients I have never seen. With reliable repetitiveness, over the months of supervisory work in such instances, one finds that the therapist has been constricted in his therapeutic endeavor by a need to maintain under repression his own more violent impulses toward his threatening patient, and the treatment regularly goes better when one is able to help the therapist to become aware of his more rageful feelings, as so clearly occurred in the treatment of Mrs. Glaser.

Surely Rosen does not believe that I am advocating the talionic principle as any informed way of dealing with murderers or potential murderers, who of course need psychotherapeutic help in integrating, and thus gaining mastery of, their violent proclivities. To say that it is desirable that the therapist become conscious of his repressed murderousness toward the patient clearly implies, to my way of thinking, that the therapist should *not* act out his own murderous reactions to the patient. But, as I hoped to have made clear, the eminently desirable feeling of personal forgiveness toward a murderous, or potentially murderous, person is hypocritical and spurious rather than genuine if one has not gained access to one's own understandably violent condemnatory feelings toward him on this score.

Brand begins, "The main purpose of the case interviews recorded . . . is to initiate therapy, to draw out some reality factors of the case and some of its emotional tone, and to prepare the patient for rapport with the doctor to whom he or she will be assigned. With that understood, there is no need to be critical of the interviews as therapy sessions." Brand is letting me off a hook here which I am prepared to remain upon, for although these interviews are intended to be useful for teaching, they are intended even more to be of immediate therapeutic value for the patient. I have been asked many times if I would have behaved differently if the patient I had just interviewed were one of my own therapy patients whom I was seeing in my office. My best impression is that the similarities far outweigh the differences, the main difference being that in my office I would often say less, for in the teaching interviews I am frequently trying, through my verbalizing, to make relatively subtle nonverbal events more explicit and perceptible to the audience. In short, these teaching interviews are intended not only to have a catalytic effect upon the patient's therapy—which, I remind Brand, was in each of these three instances (as usual) well under way at the time the interview took place—but also to *be* a form of therapy for the patient.

To Brand's objection, like Rosen's, that the patient in each instance is in complete verbal contact, unlike more severely schizophrenic patients, again I wish to point out that typescripts of interviews like those in this paper are ill suited to convey the predominantly nonverbal essence of that which proves therapeutic in one's work with the more deeply ill patients. In my previous writings there surely is no lack of detailed descriptions of such work, largely during my 15 years on the staff of Chestnut Lodge, with patients severely ill enough to fulfill Brand's most stringent criteria of massive regression. My first book (1960), concerning the role of the nonhuman environment in schizophrenia and in normal development, consists essentially of clinical examples, from my work and that of colleagues on the Chestnut Lodge staff, of the patient's and the therapist's reacting to one another as essentially nonhuman. Two of my recent papers (1972a, 1972b), by way of additional examples, detail my therapeutic approach in working with two chronically schizophrenic women, both of them far more ill than any of the three patients described in this paper.

In reference to the relatively moderate degree of illness in these three patients, Brand comments, "It may be for this reason that Dr. Searles does not assume a role of omnipotence, of the powerful parent able to bring his child up all over again, this time under truly loving and beneficent auspices." Here, in advocating what is well known to be a dimension of Rosen's therapeutic orientation, Brand touches upon the area of my main theoretical differences from Rosen, which is dealt with in my paper "Scorn, Disillusionment, and

Adoration in the Psychotherapy of Schizophrenia" (1962b), in which I report my experience that the patient's genuine feelings of adoration toward the therapist supervene only after the patient's initially predominant feelings of scorn, and subsequent feelings of disillusionment, have been largely worked through.

My paper "Dependency Processes in the Psychotherapy of Schizophrenia" (1955) emphasizes the importance of the therapist's feelings of dependency upon the patient (an emphasis which, so far as I know, Rosen's writings have not included), and my many published discussions (1959b, 1965a, 1973a) of therapeutic symbiosis, of which I began to speak in 1958, describe the mutuality of feelings of adoration in that crucially therapeutic phase of the treatment. Also, in two recent papers (1973a, 1973b) I discuss the patient's therapeutic strivings toward the analyst, a major dimension of this area with which again, so far as I know, Rosen's and Brand's theoretical concepts do not deal.

For many years, as for example in my paper "The Evolution of the Mother Transference in Psychotherapy with the Schizophrenic Patient" (1961a), I have emphasized the necessity of helping the patient to resolve his transference to the therapist as a malevolently omnipotent mother, rather than trying somehow to override this transference by functioning from the outset as a benignly omnipotent mother in the manner which, it seems to me, Rosen (and, I suppose, Brand) would advocate. Lastly in this regard, in two recent papers (1970, 1971) concerning autism, I have described the therapeutic value, for the patient, in the therapist's becoming able to experience the patient as constituting his, the therapist's, meaningful whole world in the context of the therapeutic session. So it can be seen that my theoretical concepts are in major ways very different from those of Rosen and, I gather, of Brand.

Brand's statement that "Psychosis is, in its beginnings and in its depths, an oral problem" I find hard to gainsay; my first published paper, "Data Concerning Certain Manifestations of Incorporation" (1951), had to do with oral-incorporative processes, although in trying to understand those most primitive processes which one finds in autism I find it less helpful to think in terms of mouth and breast than in terms of the much less well-differentiated *world* in which the individual is so completely immersed, or with which, alternatively, he is so bleakly out of contact. Little's (1960) writing on undifferentiatedness and Milner's (1952, 1969) writings about her work with deeply regressed patients have proved particularly congenial to my own experience with such patients.

I fully concur with Brand's statement, "Aggression in a parent may be healthy; it may have nothing to do with violence."

Malin says, "I believe that it is extremely difficult for most psychoanalysts to allow their feelings to be expressed in the therapeutic relationship on the level that Dr. Searles suggests is natural for him." I wish to emphasize in this connection that the kind of interaction described in this paper by no means came naturally and easily to me; it was achieved, bit by bit, only in the course of years of great difficulty with constrictingly obsessive-compulsive defenses from which, as I am sure is clear to the reader, I am still far from free. Several of my earlier papers have detailed aspects of my struggle to gain greater freedom, analogously, from the role of conventional psychiatrist and "dedicated physician" in my work with patients, a role which is tailor-made to dovetail with, and thus perpetuate, the schizophrenic patient's sadistic mockery of the therapist who is trying, without descending into such ugly emotions as hatred, to rescue him from his suffering.

When Malin says that "Most analysts . . . would tend to regard [these feelings] as countertransference phenomena best handled in self-analysis, or perhaps in a supervisory situation," I quite agree; but this, more than anything else, is what my writings are endeavoring to change. I do not hold a brief so much for the analyst's becoming more verbose, say, or very much more expressive of his immediate feeling-reactions to his patients. But I do strongly believe that "most analysts," to use Malin's phrase, very much underestimate the extent to which their own feelings, in the course of the analytic session, will prove to be priceless data in the analysis of the patient—if, that is, the analyst regards them primarily as valuable clues to what is transpiring at nonverbalized, unconscious levels in the patient-analyst relationship and within the patient himself, and does not assume, guiltily and anxiously, that these feelings are primarily intrusive countertransference reactions stemming mainly from his own unexplored childhood. It is only as I have come to see—over the years and from an initial base of great caution and undue readiness to write off many of my emotional reactions as aberrant, crazy, and irrelevant to what was going on in the patient—how very frequently such authentic informational value concerning the patient's psychodynamics is inherent in these reactions of mine, that I have moved more and more freely into the kind of interaction this paper details. No, it by no means came naturally to me; but I do hold that the primary value of a training analysis, in its aspect of equipping the analytic candidate to function effectively as an analyst, consists in helping him to become sufficiently in touch with his own emotional life so that when one or another area of this is evoked in his work with a patient he can feel sufficiently at ease with it to remain interested in discerning what subtle but real processes at work in the patient, heretofore unanalyzed, have provided the stimulus for this evocation.

It seems to me that Malin and Grotstein have made an excellent point in suggesting, in their 1966 paper to which Malin refers, that it is the way in which a therapist responds to the projection of the patient that allows for modification of these projections to occur. But I wish to reassert here, as I have many times in previous papers, my experience-based conviction that patients' projective (or introjective) reactions (and of course by the same token their transference reactions), no matter how psychotically distorted these may seem, can be discovered to be founded in part upon some element of reality. In my very first analytic paper (1949), I suggested that "all projective manifestations, transference reactions included . . . have some *real* basis in the analyst's behavior, and therefore represent distortions in degree only." A paper, "The Function of the Patient's Realistic Perceptions of the Analyst in Delusional Transference" (1972a), concerning my work over more than 20 years now with a remarkably delusional woman, discusses, as the title suggests, my discovering to what an extraordinary degree her delusional transference reactions, no matter how incredibly exaggerated or otherwise distorted, proved to be responses to one or another heretofore largely unconscious aspect of my own personality functioning during the sessions.

Malin comments, "I do not agree that Searles's particular approach to the schizophrenic patient is always very helpful. In my experience there are a number of schizophrenic patients who will become very frightened by what would appear to them as a loss of control on the part of the therapist." I am well aware that I myself am not always very helpful to patients, schizophrenic or otherwise, and if on balance the evidence is that I am doing more good than harm, I rest relatively content with my efforts. As for psychiatric residents who, after seeing me do interviews, have endeavored to utilize my approach in their own work with their patients, I am aware that this attempted identification with me sometimes does not go well—although more often than not it does prove useful, or my teaching interviews would long since have ceased. This difficulty tends to arise when a resident endeavors to employ the open bluntness which is one of the characteristics of my approach without having first acquired the requisite personal acquaintance with his own unconscious and the requisite degree of clinical experience. I think that one of the reasons why this at times does not go well is that the therapist in this instance is not equipped to deal with the consequences of his intervention—with, for example, the patient's reacting with increased anxiety and often with the conviction that the therapist is being the equivalent of the psychotic, sadistic (and so on) parent of early childhood. Some residents find that such reactions in the patient make them increasingly anxious and guilty, and the whole relationship quickly becomes permeated with inadequately dealt-with anxiety. I shall have more to say about this matter in responding to Flarsheim's discussion.

The most difficult thing for me personally in doing teaching interviews with schizophrenic patients is knowing how to cope with the frequently intense threat—how, that is, not only to tolerate it, but to utilize it as communication, as information concerning unconscious processes at work in the patient—that one will come, by reason of one's responses or lack of responses during the interview, to be viewed by patient and audience members alike as something other than human, far more dreadful than a terribly lonely person—something inherently outside the human pale because of a lack of the kind of emotional equipment (compassion, kindness, and so on) requisite for membership in the human species. It is precisely this kind of subjective identity experience against which the schizophrenic patient's delusional experiences are serving as unconscious defenses. Just as I find this sort of identity experience difficult in a teaching interview, so may the resident find it impossibly difficult, on venturing a bit out of the relatively safe (for himself) conventional-psychiatrist role in his work with the patient and participating with him in a more tangibly affective manner. But I cannot see how we can help the patient with his largely unconscious, fearful conviction that he himself is something other than human if we remain too entrenched in having to demonstrate that we (the therapist) are the kindly, intendedly helpful, rage-free *one* in the relationship.

Malin writes of "The angry, violent attitude that is demonstrated by the violent schizophrenic patient and projected into the therapist . . ." Here is an area in which I sense a fundamental difference, as I have already mentioned, between his concepts and mine. I surmise that he tends to assume that the patient is purely projecting, whereas I always assume the patient's projection to be based upon some increment of reality in the therapist, no matter at how unconscious a level in the latter. I have cited many times in this connection Freud's (1922) drawing attention to the basis in reality of projection: "We begin to see that we describe the behaviour of both jealous and persecuted paranoics very inadequately by saying that they project outwards on to others what they do not wish to recognize in themselves. Certainly they do this; but they do not project it into the blue, so to speak, where there is nothing of the sort already" (p. 226).

Malin makes an excellent point when he suggests that the negative therapeutic reaction on the part of a violent schizophrenic patient can be a way in which the patient is hanging on to the only internal object situation he can handle, that is, the relationship to the primary objects, the breast-mother. Malin perceptively asks, "Are we perhaps dealing with the situation in which any attempt at growth and development means to the patient that this breast-mother must be relinquished, which he perceives as a fragmentation of all inner psychic contents and a disappearance of the self?" This I find a valuable way of describing the importance the patient comes to have for the therapist also, in what I describe as the phase of therapeutic symbiosis. It is the therapist's need to maintain under *repression* his experiencing the patient as being of such a primitive kind of maternal significance to him that accounts for his own unconscious resistance to letting the consciously desired maturational changes occur in the treatment relationship. From what I have seen both in my own work and in that of supervisees, it is only insofar as the therapist becomes *aware of* this kind of early-mother significance that the patient has for him (as well, of course, as he for the patient, which is much easier to recognize) that he becomes able, more wholeheartedly now, to work toward the patient's further recovery, which, as is now evident, will involve deep feelings of infantile loss not only for the patient but for the therapist also.

Little's comments I find, as in all of her papers which I have read, illuminating and informative, especially her thoughts about the varying degrees of differentiation in each of the patients described here and about the problem, therefore, of differential diagnosis and prognosis.

I know of no other writer besides Little who accepts as fully as I do that what I term a phase of therapeutic symbiosis (or, in Little's phrase, of undifferentiatedness) is essential in successful therapy. It is powerfully strengthening to me to read her statements (in marked contrast to Malin's views, for example, as I see it): "I agree entirely with Searles that the reactions brought about in the therapist are of prime importance. The ability to allow his ego boundaries to dissolve temporarily—to let himself become merged with the patient, and to permit reality and delusional or hallucinatory experience to become indistinguishable—is the only route by which real contact, understanding, and ability to share in an experience can develop." I fully agree, likewise, with her emphasis in the

very next sentence: "But equally important are the ways in which
the boundaries can be re-established, and the speed and progression of the resynthesis, when it is appropriate." Little's own writings
have been most helpful to me in this latter connection, and I wish
to recommend Jacobson (1964) as also providing highly valuable
formulations concerning the progressive differentiation of the various psychic structures.

Upon reading Bychowski's discussion I had intended to make a
spirited response to some of the more savage of his comments, but
having heard more recently the sad news of his death I feel that a
more moderate tone is in order here.

When he says that "apparently his entourage is also filled with
all sorts of violent feelings toward the patients," he was apparently
attributing to me, as I mentioned earlier, a sycophantic following
which does not in actuality exist. As I have said already, the colleagues who observe my interviews are, on balance, more critical
than these discussants are collectively, and I doubt that anyone
would regard any of them as sycophantic.

I hope few readers will respond to Bychowski's call for the
abandonment of an essentially psychoanalytic approach to such
dangerous patients as Mr. Delaney: "One has to ask whether some
other therapeutic method, such as conditioning or retraining, based,
of course, on the dynamic insights, might not be more appropriate."

The gulf between Bychowski's views and my own is so wide that
I cannot attempt to bridge it in this brief space. I am content to
leave it for readers of his work and of mine to take from it what
they find useful and relevant, and discard the rest. The dimensions
of the gulf are suggested not only by the excoriating nature of
some of his remarks here, but also by a statement he makes in his
book *Psychotherapy of Psychosis* (1952), near the beginning of the first
chapter on "The Personality of the Psychiatrist": "not only should
he not respond with overt hostility to aggressive manifestations of
the patient, *it is also necessary that he should be sufficiently mature so as
not to harbor any resentment toward him*" [p. 1; italics mine]. This point
of view, which would require that a therapist of integrity be either

obsessive or schizoid if he were not to disqualify himself from attempting this kind of work, was precisely my emotional orientation toward patients, neurotic as well as psychotic, 27 years ago. As I have already mentioned, I have been spending all these years primarily in a difficult struggle to become less constricted, more open to communications from my own unconscious, and, by the same token, from the patient himself.

I was amused at Bychowski's extending me his "sympathy" for my troubled inner state; well might I need sympathy, after he got through with me. But I am not to be pitied for having become able to let a patient become lastingly a part of me; for me, that is a hard-won accomplishment.

Wexler is a man from whom, I am sure, I can learn much. All that he says concerning efforts at reparation make a great deal of sense to me, and his statement that "no single formulation serves to explain the violence of the schizophrenic patient" is incontestable. I hold that my capacity for integrated ego functioning is not as fully in chaos as he apparently regards it; but, after Bychowski, Wexler's comments made relatively light reading for me, such that I feel moved only to express the hope that we shall have a chance, sometime, to compare clinical experiences at leisure.

In his description of his treatment of the woman doctor who suffered from an at times delusional syphilophobia, Rosenfeld mentions, "In the countertransference I never felt that I was the murderous mother, but I was aware of an intense pressure coming from the patient to change me into a punishing, frightening superego which threatened her with death and accused her of not being human." Here I wish to emphasize that, in my own analytic work, neither do *I* feel that I *am* the murderous mother; I definitely am not recommending that the analyst be, or transitorily become, psychotic (i.e., come to misidentify himself as being the patient's mother, for example) in working with these patients.

But I definitely would find it mystifying if the analyst were entirely a stranger to murderous feelings within himself toward such difficult patients as Rosenfeld has treated. Rosenfeld, whose writings have taught me much, as I have many times acknowledged, nonetheless is a prime example of those colleagues who, in my opinion, portray psychoanalytic treatment as though the patient's transference is "pure transference" and the latter's projection "pure projection," without these reactions being based upon any reality in the feelings—murderous feelings, for example—which the analyst indeed comes to experience toward the patient over the course of the often difficult treatment.

Similarly, while Rosenfeld makes a useful point about the importance of assessing the strength of the patient's murderous intent versus the strength of his fear of it and wish to become able to control it, his comment that it may or may not be a "real" desire to kill reflects, in my opinion, his tendency, repeatedly manifest in his writings, to imply that some feelings are not "real." It is important that we regard both sides of the patient's conflictual feelings as *real*, for otherwise we fail to appreciate the intensity of his genuine conflict.

In hypothesizing about the situation where the small infant projects his destructiveness and his fear of it into his mother, Rosenfeld suggests, "It is the mother's capacity to contain both the aggression and the fear of disintegration (Bion) which gradually leads to a lessening of the sense of danger and to a strengthening of the infantile ego in coping with the aggressive impulses." Here again, in line with my foregoing commentary about Rosenfeld's views, I suggest that the mother's capacity to contain the aggression consists in part in her being conscious of, rather than needing to repress and project upon the infant or other persons, the murderous component of her actual feelings toward him.

I concur with Rosenfeld's well-stated emphasis upon the importance of distinguishing between neurotic countertransference on the analyst's part and "countertransference" that is essentially an empathic experiencing of feelings communicated from the patient. This indeed is an ever-present, never completed, and most important task. As I have already said, concerning the evolution of my own analytic position over the years, it is only as I have gained, bit by bit, a degree of increased freedom from an initial too-great readiness to *assume*, guiltily and frightenedly, that this or that emotional response within myself was predominantly of the former (true countertransference) variety, that I have become increasingly able to appreciate the richness and accuracy of the information, at times no less than amazing, which flows from the patient to oneself, largely by nonverbal avenues, and which is made available by largely unconscious empathic processes. In order to come to understand the workings of these processes better than we do at present, it is essential, in my opinion, that we react to such "personal" responses within ourselves not by self-condemnation but by regarding them, until proved otherwise (until proved, that is, more properly a function of the analyst's own unanalyzed childhood history), as inherent and priceless data of the patient's analysis, data for mutual exploration—well timed, of course—on the part of both patient and analyst, and eminently deserving of inclusion in any subsequently published account of the analysis.

Bak's discussion is brief but telling and requires, therefore, that I respond to it at relative length. It is evident that he is more conservative, analytically, than I—more cautious, more given to emphasizing secondary process. To me he represents that aggregation of relatively classical analysts who are inclined to regard me as a wild analyst and who, from hard-won positions of respect and even dominance over much of the psychoanalytic thinking in this country, have made it difficult for me to get my papers published in our leading analytic journals.

Bak makes the excellent and fundamental point (in emphasizing, as does Wexler, the patient's restitutive effort) that "It is not easy to decide whether the murderous acts represent a breakthrough of aggression with the aim of destroying a person, or whether they appear in the course of restitution, i.e., re-establishing lost contact with the world (objects)." Clinical documentation of this point is contained in a paper of mine (1958b) in which I describe at considerable length some of the clinical events of my work with a murderously rageful and frequently hallucinating hebephrenic man, and summarize the description by saying, "It was both fascinating to me in a research sense, and deeply gratifying to me as a therapist, to find that, by the end of two and a half years of both his, and my own, becoming more fully and consistently aware of our respective feelings of intense contempt and rage, his hallucinating had now all but disappeared from our sessions" (p. 204). We had become, that is, much more real interpersonal objects to one another. Similarly, in recent years I have come to realize with increasing frequency that urges toward physical violence, on the part of either a patient or myself, are in the service of our effort to make some human contact with one another in the face of the chilling weirdness attendant upon his most severely schizophrenic ways of relating to me and to others.

Bak's statement that "The lack of differentiation between animate and inanimate objects is not a cause of violence but in a way a consequence of it" might better be expressed, I believe (as I endeavored to describe in this paper), as *both* a cause *and* a consequence. My previously mentioned paper (1972a) concerning delusional transference contains much data from the account of the chronically schizophrenic woman whose analysis is detailed there, clearly showing that her awesome degree of nondifferentiation between animate and inanimate objects is both a cause and in part a consequence of her violence.

Bak comments that "one cannot help feeling that these subjective reactions of the therapist and supervisor are overdrawn. Instead of using them as *signals* for intellectual awareness, they may be *lived* for longer than necessary." This is a sobering point, with much riding on it—the whole question of whether I do wild analysis and indulge in being crazy along with the patient. I genuinely do not believe that I do, and I believe that Bak, like other persons who have made comparable comments about my interviews with schizophrenic patients, would feel reassured if he were present at typical sessions with neurotic patients—during, for example, the considerable number of training analyses I have done and am doing. I have been a training analyst for 15 years now, and for nine of them have spent most of my working time in that activity. In most such sessions I say little or nothing at all, and find that it is only on landmark occasions—of crucial value, nonetheless, for the analytic work—that I engage at all openly in the kind of interaction which is commonplace in my work (whether as therapist or teaching-consultant) with borderline and more severely ill patients. But I find his comment sufficiently thought-provoking to keep it very much in mind during the coming years in evaluating my own work and endeavoring to be maximally useful to and minimally exploitative of or otherwise harmful to patients.

He goes on, "Also, there is too much emphasis on subjective observation. . . . there is still room for clinical judgment and prognostication, at least partly based on experience." Here I wish to mention once again the inherent inadequacy of transcriptions of interviews. During these interviews I am responding in actuality, to a far higher degree than the reader has any way of knowing from this paper, to tangible nonverbal cues from the patient, cues which I perceive in a context of many previous interviews with other patients who, as regards the particular psychodynamics giving rise to the cue in question, are clinically very comparable with the patient I am presently interviewing. It is this accumulated clinical experience that, hand in hand with an increasingly frequent finding that my own personal responses to the patient are indeed relevant to what is going on in his unconscious, has given me the confidence to conduct these demonstration interviews in a manner that increasingly reveals my "personal" responses in the interview situation.

Another factor in this paper is that each of the three interviews it details was an extraordinarily anxious one for me personally, compared with the vast majority of such interviews I have conducted. I have had other interviews which were equally stressful, but not many. I chose these partly because of what I regarded as their relatively high dramatic potential for capturing the interest of the reader; but one of the prices I have paid by such a selection is that in them I emerge as more threatened with feelings of anxiety and isolation and less comfortably ensconced in clinical experience than is usually the case in my demonstration interviews.

Before leaving Bak's discussion I want to make a point concerning a subject upon which he touches: prognostication. It is easy for psychiatric residents to attribute prognostic omniscience to anyone who has had a great deal of experience in working with schizophrenic patients; his wealth of clinical experience is so great as seemingly to place his clinical objectivity, in handing down a prognostic pronouncement, beyond serious question. But I have found innumerable times that one of the most important lessons to be learned from these interviews, by me as well as by the residents I am teaching, is the subtly distorting impact the interviewer's unrecognized countertransference has upon the prognostication he tends so loftily to give—and which in most cases, indeed, he is called upon to render.

There is a tremendous tendency, for example, for the interviewer to remain largely unconscious of the hate the patient engenders in him during the interview, and to act out this hate during the discussion period after the interview by assigning to the patient a gloomy, basically hopeless prognosis, in a hypocritically sad or gloomy manner. In the light of the interviewer's prestige, this is equivalent to his placing a very considerably effective curse upon the patient who, during the just-terminated interview, has succeeded in doing various forms of violence to some of the interviewer's more cherished images of himself.

There is a comparably powerful tendency, on the other hand, for the interviewer not to face, during the interview, his own feelings of disappointment and disillusionment toward a patient who has proven able to maintain a façade of relative health and attractiveness. Thus, after the interview, he is likely to de-emphasize, in his comments about prognosis, the seriousness and tenacity of the pathologic process actually at work in the patient.

The interviewer's relationship with the therapist, and with the resident-group generally, is another important dimension, making real clinical objectivity most difficult to attain in this setting. The interviewer tends to be constricted, partially outside his own awareness, by a concern not to place too frighteningly somber a prognosis upon a patient about whom these other persons have high hopes, founded largely upon a transitory and superficial, transference-based symptomatic improvement in the therapeutic work thus far.

In short, where Bak reacts to what he tends, I gather, to regard as relatively wild analysis on my part, I react with comparable skepticism to his apparent assumption that clinical objectivity, acquired on the basis of no matter how many years of experience, can be maintained with relative comfort and certainty in the face of the intensity of involvement which these interviews need to achieve in order to be of maximal therapeutic and teaching value. Such supposed objectivity could well be regarded as wildly illusory.

Flarsheim comments, "I have had psychiatric residents misuse Searles's writings to justify burdening patients with their own emotional reactions, which are disruptive to the treatment." His reservations are to a degree, in my opinion, justified. In responding to Malin's discussion, I acknowledged that sometimes a psychiatric resident's attempted identification with me does not go well. In the belief that several of the discernible factors involved are not limited to my own experience but are present in the work of supervisors and consultants generally, I shall mention a number of them. I spoke before of (1) the resident's relative lack of familiarity with the workings of his own unconscious and relative lack of clinical experience, particularly with regard to the patient's responses to interpretations. In addition, there are the following factors to be considered in instances where the resident's attempted identification with me proves antitherapeutic to the patient: (2) the resident's partially unconscious, partially transference-derived competitive feelings, contempt, and rage toward me, and consequent unconscious attempt to demonstrate my techniques as being predominantly antitherapeutic; (3) the patient's unworked-through murderous rage at me, in terms of which patient and therapist in effect join together in murdering my intended image as a constructively functioning psychotherapist; (4) frustrated dependency feelings, on the part of both patient and therapist, toward me (who in reality visits their institution, if more than once only, then at best infrequently); (5) the competitiveness of senior staff members toward me, lest I acquire the role of favorite teacher-model for the residents; (6) my own competitiveness toward the resident-therapist, the senior staff members, and also toward the patient—competitiveness heightened by my own relative professional isolation as a full-time private practitioner and occasional consultant, who has found painful the loneliness attendant upon his having left Chestnut Lodge nearly 10 year ago, after nearly 15 years of work on its staff, and who has not acquired subsequently a comparable degree of group-relatedness with colleagues. I realized too, some years back, with rueful amusement, that (7) the flounderingly inept resident who is struggling to be Searles is indeed accurately identifying with an entirely real component of my ego identity—with, that is, the "me" which is struggling to be SEARLES, struggling to fulfill my own ego ideals as well as the images which the more admiringly hopeful of the audience members apparently have of me.

In this last regard, as the years go by I have become appreciably less burdened with concern about the audience's reaction. There have been many interviews which have left me aware that the audience was feeling predominantly disappointed and dissatisfied with the interview, but in which I have felt nonetheless, about myself, that given the difficulties posed by the patient's psychopathology, and given my own, to-me familiar limitations in ego functioning imposed by unresolved areas of psychopathology in myself, I have done sufficiently well to feel relatively kindly and accepting toward myself. The audience's expectations, if one is too much at their mercy as a projected, harshly demanding superego, can be cruel indeed.

I fully concur with Flarsheim's emphasis upon the prognostically differentiating role of available capacity for humor in the patient. I would add only my conviction, developed over the years, that *everyone* has a sense of humor, no matter how straight-faced, sadistically mocking, or otherwise unconventional its mode of expression, and no matter at how unconscious a level it is operating. It is relatively seldom, and in my opinion of particularly sobering prognostic significance, that one of my demonstration interviews, even with a tragically ill patient, includes no moments of shared and genuinely amused laughter. So I tend to ask myself, during the interview, not whether this patient has a sense of humor, but rather, "How is his particular sense of humor being manifested at present, and is he predominantly conscious or unconscious of it?"

I am sure that Flarsheim recognizes that, on the other hand, the patient's capacity for humor can be employed unconsciously as a powerful resistance to therapeutic progress. More than once I have seen, in my own analytic patients and others, that a patient particularly talented in the use of humor can postpone, time after time, his becoming aware of wishes to murder me, by proving reliably able to cause me again and again to break up in laughter, the unconscious equivalent of slaying me. Such interaction can serve for both participants as an unconscious means of fending off the recognition of murderous feelings, grief, and other nonhumorous emotions which need to become integrated in the course of their analytic work. The chronic schizophrenic patient's sense of humor is often manifested, in a manner largely unconscious to both participants, in mockingly sadistic, highly treatment-resistant delusional identifications with the therapist, such as I described in a recent paper (1972a).

Flarsheim's statement that "There are limits to the patient's capacity for actual, in contrast to fantasied, destruction" is surely valid, and to me seems relevant to my impression, mentioned in the first paragraph of the discussion section of this paper, that those patients who most violently damage one's image of oneself have no need to resort to physical violence toward one.

He says, "The therapist's unconscious destructiveness toward the patient can also take the form of an unconscious wish for the patient to commit suicide; this may first be experienced by the therapist as anxiety lest the patient commit suicide." Flarsheim's experience in this regard evidently corresponds to mine. As I mentioned in another paper (1967b):

> . . . the suicidal patient, who finds us so unable to be aware of the murderous feelings he fosters in us through his guilt and anxiety-producing threats of suicide, feels increasingly constricted, perhaps indeed to the point of suicide, by the therapist who, in reaction formation against his intensifying, unconscious wishes to kill the patient, hovers increasingly "protectively" about the latter, for whom he feels an omnipotence-based physicianly concern. Hence it is, paradoxically, the very physician most anxiously concerned to *keep the patient alive* who tends

most vigorously, at an unconscious level, to drive him to what has come to seem the only autonomous act left to him—namely, suicide.

Relevant here, too, are the following passages from my earlier paper (1961e), "Phases of Patient-Therapist Interaction in the Psychotherapy of Chronic Schizophrenia," concerning the phase of resolution of the symbiosis:

> On the other occasions, the therapist experiences a resolution of the symbiosis, or at least a step in this resolution process, not in this quiet and subjectively inscrutable way, but rather with a sudden sense of *outrage* [p. 544].

> . . . One now leaves in his hands the choice as to whether he wants to spend the remainder of his life in a mental hospital, or whether he wants, instead, to become well. In every instance that I can recall . . . I have found occasion to express this newly won attitude to the patient himself, emphasizing that it is all the same to me. . . . One cares not, now, how callous this may sound, nor even whether the patient will respond to it with suicide or incurable psychotic disintegration; and one feels and says this while casting one's own professional status, too, into the gamble. . . . Thus, in effect, one braves the threat of destruction both to the patient and oneself, in taking it into one's hands to declare one's individuality, come what may [p. 545].

> . . . if the therapeutic relationship is to traverse successfully the phase of resolution of the symbiosis, the therapist must be able to brave . . . the threats of suicide or psychotic disintegration on the patient's part, and of the professional and personal destruction to himself which might be a correlate of such outcomes . . . [p. 549].

I am deeply gratified by Flarsheim's appreciation of my work, and in turn find informative and congenial to my own clinical experience all that he says, in his discussion, of the psychodynamics of violence and suicide. Without the kind of professional comradeship I feel toward him, and in varying degrees toward all these discussants who have accorded this paper their thoughtful comments, psychoanalytic work with schizophrenic patients, which at best is formidable despite its many gratifications, would be quite impossible.

18

Countertransference and Theoretical Model

My working theoretical model for the treatment of schizophrenic patients includes the following elements.

1. The analyst's own more primitive modes of experience, and of interpersonal relatedness, have not been permanently resolved through his personal analysis and other maturing experiences, but are subject to being revived in the course of his ongoing adult-life experience, and this is indispensably true in his work with schizophrenic patients. His analysis is effective insofar as it has given him ready access to, rather than its having somehow affected, his capacities for primitive feelings of jealousy, fear, rage, symbiotic dependency, and other affective states against which his patient's schizophrenia typically serves to defend the patient from experiencing in awareness.

Mahler's (1968) repeated emphasis upon what the Los Angeles group call "genetically prepared tendencies" is related to her seeming obliviousness of the therapeutic necessity for the analyst to gain access to, and utilize in the treatment of the psychotic patient, his own (i.e., the analyst's) intensely bad-mother identity components.

This paper was originally presented as a discussion of the panel on "The Influence of Theoretical Model on Practice in Treating Schizophrenia," given at the meeting of the American Psychoanalytic Association in New York City on December 1, 1972. It was first published in *Psychotherapy of Schizophrenia*, edited by John G. Gunderson and Loren R. Mosher (New York: Jason Aronson, 1975), pp. 223-228.

Thus Mahler underestimates the degree of interpersonal, intrafamilial trauma the patient has suffered despite a relatively normal genetic endowment. By the same token, she underestimates the degree of personally intended sadistic and murderous trauma that the patient inflicts upon the analyst and evokes, retaliatorily, from the analyst.

2. There is thus some basis in reality for all the patient's "delusional transference" reactions, such as his perceiving the analyst as being the personification of the patient's ego-fragmented mother, or emotionally remote father, or whatever. The analyst's working in implicit acknowledgment of these nuclei of reality perceptions in the transference—rather than maintaining relentlessly an assumption that the patient embodies all the disturbingly intense ambivalence, for example, in the treatment situation—is necessary to the patient's developing a better integrated and more comprehensive reality relatedness.

3. A healthier reindividuation on the patient's part requires an experience of therapeutic symbiosis in which the analyst participates at a feeling-level, although to a manageable degree, subject always to his own analytic scrutiny, and quite different in nature from an acted-out *folie à deux*.

4. The patient's own therapeutic strivings toward the analyst, including the patient's guilt- and grief-laden feelings about his having failed to enable the fragmented mother to be a whole and fulfilled mother to him, are of fundamental importance in the therapeutically symbiotic phase of the work.

5. The most basic problem in schizophrenia is the patient's having failed to develop a human identity, either subjectively or, in the more severe and chronic cases, objectively as well. It is in the phase of therapeutic symbiosis that a process of mutual rehumanization, as well as reindividuation, is enabled to occur, through the therapeutic relationship's having become sufficiently strong to enable both participants to let come into play, in the ongoing exploration of the transference, subjectively nonhuman identity ingredients which heretofore had been split off from awareness and acted out in behavior.

Those analysts who view schizophrenia predominantly as a deficiency disease are typically needful of maintaining under repression the bad-mother components of their own identities, and of seeking to reaffirm, in their attemptedly warm and giving approach to the schizophrenic patient, their own good-mother aspects. They are in effect asking the patient to rescue them from their own feared bad-self, or bad-mother introjects.

The paper presented by Dr. Holzman (1975), although largely identical with the version sent to me, has been changed as regards some of the points upon which my prepared remarks are based. In my comments, therefore, I shall be quoting passages from the earlier version.

I, like the members of Dr. Holzman's group, have my own differences with classical analysis. Further, I have known at first hand the value, for therapy and research, of the family approach. I have seen phenothiazines, when used in a moderate and well-timed fashion, facilitate analytic therapy, although I do not employ them. In addition, I regard general systems theory as an exciting and promising new field of scientific thought.

Nonetheless, I find the Holzman paper both dangerous and disturbing. It is dangerous because, in the midst of repeated and incontestable appeals for open-mindedness, it would set schizophrenic persons apart, qualitatively and indelibly, from their fellow human beings as, in their very essence, something less than human. The paper's aura of high-sounding, up-to-date scientific versatility evokes feelings of inferiority and self-doubt in the reader who is committed to an essentially psychoanalytic endeavor, and who well knows that he has reason for humility.

Where I think of the phases of treatment in terms of patient-analyst interaction, Dr. Kayton (1975), however interestingly, conceptualizes them in terms of the patient's inner experience. It is significant that this paper, which states that "During the last two decades . . . progress has come principally from sources outside the psychoanalytic consulting room," says nothing about the analyst's own inner experience of the work. My approach focuses, by contrast, upon the countertransference realm, in the broadest sense of that term, as being of the greatest and most reliable research and therapeutic value. This focus is not intended as a means of providing narcissistic gratification to the analyst-researcher; quite to the contrary, his personality and especially his sense of identity is found, in one practitioner after another, to be a most sensitive and reliably informative scientific instrument providing data as to what is transpiring, often in areas not verbally articulable by the patient, in the treatment situation.

In my monograph on the nonhuman environment (1960) and in a number of subsequent papers, I have described the necessity of the analyst's helping the patient to become established as both subjectively and objectively human, and of the analyst's becoming able, in this process, to tolerate and even to enjoy, various "nonhuman" transference positions, positions which are experienced by him at first as a frightening threat to his own subjective humanness.

Dr. Holzman (1975) would have us join him and his colleagues in taking flight from the necessary and unremitting exploration of the so-called countertransference dimension of the intensive psychoanalytic treatment of the schizophrenic person and, to the psychiatrist's own relief, taking refuge in relegating the patient to a supposedly separate realm of existence, a qualitatively not-quite-human realm, a realm beyond the psychiatrist's human empathy. I strongly surmise that, when the therapeutic interaction starts to evoke subjectively nonhuman aspects of these analysts' identities, they would turn relatively quickly to the latest information from such scientific fields as behavior genetics, biochemistry, psycho-pharmacology, epidemiology, and so on, to find reassuring evidence that the schizophrenic patient is, after all, qualitatively different from truly human beings—so that it is pointless to risk one's own going insane by persisting in this disturbingly conflict-ridden effort to work psychoanalytically with him.

The version of the Holzman paper I received contained, for example, this passage: "Some questions thus suggest themselves: (1) Do psychotherapeutic interventions require as intensive a schedule as does psychoanalysis with nonpsychotic patients? (2) Can the same psychotherapeutic effects be achieved by paraprofessional people or even by groups of patients themselves? (3) Does the mere stable presence of other interested persons provide the necessary support for helping to order the internal disorder and thus to help restoration?" Now, each of these questions has some worth in itself; but, taken together, they are the kind of things said in this paper which, to me, seem to be a downgrading of schizophrenic patients.

Psychoanalysts are essentially the only group of therapists who, by reason of their commitment to a courageous and unceasing exploration of their own inner lives in the service of their treating of their patients, are equipped to discern, explore, and rescue the components of common humanity in the patient who is overwhelmed by a schizophrenic illness which, to less informed eyes, marks him as essentially nonhuman. The estimated 47 percent of all mental hospital patients who suffer from schizophrenia are there, many of them for decade after decade, not only because they have written off their fellow human beings as not kin to them, but also because their fellow human beings have come to accept this as functionally true. If the psychoanalytic movement itself takes refuge in what I regard essentially as a phenothiazine and genetics flight from this problem, then the long dark night of the soul will have been ushered in, not only for these vast numbers of schizophrenic patients—for the current ones who are already largely lost, and for the multitude who will follow them in the future—and for those relatively few psychoanalysts who are particularly interested in this field. It will also have been ushered in for the profession of psychoanalysis generally, and for the patients, generally borderline and neurotic and so on, whom psychoanalysts treat. For once we give up our heretofore unremitting, open-mindedly observational effort to discern, through an empathic exploration of our own so-called countertransference responses to our patient, the human essence in him which is struggling against the psychopathology besetting his humanness, there is no end to this flight on our part.

The Holzman group says that "Neurosis and schizophrenia are . . . to be conceived of not as a continuum, but schizophrenic and neurotic behaviors are uniquely different." I find this so-called unique difference to be explicable and resolvable in terms of very primitive, preindividuation, and even presymbiotic, processes—described by Mahler (1968) and others—which all human beings, including those suffering from schizophrenia, share in common, as can be discovered, with reliable repetitiveness, if we remain sufficiently open-mindedly observational of the so-called countertransference realm of clinical phenomena.

Dr. Stierlin's (1975) thoughtful paper contains many theoretical points that I find stimulating and worthy of prolonged clinical evaluation. He beautifully shows that the parents' attemptedly expelling push upon the patient does not imply real separation, but a tragic boundness. But I suggest that for a genuine loosening to occur, the binding first must develop in the transference, in what I call a "pathogenic symbiosis," so that the analyst can know both its gratifications as well as its frustrations and terrors, at first hand. This stage must occur before this mode of transference relatedness can become resolved into that which I term "therapeutic symbiosis," from which a healthier individuation can emerge.

Despite his saying that the children mold and influence their parents as much as the latter mold and influence them, and despite his saying that the therapist can empathically share the plight of the parents as victimized victimizers, Dr. Stierlin's paper is marred, nonetheless, by a recurrent note of blamingness toward the parents as being responsible for the child's schizophrenia. When he speaks of the parents as impressing their own stronger reality upon the child—a view which inherently would attribute to the parents a predominant responsibility for the child's schizophrenia—he takes either no, or too little, account of the following factors.

First, the parents' transferences to the child are such that he, little though he is, is perceived unconsciously as far more powerful than they. Second, the child derives enormous sadistic gratification from the position of being afflicted with schizophrenia for which the parents are held guiltily responsible. Third, as I mentioned earlier and as I have come to see only in recent years, the child himself has a deeply repressed sense of grief as well as guilt, in part reality-based, for his own failure in a predominantly loving effort to enable the fragmented mother, for example, to function as a whole and fulfilled mother to him. In resorting to a blaming of the parents, we underestimate not only their loving components but the child's also, and shield ourselves from the tragedy which has overwhelmed all of them.

We should not place upon the parents an onus of responsibility we are unwilling genuinely to look for in ourselves as well as in the patients. Repeatedly I have found that, when such emotions as hate, cruelty, rejectingness, and condemnation in myself and in the patient are too intense to be endured, it is momentarily alleviating, indeed, to conjure up images of the patient's parents as being—from however long ago and far away—the persecutors who are making the *immediate* situation so intolerable, rather than maintaining subjective responsibility for my own sadism, for example, and holding the patient responsible for his identifications with the parental aggressors of long ago. The analyst needs, during these stressful times, all his emotional powers at his command; nothing less will do. To displace or project upon the parents the sharpest intensity of, for instance, one's condemnatory feelings toward the patient, is equivalent to tying one's own hands. Such theoretical reasoning provides one with a rationalization for deferring an utterly essential experience of coming fully to grips with the schizophrenic patient.

19

The Patient as Therapist to His Analyst

INTRODUCTION

This paper is devoted to the hypothesis that innate among man's most powerful strivings toward his fellow men, beginning in the earliest years and even earliest months of life, is an essentially psychotherapeutic striving. The tiny percentage of human beings who devote their professional careers to the practice of psychoanalysis or psychotherapy are only giving explicit expression to a therapeutic devotion which all human beings share. As for the appreciably larger percentage of human beings who become patients in psychoanalysis or psychotherapy, I am suggesting here not merely that the patient wants to give therapy to, as well as receive therapy from, his doctor; my hypothesis has to do with something far more fundamental than that. I am hypothesizing that the patient *is ill because, and to the degree that,* his own psychotherapeutic strivings have been subjected to such vicissitudes that they have been rendered inordinately intense, frustrated of fulfillment or

A shorter version of this paper, entitled "The Patient as Therapist to His Therapist," was presented at a colloquium of the Postdoctoral Program of the Department of Psychology, New York University, New York City, on September 29, 1972, and also to the combined annual meeting of the Washington Psychiatric Society and the Washington Psychoanalytic Society, Washington, D.C., on November 10, 1972. The full version was originally published in *Tactics and Techniques in Psychoanalytic Therapy, Volume II: Countertransference*, edited by Peter L. Giovacchini (New York: Jason Aronson, 1975), pp. 95-151.

Reparation aspect

even acknowledgment, and admixed therefore with unduly intense components of hate, envy, and competitiveness. They have thus been subjected to (or maintained under, from the outset of consciousness) repression. In transference terms, the patient's illness is expressive of his unconscious attempt to cure the doctor.

When I suggest that the patient is ill because of the developmental vicissitudes of this particular striving, from among the various emotional strivings which make up the human affective equipment, I am, of course, putting the matter too simply. It is well known that any neurotic or psychotic symptom is multiply determined and surely, therefore, is any instance, more complexly, of a neurosis or psychosis. But not only do I wish here to highlight a theme—a determinant of neurosis and psychosis—which would be erased by too many qualifications; I do indeed assert that I know of no other determinant of psychological illness that compares, in etiologic importance, with this one.

There is admittedly, at a glance, a jarring note of contrivance, of artificiality, about suggesting that even a human infant can be viewed as an intended psychotherapist. It is more congenial to think simply in terms of human beings' love, or nascent capacities to develop love, for one another and of their desire to help the other to fulfill his or her human psychological potentialities. But I am endeavoring, of course, to be more specific and explicit than that, and above all I am focusing upon the situation of psychoanalytic therapy, wishing to highlight both the irony and the technical importance of the (to my mind) fact that the more ill a patient is, the more does his successful treatment require that he become, and be implicitly acknowledged as having become, a therapist to his officially designated therapist, the analyst.

Parenthetically, throughout this paper I shall use the terms "therapist" and "analyst" interchangeably—a dubious procedure in a paper about this particular subject, but necessary, in my opinion, to facilitate the exposition. I do not forget that the analyst, unlike the patient, has equipped himself with psychoanalytic training, and I shall touch later upon some of the difference this makes as regards their respective abilities to utilize effectively their mutually powerful, basically human therapeutic strivings. At this juncture I wish to mention, as regards the special case of the patient who is himself a psychoanalyst or is acquiring psychoanalytic training, that I have done or am doing by now a considerable number of training analyses, and have found that, for the purposes of this paper, the therapeutic strivings at work in each of these patients, powerful as they are, are no more so than I have found in my nontraining analysands. Just as the analysis of dreams shows that every human being is unconsciously a creative dramatist, so one finds that he is also unconsciously a psychotherapist.

Later I shall briefly discuss the relatively scanty existing literature on this subject. At the moment, it is fair to say that psychoanalytic literature is written, for the vastly predominant part, with the assumption that the analyst is healthy and therefore does not need psychological help from the patient, who is ill and therefore needs psychological help from, and is unable to give such help to, the analyst. My own training analysis was a highly classical one and I emerged from it markedly less ill than I had been at the beginning; but it is a source of lasting pain to me that the analyst, like each of my parents long before, maintained a high degree of unacknowledgment of my genuine desire to be helpful to him.

In my own practice of psychoanalytic therapy and in my supervision of such work on the part of colleagues, I have found over and over that stalemates in the treatment, when explored sufficiently, involve the analyst's receiving currently a kind of therapeutic support from the patient of which both patient and analyst have been unconscious. Thus ironically, and in the instances when this status quo does not become resolved, one can say indeed tragically, in those very instances wherein the analyst is endeavoring most anguishedly and unsuccessfully to help the patient to resolve the tenacious symptom, or the tenaciously neurotic or psychotic *modus vivendi*, at an unconscious level the analyst is most tenaciously clinging to this very mode of relatedness as being one in which he, the analyst, is receiving therapy from the patient, without the conscious knowledge of either of them.

This paper is allied with, and based upon, many of my previous writings (1965a, 1971, 1973a). In an early paper (1951), and in many subsequent ones, I tried to highlight the analyst's unconscious gratifications in a treatment-resistant mode of patient-analyst relatedness which he is making every effort, consciously, to help the patient to resolve. A still earlier paper (1949) put forward, as one of its hypotheses, the suggestion that there is an element of reality in all the patient's distorted transference perceptions of the analyst, in keeping with Freud's (1922) statement regarding projection that we do not project "into the blue, so to speak, where there is nothing of the sort already" (p. 226), but rather upon someone or something which offers us some reality basis for the projection. One of my papers (1972a), concerning my work over nearly 20 years with an awesomely psychotic woman, had as its main theme the highlighting of the reality components (each of which had long remained unconscious to me) in her highly distorted, psychotic transference reactions to me.

One might think—erroneously, I believe—of the whole subject of this paper as being understandable in terms of the patient's fulfilling, in any one current situation under study, some neurotic or psychotic need on the part of the analyst. This view is erroneous for at least two reasons. (1) It does not credit the patient with an at least potential therapeutic initiative, at a predominantly unconscious if not conscious level—the initiative, the active striving, to function or continue functioning as therapist to the analyst. (2) It does not take into the account the dimension of months and years of time. Patients manifest, over the course of the months and years of their treatment, an interest, a genuine caring, as to whether the analyst himself has been growing and thriving during and as a result of their therapeutic ministrations to him.

In 1961 I reported my experience from analytic work that, as regards the reality relatedness between patient and analyst, as differentiated from the transference relatedness between the two, "the evolving reality relatedness . . . pursues its own course, related to and paralleling, but not fully embraced by, the evolving transference relatedness over the years of the two persons' work together" (1961a, p. 378). In another paper in 1961 I reported: "It has been

my impression . . . that the evolution of the reality-relatedness proceeds always a bit ahead of, and makes possible, the progressive
evolution and resolution of the transference, although to be sure
the latter, in so far as it frees psychological energy and makes it
available for reality-relatedness, helps greatly to consolidate the
ground just taken over by the advancing reality-relationship"
(1961e, p. 557). In the present paper I hypothesize a large step further: the evolution of the transference from, say, the patient's
transference reaction to the analyst as being a harshly dominating
father to his coming to perceive the analyst as a much gentler
but threateningly devouring mother-figure, involves a crucial
element—that the patient has been *in reality* at least partially successful as a therapist who has been attempting to help the analyst to
modify the latter's *real* harsh-father identifications, and has received
some kind of feedback from the analyst in acknowledgment, however implicit and very possibly largely unconscious on the part of
both participants, that this change has occurred and that the patient has had a crucial role in bringing it about.

As in the instances of all my previous writings, I cannot hope to
"prove" anything here; psychoanalytic work is too intuitive, too
much dependent upon data which are inarticulable in spoken, and
even more so in written, words for that to be possible. But, as before, I hope that this paper, which emerges from my psychoanalytic
experience, will be sufficiently evocative, for colleagues, of their
own psychoanalytic experiences, to acquire the subjectively convincing "proof" for them also. I hope it can be seen that, if my
hypothesis is indeed valid, as I obviously am convinced it is, then
nothing less than a metamorphosis in our concepts of the nature of
the curative process in psychoanalysis flows from it.

Space here allows me to include only a very few of the clinical
experiences, from my work with neurotic and psychotic patients,
typical of those which have caused me to formulate this hypothesis.
The hypothesis is of particular significance for psychotic patients,
for psychosis involves the patient's not having achieved, in infancy
and childhood, the firm establishment of an individual human self.
In my view this tragedy is explicable primarily by reason of the par-

ticularly severe vicissitudes with which his very early therapeutic strivings were met, beginning prior to the time, in late infancy and early childhood, when he would normally have become able to achieve, and within his family setting would have been helped to achieve, individual selfhood. Instead, for him, life consisted basically in his postponement, as it were, of his own individuation, in the service of his functioning symbiotically as therapist to one or another of his family members, or to all collectively in a family symbiosis. For him, now a chronological adult in psychoanalytic treatment, the crucial issue is whether he and the analyst can function in such a manner that (1) a transference symbiosis can develop, a symbiosis which will at first be highly distorted or pathological, as contrasted to that epitomized by the healthy-mother-and-healthy-infant symbiosis; (2) the nuclei of reality in this pathologic symbiosis can become sufficiently evident to both patient and analyst that this symbiosis can gradually evolve into what I call a therapeutic symbiosis (1959b, 1965a, 1973a), which is essentially of the nature of the mutually growth-enhancing symbiosis of normal infancy; and (3) the mutual gratifications as well as, increasingly, further growth-frustrating aspects of this mode of relatedness can be dealt with, by both participants, such that a healthier individuation can occur, this time, for both of them.

In the course of phases (1) and (2) of the above-described sequence one encounters transference data, as I have come to see clearly only in recent years, which bring to light the patient's heretofore unconscious, lifelong guilt at his own failure in his therapeutic effort, begun very early in life indeed, to enable his ego-fragmented mother to become a whole and fulfilled mother to him. In my experience of recent years, it is only insofar as he can succeed in his comparable striving in the treatment, this time toward the therapist as being such a mother, that the patient can become sufficiently free from such guilt, sufficiently sure, as it were, of his symbiotic worth, so that he can now become more deeply a full human individual. In the treatment situation, individuation becomes free from its previous connotation of a murderous dismembering, or lethal abandonment, of the mother for whom the patient has not only been made to feel responsible, but whom the patient has genuinely loved and wanted to somehow make whole and fulfilled.

CLINICAL EXAMPLES OF THE PATIENT'S THERAPEUTIC ATTEMPT TO ENABLE THE ANALYST TO BECOME FREE FROM SOME NEUROTIC SYMPTOM OR CHARACTER TRAIT

Case 1

Mrs. A., a 28-year-old woman, clearly had had a strongly parental relationship with the youngest of her three siblings, a brother five years younger than herself, and it was early evident to me that there was much repressed grief in her concerning the loss of this relationship, which had been a most important area of the brother's childhood as well. During the first three years of her analysis she scarcely mentioned him from one year to the next, and then only most disparagingly and in passing, indicating that she thought of herself as having simply treated him in a disdainful, bullying manner.

But in the fourth year of the analysis, as her memories of their relationship began to emerge from repression, she recalled that the last several times she had fought with Eddie, when she was 16 or 17 years of age, he had won. "I guess that's why I stopped bringing them [their fist-fights] about. Actually, as I recall, I was quite pleased that he could beat me up. I guess that gave me some respect for him. I always thought he was a little drip; so after I found he could beat me up, I stopped— . . ." She said all this in a tone that made clear that she had had a very loving motive toward him in all this—a motive of helping him to become a man. I conveyed to her my impression of her tone, and suggested that she had been so motivated; but her dismissing response made clear that she was not yet able to accept anything like so-loving an image of herself.

Later on in the session she said very seriously, in another context, "My [eldest] sister says I was horrible to Eddie; so I guess I was." It seemed clear to me, although not yet interpretable, that she was afraid, at an unconscious level, lest she kill her sister, were she—the patient—to come to see how cruel was the self-image her sister had fostered in her, in relation to their brother. She spoke in this session of how "cruel," in retrospect, had been her sister's pitying attitude toward Eddie as being a weakling, and her fostering in the patient of such a view, likewise, of him. There were strong clues, partly accepted as such by her, that I was currently equivalent to Eddie in the transference relationship.

Later on in the session she said, again in reference to Eddie, "After we stopped fighting, we stopped having anything to do with one another. We never acknowledge one another's existence. We never talk; we never phone; we never write." It was apparent, although again not yet timely to interpret to her, that after her having helped Eddie to become a masterful male toward her, she and he had had subsequently to shun one another, partly because of the sexual temptation with which their relationship was now imbued.

This brief example is typical of those in my experience, both in terms of indicating how deeply repressed have been the patient's therapeutic strivings toward the other family member(s), and in terms of the clarification of the transference relationship.

Case 2

Miss B., a long-hospitalized woman, 40 years of age, devoted a considerable part of her time recurrently, over years of her treatment, to reacting to me as being her ambivalence-ridden, indecisive and therefore unfirm father. It was clear that her own needs included a need for me to become a stronger, more firmly limit-setting father toward her; but it was equally clear that she was trying persistently to help me to resolve the genuine flaw in myself which formed the nucleus of reality upon which that transference of hers to me was based. Through outrageously and persistently obstreperous behavior, which involved both blatant sexual provocativeness as well as physical onslaughts of various kinds, she eventually succeeded in fostering in me a degree of decisiveness and firmness, expressed in an at times masterful kind of limit-setting, which I had not achieved before with anyone, whether among my patients or other persons in my life. I worked for 13 years with this woman, the most deeply ill patient I have ever treated, and overall helped her much less than I wish it had been within my power to do. But I did help her considerably; I learned much from her; and one of the surest things I learned was that one of the important determinants of her illness had been a self-sacrificing effort to enable her father to become a man.

Case 3

Mrs. C., a 32-year-old attorney, had been beaten severely, on occasion, by her father when she was a child and he a relatively young and physically vigorous man. But in the later years of her upbringing, with the advent of adolescence on her part and aging and depression on his, his beating of her had ceased. When she began in analysis with me, he had long been old and incapacitated with arthritis. As year after year went by in the analysis, years during which her loving and erotic, as well as murderously rageful, feelings toward me as a father-figure remained largely under repression, she became increasingly discouraged. At a conscious level, her discouragement had to do with the tenacity of the symptoms for the relief of which she had sought analysis initially—namely, certain obsessive-compulsive rituals and a moderate but persistent alcoholism, both of which interfered appreciably with her professional work. Both these symptoms were expressions, in part, of her unconscious defiance toward me, whom she experienced as being her demanding, domineering father. At an unconscious level, however, her discouragement was related also to her inability to galvanize me, despite year after year of contemptuously defiant acting-out behavior and various forms of verbal inciting, into being the vigorous and virile young father who had beaten her. Her provocativeness clearly was not only expressive of an unconscious yearning for the erotic fulfillment with which her father's beatings had provided her but also was in the service of her striving to rejuvenate me, perceived as equivalent to an aging, impotent, helpless father in the transference. Meanwhile, during that phase of the analytic work, her grief about his aged and chronically ill condition was discernible directly only in brief glimpses.

Case 4

Mr. D., a 34-year-old man, said, after several years of analysis on the couch, in reference to his own resistance to the analysis, "I feel as though I won't participate—as though I sit down and refuse to take part . . ." I commented, "You say you feel as though you sit down and refuse to take part—*I'm* the one who's sitting down here." He agreed immediately, "Yeah—I've had the idea from time to time that you are depressed—and that I've got to do something to bring you out of yourself—to get you to blow up or—get you to lash out, or— . . ." A few minutes later, without any further intervention from me, he said, "When I think of my mother seated, she's always behind something [clearly an allusion to my being seated behind the couch]—behind her sewing machine, or behind her cookbooks, looking up recipes."

In a later session, he confided that he had long desired to be able to experience, and convey to me, a fantasy so vivid "that you would be able to say, 'Boy, that's a marvelous fantasy!' " It was clear that he was giving expression here, once again, to his long-familiar exasperation with himself for his relative inability to experience, and convey to me in the sessions, anything but highly reality-bound associational material. But, at an apparently less conscious level, he was alluding also to my own characterologic inability to express undisguised, unambivalent enthusiasm for the contribution the other person has made, or is making. Thus, here again, was a glimpse of his therapeutic striving on behalf of his depressed mother, as personified by me in the transference.

Upon hearing the statement just quoted, I was struck immediately by the fact of my adult-life-long inability to express such enthusiasm—an inability I had never acknowledged openly in my work with him, and an inability I manage, most of the time, to keep largely secret from myself. But I well know that it was not entirely, nor now even primarily, due to any derelection on his part, regarding his ability to experience and report fantasies, that I was unable to say, "Boy, that's a marvelous fantasy!" No matter how abundantly suitable an occasion he might provide me for saying this, I would be unable to say it. The inability emerged now, at this phase in the analysis, after considerable growth had occurred in him (in this regard as well as in other ways), as primarily mine. Although his therapeutic help had not proved sufficient to enable me appreciably to resolve the problem, he had helped me to confront it much more clearly than I characteristically do—and that surely is a help toward its eventual resolution.

I have dwelt at some length upon this brief clinical vignette, for it constitutes a typical example of how the analyst's psychopathology can remain masked—by introjective processes within the patient and projective processes within the analyst—within the patient's psychopathology. By the same token, it indicates how subtle is the presence of the patient's therapeutic striving—largely unconscious to him, remember, until much analysis in this regard has been accomplished—to cure this aspect of the analyst that he, the patient, has taken into himself, as it were, in his effort to heal the analyst.

One might believe that this therapeutic striving on the part of the patient is newly developed in the analysis; but my experience consistently has indicated to me quite otherwise—namely, that it has significant transference connections to his earlier life experience, and that it was indeed at work in him, though at an unconscious level, at the beginning of the analysis. When it emerges most clearly in the course of the analysis, the transference connections between the analyst and earlier figures in the patient's life, toward whom this therapeutic striving on the patient's part has been devoted, are convincingly tangible.

Case 5

Mrs. E., a 45-year-old woman, was sneezing, blowing her nose, and clearing her throat frequently in one of her analytic sessions. For years she had suffered from multiple allergies, and frequently had sinusitis with postnasal discharge, as she evidently did now. I felt, as I had felt during earlier years of her analysis with regard to a variety of her allergic symptoms, that her physical discomfort was being used unconsciously by her in a neurotically hostile manner. In the course of this session she commented, while clearing her throat for the nth time, that she had many times to make a heroic effort to keep from vomiting in my office. I was familiar with such comments from her (as well as occasionally from other patients), and she seemed, as usual, quite unconscious of any sadistic gratification in making me feel recurrently threatened lest she suddenly vomit copiously all over my couch, carpet, and God knows what else in my office.

There emerged during this session data indirectly indicating that the theme of whether she were able to *feel* was unconsciously at work. Once, for example, she commented, in reference to pain in her sinuses exacerbated by her violent sneezes, that she evidently is able to feel, all right. Upon hearing this I felt like mentioning to her tartly that she was functioning, however, in a way that made *me* feel very *un*feeling toward *her*; I felt convinced that she was projecting upon me her own subjective callousness and indifference to human suffering. I more than once felt like telling her that I found myself feeling that she could sneeze her goddamn head off, for all I cared. I was reacting to her enormous, but still largely unconscious, demandingness—demands for sympathy, admiration, and so on; any list would be endless—and to her also largely unconscious hostility and threateningness. The implicit threat lest she vomit was only one among a constellation of threats being conveyed to me. She gave me reason to feel intimidated, still, lest she suddenly sever the analytic relationship in one of her unpredictable episodes of furious impatience; and I feared, as well, her long-familiar capacity for character-assassinating me among her many social acquaintances, some of whom knew me personally. Thus on more than one count I felt unfree to use, as shared investigative data, my "unfeeling" reaction that she could sneeze her goddamn head off, for all I cared.

Driving home at the end of the day I realized, with great relief, that my being "unfeeling" is *one* among the gamut of emotional responses available to me in my work with patients, and that this reaction can be as useful, for mutually exploratory analytic work, as any others among the many emotional reactions (jealousy, anger, tender feeling, sexual feeling, and so on) which I long ago had become accustomed to utilizing in my psychoanalytic work in that fashion—as data of the patient's analysis. The relief accompanying this realization was tremendous, for until then I had found reason to fear, for several decades at crucial junctures in my personal and professional life, that I "really am" unable to feel, to care. That is, I had feared that this unfeeling one, subjectively not human, was the only real me—the only way, deep down in my core, that I really am.

In earlier years of this woman's analysis I had become aware of important ways in which the work with her was proving of unusual therapeutic value to me (as well as of considerable value, certainly, to her), and had found much evidence of powerful, and by no means entirely unconscious, therapeutic strivings on her part toward me. During the ensuing few days after this realization, which I had experienced while driving home, I came to feel sure that it, like a number of analogous insights earlier in our work, had been predominantly a result of her therapeutic strivings on my behalf— in this instance currently largely unconscious, so it appeared. My feeling in those ensuing few days was one of deep gratitude toward her. No one could possibly have helped me, so I felt, with anything more personally significant to me than this; this is where I had most been needing someone's help.

I am not unmindful of, although I consider it irrelevant for this paper to discuss, the transference aspects of the material of the session I have mentioned. I at no time lost sight of the fact that, however real my own concerns were lest I were indeed being unpardonably unfeeling in my responses or lack of response to her, I was personifying for her a number of figures from her past—notably her mother, whom she tended to experience as being indifferent to her suffering. As I mentioned earlier, in this paper I do not intend to focus upon transference phenomena per se, but rather upon those real increments of the analyst's personality functioning which serve, for the patient, as the nuclei of external reality that evoke his transference reactions.

CLINICAL EXAMPLES OF THE PATIENT'S THERAPEUTIC STRIVING TO ENABLE THE MOTHER TO BECOME TRULY A MOTHER

The healthy infant-mother symbiosis, which normally provides the foundation for later individuation, under tragic circumstances fosters the child's becoming not a truly human individual, but rather what one might call a symbiotic therapist, whose own ego wholeness is sacrificed, ongoingly throughout life, in a truly selfless devotion, to complementing the ego incompleteness of the mothering person, and of subsequent persons in his life who have the emotional meaning, in his unconscious, of similarly incomplete mothers whose ego functioning is dependent upon his being sustainingly a part of them. Such "negative" emotions as hatred and guilt, often cited in the literature on early ego development and the family dynamics of schizophrenia, are indeed a significant part of this etiological picture; but it is, I suggest, more than anything the patient's nascent capacity for love, and for the development of mature human responsibility, that impels him to perpetuate this mode of relatedness.

Whereas the foregoing clinical examples, predominantly from neurotic patients, attempted to illustrate the patient's therapeutic effort to help the analyst to resolve more fully some neurotic symptom or character trait, in the following examples, from patients suffering from some degree of schizoid or schizophrenic illness, the patient's therapeutic striving is referable more to a preindividuation than postindividuation developmental era. His therapeutic striving is essentially to function as mother to his biological mother (the latter's own ego development having been fixated at, or in her own mothering effort having regressed to, an infantile level) so as to enable her to become sufficiently integrated and mature that she will become able to function truly as a mother to himself. This striving on his own part is both "selfish" and "altruistic" in nature, and both aims are, at this level of primitive child-mother functioning, not at all well differentiated as such.

In a recent discussion (1973a) of autism, I suggest that for the analyst to help the autistic patient to become able to participate in a therapeutic symbiosis (i.e., a symbiosis similar in nature to a healthy infant-mother symbiosis), the analyst must first have become able to immerse himself in, to an appreciable degree, the patient's autistic world as being the analyst's own functional "outer world." This then fosters the patient's identifying with the analyst who can so immerse himself in the other's world: the patient, partly through such identification, becomes increasingly able to immerse himself in the analyst's more usual "own" world, and the rapid flux and interchangeability of a therapeutically symbiotic kind of relatedness flow from this. Where Khan (1963, 1964) has described the necessity for the analyst to come to function as the maternally protective shield (in my term, world) for such a patient, I suggest that the analyst must first have come to accept the patient as constituting his (the analyst's) maternally protective shield (= functionally "outer world," much as the womb is the outer world for the fetus).

Case 1

Mrs. F., a 30-year-old schizoid woman, early in the third year of her analysis mentioned that her parents were currently visiting her and her marital family. Mrs. F. had learned that her mother, in her life in Mrs. F.'s distant home city, spent her time by watching television or going to movie matinees. Mrs. F. said that her mother found her (the mother's) life boring; yet, Mrs. F. commented during her analytic session, she watched television and went to the movies rather than, for example, getting an at least part-time job as a saleslady or secretary, or joining some women's social organizations. "Somehow that seems to me such a waste; yet it's what she did so much of when I was a child," Mrs. F. reminisced, in a tone of regret and longing, "—movies and occasional romantic novels; I guess those were her only real interests . . ."

This was a glimpse, of which I came to see convincingly many, of her feeling of having failed to enable her mother to fulfill herself as a mother to her. (Regrettably, I never found it possible to interpret these feelings to Mrs. F. as such.) The oedipal-rivalry component in this material is also, of course, obvious.

In the preceding day's session Mrs. F. had mentioned learning from her mother that she had given to the church library all the books the daughter had acquired and treasured during childhood and adolescence, and thrown away all the daughter's stored clothing. "I had the feeling of being disposed of as deceased," she commented. The mother was showing her usual selfish-child concern with feeling inhospitably and inconsiderately treated by her husband and various of his relatives; and the patient added, in a tone more of genuine regret and sadness than blamingness, that on her own occasional trips with her husband and children to her parental home, "She [her mother] has *yet* to prepare a nice supper for us."

A few sessions still previously, there had occurred, as there had a great many times before, a predominantly silent session. But this one had been different in quality. Before, the silences were extremely tense ones which had often involved my having exasperated, frantic feelings of the sort which, I surmise, were largely at work in her emotionally rootless, discontented mother. During this particular session, she indicated that she was feeling unusually calm and relaxed, and asked whether I reacted differently when she is feeling so. Indeed I did, though I did not tell her so; I felt calm and relaxed, and experienced her as a source of nonverbal strength and solidity. In the course of this session she commented, "I can imagine my father holding me on his lap and cuddling me; but I can't imagine my mother." I had much misgiving, after that hour, about not having told her—confirmed for her—how I was feeling; I had never felt so with her before. Always before, her silences had been unpleasurable to me in one way or another.

In retrospect, I feel that I had withheld from her, unwisely and hatefully, a vitally needed confirmation of her at least partially successful mothering of me. Probably wisely, she discontinued our analytic work not many months thereafter.

Her having said ". . . but I can't imagine my mother" is a testimony of the crucial significance, in one's therapeutic striving, of one's ability—or in this instance, inability—to achieve a fantasy of the other person's functioning in the striven-for manner, the manner fulfilling both for the other person and oneself. In my work with hospitalized schizophrenic patients, and in what I have heard from colleagues of their work with similar patients, one's coming to experience nighttime dreams and daytime fantasies of the patient, in which the latter—who in daily life is still very ill—is perceived as functioning as a healthy person, are crucial criteria of successful treatment.

Case 2

In the instance of Mrs. G., a 34-year-old woman whose psychodynamics are in some respects very like those of Mrs. F., and whose analysis proceeds with strikingly little change year after year, I am becoming gradually much more receptive to her maternal effort to enable me to function as mother to her. Her effort is, as in all such instances, a highly ambivalent one, with strong components of a rivalrous determination (on negative oedipal but also infantile omnipotence grounds) to demonstrate that the mother is incapable of functioning as mother. But the issue is proving in her treatment to be more amenable to analysis than it was in the instance of Mrs. F. The resolution of particularly stalemated phases of the work involves my coming to realize, for example, how genuinely gratifying it is to me to go on being one of the fruits borne by the fruit tree—one of her early-mothering images of herself. My often-exasperated efforts, that is, to encourage and insist upon her functioning more productively and spontaneously as most neurotic analysands usually do, run aground upon the fact of my having such erstwhile unconscious stakes as this in her continuing to maintain her usual early-mother orientation in the transference, as in her daily life.

Case 3

Mr. H., 42 years of age, was suffering from ambulatory schizophrenia when he began analysis 15 months ago, but has improved to the point that his ego dysfunctioning has been of no more than borderline schizophrenic severity for some months now. Previously filled with hatred to a degree potentially dangerous to himself as well as to others, he has now become capable, relatively sustainedly, of predominantly loving relatedness with his wife and children, as well as in the analytic setting; and he is manifesting a steadily strengthening kinship with his fellow human beings— although, in all these respects, such developments still encounter considerable disavowal on his part by attemptedly persistent hostility and rejectingness.

His upbringing, like that of his older brother, with whom a powerful and largely unconscious symbiosis prevails, was left largely to servants, and an abundance of evidence, from the beginning of the analytic work, indicated that their mother was strikingly deficient in motherliness. Mr. H. was convinced that not only his nursemaids, but his mother as well, "despised" both himself and his brother; and he soon manifested, in our analytic work, a conviction that I, likewise, equivalent to such a mother or nursemaid, despised him.

The particular point I wish to make here is that when, in a recent session, the patient said, "Mother didn't want anything to do with us," although this was said in an offhand, attemptedly glossing-over manner, there came through in it a feeling of deep, pervasive, and subjectively ineradicable shame. Moreover and most significantly, the shame had in it a perceptible quality that this was shame not so much that he and his brother had proved unworthy of the mother's caring for them but, much more meaningfully, that the two brothers had failed shamefully in their long-sustained effort to enable the mother to become, and to know the fulfillment of being, truly a mother. Space does not allow me to include the corollary data—abundant but significant mainly for the nuances of feeling which cannot be conveyed fully convincingly in a written report such as this—data which reassure me that his analogous effort in the transference situation is proving, this time, much more successful.

Case 4

Miss J., a 42-year-old spinster who had become schizophrenic in the course of decades of living largely as a recluse in the service of her widowed and eccentric mother, became during the first year of her stay at Chestnut Lodge so emaciated, mute, and motionless that I, like the others concerned with her care, feared that she would die. The psychoanalytic contribution to the favorable change in this state of affairs consisted essentially, I believe, in my coming to function, over a period of some months, very much as a comfortably silent and unmoving inanimate object during our sessions. This seemed to provide her with a context in which she could become alive again. In retrospect, I now see that in order for me to have become able so to function, I had to become immersed, in a relatively unanxious, contented, self-gratifying way, in her seemingly so-inanimate world.

Over the ensuing months and, in fact, for many years, we had many stormy sessions, sessions in which she often reacted to me as being crazy, confused, and disorganized, meanwhile acting out, herself, a great deal of such psychopathology. During one phase of about two years in length, in about the fifth and sixth years of her treatment, the therapeutic sessions all took place in her room. They were therapeutically symbiotic in quality to the greatest degree that

I have ever experienced with any of my patients; this, I feel sure, is not coincidental to the fact of her having had a better outcome than any others among my chronically schizophrenic patients have thus far achieved. During those two years I experienced her as winning a gentle victory over me: my earlier fury, contempt, and other "negative" feelings toward her for her inability (seemingly, her refusal) to come to my office for the sessions, gradually gave way to an atmosphere of the utmost shared contentment, in which I was receptive to and appreciative of her good mothering of me, and she, likewise, basked and throve in this symbiotic atmosphere. There were abundant indications of symbiotic processes at work during this time. Meanwhile her social worker, who had worked with her throughout the several years since Miss J.'s admission, told me one day in astonishment that she had had a dream the previous night of Miss J., in which Miss J. was a mother happily nursing her baby. Several other personnel members told me how amazed they were at the favorable changes they saw in Miss J.

One of the tenacious forms of resistance in Miss J.'s treatment has been her idealization of her upbringing. After many years of treatment, despite her having long ago become healthier than her family had ever known her to be, her having become relatively well established in outpatient living, and her functioning much of the time during the sessions more in a normal-neurotic fashion than a borderline schizophrenic fashion, she is still almost totally unable to remember and report any but conventionally "nice" memories and feelings about her parents and other family members. Meanwhile there has been no lack, of course, of negative transference phenomena, in which she has reacted to me as being essentially a crazy mother whose craziness is known only to Miss J. herself.

Her very first reported memory of her mother that I heard as being a realistic one, rather than one of her usual saccharine, idealized images, occurred after some three or four years of analysis. The content of the memory was mundane enough; but I thought it highly significant that it was reported during a session in her room (as usual in that era) when the female patient who occupied the adjoining room, and who for weeks had frequently stormed in loud and overwhelming rage, was raging more loudly than I had ever heard before. Whether Miss J. will ever be able to integrate her past experience of the mother's comparable behavior into a more realistic image of her mother, now long dead, I do not know. A "nervous breakdown," in the phrase of her siblings, which had incapacitated the mother for many months following the father's death, and had required the patient to leave high school and begin taking care of her, has never been remembered or acknowledged in any way by Miss J., despite many years of analysis.

Her move to outpatient living was very slow in coming about, and it gradually became clear that one of the many sources of her unconscious resistance to this move was her equating it, unconsciously, with a mother's abandoning her little child. For example, my notes following a session early in the fifth year include this paragraph:

> She spoke with great disapproval of how mothers in effect abandon their children, as she sees in her trips into Rockville [the small city in which the sanitarium is located]. There, she said, she sees mothers leave their children at loose ends, playing near the streets and so on, while they (the mothers) do their shopping. This I have heard a number of times before. But I was greatly interested when she said, this time, that she herself does not have a child, but that if she had one, she wouldn't want to "keep running back" to the child. She would want it so well taken care of that she wouldn't "have to keep running back." This happens to be exactly the same terminology she has used [for years] in expressing her objection to moving out— namely, that such a move would be pointless because she "would have to keep running back to the hospital." I now realize that for her to move out of the hospital is unconsciously equivalent to a mother's abandoning her child (the child being me and, no doubt, various other persons in the hospital). [I would now add that the child was, much more largely, the sanitarium or "hospital" as a whole.] I recall her saying recently that as a person gets older they become like a child, and agreeing with my comment, in response, that one may feel like a mother to one's own mother.

As her years in the sanitarium went on, she had a series of roommates in the various double rooms in which she lived. A number of these persons were highly psychotic and openly disturbed, and at least a few of them sufficiently homicidal that I was impressed with her ability to live with them in an increasingly firmly assertive and forthright manner. Although I have not the slightest doubt that her own poorly integrated, infuriating qualities accounted for many of the upsets on the part of these various roommates, her components of conscious therapeutic concern for them seemed to me unmistakably genuine. And whereas a full four years elapsed, in one of the sanitarium cottages where she lived, before she ever set foot in the living room (lest, upon doing so, she immediately be held totally responsible for all that transpired there), she came to do so freely, and to participate in a generally much-appreciated and constructive way in the weekly or biweekly unit meetings of patients and staff together, which were held there.

The last roommate she had, for about a year before moving to an apartment of her own in Washington, was a highly psychotic woman whose verbal and physical behavior was often highly disorganized. Miss J. would describe Edna as being, once again, "in a whirl." In one of her analytic sessions with me during that year, she asked me whether it would be all right with me for her to go to New York City on the following Sunday, to visit her female cousin there, and to miss her Monday hour. I said that it was all right with me; for reasons I shall not detail here, I did not respond in an analytic-investigative manner, as I would do in working with a neurotic patient. She then said something about not being sure she could do it—i.e., make the trip to New York City alone. "I feel so little in New York. . . . I guess I always think of New York as a big city in a whirl."

The idea that struck me, upon hearing this, is that she projected onto New York City her own still largely repressed confusion, and tended to feel responsible—a responsibility overwhelmingly awesome to me as I sensed it—for the whole gigantic, perceivedly confused city. Her psychosis had first become overt, many years before, shortly following a visit to this cousin in New York City, and I felt that here I was being given a brief glimpse into the nature of her psychotic experience then. Later on, in looking over my notes on this session, I realized that New York City was unconsciously equivalent, for her, to her overwhelmingly confused mother, for whom the patient felt so totally responsible.

About two years later, in a relatively recent session, she was describing to me her weekly visit to her current social worker at Chestnut Lodge, a woman toward whom Miss J. has a mother-transference which involves, amidst clearly ambivalent feelings, a great deal of admiration, fondness of a sisterly sort, and a maternal caring for the social worker. She said, "Recently she's been so busy, her office looks like a whirl!"—making an illustrative whirling gesture with her arm as she said this.

Case 5

Mrs. Joan Douglas (a pseudonym, of course), whose history and course thus far in psychotherapy I detailed in another paper (1972a) and therefore shall touch upon only briefly here, was chronically and severely psychotic at the time I began working with her, nearly 20 years ago. I have seen her for four hours per week since then. For various reasons, carefully and recurrently considered, tranquilizing drugs have not been used in her treatment. For the past seven and a half years I have taped (with her knowledge) all the sessions, have earmarked and filed all these tapes, and have spent dozens of hours in careful playbacks of selected ones among them, in my attempt to better understand the processes, destructive as well as constructive, at work within and between us.

From the outset her ego fragmentation was enormous and her delusions were innumerable and ever-changing. For a long time, for example, she was convinced that there were 48,000 Chestnut Lodges among which she was constantly being shifted; that there was literally a chain on her heart and machinery in her abdomen; that her head, as well as mine and other persons', was repeatedly being replaced by other heads. She often experienced both herself and me, bodily and *in toto*, as being replaced by a succession of other persons during the psychotherapy hours. She was so vigorously and tenaciously opposed to psychiatry that for several years she refused steadfastly to come to my office at Chestnut Lodge, and by the end of about ten and a half years had been there only some three or four times, when she finally began to come with some regularity. During the past nine years, since I left Chestnut Lodge, she has been coming by taxicab to my office, some ten miles from the Lodge, and for the most recent several of those years, has been sufficiently reality-oriented and collaborative, despite continued severe psychosis, as no longer to need a nurse or aide to accompany her on the journey.

As regards her history, she apparently suffered from a significant degree of schizophrenia in childhood. Her mother, in the words of her eldest brother, had "loved to dominate" the girl, had beaten her brutally on occasion up into the girl's teens, and overall had had an intensely ambivalent and therefore highly unpredictable relationship with her. As an example of the mother's unpredictable moods, which included both manic and depressive episodes, the brother described how she would return from Mass in a beatific mood, and within moments would be furiously throwing a kitchen pot at one or another of the children.

Although the patient was able to complete high school with a brilliant academic record, to become accomplished in various athletics, and to marry and bear four children, she gradually became overtly psychotic at the age of 33, within about a year following the death, from natural causes, of her mother. She had been overtly psychotic for about four years when I became her therapist. I was to learn that her relationship with her emotionally remote father had contributed importantly, also, to the foundation of her awesomely severe psychosis; but that relationship is less clearly relevant to the theme of this paper.

For many years in my experience with her, her real identity was anathema to her to such a degree that, when one addressed her by her own name, one was met by a degree of unrelatedness from her which was often intolerable to me. She experienced a succession of personal identities, many of them nonhuman, and frequently changing *in toto* in the midst of a session, just as she usually perceived me as multiple at any one moment, as changing unpredictably, and frequently as being nonhuman. All these delusional experiences, while appreciably lessened in severity, are still present to a formidable degree.

In one session after some half dozen years of work, she explained to me, "You see, my mother was my mind." This was said in such a tone as poignantly to convey the implication, "—and when I lost her, I lost my mind." It was painfully clear during the hour to what an awesome extent she indeed had lost her mind, as measured by the incredible depth of her confusion, quite unreproducible here. For years she had been performing various crazy actions, and had come to reveal more and more clearly that, in doing so, she was following obediently the directions she heard coming from "that woman in my head," evidently an introject, no matter how greatly distorted by the patient's own anxiety and hostility, of the crazy mother of her childhood.

In one of the more amusing of our sessions in that era—sessions which much more often were far, indeed, from being amusing— she suddenly reported to me, "That woman in my head just said, 'Don't have anything to do with that frump out there.'" She confirmed my amused assumption that "that frump" referred to me. At another point in the hour when I suggested, as had long been my custom, "Let's see what comes to your mind next," she protested vigorously, "You keep asking me what's in my *mind!* She's in my mind; but *she* has nothing to do with *me!*" She went on to make it evident that she herself felt utterly ignored and unrelated to by me whenever I would endeavor, with those words, to encourage her to express what she was experiencing. Usually we think of the person's mind as the locus and core of his self; but she made clear that such was by no means true for her. It was now evident in retrospect that when, all along, I had been endeavoring, over the years, to help her to explore and articulate what was in her mind, she had been reacting as though my effort had been to stamp out finally her upward-struggling autonomy—to castrate her individuality, so to speak (she had accused me on innumerable occasions of doing all sorts of physical violence to her)—by rendering permanent and total the sway the introjected mother-image already held over her ego functioning.

By the tenth year I had long become impressed, in my work with all my schizophrenic patients, with the power and depth of the positive feelings between the to-become-schizophrenic child and his mother. My notes made following one of the sessions with her in this era include the following:

She was incredibly confused, as usual, throughout this hour. That is, she was no more confused than usual; but the degree of her confusion, present for several years now, I still find quite incredible. The bulk of it has to do with a tremendous confusion about identity.

I bluntly mentioned to her, somewhere along midway through the hour, that I found something like 90 percent of what she told me to be gibberish, or words to that effect. My saying this was no doubt related to the significant things she came to say to me at the end of the hour, and I feel that my increasing bluntness is a useful part of the work. In this regard I recall that about six weeks ago I told her bluntly, "You're a silly woman who is spending her life here in this looney bin, talking nonsense, while your life goes down the drain."

Despite her great confusion she did manage to bring out, in a confused and indirect and displaced kind of way, the fact that her mother had run her life in an utterly singlehanded and autocratic fashion up until Joan "went into St. Thomas's Hospital," which I assume was at the age of eight when [as I had long known] she had had her mastoidectomy [the first of a series of surgical operations]. She went on to make clear that thereupon the doctors had taken over the management of her life, and that they had done a highly inefficient job of it. She had been speaking of her mother in the same admiring, loyal spirit as she has shown rather consistently in her references to her mother for several weeks now, while speaking in the same spirit of her older and only sister, Ellen. I then said to her, "So perhaps, when you went into St. Thomas's Hospital and the doctors took over the management of your life, you couldn't help feeling guilty, couldn't help feeling that you were being disloyal to your mother, simply because these doctors were running your life now, instead of she." Joan clearly, verbally, and explicitly agreed with this point in a way which was fully convincing to me.

At the end of the hour as I went downstairs, she called after me loudly and defiantly, "The doctors here haven't done a *goddamn thing* for me: I'm *still* a blithering idiot!" I heard this as an expression of her loyalty to her mother, and of her determination not to let me and the others on the staff here be useful to her, because this would be tantamount to disloyalty to her mother.

Also in the course of this hour, I was struck once again with how terribly confused a person the mother must have been; I felt that Joan's own confusion is largely on the basis of introjection of this confused mother. At a point when she was describing things that the mother used to say, I said, "I suppose it would be hard for you to think that she may ever have been susceptible to being confused," and Joan flatly disclaimed any such possibility. This is an indication of how Joan is struggling to maintain a picture of her mother as a very strong person [an effort to ward off unconscious disillusionment, guilt, and grief in relation to the mother].

But I do suppose that the great fearfulness that one sees more and more clearly in Joan is referable also to this introject of the so very powerful mother. She has told me for many months now that she herself has died, and only within the last few days have I sensed that what she "dies" of is, quite specifically, terror.

Some three weeks later, I came to her room for the session feeling fatigued and about half-sick with hay fever and an external auditory-canal infection. I was therefore relatively free from the compulsively competitive, drivingly coercive orientation which has been among the tenacious countertransference difficulties in my work with this woman, who, by reason of her upbringing, is so attuned to, and provocative of, attempts on anyone's part to dominate her. She, I am sure not coincidentally to my own changed feeling-state, was looking settled comfortably in her chair, and spoke unanxiously of feeling "set." She said, yawning comfortably, "I'm certainly a woman and I'm never going to be a men." For all the years, her confusion about her sexual identity, as well as mine, had been enormous; a man was, to her, still multiple, as I was usually a multiple transference-figure to her—hence her saying "a men."

Later in the same hour she told of a time when "my mother . . . was having a nervous breakdown . . ." This was, for me, a landmark dénouement. She described vividly her mother's having talked vehemently about " 'When you were in Spain,' " where the girl in actuality had never been, and her mentioning something about " 'saving England,' " and much other material on a par with the patient's own delusions. Joan went on, "I told her, 'You can't bear to have all those thoughts in your mind!' " (said in a tone of earnest and urgent solicitude). I suggested, "You wanted to relieve her of some of the burden of them." She promptly confirmed this, nodding and saying, "I was *trying* to." It was evident that she had been precisely as nonplussed, helpless, and concerned as, so much of the time, I have felt with her.

By this time, I had become aware of a number of instances in which her own somatically experienced suffering was based on her perceiving various persons about her currently—for example, staff members and fellow patients in the cottage, or townspeople seen during her escorted trips into town—as suffering various forms of physical anguish, and her unconsciously taking those percepts into her own body-image, in an attempt to heal them within herself. Despite the obvious defense this represented against her own largely unconscious sadism and murderous hostility toward these persons, it had become clear to me that her loving solicitude and therapeutic concern had an element of indubitable sincerity and genuineness.

Parenthetically, some three years later, during my supervision, at another hospital, of the psychotherapy of a borderline schizophrenic young man, I was reminded of Joan when the therapist described the patient's, as the latter had put it, "wanting to sever the bonds of sickness to Mother. The way I'm bowing my head now is the way she does. It's like I have the struggles of a child still inside me." I regarded the image of the child, struggling within him, as comprising not only elements of his own childhood-self, but also elements of the child in mother, struggling against sickness, elements of which had been taken, partly for an intendedly therapeutic motive, into the boy's own self-image. One of the recurrently striking aspects, to me, of the theme of this paper is how extremely immature are the areas of the parent's ego which are involved in these kinds of symbiotic transference to the child, and how ex-

tremely early in life is the patient called upon, therefore, to try to
function parentally and therapeutically to the parent. Joan's confused inability to differentiate actual adults from actual children
was extreme. One of her tenacious delusions was that children are
"arrested adults." For several years she recurrently termed our sessions, derisively, her "baby-sitting" with me, and in more recent
years she has made it clear that a major source of contention between herself and her mother, beginning in Joan's early childhood,
was the girl's insistence that *she* was the mother, and that her
mother was the child or baby. Joan shows, to this day, much of the
kind of cynical-child quality that I have come to see as a characteristic defense against dependent needs, on the part of the person
who has had so prematurely to function as parent to the parent,
and who has had, therefore, so little of a childhood of her own.
Joan once told me, "I grew up at the age of eight."

In the seventeenth year of our work there occurred a session
typical of that era, in which her consciously lovingly concerned, and
unconsciously murderously competitive, efforts to bring surcease to
various mother-figures were evident. (Most of this session is too delusionally distorted, too bewildering, to warrant reproducing here,
even if space allowed.) It was beginning to dawn on me that she
tends to feel so overwhelmed by my intendedly therapeutic devotion to her—devotion which presumably contains more of murderous competitiveness than I can yet integrate (although I have long
been familiar with sustained urges to murder her)—that, identifying with the aggressor, she spends most of the therapeutic sessions
preoccupied with how to rescue her delusionally distorted, gigantic
but victimized mother. She incessantly feels unappreciated, unsuc-
cessful, and worst of all unacknowledged in her endless striving to
be of use, of help, to her mother.

She was looking tearful throughout most of this session in question. A very slowly developing capacity to grieve, bit by bit, had
been one of the major aspects of her therapeutic progress in recent
years. It stood in marked contrast to the paranoid grandiosity
which formerly had shielded her utterly against feelings of loss; but
the increments of healthy grief were accompanied by such intense

affects of depression that I recurrently felt threatened lest she commit suicide. She was looking very earnest, very serious, in what she was saying in this session.

At the beginning of the session she refused, as usual, to accept the name Joan, identifying herself as Barbara (one of innumerable names she applied to herself). Midway along in the session, speaking of multiple, highly delusionally distorted fragments of her image of her mother, in the form of various fantasied persons, she said, "I gave them to you [i.e., put them into me literally, a familiar delusion], and you didn't help them. *I* couldn't; they hated *me*." She went on (and this clearly now had reference to her roommate, a highly psychotic young woman who often needed to be placed into cold wet-sheet packs, as I had learned from the ward personnel), "I didn't want to make her *more* tense. . . . A couple of times I had to put them in straitjackets. . . . The way Mrs. Schultz[1] talks about her life, it's always been terrible; she's always been the rubber outside the hemisphere, and rubber's always been hard to cure [a glimpse, here, of her irrepressible, usually caustic and mocking wit]. . . . I spoke to Dr. Mitchell[2] about them; *he* didn't make them any better."

At one of the junctures in the session when I felt sure she was alluding to her current young roommate, she made the following statements. (In the excerpts given below, my comments to her are enclosed in parentheses.)

> . . . And that kid was in the room yesterday, and she wanted to behave well, I guess, and I started to talk to it [her hostility was often expressed in her experiencing others, including me in the sessions, as being nonhuman, and even inanimate], and somethin' grabbed it, 'cause it looked like *that* at me [she demonstrated a shocked facial expression]—like a real baby. [She explained this in a momentary tone of amusement; parenthetically, her saying "and somethin' grabbed it" is related to her

[1] This was the name of her long-deceased mother. Her mother-transference to her roommate—her misidentification of her roommate as being literally her mother—had been evident before.

[2] Dr. Mitchell was the ward administrator many years before; she experienced him as still being present.

enormous denial of the often-shocking impact of her own words upon other persons]. (Kid—"Kid"—ya mean the kid [realizing only now that she was speaking of her young roommate; one often had no way of knowing whether she was, for example, describing interactions with hallucinatory figures in her room, which were experienced by her as fully real persons].) Yeah; the one who's knifed me to death. (Looked at ya very wide-eyed.) I have *never*—uh—*felt* as *much antagonism*, and *hate*, and *loathing*—and I *grabbed* it by the shoulders, you know, and I said, "Now, your *mother* wants me to help her fix your head! And *she* doesn't have a license. *I* have a license." I tried to reason with her, and at the end of that he [N.B.] *gave* me such a *sock*; he practically knocked my *head* off my *shoulders*! Now whaddya make of that?—and *no conversation, ever*. (From—The Kid?) Um [confirmatorily]. A real baby . . . and [speaking now of some other delusionally distorted mother-figures] I gave them you as a doctor; but *you* didn't make them any better. You made them terrible—(Well, in a way that was a relief, wasn't it?) No. (*You*'d been trying *so* hard to help them. It would have been distressing if *I* had been *able* to, and *you* had *not*.) *Oh, no*, because I had to rely on *other* people to *help* them. They *really hate me*; they did *not like* me. (Spite of *all* your efforts, huh?) Yeah; I was just trying to make them feel more comfortable, less aggressive, and I couldn't understand why each person that went in there [i.e., went, miniaturized in size, literally and bodily into the body of the person he or she was endeavoring to cure] had to make them *worse*. . . .

Later in the session she said, "The mother is at Chestnut Lodge, of course. . . . The mother doesn't want to be alone. . . . The women at the Lodge need a doctor." This was one of the innumerable sessions during which I felt concern to be careful with my interpretations lest I say something that would lead to her suicide; her shockingly intense murderous hostility still tended to be directed, suicidally, against herself, in this era when her predominantly paranoid murderousness had shifted gradually more into depression. Previously my concern had been, rather, lest she kill me or, on occasion during particularly stormy and enraging sessions, lest I kill her.

In a session 17 months later (during the nineteenth year of our work) she made a number of communications which were unusually clearly expressive of her therapeutic strivings.

When I indicated for her to come into my office for the session, from the waiting room, as usual I did not address her by name. For the first ten minutes of this session she was silent, as was not infrequent in this era. She seldom looked at me. Her demeanor was one of helplessness, troubled feeling, bewilderment, vulnerability to hurt, and uncertainty as to whether to trust me. She seemed more to be listening to hallucinatory voices than thinking—many times before she had flatly stated that she had no mind, and was instead a radio through which people in the walls, for example, expressed themselves. A couple of times she nodded obediently, apparently in response to hallucinatory voices.

Thereafter she was verbal throughout the session, and I experienced her as giving me a tremendous working over, saying many caustically depreciatory things in a highly delusional way; but I had long ago come to realize that everything she said, no matter how delusional, had in it allusions, conscious or unconscious, to us in the immediate situation. Her repeated implication, as usual, was, "If the shoe fits, put it on." Recurrently I realized, with feelings of guilt, inadequacy, and self-condemnation, that the shoe fit all too well and, partly because her accusations were so indirect, I felt unable to retaliate with sufficient savagery to free my hands.

Nonetheless this session proved to be, overall, more collabora tive than many. She seemed clearly largely unconscious of how much she was doing to make me feel discouraged and depressed; but an important revelation was her managing to convey her feeling that I did not need her in any way, even to feel entertained by her. Despite the working over (accusatory, reproachful, condemnatory, competitive, mocking, and beseeching) she gave me, she was, I privately felt, particularly entertaining in this session, by reason of her caustic wit and her fabulously creative imagination which, still, possessed her more than was possessed by her.

The collaborative yield of the session was evident in a number of regards. She made many realistic references to Chestnut Lodge—which, for her, was unusually good contact with reality. Parenthetically, during the past few years she has become aware that there is but one Chestnut Lodge, where—she now realizes—she has lived for years.

Forty-two minutes along in the two-hour session, she spoke, accusingly and reproachfully, of ". . . the way you hold onto me and push me away all at the same time . . ." This was a highly perceptive and succinct statement of reality (as I knew also from having listened carefully to playbacks of tapes from earlier sessions), in addition to being a transference reaction to me as the personification of her mother, who had simultaneously held her close while pushing her away. A couple of minutes later she protested, "You keep talking to me like my mother!"

Fifteen minutes later she said, despondently, "My mother . . . she doesn't seem to need me for nothin' . . ." And six minutes later, she said of someone else she had invoked, "I amuse *her*," with an implicit reproach toward me (equivalent to her mother) that, whereas she *is* able to amuse this other figure, she fails in her therapeutic attempt to amuse *me* (= mother).

She also made, during this session, several realistic new comments about her ex-husband, of whom for many months at a time she had never spoken. At another point she said, "I would *like* to engage a psychiatrist . . ."—which was perhaps the greatest degree of verbal acceptance of psychiatry I had ever heard from her, apart from the marital connotation of the word "engage."

Among the data I have mentioned from this session, those having to do with her effort to entertain me, as the personification of her depressed mother, are what I wish to highlight here. That session occurred, as I mentioned, in the nineteenth year of our work. Throughout those years, confusion had been her predominant symptom, confusion defended against by innumerable and everchanging delusions. Only after some dozen years of my endeavoring primarily to rescue her from a life filled with manifold anguish, realistic as well as psychotic in nature, and permeated by this confusion, did I gradually come, bit by hard-won bit, to experience a kind of aesthetic appreciation, at first highly guilt-laden and furtive, of her confusion. As I came more and more clearly to see, from another point of view her confusion was a truly breathtaking creativity, far more fascinating, wondrous and, of course, alive than, for example, a beautiful and intricate Persian rug. With this gradual change in my orientation, which required some few years to become really well established, I became also more receptive to, and appreciative of, her tremendous wit and her indomitable sense of humor. Of both her wit and her humor I had been well aware from the beginning; but earlier I had been so desperately concerned to help her that I had been largely unaware of how basically concerned she was with trying to be helpful and alleviating to me—if only by entertaining me with the schizophrenic confusion which, in a sense, was all she had, for many years, to give me to relieve my depression. My depression was to a degree real but tremendously intensified, in her perceptions of me, by her depressed-mother transference to me. In its real components, it was accentuated by much that she herself said and did, largely unconsciously I believe, which would be enough to greatly depress any psychotherapist.

In the next session, two days later, she said, "The human race is in a shambles," but was able to recall realistic memories of her childhood, in which her mother had made repeated trips to Italy, evidently in line with the mother's operatic ambitions, while leaving Joan and her siblings in the care of a succession or, more accurately in terms of her memories, a chaotic myriad of ill-remembered parent-figures. The feeling-tone of the session, significantly for this paper, was mutually enjoyable. I had long ago come to see that she throve in sessions that—however much reason for despair—we both were able genuinely to enjoy.

Two sessions and five days later in this so-changeable work, I confided briefly to my tape recorder, before inviting her in for the session, my anxiety lest she invade my life so thoroughly that I would go crazy; the preceding session with her had been more disturbing to me than usual. But this session, a two-hour one (as has been the case once each week for years), proved to be relatively collaborative and therapeutically fruitful. I was slowly becoming more appreciative of the healthy ingredients of her delusional thinking. For example, she expressed a delusion that she had been an architect in New York City and had designed many buildings there. Instead of my responding, as I usually had before, to the arrogant grandiosity of her tone in saying this, I asked her what buildings, for example, she had designed. I was impressed when she then named realistically a half-dozen well-known buildings there; this was, for her, a rare nugget of reality relatedness.

Later in the session I had occasion to suggest to her that maybe, while she is here in the office, she is missing her current Chestnut Lodge roommate. To this she replied, seriously and thoughtfully, "Maybe so"—a rare acknowledgment from her. For years I had seen evidence, always loftily dismissed by her as such, that the form and content of the session were being enormously influenced by her unconscious separation feelings in relation to the cab driver or the nurse or aide in whose presence she had been on the way to the session, or in relation to the familiar scene in the living room of her cottage at Chestnut Lodge from which she was now, however briefly, severed, or in relation to me when I would leave the office for a couple of minutes to go to the lavatory.

Also in this session, the role in her psychosis of her terror of her projected envy became clearer. She said, for example, ". . . this head [gesturing toward her head]—of course, it's not a head; it's just a piece of paper— . . ." In earlier years I had been sufficiently preoccupied with my own actual feelings of envy of her, for many well-founded reasons, and so burdened with guilt about that envy that, while largely aware of how tremendously envious a person she was, I had not seen that among the reasons for her apparently never experiencing, year after year, her head as being her own head, was her fear of the envy on the part of the mother who in various ways had lost her own head—in, for example, legendary outbursts of volcanic fury, and in being carried away by beatific and other fantasies. With this fear of the mother's envy there was, also, Joan's therapeutic effort to protect the mother from the realization of the mother's own state of deprivation. In the transference I, perceived at this juncture as not having a head of my own, need not feel myself to be deprived in contrast to her for, as she assured me, "this head . . . is just a piece of paper."

Three weeks later, in a session in which she was looking tearful and sad, there was a repetitive theme of her feeling burdened and intruded upon. There were indications that her identity at this point was predominated by her identification with her mother at a juncture in Joan's childhood when the mother was more disorganized than usual, following the birth of twins. Only one of these twins, a male, had lived, while the other, a female, had died shortly after delivery. During the session she made references to "the baby," a concept encompassing both the dead baby girl and the live baby boy, and I had reason to know that she, as a child, had not only been invaded by this psychotic introject from the grief-crazed mother, but had striven thereby to rescue the mother by taking into herself the mother's burden of psychotically dealt-with tragedy.

Three weeks later she stated with conviction, as she had before not infrequently, that she is dead, this time explaining that she had died the night before in order that her mother not be killed. She stated that Daddy had killed her over and over; innumerable times in previous years she had accused me, perceived as a remote and murderously omnipotent father in the transference, of murdering her. She experienced herself and her only living sister as being in effect, artifically conglomerated Siamese twins: she showed me one hand, saying, "That's me," and the other "is Mrs. Bradley" (her sister's married name). Never before had she conveyed so tangibly how important to her, how much a part of her, is the sister, the only one among all her numerous relatives who has found it endurable to keep on visiting Joan during the past ten years. (She visits for a few days once or twice each year.)

In the next session, two days later, as she walked into my office from the waiting room, I privately thought that she looked like hell. She was wearing no lipstick; she looked pale and old; her hair was unkempt; there was a button off the top of her familiar and unbecomingly tentlike, navy blue jumper; she was wearing sneakers rather than the reasonably attractive leather shoes she often wore, and no stockings. I thought, with a familiar dull hopelessness, of the setting in which she had lived her daily life for many years, amidst other chronically schizophrenic patients, and with a highly psychotic roommate—a setting where, despite the best efforts on the part of the administrators, nurses, aides, and other staff members, the alleviating of such chronic self-neglect seemed hopeless. Throughout the whole hour her demeanor was one of tearfulness, vulnerability, and hurt; meanwhile, in her verbal communications, she was being her usual extremely formidable self, giving me the usual tremendous working over throughout nearly the whole session.

Nonetheless, during the course of the session her communications provided realistic new glimpses of her parents' marriage, and valuable evidence that her tenacious self-neglect was part of an effort to invoke her mother who, as I knew, had striven incessantly and coercively to groom her in, for example, the care of her clothing. It was apparent that she was trying to evoke this mother in me not only because she, Joan, needed that mother, but as a way of resuscitating this mother who in actuality had been dead for 23 years.

She spoke, too, of "Ma" as being a "tempestuous woman," and indeed she had been. "He brawls," she went on; the mother indeed had had a strongly phallic quality, and had often run the home in a brawling manner. "I had a daughter," she later said, as indeed she has—a daughter as anathema to her as is her own real identity, for between her and this daughter Joan's conflicts with her own mother had raged, during the daughter's childhood, to such a degree that years ago the two reached a point of mutual denial of one another's existence. She later said, "I honestly don't know where my mother is"—a strikingly realistic statement for her. Still later she referred to ". . . that Mrs. Schultz [her mother] who was a good friend of mine" (a memorable expression of positive feeling for her mother). She went on to say, "I lived for centuries as an element" (in earlier years of our work she frequently had identified herself as being a boundless element—light, electricity, and so on—or as being filled with radioactive material). She then stated, with a tone of partial accomplishment, that she has now become an animal, but is not yet a human being.

A prominent aspect of this session was my proving able not to fall for her setting me up, recurrently, to pursue eagerly the bits of more realistic reporting on her part. I came, later on in the work, to understand this effort on her part as being not only one of her ways of sadistically tantalizing me, but also one of her efforts to mobilize me as her mother, in a manner intendedly therapeutic for this mother overwhelmed by depression and apathy, into trying coercively to put her together—to put together the fragments of her healthy ego functioning, out of the welter of psychotic material.

Five days later she was looking tearful and pensive. I felt that she was reacting primarily to the fact that Thanksgiving, with all its nostalgic connotations, was but two days off; only after the session did it occur to me that her sadness probably had more to do with the fact that Thanksgiving meant, also, the missing of our usual two-hour Thursday session. During this session it was evident that she was tending to grieve, particularly, for the relationship with her daughter—new material, indeed—and she spoke repeatedly and realistically of her sister, also. A part of her multiply delusional subjective experience, during this session, was her experiencing us as being in a gigantic statue. Someone was able to see out from the eyes of the statue and reported that there wasn't any coast guard ship approaching, after all; the bleakness and remoteness of the scene, viewed from the eyes of the statue, was powerfully conveyed by her to me.

She said of her mother, "Is she dead?" in full seriousness and as though this were the first time any such intimation had come to her, although many times for many years I had come to tell her, at times gently and at times with scornfully impatient harshness and bluntness, that her mother had died many years ago. "There's a lot of water behind the eyes" of the statue, she said movingly.

She said at another point, "People who have murdered may pretend to be crazy," which clearly had reference to each of us. Many times in past years she had accused me of having murdered her mother, and clearly feared still, at an unconscious level, that if her mother was indeed dead, then it must be that she had killed her mother—either in murderous rage toward the mother, or, more likely, through neglect of this mother whom Joan had felt to be her own lifelong and total responsibility.

Nine days later, as I was returning from the men's room in the middle of a two-hour session, I had the thought that I have been having my psychosis vicariously, in a controlled way, through her, over the years, with my being safely apart from it, and that the hundreds of tapes of our sessions in my storeroom represent this psychosis of mine. Half an hour later in the resumed session she said, while wiping her face with her palms, pushing against her cheeks in a pathetic way, "I don't know how to run my expression." There was transitory, powerful, submerged anger detectible in her facial expression on occasion; but she was pathetically not in contact with it. A few minutes later she spoke of a "machine supposed to represent the mind of God" (since the early months of our work she had on occasion described either herself or me as being, quite concretely and literally, a machine).

Fourteen days later, in the course of the session I began feeling, within myself, overwhelmed for a few seconds, with accompanying feelings of panic, when I realized how *many* of the things she was saying and feeling were based upon lampoons or satires, some conscious and many unconscious, of various aspects of me as she perceived me. This submerged feeling arose in me after a sequence of several such communications in the midst of her usual delusional outpouring, an outpouring which on a later occasion I told her I felt as an avalanche. She seemed, still, massively unknowing of the enormous impact her verbally expressed delusional thinking had upon me, as well as upon other persons in her daily life, who many years before had come, therefore, largely to shun her as someone too disturbing to attempt to relate to more than briefly. She often identified herself as a leper.

In essence, it was evident in this session, once again, that I was still emotionally unprepared to occupy the transference role she so desperately needed me to occupy, as a gigantic but psychotically fragmented mother.

Five days later, in a session only two days before Christmas, she looked very sad, unhappy, and tearful, recurrently throughout most of the session. She made clear, as she had before, that people cannot have any emotional relatedness with one another unless they are members of the same parental family, related by blood; her compulsive family loyalty had been, throughout, among the most powerful sources of her resistance in the psychotherapy. But in this session, for the first time, she indicated that she had given over her own four children, from whom she had severed all ties many years before, to her mother, in order to provide the latter with fulfillment, at last, as a mother; it had long been evident, of course, that the mother had not found fulfilling her own mothering of Joan.

During this session, in which her rapidly changing perceptions of me—her seeing, for example, the eyes of many different persons fleetingly in my eyes—were even more delusionally distorted than usual, I experienced within myself a submerged and disturbing agitation to an unusual degree. So far as I could discern, during the session, this had to do with the intensity of the reality unrelatedness between us. Only after the session did it occur to me that she had been more resistive—more hostile, rejecting, and emotionally unrelated toward me—than usual because of a Christmas-holiday-impelled need for closeness—closeness permissible, according to her superego standards, only with members of her family. Many years before I had chanced to see her and her sister rush warmly into one another's arms, on one of the sister's visits, in a manner expressive of utterly genuine familial love. In retrospect, I could see that during this session Joan had had to remain vigorously defended against the expression of such feeling toward me, at this Christmas time.

A week later I found her to be more psychologically *here* in the session, more tangibly related to me, than she had been in a very long time—perhaps *ever*. Further, and significantly for the theme of this paper, she made clear that she had found that both her mother and father (each clearly related to me in the immediate transference situation) had regarded her as worthless, as contributing nothing worthwhile to either of them.

Three weeks later, I learned from the nurse in charge of her unit that Joan had cried upon returning to Chestnut Lodge from the session with me on that day and had talked, at the same time, of her mother's death—for the first time ever in this nurse's several years of experience with Joan. Two sessions thereafter, she was speaking very realistically of her mother's hatred of her: "But I can't get over why she hates me so much . . . my mother doesn't like me."

Five days later she said, gesturing toward her head, "I think I usta run in and out of myself," which I understood to mean "in and out of fantasy"; one of my efforts with her for many years had been to help her to become able to differentiate between fantasy and reality, and this was a welcome indication of progress in that direction. She referred to herself at another point in the session as being an "earthquake"; I mention this as a sample of her still-incredible degree of identity distortion.

As regards her going in and out of fantasy, I had much evidence, from both the events of her psychotherapy as well as the historical data provided by one of her siblings, that her mother had gone in and out of fantasy a great deal. Some four months later on, the patient came to say, "My mother feels she can't survive unless she's playing a part." It was evident that Joan's childhood participation in the mother's fantasies, a result not only of the mother's domination of her but also of the girl's effort thereby to help the mother to survive, had been one of the main sources of Joan's chronically fantasy-ridden, schizophrenic mode of existence.

Meanwhile, four days after the session I mentioned, I had just returned from a professional trip to another city, a trip I felt had been nothing less than triumphant for me in my part-career as an authority on the psychotherapy of schizophrenic patients. Now, in my session with Joan on this day, I found myself feeling, as usual in my work with her, completely inept and fully deserving of her delusionally expressed but demolishingly effective scorn toward me. It was becoming increasingly clear to me that I had been needing for her to confirm, recurrently over the years, the lowest areas of my self-esteem—to reassure me, as it were, that I am indeed worthless, as I often privately feel. To be sure, I could see transference connections between myself and her head-in-the-clouds mother who needed recurrently to be deflated down to earth, as well as between myself and her remote, cerebral father who so tenaciously ignored the interpersonal work at hand that desperately needed getting done; but there has been this significantly real core in her transference perceptions of me. In more recent times, as for various reasons my hunger for vilification has lessened somewhat, I gradually have become better able to weather her insults and hold her to our realistic collaborative task.

A week later, in the early part of the session, she suddenly, unexpectedly, and very movingly to me, became unusually tearful in protesting, "You keep looking at *me* so much, when there is someone in your right eye who needs your attention!" It seemed clear, as she had made known many times before in other ways, that she felt undeserving of my interest. A half-hour later in the session she spoke about an overzealous doctor, clearly in part at least a reference to the way I was then functioning. It seems that among the reasons why she has had, for so many years, to defend herself so vigorously against my therapeutic dedication, is that as long as she felt herself to be so therapeutically ineffective toward me as a transference-figure, it only augmented her feelings of guilt and worthlessness whenever she did get a glimpse of me as being genuinely intendedly helpful to her.

She maintained at another juncture in the session that her mother is not dead, and that she herself is dead, having been murdered. This I heard as based typically upon her unconscious guilt about her mother's death, but also upon a genuinely loving devotion to the mother and a readiness, therefore, to sacrifice her own life in order that the mother might live. Repeatedly in the session she perceived "that man from Tunis" in my left eye—the origin of this perception, like that of most of her perceptions, I had no way of knowing ("Tunis" = two-ness?). She saw Al Capone in my right eye, and repeatedly and forcefully accused me of multiple murders and other evil deeds. At one point I felt a rageful urge to beat the craziness out of her, and I sensed this urge as presumably akin to those which had impelled her mother to subject this daughter to repeated and brutal beatings. One of the currents at work in this surely complex interaction was, I remain convinced on the basis of much corollary data, Joan's struggle therapeutically to resuscitate her dead (= depressed) mother, as personified by me.

Three weeks later she said to me, in the midst of the session, "You're the man from Pakistan." I had been confronted with such communications from her innumerable times before, and this, like so many of the others, was said to me very decisively and directly. The new aspect in this instance is that I immediately asked, "Is this what the *voices* just told *you*?" and she convincingly confirmed this. I gained with this a deeper appreciation of the havoc wrought upon her sense of personal identity through her being assailed by such unexpected, forceful, and unequivocally emphatic hallucinatory voices, and realized, more clearly than before, that her own incessant verbal barrage against my sense of personal identity contained an increasingly large element of her faithfully and collaboratively reporting to me what was happening to her in the session.

On the other hand, in the same session there emerged much data highlighting various of the gratifications afforded her by her having essentially no mind of her own—notably a freedom from feeling responsible for what would otherwise be her own thoughts. I had been familiar, from previous sessions, with her experiencing herself as a radio through which people in the walls, for example, were communicating. On some of the occasions when she had said such things—which of course tended totally to nullify my efforts with her—I had reminded her, ironically, that of course she realizes that I, too, am but a radio.

Eight days later, in an unusually collaborative and useful session she said, "You don't seem to realize you've interviewed nine hundred quaduary trillion people in this chair," gesturing toward her chair, which seemed only somewhat of an exaggeration of the stream of ego-identity fragments which successively had predominated in her over the years. Also, she was able to say, at another juncture in this session, ". . . but I got it all mixed up, I guess, in my mind. . . ," which was a most rare acknowledgment of the fact of her own confusion.

Eleven days later, a major theme which ran through the session was her reproach toward me, and others, as being callous and brutal with extremely vulnerable, delicate structures. For example, she pointed out that the people at Chestnut Lodge are living inside a baby; as usual with her delusional thinking, this was referred to as an entirely obvious fact. She stated that she herself stays in her room there most of the time, and remains very quiet, so as not to do damage to the baby. Parenthetically, for years the ward staff has been concerned about her massive self-isolation there. This building, likewise, she went on, is the inside of a baby. She was immensely harsh with me, as so often before, for being so unfeeling; there were innumerable direct reactions, as well as allusions, to my being callous and brutal, as well as inept. A second and interrelated main theme emerged in the session with equal clarity: she was desperately in need of maternal assistance from me (as well as from others in her daily life), but manifested a fiercely destructive competitiveness with anyone's endeavor to provide such assistance to her. Early in the session there were unusually clear depictions of her childhood rivalry with her own mother; between the two there had developed a chronic and unresolved power struggle as to who was the mother and who the child. Again, it was evident that the prize at stake was omnipotence, as well as the more conventional oedipal goals; and, for the girl, there was the motive of recurrently rescuing the mother from depression by enraging her through outrageously insolent and arrogant behavior.

A month later, in a session during which, as was customary, she seemed largely unaware of her castrative rivalry toward me and of the impact, therefore, this was having upon me, she was able to say, "My mother has always been disgusted with me," a highly accurate statement of one dimension of her childhood. She had given me to know, for example, in our work, that for a prolonged period in her childhood she had suffered from vomiting, and that her mother's fury at Joan's recurrent vomiting had precipitated some of the beatings the girl had received. Joan's vomiting had served, I believe, to bring the mother back to earth, recurrently, from her own (the mother's) fantasyland. In a much earlier session, Joan had conveyed a hilarious description of the shock a fellow patient perceptibly experienced each time he returned from a walk on the sanitarium grounds, with his head immersed in Napoleonic fantasies; he was obviously thunderstruck upon coming back through the front door of the cottage and being met by the usual turmoil within it.

Some 15 minutes along in this same session she concluded one of her usual bewilderingly delusional, dreamlike narratives with "—so that's where we are now," which gave me the useful realization that this meant that she was at this particular juncture in an ongoing fantasy. The significant new development here, I believe, is that her intrapsychic life was becoming sufficiently coherent, in contrast to its earlier seemingly patternless chaos, so that I could sense now that her days were dominated by ongoingly developing, continuing fantasies. Half an hour later in his same two-hour session, she spoke of "mother's . . . sublime . . . ethereal" qualities, so reminiscent of her brother's description of the mother's coming back from Mass in a beatific mood, and a glimpse, therefore, of the identification-with-mother aspect of her own fantasy-dominated mode of living. Twenty minutes later, she said thoughtfully and simply, "Mrs. Schultz raised her children," a comment full of tremendous implications of grief and guilt, for she, by contrast, had abandoned, in her psychosis, her own four young children to be raised by others. But here, too, emerged hints (like those I reported from an earlier session) that she had done so partly, if not primarily, to provide, in this manner, maternal fulfillment to other mother-figures.

It occurred to me immediately following a session three weeks later that she cannot come to occupy her own real identity so long as I cannot become, at a feeling-level, her perceivedly gigantic mother. Parenthetically, a month later I noted, after the session, "The main value of the session is that it is dawning upon me increasingly how *many*—I *now* surmise *all*—of her responses are founded predominantly upon identifications with me as she perceives me. It is dawning upon me how amazingly much she needs for me to be her *world*, in the transference relationship, for her to become well, and it seems to be exclusively interpretations of *this* that prove to be useful interpretations."

Perhaps the main reason why this has been so difficult for me fully to experience is that it has required, in light of the symbiotic nature of the relationship between her and her mother, a feeling-acknowledgment, to myself, of her fully comparable degree of importance to me in the context of the transference-countertransference relatedness—with her being equivalent, in countertransference terms, to my own early, symbiotic mother. I am convinced, not only from my own work with Joan and other schizophrenic patients, but also from my supervisory experiences with many therapists who were treating such patients, that the more readily accessible to himself are the therapist's own symbiotic-dependent feelings, the better is he equipped to help the patient to become conscious of the latter's own feelings of this nature, so that the patient need no longer act out the symbiotic yearnings through the schizophrenic postponement of individuation.

A month later Joan made clear, within the first five minutes of her coming into the session, that her head at present was that of Anne Greenstein, a fellow patient in her cottage whom I knew to be chronically schizophrenic. She described in detail that the head contained a man in a bizarre position which was causing him much physical suffering. It was apparent that this distortion of her body-image, typical of innumerable ones I had heard before, but more clearly expressed than most, was based at least in part upon her primitive attempt to bring her fellow patient's suffering in for me, she hoped, to cure. As usual I felt mocked for my ineptitude as a therapist, but was impressed once again with how thoroughly her existence was given over to attempts, as a subjectively omnipotently responsible therapist, to cure all her fellow patients, not to mention mankind generally.

Her sister visited her a month later for two or three days, for the first time in some eight months. In the sister's usual interview with me toward the end of her stay, she documented impressive indications of progress on Joan's part, while not disregarding the still-present manifestations of her tenacious psychosis. In my interview with the patient a bit later still during these same days of the sister's visit, I was both amused and impressed that Joan, for her part, was equally oriented toward evaluating how much progress her patient, namely her sister, had made in the interim of several months since the previous visit. She detailed and caricatured, with consummate perception and mimicry, certain of the sister's lifelong compulsively driving aspects, so like some of my own qualities, and expressed genuine distress that the sister still proved incapable of sharing Joan's own current orientation, of taking life as it comes. Two days later it was apparent that her having taken "the Mrs. Bradleys"[3] into her own body-image, protectively and restoratively, as had quite evidently occurred, had been done less out of lovingness toward the sister, than as a defense against her largely psychotic and projected, but quite evident, murderousness and contempt toward the latter. Toward the end of this same month, she said of herself, "We're virtually the whole human race," in a tone both grandiose and burdened, as well as simply human in quality. I heard this as an expression of simple and profound truth on the part of one who had come, after long and tragic struggle, into kinship with her fellow human beings, but had yet to come to nonpsychotic terms with the conflict between her omnipotence-based murderousness toward her fellow human beings, and her at least equally intense loving and therapeutic concern for them.

DISCUSSION

Goals and Techniques Involved in the
Patient's Therapeutic Strivings

The clinical examples have been presented in my attempt to portray various facets of the goals and techniques involved in dealing with the patient's therapeutic strivings. More comprehensively, as I mentioned in the introduction, the patient's striving is to help the other person (in the treatment situation, the analyst) to fulfill the latter's human psychological potentialities. The patient strives to help the analyst to share those modes of interpersonal relatedness which are relatively anxiety-free for the patient, and anxiety-laden

---

[3] This was her sister's married name. She perceived her sister as being, as usual, multiple figures rather than one person.

for the analyst; a simple example is the nonobsessive patient's teasing the analyst, in a basically intendedly helpful, "come off it" manner, about the latter's obsessive fussing with the ventilation, or lighting, or whatever, of the office. Another way of putting it is that the patient endeavors to help the analyst to share in the former's relatively non-neurotic areas of ego functioning. He is endeavoring to contribute to the analyst's emotional growth, integration, maturation. He is endeavoring to help the analyst to fulfill the latter's emotional potentialities and healthy ego ideals.

Particularly in the instances of the more ill—schizoid or schizophrenic—patients, such goals are relatively undifferentiated from the goal of the patient's endeavoring to provide himself with an increasingly constructive identification model, in the person of the analyst, for the sake of the patient's own further maturation.

The psychotherapeutic techniques the patient utilizes frequently include one or another form of catharsis and various forms of verbal, and much more often nonverbal, reassurance. Most important are the primitive, long-unconscious processes of introjection of the analyst's more ill components, and projection upon the analyst of the patient's areas of relative ego strength (Searles, 1972b), whereby the patient attempts to take the analyst's illness into himself and treat the "ill analyst" there, within the patient, so that a healthier analyst can eventually be born out of the patient. This is a dimension of what does, indeed, take place during the course of, and as a result of, the therapeutically symbiotic phase of the treatment.

It is obvious that the patient is relatively unequipped, either consciously or unconsciously, to carry out the primary and paramount goal of the *psychoanalytic* psychotherapist—namely, the analysis of the transference. I shall touch on this matter again in the third part of this discussion.

Technique of Interpreting, or Otherwise Acknowledging the Presence of, the Patient's Therapeutic Strivings

This is so complex a matter, so much a function of therapeutic intuition and timing, as to render unwise any attempt to generalize about the subject of when, and how, and to what extent, and whether, one acknowledges to the patient that the latter has been and is endeavoring successfully to provide therapeutic help to oneself. I rarely if ever acknowledge, in any explicit way, and surely not in any formal way, that I am receiving, and long have been receiving, such help from the patient. The more I have come to accept comfortably this dimension as inherent to the treatment process, the more, I feel sure, does my whole demeanor in the work with the patient come to include an implicit acknowledgment that the therapeutic process at work between us is a mutual, two-way one. Surely I make *transference* interpretations, not infrequently, of such strivings on the patient's part, and these interpretations convey implicitly my acknowledgment that the patient's endeavor to be therapeutically helpful (and in my interpretations I use no such stilted a word as "therapeutic") to the mother, for example, is at the same time an endeavor on his part to be so toward me as the personification of that mother.

It seems to me that any indications the analyst gives that he finds what is transpiring to be personally helpful to him are on relatively solid ground, technically, if given in a relatively nonanxious, nonguilty, and therefore nonconfessional way, as data being shared with a collaborator, primarily in the service of the ongoing exploration of the transference neurosis or transference psychosis.

Against the hazards of failing at all to see and interpret the patient's therapeutic strivings is the hazard of prematurely interpreting these. In general, it seems to me that as long as a patient remains very much caught up in feelings of guilty responsibility, he reacts with intensified guilt to any intimation from the analyst that the latter is finding the sessions to be personally helpful in some way. It is as if the patient, in addition to all his other burdens of guilty responsibility, has now become responsible, too, for the analyst's life, or for that particular aspect of it which the analyst has just revealed.

I cannot say simply that interpretations of the patient's therapeutic strivings should be reserved for relatively late in the analysis, for as a generalization I think that untrue. But I can say that, in most instances, it is only after some years of analysis that one comes to find the following shift in the feeling-tone with which the patient speaks of the psychopathology that had prevailed in his parental family. His feeling-tone, which in the earlier years of the analysis portrayed the etiologic family events or situations as involving burdens of psychopathology being *imposed upon* him, unwantedly, by the other family members, gradually shifts in quality, as his more deeply repressed emotions of grief and loving devotion come to the fore, so as clearly to convey that these burdens had been, nonetheless, also taken upon himself in an active and lovingly devoted—what I am here terming therapeutic—spirit. Surely transference interpretations of the patient's therapeutic strivings toward the analyst now are unlikely to intensify the patient's anxiety, confusion, or guilt. But I question whether this phase in the analysis could have been reached, had the analyst not engaged in interpretative activity at an earlier time, when it involved speaking with courage in the face of perceivedly appreciable risk.

Relatively late in my preparation of this paper, a simple clinical vignette served to remind me how important is the matter of timing in the analyst's interpretation of the patient's therapeutic strivings. A borderline schizophrenic woman, from whom I have long been receiving therapeutic help of various kinds, made me realize, in essence, that it is not yet timely for me to begin interpreting this aspect of her ego functioning in the transference situation. She was reminiscing, as she often had before, of experiences with a previous therapist in which, seemingly at her initiative, he would soothingly hold her hand. This time she said, "On other occasions he very much wanted to hold my hand, and I was very much aware that it wasn't all what *I* needed; it got mixed up with what *he* needed . . ." She said this with, significantly, a tone of distinct regret.

She want on a moment later, "He seemed to believe in interaction; he wasn't like you at all. With you, nothing I do seems to matter; you're always the same way. I couldn't have *abided* someone like you [seizing her head in furious exasperation, as she had many times before in our sessions]—you'd have driven me *crazy!*" I felt convinced (particularly by her regretful reference to her previous therapist's need) that it was not yet timely for me to interpret her still largely unconscious therapeutic strivings toward me (in the transference, variously her mother and her nursemaid, both having been highly impersonal individuals toward her).

In general, to the degree that a patient is functioning in the treatment sessions in an autistic, infantile-omnipotent manner, he, like the woman just mentioned, is intolerant (despite all his complaints of the analyst's unresponsiveness) of the analyst's functioning in a tangibly alive and participative manner during the sessions—of the analyst's discernibly *contributing anything to* the analytic work, let alone *deriving anything from* it, in which latter event the patient's infantile omnipotence would be even more greatly outraged.

At a somewhat later phase of the patient's ego development, one finds instances in which the patient manifests a transference to the analytic *situation* as being a nursing mother, and to the analyst *himself* as being a sibling rival whom the patient is determined to keep barred out of this cherished situation of having mother all to oneself. But once this degree of object relatedness has been achieved, the transference is more subject to interpretation.

In any event I hope to have indicated here, however briefly, my cognizance of the fact that the patient's therapeutic strivings are not simply to be interpreted, or otherwise, acknowledged, willy-nilly. The main theme of this paper, after all, has to do with the loss to both participants in the analysis if the analyst, like the patient, remains unconscious of this dimension of the relationship and therefore fails to deal with it consciously at all.

Regression on the Part of the Analyst, as Regards His Own Therapeutic Strivings

In a paper (1967b) which included some mention of patients' therapeutic strivings in the course of my developing another theme, I wrote of some of these patients:

> Their therapeutic techniques are outwardly so brutal that

the therapeutic intent is seen only in the result. One apathetic, dilapidated hebephrenic patient of mine received considerable therapeutic benefit from a fellow patient, newly come to the ward but, like him, a veteran of several years in mental hospitals. This fellow patient repeatedly, throughout the day, gave my patient a vigorous and unexpected kick in the behind. From what I could see, this was the first time in years another patient had shown any real interest in him, and my patient emerged appreciably from his state of apathy and hopelessness as a result.

During moments or even long phases of particularly intense anxiety in his work, the analyst undergoes regression, such that his own analytic orientation becomes primitivized (desublimated) to the level of relatively raw aggressive and sexual urges which are the hallmark of his patients' own therapeutic strivings. In my work with the hebephrenic man mentioned in the above-quoted passage, for example, it was only after some years of four hourly sessions per week, sessions filled with apathy and unrelatedness punctuated only by moments of murderous rage, violent sexual urges, and acute fear, that I finally realized that it was possible for me to relate to him in some fashion other than the only two potential means heretofore available, those two means being, so I had thought of them, fucking him or killing him. To my enormous relief I realized that I could now be related to him without having either to kill him or fuck him.

It has long been my impression that a major reason for therapists' becoming actually sexually involved with patients is that the therapist's own therapeutic striving, desublimated to the level on which it was at work early in his childhood, has impelled him into this form of involvement with the patient. He has succumbed to the illusion that a magically curative copulation will resolve the patient's illness which tenaciously has resisted all the more sophisticated psychotherapeutic techniques learned in his adult-life training and practice.

In my own clinical experience, the temptation toward such activity is most intense in my work with patients whose childhood histories include the patient's having been involved in a relationship with a parent in which the child had been given to sense that incestuous fulfillment would provide the parent, in the same process, with a specific relief from the latter's neurotic or psychotic suffering. That is, there evidently was a large component of hysterical, sexual-frustration psychodynamics in the parent's illness. In such a childhood family situation, it is inordinately difficult for the child's therapeutic striving to become differentiated from, or sublimated beyond, his or her sexual strivings. All this becomes re-experienced in the transference relationship, with the analyst becoming the personification of the patient's child-self, and thus feeling impelled to try to resolve the patient's neurotic or psychotic parental identification (introject) as it were, through actual sexual activity.

In these instances where there has been such a degree of oedipal sexualization of the therapeutic striving in the patient's childhood (and adolescence), not only does the concept of a successful outcome of the therapy have an inherent connotation of incestuous fulfillment (until that connotation has become resolved through the analysis of this aspect of the transference), but also the therapist, precisely because he is established and acknowledged officially as therapist, is hated by the patient as being the latter's successful oedipal rival (unconsciously, for the patient, the desired parent's "sexual therapist"). Hence the transference is a mixed and highly ambivalent one, such that the patient who succeeds in seducing the therapist is winning one oedipal sexual object in the therapist, and at the same time destroying the oedipal rival in the latter.

It is transparently obvious that unacceptable incestuous urges become acceptable to the therapist's superego by clothing themselves in an intended-healer guise. But what I wish particularly to stress is that these primitive therapeutic strivings are no less powerful, in themselves, than are the sexual strivings. I can believe that in many instances, the therapeutic strivings are most powerful of all in bringing about such a tragic deforming of the therapeutic endeavor. I believe that just as sexual predatoriness on the part of the therapist can wear the guise of the emancipated-healer role so, too, can a basic problem of therapeutic omnipotence on his part lead him to seize upon any available, intendedly therapeutic measures, including those of actual sexual involvement with the patient.

I touched upon this problem of regression, on the part of those responsible for the patient's treatment, in an earlier paper (1959c) concerning integration and differentiation in schizophrenia. In discussing the group symbiosis which develops in the ward life of the hospitalized patient, I stated:

> In the face of the increasingly intense conflictual feelings which permeate such a group symbiosis, regression deepens, not only in the patient's behaviour but in that of the staff members as well. Not only do his demands become more infantile, but the personnel's mothering, good and bad, tends to assume more and more primitive forms. Just as he tends to become a suckling, demanding infant at the breast, they tend almost literally to offer him a breast, 'good' or 'bad' as the case may be, rather than provide more adult forms of mothering [pp. 332-333].

At that juncture I referred to one of Knight's (1953b) articles on borderline psychosis, in which he described the treatment a borderline psychotic college girl had received, from a woman dean and self-styled psychotherapist, prior to the girl's hospitalization. As the dean felt progressively cornered by the girl's demands, she allowed the sessions to go overtime; she allowed the girl to have sessions in the dean's home in the evenings and on weekends; she allowed the girl to use the dean's car; she allowed her to stay overnight in her home and, still later, to sleep in bed with her. Knight writes of the patient:

> . . . At times she expressed irrational hatred of the dean and pounded her with her fists. At other times she wanted to be held on the dean's lap and fondled, and this wish was granted also. No real limits to her regressive behavior were set until she expressed a strong wish to suckle the dean's breasts. Here the dean drew the line . . .[p. 120].

Parenthetically, I now see in that material an element I did not see when I wrote that paper and which Knight also did not mention: the patient's own therapeutic striving to enable the dean to become strong and decisive enough to draw a line when sufficiently cornered by the patient's demands (and, more importantly of course, by the dean's own unconscious ambivalence). But to provide another clinical example of the point I am presently making, namely, the regression that becomes manifest in the nature of the doctor's own therapeutic strivings, I mentioned in a paper (1970) concerning autism and therapeutic symbiosis:

> I have been amused in retrospect—but only in retrospect— at something I would do from time to time when I would be feeling helpless in my work with one or another chronically paranoid patient who was sure I possessed the magic cure for his or her suffering, if I would only "think nice thoughts about me," or "want me well." I would have come, long since, to experience much fondness for the patient; but all my conventional analytic armamentarium had failed to help her resolve her psychotic symptoms. Now I would find myself smiling helplessly and pleadingly at the patient . . . with a feeling of wanting desperately to cure her, somehow, with my love. This, of course, like everything else I had found myself doing, did not work, and the intendedly magical love would be replaced by an equally omnipotence-based hatred, such that I would glare at the patient with, for example, a fantasy of burning out the inside of her skull.

To rephrase this point before going on to the next topic in this discussion, I am suggesting in essence that many instances of therapists' sexual acting out with patients are motivated predominantly by the thwarting of the therapist's omnipotent-healer strivings toward the patient. Surely this matter is related to a high percentage of negative therapeutic reactions: the so-resistive patient is holding out for the time when the therapist, out of his by-now-intolerable frustration and despair with the unceasingly futile results of his more conventional therapeutic efforts, will resort to throwing his sexuality onto the balance.

As it is with the therapist's sexual urges in his regressed omnipotent-healer state, so, I suggest, it is with his aggressive urges also. At times my murderous urges toward a patient have taken the form of intended euthanasia—a rock-bottom urge to put him out of his misery. Since instances of therapists' bare-handed murdering of patients are surely rare, indeed, by contrast to the apparently not-so-rare instances of sexual involvement between the two, one can surmise that the sexual involvement gives unconscious release, as well, to the two participants' murderous urges toward one another. I have worked analytically with only one patient who had had an affair with a previous therapist, and I was not surprised to learn that powerful murderous urges evidently had been at work in both of them in the mutual omnipotent-healer strivings toward one another which had impelled them into that involvement.

To write now in a less sensational vein: we have the extremely frequent instances, seen in the course of one's own work and in supervising the work of colleagues, wherein a typical earmark of regression in the therapist, under the stress of his efforts to cope with his patient's intense ambivalence and his own responsive ambivalence, is that he, the therapist, has lost touch with the transference context of what is happening. His vision is so narrowed by the anxiety and guilt aroused in him by his awareness that he indeed possesses, as parts of his real self, increments which give immediate reality to the patient's transference to him, that he cannot achieve sufficient emotional distance from the immediate interaction to see what is happening as being a part of the patient's overall life history, with clear links between himself and earlier important figures in the patient's life, links between himself and the patient's childhood-self, or evidence that the patient's present way of responding to him represents the activation of an important identification on the patient's part with some parent-image from the latter's childhood.

Here again, then, the therapist, in trying to carry through his therapeutic endeavor without, at this stressful time, the aid of his usual working knowledge and awareness of the dimension of transference, is himself very much in the category of the typical therapeutically striving patient in childhood who, in his or her efforts to bring therapeutic help to another family member has, of course, no awareness of the dimension of transference—a dimension which Freud, among his other fundamental contributions to mankind, discovered and enabled us, in turn, to recognize.

Additional Aspects of Childhood Family Etiology

Any full description of the parental-family warping of the child's therapeutic strivings would require a book in itself. I shall add here only a few comments to the brief mentions I have made of this subject earlier in the discussion.

Typically, the more ill the adult patient is when he comes into treatment, the more powerful have been the parent's or parents', transferences (largely unconscious, of course) to him as being the latter's parent(s). Thus, any therapeutic concern the child manifested, relatively undisguisedly, toward the parent was immediately reacted to, by the latter, as something *parental* in nature and as threatening to undermine the parent's status as parent and bring about a perceivedly rivalrous turning of the tables. For many reasons—including (a) the parent's need to keep rigidly under repression his or her deeply dependent needs for a parent, and (b) the pervasive threat in the family lest actual displacement of the parent, and fulfillment of incestuous aims, occur—the child's therapeutic striving (inevitably, in this context, impelling the child toward fulfilling a *parental* role in the family) had to be subjected to, or remain under, severe repression and be acted out, within the family, in a manner largely unconscious to all the family members, including the child himself.

In a high percentage of the hundreds of teaching interviews in which I have participated, at various hospitals, with adolescent or young adult patients who have become psychotic in the course of attempted emancipation from their families (through going away to college or making similar attempts to become established as separate individuals), I have found evidence that the patient had become overwhelmed with psychotic defenses against unconscious rage, guilt, anxiety, and grief at having proved unable simultaneously to be (a) a successful young college student (or whatever), and (b) a transference-mother, who in this same process of going away to college has abandoned her children back home (namely, the parents and other family members). The young person's individuation needs have come into unbearable conflict, that is, with his therapeutic strivings toward his family members.

It has further seemed to me—although this, now, is somewhat more conjectural—that the same course of events has involved the parents (and other family members) at home in responding to the youth off at college (let us say) as being an unconsciously hated (as well as loved) parent-figure, a feared and hated *parental* (i.e., father or mother) oedipal rival. Hence the parents have seized this very time, when the offspring is making tenuous and of course ambivalent efforts to become established as an individual, defiantly to cast him off as being a hated authority-figure to them. Thus, partly in their unconscious rage and hurt at this mother or father who has abandoned them, they have severed him from the genuinely parental support which he needs, and which most young people evidently receive in sufficient measure. The more one comes to appreciate the family-wide, overwhelming tragedy in these situations, the less one feels a sense of blaming any one or ones among the family members.

Concerning Gratitude

More and more during the past several years, I have come at last to see something of how frequently the analyst has cause to feel gratitude toward the patient. Any discussion of gratitude, in the psychoanalytic literature, usually is conducted in the implicit assumption that gratitude is inherently, predominantly if not exclusively, unidirectional in nature: the *patient*, over the course of successful treatment, has reason increasingly to experience gratitude toward the *analyst*, and if the former does not manifest this, he remains to that degree neurotic or psychotic. Hill (1955), for example, in the final chapter of his book concerning the psychoanalytic therapy of schizophrenic patients, notes that ". . . one hears very little about gratitude from these patients" (p. 206). Surely one hears little, likewise, of an analyst's gratitude toward his patient, and it has been only after decades of work in this field that I am becoming at all accustomed to such an emotion. I was still relatively rigorously defended, unconsciously, against experiencing gratitude toward patients when I discussed (1966-1967) the sense of identity as a perceptual organ:

> . . . Following a single consultative interview [several years previously] with a schizophrenic man—one who had been making a thoroughgoing ass of himself with certain hebephrenic symptoms—I experienced myself, as I drove away from the hospital, as being an incredibly gifted and perceptive consultant. But then I caught myself and wondered what this was saying about the patient's dynamics. I was immediately struck with the likelihood that he tended to project onto other persons, including me, his own best ego capacities. This man, who had done such wonders, transitorily, for my self-esteem while abasing himself, committed suicide about two months later. We never know why these things happen; but among the likely causes is the possibility that he came to find insupportable the burden others placed upon him in their unconsciously exploiting him for the enhancement of their own subjective identities.

I am sure that I experienced, during that interview, no gratitude toward that man; one has no reason to feel gratitude toward someone whom one perceives as being, whether consciously or unconsciously, victimized, exploited. It is only as I have come to sense and perceive the lovingly devoted, self-sacrificing, therapeutic-striving determinant of such behavior as he had manifested, that I have found reason to experience gratitude toward the patient. Nowadays, during and following sessions—whether with my own analytic patients or with patients seen in single consultative or teaching interviews—which have proved to be unusually fulfilling for me both personally and professionally, I find in myself feelings of heartfelt gratitude.

For example, during my teaching interview with a borderline schizophrenic young woman at a nearby hospital a year ago, I quickly began feeling that the interview was not only of unusual therapeutic value for her, but was, in the same vein, deeply fulfilling and confirming for me in my identity as an intendedly useful psychoanalyst. I was sure that I was being of use to her and to the several psychiatric residents who were observing the interview. I felt that she and I both were being of rare growth-value for one another. I have no doubt that my keen appreciation of her was evident in my demeanor, and the group of staff members present fully shared, as was evident in the post-interview discussion, my appreciation of how much this patient had done for all of us. It struck me how illusory is any assumption that a therapist experiences such professional gratification as any expectable, everyday, mundane part of his work; I am trying here to suggest that the therapist has reason to feel as rare and memorable and intense a form of gratitude as has the patient whose therapist has effected, so we conventionally say, a remarkable cure.

On the very next day I had, at another nearby hospital in the presence, again, of a group of staff members, an interview with a young man who was suffering from schizophrenia and drug addiction. This interview was in quality more like those to which I am accustomed, although this was one of the more extreme examples of its species. This interview gave me fantasies and feelings of giving up this profession entirely, as a useless endeavor. The patient seemed to feel called upon chronically to justify his existence, his having been born, and to feel unable to justify it. His impact upon me and upon the audience was as one unfit to attempt to save, not worth trying to save; and no one (with the possible exception of myself, certainly not his therapist whose initial presentation of the case, prior to the patient's coming into the room, showed thoroughgoing disdain for the patient) seemed to feel at all interested in trying to save him. This interview served to enhance my gratitude toward the young woman I had interviewed on the previous day.

REVIEW OF RELEVANT LITERATURE

I cannot claim to have done an exhaustive review of the psychoanalytic and general psychiatric literature; thus this review cannot be considered comprehensive. But I feel able to say with confidence, after at least a decade of interest in this subject and alertness, therefore, to published material about it, that the existing literature concerning it is scanty indeed.

In a sense any relatively classical psychoanalytic paper concerning the analysis of a nonpsychotic patient is relevant literature, because this particular subject is so conspicuously absent from such a paper. But for reasons of space I must resist quoting, by way of contrast, passages from such articles that would highlight their striking absence of acknowledgment of any therapeutic strivings, whether conscious or unconscious, on the part of the patient.

Even in the literature concerning schizophrenia, in which illness the patient's therapeutic strivings are overwhelmingly significant and relatively easy to discern, most authors continue, seemingly, to view schizophrenic patients as being basically parasitic. Typical of the abundant literature which views the patient as suffering from a crippling ego defect, as needful primarily of supplies from without, and as being oriented, therefore, toward receiving from, rather than giving to, his environment, is the volume by Burnham, Gladstone, and Gibson (1969), *Schizophrenia and the Need-Fear Dilemma*:

> . . . a key element of our theoretical system . . . is the proposition that the schizophrenic person, because he lacks stable internal structure, is exceedingly dependent upon and vulnerable to the influence of external structure [p. 13].

> We turn now to discuss the schizophrenic person's disordered object relations, particularly his intense need-fear dilemma. Because he is poorly differentiated and integrated, he lacks reliable internal structure and autonomous control systems. Accordingly he has an inordinate need for external structure and control. He requires others to provide the organization and regulation which he is unable to provide for himself. . . .

> The very excessiveness of his need for objects also makes them inordinately dangerous and fearsome since they can destroy him through abandonment. Hence he fears and distrusts them. He may attempt to alleviate the threat of abandonment by repeated pleas or demands for proof of the object's constancy. Such pleas are insatiable because much of the incon-

stancy of his percepts of objects stems from his inner instability. Another defensive tactic, also of limited value, is the attempt to deny his need and his fear of separation [pp. 27-28].

The authors describe the patient as attempting to cope with his need-fear dilemma by object clinging, object avoidance, and object redefinition. Concerning object clinging, for example, they say:

> In this attempted solution . . . the patient, in effect, gives himself over to the need side of his conflict. He abandons efforts at differentiation and independence and attempts to fuse inseparably with others. A bewildering variety of terms has been employed to describe this type of relationship: symbiotic, narcissistic, orally fixated, object-addicted, anaclitic, self-centered, unilateral, possessive, overdependent, receptive, demanding, devouring, hunger-fulfilling, and others. These terms share common reference to the excessive need for supplies from the object, with little regard for the reciprocal needs of the object; in other words, a wish to receive but not give. . . . The schizophrenic person wishes the object to provide the inner balance and integration he has been unable to achieve for himself [p. 32].

Similarly Gibson (1966), in his paper "The Ego Defect in Schizophrenia," while documenting a remarkably impressive degree of clinical improvement on the part of a chronically schizophrenic woman still in treatment with him, consistently portrays the patient as improving on the basis of strength borrowed from the therapist, who is portrayed as vastly more powerful than herself:

> This patient was struggling with a basic dilemma—the *need* for an object from which to borrow ego strength, and the *fear* of the same object because of its threat to ego organization. . . . The need-fear dilemma arises out of a deficit in ego functioning. I do not think of this defect as limited to a specific area of ego function; so perhaps it would be more accurate to speak of ego weakness rather than defect [pp. 88-89].

Writing in general of the schizophrenic person, Gibson says:

> . . . His vulnerability to disorganization of ego functions makes him desperately need objects to provide the support and structure which he lacks. His lack of ego autonomy leaves him

unable to resist the influence of objects and thus makes them frightening to him. The poor reality testing of the schizophrenic makes all object relations extremely tenuous [p. 89].

Concerning the particular patient upon the treatment of whom his paper is mainly based, he says:

> I believe, to recapitulate, that this schizophrenic patient had an inordinate need for objects to compensate for an ego defect [p. 92].
>
> . . . At times, her prevailing feeling was one of extreme gratitude to me, and she took pleasure in our relationship. But, quite regularly, she felt threatened by the thought that she might lose it. At other times, she resented the enormous power over her that this gave me. She also feared that she would have to satisfy my dependency needs just as she had those of her parents. . . .
>
> The inevitable vicissitudes of object clinging are illustrated by this sequence of events. Object clinging occurs as a response to the need-fear dilemma in the schizophrenic when the need is dominant. An effort is made to compensate for the ego defect through fusion with an object. The object becomes an auxiliary ego that shares the responsibility for organizing behavior, managing and controlling drives, and testing reality. This device may work remarkably well. Superficially at least, patients may seem fully intact so long as this kind of a relationship to an object is maintained.
>
> . . . The patient will see in the therapist an object to which he can cling to strengthen his weakened ego, but this can rouse all of the fears I have just described. In addition the therapist may be seen as a controlling agent that will threaten the patient's autonomy [p. 94].

Gibson describes the mother as having been extremely dependent upon the patient during the latter's childhood:

> The patient and a sister (younger by three years) grew up with the mother, who was extremely dependent on both of her children, especially Eileen [the patient], and did everything she could to keep them from becoming independent [p. 90].

But, although he writes that "She . . . feared that she would have to satisfy my dependency needs just as she had those of her parents"

(p. 94), his account includes no acknowledgment of any personal dependency feelings on his part toward her, of any anxiety lest he lose her, nor, by the same token, of any therapeutic strivings on her part toward him. It seems to me probable that such factors help to account for her maintenance of a predominantly positive transference toward him, of which he takes note in his account:

> Eileen required a fair degree of selective inattention to maintain the idealized view of me as an entirely benevolent helper. . . . By always displacing negative transference feelings onto someone other than the therapist, she was able to avoid any feeling of hostility toward the therapist that might have led to thoughts of terminating treatment. Such thoughts were intolerable to Eileen when she had to rely completely on me to serve as an auxiliary ego [p. 96].

It is only in the most general terms that Gibson alludes to a conjectured dependency on the part of the therapist toward the patient. Early in his paper, he comments: "To some extent, this need-fear dilemma is a part of the experience of all human beings capable of relating to an object" (p. 88). In his closing sentence, he conjectures, concerning what the therapist offers which proves therapeutic in this regard: "Perhaps most of all, the psychotherapist shares in the need-fear dilemma, and in so doing establishes a new kind of relationship for the patient—a relationship that nurtures ego growth" (p. 97).

As a portrayal of an important part of the state of affairs which one finds at work in the schizophrenic patient, the above-quoted descriptions by Burnham, Gladstone, and Gibson seem to me accurate enough. But the basic psychodynamics of such schizophrenic phenomena warrant, in my clinical experience, an utterly contrasting emphasis as being the truer one, and this emphasis is crucial for any successful psychotherapy of the schizophrenic person. His impairment in whole ego functioning, his inability to function as a whole individual, is due most fundamentally to a genuinely selfless devotion to a mother, or other parent-figure, the maintenance of whose ego functioning required that the child not become individuated from her (or him). In the course of our work with him as a chronological adult in psychotherapy, we entirely miss the main point, in my opinion, if we regard him as suffering most fundamentally from a crippling ego defect, a result of early deprivational trauma, and as needful of receiving supplies of various sorts from our whole and intact ego. Ironically, the crucial issue is, rather, whether *we* can become and remain conscious of the symbiotic (preindividuation) dependency which *we* inevitably and necessarily (for the successful outcome of "his" treatment) develop toward *him*.

In this regard we personify in transference terms the parent whose relationship with him over the preceding years has been fixated at a symbiotic level; but, as I have emphasized repeatedly, it is not "only transference." The therapist comes to feel that he *really* is, to a significant degree, at one with the patient, and to experience it as becoming a *real* issue whether he, the therapist, can bear the loss, to his own ego functioning, of the individuation toward which the therapeutic endeavor is directed. Thus, in retrospect, the schizophrenic patient's "ego defect," toward which it is so easy to feel a kind of pitying condescension, becomes translated as having a "frightening degree of personal importance to the therapist's very self" (with the patient being equivalent to the therapist's heart or mind, for example). The more *conscious* the therapist becomes, and remains, of these processes, the less likely is any acted-out *folie à deux* to occur. If we never become conscious of them, we remain relatively comfortable in our condescending view of the schizophrenic patient, and he retains his usual status of a perceivedly pathetic and needful cripple. I can confidently say that the great bulk of our psychoanalytic and psychiatric literature is such as to make our recognition of the patient's symbiotic-therapist-striving orientation toward us more, rather than less, anxiety-arousing, embarrassing, humiliating, and otherwise difficult for us.

To enlarge the focus of these remarks to include, once again, psychotherapeutic patients generally and not merely those suffering from schizophrenia: that literature which acknowledges patients' contributions to our understanding of psychodynamics and of increasingly effective techniques of psychotherapy, while stopping far short of perceiving the patient as being an intended therapist, can be looked upon as a forerunner to literature concerning that latter subject itself. It is not uncommon for books to be dedicated gratefully, in this regard, to one's patients, though few are so explicitly acknowledging as is Milner's (1969) dedication: "To all my teachers in psychoanalysis especially my patients."

Jones (1953), in his biography of Freud, describes the following event as one of the landmarks of the Breuer period: "Freud was still given to urging, pressing, and questioning, which he felt to be hard but necessary work. On one historic occasion, however, the patient, Frl. Elisabeth, reproved him for interrupting her flow of thought by his questions. He took the hint, and thus made another step towards free association" (pp. 243-244).

Although this so-fundamental technical refinement which Freud and his patient achieved together occurred in 1892 or shortly thereafter, it is commonplace still to find classically psychoanalytic discussions of technical matters written without acknowledgment of patients' therapeutic strivings, which seem to me so inherently at one, properly, with any adequate treatise on the subject of analytic technique in a truly interpersonal context. For example, Olinick et al. (1972), in their paper "The Psychoanalytic Work Ego: Process and Interpretation," state:

> . . . The timing of an interpretation is an acquired art that involves the synthesis of empathic and cognitive processes [and is in part, I suggest, the analyst's response to the patient's therapeutic strivings to enable the analyst to function, for example, as a successfully nursing mother or as a sexually potent father]. Partial and spontaneous interventions, of the kind described, are then further elaborated in the course of subsequent working through [which subsequent working through, I suggest, presumably consists in part in the consolidation of the analyst's therapeutic benefit at the hands of the patient].

In the above-quoted passage, my admittedly rude intrusions with my own thoughts are attempts to depict how pervasively significant, to *any* of the much-discussed psychoanalytic topics (such as interpretation and working through), is our cognizance of the patient's own therapeutic strivings toward the analyst. Similarly as re-

gards the literature on the "therapeutic alliance" (for example, Zetzel [1956] and Greenson [1965, 1967]), where such writings imply
that what is being discussed is alliance for therapy for the *patient*, I
hold that what is actually at work is an alliance for therapy for *both*
participants in the treatment situation.

The first writing, to my knowledge, which at all explicitly describes the patient's functioning as therapist to the doctor is Groddeck's (1923) *The Book of the It*. It is noteworthy that even this
courageously pioneering statement portrays the therapeutic process
at work as being, in essence, therapy *for the patient*, exclusively, in
the long run; nonetheless, Groddeck is a pioneer of high courage
in his reporting:

> . . . Her childlike attitude towards me—indeed, as I under-
> stood later, it was that of a child of three—compelled me to as-
> sume the mother's role. Certain slumbering mother-virtues
> were awakened in me by the patient, and these directed my
> procedure. . . . And now I was confronted by the strange fact
> that I was not treating the patient, but that the patient was
> treating me; or to translate it into my own language, the It of
> this fellow-being tried so to transform my It, did in fact so
> transform it, that it came to be useful for its purpose. . . . Even
> to get this amount of insight was difficult, for you will under-
> stand that it absolutely reversed my position in regard to a pa-
> tient. It was no longer important to give him instructions, to
> prescribe for him what I considered right, but to change in
> such a way that he could use me [pp. 262-263].

Whitaker and Malone (1953), in discussing the motivations of
the therapist, suggest: "The enthusiasm and elation felt when con-
templating the possibility that schizophrenic patients may be amenable to psychotherapy may reflect a perception that some residual
needs can perhaps be answered only in therapeutic experiences
with the schizophrenic" (p. 101). Later on the authors go far beyond this statement, which does not explicitly attribute a therapeutic motive to the patient and which—with its implication that certain
therapists, presumably more ill than most, may therefore somehow
find therapy for their own aberrant needs in this work with
schizophrenic patients—is much more at odds with, than consonant

with, the theme of this present paper. In an extremely interesting chapter entitled "Patient-Vectors in the Therapist,"[4] they make the following statements, clearly in reference to patients generally (rather than exclusively schizophrenic patients) and to healthy therapists:

> ... the bilateral character of therapy constitutes its most effective dynamic basis. ... In the best therapeutic relationship, the therapist recurrently brings his own patient-vectors to the patient. ... Indeed, a therapeutic impasse can often be resolved only by the therapist's willingness to bring his patient-vectors to the patient quite overtly. This principle implies that were the therapist free of all patient-vectors, he would be no therapist at all [p. 165].

They do not give any details as to how the therapist may usefully "bring his patient-vectors to the patient quite overtly." If by this they mean to recommend that the therapist on occasion share with the patient information about the therapist's own personal life, I must part company from them, for in my own work I probably do little more of this than does any classical psychoanalyst.

In 1968, Marie Coleman Nelson et al. published their volume *Roles and Paradigms in Psychotherapy*, describing a method of psychoanalytic psychotherapy they had developed during the previous ten years, which they call paradigmatic psychotherapy. A paradigm is defined as a showing or saying by example, and paradigmatic psychotherapy is the systematic setting forth of examples by the analyst to enable the patient to understand the significant intrapsychic processes or interpersonal situation of his life, past and present. The authors see this technique as most appropriate for borderline patients who are unable to utilize the verbal interpretations basic to the usual psychoanalytic approach; but it is a technique the authors convincingly demonstrate to have implications for the treatment of virtually every patient.

---

[4] By "vectors" they mean, I gather, forces. They consider this an operationally more meaningful concept than the concept of countertransference—a view I do not feel moved to embrace, incidentally.

One of these authors' standard techniques they term "siding
with the resistance," which they further define as:

> . . . joining with the irrational aspects of a patient's responses
> and thus inducing him to oppose his own pathology, which the
> therapist has now taken over. When this technique is followed
> persistently, it soon appears that the patient is much more
> reasonable and healthy than the therapist, who then appears as
> a paradigm of the patient's own presenting pathology [p. 75].

At the end of one of the clinical examples of the use of this
technique, the author (Strean) formulates:

> Joining the patient's resistance in the above instance was
> narcissistically enriching [for the patient] instead of depleting.
> The patient and therapist were colleagues, with the former
> helping the latter. As the therapist enacted the role of the pas-
> sive, naïve, ignorant child, Mr. B. was in no way threatened by
> potential attack [whereas he had so reacted to more conven-
> tional psychoanalytic responses]. On the contrary, he could
> teach the therapist psychological facts. The therapist's role (the
> naïve, ignorant part of Mr. B.) stimulated the patient to educate
> the therapist. For Mr. B., educating the therapist was, in effect,
> educating that part of himself which needed enlightenment but
> resisted it [p. 183].

Despite a recurrent note of game-playing superficiality, which in
my opinion does far less than justice to the patient's genuine importance as therapist to the therapist, these authors' work is of
much significance and value for anyone who wishes to pursue further the theme of my paper. On occasion these authors' accounts of
their work convey a movingly genuine portrayal of their patients'
functioning as therapists in the treatment situation, beyond what I
can capture in these necessarily brief excerpts. For example, Strean
(pp. 233-237), in his account of his work with a very withdrawn
14-year-old boy who could not read and who had been involved
unsuccessfully with several previous therapists, describes his approaching the patient as being a consultant, whereby the patient
was in a position of "self-dosing," that is, of providing his own pre-
scription in the treatment situation. This came to involve the patient's functioning as teacher to the therapist:

... in the first interview ... The patient was asked by the therapist, "What should I do?" ... Possibly he could teach the therapist techniques of passive resistance? ... Joe stated that he might try for a little while to teach the therapist to be silent.... However, the patient insisted, "You have to promise to say nothing. I'll be the boss around here." ...

Several interviews passed uneventfully. Joe, instead of talking and teaching, remained silent. The therapist and patient merely looked at each other with no exchange except, "Hello" and "Good-bye."

... When the therapist wondered if Joe could teach him something about electricity [in which he knew the boy was interested], Joe got up, walked out of the interview and stated dryly, "You've got a lot to learn. I'll think about coming back and showing you."

Joe did return for two silent sessions, but without encouragement soon delighted in showing the therapist several electrical plans. Electricity became the sole mode of communication for several months, with Joe as teacher and the therapist as pupil....

... Eventually, Joe entered a vocational school and specialized in electricity....

As he learned how to read and attained other academic and social successes, Joe suggested that "the case be closed." He wrote in his own handwriting, "A Closing Summary on Mr. Strean" in which he both criticized and praised the therapist, giving a colorful picture of the treatment process....

For the therapist, the relationship had enormous meaning [pp. 235-236].

In 1969 Milner published her previously mentioned 412-page account of her psychoanalytic treatment, extending over nearly 20 years, of a schizophrenic woman. Milner's volume is richly creative, scholarly in its evaluation of the many dozens of psychoanalytic writings she found relevant in the course of this long treatment endeavor, and inspiring in terms of the author's clinical devotion and the patient's clinical improvement. One of the many fascinating aspects of her book, to me, consists in Milner's very long-delayed, but eventually at least partial, recognition of the patient's therapeutic strivings toward her.

On page 107, for example, I noted that, thus far, one could

find no evidence that Milner was yet aware of the patient's therapeutic strivings toward her, though such strivings were implicit in much data she had been presenting from the patient. On page 120, although she surmises that the patient had endeavored, during the latter's upbringing, to cheer up her depressed mother, Milner shows no evidence that she finds this to be a factor in the transference relationship. On page 130, I noted that, throughout the abundant data concerning mother-infant transference relatedness thus far, Milner assumes consistently that she is in the transference role of mother, and the patient in that of infant, whereas the reverse is often implied in the data from the sessions.

Referring to a time near the end of the seventh year of the treatment, Milner says:

> During the eight weeks of my summer break Susan wrote frequent letters to me from the hospital, sometimes four posted by different posts all in one day, calling me by my first name and ending 'with love'. . . . In the letters she said she was feeling quite terrible and was angry with the psychiatrist in charge, who, she said, had been tough with her and done nothing to help [p. 171].

Milner seems to continue, here, to perceive the patient as being equivalent to a needful infant or child in relation to her as a mother, and not to perceive the aspect in it of the patient's implicit maternal concern for the therapist as abandoned child—the patient's anxiety lest the therapist not be able to endure this separation, and her striving to assuage the therapist's loneliness and to reassure the latter of her (Milner's) indispensability.

Later, concerning a session in the fourteenth year, Milner makes a statement, for the first time in her account, which takes relatively full cognizance of the patient's therapist potentialities, and which is fully consonant with my own concepts about therapeutic symbiosis: "What I seem to have said in the session was that she had difficulty in believing in a way of coming together with me that is psychical and not erotically physical, and which could lead to something new being created, her new self *and mine*" (p. 289; italics mine).

The author notes a theme, evident at that juncture (the fourteenth year of the treatment), "of her attempt to avoid dependence on me by feeling she herself has all that she needs—and what I need as well" (p. 292). But the reader has no way of knowing, here, whether Milner conceptualizes "what I need as well" to be purely a distorted transference perception on the patient's part (if such were indeed possible), or whether there is a nucleus of reality in the patient's perception, here, of the analyst.

Concerning a session a bit later in the fourteenth year, in which the patient did a drawing of a baby duck within a larger duck, Milner notes: ". . . there was not only the question of the part of herself, as the baby duck, being ready to come out from inside me, there was also the related task of her becoming able to let me out, let me be born out of her" (pp. 302-303).

Still later in the fourteenth year, when the patient continued to be involved in a process, lasting more than ten months, of becoming ready to be born, Milner reports: "On 27 July she says she remembers sitting on her mother's knee and feeling so depressed, and how her mother was always saying she [the mother] was going to die. Now she wonders if she was always trying to stop her from dying" (p. 322).

When, a few months later, the following material emerges, I would infer that the patient is concerned therapeutically to provide life to the analyst, a depressed mother in transference terms but, I would assume, to a degree *really* depressed also. Milner, however, does not:

On Thursday 25 November she brings a dream:

> It was that I was telling her how my husband had left me his mummied heart, in his will, and I was crying and so was she. But we were both quite separate from each other.

Her own association to the dream . . . was that she could only give me a dead heart, which means that she will never get well. I said that in the dream she does seem to have a heart, because she is crying and feeling sorry. I said I thought the dream was more about artifically keeping a live heart dead than artificially preserving a dead one; that is, she has been trying to blot out the inner movement of feeling to do with love and sadness [pp. 347-348].

By contrast, in my own similarly prolonged work with Mrs. Douglas (some aspects of which I have described at length earlier in this paper), I found that my awareness of real feelings of depression on my part (in addition to—or, in my terms, as a nucleus of—the patient's long-familiar transference perceptions of me as being the personification of her depressed mother, or of her depressed self) helped greatly to account for the tenacity during the sessions of her "crazy talk" (as it for many years has been referred to in the sanitarium where she lives).

Specifically, innumerable times during recent years, as she has become more able to face her tremendous and long-repressed feelings of grief, this has involved our having to face, concomitantly, a very considerable risk of suicide on her part; that is, the feelings of healthy grieving are not yet well differentiated from those of a psychotically depressive nature. Partly as a function of this phase of the work with her (as well as from various other sources in my current life), I have found myself experiencing, concomitantly, feelings of depression of a formidable degree during our sessions; in fact, during at least one of our sessions some two years ago, I experienced considerable fear lest *one or the other* of us commit suicide immediately following the session.

Hence it is to a degree understandable to me that the following sequence occurred innumerable times in recent years, during a phase which now seems largely behind us, as she has become better able to grieve. She would come into the session and, instead of starting to pour forth her usual appallingly fragmented, yet irresistibly fascinating and in a sense entertaining "crazy talk," she would sit silently, looking filled with mute grief and despair. Consciously I welcomed this development in each such session; but each time when, after a few or many minutes of silence, she then started verbalizing her usual "crazy talk," and her demeanor came within a few minutes later still to show little if any of the feelings of grief and despair, *against my will* (so it felt) I would find myself feeling relieved at her being her long-familiar, chronically crazy self. There were abundant data, in such sessions, indicating that she tended to feel that by this craziness she was keeping her mother (= HFS) alive, or bringing her mother back to life. If I had thought of such perceptions on her part, of me, as being "just transference," the remarkable tenacity of her craziness would have been much less understandable to me.

For a great many years following her admission to Chestnut Lodge, it was clear that her social role at the Lodge was of one whose craziness seemed designed to relieve depression in others about her there. It was typical of her that when, a few days before a Christmas during the early years of her stay at the Lodge, the patients in the recreational therapy center were reacting with an intensely depressive pall to efforts on the staff's part to encourage them to join in carol-singing, Joan's caustically scornful voice came loud and clear and masterfully sure over the group's tragically depressed and nostalgic efforts at singing: "What's the *matter* with you *idiots*, singing *Christmas carols?*—don't you realize it's *March the tenth?*" This broke up the crowd, staff members and patients alike, with relieved laughter at her craziness.

In the course of my careful reading of Milner's book, I recall no mention by the author of her feeling any such despair as has been so familiar to me in the work with Joan. Milner describes her realization, in retrospect, of how caught up she had been in a compulsion to be helpful to her patient,[5] in which state one is in no position to discern the patient's therapeutic strivings toward oneself. She notes ". . . my early tendency to do too much for her and to interpret too much in terms of the 'good object', not taking enough account of the 'good subject' . . . my over-anxiety to be a 'good' analyst in those early years of my practice, over-anxiety leading to giving too many interpretations . . ." (p. 366).

The following passage, concerning a dream the patient reported early in the sixteenth year of the analysis, shows how much more clearly the author has come to recognize the significance of the pa-

[5] Much as I described in a paper in 1955.

tient's own love—highly relevant, of course, to the theme of my paper:

> . . . So now I see the . . . dream as expressing this basic conflict she has been battling with all these years, the issue of whether she can accept any limitations on her loving, both in how she gives or how she takes; whether she can give up her belief that she can make herself one with what she loves by eating it, accept the fact that the food she eats is not actually the same as the breast that she loved, that she wished to become one with by eating; and also whether she can accept limits in her giving, accept something less than an actual giving up her life; and find instead, by discrimination between inner and outer, a surrender that is not physical death [p. 370].

Somewhat later in the sixteenth year of the analysis, Milner describes:

> A few months after Susan's getting a room of her own her mother died; it was the ending of a long illness during which Susan had been very good to her, in spite of the fact that her mother could never recognize her devotion or give her any thanks; for instance, in the last year of her mother's life Susan would often visit her, taking her a box of chocolates, and her mother would eat them without ever offering Susan one. And when the nurse looking after her mother said, in front of them both, 'You have a very good daughter', her mother had said nothing [p. 388].

In a footnote to the above, Milner comments:

> This inability on the part of her mother to acknowledge her daughter's reparative activities high-lighted important aspects of Susan's account of her childhood . . . [and] certainly tended to confirm the psychoanalytic view that the lack of opportunity for and recognition of reparative activities can greatly encourage psychotic states of mind [p. 388].

It can be seen that what Milner (following her usual Kleinian conceptualization) terms reparative activities, I would term therapeutic strivings, regarding these strivings as being more primarily a part of the infant's potentialities for giving love, than secondary to the individual's hostile strivings (and therefore expressive, in Kleinian terms, of an attempt at reparation for the fantasied damage wrought upon the mother, in past experiences with her, by one's own hostility).

It is my impression that an analyst's rigid adherence to a classically psychoanalytic orientation, his remaining oblivious and unacknowledging of the nuclei of reality in the patient's transference responses to him, fosters his being precisely as unacknowledging of the patient's therapeutic strivings toward him as Susan's mother was being, apparently, toward Susan in the above-described situation. One is left with a nagging sense of doubt as to whether, or to what extent, Milner regards her patient's transference reactions to her as being based in an increment of reality when, in the following passage in her closing pages, she implies that a psychotic patient needs to create the analyst—*really* needs to, to a very significant and crucial degree, I would say—in order to become free of psychosis:

> . . . although I had myself been convinced through my own enquiries into painting [1957] that the 'other' has to be created before it can be perceived, I had yet taken so long to realize the implications of this in clinical work, the full extent to which she had to be allowed to contribute from herself before she could feel that I was truly real for her [p. 404].

The recent paper by Singer (1971), "The Patient Aids the Analyst: Some Clinical and Theoretical Observations," because of its high degree of consonance with the theme of my paper, merits my quoting from it at length. Singer begins:

> From their very beginnings most publications on psychoanalytic technique have stressed at least implicitly a dominant theme: that the analyst derives little personal satisfaction from his work other than the gratification the healer inevitably derives from the sense of a job well done and, of course, from the financial rewards attending his efforts. All other satisfactions arising in his working day have been suspect of countertransference tendencies rooted in the analyst's unresolved conflicts.
>
> Structuring the psychoanalytic relationship in these terms molded the process into a one-way street: the helping relationship was to be one in which the analyst aided the patient, in

which he could not and should not expect any comparable aid from his client. . . .

It is the purpose of this paper to explore . . . the potential power of the analyst's revealing his own life situation, thereby making it possible for the patient to be realistically helpful; and finally, as its main contribution, to support implications for a theory of personality development derived from these observations, implications at variance with those traditionally advanced in the psychoanalytic literature.

. . . unbending anonymity, while furthering the denouement of hidden destructive and other primitive tendencies, does not promote and activate reality-oriented and constructive qualities [pp. 56-58].

Singer's paper resulted from the fact that his wife suddenly became seriously ill, which required him to cancel, with a demeanor he knew his patients had reason to detect as uncharacteristically anxious, all his appointments until further notice.

. . . My patients . . . sensed from my voice that this cancellation did not reflect a frivolous impulse and spontaneously inquired, "What's up?" Too troubled to engage in lengthy conversations and hesitant about how much I wanted to say, I merely replied that I would explain when I saw them again. . . .

With some trepidation I decided [in the interim] to tell them the truth. . . . I informed all patients about the reason for my absence.

Their responses seemed to be astonishing, and that I was astonished reflected poorly on me. Concern, genuine sympathy, eagerness to be helpful with problems likely to arise, and above all efforts to be supportive and comforting—these reactions were eye openers. As I listened, deeply moved and profoundly grateful, to the patients' efforts, it became apparent that each person expressed his desire to be helpful in his particular style, a manner which often, when occurring under different circumstances, had been identified as reflecting a pathological character orientation. I will give a few illustrations . . . [pp. 58-59].

I hope that these vignettes illustrate what I have learned: that the capacity to rise to the occasion when compassion and helpfulness are called for is part and parcel of the makeup of all human beings. Importantly, in no single instance did my disclosures have any ill effects; on the contrary, the insights, memories, and heightened awareness which followed my self-exposure proved remarkable, and I have the deep conviction that my frankness accelerated the therapeutic process in several instances.

. . . Strict psychoanalytic anonymity would have reduced my patients' opportunities to see their own strengths; and certainly it would have limited my knowledge of their caring and compassionate capacities. . . .

My patients' efforts to search themselves, much more seriously after my disclosures than ever before, brought to light certain themes which up to now had never emerged or had at best been mentioned only fleetingly.

Mrs. N., for instance, now genuinely attempted to grasp the truth of critical experiences and of the affect associated with certain of her present-day reactions to them. . . . With great pain Mrs. N. now began to reexperience instances of feeling totally unable to make any meaningful contributions to these all-knowing, all-successful, and seemingly "need-less" people [i.e., her mother and her father]. . . . there is little doubt in my mind . . . that the admission of my pain made the vision of genuine usefulness a realistic possibility for her [pp. 62-63].

. . . much of the neurotic distress experienced by my patients seemed associated with their profound sense of personal uselessness and their sense of having failed as human beings because they knew that the only contributions they had made were embodied in nonconstructive reactions and behavior responding to equally nonconstructive demands. . . .

. . . those concerned with the origins of psychopathology and with efforts to rekindle emotional growth must give serious attention to the possibility that the most devastating of human experiences is the sense of uselessness [p. 65].

This lack of authenticity in parent-child relations, the child's inadequate opportunities to express constructive relatedness, finds an analogue in the traditional analytic relationship. . . .

. . . For some patients the events described here accelerated a process of growth well underway. But others were reached emotionally for the first time in therapy by my disclosures and willingness to accept their help [p. 67].

I have already indicated that my own views are at variance from one of Singer's main conclusions, namely that "... a marked reduction of the analyst's anonymity is essential to therapeutic progress" (p. 67). In my own work, while being relatively freely revealing of feelings and fantasies I experience during the analytic session itself, I tell patients very little of my life outside the office. But I feel sure that even the most critical reader of Singer's paper will find it difficult to write off his work as "wild analysis," for throughout the paper he manifests, recurrently, a commendably detailed, serious, and genuinely humble acknowledgment of the potential hazards of the departures from classical analysis he is advocating.

I myself regard the theme of my paper as being one fraught with complexities; but it seems to me imperative that we enter this thicket and carve out, in it, some solid theoretical and technical area for our functioning as analysts, for in my opinion the classical analytic position, containing an element of delusion to the effect that the analyst is not at all a real person to the patient, simply will not do. I find an analogy to this latter point in the point Lewin (1958) makes in his charming little monograph, *Dreams and the Uses of Regression*. Lewin begins by saying, "Around the year 500 B.C., natural science began with a repudiation of the dream" (p. 11). And then, toward the end of his essay, Lewin discloses the delightful irony that the view of the world as conceptualized by Descartes, the epitome of the natural scientists, is essentially dreamlike in nature:

> In short, I should like to hazard a hypothesis: when Descartes came to formulate his scientific picture of the world, he made it conform with the state of affairs in an ordinary successful dream. The picture of the dream world that succeeds best in preserving sleep ... came to be the picture of the waking world that succeeded best in explaining it scientifically [p. 50].

So, I feel, it is with classical psychoanalysis: to the degree that it is rigorously classical, it is essentially delusional.

Space does not allow for my trying to recapitulate all my own previous writings about the theme of my present paper; several of those have already been touched upon as I have gone along. One of the earliest is my paper in 1955 concerning dependency processes in the psychotherapy of schizophrenic patients, which includes a description of the role of the therapist's real dependency upon the patient.

SUMMARY

This paper advances the hypothesis that innate among the human being's emotional potentialities, present in the earliest months of postnatal life, is an essentially psychotherapeutic striving. The family-environmental warping of that striving is a major etiologic source of all psychopathology. The analyst's failure to discern that long-repressed striving in the patient accounts, more than does any other interpersonal element in the treatment situation, for the patient's unconscious resistance to the analytic process. Despite the acknowledged complexities involved in our departing from classical psychoanalytic theory and technique in this regard, it is essential that we do so.

Special emphasis is placed, in this paper, upon the psychotic patient's therapeutic effort to enable the mother (and analogously in the analytic context, the analyst) to become a whole and effective mother (= analyst) to him.

20

Dual- and Multiple-Identity Processes in Borderline Ego Functioning

The main emphasis of this paper is upon the internal world of the borderline patient. This theoretical vantage point for the study of emotional illness rests first and foremost, of course, upon the work of Freud. Melanie Klein (1946) and her followers deserve acknowledgment for increasing greatly our theoretical understanding of this realm of the patient's internal world (the never-ending controversies between Kleinian and non-Kleinian analysts notwithstanding); Segal's (1964) recently revised *Introduction to the Work of Melanie Klein* includes a fine survey of Kleinian contributions in this regard. Wexler's (1951) paper, "The Structural Problem in Schizophrenia: The Role of the Internal Object" is relevant here, as is Coleman's (1956) paper, "Externalization of the Toxic Introject: A Treatment Technique for Borderline Cases." Roy Schafer's (1968) volume, *Aspects of Internalization*, provides a richly detailed background of theory here, and Kernberg's superlative works on borderline patients (e.g., 1972) are focused essentially upon his understanding of the patient's internalized object relations. Volkan's (1976) recently published volume, drawing heavily upon the work of Kernberg, explores the psychodynamics and analytic psycho-

First published in *Borderline Personality Disorders: The Concept, the Patient, the Syndrome*, edited by Peter Hartocollis (New York: International Universities Press, 1977), pp. 441-455.

therapy of patients with borderline personality organization, as well as those with narcissistic personalities, and those manifesting frank psychosis. Volkan's basic focus is expressed in his book's title, *Primitive Internalized Object Relations.*

The psychotherapy of schizophrenia program, organized by Mosher and Feinsilver of the NIMH Center for Studies of Schizophrenia, has yielded the following working definition of schizophrenia; note particularly the focus upon internal mental representations of the outside real world:

> Schizophrenia is a disorder of ego functioning caused by developmental parent-child experiences (which may include biological-constitutional elements) which results in a deficit in the ability to separate out and maintain accurate internal mental representations of the outside real world. This deficit, in turn, causes the production of restitutional symptoms (delusions, hallucinations) which are most prominent when the individual is confronted with the stresses of developing independent, mature, trusting adult relationships [Friedman, Gunderson, and Feinsilver, 1973; also cited in Gunderson and Mosher, 1975, p. 675].

Various of my own previous writings have much to do with the internal world of the schizophrenic patient. These include: "Data Concerning Certain Manifestations of Incorporation" (1951), "The Schizophrenic Individual's Experience of His World" (1967a), "Autism and the Phase of Transition to Therapeutic Symbiosis" (1970), and "Pathologic Symbiosis and Autism" (1971).

The specific title-subject of this paper, dual- and multiple-identity processes in borderline schizophrenia, has its earliest theoretic antecedent in Freud's (1940) paper, "Splitting of the Ego in the Process of Defence." Helene Deutsch (1942), Klein (1946), Rosenfeld (1947), Fairbairn (1952), Knight (1953a, 1953b), Winnicott (1958), Guntrip (1961, 1969), Modell (1963, 1968), Segal (1964), and Khan (1974) are among those writers (I am not attempting here to be comprehensive) who have discussed the phenomena of splitting in the ego functioning of the borderline patient, or processes highly relevant to that splitting. *The Borderline Syndrome* by Grinker, Werble, and Drye (1968) provides a helpful review of some of the literature which is relevant to my subject.

Perhaps due in part to a too-literal interpretation of some of Erikson's (1956) early writings concerning ego identity, I long thought the sense of identity in a healthy individual to be essentially monolithic in nature, consisting in large part of well-digested part-identifications with other persons (I omit discussion, here, of the nonhuman environment, as irrelevant to the specific theme of this paper). But in more recent years, especially in the course of my exploring the psychodynamics of the borderline patient, in whom the sense of identity coexists simultaneously in two or more internal objects, I have come to see that the healthy individual's sense of identity is far from being monolithic in nature. It involves, rather, myriad internal objects functioning in lively and harmonious interrelatedness, and all contributing to a relatively coherent, consistent sense of identity which springs from and comprises all of them, but does not involve their being congealed into any so unitary a mass as I once thought. I have come to believe that the more healthy an individual is, the more consciously does he live in the knowledge that there are myriad "persons"—internal objects each bearing some sense-of-identity value—within him; and he recognizes this state of his internal world to be what it is: not threatened insanity, but the strength resident in the human condition.

EXAMPLES OF THE PATIENT'S PHRASEOLOGY WHICH IS SUBTLY REVEALING OF MULTIPLE-IDENTITY FUNCTIONING

Often the content of the patient's remark seems ordinary enough; but the feeling-tone conveyed in it gives the analyst a glimpse of the patient's functioning, unconsciously, in terms of a dual or multiple identity.

A married woman comments, "I suppose the most tolerable compromise with these hungers of mine is to go with another couple, so I'd have a chance to share ideas with another man." Here she reveals both her unconscious image of herself as being a man, as well as that of her being a couple. On another occasion she describes: "One time when I was smoking some grass, and *Bill were* [my italics] having—and Bill and I were having an argument . . ." Her slip here reveals her unconscious image of Bill as being two persons (which involves a projection of her own internal state). A male patient makes a similarly meaningful slip in speaking of one of his several cousins: "He's the *ones* [my italics]—the one who's a lawyer." An attorney says of his opponent in a forthcoming case, "He's filled with vindictiveness; he's determined to *kill me off* [my italics] during the trial." Common usage tends to confine the phrase "kill off" to references to doing away with multiple foes rather than a single one.

A woman patient reproaches me with, "You *overran* [my italics] me yesterday," unconsciously projecting upon me her own multiple-ego functioning in alluding to me, here, as though I had been a herd of stampeding horses, or, equally likely, a horde of insects. Another woman's statement that "My mother has a large head, y'know" seemed in content mundane enough; but it was said with such an intonation as to convey the unconscious meaning, "My mother has a large head, *among other* heads in her possession"— reminiscent to me of a frankly psychotic woman's delusion that either her head, or mine, was replaced by a succession of other heads on innumerable occasions in the course of our sessions.

Within another woman's ordinary-seeming statement that "I feel terribly uneasy in my family, in my marriage, in my home" was a certain feeling-tone which revealed the existence, at an unconscious level, of three separate identities in her—one having to do with her family; a second, with her marriage; and a third, with her home. A much traveled woman says, "I feel more disturbed in England than I do in other countries. . . . I feel more comfortable in Italy; I feel more comfortable in France. I used to feel all right in Canada." This innocuous-seeming statement was said, again, in a curious manner which conveyed the unintended meaning that, at an unconscious level, she was living at the moment, and simultaneously, as several different selves, in England and in other countries, including Italy and France.

The many patients who habitually and frequently add parenthetically, in the course of their reporting, "Y'know," are revealing the unconscious meaning: "You know, because you are having or have had the same experience as the one I'm telling you about; your experience is always a twin of mine."

Equally frequent is the patient who, in reporting some recently past incident, expresses puzzlement about some aspect of his own behavior, either implying (or, much less often, explicitly stating), "It wasn't like me to react as I did." Here is an allusion to the presence of another "me," this one unconscious, who had been governing his behavior in that past incident. This is a very muted variation upon the frankly paranoid individual's delusion that occult forces were governing his mind and behavior. One paranoid patient was convinced, for years, that innumerable "doubles" of her self existed, and that supernatural forces replaced her self, unpredictably, with one or another of these doubles, which then carried out destructive behavior for which she herself was later held accountable. A borderline young woman revealed only a subtle hint of paranoid reaction to one of her internal objects in saying, of her having found herself uncharacteristically late for her college classes recently, "So I wonder if there's something cooking," clearly meaning, here, something at work in her own unconscious, but with the aforementioned, unintended paranoid-flavored allusion to the possibility that external forces were influencing her. She added, in the same vein, "I wonder if there's something going on. It's not like me to be late for classes."

THE PATIENT WHO SAYS, "I DON'T KNOW WHERE TO BEGIN"

It may not be deeply significant if a patient occasionally begins a session with the statement, "I don't know where to begin." It may be simply a realistic attempt to cope with, for example, the fact that much has been happening around him and within him of late. But I began to realize, some two years ago, that the patient who more often than not begins the session with this statement (or some variation upon it) is unconsciously saying, "It is not clear which one of my multiple I's will begin verbally reporting its thoughts, its feelings, its free associations, during this session." That is, it is not basically that there are too many competing subjects for his "I" to select among, to begin the reporting, but rather that there are too many "I's" which are, at the moment, competing among "themselves" as to which one shall begin verbalizing. One such patient explained, after an initial silence in which his physical demeanor was expressive of "I don't know where to begin," that during that silence he had been feeling partly like Jimmy, a boyhood friend who was given to temper tantrums—and, evidently, partly like a much more adult, and quite different, person. A woman who had become able, over the course of her analysis, to integrate into her conscious sense of identity many previously warded-off part-identities began a session by saying, in a relaxed way and in a manner which I felt expressive of much ego strength, in a kind of confident good humor, "Now let's see; which one of my several identities will materialize today?"

CERTAIN SIGNIFICANCES OF THE USE OF THE WORD "WE"

First to be noted are those patients whose reminiscences about childhood are expressed not in terms of "I" but rather in terms of "we." Such a patient recalls almost invariably that "we" used to do this or that. He scarcely ever says "I" in this connection, and the analyst is left largely in the dark as to whom "we" is meant to include. My impression, developed in the course of working with a number of such patients, is that the patient's sense of identity is essentially symbiotic in nature (as is, or at the beginning of treatment was, that of each of the patients mentioned in this paper), with the sense of identity being either dualistic or multiple and with an ever-changingness as regards the shifting of the symbiotic partner(s) in that sense of identity.

Several years ago I encountered comparable data in a supervisory session, in which the female supervisee was describing her work with a hospitalized, frankly psychotic man who showed an extraordinarily severe problem in terms of multiple-identity functioning and, by the same token, symbiotic interpersonal relatedness. Time after time, as the supervisee herself reported to me that "We decided to meet on the sun porch," or "We talked for a few minutes about that," or "We discussed that for a few moments," it was proving impossible for me to know whether "We" referred to the supervisee and the patient, or to the supervisee and one of the ward staff members, or to the supervisee and the whole ward staff collectively, or whomever, and I began to realize how impossible it was for the deeply confused patient to discern with whom he was dealing in the supervisee who was so immersed in so ambiguous and shifting a "we"-identity.

A few weeks ago, in my third session with a male patient who was still occupied mainly with presenting details of his history, I suddenly realized that he was using the word "we" with the significance I am describing here. I had become accustomed already to his presenting himself more as a married couple than as an individual; he spoke of his wife nearly as much as he did of himself, such that it was much as though the wife were ever-present in our sessions. In this third session, I noticed that he would describe the events over a relatively long stretch of the marriage, detailing what "we" had done during that time, then mentioning relatively briefly that his mother-in-law had intruded briefly but disruptively on the scene, then resuming his narrative that "we" had moved to another part of the country, then detailing at length what "we" had done there, then mentioning a brief affair he had had, then resuming his narrative of what "we" had done in subsequent years. I am oversimplifying here; but, in essence, I realized that at an unconscious level, "we" did not refer consistently to his symbiotic identity comprising himself and his wife. Rather, at the time when the mother-in-law had come upon the scene, she had replaced his wife as his symbiotic partner, so that the "we" who had moved to another part of the country had been, in his unconscious experience, himself and his mother-in-law. Similarly, later on his mother-in-law had been replaced by his mistress, such that it was a symbiotic himself-and-his-mistress, not a symbiotic self-and-his-wife, who had participated in the things "we" had done in subsequent years. These were simply three among many symbiotic partners whom he evidently had had at an unconscious level.

Patients' use of "we" as having an unconscious symbiotic-*transference* significance is a phenomenon I find particularly valuable to note—privately, that is; I do not recommend any early interpretation of this phenomenon, lest a premature interpreting of it interfere with the development of the nondefensive, healthy-identification aspects of this phenomenon (those aspects which relate to the patient's development of a constructive introject of the analyst).

A female patient, for example, comments at the beginning of the session, "Why did you move that plant over there?" and, after a very brief silence (my having made no reply), she goes on, "*We* [my italics] were invited out to a Chinese dinner with some people last evening, and went to the Kennedy Center afterward . . ." "We" consciously referred to herself and her husband, as from long-established custom I was assumed to know; but unconsciously it referred, as I had come by now to realize from this and other transference data, to herself and me (a father-figure in the transference) as a symbiotic-marital partner.

A male patient details for several moments, at the beginning of a session, his feelings about what he experiences as the combative relatedness between us of late, making a number of references to our session of the preceding day; then, after a pause of only a couple of seconds, he goes on, "I was thinking about yesterday *we* [my italics] took the children to the zoo— . . ." Later in the session, referring to a girlfriend he had had in California prior to his meeting his wife, he says, "When I think about her, and then I think about myself *here* [my italics], married and with three children . . ." Data from many sessions substantiated my impression that the "we" who had taken the children to the zoo had been, at an unconscious level, himself and me as his transference-mother.

Another male patient characteristically asked, at the end of each session, "Time to go?"—with such an intonation as to convey, "Time for us to go?" It had become clear to me, long before, that he carried an internal image of me within him between (as well as during) our sessions. He frequently began sessions by saying that "We" did thus-and-so with the children over the weekend, or that "We" had another nasty argument last night. It became more and more evident to me, as the analysis went on, that these communications, such as his beginning a session with, "Night before last we had sex. . . ," contained unconscious references to me as his symbiotic-identity partner; in the transference, in this regard, I represented mainly aspects of his symbiotically-related-to mother.

The psychodynamics described by Freud (1917) in his "Mourning and Melancholia" (including the phenomenon of identification with the lost object, and the venting of hostility upon the self as a representative of that ambivalently love-and-hated lost object), when applied to the symbiotic transference phenomena described here, help to illuminate innumerable instances of patients' acting out.

For example, one female patient says, near the beginning of a session, "If I seem relatively unanxious to you this evening—I don't know whether I seem so to you or not; I feel relatively unanxious—it's probably because *we* [my italics; this ostensibly referred to herself and her husband] didn't do any acting out last night" (i.e., any tirading at their poorly disciplined young children). In dozens of instances from my work with several to many patients over the years, it has been apparent that a patient's acting out (during my or his vacations, or in the usual interims between scheduled sessions) in the form of reckless driving, or excessive drinking of alcohol, or self-detrimental behavior at work, or whatever, represents, to a significant degree, his rageful subjecting not of himself but of me, his symbiotic-transference identity-partner, to such punishment. Sometimes such a patient is conscious of his trying to emulate the analyst (or, in some instances, someone ostensibly outside the analytic situation) but then, time and again, he feels unable to carry through the identification successfully; he keeps falling on his face. He long represses the fact that, at an unconscious level, it is not that he is so much "unable" to maintain the identification, but rather that he keeps on, as it were, burning the other person in effigy within himself; he keeps throwing the internalized analyst upon the latter's face, within himself.

The Analyst's Feelings and Fantasies as Clues to Dual- or Multiple-Identity Functioning on the Part of the Patient

In a discussion (1973a) of the role of jealousy in the fragmented ego, I wrote, concerning my work with a schizoid patient:

> . . . For several years I found this man infuriatingly smug. But the time came when, to my astonishment, I realized that what I was feeling was jealousy; *he* so clearly favored his *self* over *me* that I felt deeply jealous, bitterly left out of this mutually cherishing and cozy relationship between the two "persons" comprising him. . . . In retrospect, I saw that I previously had not developed sufficient personal significance to him . . . to sense these two now relatively well-differentiated "persons" in him and to feel myself capable of and desirous of participating in the "three"-way, intensely jealousy-laden competition. It is my impression that such schizoid patients usually prove so discouragingly inaccessible to psychoanalysis that the analyst and the patient give up . . . before they have reached this lively but disturbing . . . stratum in which the patient's ego fragmentation becomes revealed and the nature of the transference becomes one of a murderously jealous "three"-way competitiveness.

Since then I have collected many examples, largely from my work with borderline, schizoid, and narcissistic patients, concerning this phenomenon, which I have thought of as "intrapsychic" jealousy, or jealousy involving an internal object in one or the other of the two participants in the analytic interaction. Recently, for instance, when a woman suddenly interrupted her own reporting by telling herself with intense impatience and exasperation, in an appreciably different tone of voice, "Oh, *shut up*, you *idiot*!," I experienced that by now familiar feeling of jealousy of this idiot-"person," for her tone, despite all its furious impatience, was filled with possessive fondness. The "idiot" to whom she spoke was clearly mother's cherished little idiot.

In my sessions with a number of patients, one of the means whereby I sense that the patient is functioning unconsciously in a multiple-identity fashion is that I have come to realize that I feel often not simply intimidated or overwhelmed by this overbearing patient but, curiously and more specifically, *outnumbered* by him or her. In the instance of one such woman, relatively far along in her analysis I had the thought, accompanied by a feeling of gratification and fulfillment in the analytic work, "She is moving." But there emerged in me, along with this freely conscious thought and feeling, an entirely unbidden fantasy: in my mind's eye, I saw some 50 to 100 people on foot in a caravan, moving in a straggling, undisciplined but clearly peaceable fashion across a landscape, and all going essentially together in the same direction; they were clearly all related to one another, and it later occurred to me that the word "tribe" described that relationship. The fantasy was accompanied by a distinct sense of awe at the realization that, evidently for a long time, I had been perceiving, unconsciously, this woman as made up of so many "persons."

During the long years of the analysis before so coherent an internal object relatedness has developed within such a patient, she is unconsciously defended against the recognition of this internal state, partly through the utilization of projection of this or that internal object upon the analyst at the slightest opportunity, as it were. The analyst comes to feel that he is interrupting, somehow, her train of thought, even though he is being totally silent; it eventually becomes clear that, to her, if he is "allowing" her to digress from her intended main path, he is thereby guilty of interrupting her. If he moves slightly in his chair, this tiny sound is reacted to as a gross interruption. She reacts fully as though a third person had come upon the scene, or as though this sound was the surreptitious one made by a copulating couple (another form of unconscious relatedness of her own internal objects), or, at times, as though a part of her own body-image had suddenly and dismemberingly separated itself out from the rest of that body-image.

Such patients are, in my experience at least, by no means rare. The intensity of their projection of the internal objects which interfere, at an unconscious level, with their more conscious ego-identity functioning tends to have a severely constraining effect upon the analyst's functioning at all overtly as an analyst during the sessions. In the instance of one such patient who indicates that I am an enormous interference with his attempts to free associate, I often think of his silent and agonized demeanor as being that of a fly imprisoned in amber; and, further, I have noted privately that more often than not, when I venture some intendedly liberating brief interpretation, it is as if the fly in the amber now manages to appear, somehow, even *more* cramped than it was before.

As the patient becomes more aware that the interruptions come primarily from within, he will speak, for instance, of ". . . what I was going to tell you when I was interrupted by that remembrance of the fantasy I had on the way here," or he may explain that the reason he is silent so much of the time here is "because I can't stand the sound of my own voice. . . . It is so grating; it sounds exactly like my mother's voice . . ." Such patients make clear, on some of these occasions, that their "own" voice is being experienced by them as thoroughly alien, fully equivalent to that of an antagonizing and entirely separate other person.

DEFENSIVE (TRANSFERENCE-RESISTANCE) VERSUS EGO-INTEGRATIVE ASPECTS OF THESE PHENOMENA

Any one of these clinical phenomena, when it appears in the context of the transference, needs to be evaluated in terms of whether it is predominantly a defensive phenomenon, an instance of the patient's characteristic borderline, symbiotic mode of ego functioning in relation to other persons over the years, or whether it is a predominantly healthy new development, signifying (among other things) the patient's having managed to develop a healthy internal object representation of the analyst in the latter's own right, beyond his transference significance to the patient. Presumably any one vignette represents to some degree a mixture of both kinds of elements.

As for the defensive functioning of these phenomena, much of the clinical material presented in my 1951 paper on incorporation is relevant; this material shows patients' unconscious utilization of incorporation as a mode of defense to maintain under repression, for example, feelings of hostility and rejection. On the other hand, most of these examples of dual- and multiple-identity processes described here are of essentially the same nature as those encountered in what I (1961e) have termed the phase of ambivalent symbiosis, a phase I have described as one traversed by the schizophrenic patient in the course of his improving ego integration as his treatment progresses. To my way of thinking, the ambivalently symbiotic, dual- and multiple-identity processes so characterologically typical of the borderline patient will give way, over the course of psychoanalytic therapy, to better integrated functioning on the patient's part only if the therapist becomes able to function during the sessions in a fashion which allows for the ambivalent symbiosis in the transference to become replaced, gradually, with a therapeutic symbiosis, the characteristics of which I have described in a number of papers (1965a, 1973a).

Space allows me to touch only briefly upon the defensive aspects of the processes under discussion. Time after time in my work with borderline patients, I find that the patient's not responding to my greeting upon his entering the office has come to infuriate me so much that I no longer greet him, either; this is one of the ways in which we come to function as alike or as one. Such behavior on the analyst's part is clearly a fostering of symbiosis (or a succumbing to the patient's coercion toward symbiosis), but of a symbiosis which is defensive against antagonism.

A patient who says that "Yesterday when I walked in, you looked as if you were afraid I was gonna attack *me* [my italics]" is clearly fusing with me, unconsciously, at the moment of this slip, as a defense against his anxiety concerning his perception of me as being afraid of him; it is less threatening to him, unconsciously, to be the attacked than the attacking one.

A married man showed, relatively early in his analysis, a multiple-identity mode of ego functioning at an unconscious level.

In reminiscing about his childhood, for example, he was describing the struggles that took place between an alcoholic uncle and the patient's three older brothers who had attempted to keep the uncle from drinking. *"I can remember fighting with him* [my italics]—not me personally but my three brothers . . ." The italicized portion was said *fully* as though he personally had fought with the uncle; it was clear that "I" included his three brothers as well as himself. Incidentally, I was reminded, upon hearing him say this, of a chronically schizophrenic woman who had two sisters, two and four years younger than herself. She once said, in reminiscing about something in her childhood, "When I was six-four-and-two—," then corrected herself, "When we were six-four-and-two . . ." The man whom I was just discussing soon established, in the treatment sessions, a defensively symbiotic mode of ego functioning which proved for years highly resistive to analysis. He essentially presented himself as a couple consisting of himself and his wife. This had, of course, various genetic roots; for one thing, he was identifying with a mother who had functioned, in his upbringing, as both mother and father. It gradually became clear that he was enormously threatened, at an unconscious level, lest I replace his wife as his symbiotic-marital partner, which would mean that I would become not merely, so to speak, his mate in a truly separate object relationship, but that I would become the other half (so to speak) of the only ego identity he possessed.

A woman patient came, over the course of many months of analysis, to tell me during one of our sessions, "You are my self," in a way which I found very moving. She then added with a kind of small-child shyness the qualification, as though not to frighten me,"—not *all* the time . . ." The affective quality of this communication was such as to make me feel that it was not predominantly treatment-resistive in nature, but rather a manifestation of healthy growth in her, made possible partly by my no longer needing to shy away from a more therapeutically symbiotic mode of transference relatedness with her.

In my work with each of several patients, after a number of years of work the patient has come finally to ask me, with unusual simplicity and directness, "What's the matter with me?" or "What's wrong with me?" In each instance this question seems expressive consciously of feelings of futility, helplessness, mystification, exasperation, discouragement, and so on, because of various tenaciously treatment-resistant symptoms. But in each instance the question proves to have been expressive, at an unconscious level, of oedipal longings; the patient in this regard is asking me why she or he still does not qualify, in my eyes, to become my romantic and sexual partner. But at a still deeper level the question conveys the meaning, "Why have you still not accepted me fully as your symbiotic-identity partner, and by the same token surrendered fully your individual identity and entered fully into a symbiotic identity with me?"

THE PATIENT'S MONOLOGUE AS BEING, UNCONSCIOUSLY, A DIALOGUE

Some time ago I devoted a paper (1972a) to reporting a few of the developments in my psychoanalytic therapy with a deeply schizophrenic woman with whom I have been working for 23 years at this writing. For at least 15 of those years I have been accustomed to her spending the bulk of many of her sessions in dialoguing vehemently with one or another part of herself, thus shutting me out, to a high degree, from talking at all directly with her. In about 1962 I heard M. A. Woodbury describe, during a staff presentation at Chestnut Lodge, that the auditory hallucinatory experiences of a chronically schizophrenic woman with whom he was working functioned, during the therapy sessions, to provide her with responses from another person, so to speak, at a time when he was not supplying any comments to her. A paper of mine (1976) contains comparable data from another patient of mine, much less ill than the one mentioned above, but who has experienced auditory hallucinations for many years. As a brief example, among many available ones from my work with this woman, she came into a session deeply worried about the persisting, and apparently as yet undiagnosed, illness on the part of a cousin. She asked, "What do you think Paul has, Dr. Searles?" I made no direct answer, but endeavored to elicit more of her thoughts in this regard. Within a few seconds, she reported, seriously, "I heard the voices say, 'It's a reaction.'" She quoted the voices as speaking in an explanatory tone, as if providing, authoritatively and decisively, the explanation she had sought in vain from me.

But many years of experiences such as those just mentioned did not lead me to recognize, until a very few years ago, how frequently the borderline patient's monologues during the session prove to be, on closer examination, unconscious dialogues—dialogues between two parts of the patient's self, one part comprising the introjected analyst, a symbiotic-identity partner, at an unconscious level, in the transference. I emphasize that the fact that he is involved in a dialogue is genuinely unconscious to the patient.

It is important that the analyst become aware of what is happening primarily because otherwise this symbiotic transference functions as a powerful resistance to further analysis. In addition, from the analyst's observing in detail the nature of the dialogue role which he is being unconsciously assigned, he can see whether the patient tends to perceive him as being, say, an enthusiastically interested parent or a parent ridden with futility and having essentially nothing to offer him—to give but two rudimentary examples.

In one instance after another, subtle shifts in the patient's tone (extremely muted versions, indeed, of the strikingly different part-identities involved in the chronically schizophrenic woman's dialogues mentioned above), as he vocalizes first one·side of the dialogue and now the other, help one to detect that this unconscious dialogue is occurring. I shall present a few among a great many available examples, examples which emerge in relative profusion in any average working week for me.

A woman reports a dream in some detail. I say nothing, as usual. After a few seconds of silence, she comments in the tone, now, of an interested observer, "Rather interesting dream," and goes on with her seeming monologue.

Another woman complains, "... the *boredom* of the analysis is what gets me down . . . I wonder [tone of discovery] if that's why I've been getting into all these social activities lately?" Then, after a momentary pause, she says in a rather different tone of voice—one, now, of an interested rejoinder, "Hm!—could *be*!" I distinctly feel that in saying those last three words, she has been functioning unconsciously as though she were me, an interested symbiotic-mother in the transference, responding with vocalized interest and acknowledgment of an interesting new idea on her part.

A man reports a detailed précis of a play he has attended the previous evening, and which he has found very interesting. After having completed this précis, he is silent for a few moments, during which I say nothing. He then gives an interested-sounding, emphatic grunt, and resumes his seeming monologue.

Another man speaks animatedly throughout the session, as usual, while I as usual say little or nothing. Near the end of the session, he pauses briefly, then says in a tone which now is relatively unanimated, futile, empty, "I don't really know what to say." I sense, here again, that in saying this he is speaking unconsciously as me in the transference—the personification of his own schizoid-depressed mother-identification qualities.

I can merely touch, here, upon the matter of interpreting these symbiotic-transference phenomena to the patient. In general, I do not attempt to interpret them at all early. In line with my concepts about therapeutic symbiosis, it seems to me essential that the analyst come to recognize that these phenomena are representative not merely of unconscious defenses on the patient's part, but also of a need on his part for an appreciable degree of symbiotic relatedness with the analyst, relatedness having both reality as well as transference aspects. A too-early attempt at interpretation tends to make the patient feel dismembered. For example, in one instance I suggested to a patient, "When you say ' —— ,' are you speaking for me?" She replied, "For *you*? [her tone clearly indicating that she found this suggestion preposterous] *No*; I have enough trouble speaking for *myself*." "Why should I speak for *you*," she added, not really asking a question, but making a bluntly decisive statement. But a few moments later she was showing interest in my suggestion.

"You mean that if you don't answer, I have to supply an answer?" I replied, ambiguously, "Mm." She did not go further with this matter directly, but within a few moments said, in reference to her brother, "Ed is *torn in two* [my italics] these days about whether to move to Massachusetts." In saying this, she evidently was projecting upon Ed her own unconscious feeling of having been dismembered (by my premature attempt to interpret the symbiotic transference).

SUMMARY AND CONCLUSION

This paper is written with the assumption that unconscious dual- or multiple-identity processes are among the fundamental features of borderline ego functioning, and with the additional, implicit assumption that such processes can be found to some detectable degree in the analysis of any patient with an illness of whatever diagnosis. Most of the patients whose clinical material is included here were functioning, to a superficial view, as normal-neurotic individuals; their dual- or multiple-identity functioning was at first subtle indeed.

Examples are presented of patients' phraseology which is revealing of multiple-identity functioning. Patients who characteristically begin a session by saying, "I don't know where to begin" are shown to be revealing, thereby, the presence of such identity functioning. Certain relevant significances in patients' use of the word "we" are described, with particular emphasis upon the symbiotic-transference connotations of such usage. Examples are included of the analyst's feelings and fantasies as containing clues to dual- or multiple-identity functioning on the part of the patient. The defensive (transference-resistance) versus ego-integrative aspects of these multiple-identity phenomena are discussed briefly. Finally, the borderline patient's monologue is shown to be, unconsciously, a dialogue with the internalized image of the analyst as being a symbiotic-identity partner in the transference.

Work with patients such as these, who have helped me to realize that the normal-neurotic individual may be unconsciously reacted to by the other person as comprising, and may unconsciously experience himself as comprising, two or a group or a tribe or a multitude of persons, has helped me to realize, in the same process, that individual psychoanalysis and sociology are, at base, essentially one field of study. This psychoanalytic work has given me also a deeper appreciation of the multifarious creativity of the human being's unconscious t 1an I possessed even a few years ago.

21

The Development of
Mature Hope in the
Patient-Therapist Relationship

Hope is generally assumed to be a "good" emotion, just as hate is
assumed to be a "bad" one. We as adults cling to our cherished illusion that our hope is innately as good—as pure, as virtuous—as is
that of the infant or little child who, at least so our concept would
have it, is hoping that his momentarily absent good mother will
imminently return. The realm of hope seems to us a last repository
of such innate goodness as human beings possess. One of the
harshest maturational tasks the individual must accomplish, to become truly adult, is to realize and accept that his hope is "impure"
in two vast ways: first, it is not unitary in nature but multifarious
and permeated with ambivalence, with conflict (such that no one
hope or set of hopes is completely fulfillable, for it is opposed by
powerfully contrasting hopes); and, second, many of these hopes
are devoted not to loving, but rather to destructive ends.

Thus, since hope tends to be a realm into which we are most
reluctant to allow, so to speak, our conscious ambivalence to enter,
it is one of our most tenaciously clung-to refuges for our repressed
fantasies of omnipotence. One of the major dimensions of genuine

First published in *The Human Dimension in Psychoanalytic Practice*, edited by Ken-
neth A. Frank (New York: Grune and Stratton, 1977), pp. 9-27.

adulthood is living in the full knowledge that many of one's private hopes are mutually irreconcilable, and are far less loving in nature than one's ideal self would have them be.

Realistic hope can come into existence, be maintained, and grow only insofar as one has become able to integrate one's multifarious, and in many areas conflictual, hopes into a more coherent and predominant hope nucleus. This aspect of ego integration involves our working through our disappointments, and above all our infantile omnipotence-based frustration-rage and grief, as regards those of our hopes we have had to relinquish. Put somewhat differently, this hope aspect of ego integration requires our working through our rage, grief, disappointment, and so on, at having to recognize, and accept, that human relatedness inescapably involves ambivalence.

This is a never finally completed maturational process but, rather, a route every therapist, for example, traverses in terms of the evolution of his own personal feelings in relation to each of the patients with whom he becomes deeply and sustainedly involved.

If the therapist's and patient's mutual therapeutic endeavor is to prove successful, the patient must come to discover in himself heretofore unconscious hopes which do violence to his long-conscious hope for relief from his symptoms, or for personal fulfillment in life; and the therapist himself must discover, over and over again, repressed hopes within himself which are violently at odds with his conscious hope of becoming a successfully and lastingly helpful therapist for the patient.

I have a vivid memory of an experience of mine as a patient in analysis, more than 20 years ago, when I become conscious of a previously repressed hope entirely at odds with what I had felt to be my single-mindedly hoped-for goal—namely, my parting from the analyst.

From very early on in the analysis, my feelings about being there had oscillated between two extremes. On the one hand, I was convinced that I was on the verge of such overwhelming insanity that, as I frequently admonished the analyst, "You'd better get a bed ready for me at Chestnut Lodge" (one measure of my true nuttiness being that I assumed that, for anyone so special as an analytic candidate, the Institute would arrange free treatment at that expensive place, where I had not yet gone to work). On the other hand, I was convinced that I was so manifestly and totally well that the analysis had now become absurdly superfluous.

At the time the incident in question occurred, my self-evaluations had pretty much stopped oscillating and I had settled into a consistent, unremittent bellyaching that the analyst was refusing to let me have done with this idiotically unnecessary analysis. He indicated the end of the session during which, for the nth time, I had been carping thus throughout. I got up from the couch, as usual.

The next thing I knew, I was walking toward him; he was standing by his chair, no doubt preparatory to my walking out the door as usual. As I walked the couple of steps to him, I did so suffused with romantic love of which I had been entirely unaware, but which had a quality of having been there all along. I embraced him and said, fondly, pleadingly, companionably, and above all romantically, "Ernest, *when* are we going to get this analysis over with?" I referred to the analysis clearly, here, as being in the nature of some inherently meaningless courtship ritual which was being imposed from without upon both of us, and which we had to get behind us in order, at long last, to consummate our fully mutual love for one another.

For all my gripingly impatient hope of getting the analysis over with, it was now immediately clear to me, in other words, that I unconsciously had not had the slightest intention of leaving him; my unconscious hope had been, on the contrary, for us fully to possess one another.

Incidentally, I give him high marks, indeed, for his reaction to all this. His neither returning my embrace nor saying a word left me free to make this discovery without his being, on any mature and realistic level, rejecting or scornful of me, or threatened by what I was doing. I assume that he had long been aware of my unconscious romantic attachment to him, for he showed not the slightest trace of surprise.

Before going on to the next aspect of this paper, I shall present a second bit of relevant patient-data from my own analysis.

When I went to Dr. Ernest Hadley for my initial interview with him, I went in the conscious hope of finding relief from a great deal of severe anxiety and despair and, far less importantly to me, of discharging successfully the training-analysis requirement for graduation from the analytic institute. He was standing outside the door of his analytic office when I walked toward it from the waiting room. I had the distinct sense—not a delusion, but a nonetheless vivid fantasy—that he, standing there, was Cerberus, the three-headed dog guarding the entrance to Hades.

I have remembered this impression many times during the more than quarter century since then, and have never thought much about it, beyond preening myself a bit at this evidence of some familiarity with mythology. Only during the last few years have I found it significant that I was not so afraid, after all, that Dr. Hadley would not let me *escape from* his office (= Hell), but rather that he would not *let me into* it. You see, my first training analyst had suddenly stood up, early in our third session, and permanently dismissed me. The despair I brought into the first session with Dr. Hadley was despair lest I prove hopelessly unable to communicate my innermost feelings to any human being. At the end of the first session, during which I had sat, following his direction, in a chair opposite him, I asked, "Do you see any reason why we can't work together?" He assured me, briefly but emphatically, "Hell, no!"

The point I am trying to make here is that it was only a few years ago that I realized that the Cerberus-Hell imagery indicated that, at the time, I unconsciously *hoped* the analysis would prove to be hell, a sought-for hell which I feared that its guardian, Cerberus, would prevent me from entering.

It would take me too far afield, here, to pursue in detail the determinants of my hope that the analysis would be hell. My often terrifyingly raging mother made life hell for me much of the time in her kitchen and environs, where I cowered like a frightened animal in a corner at the end of an alley under her cook-stove, a refuge where I could be near her but where she could not readily get at me. Although much of the time loving indeed, she was often, particularly when I was a very small child, hell to live with. Thus any longing to recapture my early-mothering experience was impossible to differentiate from a hope to be living again in hell. Further, during much of the time in the subsequent years of my upbringing, when I was more in the orbit of my father, I found him to be living largely in his private hell—a hell comprised of an endless succession of excruciatingly painful psychosomatic symptoms, depression, fear of insanity, and other torments. As regards my analysis, I do not doubt, in retrospect, that I hoped fully to join my father in hell, not only because I hated him and had much unconscious guilt to atone for, as regards his suffering, but also because I loved him and wanted to rescue him from his hell.

The next general point I want to make is that a healthy hopefulness needs to be distinguished clearly from an essentially manic repression of feelings of loss and despair. In one of the most tragic families I have ever encountered, in which one after another of the children grew up to meet suicidal, chronically psychotic, and similarly tragic ends, the mother had written a book entitled *Joy Is the Banner*; it seemed clear that she unconsciously had instilled her despair into her children, who came in course of time to provide her with the ground of tragedy above which her joyful banner could continue, by way of contrast, to fly undyingly high. The determinedly optimistic therapist coerces, similarly, his patients into experiencing the depression which he is too threatened to feel within himself.

A healthy capacity for hope is founded, quite in contrast to a manic denial of depression, in past experiences of the successful integrating of disappointments—past experiences, that is, of successful grieving. Hope emerges through the facing of feelings of disappointment, discouragement, and despair. This is analogous to the kind of archaeological uncovering of successive layers of affects which I described in my paper "Scorn, Disillusionment, and Adoration in the Psychotherapy of Schizophrenia" (1962b), in which I reported that one helps the schizophrenic patient to achieve a derepression of his feelings of adoration only by traversing first, in succession, the strata of his scorn and his feelings of disillusionment.

In other words, any realistic hope—as contrasted to unconscious-denial-based, unrealistic hopefulness—must be grounded in the ability to experience loss. One who has survived the griefs over losses, over disappointments in the past has known what it is for hope to triumph over—to survive—despair. Also, he knows that hoped-for changes which the future may bring, no matter how "favorable" or "healthy" (in psychotherapeutic terms) these changes may prove to be, inevitably will bring a concomitant sense of loss in various regards—since, as he knows from his past experiences, the fulfillment of one hope is accompanied by loss feelings stemming from the necessary discarding of the hopes which have been opposing it.

In this same regard, hope comes into being when one discovers that such feelings as disappointment and despair can be shared with a fellow human being—when one discovers, that is, that the sharing of such feelings can foster one's feeling of relatedness with one's fellow human beings, rather than stigmatizing one as something less than human, something alien and unqualified to be included among human beings.

At Chestnut Lodge, many of the schizophrenic patients with whom my colleagues and I worked would have been considered to be, by reason of the severity and chronicity of their illnesses, hopeless. One of the lessons my experience with these patients taught me is that *any* gratifications the therapist can come to experience[1] in his work with the patient—no matter how lustful or sadistic or murderously rageful or whatever these gratifications may be in nature, nor how largely they spring from countertransference sources in the therapist (as long as the therapist proves capable of gaining access to the relevant areas of his own repressed memories)—engender hope in both participants that the therapy will prove meaningful and will eventuate well and relatively successfully. It is

---

[1] Here I am referring primarily to the realm of feeling, rather than that of observable behavior.

essential, therefore, that the therapist become as open as possible, within himself, to the experiencing of whatever gratifications this work, which innately tends to be so deprivational, so engendering of feelings of futility and discouragement, can come to afford him, no matter how tabooed such gratifications are in relation to our time-honored concept of the analyst who experiences in response to the patient naught but affective neutrality and evenly hovering attentiveness.

Two of the ways in which hope (or hopefulness) and sadism are related deserve to be detailed here. First, one of the more formidable ways of being sadistic toward the other person is to engender hope, followed by disappointment, in him over and over. Second, the presenting of a hopeful demeanor under some circumstances can constitute, in itself, a form of sadism toward the other person, for it can be expressing, implicitly and subtly, cruel demands upon him to fulfill the hopes written upon one's face. One finds both these forms of sadism at work in many patients, whether schizophrenic or neurotic, and in many therapists also.

For many years now I have stressed, in my writings, that the chronically schizophrenic patient derives enormous gratification, sadistic in nature, from watching the recurrently hopeful therapist make eager and vigorous, but increasingly anguished, attempts to rescue the seemingly so-tormented patient from the latter's schizophrenia. By now I have learned that, whenever I am finding the course of work with any patient (whether psychotic or nonpsychotic) recurrently and painfully disappointing to me, I am alerted to the presence of more sadism in the treatment relationship than I had suspected previously.

I have come also, with some regret, to be conscious of the likelihood that if a person walks into the interview room with a too naïvely hopeful look on his or her face, and particularly if I know the person to be a borderline schizophrenic patient who is a veteran of a number of treatment efforts, I am perceiving not merely a youthfully and healthily hopeful person, but an accomplished and formidable sadist. I came to this rueful conclusion in the course of several hundreds of demonstration interviews at a number of hospitals, particularly at Sheppard Pratt, interviews held in a one-way-mirror viewing room and observed by the residents and other staff members. Stressful as many of the interviews with, for example, dilapidated, manifestly psychotic, hopeless-appearing patients have been, even more stressful in some regards have been those interviews with relatively youthful, healthy-appearing patients who have been diagnosed accurately as schizophrenic, but who come into the room appearing filled with hope that I shall somehow put, in that single interview, the specter of mental illness out of their lives. I know, when I see one of them walking into the room with such a demeanor, that by the end of the interview I shall have been led to feel that I am an inhuman monster for having so cruelly disappointed him or her.

Only about six months ago did I realize that I had been doing this often, unconsciously, to a chronically schizophrenic patient who has been in intensive psychotherapy with me, four hours per week,[2] for more than 21 years now. I had noticed that frequently, when she looked at my face upon my showing her into my office from the waiting room, she would give a helpless shrug. It finally occurred to me that this was her reaction to the radiantly hopeful expression she saw on my face.

In the instance of another, much less ill, but highly sadistic woman, with whom I have worked for several years, it recently occurred to me that the vigorously hopeful manner I presented on inviting her into my office from the waiting room on one occasion, a manner so inappropriate to the glacial slowness with which the analysis advances, was in essence a hopefulness that I would succeed, this time, in giving her the sort of anguishedly difficult time—particularly as regards a torture of disappointment—which she had given me, innumerable times, over the past years of our work together.

A 37-year-old divorced woman, upon her transfer to Chestnut Lodge after a year in another hospital, although clearly suffering from paranoid schizophrenia seemed, nonetheless, far less ill than

---

[2] This is the usual frequency for Chestnut Lodge patients.

most of the patients with whom I worked there. Only gradually did the true depth of her illness become evident and likewise the integral role, in her psychodynamics, of tantalization and disappointment.

Her verbally expressed emotions were largely limited, for at least two years, to expressions of her feeling threatened in a paranoid fashion, and, in particular, to her intense, bitter, and often acid disapproval and condemnation, always self-righteous, of practically everyone and everything about her. Only after some two years did I begin to see, during our sessions, that the paranoid hate and fear she typically expressed were subtly becoming differentiated into a wider gamut of underlying feelings, feelings against which her paranoid ways of relating could be seen to constitute an unconscious defense system. In particular, such emotions as *disappointment*, hurt, and grief began to be discernible in her. That is, I found I was no longer met by a demeanor of unbroken, threatened (and at times threatening) paranoid hate, but could detect that she tended to feel disappointed or hurt by something I had just said or failed to say. But rather than her experiencing, as yet, the fullness of these human emotions, she evidently experienced instead, on such occasions, a heightened perception of me as being hateful and threatening.

Incidentally, I have found reliably in a number of much less ill patients—patients with, variously, borderline ego functioning or a schizoid or narcissistic ego structure—that only after several years of analysis, during which an essentially paranoid blamingness and reproachfulness and hostile passive-competitiveness holds sway in their relationship to the analyst, do they finally start experiencing the fullness of their long-repressed disappointment—disappointment with the analyst, with the significant persons in their childhood, and with themselves.

In the early stages, then, of the derepression of the feelings of disappointment, one can at times clearly see these feelings to be in conflict with the more usual paranoid way of responding. For example, one woman, whose expressions of emotions had been largely limited, for years of analytic work, to a monochromatic, paranoid-tinged ragefulness, resentment, and dissatisfaction, came to say of her young son, "Billy—goddamn dirty trick that he was born a boy . . ." There was *some* note of disappointment in her tone as she said this; but there was, still, a much more predominantly paranoid note in it—an implying that Billy had played, omnipotently, a viciously dirty trick on his mother by causing himself to be born a boy rather than a girl.

A man whose ego functioning was essentially similar in this regard had recounted many things in a session when, characteristically for him, he suddenly became intensely exasperated and said, "Oh, I'm all mixed up!" In the past, on such occasions, his exasperation would be so overwhelming that he would beat his head with his fists; but his self-destructiveness had decreased somewhat by now. I suggested, ironically, "I've spoiled everything by not responding at the right times?" He replied, "No. . . . You spoil everything by *being* here! . . . *People* ruin *everything*; they really *do*! They have *nothing* to recommend them— . . ." When he said, "*People* ruin *everything*; they really *do*!" his tone was one of intense disappointment—a significant sign of analytic progress—but at the same time I could discern a paranoid element, expressive of his semiconviction that all the rest of humanity was in a plot against him—a plot to ruin everything he cared about.

The previously mentioned divorced woman became relatively soon—for Chestnut Lodge patients—sufficiently well to seem tantalizingly on the verge of being able to move to outpatient living, and I was highly aware of needing, for statistical as well as for many more personal reasons, one of my current bevy of Chestnut Lodge veterans to become an outpatient. Finally, after three years she was moved out into a long-ready apartment nearby in Rockville, but almost immediately became frankly psychotic again, and was back in the sanitarium within less than 24 hours. She quickly regained her previously achieved level of ego functioning, and resumed her snail-like progress. In one building, for example, at Chestnut Lodge where relatively well patients were housed, she refused for three full years ever to set foot in the living room of the building, sure (for reasons well-founded, indeed, in her childhood family life) that, were she to do so, she would instantly be held responsible for all that was transpiring and would transpire thereafter in that room.

Not until more than 12 years after her initial Chestnut Lodge admission did she again move out; this time successfully.

Those 12-plus years had involved a succession of some eight or ten administrative psychiatrists, each of whom found reason to hope, as I did, that the carefully made plans for her moving out would imminently be crowned with successful fulfillment. Each administrator in turn was disappointed. For most of those years I, slowly becoming acquainted with the existence and subtle workings of her sadism, subsisted on the aphorism, which occurred to me in innumerable sessions, "Most men live lives of quiet desperation." I looked up this quotation in preparing these comments, and found that it was Thoreau who, in *Walden* (1854), first opined this, and that I unknowingly had been misremembering, for years, his precise statement, "The mass of men lead lives of quiet desperation." But then, as I really still can't accept, nothing is perfect.

I regard it as significant that, some time prior to her becoming established in outpatient living, I had become able sufficiently to integrate my essentially infantile omnipotence-based disappointment, as regards the lack of fulfillment of my multifarious goals in my efforts with her, so that I was no longer threatened by the possibility that she might never be able to live outside the Lodge. By now I have experienced analogous turning points (or, better, phases) in my work with one patient after another. It seems in each instance that the patient's successful individuation cannot occur until it has become clear that the patient's life is, in a sense, in his own hands: the contemplated next major move (whatever it is in any particular case —whether graduation from the analytic institute, or marriage, or termination of the analysis, or whatever) is experienced by the patient not primarily as some feather in the cap of the analyst's narcissism, coerced out of the patient in conformity to some omnipotence-based ego ideal on the analyst's part, but primarily, rather, as a step in fulfillment of the patient's individual self.

A 40-year-old man, whom I shall call Bill, had been hospitalized constantly for eleven years, including five years at Chestnut Lodge, when I became his individual therapist. He had long ago established a durable social role there as a chronically hebephrenic patient who seemed to remember nothing of his prepsychotic past, a past which I knew from other sources to have been marked by promiscuous homosexuality, transvestitism, physical violence, alcoholism, and reckless driving. Over the years at the Lodge he had lived a highly stereotyped life largely as an apathetic vegetable, lying on a couch at the end of the ward corridor and leaving it only briefly to walk rapidly, with an effeminate gait, to the nurse's station, swearing explosively on the way at, apparently, random hallucinatory figures, and then getting a cigarette and returning to his couch. He was generally looked upon as being one of the least promising among the Lodge's nucleus of severely and chronically schizophrenic patients.

During approximately the first two years of our work, while he spent the sessions lying or sitting on his bed, silent except for his frequently farting loudly and occasionally launching into frighteningly unexpected, brief, but vitriolically furious tirades at me, neither of us seemed to find any great reason for hope. But over the total of nine and a half years of our individual psychotherapy together, prior to my leaving the Chestnut Lodge staff, he manifested really memorable progress. This progress occurred in proportion as I became able to recognize, within myself, a succession of intense feelings regarding him, feelings each of which was at first formidably opposed to my superego standards and my sense of personal identity. These feelings included intense envy of his inherited millions of dollars and of the various forms of contentment his hebephrenic mode of living afforded him, as I perceived that mode of life; murderous rage toward him, rage born of his behaving in a psychotically violent way toward me on innumerable occasions (an atmosphere of intense murderousness permeated the room for a number of years); unmistakable indications (from my dreams and various daily-life data) of feelings of violent sexual lust in myself toward him; and, in the later years of the work, increasingly freely conscious romantic feelings toward him, as well as dependent feelings toward him as a good mother, and friendly, brotherly feelings.

Early in our work his vitriolic tirades at me had typically been of this order: "Shut up, you black bastard!" or "Shut up, you slimy son of a bitch, or I'll knock your teeth out!" His contempt, as well as his fury, was barely controllable. After some years, during which I had become relatively well aware of my own contempt and rage toward him, I took to resorting, with excellent therapeutic results, to goading him, contemptuously, about his defiant pseudo stupidity. When he would utter some verbal stereotype in a spirit of being defiantly idiotic—when, in short, he would play dumb—I would inquire with ironic politeness, "Do you find that it [your head] echoes when you talk?" On other such occasions I would remind him, ironically, "The trouble with *acting like* an imbecile so much is that you're apt to really *become* an imbecile." On one occasion when his long silence was broken by a loud fart I said to him in furious contempt, "Why don't you just *shit* here on the floor? Why don't you just make yourself comfortable? I don't understand why you go to the toilet if you're trying to be an animal." After years of his threatening furiously to knock my teeth out, I replied with equivalent rage, "You'd better *not* hit me, or I'll knock you right through that wall there!"

As his psychotic ragefulness found thus an interpersonal context for its expression, so over the same years did his hebephrenic manifestations of homosexual lust evolve into something finer. Early in our work he asked invitingly, while lying in his bed, "Do ya wanta see my banana?" I politely declined this offer in my most conventionally obsessive-compulsive manner. A bit later in the work, he sat on his bed open-mouthed, leering at me, with a wad of sputum on his tongue. On another early occasion, he sat on his bed looking like a fat, veteran prostitute, and I heard him murmur voluptuously to himself, "Mm—it's a beauty; shove it up!" He frequently appeared close to panic, on the other hand, lest I had come there to homosexually assault and/or kill him. He misidentified me more than once as being "Pretty Boy" Floyd, a notorious gangland killer of the 1930s, and on one occasion he said to himself in quick reassurance as I walked into his room, "That's all right, Dearie; that ain't one of them Fuller Brush ones."

It required some years before I realized, sitting in one of the silences which still predominated during our sessions, that it had now become conceivable for me to be tangibly related to him without my having to either fuck him or kill him. It was some time thereafter that we went through a phase of predominantly romantic feelings toward one another and mutually experienced fantasies of becoming happily married to one another. I believe that he was fairly consistently the bride in these hopeful fantasies. In my actual marriage during that era, I most uncharacteristically forgot, until the following day, my wife's and my fourteenth wedding anniversary, and my first thought as to why I had forgotten it was a feeling that my wife stood between me and Bill, a feeling of sufficient power that, although I had been aware for some time of romantic feelings about Bill, the realization hit me very forcibly.

In a staff conference five years after my having become Bill's individual therapist, his then-current administrative psychiatrist reported:

> I do feel he's changing. . . . Certainly his relationship to me is quite different. In the first year I was administrator [of his ward] he never spoke to me, and regarded me as more not there than anything else. He was the only patient who never attended the group meetings. Now he's one of the most faithful patients; he never misses a group meeting. He enjoys it a great deal, and participates, verbally, as well as listens. A lot of humor comes out, which is quite new . . .

Two years later still, his younger sister and her husband came to visit him for the first time in several years; he had received no visits from relatives in that interim. His sister and brother-in-law were nothing less than astonished at how much more healthy they found him to be, this time, and they began to give serious consideration to the possibility of his coming to visit them at their distant home. Meanwhile during these later years, Bill—who used to be unable to endure any sustained physical proximity to me—had come to spend at least 80 percent of the time during the psychotherapy sessions sitting in his room with me, within arm's length, and with the door to the corridor closed. His demeanor clearly was one of attaching great importance to our sessions, and of being very attentive to what was occurring between us. He was able to provide sufficient meaningful data to enable me to make transference interpretations.

During the early years of our work I—as well as various members of the ward staff—heard him say, many times, "I came here to die," and this hopeless statement seemed then all too well founded. But after a few years, during one of our sessions, he now said, "I came here to reminisce," and in the later years of our work his hopefulness had grown still further, such that he now said, "I came to join," which clearly had a connotation of joining in mature human interrelatedness.

Miss Susan Johnson was only 21 years of age—relatively young, that is, among the Chestnut Lodge patient population at that time—upon her transfer to the Lodge from a hospital in her home city to which she had been admitted six months previously. But her illness, which had developed insidiously prior to its first manifestations about two years before, proved to be more severe than that of any other Chestnut Lodge patient with whom I worked. She had, on admission, the appearance of a hopelessly chronic, backward hebephrenic patient, was said by her Lodge administrative psychiatrist—a man with decades of mental hospital experience—to be the sickest patient he had ever seen, and was reported by the nurse or attendant assigned initially to "special" her to look "at times like a demon." I found her appearance and behavior initially to be grotesque, indeed, and only after a number of years did her sense of identity as a human being come to prevail at all durably over a galaxy of "nonhuman" identity components—whether as some kind of demon, or a circus freak, or a horse, or a dog, or whatever. When after 11 years of my work with her I left Chestnut Lodge, she was still—despite a number of dramatic but transitory periods of improvement—deeply schizophrenic.

At the time of her admission to the Lodge, it was learned that each of her parents had confided to her, during the previous few years, the hope that she would never marry, for the expressed reason that the three of them—the girl and her parents—had such good times together. She had been in many ways popular, socially; but both her parents had disapproved of each one of her several successive boyfriends. I found it shockingly incongruous when the father of this grievously ill young woman, housed in a seclusion room some floors above my office, told me thoughtfully, "My daughter has had two love affairs that didn't materialize, I think fortunately for her," and went on to speak critically of the two young men in question.

There was abundant case-history data to indicate that she and her parents were involved in a deeply pathological, symbiotic relatedness. But I, and the other personnel members who worked with her, had little reason to feel superior to her mother and father in this regard, for she was to become involved, over the years of her hospital stay, in equally formidable, pathologically symbiotic modes of relatedness with us as well. Of specific relevance for this paper, I learned over and over, in my work with her, that at the heart of my own recurrent feelings of hopelessness about her was a symbiotic infantile dependency on my part, toward her, which I found appalling in its depth and power.

It was relatively easy, of course, for me to see the other personnel members' symbiotic dependency upon her—to see, that is, their unconscious stake in her remaining ill. One of the veteran female aides, for example, who worked much with her, over the course of the early years, said to me with enthusiastic warmth and fondness, one day when I came upon the locked ward for my session with Susan, "All of us up here love Susan so much. . . ," detailing something about the endearing things she did there with them. She then added, with an intonation of intended sadness about the tragedy of Susan's long illness, "You don't think she'll ever get well, do you?" But the way this question actually was said was in the form of a request for reassurance from me—reassurance that Susan would never become well and reassurance, therefore, that this aide (and the others among the ward personnel) need not fear losing her.

I well remember one session, which occurred after several years of my work with her, at a time when the ward administrator was planning to move the majority, and it was hoped all, of the patients to a nearby small building which had been readied for them, and where, it was hoped, they would come to live in a generally less regressed, more autonomous fashion. It had not been decided whether Susan was sufficiently well to make this move. I realized, sitting there in her room, that I was *unable to want* her to be able to make this move. This realization was accompanied by intense feelings of personal humiliation and helplessness, for it ran entirely counter to my better judgment—namely, that the move would be conducive to her recovery. I still believe, in retrospect, that this reaction of mine was less a function of my hatred toward her—I was quite accustomed to hating her with at times shocking intensity—than of the enormous loss feelings, at a repressed level, which the prospect of the move aroused in me. Incidentally, she did make the move, along with all her fellow patients.

There emerged much evidence that Susan had functioned as a kind of unofficial and unacknowledged family therapist in her family, just as she did on the ward. I remember my amazement at the demeanor of her mother upon the latter's return from a visit which she and Susan's brother had just had with her grotesquely and tragically ill daughter. The mother was laughing gaily and exclaimed delightedly, "She just kept us in stitches!" Nearly three years later, at a time when Susan was very markedly improved, her mother was looking, in my office, very like a little girl who has lost her mother. This was at a time when another therapist on the staff conveyed to me his astonishment upon noting, during his own visits to the locked ward for interviews with a patient of his there, that Susan appeared no longer grotesquely ill but, instead, "like a girl from a fine Eastern school," as she indeed was.

The father's symbiotic stake in her illness became revealed in the evolution of the transference, as well as elsewhere. In one of our sessions, for example, Susan clearly perceived me as being dead, and said of her father later in the session, "He's alive when he gives to me." I had become, indeed, deeply dependent upon her allowing me to give something to her—if not an interpretation, then at least some orange juice; it is hardly an overstatement to say that it felt to me that my life depended upon her being willing to accept *some*thing from me.

It was commonplace at the Lodge to find that marked improvement, in this or that patient, was reacted to by manifestations of repressed loss reactions on the parts of those most concerned with the patient; but this was true with extraordinary intensity in Susan's instance. For example, at the end of the fifth year of Susan's stay at the Lodge, both the head nurse of the ward and a nighttime attendant, on the same day, expressed to me their feelings of being *stunned* by her improvement.

In sessions when she was appearing markedly more healthy, I myself reacted, more often than not, with feelings of overwhelming awe and envy of her healthy-young-giantess quality, her Junoesque quality, her quality of radiating an innate social superiority over me. On such occasions I would feel personally, in contrast to her, overwhelmingly puny and socially inferior, and would have no sense whatever that I had made any contribution, however small, to the improvement in her.

On an occasion in the middle of the fifth year I realized that my then-prevailing feelings of hopelessness about her prognosis were springing, at least in part, from previously repressed feelings of hopelessness about my ever being able to satisfy my sexual desires toward her—she being, in this regard, I realized at the same time, the personification of my early mother. Presumably until then I had been hopeless about ever becoming able to *acknowledge* to myself such a desire.

Sometimes she clearly manifested all the loss feelings, herself, in our symbiotic relationship, in reaction to clinical improvement in her which I consciously welcomed. When, for example, early in the fifth year, she had improved sufficiently to be able to spend the entire session in my office for the first time in all our work, I felt jubilant about this development, while she clearly was bereft. On another occasion she let me know that the loss of her accustomed room, when she came over to my office for the session, was equivalent to the loss of her *self*. I strongly surmise that it was this very kind of primitive loss reaction, on my own part, which rendered me unable to want her to be able to make the above-mentioned move to the other building: her accustomed room on the locked ward, where our sessions had long been held, presumably had become, at an unconscious level in me, equivalent to my self.

I am implying with these clinical vignettes the principle that the better aware the therapist can become of his heretofore repressed emotional investment in the perpetuation of the patient's illness, the more a realistic hope for the patient's recovery will grow. I am trying to show that this unconscious investment can exist in many forms, whether in the form of symbiotic dependency, or sexual lust, or vindictiveness and envy, or whatever. It is obviously well for the other staff members also to become as aware as possible of their respective, heretofore unconscious investments in the perpetuation of the patient's illness. The patient's own most crucial unconscious stake in his remaining ill cannot become conscious, and eventually resolved, if the therapist, at least, cannot face his own hopes for the illness to continue.

My infantile omnipotence-based feelings of personal guilt, concerning Susan's illness, impelled me unwittingly to make enormously heavy, coercive demands upon her toward improved functioning, and to remain largely oblivious of the progress which, in her individual way, she was actually making. I expressed the latter aspect of this realization in a staff conference near the end of the third year. As I told my colleagues, I had realized recently:

> I have been underestimating how much she has put into her therapy—how much progress, relatively, she has gained. I have been so awed by the depth of this illness. For instance, two or three months ago, I came up to see her at five o'clock and she was lying on the floor [in one of the ward's few seclusion rooms] in her slip and menstrual blood was all over her—she was reeking with menstrual blood—and things like this are such that I haven't realized how badly she needs acknowledgment for what [i.e., what forward moves] she *has* been doing.

The above-quoted realization had come only a week before when, in a session which involved little meaningful verbal contact, she had asked me laconically, in a shy, eagerly hopeful way, "Strides?" I heard this as her first clear request for recognition, from me, that she was making strides in overcoming her illness. I could see, upon hearing this, that she was indeed making strides, in various subtle and seemingly small ways; but I had been feeling too burdened, in an agonizedly guilt-ridden way, at the immensity of the task yet before us to have paid any heed to these "little" steps of hers.

During one of the infrequent walks we took together—not really much together, actually—on the hospital grounds during the early years of her treatment,[3] she suddenly dragged me by the hand while she went racing through a kind of dense thicket of low, over-hanging tree branches which whipped against me. It was a frighten-ing and confusing experience for me; but she managed, thus, to communicate to me the idea that this was characteristically the way I made her feel in our sessions, in which I tried—without realizing it—to drag her pell-mell and headlong toward health.

On one occasion in those early years, she was able to make a verbal communication of the same order; I was shocked at hearing her say, "Bob [her father's nickname], he dragged me behind a car." This statement, like so many of her cryptic comments, seemed to have a myriad of meanings, many of them unfathomable; but the one shockingly clear meaning it conveyed was that he had (figuratively speaking) dragged her, on a rope, from a car which he was driving. I had long known that all her many accom-plishments—athletic, social, and so on—prior to her psychosis had fallen far short of his perfectionistic goals for her. What shocked me in her statement was, more precisely, the realization that my own demands upon her, in her psychotherapy, were felt by her to be fully as callous, impossible, and dangerously uncontrollable.

In this era, my enormous superego-based demands upon her in-terfered with, if not precluded, the development of realistic hope-fulness in her. But, to say a word here on my own behalf, I could not realistically hope to satisfy the so-ambivalent demands she was making upon me, for whereas on the one hand she made me feel that I was placing cruelly impossible demands upon her, on the other hand, in ways too numerous and varied to elaborate here, she conveyed to me urgently anguished pleas *for* me actively to inter-vene in her so-tragic plight.

---

[3] She had been quite unable even to attempt such walks during the first several months.

I must have become appreciably less superego-tormented for the following development to have taken place in her, during the seventh year of our work. She had moved to the previously mentioned small building something like a year before, and the session was being held, as usual, in her room there. She was lying on her bed, as was often the case. The notes I dictated (as was customary) immediately after the session reported:

In this hour occurred a beautiful example of the development of autonomy [partly through, I would now add, the formation of a healthy identification].

We were on relatively close and friendly terms in this hour, as has been the case now for some weeks. . . .

In the course of this hour she got to talking about Emily, the [black] maid, and mentioned Emily's last name, which I had not known—"Miller." She said, "Her job is not hard," indicating that she, Susan, has lain there watching Emily do her job. There was no criticism implied in Susan's remarks. She feels fond of Emily, as I have known for several weeks or months, and I, also, admire Emily. Emily, it has seemed to me, has stood in refreshing contrast to my conceited self, from Susan's point of view. Emily is a mature, unassuming, friendly person whom it is easy to respect as a human being.

A bit later on in the hour (there being verbalizations from both of us pretty much throughout the hour), she said something about "dust on the table," indicating the table in her room—or dresser, or something like that—to which I replied, "Yes, that's Emily's job: dusting," again without any criticism of Emily in my tone, simply an acknowledgment that that is Emily's province.

A few minutes later, after other verbalizations about apparently other subjects from both of us, she said, "It's *my* job, *my* place, to grow up, as the years go on," in a tone of quiet, prideful assertion of autonomy, a tone of pleasureful self-possession. There was no defiance implied in this, nor any kind of stiff-arming me away as though to say in any defiant tone, "You stay out of my business." One of the components of this remark was a realization that this is not going to be accomplished in a day or a month, but that it is within her capacity and that it will happen. This struck me as a beautiful example of her identifying usefully with the maid, who has a job which is within the latter's own capacity.

Needless to say, I was tremendously pleased to hear this, and felt at the end of the hour, not many minutes later, like giving her a very warm hug and kiss on the cheek.

This represented a tremendous advance beyond a session in which, while lying hopelessly on the same bed in the same room, she had asked me in despair as I walked in and sat down in my usual chair, "Did you come to look at your hole?" This remark had much less of an adult sexual meaning than a meaning referable to the pathologically symbiotic components of our relationship, in terms of which one of her meanings to me was as the personification of my own hopelessness about myself, my feelings of being empty of any personal worth. It seems to me that I must have become, at the time of the above-cited session, at least to some limited degree assured that the function of being psychotherapist to her was within my capacity, or she could scarcely have felt, and said, what she did.

Speaking more generally for a moment, it seems to me that the realm of realistic hope, in the doing of psychoanalysis and intensive psychotherapy, becomes more tangible insofar as the therapist can discover meaning, or previously undiscerned meanings, in what is transpiring during the session. In the instance of so tragically ill a patient as Susan, the therapist tends to feel too guiltily and anguishedly enmeshed in the patient's illness to be able to achieve enough separateness—objectivity, distance—to be able to see the meanings in the processes which hold both the patient and himself in their grip. In another session in Susan's room, she was standing near her bed, by which I was sitting as usual. She reached down and touched her patterned bedspread and said to me quietly, "Patterns?" Ostensibly she was asking whether I saw the patterns in her bedspread; but I realized that she was asking also whether I was aware of the patterns, in our ways of relating to one another, which were evident to her. She was not yet well enough to verbalize in more detail about this; but the fact that she had become able to communicate on such a level of differentiation surprised and impressed me.

This young woman's illness proved tenacious and severe despite brief improvements which enabled her, for example, successfully to visit her distant parental home and function capably as hostess at a large cocktail party attended by some 50 of her former friends and acquaintances—a visit from which she had returned to the locked ward looking like the sole survivor of a mining disaster. I finally sought, some several years along, weekly supervision—something I had not done at the Lodge, or elsewhere, in several years. I began meeting with one of the few persons higher in the sanitarium staff hierarchy. One of Susan's more troublesome symptoms at the time was her pulling out her scalp hairs, one by one, in patches, and eating them. This had gone on for years, and contributed greatly to her circus-freak appearance, as well as to my own feelings of helplessness, embarrassment, guilt, and hatred of her.

The supervision had been going on for a few months when I reported a new development in my work with Susan. Susan, while sitting on her bed, had quietly leaned forward, so that I could readily look directly at her present bald spot; I had no doubt that she was carefully showing it to me. I noticed that it was an amazingly perfect square. Parenthetically, at this writing I have little doubt that she was nonverbally conveying to me—among whatever other meanings—her conviction that I am a square; another chronically schizophrenic woman, this one from New York City, used to speak in passing of Herald Square with, I thought, more than merely passing significance.

At any rate, what was new in my work with Susan was that I had become sufficiently free from being enmeshed in guilt so that I could view this symptom from a vantage point, now, of a kind of aesthetic interest, although I did not spell all this out to the supervisor.

When I reported to him my amazement at seeing how perfect a square she had created, currently, on her scalp, his response was to push himself back from his large desk where he sat, across from me, look at me condemningly, and ask, heavily, "Just what do you regard as your responsibility to this woman?" With that, I stopped getting supervision from him for, after my having suffered for years from a kind of malignant overconscientiousness in the work, this response was precisely what I did *not* need. To his credit, he did not take steps to discharge me from the case; but I have never found reason to seek any formal supervision, from anyone, since then.

SUMMARY AND CONCLUSION

Maturation involves one's coming to realize and accept that one's hopes are multifarious, devoted variously to destructive as well as constructive ends, permeated with ambivalence, and in many regards mutually irreconcilable, and inherently, therefore, far from wholly fulfillable at best. Thus the accomplishment of this maturational task requires one's recognition and large-scale relinquishment of one's erstwhile unconscious fantasies of omnipotence.

The integration in awareness of previously unintegrated, and largely unconscious, feelings of hopefulness proceeds in pace with the working through of progressively intense feelings of disappointment, discouragement, despair, grief, and infantile omnipotence-based frustration-rage. This is a maturational process which is never finally completed, but which comprises, rather, the route traversed by every therapist, for example, in terms of the evolution of his own personal feelings in relation to each of the patients with whom he becomes deeply and sustainedly involved.

In the therapist's work with those patients who are initially largely without hope, and who give him much reason, indeed, to write them off as "hopeless cases," it is essential that he become as open as possible, within himself, to the experiencing of whatever gratifications this work, which innately tends to be so deprivational, so engendering of feelings of futility and discouragement, can come to afford him. This is true no matter how much such gratifications may conflict with our time-honored notion of the analyst as maintaining a consistent affective neutrality and evenly hovering attentiveness in response to the patient. The therapist's becoming aware of these gratifications comes to engender hope in both participants that the therapy will prove meaningful and will eventuate well and relatively successfully.

22

Transitional Phenomena and Therapeutic Symbiosis

INTRODUCTION

In 1958 I postulated that symbiotic relatedness constitutes a necessary phase in psychoanalysis or psychotherapy with either neurotic or psychotic patients, and introduced the term "therapeutic symbiosis" for this mode of patient-analyst relatedness (Searles, 1959b). In my monograph concerning the nonhuman environment (1960) I emphasized that in normal ego development, the infant is subjectively undifferentiated from his nonhuman environment as well as from his human environment, and suggested that throughout subsequent life we all struggle against deep urges to yield up our identities as individual human beings and to regress to subjective oneness with our nonhuman environment, as a means of escaping from various conflicts inherent in our living as human individuals. In 1966-1967 I suggested, "It may well be that the predominance of personality functioning, even in healthy adult persons, is subjectively undifferentiated, at an unconscious level at least, from the great inanimate realm of the environment," and stated, "The very fact of one's preoccupation with the uniqueness of one's own identity is likely to be serving as a defense against one's unconscious fear of recognizing that human existence is lived largely at a symbiotic level of relatedness."

First published in *International Journal of Psychoanalytic Psychotherapy*, 5:145-204 (1976).

In my monograph (1960) and in various subsequent writings, I have described instances of the patient's transference to the analyst as being something other than human—as being, for example, the pet dog from the patient's childhood, or a tree, or an inanimate object, or whatever. In 1961 I wrote concerning schizophrenic patients:

> . . . each of these patients—and, I think, this is true to a lesser degree of the neurotic patient also—needs in the course of the therapy to project upon the therapist the subjectively unfeeling, non-human and even inanimate, aspects of himself, and thus to see his therapist, in the transference, as the representative of the parents who were, to the child's view, incapable of human feeling, as has been the patient himself in his own [repressed] view [of himself]. . . . Only by thus re-externalizing his pathogenic introjects can the patient make contact with his own feeling-capacities and come to know, beyond any further doubt, that he is a human being. This aspect of the transference, this aspect of the healthy reworking of very early ego-differentiation, cannot be accomplished unless the therapist is able to be self-accepting while spending hour after hour without finding in himself any particular feeling whatever towards the patient. He must be sufficiently sure of his own humanness to endure for long periods the role, in the patient's transference experience, of an inanimate object, or of some other percept which has not yet become differentiated as a sentient human being [1961e, pp. 558-559].

In 1973, paraphrasing comments from some of my earlier papers, I said of the patient—either psychotic or nonpsychotic—that "the individuation which he undergoes more successfully this time, in the context of the transference relationship, is in a real sense mutual, in that the analyst too, having participated with the patient in the therapeutic symbiosis, emerges with a renewed individuality which has been enriched and deepened by this experience" (1973a). In one or more of my earlier papers, I had described the phase of therapeutic symbiosis as involving not only the patient's, but also the analyst's, enhanced ego integration of previously repressed, subjectively nonhuman identity components, such that a deepened sense of humanness evolves in analyst as well as in patient.

In my monograph (1960), in discussing the role of the nonhuman environment in the development of object relations, I devoted a number of pages to excerpts from, and comments about, the work of Winnicott (1953) and Stevenson (1954) concerning the role of transitional objects in the life of the infant and young child. These comments included the following:

> I believe . . . that this work by Winnicott and Stevenson provides a valuable frame of reference for the further investigation of various manifestations of schizophrenia. In my own experience I have seen, for instance, that some schizophrenic patients show "objectless" behavior [referring here to Stevenson's having found children in a residential nursery setting whom she called "objectless"—that is, devoid of any transitional-object attachments]; some are strikingly destructive of all inanimate objects which come within their reach; and others cherish certain inanimate objects for long periods of time. Each of two of my [chronically schizophrenic adult] patients who manifested at first a particularly conspicuous noncherishing of inanimate possessions came to show an intense cherishing of such objects as therapy progressed. . . .
>
> It is evident that the above-described "transitional objects" are transitional in two respects. First, although the teddie bear (for example) is not objectively a part of the infant's body, it is not experienced by him as coming, either, from the outside world—as are the later toys. In the same way, it still stands in a close affective relationship to mother. Thus this security-engendering object helps the infant through the transition period leading up to the recognition that there *is* an outside world. Secondly, and by the same token, the teddie bear represents a transition step in the child's becoming aware of his own aliveness, for here we see that an inanimate object is experienced as being a part of the infant's body, to a degree at least approximating that of his own thumb, before the next phase is reached when inanimate objects (toys, blankets, and so on) are experienced as coming from, or "belonging to" the outside world rather than being a part of his own alive self [1960, pp. 69-70].

Since Winnicott's pioneering work on transitional objects and transitional phenomena appeared in 1953, the wealth of related findings has attested, and continues to attest, to the seminal nature of his discoveries in this regard. For me, however, the psychoanalyst or psychotherapist can best understand transitional-object phenomena as being tributary to, or consisting in various different facets of, the—for him in his work with patients—more comprehensive realm of therapeutic symbiosis. As he comes to discover how pervasive, at largely unconscious levels of ego functioning, is symbiotic relatedness not only with one's fellow human beings but also with the totality of the "outside" world, including the vastly preponderant nonhuman realm of that world, he becomes progressively less amazed to discover, as many of the writers since Winnicott have discovered, that this or that particular additional increment of the objectively nonhuman environment is also being experienced by the patient as a "transitional object"—as existing, that is, in the transitional realm between no longer fully inner, and not yet fully outer, reality.

Thus I find much of the literature on transitional objects to be too particularistic, too phenomenological, and I cannot help believing that not a few of these writers are still unconsciously staving off, while gingerly approaching, the degree of recognition of the pervasiveness of symbiotic phenomena, involving nonhuman as well as objectively human realms of existence, which my long-term work with chronically schizophrenic adults compelled me, against tenacious unconscious resistance on my part, to see.

In this paper I shall dwell particularly upon data concerning objects or phenomena that are transitional—if one must use that word; the word "symbiotic" is more appropriate to the patient-therapist context—for both patient and therapist concomitantly. By seeing the development of the phase of therapeutic symbiosis as one in which the patient's symptoms have become—if you will—transitional objects for both the patient and the therapist simultaneously, I hope to contribute to our increasing understanding of the nature of the therapeutic process in psychoanalysis.

As I write this paper I am conscious once again of my debt, acknowledged more than once before, to Harry Stack Sullivan (1940), whose lectures and writings helped to drive home to me the

indispensability of our keeping in view, in our attempting to understand seemingly exclusively intrapersonal phenomena, the interpersonal frame of reference. That frame of reference does not provide, all by itself, an adequate conceptual framework; but to the extent that the analyst is ever-mindful of it, he rarely indeed would
equate himself, even in working with the most ill patients, with a
visitor strolling through a zoo. My own writings have stressed repeatedly the increments of reality in even the most delusionally distorted of my patients' transference perceptions of me. A paper in
1972 (presented over some eight years previously as a lecture in
several different educational settings) described nearly seven years
of intensive psychotherapy with a chronically schizophrenic woman.
It gives some hint of the extent to which I believe the analyst's own
unconscious processes are involved in such matters as transitional-
object phenomena, or subjectively nonhuman experiences, in the
context of psychotherapy:

> Two weeks later I had occasion to see, still more clearly, that
> in back of the patient's rages stood *terror*. During this particular
> hour she came to tell me, "There is a vapor over people some-
> times." She added that there is sometimes one over me as well
> as over other people. It is difficult to describe her tone when
> speaking of this "vapor," but it was one that clearly conveyed
> terror and weirdness. . . .

> As the work with her went on, she became more and more
> able to tell me at what point she was experiencing me as having
> a vapor over my head, and there were times when she let me
> know that instead of seeing my face she was seeing a death's
> head. On one occasion I got the *feeling*, from the way in which
> she was looking at me, that my face was made up of hooded
> cobras. I hope that I am conveying some idea of how extremely
> uncomfortable this was for me; but I want particularly to em-
> phasize my belief that my ability to endure such nonhuman
> transference roles—to endure such projections of her own sub-
> jectively nonhuman components upon me—helped greatly in
> her becoming sure that she is a human being. Another way of
> thinking about this is that I had to become sure—on my *own*
> part—that my own humanness would assert itself over such sub-

jective nonhuman components of myself. From this latter point of view, we see how in successful therapy the patient eventually confirms, at a deeper level, the therapist's own humanness [1972b].

THE ANALYST'S RELATIONSHIP TO THE PATIENT'S SYMPTOMS

Instances in Which the Analyst Feels That the Patient's Symptoms Are Being Inflicted upon Him (the Analyst)

As a third-year medical student I chose a one-month elective in psychiatry, and it happened that each of the two patients assigned to me for psychotherapy during that month was suffering from depression. Toward the end of the month, my roommate commented that he had not seen me smile during the whole month. I had been largely unaware of how greatly the work with these two depressed patients had been depressing me.

In later years I became aware of how commonplace is the difficulty, in the training of psychiatric residents and of analytic candidates, of the doctor's unconsciously overidentifying with his patient. But I have seen, too, that all too often the analytic candidate (for example) is given by various of his teachers, and by his readings in the psychoanalytic literature, to assume that any intensely felt, conscious sense of oneness with the patient is a countertransference (in the classical sense of the term) intrusion into his attempted maintenance of a neutrally hovering attitude toward the patient. That I long ago departed from such a classically psychoanalytic view, in this regard, is indicated by the following comments, concerning the sense of identity as a perceptual organ, in a paper published in 1966-1967:

> During the past two years I have had occasion to do single interviews for teaching and consultative purposes with a relatively large number of hospitalized patients. In this work I have encountered the well-known problem of how best to cope with massive amounts of data which need to be assimilated quickly—what criterion, what point of orientation to employ in

order to find coherence and meaning in all that transpires. I have found that the most reliable data are gained in these necessarily brief contacts from my noticing—and, increasingly, sharing such information with the patient—the vicissitudes in my own sense of identity during the session. It is thus, I have found, that I can best discern what are the patient's most centrally important transference distortions in his reactions to me, and what are the aspects of his own identity he is repressing and projecting upon me.

I cannot claim to have achieved an unbroken sense of inner harmony in this regard (if such equanimity is possible for anyone to maintain, and I am confident that such a state is more a cruel and analytically stultifying illusion, essentially autistic in nature, than a desirable goal). For instance, I wrote five years later (1971):

> On numerous occasions, for example at the Sheppard and Enoch Pratt Hospital in Baltimore, I have had teaching interviews during the course of a day with two or three schizophrenic patients, each of whom tended powerfully to deny, unconsciously, the presence of the crazy, sadistic introjects within him, to attribute these instead to me—to, quite literally, experience them as residing within me—and to leave at the end of the interview with its having been formidably established, not only in his mind but in the minds of the onlooking staff and in my own mind, that he is the human being deserving of compassionate rescue from the inhuman, unfeeling monster of schizophrenia personified by myself. Then, at the end of the day, during the hour and a half of high-speed and hazardous rush-hour beltway driving to my office in Washington to see training analysands in the evening, I would feel one or more of those patients as disturbingly present within myself.

It would be simple to say that I was overidentifying with the patients in these particular instances; most of my return-trips from that hospital involved no such degree of inner turmoil. But part of the difficulty in the overall field of the psychotherapy of schizophrenic patients consists in *under*identification on the therapist's part with the patient. Relatively few psychiatric residents, for example, develop sufficient ability to identify with schizophrenic patients so as to become much interested in this aspect of psychiatric practice.

Part of the difficulty, in this regard, is that there is an all-too-prevalent tendency, among psychiatric colleagues, to regard as crazy any therapist who experiences such identification phenomena as those I have just described. Most psychiatric residents tend to be afraid to report analogous treatment experiences to their supervisors, for example.

Several years ago, for the first time in more than 50 years of remembered experiences, I had the sense of a sudden, entirely unexpected explosion somewhere in my torso. I could not locate it more precisely than that; it did not feel, for example, located specifically in my cardiac region. This was more than a mere fantasy; there was enough feeling of bodily participation in the mental imagery that I found the experience distinctly disturbing, and even frightening, although not to the point of panic. This experience recurred on some half-dozen occasions, at seemingly random times and in seemingly random circumstances, over the next few months. At this writing I still rank these experiences as being among the most upsetting ones of a predominantly psychological causation that I have ever had.

With the very first of these experiences, as well as with the subsequent ones, I almost immediately felt sure that what I was experiencing had its predominant causation—however multiple might be its determinants from other sources—in my relationship with one or another of my patients. Although I myself have had an explosive temper throughout my life, this particular experience was so foreign to me that I felt sure that it represented—among, as I say, whatever additional meanings it had—a reaction to some otherwise undetected component of my relationship with one of my patients. Had this happened some years earlier, I would have assumed, equally promptly, that here was one more evidence of my craziness, and that I really must get back for more analysis.

The task of ascertaining which one among my patients was involved in this experience was not easy, for I was seeing more than one in whom there was the symptom of poorly controlled (because largely repressed), explosive, murderous rage, and more than one whose youth had been characterized by a notable preoccupation with the contriving and setting off of explosives. A chronically schizophrenic woman whom I have treated for a long time had expressed more than once the delusion that we are living in a bomb, and on other occasions had experienced herself as being, essentially, a bomb, filled with radioactive material. Incidentally, she has spoken more recently, many times, of people being "exploded," and of having been herself "exploded."

The detective work required great patience, and went on while many other analytic-detective works were simultaneously in process and were holding, nearly all the time, the major foci of my interest. It was actually not until some few years later that one of my patients came to express, over the course of many months, previously repressed transference feelings and attitudes toward me which dovetailed so precisely with these now long-past experiences within me that I felt thoroughly convinced that she had been the one most involved in them. If space here permitted me to quote many of her detailed comments in this regard, I am confident that the reader would share, to a considerable extent, my feeling of conviction in this regard. Parenthetically, at no point have I ever confided to her the feeling-experiences I have described; had any one of these delayed time-bomb experiences occurred during one of my actual sessions with her, in all probability I would have reported them to her as being data of obvious relevance for her analysis.

Another example of my experience of certain thoughts and feelings referable to a patient's unconscious (or, in the following instance, perhaps preconscious) contents, comes from my work with a male patient in analysis several years ago. This man at the beginning of his analysis was so maddened, at times, by his own thoughts that, while lying on the couch and trying to report what he experienced to be going on in his head, he would suddenly feel driven to desperation and begin beating his head fiercely with his fists. I of course not uncommonly felt maddened also in trying to fulfill my function as analyst; the interaction between this man and me often reminded me of my paper "The Effort to Drive the Other Person Crazy" (1959a).

In the course of my work with him, some time after his own

head-beatings had for the most part ceased, I began to experience
within myself a phenomenon I could not remember having experienced before in relation to anyone. My earliest note in this regard
was made in a session during which he was reporting his thoughts
about four different situations, in recent weeks, in which he had
felt unaccountable anxiety. He described his having come to realize
that some particular aspect seemed central to all four situations. As
he put it, "That was a common—[momentary pause] well, something common to the four of them— . . ." My notes describe, with
regard to that pause: "Here is one of the many times in the past
several sessions when I think of the obviously missing word, and on
some of such occasions the word has come to be present in my
mind with somewhat disturbing force—sort of pulsating or reverberating, with almost explosive force. In this particular instance the
word is 'element.' "

In a session nearly two months later, he was speaking of his
wife's childhood, saying, "It seems as though her mother really
doted on Alice when Alice was a baby, and then after that just—
[momentary pause] had nothing to do with her for the rest of her
life . . ." Of the pause, my notes record: "Here the word 'dropped'
comes to my mind, and I have a fantasy of its echoing in my mind
all the rest of my life, with me helpless to stop it from doing so."

A couple of weeks later, my notes include the comment: "The
phrase 'window-dressing' is still reverberating sporadically in my
mind from one of his manipulative omissions about 20 minutes
previously."

A few days later, in describing a running battle which one of his
sons, a high school student, was having with his French teacher,
and after mentioning some of the teacher's complaints, he expostu-
lated, "But *he* [the teacher] is a—[momentary pause]. Why does he
subject himself to that?" Concerning the pause, I wrote in my notes,
"Here the phrase, 'bitch on wheels,' starts repeating in my mind."
Later on in the same session, speaking again of his wife's
background, he said, "So that's what she got from her mother.
That's her—[momentary pause]. That's what she brought with her
when she left her mother's home for good." Of the pause, my notes

mention: "Here the word 'legacy' repeats a few times, vividly, in my mind."

During the following week, while recounting some of the experiences a colleague had had during a visit to Alaska, he commented, "Alaska *does* seem— . . ." My notes mention: "Then he veers off into other content, such that the word 'primitive' starts booming slowly in my mind, for several moments (causing no more than mild discomfort in me)."

Instances in Which the Analyst Fears That He Personally Is Inflicting the Patient's Symptoms upon the Latter

These are instances in which the analyst is reproached, whether explicitly or implicitly, as being to blame for the patient's symptoms, and in which the analyst experiences anxiety, guilt, and remorse in this regard. Since such transference situations, with illustrative clinical details, have been reported many times in my previous writings, I shall limit myself here to a presentation of a few of my previously published summarizing comments about this topic.

In my paper "Phases of Patient-Therapist Interaction in the Psychotherapy of Chronic Schizophrenia" (1961e), in one of the passages descriptive of the phase of ambivalent symbiosis, I stated:

> At its fullest intensity, this phase is experienced by him [the therapist] as a threat to his whole psychological existence. He becomes deeply troubled lest this relationship is finally bringing to light a basically and ineradicably malignant orientation towards his fellow human beings. He feels equivalent to the illness which is afflicting the patient; he is unable to distinguish between that illness and himself. This is not sheer imagination on his part, for the patient is meanwhile persistently expressing, in manifold ways, a conviction that the therapist constitutes, indeed, the affliction which threatens to destroy him and with which he, the patient, is locked in a life-and-death struggle. In my theoretical view, the therapist is now experiencing the fullest intensity of the patient's transference to him as the Bad Mother [p. 533].

In my paper "Feelings of Guilt in the Psychoanalyst" (1966), I suggested:

> . . . our most troublesome guilt reactions are a function of our having regressed, in our relationship with the patient, under the impact of, and as a defense against, the helplessly ambivalent feelings that our work with him tends to inspire in us, to a defensively symbiotic relationship with him, in which our view of ourself and of the world is an omnipotent view. In this state of subjective omnipotence, we are totally responsible for all that transpires in the analysis, for there is no world outside us; there is no real, flesh-and-blood other person. Hence all our erotic and angry responses to the patient are felt by us as crazy, for we fail to see their interpersonal origin; they are felt instead as being exclusively crazy and frightening upwellings from within us, threatening irreparably to damage or destroy the patient, who seems so insubstantial and fragile. Since we do not experience any clear and firm ego boundaries between ourself and the patient, his acts are, in their guilt-producing capacity, our own acts; we feel as guilty, about his sexual or aggressive or other kinds of acting out as if we ourself had committed and were committing those acts.

In a paper (1972a) concerning my long-continued work (18 years at that writing) with a chronically schizophrenic woman, I reported:

> The most difficult aspect of the work . . . is the enduring of a quite terrible feeling of unrelatedness between us. . . .
> . . . Moments of feeling related to her, of seeing where her delusionally expressed views are linked up with my own view of my reality, have aroused . . . in me a deeply guilty sense of my being totally responsible for her plight. This subjective omnipotence-based sense of guilt seems clearly a sample of that against which she herself has been defended, unconsciously, over the years, by reason of her psychotic mechanisms such as projection and introjection, dedifferentiation, splitting, and denial.

The contributions from Kleinian analysts, while describing little or nothing of the *analyst's* feeling-experiences which are my main topic of discussion at the moment, contain some vivid examples of the kind of *patient* behavior that tends to give rise to such feelings in the analyst as I have detailed. For example, in the following excerpts from Rosenfeld's (1962) paper "The Superego and the Ego-Ideal," I find what he says concerning persecutory anxieties in the patient to be particularly relevant here:

> ... I am following Klein's work on the early superego (1933). In her view the earliest beginnings of the superego contain mainly idealized and persecutory aspects of the breast, soon including aspects of the penis and, with the beginnings of the early Oedipus conflict in the middle of the first year, aspects of the oedipal parental figures [p. 145].

> About six to eight weeks after the rabbit dream [a particular dream reported by a patient from whose analysis Rosenfeld's paper mainly derives] I had to change some of the patient's sessions. Her anger about this was first analysed as a disappointment in the analyst as a father figure, but she continued to regard the change as a cruel persecution and a sign that the analyst could not be trusted, and it became clear that it had reactivated early infantile experiences. The patient had been weaned when she was about ten months old and afterwards developed severe whooping cough. During this time she rejected her mother, and her father fed her and apparently saved her life. She dramatically re-experienced much of this early situation in the transference by accusing the analyst as the mother figure that he was letting her starve to death. It seemed that the change of time meant that the analyst/mother was taking away her food, but the sessions themselves also seemed completely altered in substance; they had become bad, poisonous and persecutory [p. 149].

> The role which the sadistic father played in her early superego remained hidden in the analysis for some time [p. 150].

> ... The analysis of the weaning situation and the superego built round this experience which I have discussed in some detail, brought the early persecutory superego right into the analysis with convincing dynamic force. The analyst was experienced again and again as a sadistic, critical superego figure who took pleasure in destructively criticizing everything the patient was doing or saying, or who took everything out of the patient,

enriching himself and leaving the patient empty and destroyed. At the height of the persecution the patient would often threaten to kill herself . . . [pp. 151-152].

At this juncture I wish to emphasize that, although I have just quoted material having to do with persecutory anxieties, I would not want the reader to infer that, either in this portion of the paper concerned with the analyst's relationship to the patient's symptoms, or in the larger subject of the paper as a whole, I am concerned exclusively, or even predominantly, with schizophrenic patients, for that is not the case. Each of my points concerning psychodynamics is something that, so my experience has indicated to me, is valid for any patient, to a varying but nonetheless significant degree, at one or another phase of his or her psychoanalysis or psychotherapy.

Instances in Which the Analyst Has Come to Feel That the Patient's Symptoms "Couldn't Be Happening to a Nicer Guy"

In my experience with patients of whatever diagnostic category, I find that a phase of the work develops during which I no longer feel helplessly inflicted with the patient's symptoms, nor anguished at my inability to rescue him from them, nor deeply concerned and guilty lest I be somehow the primary cause of his symptoms, and even personally equivalent to his symptoms, his illness. Now, instead, when he anguishedly or reproachfully or furiously reports his symptoms, for the nth time, I experience a freedom from these long-accustomed forms of personal suffering, and I think to myself, as I listen to him, "It [whatever tenacious symptom of which he is complaining at the moment—whether a headache, or suicidal urges, or various forms of marital-family anguish, or whatever] couldn't be happening to a nicer guy." The feeling is one which involves, obviously, irony and a sense of vindictive, sadistic gratification derived from a degree of my identifying with the symptom which is affecting him in the manner of which he is complaining.

In my paper entitled "Phases of Patient-Therapist Interaction in the Psychotherapy of Chronic Schizophrenia" (1961e), in my discussion of the phase of resolution of the therapeutic symbiosis, I described the therapist's experiencing his newly-won sense of individuation from the patient in terms somewhat analogous to those I am using here. But in that earlier paper I was discussing, in particular, treatment situations in which the therapist has come to terms with his erstwhile feelings of concern lest the patient commit suicide or remain chronically psychotic for the remainder of the latter's life. At that time I did not yet see as clearly as I have come to see in more recent years that it is an inherent part of the psychoanalytic process, in one's work with a patient of whatever diagnostic category, that one develop, among one's other feelings toward the patient, the kind of hard-won and only ostensible callousness I am describing here.

From a theoretical point of view, I have come to believe that when the analyst has developed this "It-couldn't-be-happening-to-a-nicer-guy" internal reaction to the patient's symptoms, one could say that the patient's symptoms have become transitional objects (to employ Winnicott's term) for the analyst as well as for the patient himself. In the theoretical terminology more congenial to me, I would say that the phase of therapeutic symbiosis is now relatively near, with the unhealthy pseudo individuality crystallized in the patient's symptomatology soon to be relinquished by both participants in the analytic situation.

A few years ago, as I was becoming aware of the apparently general relevance of the analyst's development of the kind of feeling-orientation I am discussing in this section of this paper, I made the following notes concerning a session with Mrs. Jones:

> . . . In essence, I had just come to feel a change in myself, from the state of feeling which had obtained almost from the beginning of the work with her, predominantly a guilty, anxious, intimidated feeling of trying to *provide* her with enough supplies to relieve her dissatisfaction, her anxiety, her fury— always with a feeling that I *owed* her much more than I was giving her. Such feelings have become interlarded, increasingly, with resentment and rage at her for browbeating me, but with no *direct* expression of this rage visualizable in the work with her, because of the likelihood that the treatment relationship

would be severed, or that I would lose face in my own eyes—lose stature—through having, essentially, a temper tantrum.

All this has evolved such that as she continues to report or express such symptoms as sexual frigidity, or anxiety, or intense dissatisfaction, or fury, I have come more and more to find myself feeling a vindictive satisfaction, a grim relish, above all a calm kind of neutrality, in hearing about it—a kind of calm balance between my urges to try, once again, to bring her relief, and my sadistic gratification at the evidence that her symptoms are wreaking upon her a savagery which I am not free to wreak more directly. Most of all, I feel a sense of conviction that all this change in me is very *necessary* and useful in her analysis, for it enables me to achieve a very useful overall analytic neutrality toward her, such that, for example, I no longer intervene in her many silences of a few minutes in length—silences into which I used anxiously and guiltily to intrude with attemptedly relieving interpretations or other comments.

Somewhat to my surprise, all this seems to be working relatively well. For example, she becomes verbal again each time after one of her silences, reporting the fantasy in which she had found herself immersed during it. I get the distinct impression that the more schizoid aspect of her, which is formidable, finds more comfortable the kind of analytic neutrality I have achieved, whereas her more hysterical aspects previously had been very provocative of my doing much interacting with her.

The theoretical view that the patient's symptoms have come to have the meaning of transitional objects for the analyst (as well as their having come to have such a meaning for the patient) is supported by a number of familiar clinical phenomena and relatively well-established theoretical concepts, not all of which can be encompassed here in an attempt conclusively to "prove" my hypothesis.

First, there is the analyst's subjective experience that the patient's symptoms are enabling him vicariously, as it were, to have a significant effect upon the patient, whereas he had come, long before, to feel helpless to have any more direct effect, and above all any symptom-relieving effect, upon the patient. He feels now, in other words, clearly partially identified with the patient's symptoms, and I think it a clinical experience familiar enough to us all to find that the patient's symptoms not only develop such sadomasochistic transference meanings as I have been implying, but come to represent, also, the bond of mother-infant dependency between patient and analyst. I surmise that many analysts, nowadays, are receptive to the idea that just as a patient's illness can come to be seen as a kind of security blanket for the patient (personifying both the early mother and the rudimentary own ego), so can the patient's illness develop the meaning to the analyst, in the course of the transference evolution, of a security blanket for him also, with the result that the eventual resolution of the patient's symptoms gives cause for feelings of loss, as well as of rejoicing, on the part of analyst as well as patient, just as the mutual individuation which develops from a healthy mother-infant symbiosis, in normal development, gives mother as well as infant occasion for feelings of loss as well as of personal fulfillment.

My hypothesis concerning the patient's symptoms as transitional objects for both analyst and patient is buttressed, also, by the familiar clinical finding that each of the patient's symptoms can become discerned, over the course of the analysis, as referable to some pathogenic introject or introjects, undigested and distorted internal-object representations of part-aspects of mother and other persons significantly involved in the child's earliest years. These introjects need to become reprojected upon the analyst, in the course of the transference evolution, in order for them to become resolved into an increasingly healthy own ego on the part of the patient.

From among the whole range of symptomatology, it is the category of psychosomatic symptoms which most commonly and readily make the analyst realize what I believe to be a general truism—namely, that the long-manifested symptom comes to have a meaning, as the transference neurosis or psychosis becomes established, of an introjective representation of the analyst (who is being unconsciously reacted to by the patient, here, as personifying some part-aspect of mother, or father, or whomever). Thus, for example, when the patient complains of "my sore asshole"—or of his excruciating headache, or bellyache, or whatever—the analyst soon finds reason to surmise that this is an unconscious transference reference to himself, but that the patient is not yet able to experience the contempt and rage toward him, as well as the body-image degree of dependent symbiosis with him, which is crystallized in the symptom in question.

In my monograph in 1960, I stated:

> . . . For the deepest levels of therapeutic interaction to be reached, both patient and therapist must experience a temporary breaching of the ego boundaries which demarcate each participant from the other. In this state there occurs . . . a temporary introjection, by the therapist, of the patient's pathogenic conflicts; the therapist thus deals with these at an intrapsychic, unconscious as well as conscious level, bringing to bear upon them the capacities of his own relatively strong ego. Then, similarly by introjection, the patient benefits from this intrapsychic therapeutic work which has been accomplished in the therapist [pp. 421-422].[1]

In a paper in 1959, I mentioned:

> Coleman (1956) and Coleman and Nelson (1957) have described a psychotherapeutic technique, which the former has employed with borderline patients, termed 'externalization of the toxic introject'. This technique consists in the therapist's deliberate impersonation of—conscious and calculated assumption of the role of—a traumatic parent, or other figure from the patient's early years, the long-standing introjection of whom comprised a 'toxic introject,' the core of the borderline schizophrenic illness. The authors' psychodynamic formulations are of much interest. . . .
>
> The great difference between Coleman and myself, however, is that in my experience the therapist does not express, in such situations, affects which are merely a kind of play-acting,

---

[1] I acknowledged that "John L. Cameron, a colleague on the Chestnut Lodge staff, has helped me to see" this. On this point I always have felt, subsequently, that I was less than candid. To put it more simply and honestly, he taught me this, as a teacher does with a pupil. The remainder of that paragraph, not quoted above, is so far as I know my original contribution.

Incidentally, as regards all these excerpts from my previous writings, I undoubtedly would phrase them somewhat differently, and to my present way of thinking more adequately, now; but I cannot devote these pages to doing so in the present paper.

deliberately assumed and employed as a technical manœuvre indicated at the moment. Rather, in my experience [with frankly schizophrenic patients], the affects are genuine, spontaneous, and at times almost overwhelmingly intense [1959c, pp. 345-346].

Marie Coleman Nelson et al., in their volume *Roles and Paradigms in Psychotherapy* (1968), report upon the further development of their technique of externalization of the toxic introject, and related techniques for the treatment of patients in general, with particular emphasis upon the treatment of borderline individuals. In a subsequent review of this book, a highly favorable review in the main, I took issue with Marie Coleman Nelson's opinion that "genuineness as a therapeutic quality *per se* has no intrinsic merit, is often lost upon the patient and may even be felt as artificiality." I commented:

> ... I, for one, cannot believe that the therapist or analyst can set aside his *real* feelings and still function effectively with the patient. But the authors are highly aware of the crucial significance of this question, and one finishes the volume with a sense of admiration of them for dealing recurrently, candidly and in thoughtful detail with this question in various contexts [1968-1969].

In any event, irrespective of this particularly controversial facet of the matter, the technique detailed by Marie Coleman Nelson and her colleagues, of "externalization of the toxic introject," is relevant to the present subtopic of my paper, namely, the analyst's "It-couldn't-be-happening-to-a-nicer-guy" response to the symptom-ridden patient.

Another brief example from my own clinical work concerns a man whom I analyzed for a few years, who on the one hand seemed endlessly reproachful of me for not freeing him from the symptoms which had brought him into analysis, often demanding that I give him relief from them, but who on the other hand clearly derived enormous grandiose satisfaction from the abundant evidence that I seemed incapable of having any effect upon him whatsoever. In the course of time, after my having gone through much feeling of analytic devotion to him, anguished efforts to help him through carefully formulated interpretations which he derisively rejected as futile, and largely suppressed feelings of hurt and rage at him for his tenaciously maintained resistance in the analysis, I came to a relatively stable orientation of feeling, when he would once again anguishedly demand relief from his symptoms, that these couldn't be happening to a nicer guy.

Since I long before had come to feel unable to have even a successfully aggressive impact upon him, let alone an effectively psychoanalytic participation with him in any more conventional sense, it gave me a kind of vicarious sadistic pleasure that, even though he had demonstrated, over and over, that I personally was incapable of drawing blood from him, at least his symptoms were capable of doing so. In the sadomasochistic transference relationship which had come into being in the treatment situation—so typical of those I am describing in this section of the paper—"his" symptoms of which he was complaining could be regarded as either transitional objects of his in terms of his masochism toward me or transitional objects of mine in terms of my sadism toward him. Kafka's (1969) comments concerning sadism and masochism, to be quoted in my review of the literature toward the end of this paper, will be seen to be relevant to my work with this man.

For myriad reasons which would take me too far afield to detail here, it was not yet timely for me to report to him this feeling-orientation which had developed in me. But there was solid evidence that it was accurately attuned to the etiology of his own illness. His own marriage was rendered neurotically miserable partly because of his inability to achieve this kind of feeling (among others, of course) toward his wife. She suffered from chronic alcoholism which, it was clear to me, the patient was helping to perpetuate, through his acting out, in the marriage, of unconscious death wishes toward his wife as a mother-figure.

For example, in one session he described his feelings the previous evening, while his wife was drinking once again. "I have this terrible feeling that Clara is slowly being destroyed—not by me, so much as by herself; but I feel helpless to do anything about it." I found it notable that he showed, in this session, no awareness whatever of any vengeful satisfaction in the thought that his wife was drinking herself to death—notable in particular because he had spent the previous day's session, as so frequently before, in expressing resentment, bitterness, and contempt about her perceivedly selfish, inconsiderate, demanding (and so on) behavior. He had punctuated that flow of predominant hatred and contempt with a few moments of a crocodile-tears kind of "pity," as he had called it, for her, whom he termed, in a most unconvincing way, "pathetic." In the current day's session, then, he went on, regarding her, "We're just on separate planets"—a statement expressive not only of his conscious despair about his marriage, but also of his unconscious need to disclaim any responsibility for his wife's neurotic illness.

The analysis came to reveal much data that this patient's "It-couldn't-be-happening-to-a-nicer-guy" feelings were so deeply repressed primarily because the circumstances of his childhood had left him convinced, at an unconscious level, that he himself had been responsible for the prolonged physical illnesses, and eventual deaths, of both his mother and an older sister. Until he came into analysis, just as he had never grieved at all fully over their deaths, neither had he been able to become conscious of the extent of his contempt, hatred, and death wishes toward each of them. In the evolution of the transference, I was much of the time in the position of a parental figure from whom he consciously and anguishedly sought rescue from his symptoms, but at the same time I was a mother or older sister whom he unconsciously had written off, hatefully and scornfully, as being as good as dead. To the extent that, in my own private feeling-orientation toward him, I could experience such sadistic feelings, contempt, and death wishes as he had been repressing, I became able to help him gain access not only to comparable feelings in himself, but also to the feelings of love and unworked-through grief which had been repressed along with those negative feelings.

The kind of patient-analyst relatedness described in the clinical example above, in which the patient's symptoms may be discerned to be transitional objects for the analyst as well as the patient, can be seen to be on a continuum as regards symbiosis and individuation. The more predominant interaction is the symbiotic one, as mentioned earlier, respecting the phase of ambivalent symbiosis in the treatment of the chronically schizophrenic patient. Here the analyst becomes unable to maintain a clear differentiation between the patient's illness and the analyst's own self, to such a degree that he feels on occasion fully and directly—not merely partially and vicariously—responsible for the patient's illness, by reason of his subjective experience that he personally *is* that illness. As I described this latter, more predominantly symbiotic transference relatedness in a more recent paper (1973c) concerning schizophrenia: ". . . the analyst . . . may come to experience himself, as I have done more than once, as being indistinguishable from the terribly malevolent affliction from which the patient is suffering."

Now I must step back a bit from this specific topic, to comment more generally about the analyst's emotional neutrality, as related to the need for him on the one hand to be emotionally involved, to a degree, in the analytic relationship with the patient and on the other hand not to be overly involved—overidentified—with the patient.

A year ago I made this note:

> It occurred to me today [as I found myself thinking of all my current patients collectively], while driving over to my office, how important it is for an analyst not to try to beat each of his patients at the latter's own game. My feeling is that one of my greatest difficulties in doing psychoanalysis is that I do get very much involved in just that—trying to out-passive-aggressive Jenkins, out-tough and out-humor Bradley, out-granite Weiss, out-insult Clara, and so on. It is folly for an analyst to fight with the patient's choice of weapons, for the patient has spent a lifetime in becoming adept with these.

. On the other hand, the following comments made in my recent paper (1973c) concerning psychoanalytic therapy with schizophrenic patients are, in my experience, to a significant degree valid for one's psychoanalytic work with neurotic patients also. In discussing many analysts' attempts to maintain, from the beginning of their work with such a patient, a demeanor of evenly hovering, benevolent neutrality, I suggested:

> . . . That . . . classically analytic position is indistinguishable from the omnipotent parental transference position which the schizophrenic patient tends so powerfully to lure, and demand, the analyst to occupy, while making life hell for him to the degree that he attempts to acquiesce to this tantalizing transference demand.

> . . . the emotions which schizophrenic patients foster in the analyst are so intense, and conflictual or discoordinate, that it is quite untenable for one to attempt to carve out such a position for oneself at the beginning; this can only become established much later, after many stormy interactions, in proportion as the patient's ego functioning becomes predominantly normal-neurotic in nature. Further, any such early attempt involves . . . an offensive condescension on the part of the analyst, who is being so presumptuous as to imply that nothing within the patient, either now or in the future of their work together, can ever seriously discommode the analyst. . . . The patient can only become increasingly determined to be taken seriously by the analyst, and make intensified, and surely eventually successful, efforts in that direction. As for the analyst, his attempt to maintain a dispassionate stance surely is serving as a defense against the activation, within himself, of reality nuclei for the patient's various and discoordinate transferences to him—transferences which need to become perceived by both participants, and their reality-nuclei basis in the analyst (as well as in the patient) perceived by both participants, in order for the transference psychosis to become manageably evident and to evolve into a transference neurosis of anything like the usual analytically explorable proportions.

Of some relevance for psychoanalytic work with neurotic patients is the following observation, from the same paper:

> The passively aggressive, sadistic gratifications afforded the chronically schizophrenic patient, in response to the anguished efforts of the analyst and others to bring him relief, are limitless. A typical dilemma for the analyst is how to achieve ways of functioning, during the session, which will make it possible for his own personal suffering to become less than that of the patient; in my own experience, the treatment cannot proceed use-

fully for either patient or analyst as long as the patient's
schizophrenia is inflicting, evidently, more conscious suffering
upon the analyst than upon the patient.

... Any such patient derives enormous sadistic gratification
from watching detachedly while the well-intentioned analyst
endeavors, valiantly but with intensifying despair and anguish
and repressed infantile omnipotence-based murderous rage, to
rescue the patient from the grip of the schizophrenia which
seemingly—and of course in various regards really—is causing
the patient such intolerable suffering.

I regard it as inescapable, and inherently necessary to the
psychoanalytic treatment process, that the patient's transference responses and attitudes will become focused upon, and will mobilize
to a degree, corresponding components of the analyst's actual personality. Both in terms of his coming to experience feelings, such as
the patient as a child had found in the particular parent relevant to
the current transference phenomenon, and in terms of the analyst's
inevitably becoming at times involved in some identifying (whether
unconsciously or consciously) with the patient as an aggressor, the
analyst feels involved in a degree of struggle with the patient as to
which one of them is going to succeed in imposing the symptoms in
question upon, or into, the other participant.

Rosenfeld's (1952a, 1952b) writings contain, as I have mentioned, excellent examples of this situation as regards the processes
at work in the *patient*.[2] But to comprehend more fully and deeply
these patient-analyst phenomena, we need to see that the analyst's
feelings are by no means so consistently and fully detached from
what is transpiring as Rosenfeld's clinical portrayals would suggest.

I have found, many times, that in my work with patients whose
marital-family situations were severely and chronically disturbed,
my own marital-family situation has become disturbed perceptibly.
In such instances, usually in a treatment atmosphere of long-
maintained and nearly intolerable suspense, what I have felt to be
at issue is not merely upon whom—patient or analyst—the *indi-*

---

[2] See, in particular, the passages cited in my own paper (1963b, pp. 664-665).

vidual psychopathology will be inflicted permanently, but whose *family*—the patient's or the analyst's—will be destroyed by a family-engulfing kind of psychopathology.

I hope it is clear enough that I do not recommend that the analyst attempt actually to bring about the destruction of the patient and/or the latter's whole family in order to preserve himself and his family relatively intact. What I am trying to describe is an aspect of one's work with particularly difficult patients, and a corresponding aspect of one's work with any patient during more particularly stressful crises, whereby both the patient and to a significant degree the analyst as well are involved in a struggle as to whose will be the psychopathology in question. I suggest that some degree of this kind of really mutual struggle is not only inherent in the analyst's becoming able to develop and maintain a *predominantly* neutral emotional orientation toward the patient and the latter's symptoms, but also necessary to both participants' coming to accept the symptoms as "belonging" functionally to both of them—as being equivalent to transitional objects for both of them—prior to the development of a stratum of more directly and unimpededly therapeutic symbiosis in the transference relationship.

Thus, for example, in my work over several years with a woman whose recurrently psychotic mother had threatened repeatedly to burn down the family home with the whole family in it, I remember a time when the patient's mother-identification in this particular regard had been ragingly at issue in the analysis for many months (I say "ragingly" even though, while the patient indeed raged much of the time, I said little or nothing in session after session; the struggle between us was predominantly subterranean). One of the turning points in the work occurred when my feelings had finally become sufficiently firmly integrated that I told her grimly, "If one of us is going to go home and burn down our family home, it's not going to be me." No discernible harm resulted from my having expressed verbally to her my hard-won determination on this score; but I think one could make a good case that it is superfluous to say such a thing to the patient. The main thing is to achieve the necessary bedrock of feeling of determination which such words bespeak. In my clinical experience, in marked contrast to that which Rosenfeld reports, such a feeling is not merely to be assumed as a given in the well-analyzed and experienced psychoanalyst, but is something that develops in him, over and over, in relatedness with one individual patient after another.

In my view, the deepening spiral of the patient's coming to experience the increasingly intense fullness of the transference neurosis (or psychosis) is a function not only of the *patient*'s becoming gradually able to withstand the intensity of such experienced feelings, but also of the increasing strength of the patient-analyst relationship, which involves the *analyst*'s becoming (predominantly through finding that the patient and he have been able to deal successfully with increasingly intense transference phenomena) increasingly able to endure his own being the object of such intense transference responses on the patient's part. His "enduring" such experiences is, for me at least, often just that in feeling-tone: far from finding myself immersed predominantly in an emotionally neutral apartness, I have to learn to be at home with various inner emotional reactions to the patient for which my early readings in the classical psychoanalytic literature, and my classically psychoanalytic training analysis, ill equipped me.

Many years ago, in working with one or another chronically schizophrenic patient, during some of the most stressful of the sessions with him (or her), I felt on occasion (and came to confide so to the patient, usefully) that the *only* appropriate response to the way he was behaving at the moment would be for me to beat the hell out of him. To include the erotic realm in this discussion, in the instance of my work with one hebephrenic man, as I reported in a recent paper (1974): "It required some years before I realized, sitting in one of the silences which still predominated during our sessions, that it had now become conceivable for me to be tangibly related to him without my having to either fuck him or kill him."

I had many stormy sessions with this man, whose history was marked by murderous violence and innumerable sadomasochistic homosexual conquests. It is only in more recent years, during which I have subjected myself to relatively little work with patients of this degree of illness, that I have become able to indulge myself in the luxury of doubting whether increments of raw emotion are *ever* needed, by any patient, from the therapist or analyst. Theoretically at least (although I still do not believe this can obtain in the actual clinical work with hebephrenic patients, for example), the analyst's functioning consistently in a self-possessed "neutral analyst" demeanor should provide him an effective outlet, in sublimated form, for all the sadism, vengefulness, sexual lust, tenderness, and so on, which he finds engendered in him in response to the patient's transference reactions and attitudes toward him.

In this same spirit, it has occurred to me, as regards my long-continued work with a chronically schizophrenic woman, that whereas I used to feel immobilized at times when it felt to me that the only appropriate response to her infuriating behavior would be for me to beat the hell out of her (as her mother used frequently to do during the patient's childhood, but as was barred, of course, to me), I have become more interested in the technical problem of *how* to beat the hell out of her in a sublimated and psychoanalytically effective fashion. Of such sublimations, I surmise, is the analyst's "neutral position" constituted—not, as I say, constituted early and permanently back in the years of his psychoanalytic training, but constituted anew, in a far more dynamic fashion, with each patient in turn, largely as a function of the transference evolution in each instance.

Two years ago I made the following note:

> This idea has occurred to me several times, in sessions with one or another patient, for perhaps a year or two now: the worst thing I can do to the patient (Connolly, for example) is to analyze him successfully. This serves as a beautiful avenue or context for the sublimation of my hatred toward him, because analytic progress brings with it, for him, the experience of feelings of loss, grief, deflation of grandiosity, and so on. This idea is amply supported by data from past years (in the work with Connolly, for instance) which indicate that the analysis, to the extent that it has been successful, indeed has opened him up to the awareness of suffering of various forms—anxiety, disappointment, jealousy, and so forth.

Significantly, a note I made only four days later, concerning that day's (Tuesday's) session with Connolly, mentions:

> . . . On Sunday I was looking forward with pleasure to the hour with him on the following day—a pleasureful sense of interest in the work with him, of companionship with him—for the very first time in all our work together. There have been many times in the past when I've looked forward to the next hour with him in a spirit of vindictive determination, but never before in this manner.

Connolly, with whom I worked altogether for more than six years, early had proved to be a highly sadomasochistic, remarkably murderous-hate-engendering person with paranoid psychodynamics of a borderline schizophrenic degree of severity. It is apparent that my above-quoted notes indicate that only now had my previously relatively raw, unintegrated feelings of murderous rage and hatred toward him become sublimated into a *relatively* neutral analytic orientation. In subsequent months of his analysis, he came to express feelings of heartfelt gratitude to me for the help I had given him; he expressed at the same time feelings that this help had also been in the nature of an affliction, for I had helped him to come to experience many emotions against which his former autistic grandiosity had shielded him effectively—such emotions as loneliness, anxiety, grief, and gratitude. While expressing gratitude to me, in short, he was also providing strong confirmation of my previously noted realization that the worst thing I could do to him was to analyze him successfully.

Instances in Which the Analyst Reacts to the Patient's Symptoms as Being His—the Analyst's—Allies

When I was working in a V.A. outpatient clinic many years ago, before beginning my psychoanalytic training, I made an interpretation to a belligerent young man, who thereupon was obviously hard put to keep from hitting me. I dreaded the next week's session with him, for he had left so very angry that I feared that next time he indeed would physically attack me. To my great relief—and clearly to his, also—when he did appear for the following week's session, he had a large bandage on his right hand. It turned out that he somehow had cut his hand, quite severely, with an axe. This piece of undoubted acting out on his part proved at least temporarily to be an ally of the treatment process—an ally of both his and mine. I still believe that, had this fisticuffs-precluding accident not happened, our work together would have been destroyed by his previously barely suppressed rage at me.

In one of my supervised cases during my analytic training a few years later, the patient was a borderline young woman whose impulsivity, involving of course erotic as well as aggressive impulses, I found frequently placed a barely tolerable strain upon my ability to maintain the relatively classical analytic position I was struggling to fulfill. I could not help feeling relief, as well as concern, when the intensity of the transference relatedness was decompressed for a few sessions by her having acted out, once again, her poorly integrated sexual and aggressive impulses outside the office. I typically was able to report to the supervisor: "We've been making pretty good headway even though she has been continuing to act out"; but I doubt that I was as free then (partly because of the analytic-training context) as I have since become, to recognize that analytic progress is being made not so much despite, but because of, continued acting out on the patient's part. I do not mean to suggest that acting out is inherently a good thing; but as the years go on I find less and less cause to wonder at the analyst's temporarily reacting to this symptom on the patient's part, like others among the patient's symptoms, as serving as an ally to each of them during otherwise intolerably intense times in the course of the analysis of the transference.

Six months ago I made a note, in this same vein, concerning my work with Mrs. Lombardi:

> . . . I feel a kind of co-worker, or ally, feeling toward her acting-out symptoms (drinking, overeating, and shopping sprees) which help to stave off psychosis—very much as I felt with Bryant [the above-mentioned supervised case]. It is to be emphasized that my comrade-in-arms feeling toward such

symptoms is a furtive, guilty one; I feel that if only the caliber of my analytic work were what it should be, my work wouldn't need any such allies.

Instances in Which the Patient's Symptoms Are Experienced as Transitional Objects by Both Patient and Analyst

For the past 11 years, in lectures concerning psychoanalytically oriented intensive psychotherapy with schizophrenic patients, I have included comments, relevant here, concerning the therapist's participation in the resolution of pathogenic introjects in the patient. I have emphasized the importance of the discovery, by both patient and therapist, that these introjects in the patient have both a root in what might be called his inner reality—that is, a link to repressed components of his own identity—and an external root, traceable to unconsciously denied perceptions, on his part, of the therapist (perceptions much distorted and exaggerated, of course, by transference factors, but with nuclei of reality in them as regards the actual personality functioning of the therapist):

> . . . Over the long course of the therapy, the patient needs to become able to discover a sample of everything [that is, of every conceivable kind, and combination, of feelings and attitudes] in the therapist, and in himself also. During the phase of therapeutic symbiosis, the patient comes to see in the therapist all the figures from his [the patient's] own past, and these percepts become now so free from anxiety that the patient can [partly by identification with the therapist who can accept within himself the reality nuclei for his being so perceived] discover them in himself, too, with a freedom which enables him now to experience them as really acceptable components of his own self. Thus they need no longer be defensively either projected or introjected.
>
> With one schizophrenic woman in particular, I learned this lesson: whenever any murderous feeling, for example, arose during a session, it was important that each of us become able to acknowledge murderous feelings in ourself and in the other, and likewise with envy, or adoration, or contentment, and so on, over the whole range of feelings [referring here to many months, collectively, in the overall treatment]. So very often she

saw, for instance, murderousness in me, and was able to discover the projectional element in her perception only after I had become able to recognize, and acknowledge in one way or another, that there was and is, indeed, murderous feeling in me. Comparably, many times she would experience as being exclusively a feeling-attribute of herself [i.e., she would be manifesting now introjection, rather than projection] something that had a counterpart in me also, and I found that her ego boundaries could become healthily established only in this setting of a free intercommunication of emotion over the whole gamut of feeling. An identity which grows out of such a variety of mother-child symbiosis, or in the treatment-situation therapeutic symbiosis, is not a defensive identity but an identity emerging out of the reality of both participants' own feelings [1963c].

I have already mentioned, earlier in this paper, how difficult it is for the therapist to endure various "nonhuman" transference roles—roles in which he is reacted to by the patient as being nonhuman—particularly when his conscious sense of his own identity is such as to require him to keep repressed, subjectively, as being indeed horrifyingly nonhuman, those components of his (unconscious) identity which are forming the reality nuclei for the patient's particular transference response to him.

For many years I have seen, over and over during supervisory sessions or while listening to colleagues' case presentations, that the most effective therapists of chronically schizophrenic patients are persons who have unusually free access to their own sadistic identity components—who do not easily or frequently become inhibited, that is, by guilty fears that their patient's perceptions of them as being diabolically nonhuman, at times when the negative transference is in full sway, are overwhelmingly and unanalyzably accurate perceptions. It seems to me that the chronically psychotic patient can be helped back to the world of reality only by a therapist who is able relatively comfortably to participate with him in a transference relatedness in which the patient is experiencing a kind of half-reality, a kind of twilight or purgatory state. This is the greatest degree of experienced reality that the patient can yet tolerate, in actuality, because of his enormous unconscious ambivalence as to whether to become more fully reality-oriented or to return to his erstwhile more fully psychotic state, in which the therapist is perceived by him as being a diabolically sadistic, nonhuman creature who is playing tantalizing, tormenting games with his (the patient's) as yet unfirmly established sense of reality.

Parenthetically, the transference atmosphere to which I am referring here is one in which not only is the patient reacting to the therapist as being a transitional object for the former, but also the therapist is not frightened off by indications that, to a subtle but detectable degree, the reverse is true also: patient and therapist are functioning as transitional objects for one another. In other words, then, for the therapist to become able to foster this so-necessary transitional-object atmosphere in the sessions, he must gain unusually free access to his own sadism—as well as to his own feelings of symbiotic dependency toward the patient as being a preindividuation mother-figure to him.

In my work, extending now for more than 22 years, with a severely ego-fragmented woman,[3] it has seemed to me that, of all the etiologic factors in her childhood, none was more conducive to later schizophrenia than the experience, on her part, of finding that those figures upon whom she had to depend for her development of reality relatedness had an investment (presumably a largely unconscious investment) in playing games with her not yet well established, and therefore highly vulnerable, sense of reality. The analysis of her corresponding transference reactions to me has required me to become somewhat accustomed to, and to find in myself reality-nuclei bases for, her perceiving me as correspondingly shockingly sadistic and nonhuman in this regard. She has thrived to the extent that I can participate in such sessions in a game-playing kind of spirit, really enjoying the seeming violence that is being done to any conventional concepts of reality.

Marie Coleman Nelson, writing of the therapist's deliberately functioning in an ambiguous manner, as one of the frequently employed techniques of what she terms paradigmatic psychotherapy (a

---

[3] Some aspects of this work were described in another paper (1972a).

treatment approach she and her colleagues have utilized much with borderline—as well as other—patients), says:

> . . . the atmosphere most conducive to the treatment of the borderline patient . . . is one in which the patient remains slightly mystified concerning the motivations underlying the analyst's *overdetermined* interventions, somewhat intrigued by the analytic process . . . [Nelson et al., 1968, p. 178].

An outstanding characteristic of the paradigmatic intervention is its selective avoidance of direct interpretation of the problem centrally in focus at any given time. This avoidance may be manifested, for example, in the analyst's pursuit of some theme other than the one consciously selected by the patient, by diversions such as word play, puns, jokes or nursery rhymes, by deliberate attention to subordinate notions and phrases and by oblique, multiply-determined comments on the patient's productions. . . . The conventional therapeutic situation, wherein the content of the presenting problem constitutes the figure and the associative material the ground, is reversed; the peripheral material is encouraged to occupy the foreground of attention and the presenting problem is relegated—in the *conscious* interchange, that is—to a peripheral position [Nelson et al., 1968, p. 37].

There have been times, in my teaching interviews with borderline patients, such as are many of those of whom Marie Coleman Nelson writes, when I have had the delightful experience of the patient and myself as being two subjectively diabolical sadists fully enjoying ourselves in childlike playfulness which clearly is doing both of us a great deal of good. Such experiences are a far cry from, and represent a kind of resolution of, one's experiences with more deeply ill patients wherein one has horrifying fears lest one be equivalent to the schizophrenia with which the patient is afflicted.

Modell (1963) says, of borderline patients:

> The relationships established by these people are of a primitive order, not unlike the relationship of a child to a blanket or teddy bear. These inanimate objects are recognized as something outside the self, yet they owe their lives, so to speak, to processes arising within the individual. Their objects are not perceived in accordance with their 'true' or 'realistic' qualities. I

have borrowed Winnicott's concept of the transitional object, which he applied to the child's relation to these inanimate objects (Winnicott, 1953), and have applied this designation to the borderline patient's relation to his human objects. . . .
. . . The relationship of the borderline patient to his physician is analogous to that of a child to a blanket or teddy bear.

In a similar vein, he says:

A defective sense of identity in borderline and psychotic individuals is, I believe, a major element in the creation of the qualitatively different transference relationship that occurs in these patients (see also Zetzel, 1956, 1965). It is not true, as Freud once believed, that the psychotic remains inaccessible to the psychoanalytic method because he is incapable of forming a transference. For we now know that psychotic people do in fact form a transference relationship of the most intense sort, a transference corresponding to the mode of the transitional object relationship—the person of the analyst becomes a created environment [1968, pp. 45-46].

My concept of the therapeutic symbiosis is fully consonant with Modell's view that the borderline or psychotic patient forms a transitional-object form of transference relationship with the analyst. But, as I have indicated in my several papers about the therapeutic symbiosis, it can equally well be seen that the analyst manifests, in that phase of the work, a transitional-object relatedness with the patient—and, in fact, a considerably deeper degree of symbiotic relatedness than that. Moreover, as I have reported in various earlier papers (1965a, 1973a), I regard the phase of therapeutic symbiosis as being present—though less prominently— in the analysis of the neurotic individual also, particularly as regards the areas of autism which are to be found in any such individual. Where Modell says in the above-quoted passage, concerning psychotic people, that the person of the analyst becomes a created environment, I have indicated in a recent paper on therapeutic symbiosis that this is true in the reverse direction also. Writing of the resolution of autism in patients—whether schizophrenic, borderline, or neurotic—I reported:

In my experience, for the resolution of the patient's autism to occur, the analyst must do more than function as a more reliable maternally protective shield for the patient than the latter's biological mother was during his infancy and early childhood, in the manner Khan (1963, 1964) has described. First the analyst must have become increasingly free in his acceptance of the *patient's* functioning as *his*—the analyst's—maternally protective shield. In my own way of conceptualizing it: to the extent that the analyst can become able comfortably and freely to immerse himself in the autistic patient as constituting his (the analyst's) world, the patient can then utilize him as a model for identification as regards the acceptance of such very primitive dependency needs, and can come increasingly to exchange his erstwhile autistic world for the world consisting of, and personified by, the analyst [1973a].

It seems to me probable that, in order for any effective transference analysis to occur with any patient, whether neurotic, borderline, or psychotic, the analyst must have come to accept at *least* a transitional-object degree of relatedness with the particular transference image, or percept, which is presently holding sway in the analysis. I myself characteristically feel a much clearer and more tangible correspondence than that with components of my own identity as I customarily know it in daily life. It seems to me particularly unworkable to relate to a psychotic patient as though his transference reactions to me were "purely" transference, and his projection-distorted perceptions of me were "pure" projections; he needs some acknowledgment, no matter how implicit, from me that his perceptions of me are not purely and completely crazy. But even a neurotic patient must be receiving, from his analyst, some kind of implicit acknowledgment that the patient's transference responses are not as "purely"—essentially, that is, delusionally—transference as is indicated in classically analytic writings. (For example, in the passage quoted above, Modell [1963] states flatly concerning borderline patients, "Their objects are not perceived in accordance with their 'true' or 'realistic' qualities.")

Under the impact of particularly intense transference responses from the patient, on occasion I find that something occurs in me whereby I disavow any reality nucleus for the patient's particular transference perception of me, whereby in other words I temporarily flee from the erstwhile degree of symbiotic relatedness with her in which her symptom—in the particular instance I am about to describe, her symptom of murderous paranoid hate—has been serving as something like a transitional object for myself as well as for her. Now, instead, I find immunity from such relatedness by regarding her as being the bearer of all the psychopathology in the situation—as being, in short, crazy. The following notes were made during a Friday session several years along in this woman's analysis:

> Two days ago . . . I had been feeling relatively free of any animosity toward her, and therefore was much jolted to find that, on her arrival, she was filled with murderous rage at me because of some minor litter she had seen in the corridor outside my door. . . .
>
> In that session two days ago, as many times before over the years, I was conscious mainly of the remarkably intense hate which is the atmosphere in which her analysis takes place, or proceeds—murderous hate, mutual murderous hate. Innumerable times, I have had fantasies that she would come here and, in cold-blooded paranoid hate, shoot me. Lately I have not been feeling frightened of her, but have felt—two days ago—what a strain it is to experience, sustainedly, this extremely intense hate.
>
> There are more positive aspects, too, and as a matter of fact on Sunday, for the first time, I found myself looking forward with comfortable pleasure to the session with her on the following day.
>
> Yesterday she was being her usual schizy self in reaction to the death, earlier that day, of her elderly aunt.
>
> Today she was a few minutes late in arriving, and meanwhile I found myself feeling very angry at her—feeling the violent, murderous hate—and then when the door from the corridor opened with (as usual) infuriating violence, I felt even more violently murderous rage at her.
>
> Then, as if by a conscious decision which emerged out of my being unable to tolerate, or unwilling to tolerate, that degree of violent, murderous, sustained hate toward her, I decided to regard her as schizophrenic (as yesterday's session had served once again to highlight her to be), and said to her,

"Hello, Bernice," in a very conventionally friendly tone as she walked in. She was looking pale, extremely tense, schizy (as she very frequently does).

I found this a striking example of how one's view of the patient as being schizophrenic serves as an unconscious defense against one's intolerably intense *personal* feelings toward her.

There is a definite balance in this regard which a skillful analyst must achieve. During the past few days in my work with the fantasy-immersed Mr. Marshall, I have come to feel that I take my patients' symptoms too personally. The steady analysis-of-the-transference focus does foster one's taking the patient's symptoms personally, in a sense.

All this is a very complex and most important question.

It seems to me that any symptom on the patient's part which proves, over a long course of time in the analysis, highly resistant to further analysis, is apt to have developed an unrecognized transitional-object function for the analyst as well as for the patient. The problem is not that the symptom has *developed* this function, but rather that both participants have had to keep under *repression* this mode of relatedness with it. This transitional-object mode of their relatedness with the symptom in question has proved not to be a preliminary to the necessary degree of therapeutic symbiosis between them, but rather to have become an unconscious defense, for both of them, against a more free, constructively therapeutic symbiosis. In such an instance—and, in my experience, such instances are very common, indeed, in psychoanalytic work—the tenacious symptom in question, unconsciously related to by each participant as being a transitional object for himself or herself, can be seen to be in the nature of an autistic, essentially paranoid, defense against the development of therapeutic symbiosis.

A common example of such a treatment-resistant symptom is a patient's obsessive preoccupation, throughout seemingly endless analytic sessions, with the unsatisfactory qualities in his or her spouse. Notes I made some seven months ago concern such a situation:

In yesterday's session, Mr. Robinson spent the session in a way highly typical of him—vituperating about his wife, Edna, as being so insensitive, unhelpful, selfish, sitting on her ass and not helping sufficiently in the care of their young sons, almost never showing any sexual interest in him, and so on.

As in many dozens, if not hundreds, of sessions previously, I felt much exasperation and futility at his massive resistance to becoming aware of the very clear displacement of his unconscious transference feelings toward me, onto Edna; and the almost equally clear parallels, for a very long time now, between his own ways of functioning during the session and the way the unhelpful, selfish Edna functions at home. [For years, it had become increasingly clear to me that he typically treated me, unconsciously or preconsciously, in ways remarkably like the ways he found so offensive in Edna's treatment of him; and increasingly clear, likewise, that Edna was often an only slightly displaced transference image of me. But many dozens of interpretations, over the years, about various aspects of this, as well as of its totality, had proved completely unavailing.]

What was very evident to me in the session yesterday—not entirely new, but clearer than previously—was the extent to which the "Edna" of whom he talks in the session (devoting most of his analytic time to such talk, year after year) needs to be seen as having parallels in both himself and in me [as was accomplished successfully in my work with the schizophrenic woman mentioned at the beginning of this subsection]. What was a new idea to me, during the session yesterday, was that the "Edna" he talks of during the session is an unconscious defense against the symbiotic linkage between himself and me. That "Edna" is the area of symbiosis between us.

In the last sentence above, where I wrote of "the area of symbiosis between us," I was referring to that area of our relatedness wherein he was unconsciously in symbiosis with me, and wherein I was, as I was only now becoming aware, symbiotic with him. I recall its becoming vividly clear to me during this particular session that for all practical purposes, as regards his functioning during the analytic sessions, this "Edna" of whom he spoke was only seemingly a third *real person*. This "Edna" needed to be seen, for analytic purposes, as predominantly an *unconscious construct*, constituted largely through displacements and projections on his part—and on my own part. One of the clues that "Edna" came to play a significant role in my own unconscious functioning is that many times, over the years, I found myself making some comment which served to bring him back to the subject of "Edna," at times when he was functioning relatively freely and was able to do without "her" for the moment.

At this juncture, it seems to me accurate to hypothesize that, as with tenaciously treatment-resistant symptoms in general, so with persistent transference images which the patient maintains in his response to the analyst: in order for these to become resolved, they must go through a phase of functioning as transitional objects for both patient and analyst, and of being acknowledged, no matter how implicitly, by both participants as having developed this status in the relationship between the two of them.

The following detailed material is from my work with a middle-aged single woman, Miss Bryant (a pseudonym, of course), whom I have been analyzing, four hours per week, for more than 22 years at this point. During the past few years she has been able to live alone outside the sanitarium.

During the past several years her experiencing auditory hallucinations, which she had begun experiencing some time prior to her hospitalization, has proved to be an analytic theme of paramount value for her ego differentiation and integration.

Early in our work, whenever she "heard voices," she evidently experienced these as emanating from some weirdly nonhuman source; she spoke of them, with a psychotically threatened demeanor, as being "an electric voice." During the early years more often than not she reacted to me, also, as being something other than human—as being, very often indeed, either inhumanly unfeeling or a frighteningly crazy sex-fiend.

As the years went on, she became able gradually to work collaboratively with me during the sessions in this as well as in other regards, reporting to me during the sessions whenever she heard the voices. Gradually these were taking on, evidently, more and more human characteristics, as I helped her to become able to identify with these previously unconscious and projected components of herself. Concomitantly and equally much, I helped her to see them as being, at the same time, unconscious transference perceptions of components of myself, perceptions which did not fit with her conscious images of me, and which therefore were being displaced onto these hallucinatory experiences.

In the chronologically arranged excerpts given below, one can readily see instances in which the voices say things to her—helpful, explanatory, sympathetic, or confirmatory things which, at an unconscious or preconscious level, she wishes I would say to her. Increasingly, the voices can be seen as referable to either her own conscious identity, or to her consciously perceived image of me. The voices become more and more simply human in quality, and at times difficult or impossible for her to distinguish from her "own" thoughts and feelings.

Friday, June 6, 1969. She reported having heard, in a store where she was shopping on Wednesday, "so many voices . . . I thought [tone of helplessness], 'Hafta talk to my doctor and tell them—" At this point I interjected, "Tell *them*?" She agreed that this was the way she had said it. She then "corrected" this slip of the tongue, "—talk to my *doctor* and tell him to tell them to go away—well, maybe when I talk to my doctor I think it *is* them— connected to so many doctors—aren't ya, Dr. Searles?—connected to so many doctors?" While saying these last few phrases, in a very intimate, teasing tone, she leaned over toward me. This was the most intimate few moments we'd had in years, in terms of physical proximity and atmosphere of intimacy. (As regards this paper, her slip of the tongue, in which she said "tell them" instead of "tell him" seemed to me a strong clue that she was equating me, unconsciously, with the voices.)

As the session went on, much data emerged which indicated that the voices were unconsciously equivalent, also, to the subjectively unwanted-by-other-people parts of herself. For example, it was clear to me, from her description of her attendance, yesterday, at the weekly hospital-unit meeting (where there are relatively few outpatients), that she had felt much more isolated, unwanted, and lonely there than she had been aware of feeling.

Some minutes later she said, decisively, "I just don't want those voices." I suggested, "You are surer of that than you are of what you *do* want," to which she responded promptly, "I'd like life to be a *little* easier than it is. . . . I think people are shown too hard a time. . . . I heard the voices say, 'It's true; things *don't* have to be so difficult' " (said in a strongly confirmatory tone).[4] Then, after a few seconds of silence, she continued, "I heard the voices say, 'People don't have to be so nasty' [said in a companionable, consoling tone]. I don't know what they're referring to. . . . It's something I don't understand—voices in the air that I'm—that come my way—the voices say, 'You know why this occurred?—Something happened to you' " (said in a helpfully explanatory tone).

In this session she went on to report some new and important material about the initial onset of her overt psychosis, many years ago. Also, she proved to be more than usually accepting of my suggestion to her that she is more lonely than she had realized.

Friday, December 12, 1969. In the middle of our usual weekly two-hour session,[5] during which we had been arguing a great deal (as not infrequently has happened over the years), I made my usual brief trip to the men's room across the corridor. She reported, as I returned and sat down again, "I just heard the voices say, 'Dr. Searles has realized that you've had enough of his fussing around with you' " "You open the door and let the voices in," she added, laughing warmly. I asked, "It's as though they come in at the same time I do?" She nodded, explaining, "When you opened the door to the hallway"—on, she later made clear, my way back into the office.

Friday, January 16, 1970. When, on coming from the corridor into the waiting room where she was sitting waiting for her session, I opened the door, she whirled and looked at me in a psychotically fearful way. Then five minutes along in the session, after talk about other matters, she explained, "When you opened the door, it seemed like you let some voices in, and they said, 'Don't worry so much; you're a very sweet woman.' "

[4] My description of the tone used refers to her imitation of the voices.
[5] I was seeing her, each week, for two sessions of one hour each and one session of two hours.

Then after about one and a half hours of this same two-hour session, within a few seconds after my return from the men's room, she reported hearing the voices say, "Why do you refuse to learn? Do you think your father doesn't know you're nervous with him and Eddie [her brother]?" Here, the tone used was one of such warmth, intimacy, and liveliness that I burst into laughter. The tone was entirely that of a family member. I told her that I thought of her mother (who had died many years ago). She replied, "Well, she thought I was a very sweet person by nature," in a confirmatory tone, and went on, "Yeah; but this voice didn't sound like her voice—I just heard the voices say, 'Guess what's gonna happen with you and Bill [her brother-in-law]!'" Again the tone had the same heart-warmingly intimate, family-member quality. I suggested, "Pauline, one of the ways I think is that if you can ever find someone to share your life as warmly and intimately as the voices do, you won't need the voices." She laughed warmly on hearing this. (It had been most rare for her to be so receptive to any interpretation wherein I cast the voices in so benign a light. One of the, to me, interesting features of this excerpt is that it gives some glimpse of the intense ambivalence so characteristic of her—at one point psychotically threatened, at another point overwhelmingly warmly intimate.)

Friday, April 3, 1970. Toward the end of the first half of a two-hour session, she said, "I worry about those voices," in a tone clearly conveying that she unconsciously was concerned about their welfare. Within at most two minutes later, she talked about having seen a TV documentary which included interviews with some of the wives of P.O.W.'s before they were returned from Korea. Her "I worry about the voices" had been said, I thought now in retrospect, *very* much the way a P.O.W.'s wife might worry about her husband. At the time I first heard it, she had sounded more like a worried mother, speaking about her children.

She went on to speak of various deceased parental-family members who had died during the spring months (such as this). "I feel they went through a winter that wasn't good for them," she said.

A bit later, I suggested, "Your tone in saying that you worry about those voices was that you worry that they may be dying." At this, she immediately made a disgusted, annoyed, rejecting wave of her hands at me, and plunged down on the couch pillow (she had been sitting up on the couch, as she usually does.) All this she did with such warmth and intimacy that I laughed happily.

In subsequent minutes, she made comments which contained evidence that the voices, in this regard, were equivalent not only to long-lost and long-feared-dead P.O.W. husbands, to cherished and long-dead family members, but also to the long-known fellow patients who were still inpatients at the sanitarium to which she returned each week for a visit. She spoke feelingly of how sad the atmosphere was in the ward meeting which she had attended there yesterday. She learned yesterday that Dr. —— is leaving Chestnut Lodge. She described, during the session today, his first coming onto her ward, years ago, as her new administrator (to be succeeded, in due course, by the next one in her long series of administrative psychiatrists). Her description was full of liveliness and warmth, with implications of tremendous nostalgia for her inpatient life on that unit. But she clearly had very largely to repress, still, such nostalgia and loss feelings. The voices she described having heard yesterday, on returning to her apartment in the city after her weekly visit to the Lodge, clearly had served as an unconscious defense against her longing for the so-lively group relatedness she had enjoyed on that unit.

At one point in this session, she said about the voices, while glancing rapidly around at the floorboards in the office, "*I* think it has something to do with a radio or something like that—or caused with a battery, something electrical. *I* don't know; I'm just guessing—I heard the voices say, 'It has something to do with money.' "

Friday, May 29, 1970. In expressing fond memories of her mother, she said, "She was a nice woman—she always worked hard—I always thought she worked too hard and I wanted to help her. . . . I used to say my mother was very close, my best friend. I always loved her so; we always wanted to be close together—[few seconds of silence]—I heard the voices say, 'She loved you, too.' " (The tone here was one of gentle assurance.)

Tuesday, June 9, 1970. After having reported that she had just heard the voices again (their content being usual enough), she said, "Oh, the voices, Dr. Searles, I hate 'em!"—plunging her head down on the couch pillow from her previous sitting position. This was said with no more than moderately hateful intensity. The striking thing, to me, was the " 'em"—so close to " 'im"—so close, then, to the meaning, "Dr. Searles, I hate 'im!" (That is, I felt that the displacement of her unconscious hatred of me, onto the voices, was here unusually transparent.)

Several minutes later in the session, she confirmed my impression that she had felt frightened on seeing my pen, with which I had written down the date. "Sometimes I don't feel that my mind is my own." After a few seconds of silence I said, in a manner intended to encourage her to elaborate further, "Sometimes you don't feel that your mind is your own?" She agreed, adding only, "Sometimes I wonder." (I would assume that she was unsure whether her mind was being controlled by my pen—a kind of paranoid experiencing which would be fully in accord with that which had been so predominant in the first several years of our work.)

Tuesday, July 21, 1970. During the first several minutes of the session, she reported, several different times, having just heard the voices, and quoted what they had said to her. On most of these occasions, in my private opinion, the voices had said things to her which she very likely might have wished I would say, but which are not typical of me—more the kind of things a friend, or a person involved in doing supportive psychotherapy, would say. I had been remaining silent throughout. After seven minutes of this, she said after a minute or so of silence, "You haven't any comment to make about what I've said, have you?" to which I made no reply. (I regard this vignette of relevance here because of the evidence, in it, of her experiencing me, in terms of "interpersonal" cathexis, as being on a par with the hallucinatory voices. It was much as if she had said, "The *voices* have been making comments, several times, about what I've been saying. *You* haven't any comment to make about what I've said, have you?")

Tuesday, August 4, 1970. At the beginning of the session, she said she had been quite pleased yesterday at not hearing the voices. But then today, after sitting downstairs in the lobby of this building for a time, when she had gotten up to walk to the elevator, to come up to her session, "I heard the voices say, 'It's not because you're bad, I guarantee ya'—" Her facial expression while she recounted this was complex—mainly, I would say, tortured, helpless. I commented, "Those voices really tease you cruelly, don't they?" I was planning here, assuming—as I fully assumed—that she would agree, to next suggest to her the possibility that there is an aspect of her*self* fully as cruelly tantalizing as these voices. (I personally have felt the impact of this aspect of herself innumerable times over the years.)

But she promptly retorted, with conviction, "What about your*self*?" I replied, "Are you referring to what I said on Saturday?" (I had in mind the following incident. She had asked me what the little slabs in my new mobile were made of, and I had said, "Petrified wood," then added, teasingly, "Did you notice that I avoided looking directly at you when I said, 'Petrified wood'?" Thereupon she had looked—naturally enough—very hurt, very cruelly teased by me, and I felt I had been very mean, very cruel to her. Parenthetically, I generally feel that my own sadism is in evidence much less often than hers during the sessions; but hers is still largely unconscious.)

She interrupted me vigorously by saying, decisively, "I'm referring to right now," with considerable antagonism, although I did not feel, this time, that the retort was at all fully deserved.

Later on in the session, after she had commented about something, she said in an unusually spontaneous, good-naturedly teasing way, "As my analyst, what d'ya say? . . . I think that's a good joke, don't you?" She said this with amused laughter which I shared. (She regarded this as a joke because, in her opinion, an analyst is by definition someone who never responds when asked to do so.) "Couldn't help saying what came to mind," she added with a half-sarcastic, but half-serious note of apology; it was apparent that to permit herself even this bit of conscious teasing of me caused her to feel a bit guilty.

After a brief silence, she reported, "The voices just say, 'If ya had any sense, ya'd leave Washington.' " I suggested, "They talk as though that's what *they* would do if *they* were in your position?" She replied, less rejectingly than usual of such comments from me, "Maybe they wanta travel; I don't know. . . . If I go somewhere ya think they're gonna come along?—Dr. Searles?" I said nothing.

Shortly thereafter, she said, "I just heard the voices . . . and I was getting along *so well* yesterday—" Whereupon I interrupted, suggesting, "It's as though you're hardly the same *person* ya were yesterday?" She agreed promptly and emphatically, "*Yeah, yeah.*" I found it impressive, indeed, that she was able so fully to accept this comment.

Later on in the session she said with an impressively healthy, spontaneous rapidity and fluidity of feeling, "I was thinking of the [ornamental] rocks I saw in Camalier and Buckley [one of the local stores she frequents], and I was thinking, 'My doctor doesn't have any,' and I heard the voices say, 'He doesn't want any'—I think that's funny," and indeed she sounded genuinely amused.

Friday, September 11, 1970. She described a bus ride yesterday during which another passenger commented, about a talkative young man a few seats away, "He has a need to talk." I suggested to her, "Perhaps, too, those voices have a need to talk." (I thought of them as being, in this regard, a projection of an unconscious aspect of herself.) She replied promptly and spontaneously, with an amused laugh, "Maybe so—I wish they'd go away from *me*, though."

Friday, November 27, 1970. About 15 minutes before the end of this two-hour session, she said that she had just heard the voices for the first time in the session. "I heard the voices say, 'You're getting older, you know; but aren't we all?' [the tone here is a gentle, friendly one]—Now, *that's* the way *I* very *often talk*, isn't it?" I replied, "Yes—but it didn't sound like your voice?" She responded, "No; [but] it's the way I very often talk."

Thursday, January 7, 1971. She was speaking of the "Peanuts" comic strip (which I had not read in many years), and said, "I was trying to think of the dog's name and I heard the voices say,

'Snoopy' . . ." I asked, "*Is* that the dog's name?" She replied, "Snoopy, yeah— . . ." She had said all this in a relatively comfortable-sounding tone, indicating the voices to be as comfortably companionable with her as I had ever known her to indicate.

Friday, January 15, 1971. After we had been discussing the Library of Congress, on the basis of our each having been there on various occasions, there was a silence of perhaps half a minute. She then reported, "I heard the voices; but they were very far away. I don't know if I really heard them or if it was in my mind. They said, 'Do you know why he *really* went there?' . . . I don't think I really heard the voices; I think it was in my mind . . ."

Friday, January 22, 1971. She described how complex her life becomes, repeatedly, just at times when she is feeling most secure. She said this with exasperation but also with amused laughter. She then asked, in a half-teasing, half-serious way, "How'm I doing, Dr. Searles?—*You're* my psyche." I replied, in a manner neither challengingly questioning nor fully confirmatory, "I'm your psyche," and she agreed. I did not reply to her question as such. A few minutes later, after more back-and-forth conversation between us, she reported, "I heard the voices say, 'You *are* a nice lady' " (said in a reassuring tone).

Tuesday, February 2, 1971. About 15 minutes along in this session she said that just then, "I heard the voices say, 'It's true—people should be more considerate.' Now, I don't know if it's actually a voice or in my mind—it's close to my feeling about it . . ."

Tuesday, February 16, 1971. She said that today she was starting to get on a bus, when she heard a (real) woman and a man talking to one another, "—and somehow through that I heard some voices." Because of this, she decided not to get on that bus, but waited for the next bus, got on that one, and did not hear voices. "Somehow I felt that if I had got on that other bus I would have heard voices. . . . I heard, just now, 'It's true; there's something about you that looks very worried.' " Later in the session she mentioned that, upon having heard those voices at the bus stop, "The first thought I had was, 'Why should I go on that bus to hear voices?—and it's crowded!'—so I didn't go . . ." (I include this item partially to indi-

cate that the hallucinations are still influencing her daily-life behavior, although far less constrictingly than used to be the case
years before, when she led a severely cramped life, afraid to venture into, for example, certain stores where she had heard the
voices terrifyingly loudly and "thick and fast" when she had last
dared to go in there.)

Friday, February 19, 1971. This was a chilly, overcast day, with
combined snow and sleet predicted. About 50 minutes along in her
two-hour session this morning, she reported, "It seemed to me that
a voice has been trying to come through and I get very nervous
with it. I didn't actually hear it; it's very distant." I commented,
"You're not aware, I gather from what you say, of feeling at times
distant from me, or that I seem at times distant from you." After a
few moments of thought she responded, with a warmly amused
laugh, "I don't know about *distance*—you know I don't like to compare." (She smiled in an empatic way in making this aside; she is
alluding here to the major area of dissension between us in earlier
years—my talking in comparative terms, often—not excessively so
by any usual standards, in actuality—and her having only relatively
recently become largely free of her long-held conviction that this
was frightening craziness on my part.) "But," she continued, "I feel
you're like the weather—you're about the same temperature toward
me as the weather—cold." (I found very impressive, here, the degree of ego differentiation involved in her being able to liken to the
weather my feeling-attitude toward her. For years I had endeavored, in vain, to help her to come to know that she was experiencing as purely weather phenomena—she talked endlessly of the
weather in those years—phenomena which basically had to do with
the complex and changeable emotional climate of the relationship
between us. For years, in short, she had projected onto the weather
many of her unconscious feelings, and had displaced onto it many
unconscious transference perceptions of me.)

Then a few moments of silence ensued, and she said, "I was
thinking it's nice to know that the voices have stopped, and I heard,
'You've won'" (simply said), and she laughed with amusement
which I shared.

Tuesday, March 2, 1971. This was our first session in a week, for I had been out of town. (This I assume to be significant for what had occurred during my absence.) She said that on Friday she had had to spend two and a half hours in a beauty parlor, having repeatedly to wait for the different steps in the procedure to occur, and had heard voices while there. "I was really *very* frightened [said with unmistakable seriousness] . . . I never heard them so loud— kept telling me, '*Leave!—leave!*—ya don't like it here—leave—why don'tcha leave *Washington?* . . .'" She had stayed, obviously, nonetheless, but said, "I'm very hesitant about going back there. I like the way they fix my hair; but I *didn't* like those voices. . . . Seems to me I was *detained* there especially to hear the voices; I can't help feeling that. . . . And it does seem a shame; the work was really very well done—matter of fact, better than ever before," but because of the voices, she re-emphasized, "It made me *very* nervous . . . I have this frightened feeling that it may return . . ." (I include this material to show that on occasion still, as during an unusually long separation between us, she experienced the hallucinatory voices with frightening intensity. She was still not ready for any interpretation from me that the voices had been, in part, projected expressions of her unconscious and intense wishes that I, as a hated and unwanted transference-figure—and of course in any case I would not employ such technical terminology—would leave the city permanently and never return. Nor that they had been, in part, displaced unconscious perceptions of me as trying to send her into exile.)

Much later in the session she returned to the incident at the beauty parlor. "Other people get provoked, too; it's just too long to wait. . . . I heard the voices say, 'It's true; things don't hafta be so hard for you.'" I suggested, calmly, "Sounds as though that's said in a very sympathetic way." She responded, assertively but unangrily, "Very matter-of-fact, I'd say. Not unsympathetic; but not so sympathetic."

Friday, March 5, 1971. She mentioned that she hadn't heard any voices yesterday—or today—until she reported hearing them briefly, a time or two, relatively early in this two-hour session. Then much later in it, after we had been discussing some of the ways she had felt very early in her long hospitalization, there was a pause of a few seconds, and she then said, "I just heard, 'That's true; you've had plenty of problems' [the tone was a mild, somewhat offhand, not actively sympathetic one]—but not very loud, almost like it was *my* mind. . . ." Her tone in saying "almost like it was *my* mind" was one of pretty much accepting that it probably *is* her mind; there was no note of surprise, nor any anxiety, in her voice.

Tuesday, July 6, 1971. Upon coming into the office, and before sitting down on the couch, she said, "I just heard the voices say, 'You're a very nice woman.' I was going to tell you I felt so good because I didn't hear the voices all weekend or yesterday—so, this [tone of mild exasperation] is what I get . . ."

I found this interesting because, in the same process, the voices had behaved in a tantalizing way toward her and she had behaved in a tantalizing way toward me. That is, I felt, ironically, as she was telling me all this, how close I had come to hearing her make a gratified and gratifying, rather than a complaining, report about the days since the last session. The ironic aspect of my feeling had to do with my seeing clearly her largely unconscious investment in tantalizing me.

The Functioning of an Appurtenance, in the Analytic Situation, as a Transitional Object for Both Analyst and Patient

I shall give but a few examples from a presumably wide range of possibilities—which surely would include the analytic couch, for instance.

A Tape Recorder

Mrs. Joan Douglas (a woman much more deeply ill than Miss Bryant), whose history and course in psychotherapy I have reported elsewhere in some detail (1972a), has been working with me for nearly 22 years, four hours per week, at the present time. For the first 11 years I met with her at Chestnut Lodge, and since then she has come by taxi to my office in Washington several miles away. Although she has improved in a number of important regards over this tremendous span of time, she has continued to manifest an extremely severe degree of ego fragmentation and unrelatedness—experiencing herself and perceiving me, more often than not, for example, as comprised of multiple and unrelated persons or fragments of persons.

Then years ago I began audiotaping our sessions, openly and with her knowledge, and have taped all of them for the past nine and a half years, on seven-inch reels, all of which I have kept on file. Occasional playbacks of these tapes, privately, have confirmed my conviction that they are of immense research value as regards the psychodynamics, and psychoanalytic therapy, of schizophrenic patients.

With only a dozen or so exceptions I have used the same recorder, throughout, for taping all these sessions, and this recorder long ago acquired enormous personal feeling-value for me. Among other meanings for me, it is a link to her, a link to Chestnut Lodge, a link to my cherished collection of tapes; and it is symbolic, too, of the scientific and the academic life, for one who feels all too burdened, these days, with workaday clinical responsibilities.

When I began audiotaping the sessions I began augmenting this form of data collection by noting down briefly, during the hours, data concerning some of the nonverbal processes which the recorder could not register—such as, for example, whether she nodded in agreement or shook her head in disagreement in response to a comment of mine.

Between one and two years ago I began, very tentatively at first, to try to dispense with this note-taking and to make, instead, comments to the nearby microphone on my desk which led to the recorder over on the other side of the desk. I did this partly in an attempt to make the situation a bit less artificially encumbered by data-collecting, and also because it seemed less of a bother for me.

Throughout all the foregoing years I had had a persistent difficulty which consisted in my pulling my punches with her, fearing her apparent fragility and vulnerability, while she rode roughshod over me, doing unfettered violence to my own sense of reality. Similarly with my beginning, in a gingerly way, to make brief asides to the tape recorder, I was concerned lest she be jarred and offended, even though one of my most frequent experiences with her, over the years, had been for me to sit helplessly by while she was immersed in a vigorously lively dialogue with one or another projected internal image—of, more often than not, some mother-figure giantess—during which she vocalized, in different voices, both sides of the dialogue.

Moreover, anything resembling play therapy has always come to me with great difficulty. Bit by bit over several months, however, I dispensed more and more with my note-taking, and became able to utilize the tape recorder with some relative versatility in my relationship with Mrs. Douglas. For example, when I was feeling particularly furious at her and determined to hurt her in retaliation for what she had been doing to me, I would deliberately talk, in a coldly clinical, lecturing fashion to the tape recorder, about her diagnosis of chronic schizophrenia. And when I was feeling particularly warmly fond of her, and sensed that she was suddenly being frightened away by this response from me, I would turn, with a barely perceptible change of tone or volume, and talk in an intimately companionable way with my recorder, with which she could identify in proportion as she became able to do so.

In a paper (1973a) I mentioned: "In my work with . . . [a hebephrenic] man, as well as with another patient earlier and many subsequently, I have seen that ambivalently symbiotic relatedness often comes to have, at first weirdly, a quality of *group* relatedness, with jealousy a most important and difficult complicating factor." This had been true, for some years, of my work with Mrs. Douglas—prior to my starting to talk with my tape recorder. Now it became commonplace for a quality of group interaction to be present in the room while she was talking with some projected mother-image up toward the ceiling, and I was talking simultaneously with my tape recorder.

As for her own responses to the tape recorder directly, she seems to this day convinced that there are people in it who have been shrunken and placed there. On occasion, at her request, I have played it back for a couple of minutes or so during a session, and although she has come regularly to confirm that my voice, from it, does indeed sound like my voice, she is firmly convinced that her voice, from it, is not hers. She is aware of my attachment to the recorder; I was once baffled at her referring to it as "your daughter," in all seriousness, until I remembered that, in both her marital family and in her parental family, the daughter was the apple of the father's eye.

I am convinced that my way of utilizing the presence of the recorder has been promoting, in this atmosphere of group relatedness, her increasing ego integration. In a session on April 3, 1974, for example, in which I was weaving many comments to the tape recorder into the interaction between her and me, she said with an amused laugh, of some person who had just occurred to her, "She can come and join our group therapy." A few minutes later she, who seldom had mentioned realistically any of her fellow patients at Chestnut Lodge, and who rarely indeed had spoken of the group of them in her cottage as a whole, said in regard to the question of whether one has to eat to stay alive, "The group we have at the Lodge now is disputing that. They say, 'You *do not*; you *do not eat ever* in your whole life.' . . . Millie and Betty [real names of two of the other patients in her cottage] believe you *have* to eat."

In the July 17, 1974 session she referred to herself as "this group," and clearly confirmed, when I inquired, that she was experiencing herself as being a group. This was merely one of many indications that a change was taking place, from her more customary sense of her own identity as discontinuous and unrelated over the course of time, shifting unpredictably from one day to the next or even from one moment to the next, to a sense of identity which, while still multiple, involved a sense of a group of "selves" simultaneously existing in group relatedness with one another. Similarly, a careful study of this session shows her being able to be more collaborative with me, more related realistically with me, in a setting of my repeatedly interspersing brief asides to the tape recorder into moments of unrelatedness between us. To me it seems clear that this "group" relatedness involving us threatens her less with devouring or being devoured, than does my erstwhile attempt to focus my attention single-mindedly upon her.

In the preparation of this present paper, I came upon Ekstein's (1965) paper "Puppet Play of a Psychotic Adolescent Girl in the Psychotherapeutic Process." His paper, in which he portrays the puppet as functioning as a transitional object for the girl, is one which I find in many details reminiscent for me of my work with Mrs. Douglas, work during which the tape recorder serves as a transitional object for me and, increasingly, for her, as she is increasingly able to let herself be the object of various responses which I have diverted temporarily to the recorder, until such time as she is able, through identification with that quasi-person, to endure and enjoy being comparably related to, directly, by me in the transference situation.

The Analyst's Notes

A borderline paranoid woman, who had been in analysis for a number of years, commented, after I had quoted back to her something from the notes I had been taking during the session, ". . . as you read from your notes . . ." To myself, as the session went on, I privately noted the following thoughts:

> She did not especially emphasize the word "your"; but I was struck that there could well be an underlying confusion in her mind as to whether my notes are *mine* or *hers*, since what I quote—and have obviously noted—are statements *she* has made. Thus it seems to me the notes *could* be reacted to unconsciously by *each* of us as being in the uncertain realm that is neither clearly "me" nor clearly "not me."

Some six months after the above incident, during a session in which she was expressing newly derepressed murderousness of the kind which I had perceived in her for years, but which only recently had become possible to interpret with any success, I made the following notes:

> One thing that interests me about the above [referring here to many verbatim notes, setting down her reporting of this newly derepressed material] is that it provides confirmation of my *many* threatened fantasies [which I had experienced for years]—still present at times—lest she shoot me, or destroy me by lawsuit. Ever since the last session—on Saturday—I recall having had the fantasy of her refusing to use the couch, my suddenly quitting with her, her vowing to destroy me—implying, by legal means—and my hastily renting a safety-deposit box big enough to hold the notes at least from the first couple of years of her analysis, and my putting them there—or—I also recall fantasying—secreting them in one of the boxes labeled "JD Tapes." My fantasy was that she broke into the storeroom, determined to get her notes—I'm struck by my calling them here "her" notes, rather than mine, which to me indicates symbiosis between us, and my unconscious anxiety at the prospect of loss of this symbiosis, anxiety defended against by paranoid fantasies and feelings on the part of myself as well as of the patient—and she overlooked this portion of her notes, because they were in the box so labeled. . . . One of the valuable aspects of this material is that the notes are so likely (in psychoanalytic work in general) to be, as I feel reasonably sure they are here, a transitional object for both analyst and patient. . . . I do not trust her sufficiently to tell her my fantasy since the Saturday session—not even *nearly* enough to do so.

The Couch

A woman who characteristically reacted intensely to even brief absences on my part had been saying, for several sessions, that when she comes here and sees me, she remembers that I am going to be away on Saturday of next week. Then, at the beginning of the week in question, she revised this:

> . . . It's when I come in and sit on the couch that it occurs to me that you won't be here on Saturday; it's not when I look at you, but when I sit on the couch. . . . This couch has more—something—more substance. It's more real to me than you are;

it really is. . . . This couch is even more than you—it has something more—it's because I lie on it and touch it and I do things
to it, and I can't touch you, I can't do things to you. . . . This
couch stays here and it's nice and certain. . . . It's no wonder
people get attached to their furniture, their belongings
. . . . That's why the couch is more important than you are—

Later in the same session I set down some of my own thoughts as
follows:

> I sense that the time will shortly come—though it is not yet
> here—when it will become a moot issue whether the couch is
> *hers* or *mine* (i.e., when the couch will have the function of a
> transitional object for each of us). In this session I referred to it
> [in speaking to her] as "my couch," without feeling that she is of
> a mind to make any great issue of it; but it is noteworthy that
> she doesn't refer to it as "your couch," but "the couch" or "this
> couch."

About three weeks later, the day before I would be away again
for a day, she got up at the end of the session and, while tidying up
the two small rugs I have over the foot of the couch, said in a
warmly possessive tone, which I felt sure was expressive of feelings
displaced from me, "If *this* were *my* couch, I'd have one large—
instead of two small." I replied, "I'll see you Friday," to which she
replied, with warm fondness, "Don't forget," and I replied in the
same tone, "I won't forget."

As for the meaning of the couch to me in terms of my relationships with my various patients, I find it easy to believe that it often
comes to function as a transitional object; for one reason, I feel toward it, while tidying it up, so much of the fondness, tender feeling, contempt, fury, or whatever, which I have toward the just-
departed patient (whom the couch represents, fleetingly, to me).
Parenthetically, as regards my feelings toward one patient after
another in sequence in the course of the day's work, in the relatively infrequent instances when I tend to confuse one patient with
his or her predecessor, the image I have of the just-departed patient is serving me momentarily as a transitional object toward the
establishment, or re-establishment, of my relationship with the
newly arrived patient, while at the same time shielding me from the

fullness of my loss and relief feelings at the departure of the one who has just left.

Psychotropic Drugs

Thus far, despite many recurrent conflicts, I have never prescribed psychotropic drugs for my patients, and shall only touch here upon this vast and complex subject.

Following my presentation of a paper on another subject a year ago, during the discussion period the question came up as to whether the treatment of chronically schizophrenic patients can be speeded up with the aid of one or another mechanical contrivance—such as, I gathered, the use of bottle-feeding reported by Duhl (1951). I told the audience that if they indeed were referring to such mechanical contrivances, I reacted against such techniques as being expressive, in my opinion, of unconscious contempt on the therapist's part toward the patient, and as putting unhelpful distance, emotionally, between therapist and patient. I mentioned to them, in a spirit of not knowing whether it were relevant to that discussion, my experience with the tape recorder in my work with Mrs Douglas. I suggested that maybe the tape recorder functions as a transitional object for me, noting that just as she had for a long time talked with her hallucinated, and delusionally distorted, mother-image (for example) during the sessions, I had come, more recently, to talk more and more with my tape recorder, such that there was at least a four-"person" conversation going on during the sessions.

At this juncture, Jerry Morrow, a psychiatrist, contributed the valuable thought, "You have made clear, perhaps, what is the essential difference: *if* the mechanical contrivance, whatever it is, is being employed the therapist as a transitional object of the latter, and as being the only way he knows of reaching the patient, then it is useful, rather than it's being expressive of any alienating scorn on the therapist's part."

It occurred to me subsequently that the point Morrow made may be applicable, also, to the therapist's (or analyst's) utilization of

a psychotropic drug in the treatment of one or another of his patients: if the drug is of sufficient affective meaning for the therapist
to have the function for him (and, presumably, for the patient also
during some phase of the work) of a transitional object, then such
drug therapy need not necessarily represent the kind of subjectively
nonhuman intrusion into the psychotherapeutic or psychoanalytic
relationship which I have tended to regard it as being.

Of interest in this connection is Berman's (1972) paper on "The
Role of Amphetamine in a Case of Hysteria," in which he describes
the symbolic meaning of this drug to the patient, and the role it
played in her symptom complex as revealed in the course of her
analysis. His summary includes the statement: "As an emergency
narcissistic supply to relieve her feelings of separation anxiety, it
served as a transitional object" (p. 340).

Review of Literature

Taken with the items already mentioned, I can include here
only a sampling of the literature concerning transitional objects and
closely related phenomena, not only because of limitations of space,
but also because I cannot claim to have read the greater part of it. I
shall not even touch, here, upon another section of literature which
is of hardly less relevance to the present paper—namely, that having to do with the psychodynamics of the therapeutic process in
psychoanalysis; some of my previous writings (1965a) have dealt
with that subject.

Much of what I have written here has implications concerning
disturbances in the body-image—for example, the transference
meaning of the psychosomatic symptom as being an introjective
representation of the analyst, or Mrs. Douglas's speaking of herself
as "this group." In this connection, Greenacre's writings concerning
fetishism—a phenomenon analogous with transitional phenomena—are of much value. In the following passages from her article "Certain Relationships Between Fetishism and Faulty Development of the Body Image" (1953), note in particular those which

mention instability in the formation of the body-image:

> Fetishism is the result of a rather definite combination of genetic influences, in disturbances of pregenitality. These consist of (1) disturbances in the early months of life, producing instability in the formation of the body image, with uncertainty as to outline, and fluctuations in the subjective sense of size; and (2) complementary disturbances in the phallic phase, which produce an exaggeration of the castration complex. The genital area of the body image is under any circumstances less certain in the early months of life than other parts of the body except the face. Under normal developmental conditions, the genital area of the body image becomes consolidated during the phallic phase, due to the increase in the spontaneous endogenous sensations arising then. Under the disturbed conditions of pregenitality described, the overly strong castration anxiety is combined with body disintegration anxiety from the early phase, and depletes rather than reinforces the genital outlines of the body. These conditions also contribute to increase bisexuality and contribute to a corresponding split in the ego.
>
> Due to the marked pathology of the first months, there is a persistence of the unusually strong primary identification (which in many cases has played a part also in confusing the genital part of the body image). This persistent tendency to primary identification, especially through vision, again influences what happens with attempts at intercourse. Then the sight of the penislessness of the partner brings into focus the underlying feminine identification and makes genital performance impossible unless special support is offered.
>
> The support is attained through the use of the fetish; which is tangible, visible, generally inanimate, unchanging in size, also not readily destroyed. It offsets the effect of the identification with the partner, and "pegs" the genital functioning by furnishing this external and material symbol of the phallus to be reintrojected and reaffirm the genital integrity of the fetishist.
>
> Thus, while the fetish is precipitated in the situation of the need to preserve the idea of the mother's phallus and so deny anatomical differences between the sexes, it *functions* by reinstating, through visual, olfactory and actual introjection, the phallus of the individual [pp. 96-97].

Greenacre's work, as in the sample above, makes me think also, for instance, of my experience with the recorder in the work with

Mrs. Douglas. Another paper, the stimulating originality of which can only be hinted at in the following brief excerpts from it, is "Significance of the Body Image in Schizophrenic Thinking" by Torsten Herner (1965). Herner's paper is an outgrowth of his psychotherapeutic work with chronically schizophrenic patients—in much isolation from his colleagues, since nobody else in that Swedish hospital was engaged in such work. He says:

> Because of my nearly complete isolation, I felt committed to an especially intense, intellectual working through of the material. Most of it came from the countertransference, which constitutes the "royal road" to an understanding of schizophrenic phenomena [p. 458].

> On the most primitive level, the body which constitutes the "world" is not, *nota bene*, the body as usually perceived but a very strange body *image*. Of all the bizarre ideas encountered in my therapeutic work with the schizophrenic woman I have already referred to, this one was the most startling; it overwhelmed me. Ever since then, however, this particular idea has been the point of departure in all my attempts to understand not only schizophrenic thinking, but all sorts of primitive thinking. Apparently, the nucleus of the problem of the ego is to be found in the stage where "world" is represented by the body [pp. 451-462].

By way of summary, he states:

> The split body image observed in schizophrenic patients is the introjected, disorganized, interpersonal relationships perceived by the infant to whom the family is the world. In therapeutic work with such a patient, unsolved problems of relationship to immature parents are delineated. He struggles for liberation from these maleficent figures, who appear in his dreams and hallucinations. In the course of treatment, the incomprehensible symptoms can be explained and a unit [i.e., unification] of the split body image effected. It is possible to meet the crippled and weak ego of the schizophrenic in a new way [p. 465].

In the following excerpts from a paper by Martin Wangh (1962), "The 'Evocation of a Proxy,'" the relevance to the present paper can be seen if we think, in retrospect, of Mr. Robinson's

"Edna," or of the spinster's auditory hallucinations, as being psychodynamically equivalent to what Wangh calls a proxy. Wangh explains: "A 'proxy' shall be defined as a person other than oneself who is used to experience feelings, exercise functions, and execute actions in one's own stead" (pp. 453-454).

In his conclusion he states,

> . . . I have hypothesized that in the cases cited, the inclination to resort to it [the evocation of a proxy] is genetically tied to a persistence of symbiotic needs and to the failure in the proper development of a sense of identity.
>
> I have postulated that the insufficient dissolution of the early symbiotic tie to the mother produces weak spots in the development of the sense of identity, of the sense of reality, and of the ability to control impulses by offering fixation points in a period when such reliance upon another individual for the exercise of these functions is quite the normal order. . . .
>
> Separation from any object that has prevalently served as a narcissistic extension of the self, that has functioned more like a transitional object and less like a true object, becomes, under these circumstances, a particularly grave threat to the integrity of the self. The "evocation of a proxy" utilizes such symbiotic and transitional foundations for defensive purposes. Another person is mobilized to function as an "alter ego." Selected superego qualities, ego functions, and id manifestations are evoked in and assigned to a partner. The anxiety aroused in the proxy stirs him—instead of oneself—to actions, emotions, judgments, and controls. . . .
>
> . . . I have tried to demonstrate at least two ways in which these patients unconsciously attempt to involve the analyst in the transference in the proxy-creating process. The wish may be to make him represent the precious narcissistic extension object which needs to be protected against the attack of an incited outsider, or the wish may be that the analyst himself become the attacking or seducing proxy [pp. 467-468].

Some of Modell's work has already been cited. His paper on "The Transitional Object and the Creative Act" (1970) also is relevant here. In this he says:

> . . . In this essay I restrict my attention to the very specific characteristics of paleolithic art that suggest a correspondence to Winnicott's concept of the transitional object.

Not infrequently the paleolithic artists made use of the natural geologic formation of the walls, floor, and ceiling of the cave itself [p. 241].

I view the transitional object as a watershed[6] concept, a great psychological divide: on one side there is a sense of connectedness of the subject to the object, a sense of connectedness that supports a denial of separation; while on the other side there is an acknowledgment of that which is outside the self; the transitional object is a thing in the environment and not entirely self-created. Therefore I would interpret the paleolithic artist's use of the actual formation of the cave walls and ceilings themselves as a concretization of the interpenetration of the inner and the actual environment, that is, the art work itself is a tangible expression of the psychology of the creative process.

What is created is not an entirely new environment but a *transformation* of that which already exists. This suggests that an essential element of creativity is an *acceptance* of that which is outside the self. . . .

. . . We have suggested that the environment itself may be equated with this, the child's first love object. . . . If we understand the transitional object concept as a great psychologic divide with a progressive and a regressive side, we can discern an analogy in creative processes between primitive and more mature modes of loving. Mature love requires an acceptance of the nonself. We believe that true creativity, whether in art or science, also requires the acceptance of a prior tradition which stands for the nonself, that is transformed by the creative act [pp. 244-245].

I have employed the analogy of the transitional object to describe the creative illusion of transference in certain borderline and schizophrenic people [1968]. In these people the element of illusory connectedness between self and object is retained to the point where the analyst's separateness, that is, his uniqueness, cannot be fully acknowledged [p. 246].

. . . culture, which is the creative transformation of the environment, bears the imprint of the psychological equation, mother[7] = environment [p. 249].

---

[6] Note that a watershed is a ridge dividing one drainage area from another.

[7] Modell explains that the mother here stands for all protective parental objects.

This interesting paper by Modell fits in beautifully, at many points, with my monograph concerning the nonhuman environment published ten years previously, which he evidently had not read.

Volkan has contributed a number of papers which are highly relevant to, for example, what I have reported here of Mr. Robinson's "Edna" and of Miss Bryant's hallucinatory voices. I find Volkan's work brilliant, but showing the limitation characteristic of classically psychoanalytic writings, in that the phenomena described as taking place in the analytic session are described as if they were predominantly autistic phenomena on the patient's part, with little or no feeling-involvement, in them, on the part of the analyst. I see subtle indications, which I shall not detail fully here, that he is moving into a more comprehensive view than this—a welcome development which, I feel sure, will strengthen greatly his already impressively creative contributions.

In his paper "The Linking Objects of Pathological Mourners" (1972), he reports:

> A study of adults involved in pathological response to the death of a loved/hated person discloses the use of controllable symbolic objects to perpetuate the link with the dead individual. Although resembling in some respects fetishes, transitional objects, and inherited items that are simply valued and put to appropriate use by a mourner, they are sufficiently specific in their function of maintaining psychophysical balance in the face of loss to be differentiated as unique entities. An externalization process is suggested by which linking objects provide a focal point in which the self-representation of the mourner merges with that of the dead person, and in which the painful work of mourning an ambivalent object relationship can be accommodated [p. 215].

> . . . The linking object belongs both to the deceased and to the patient himself, as if the representations of the two meet and merge in an externalized way. The ambivalence which had characterized the relationship with the dead one is invested in the process of distancing the object in a representation of psychic distancing, but at the same time keeping it available [p. 217].

In adult life, linking objects mark a blurring of psychic boundaries between the patient and the one he mourns, as if representations of the two persons, or parts of them, merge externally through their use [p. 220].

The linking object provides a means whereby object relationships with the deceased can be maintained externally. The ambivalence of the wish to annihilate the deceased and the wish to keep him alive is condensed in it, so that the painful work of mourning has an external reference and thus is not resolved [p. 221].

Volkan's (1973) paper, "Transitional Fantasies in the Analysis of a Narcissistic Personality" (which is, incidentally, a beautiful paper concerning narcissism), is relevant, similarly, to the productions of the two patients of mine mentioned above. He reports, of the man upon whose analysis his paper focuses:

> . . . His reality testing in intimate relationships was so blurred . . . by his protection of the belief that he had precedence over all others, that one must ask what kept him from exhibiting generalized psychotic manifestations. The answer seems to lie in his use of specific fantasies in a way that suggested my term, transitional fantasies. He employed them as intangible representations of transitional objects, regarding them as though they had lives of their own and behaving as though he were addicted to them, although they were at the same time subject to his absolute control, whereby he could maintain the illusion that he had similar control over the real environment [pp. 351-352].

> . . . At the start of the fourth year of analysis I came to understand his specific fantasies and visual images as transitional objects. . . . Fantasies and other images slowly lost their magic. He became capable of remorse and sorrow and spoke of suicide. . . . He began to use me as a transitional object more than his own productions. He then came to see me as another human being and became curious about me as a person [pp. 362-363].

> Perhaps more important than his verbal acknowledgment of the fact that he had used fantasies as transitional objects was his working through his addiction to them; this occurred in the third year of analysis when, in transference, his use of me as a transitional object became obvious [p. 374].

It is noteworthy that, in the context of the last quote above, Volkan does report a bit of his own feelings in that phase of the work: "I felt somewhat fused with him, just as he fused me with external objects" (p. 374). This is a tentative bit of the kind of reporting of the analyst's feeling-involvement which I have detailed in my papers on therapeutic symbiosis. I would assume that, in the earlier quote, where he reports that "Fantasies and other images slowly lost their magic," that these fantasies, long reported by the patient, had now lost their magic for the analyst as well as for the patient and that, in retrospect, they could be seen to have been serving as transitional objects not only for the patient, but also for the analyst—as in the present paper I hypothesize to be the case in the instance of any long-manifested symptom in the transference relationship. Similarly in the instance of the previously mentioned paper by Ekstein (1965) concerning the puppet play of a psychotic adolescent girl, the wealth of verbatim taped material which he presents from his sessions with her includes data which indicate to me that the puppet served as a transitional object not only for her—as Ekstein suggests in his theoretical formulations in the paper—but, on occasion, for him also.

Volkan and Kavanaugh, in their (1973) paper, "The Cat People," report:

> Two female borderline patients became intensely preoccupied with their pet cats when their analysis focused on their working through the severance of the symbiotic tie to the mother/analyst. For their psychotic parts their cats *became*, as presymbolic transitional objects, the me, not-me, and the link between the two. A third patient, a schizophrenic unable to differentiate between self- and object representation, in her involvement with her cats *became* her cats.

Where these authors see the patient to be relating to the pet cat, or to the analyst, as being a transitional object for the patient, in my concepts concerning therapeutic symbiosis I find—as mentioned previously—that in this phase of the analysis *both* analyst and patient relate to one another as what might be termed transitional objects for one another. Likewise, although they explain that "we will in this paper use the terms transitional object relatedness and symbiotic relatedness interchangeably" (usage which the present paper indicates to be acceptable enough to me), it has to be kept in mind, in reading their paper, that the authors do not portray the analyst as *participating in* that relatedness to any significant degree.

Marjorie McDonald's paper on "Transitional Tunes and Musical Development" (1970) applies the psychoanalytic understanding of transitional phenomena to a study of the Suzuki method of teaching the violin. In so doing, she introduces the term "transitional tune." She explains:

> It is Suzuki's goal to teach children as young as three years of age to play the violin and to do so in a manner which resembles as closely as possible the way children have learned language. Recognizing the importance of the parent in this process, Suzuki begins by teaching the parent, who plays a small-size violin such as the child will later use. As the parent plays and enjoys the instrument, the child spontaneously wants to join the activity. He then attends both private and group lessons with his parent and soon is participating himself, enjoying the violin as a new toy. As he has learned language from his parents, so he learns the violin, at first from them, and later from his teacher and from group play sessions where he is exposed to older and more advanced pupils. The emphasis is always upon having fun through playing music [p. 504].

McDonald presents the hypothesis:

> ... some children, who have experienced music from birth onward as an integral part of the loving motherly and fatherly caretaking environment, might make use of music in a very particular way. My hypothesis is that these children find in music their own special "transitional phenomenon." Some may even select from a musical repertory a special "transitional tune," just as another child selects from among his toys a special transitional toy [p. 509].

In her summary she mentions:

> ... In his original article on transitional phenomena Winnicott [1953] included sounds and tunes among the wide range of normal transitional experiences.
> Confirmation for the concept of a transitional tune comes from direct observation of young children, from biographical and autobiographical accounts of the early lives of musicians,

and from music itself, in the form of lullabies and cradle songs. . . .

Finally, I have proposed a developmental line for music, in which the "transitional tune" stage occupies an early and probably an important position. The success of Suzuki's method of teaching the violin to young children seems to be based on its close adherence to and support of this natural developmental line for music [p. 519].

Paul C. Horton, in his paper "The Mystical Experience as a Suicide Preventive" (1973), describes depressed patients' utilization of mystical states as being, essentially, transitional phenomena which protect them against suicide—a finding which seems to me closely comparable with Volkan's observation (1973) that his patient's utilization of transitional fantasies served as an unconscious defense against frank psychosis. Horton states:

Three suicidal adolescents suffering from schizophrenic reactions developed the ability to conjure up a mystical consciousness. Directly experiencing this "oceanic" state (or just its memory) provided the patients with a reliably soothing safeguard against their overwhelming loneliness and possible suicide. Recognition by the psychiatrist of the mystical state as a transitional phenomenon points the way to the most effective therapeutic stance [p. 294].

Winnicott said of the transitional object: "It's fate is to be gradually allowed to be decathected, so that in the course of years it becomes not so much forgotten as relegated to limbo" (1953). The same is true, one can hope, for the mystical experience insofar as it serves as a suicide preventive rather than as part of a healthy religio-philosophical life-style. The therapist can best facilitate this decathexis by himself becoming a transitional object, thereby providing a reliably soothing, nurturant, reality-oriented relationship [p. 296].

Horton's recommendation, above, that the therapist become a transitional object for such a patient, is reminiscent to me of Volkan's (1973) finding, in the third year of his analysis of his narcissistic patient, that as the patient's working through of his addiction to his transitional fantasies proceeded, "his use of me as a transitional object became obvious."

It can be seen that Horton's views concerning psychotherapy

with these patients have some similarity to my concepts concerning therapeutic symbiosis; but it is to be noted that when he indicates that it is well that the patient's mystical experiences be "shared" with the psychiatrist, he is using the term "shared" quite differently from my use of it in discussing therapeutic symbiosis. He clearly is recommending that the psychiatrist facilitate the patient's *telling him of* the latter's mystical experiences, whereas I would assume that in the therapeutic-symbiosis phase of one's work with such a patient, one would literally share, to a degree, in mystically felt symbiotic relatedness with the patient at times during the sessions. Further, where Horton, like Modell and Volkan, describes the patient as reacting to the therapist as being a transitional object, I suggest, as mentioned before, that there are times in the work when patient and analyst relate in terms of being transitional objects for one another.

Kafka's (1969) paper, "The Body as Transitional Object: A Psychoanalytic Study of a Self-Mutilating Patient," is not only highly relevant to my paper in general, but in particular gives a richer portrayal of the analyst's feeling-participation in the phenomena under analytic investigation than is the case with the other writings I have been citing here. I had the pleasure of discussing Kafka's developing ideas with him during several years, and in the following passages I can give only relatively meager samples from a fascinatingly many-sided paper. Kafka says:

> . . . A point to be developed concerns the notion that the patient's own body can be treated by her as a transitional object and that this can be related to the history of self-injury. . . .
> . . . My experiencing an unusual degree of erotic and sadistic fantasies found its place in the analysis as representing some repressed aspects of father's, but predominantly of mother's relationship with the patient. To be singled out for further description and theoretical consideration will be one of the many examples in the analysis, when echoing her own experience of her body, I experienced her as not quite living matter. . . .
> . . . In the course of the analysis she described how, when she slowly and deliberately cut herself (for instance, with a razor-blade or with a broken light-bulb smuggled under her bed-covers while gazing lovingly at her "favourite nurse" who

was "specialing" her) she would not feel it, but "I always stopped as soon as I did feel it" and she managed to convey the exquisite border experience of sharply "becoming alive" at that moment. This sharp sensation was then followed by the flow of the blood which she succeeded in describing as being like a voluptuous bath, a sensation of pleasant warmth which, as it spread over the hills and valleys of her body, moulded its contour and sculpted its form. Blood was described by the patient as a transitional object. In a sense, as long as one has blood, one carried within oneself this potential security blanket capable of giving warmth and comforting envelopment [pp. 207-209].

What he says above, about the patient's experience that "the flow of the blood . . . spread over the hills and valleys of her body, moulded its contour and sculpted its form" is reminiscent to me of Modell's (1970) concepts concerning paleolithic art as transitional object. Kafka goes on: "In the countertransference I experienced this patient frequently as a not quite living, not quite animate object; in other words, as a transitional one" (p. 210).

The following passage indicates a feeling on his part analogous to, although not identical with, what I have described here on the analyst's part, in regard to the patient's symptom—that "It couldn't be happening to a nicer guy":

> . . . My experience in the face of her self-mutilations was not always "don't do that . . . don't hurt yourself . . . I won't let you hurt yourself." My experience was perhaps more in line with what Winnicott (1947) has called "hate in the counter-transference" or at least my subjective feelings could have been verbalized in some such fashion as "go ahead, slice yourself to ribbons; let's find out if you're alive or not" [p. 210].

Kafka asserts: .

> On the descriptive level we are on rather firm ground in applying the transitional object concept to the situation. This patient certainly *did* treat parts of the surface of her body as though she were not dealing with quite living skin and there is much evidence to support the notion that she was much preoccupied with the, for her, very much *unfinished business* of establishing her body scheme [p. 210].

I have mentioned earlier in this paper the role of ambiguity in psychoanalytic technique, and Kafka makes some interesting comments concerning the developmental significance of ambiguity:

> . . . I have come to think of benevolent parental communica-
> tion of tolerance of ambiguity—the ambiguity, for instance, of
> pain through, but hunger for, contact—as related to the
> offspring's individuation without alienation. The dynamic
> semi-permeable membrane, which helps to define the indi-
> vidual, yet permits two-way passage from and to the social envi-
> ronment, is gradually formed by sequences of parental com-
> munications or meta-communications appropriate to the age of
> the offspring . . . to the effect that ambiguities and contradic-
> tions are tolerable. . . . This . . . tolerance of ambiguity, permits
> the gradual formation of a membrane which is ego syntonic to
> the extent to which it was not prematurely and externally im-
> posed but individually established through much active
> exploratory crossing and recrossing of the culturally poorly or
> ambiguously defined border territory [p. 211].

He closes with some comments about sadism and masochism:

> . . . While sadism and masochism are generally considered
> two sides of the same coin, it remains a fact that one or the
> other side of the coin often dominates a particular clinical pic-
> ture. The study of how one's own body can be a "not-me" ob-
> ject may illuminate the general question of the sadistic or
> masochistic preference. In a sense the cutter's choice is a transi-
> tional one between the sadistic and masochistic object, his *own*
> *not-me* skin. It is his skin—which, however, he experiences as *not*
> his own. In analysis the ebb and flow of sadomasochistic trans-
> ference and countertransference may be conceptualized as a
> factor contributing to the re-formation of a more integrated,
> more bodily-ego-syntonic membrane, and thus contribute to the
> eventual elimination of the symptom [p. 212].

Busch and McKnight's (1973) paper, "Parental Attitudes and the Development of the Primary Transitional Object," seems to stand largely alone in the literature in its focus upon the role of parental attitudes in the development, or nondevelopment, of transitional-object behavior on the part of the child. I am re-minded, here, of the rarity with which the analyst's feeling-participation in the exploration of the adult patient's transitional-object experience is reported in the literature. These authors report upon their study of 40 children from 23 different families, an investigation of the qualities of the child's relationship to the primary transitional object. Their investigation included extensive interviews with the mothers. They state:

> . . . Research on the primary transitional object has ignored the subtle interactions that occur between parents and children in the development and use of the primary transitional object. While conscious expectations of whether the child will develop a primary transitional object do not seem to be an important factor, unconscious motivations seem to determine if parents serve as either facilitators or disturbers of the child's relationship to the primary transitional object. The ways in which parental attitudes may affect the development of the primary transitional object, and the consequences of this, are described [p. 12].

> Given our agreement with Tolpin (1971) that the primary transitional object as a soother aids greatly in the separation-individuation process, we would see [arbitrary] restrictions of the primary transitional object as a disruptive factor in a critical developmental process. . . . [But] There are other times when the primary transitional object may serve other than adaptive purposes, and the sensitive mother may well attempt to interfere with this process [pp. 18-19].

In 1974, when the original draft of this paper had been completed, Khan's book of collected papers, *The Privacy of the Self*, was published and, having read only a few of his papers before, I now had occasion to become more fully acquainted with his work. His book is eminently worthy of perusal by anyone interested in matters allied to the subject of my present paper. A few quotes from his book will serve to indicate how closely related, while far from fully congruent, are some of his views and my own.

In one of the papers which his volume includes, "On Symbiotic Omnipotence" (1969), there are passages suggestive of my concept of patient and analyst as becoming, in the early phase of therapeutic symbiosis, transitional objects for one another. Khan states:

> I can express this equation of relationship only by the statement that the 'self' of the child functions as a 'transitional

object' between the child's ego and the mother. It is treated as special, idealized and, at one remove, psychically by both parties [p. 86].

Only the transference relation let my patients and me see that they were trying to *actualize* a relationship with another person where symbiotic omnipotence would be the exclusive vehicle of relatedness, where both the patient and the object would emphasize [empathize?] into a relatedness where the *special self*—object of both the patient's ego and instinctual cathexes as well as the other person—is endorsed. The situation would be of two persons (egos) devoted to the maintenance of *this special self* [p. 89].

But from Khan's writings, in contrast to mine, one gets little or no portrayal of the analyst's dependency (whether symbiotic dependency or postindividuation, object-related dependency) upon the patient, beyond that evoked purely as an adaptation to the patient's transference.

In another paper, "Regression and Integration in the Analytic Setting" (1960), Khan writes, concerning a psychotic patient who manifested manic and depressive states in the course of her illness, "The manic mental state achieved the value of an object for Mrs. X. Her whole relation was to *it*" (p. 147). I find this to be an example of my concept of the symptom as a transitional object for the patient.

Khan, in addition to being one of our foremost psychoanalytic clinicians and theoreticians in his own right, is almost certainly the foremost living authority on Winnicott's work and thought. Winnicott's final book, *Therapeutic Consultations in Child Psychiatry* (1971) reported his employing an exchange of drawings, which he called the Squiggle Game, as the basis of his technique in these consultations. Khan describes beautifully the theoretical rationale of this technique:

The essence of the therapeutic space that Winnicott establishes with the child for the Squiggle Game is that it is a transitional space, in which both Winnicott and the child are separate and private to each other, and yet through playing on the surface of the paper, find both a relating and a communication.

Winnicott makes a very specific distinction between *relating* and *object-relationship* in this context. It is because there is only relating without the sophistication of an object-relationship that he can find his access with the child to the child's reverie [1974, p. 265].

That passage is highly relevant to this paper's section on appurtenances, concerning the functioning of one or another kind, in the analytic situation, as a transitional object for both analyst and patient.

SUMMARY

The analyst (or therapist) can best understand transitional-object phenomena as being tributary to, or as consisting in various different facets of the—for him in his work with patients—more comprehensive realm of therapeutic symbiosis. Nonetheless, the concept of transitional object (or phenomena) proves a useful theoretical instrument, a kind of scalpel or microscope lens, in achieving a relatively differentiated sample of the more global theoretical concept of therapeutic symbiosis.

In the various different kinds of relationship between the analyst and the patient's symptoms (depending upon the phase of the treatment), I have found situations in which the analyst feels that the patient's symptoms are being inflicted upon him (the analyst). In other instances, the analyst may fear that he personally is inflicting the patient's symptoms upon the latter. At times the analyst may come to feel that the patient's symptoms "couldn't be happening to a nicer guy." In still other cases, the analyst reacts to the patient's symptoms as being his—the analyst's—allies. Finally, there are instances in which the patient's symptoms are experienced as transitional objects by both patient and analyst. In addition, I have found that an appurtenance in the analytic situation—such as a tape recorder, the analyst's notes, the couch, a psychotropic drug—may function as a transitional object for both analyst and patient.

I suggest that the patient's symptoms become, with the development of the early phase of therapeutic symbiosis, transitional objects for both patient and analyst simultaneously. As with the patient's symptoms, so with his transference images of the analyst: I believe that in order for any effective transference analysis to occur with any patient, whether neurotic, borderline, or psychotic, the analyst must have come to accept at *least* a transitional-object degree—if not more deeply symbiotic degree—of relatedness with the particular transference image, or percept, which is holding sway presently in the analysis.

23

The Analyst's Participant Observation as Influenced by the Patient's Transference

I never met Sullivan personally, and do not consider myself to be a Sullivanian. But the early years of my analytic training took place in a Washington strongly influenced, if not dominated, by him and his ideas; I was a student in two and a half of the courses he taught (he died midway through the last of these); and I have acknowledged in earlier writings my debt to him. His term, "participant observation," seems to me to capture well and succinctly the spirit of the analyst's functioning vis-à-vis the patient.

Concerning the psychotherapist's role, my earliest concept, developed prior to my coming to Washington, and based largely upon medical training coupled with my predominantly obsessive-compulsive psychodynamics, required me to maintain myself and my feelings in a kind of stance which had essentially nothing to do with the individual patient. My ego ideal, as regards my functioning as therapist, required that I endeavor always to be helpful to the patient, that I be unflaggingly interested in him, and that I *experi-*

This paper was the author's invited contribution, among those invited from several other authors, to a discussion of the general topic, "Sullivan's Concept of Participant Observation." It was first published in *Contemporary Psychoanalysis*, 13:347-386 (1977).

ence no negative emotions whatsoever toward him—let alone *express* such feelings to him openly. I regarded my personal identity as changeless, and my therapist-role as similarly fixed and absolute.

I have described elsewhere that, in the course of subsequent years of personal analysis and clinical experience

> ... my sense of identity has become ... my most reliable source of data as to what is transpiring between the patient and myself, and within the patient. I have described ... the "use" of such fluctuations in one's sense of identity as being a prime source of discovering, in work with a patient, not only counter-transference processes but also transference processes ... [Searles, 1966-1967].

The main point of the present remarks is analogous to the one just quoted: as with the analyst's overall *sense of personal identity*, so the *customary style of participant observation* which he has developed over the years, his observation of the ways wherein he finds himself departing from this normative style, in his work with any one patient, provides him with particularly valuable clues to the nature and intensity of this patient's transference responses and attitudes toward him. Beyond the analyst's privately observing such variations in his customary mode of participant observation, he can find it constructive, with increasing frequency as the analysis progresses, to share these data with the patient.

If one has some superego-based, professionally ingrained standard for oneself (as did I initially to an almost paralyzing degree), such as evenly hovering attentiveness or unflagging interest and helpfulness, one will fail to note those variations in one's interest, participativeness, and so on, which are due to the impact, upon one, of the patient's transference.

In one's attempt to achieve and maintain some personally idealized, superego-imposed participant-observer position, one is apt never to notice that the *patient* may be perceiving or experiencing, on the basis of his transference distortions, the analyst's position and functioning to be quite different from what the analyst is experiencing these as being. The patient may be reacting to one's subjectively helpful participativeness in terms of one's threatening to devour or destructively pervade him, and to one's observational functioning as emanating from his own projected, harshly condemnatory and omnipotently controlling superego (his own "Watcher-Machine," as one schizophrenic patient phrased it). In this connection I have found many times, both in my own work as an analyst and in my supervision of the work of analytic candidates, that when the analyst is being unaccustomedly warmly participative with the patient, we have a clue to the analyst's unconsciously avoiding the negative transference role in which the patient is tending to perceive him (as being, say, a perceivedly remote and unfeeling parent). Similarly, when the analyst finds himself being disproportionately observational and minimally participative in any tangible fashion, he now possesses a clue to the likelihood that he is unconsciously fleeing from the recognition of, say, cannibalistic urges on the part of the patient or himself, or both.

A few weeks ago, in my work with a highly intelligent, intensely ambitious lawyer who had begun analysis a few months previously, I found myself immersed in deeply troubled feelings concerning my sense of identity as an analyst. I had had a nagging feeling, from the beginning of our work, that I was unable to keep up with the rapid and abundant flow of analytic material from him. He typically reported dreams which were not only numerous but which clearly possessed much significance for the analysis, and he himself was able to perceive their significances more rapidly than I could. I felt that this man, who showed many signs of moving unusually rapidly in the analysis, was only highlighting a chronic and pervasive deficiency of mine as an analyst—a deficiency, so I felt, of underinterpreting. The work with him intensified my long-familiar concern lest I be burned out as an analyst.

It came to me as an immense relief, then, a few weeks ago, to discover that an important cause of my troubled feelings consisted in his transference to me as being his own small-child self, the youngest child among several siblings, a child who had felt chronically unable to keep up not only with his highly competitive older and larger siblings, but also with his mother, who seemed to him always in motion, always going away somewhere. I now remembered that I had gone through much this same sequence of analytic developments a few years previously with another such man, whose childhood-family dynamics had been similar to those of this current analysand.

A narcissistic man with whom I am currently working used, earlier in the analysis, to give me the feeling I was insufficiently intelligent to qualify for working as an analyst. He is a highly intelligent person and I used often to feel admiration, bordering upon awe, for his ability to make nice differentiations in his thoughts, his fantasies, his memories. The subtlety of his thought, and his ability to create beautifully apt metaphors to express his ideas, all seemed quite beyond my reach. I seldom found any opportunity to make any verbal contribution to the analysis, and he spent much time silently immersed in—so the intricate verbalizations which were the product of these silences give me to assume— thought of a subtlety and richness that I could scarcely begin to appreciate, let alone hope to participate verbally with him concerning it.

Here again, transference data which emerged subsequently led me to realize, to my great relief, how powerfully motivated he had been to project upon me the feelings of inadequacy which he had felt toward an older brother, a brother who had lived, during the patient's childhood, in a longed-for world which felt utterly beyond the younger boy's despairing reach. I now became more aware of the defensive aspects of the patient's functioning during the sessions in the way I have described, and was better able to see the narcissistic, bordering on autistic, aspects of his displaying so complex a mental activity—a kind of activity not necessarily so highly superior to my own but designed, more, to shut me out of his world. While I still can well believe that he has a mind superior to my own in important regards, he no longer makes me feel unqualified to conduct work as an analyst.

In my work with another male patient I began early to feel semi-moribund during most of each session, and for at least some months attributed this largely to chronic fatigue from an unusually heavy weekly schedule of patients. But as the analysis went on I became appreciably less burdened by such a feeling as, bit by bit, transference material emerged which made clear that he was reacting to me variously as his chronically depressed mother, and as a long-senile grandmother who had lived largely as· a vegetable, nearby, during a considerable portion of his developmental years.

Several months ago I confided to a middle-aged female analysand that she was, and long had been, my favorite patient; I told her this because I knew that this phenomenon, although in various ways pleasant to me, must indicate one of her major problems. My sharing with her this information (information which represents, obviously, an aberration in my customary participant-observer functioning with my patients collectively) had highly constructive results in terms of the emergence of a wealth of newly remembered transference material. She recalled, with intense feelings of murderous rage and grief, how all her life she had felt it absolutely necessary to be pleasing to other people generally and, above all, to her mother. Her negative mother-transference feelings toward me, largely repressed for years in our work, now emerged with an intensity which I found at times frightening and awesome. With all this, she began manifesting a coherence and a purposefulness in her ego functioning which had been largely lacking before.

Lastly, and apart from my main theme, I long ago learned that the analysand's part of the work involves something far more and other than learning to be a free-associating, and dream-reporting, machine; the analyst must both require and, primarily by collaborative personal example, help him to internalize the participant-observer activity as an ego function which he can carry away from the analysis as a part, now, of himself.

24

Psychoanalytic Therapy with Schizophrenic Patients in a Private-Practice Context

This subject, to which I was asked to address myself, highlights what I have thought of frequently and ruefully as my middle-age identity crisis. I cherish a reputation as an authority in psychoanalytic therapy with schizophrenic patients, and yet by far the majority of my time in private practice is spent in analyzing neurotic individuals, most of whom are themselves psychiatrists. Although there is of course a degree of overlap of these two clinical fields, for the most part they call for modes of participation on the analyst's part which are appreciably, and often strikingly, different. Many times, for example, I have spent an hour in highly vocal, vehement interaction with a schizophrenic patient who was sitting opposite me, followed immediately by a session of my sitting silently behind the couch while a training analysand was reporting, uninterruptedly throughout the hour, his free-associational material.

In 1949, intending to go into the full-time private practice of

This paper is based, in part, on a presentation at the Ninth Annual Conference of the Adelphi University Postdoctoral Program in Psychotherapy, "The Psychoanalytic Therapy of Non-Hospitalized Schizophrenic Patients," at Adelphi University, Garden City, New York, on Thursday, May 24, 1973. It was first published in *Contemporary Psychoanalysis*, 12:387-406 (1976).

psychoanalysis within a couple of years or so, and feeling anxiously in need of sufficient experience with schizophrenic patients to be able to cope with the at least occasional such patient I knew one would encounter in such a practice, I became a psychiatric resident at Chestnut Lodge. I found the work with such patients there to be so absorbing that I remained on that staff nearly 15 years, although spending throughout those years at least a few hours each day in analyzing non-Lodge neurotic patients. During the 10 years since I left there, I have spent a great many hours in working as a teacher and consultant at many different hospitals, focusing upon the modified psychoanalytic treatment of schizophrenic patients.

Whereas 15 years ago it seemed to me probable that I would devote the bulk of my remaining professional career to working predominantly with such patients, when I left the Lodge 10 years ago I made a point of not filling my private-practice time mainly with schizophrenic patients, and at this point I assume that the remainder of my career will be devoted largely to the psychoanalysis of neurotic individuals, while keeping very much in touch, still, with what was once my major career. At the present time I am working with one chronically schizophrenic person, one ambulatorily schizophrenic person, and several borderline schizophrenic persons, each on the basis of four or five hours per week.

This brief paper, closely related to two of my earlier ones (Searles, 1966, 1967b), will permit me merely to present in broad outline some of the major principles which govern my work with schizophrenic patients. The term "schizophrenic" is intended here to include borderline as well as frankly schizophrenic individuals.

One additional word of explanation is necessary by way of introduction. If at times here I wax—as so frequently in my previous writings about this field—preachy and superior, implying that I am delineating problem situations and typical countertransference" difficulties which I was able in my early years in this field permanently to resolve, and am now trying to help the younger colleague to become successful like me, let me hereby acknowledge that such a connotation is nonsensical, and a presumable measure of my unconscious attempt to avoid experiencing the full agony of the sub-

jective incompetence, impotence, and malevolence that my work
with these patients evokes in me. Without exception, each of the
typical analytic difficulties upon which this paper touches is one
which I myself was experiencing, if not last week, then the week
before last. It seems to me that these patients' transference responses are so intense that the evolution of the transference will
confront any analyst, of however long experience in this field, with
each of these difficulties in one or another phase of the treatment.
One learns not to try to avoid these difficulties, but to recognize
them earlier in one's work with successive patients, and with de-
creasing accompaniments of guilt and anxiety, as being developments inherent in, and indeed necessary to, the evolution of the patient's transference.

Some of my concepts can be seen to be at variance both from
the usual psychotherapeutic approaches and from the classical
psychoanalytic approach. Unlike psychotherapy as I have usually
heard or read of it, wherein patient and therapist explore together
what is going on in the patient's life outside the office, my focus is
primarily upon what transpires in the office—upon the analysis of
the transference; and whereas most psychotherapists give negative
transference manifestations a particularly wide berth, I regard it as
essential that these be confronted as squarely and explored as fully
as possible. Unlike the tenets of classical analysis, my concepts dwell
particularly upon the analyst's feeling-experiences in terms of their
welcome, informationally empathic value, inestimably so in the crucial therapeutic-symbiosis phase of the transference evolution
(Searles, 1973a). The classical analyst, in contrast, tends to react to
intense feeling-reactions on his own part as being unwanted intrusions into a necessary analytic neutrality, and as much less likely to
be priceless empathic glimpses into that which the heavily defended
patient is defending against, than disruptive messages from his—
the analyst's—own incompletely analyzed early childhood. In addition to recommending a much deeper and far more frankly
acknowledged feeling-involvement than does the classical analyst, I
take cognizance of, and in fact attach fundamental significance to,

the patient's own therapeutic strivings on behalf of the analyst (Searles, 1973a)—the latter portrayed, here again, as being to a significant degree a transference-figure to the patient, but with detectable increments of the analyst's own reality as a person serving as a basis for such transference reactions or strivings on the part of the patient.

My feeling-orientation in starting to work with any schizophrenic patient is devoid of any simple assumption that I am stronger than he. Most therapists who report their work in this field seem to regard it as implicitly, if not explicitly, understood that the therapist is endowed with basically sound reality relatedness and ego strength and is faced essentially with a rescue mission: how to help restore to health (through, to a major extent, the facilitation of the patient's identifying with the therapist's own healthy processes—and, as will be seen, I think this is indeed a *part* of what happens) a poor, fragile person severely crippled by psychological traumata, traumata both from current living and from long ago.

I have learned the hard way, by contrast, that any chronically schizophrenic patient is in, at the beginning of our work, at least as strong a position as my own. There are certain processes in him which (working in conjunction with the mores of our medical profession) render him enormously formidable, interpersonally, to any analyst who presumes to help him, and the fact that these processes are not predominantly within the patient's conscious control seems often to strengthen, rather than weaken, the patient's power position as perceived by the analyst. The latter inevitably becomes deeply embroiled, at a conscious level, in conflictual feelings including intense guilt and self-condemnation, feelings not merely of his "own" but, often more predominantly, feelings being projected into him by the patient who remains successfully defended, at an unconscious level, against experiencing these in awareness.

The passively aggressive, sadistic gratifications afforded the chronically schizophrenic patient, in response to the anguished efforts of the analyst and others to bring him relief, are limitless. A typical dilemma for the analyst is how to achieve ways of functioning, during the session, which will make it possible for his own personal suffering to become less than that of the patient; in my own experience, the treatment cannot proceed usefully for either patient or analyst as long as the patient's schizophrenia is inflicting, evidently, more conscious suffering upon the analyst than upon the patient.

Important dimensions of the treatment situation have to do with the power of the patient's intensely negative transference reactions in kindling and fanning into flame the most archaic, self-punitive increments of the analyst's own superego. One of the many typical results of this development is that the analyst, projecting these self-condemnatory superego components upon not only the patient himself but the latter's family members and his own colleagues, friends, and family members, comes often to feel unworthy, in the eyes of all these persons, to be regarded as a physician or, more basically, as a human being.

In much the same vein, as ancient hopes as well as self-condemnations are revived in the analyst, he tends unwittingly to attribute to the poorly differentiated or chaotically functioning patient the eventual realizability of all sorts of ego-ideal longings and ambitions. That is, the more ill-defined or fragmentedly unstable is the ego functioning of the patient, the more this facilitates the analyst's projecting into the latter the reification of these largely unconscious, deeply cherished, fantasized self-images of the analyst's own. In an earlier paper (1961b), I noted that the prolonged silences which characterize one's work with such patients facilitate the relaxation or loosening of ego boundaries between the two participants, promoting the kind of projection of the analyst's unconscious contents into the patient (and, of course, vice versa) which I am describing here. In short, it is easy for the analyst to go on hoping, whether at largely unconscious or conscious levels, that all his own fondest dreams will materialize, one day, out of that unformed chaos over there—over there in the patient, who is perceptibly so very far, at this moment, from functioning as a definitively mature human individual and in whom, therefore, there are no discernible limits upon what future growth, with its wondrous possibilities for ego differentiation and integration, may bring.

Essentially, the analyst looks to the patient to provide the fulfillment, at long last, of his own thwarted strivings for omnipotence. Hence the work inevitably tends to involve his placing, no matter how unwittingly, cruelly inhuman demands upon the patient, while in the same process placing into the patient's hands the power cruelly to disappoint, over and over, the eagerly hopeful analyst.

Many such past experiences have caused me to become, over the years, so keenly aware of the schizophrenic patient's endowment of transferential powers to evoke my strivings for omnipotence that this awareness affects greatly the spirit in which I have come to employ the basic rule of psychoanalysis in this work. That is, when I recommend to the patient near the very beginning of our work, and often thereafter, that he engage insofar as possible in the reporting of free associations (without my using that technical term), I am careful to make plain in my demeanor, and if necessary explicitly in words, that this invitation is not intended to imply a corollary promise that I shall respond to whatever comes from him with a demeanor of evenly hovering, benevolent neutrality. That latter classically analytic position is indistinguishable from the omnipotent parental transference position which the schizophrenic patient tends so powerfully to lure, and demand, the analyst to occupy, while making life hell for him to the degree that he attempts to acquiesce to this tantalizing transference demand.

I well know that the emotions which schizophrenic patients foster in the analyst are so intense, and conflictual or discoordinate, that it is quite untenable for one to attempt to carve out such a position for oneself at the beginning; this can only become established much later, after many stormy interactions, in proportion as the patient's ego functioning becomes predominantly normal-neurotic in nature. Further, any such early attempt involves in my view an offensive condescension on the part of the analyst, who is being so presumptuous as to imply that nothing within the patient, either now or in the future of their work together, can ever seriously discommode the analyst. Intendedly reassuring to a preceivedly fragile and fear-ridden patient, such communications are also unwittingly belittling and provocatively challenging to one whose powers arc great for rendering impotent and anguished his would-be savior. The patient can only become increasingly determined to be taken seriously by the analyst, and make intensified, and surely eventually successful, efforts in that direction. As for the analyst, his attempt to maintain a dispassionate stance surely is serving as a defense against the activation, within himself, of reality nuclei for the patient's various and discoordinate transferences to him—transferences which need to become perceived by both participants, and their reality-nuclei basis in the analyst (as well as in the patient) perceived by both participants, in order for the transference psychosis to become manageably evident and to evolve into a transference neurosis of anything like the usual analytically explorable proportions.

Schizophrenic patients by and large have a deep-seated conviction that their becoming close to another person—to the analyst, for example—will mean the destruction of the latter. I do not attempt to be reassuring to the patient about this beyond the obvious reassurance involved in my going ahead and exploring with him the nature of such fears. I have learned over and over that these fears are not to be taken lightly, as being pathetic and "purely delusional" ones based only upon tragically ill-timed interpersonal losses in the past. These fears are referable also to truly formidable components of sadism and murderous hatred and, more than anything else, to an unconscious need for experiences of a therapeutically symbiotic nature—a kind of relatedness with the analyst which only gradually, bit by hard-won bit, becomes free from intensely threatening components to both participants in the work, as it gradually becomes evident that such symbiotic relatedness does not involve the actual destruction, mentally or physically, of either or both of them.

Some of the ostensible fragility of the schizophrenic patient is due to the analyst's unconscious ambivalence about becoming and remaining emotionally related to him. Beyond the patient's own much-described evanescences of transference responses and other difficulties in establishing and maintaining precariously an emotional relatedness with any fellow human being, the analyst tends largely to repress, under the impact of the patient's transference to him as a hoped-for good mother, and under the impact of his own physicianly superego standards, much of his own misgivings about entering into this relationship, and his wishes to be rid of the patient. Hence, in this regard, it is not that the patient truly is fragile, but rather that the analyst's unconscious ambivalence about relatedness with the patient renders that relatedness fragile. At a conscious level, the analyst unquestionably assumes that, since the patient is so full of intense conflict about relatedness with him, he himself must permit himself no misgivings, of even a minor degree, in this regard.

Further, as I indicated earlier, the analyst comes to project upon the patient numerous fragile, idealized, deeply cherished, unconscious self-images (as being, for one typical example, unambivalently loving—free of hate), and it then becomes a complexly fragile thing, indeed, for the analyst as to how to function toward the patient in such a way as not to destroy those fragile and cherished projections from within himself.

For example, in my work with one chronically schizophrenic woman years ago, I found it deeply poignant, and I was filled with the most tender feelings of pity, when I heard this woman, whom I knew to be staving off vast realms of repressed grief, say that whereas birds of passage can fly safely across the ocean, swallows and other birds of short-range flight, if they attempt this, fall into the sea and are drowned. When I heard her say this, I had no doubt that she was a swallow and I (sure of my own personal identity, able to live in the world outside an insane asylum, and all that), a bird of passage. But many times since then as our work has proceeded and I have found reason to marvel at her indomitable strength of various sorts, I have seen that, of the two of us, she is the bird of passage who can cope with her grief if only the swallow, Searles, can avoid drowning in self-pitying guilt over her perceivedly tragic plight.

In beginning treatment with any schizophrenic patient, my endeavor is to explore with him what is transpiring between us, within him, and within myself in relationship to him—sharing with him the data from this last-mentioned realm to the degree I find he can utilize it in furtherance of his own integration and differentiation.

My endeavor is thus quite different from the usual psycho-therapeutic approach of the therapist who, assuming it to be generally understood that he is the healthy, strong one in the treatment relationship, is setting out to rescue the patient from the grievous illness, the schizophrenia, with which the latter is afflicted. There are a number of reasons why this latter approach, which powerful forces—notably some of the patient's characteristic trans-ference attitudes toward the therapist—coerce the therapist into ac-cepting, is folly.

1. First, it became apparent to me, within the first few months of my work on the staff at Chestnut Lodge, that we staff members had to face, and daily deal with, a basic philosophical question of whether sanity or psychosis is the more desirable mode of ex-istence. This question seems at first glance idiotic, and on more prolonged thought very disturbing. To the degree that the subjec-tively healthy therapist goes on obviously trying to rescue the per-ceivedly damaged and afflicted patient, the therapist is shielding himself from asking himself, seriously, that question.

Close up and over a long period of time it becomes quite sober-ing how many are the gratifications of chronic psychosis, not only the myriad regressive gratifications of a positive sort which it af-fords, but also those which derive from the schizophrenic individu-al's large-scale obliviousness of, apartness from, such mundane daily-life sources of frustration, despair, and grief as are involved in the maintenance of a marital relationship, the rearing of chil-dren, the paying of taxes, the living in the clear knowledge of the inevitability of one's own death and the deaths of those dear to one, and so on.

2. In the same vein, the therapist's compulsive attempt to res-cue the patient from the latter's illness serves as an unconscious de-fense, for the therapist, against his own envy of the patient for the gratifications the latter is deriving from the schizophrenic mode of

existence. The therapist's compulsive therapeutic "devotion" serves as an unconscious defense, likewise, against his hatred of the patient, his contempt for the patient, his despair lest his own goals in the work never be fulfilled, and many other emotions and attitudes which are quite at odds with the healing-physician image of himself he is struggling to maintain, both in loyalty to his long-held ego ideals which by far preceded his beginning to work with this particular patient and also, perhaps even more importantly, because of unconsciously threatening transference positions, such as that of the diabolically sadistic or heartlessly uncaring parent, into which the patient's so-powerful and tenacious transference responses and attitudes tend to coerce the therapist.

Fortunately, even though any analyst inevitably will become more or less caught up, in working with these patients, in trying to function as the conventionally healthy person, the strong one trying to help this weak, afflicted schizophrenic person, this endeavor does not really serve to ward off the development of the patient's transference to the analyst as being, for example, the depressed father or schizoid mother, or whoever. Such forms of transference relatedness inevitably develop, and this in the long run is good, for the analysis of the transference is the central treatment activity in one's work with these patients, essentially as it is in one's psychoanalytic treatment of neurotic patients.

Classical analysts often find reason to doubt that schizophrenic patients are capable of developing analyzable transference reactions, and such analysts tend as a result to place these persons beyond the pale of psychoanalytic endeavors, thus relegating them, inevitably, to such kindly modes of treatment as, in the old days, electroshock, insulin coma, and lobotomy, and, in current days, phenothiazines and so-called maintenance psychotherapy, which inevitably is consigning most of these patients to far less than half a life with regard to any fulfillment of their human potentialities. By contrast, I regard these patients as being highly capable of forming inherently analyzable transference responses and attitudes, and I find that the limitation tends rather to be in the analyst. The question is whether the analyst can achieve somehow the self-knowledge

to become able to endure, and even enjoy, the transference positions into which largely unconscious forces within the schizophrenic
patient tend to place him, and which the patient genuinely needs
for him to become able to occupy to a degree sufficient to enable
the patient and the analyst to explore, together, the childhood
meanings for the patient of these transference distortions in their
working relationship.

3. It seems to me well to assume that, with these patients collectively, there is a relatively high dropout rate. I came to believe this
partially because of my own treatment experiences at Chestnut
Lodge, but more because of how I saw treatment to eventuate at
the hands of some dozens of supervisees there over the years, a
considerable number of these being highly capable analysts. In the
instance of borderline patients, all too often the patient, being not
so ill as to be certifiable, could not be prevented from signing out
of the sanitarium against the advice of his physicians. Often, too, in
the instance of the more ill patients, there was the widely known
experience that family-dynamic forces became unmanageable and
the parents took the patient out of treatment just at a time when
highly promising results were starting to emerge. Incidentally, too
often the other family members, and to a lesser degree the patient,
are assigned the responsibility for such abortive outcomes of treatment, while the analyst's wish to be rid of the patient, or relief at
having become rid of him, remains largely unconscious. But a detailed discussion of this point would lead too far afield from the
one I am making at present.

I mention this philosophical attitude because it seems to me that
to the degree that the analyst can keep in touch with it, he functions with the patient in a fashion which is minimally threatening to
the latter. By contrast, a too devouringly, compulsively helpful kind
of orientation tends naturally to drive the patient out of treatment.
The more conscious an analyst is of his own envious hatred of the
patient, and above all of his own wishes to be rid of the latter, the
less likely he is to act out such feelings at an unconscious level, in
behavior that would realistically frighten or antagonize the patient
away from treatment. In contrast, the patient's paranoid proclivities

are intensified by an analyst who, unable at all freely to hate him and want to be rid of him, goes on hoveringly and protectively trying to keep him in treatment, despite all manner of hateful or otherwise outrageous behavior on the patient's part. The patient naturally develops, under these circumstances, deep suspicions that the analyst is exploiting, or is bent upon exploiting, him in some unacknowledged manner—whether sexually, or financially, or whatever.

Under such circumstances the analyst indeed is exploiting the patient, although doing so at a largely unconscious level: he is struggling unconsciously to bring into fulfillment, into realization, his own ego ideals of a largely infantile omnipotent nature—his cherished aspirations to be omnipotently able to resolve the patient's schizophrenia, essentially unassisted by the patient himself, to achieve and maintain a totally hate-free attitude toward the patient, to deny any infantile dependent longings within himself and any quasi-psychotic areas of nonintegration or nondifferentiation within himself; and so on. With this going on at an unconscious level in the compulsively "dedicated" analyst, he inevitably is placing, unwittingly (as I mentioned earlier) cruel, bewildering, impossible conflictual and intense pressures upon the patient—the very kinds of pressures which originally fostered the schizophrenic mode of functioning in the patient as a child, at the hands of the mother and other family members. In essence, the analyst is responding, at a largely unconscious level, in keeping with the patient's transference to him as being the "schizophrenogenic" mother of the patient's childhood. We see, here, one of the great reasons why it is so essential that the analyst become able to discern nuclei of reality in the patient's transference perceptions of him, no matter how exaggerated, or otherwise distorted, these perceptions may at first seem.

4. The compulsively devoted, attemptedly rescuing analyst is playing unwittingly into the hands of the passive-aggressive sadistic aims which are an important part of any schizophrenic individual's orientation toward his fellow human beings. Any such patient derives enormous sadistic gratification from watching detachedly while the well-intentioned analyst endeavors, valiantly but with

intensifying despair and anguish and repressed infantile omnipotence-based murderous rage, to rescue the patient from the grip of the schizophrenia which seemingly—and of course in various regards really—is causing the patient such intolerable suffering. In an earlier paper (Searles, 1967b) I suggested that the analyst who sets out to rescue the damsel-patient from the dragon of schizophrenia is failing to realize that the patient himself is both damsel and dragon. In other words, as treatment with any one patient proceeds it is important that the analyst come eventually to hold the patient's increasingly strong, healthy self increasingly responsible for the existence of, and the destructiveness emanating from, the pathogenic introjects (collectively, the dragon) which heretofore have been projected upon the analyst and others.

Meanwhile, with the deepening of the patient's transference to the analyst as being the personification of the perceivedly diabolic or heartless components of the mother and father of the patient's childhood, the analyst inevitably comes to feel, to a seriously guilt- and remorse-engendering degree, responsible for the existence of the patient's psychopathology. The patient has led the analyst to feel in any case, from the beginning, that it is incumbent upon the analyst to ensure that the treatment will eventuate successfully, and with this added dimension of transference-engendered, infantile omnipotence-based guilt on the part of the analyst, the latter feels all the more personally responsible for the patient's schizophrenia, and in fact may come to experience himself, as I have done more than once, as being indistinguishable from the terribly malevolent affliction from which the patient is suffering. When one becomes immersed in such experiences of the work, one has become out of touch with the sadistic and masochistic components, in both the patient and oneself, which are so necessary to keep in focus in this work.

In beginning to work with a patient who is too ill to seek out an analyst, such as are many of those on locked wards, one must work in an implicit acknowledgment that the treatment effort is more important to oneself than it is to the patient, for whereas one seeks him out to institute the treatment situation, the patient himself cannot do so. But as the work proceeds, there is always trouble insofar as the treatment atmosphere persists as one in which the maintenance of the treatment is more important, and the goal of the patient's eventual recovery is more important, to the analyst than to the patient. That is, so long as predominantly negative transference reactions hold sway in the patient, he has reason to know that, in the context of the therapeutic session at least, his own maintenance of a schizophrenic mode of functioning is causing more suffering to his hated and despised analyst than it is to himself. Many times I have found difficult the technical problem, mentioned earlier in this paper, of how I can become able to function, during the analytic sessions with one or another of these patients, in such a manner as to ensure that the chronically sadistic patient, not I, will at long last come to do the major part of whatever personal suffering is experienced in the room, and thus will come genuinely to desire, and work with me toward, changes in the sadomasochistic modes of functioning which have held sway in the room for months or years. Such hoped-for changes have occurred, in my experience at least, only in proportion as I have come to experience unaccustomedly intense feelings of sadistic cruelty, contempt, and other highly negative emotions toward this patient whom I have been trying for so long to help.

5. The patient who is projecting upon the analyst the former's unconscious self-images, which involve identifications with the sickest aspects of the parents and other significant persons from the patient's childhood, is not only involved in a process of getting his illness out of his own system (to phrase it colloquially), so that his own more healthy components can thrive unconstricted by such pathogenic introjects. He is also trying, once again, to cure the sick parents whom in childhood he was unable to cure. This aspect, of the patient's genuinely loving therapeutic devotion toward the parents and toward subsequent parent transference-figures such as the analyst himself, is the dimension of this work of greatest current interest to me.

In this connection, it can be seen that an analyst who becomes able to resolve his own compulsively devoted, ambivalence-

repressing attitude toward the patient, and who comes into relatively free contact with the ambivalently loving-and-hateful components, including the sadomasochistic components, within himself as
well as within the patient, is now someone whom the patient can
genuinely utilize as a helpful therapist, partly through identification
processes which assist the patient in resolving those extremely compulsive, omnipotence-based components of his own therapist-
orientation within his own childhood family. In short, the analyst
can now serve, among other ways, as a model of a human-sized,
rather than as an impossibly would-be omnipotent therapist.

As I have indicated, if the analyst can gain the courage to consider seriously and calmly the pros and cons of the philosophical
question as to whether sanity or psychosis is—not only in the
abstract, for mankind collectively, but for himself personally—the
more desirable existence, then he does not become and remain
caught up in an anguished attempt to rescue the psychotic patient
from a supposed fate worse than death. In this connection it is important that the analyst become able to perceive something that the
psychotic patient has not come to discover, and to which Harry
Stack Sullivan (1940) alluded in his statement that ". . . we are all
much more simply human than otherwise." The specific point to
which I refer here is that psychosis and sanity are not nearly so *different*, qualitatively, as the patient himself assumes, and as the
nonpsychotic part of our population, including psychiatrists who
have not worked much with these patients, assume these two con-
fluent modes of existence to be. The psychotic patient's image of
his nonpsychotic fellow human beings is that of totally dein-
dividualized beings who are incapable of fantasy or of any other
than totally reality-bound psychological activity. It is obviously important for the psychiatrist himself to realize that for the psychotic
patient to become free from psychosis would not mean the latter's
loss of creatively individual aliveness. We need to realize that any
true sanity, any true mental health, involves the individual's being
open to experiencing, at the level of feeling and fantasy and nighttime dreams, whatever exotic or unconventional psychotic contents

had previously overwhelmed the patient and become acted out in his psychotic modes of behavior.

All this is relevant to the crucial issue of *choice*—of the patient's coming to feel *in a position to choose* between continued insanity on the one hand, and healthy interpersonal and intrapersonal related-ness on the other hand. In order for the analyst to help the patient to become able to choose, the former must not only be able to ex-perience, indeed, a passionately tenacious devotion to helping the latter to become free from psychosis, but must also become able to tolerate, to clearly envision, the alternative "choice"—namely, that of psychosis for the remainder of the patient's life. I do not see how the patient's individuation can ever occur if the analyst dare not envision this latter possibility. The patient's previous life exper-ience presumably has proceeded in such a manner, and his therapy at the hands of a too compulsively "dedicated" analyst may proceed in such a manner likewise, that chronic psychosis may be the only subjectively *autonomous* mode of existence available to the patient.

This is analogous to what one finds in patients who manifest a recurrent danger of suicide. Such a patient's life experience has made him feel that the only autonomous activity left to him is to kill himself—for continued living, in whatever manner, seems to him a living out of the wishes of others and a betrayal, therefore, of his own individual, inner self. Like the chronically psychotic pa-tient, the chronically suicidal patient needs an analyst who can be-come able to tolerate the possibility of the patient's suicide, such that the patient becomes unable to tyrannize the analyst with this danger, and comes to be in a position of facing a genuine choice for himself, as to whether or not he wishes to go on living.

To return to the work with the psychotic patient, it appears to me that the analyst's becoming able to tolerate personally the possi-bility that the patient will remain psychotic for the rest of his life, and in this sense—however unformulatedly—"choose" psychosis as against sanity, is a development which must occur in the analyst not only prior to the patient's eventual healthy individuation but, much earlier in the analysis than that, prior to the development of the therapeutic symbiosis which, in my clinical experience, is a necessary foundation for the later individuation. An analyst who, for whatever unconscious reasons, cannot become able to live comfortably with the possibility that his patient may never become free from psychosis cannot, by the same token, foster the necessary emotional atmosphere in the sessions for the development of the contented, unthreatened emotional oneness to which I refer by the term "therapeutic symbiosis" (Searles, 1961e)—a form of relatedness of the same quality as that which imbues the mother-infant relatedness in normal infancy and very early childhood. Any so-called individuation in the patient that is not founded upon a relatively clear phase of therapeutic symbiosis in the treatment is a pseudo individuation, and only a seeming choice of sanity, with the urge toward psychosis, the yearning for psychosis, subjected to repression rather than faced at all fully in the light of conscious choice. Essentially, at the unconscious level, the patient chooses to remain psychotic.

Limit-setting is one of the major dimensions of therapeutic technique in this work, for the schizophrenic patient's demands, whether verbal or nonverbal, upon the analyst are intense, tenacious, conflicting, and above all are backed up by the implicit threat, inherent in various forms of negative transference to the analyst, that if he fails to meet these demands, then he fails to qualify as a human being but is exposed, instead, as being a heartlessly sadistic, nonhuman monster.

This subject of limit-setting is scarcely a change of topic from what I have been saying thus far, for all that I have been saying implies that to the degree the analyst can get in touch with, and remain in touch with, the whole range of his own emotional equipment, he will be in an optimal position to establish and maintain such limits upon the behavior of the patient as are needed in the course of the latter's treatment. But I do want to make a few more explicit comments about the matter of setting limits.

Early in my analytic career, evidently in part because I placed, unconsciously, too low a valuation upon the realm of outer reality as opposed to that of intrapsychic fantasy, I was scornful of and impatient with any limit-setting activity on the part of the analyst, in contrast to my esteem of his function of ascertaining the unconscious meanings of the patient's verbal productions, and his function of making well-founded, well-timed, and otherwise effective interpretations.

It was my experience with, more than any other patient, a borderline psychotic young man with whom I began working more than 20 years ago, and with whom I worked in an increasingly useful collaboration for several years, that made me realize that the analyst's function in setting limits calls, in its multidimensional complexity, which involves awareness not only of myriad transference but also of countertransference elements, for as much analytic sophistication, in every sense of the word, as does, for example, his function in analyzing dream material.

Early in my work with this young man, on innumerable occasions I felt relegated unjustly to the role of a truant officer, resentful of this role and impatient to get back to what I thought of as my higher and truer calling as a psychoanalyst. Those were occasions when he was tardy to an outrageous extent, or when he absented himself from sessions unpredictably, or when he caused me great annoyance and embarrassment by his seemingly inexhaustible ways of complicating the matter of paying me for my work with him, or when he harassed me so greatly, both at my home and at my office, by his use of the telephone, that the telephone itself became, for many weeks at least, to me more a fearsome torture instrument than a homely and convenient instrument of communication. These are but a few among the wide variety of activities in which this patient, a gifted and versatile person with, obviously, highly unreliable ego controls, participated which required firm limit-setting on my part in order for any of the more customary activities of transference analysis to be achieved. I eventually came to know the gratification of his working with me in a highly collaborative manner, for months on end, without any acting-out behavior on his part of a degree at all seriously jeopardizing our work. But before that became possible, I had to become able to set limits more firmly than, in my work as a psychoanalyst, I had ever before felt called upon to do and, beyond that, I had to develop a deep respect for the limit-setting function as being an inherent part of the analyst's work and, in fact, fundamental to all his "higher" analytic functions.

It is not only permissible, but in every sense desirable, that the analyst develop, and come to maintain, his own particular, individual style in setting limits, for it is through one's own manner of setting limits, valid for one's own individual self as an analyst, that the patient has the opportunity to become acquainted with the analyst as a real individual. There are, to be sure, other ways in which the analyst's individuality is made easily accessible to the patient, over the course of treatment; but the analyst's own individual gestalt of limit-setting is, surely, one of the major ways.

Obviously, we are all governed to a degree by our colleagues' customary ways of conducting their treatment of their patients; one cannot, for example, charge fees that are far above the average, for in that event, no patients would remain with one. Even more obviously, we cannot ignore the legalities that apply to all individual practitioners. But within these limits there is wide latitude for the expression of one's individuality in establishing the particular limits within which one is willing and able to work effectively.

It is well to remember this essentially constructive aspect of a limit-setting which is expressive of one's individual self in doing analysis, for the reason that these patients would have one feel, so frequently, sheepish or embarrassed or otherwise isolated and threatened, singled out from one's colleagues to whom the patient is contrasting one. Many patients are quick to point out, derisively and reproachfully, that they know of psychiatrists who are quite untroubled about certain issues wherein one feels determined to maintain firm limits. The patient would have one feel that one is being obsessive, eccentric, openly psychotic, or whatever, for maintaining the position one is struggling to maintain. This aspect of the treatment is much involved with transference reactions on the part of the patient which can be very browbeating, very intimidating, in their effect upon the analyst, whose customary abilities in setting limits may be much less than those usually available to him as he endeavors, through his attempts to set or to avoid setting certain limits, to demonstrate to this particular patient—and above all to himself—that he is not in reality the crazy transference-mother, or suicidally depressed transference-father (or whoever) whom the patient is sustainedly and overwhelmingly sure he is.

At times the analyst becomes almost paralyzedly concerned with the threat lest his colleagues come to hold a view of him which coincides, essentially, with the transference perception the patient has of him—as being an oddball, or openly psychotic, or heartlessly sadistic, or crippled with depression, or what-not.

Again, it seems to me, the matter of *choice* is relevant. Presumably the analyst would not fear so greatly such transference roles if he did not also tend to gravitate to them, take refuge in them, as seemingly his *only* available ways of relating to a patient who is offering no other choice—no discernible alternative modes for relatedness. For example, in my work with a long-hospitalized, middle-aged hebephrenic man, it was only after a number of years that I realized that it had now become conceivable to me that I could relate to him in some manner that would not necessarily involve my either fucking or killing him—the only two modes which previously had seemed imaginable for one to enter into any at all close and tangible relatedness with him. Previously, I apparently had registered in his awareness—had been part of his world—only insofar as he perceived me to be an intensely threatening homosexual rapist and/or murderer.

The analyst is able firmly to set and maintain limits to the extent that he is aware of, and accepting of, his own individual limitations. But the very nature of the work with schizophrenic patients, who themselves have so much unresolved infantile omnipotent striving, is such as powerfully to evoke the analyst's unconscious fantasies of omnipotence. That is, the patient's psychopathology is such as inherently to hold out to the analyst the lure that the latter's fantasies of omnipotence will become realized through the very avenue of his *not* needing any limits, himself, upon the suffering and deprivation he can tolerate in the service of the patient. He therefore comes to have difficulty in setting limits because he is reluctant to give up the fantasy, for example, that his family life will tolerate an endless number of off-hours phone calls from the patient, or that his financial situation will adapt to the patient's not paying him, or that his personal ego integration will survive, during the session, endless battering from the brutally condemnatory paranoid patient. Always, as I have mentioned before, it is implicit, if not made explicit, in the situation, that if the analyst cannot qualify somehow as omnipotent—omnipotently powerful, unambivalently loving, and so on—then he stands revealed, instead, as subhumanly malign or beneath contempt.

Some of my own individual limits involve my not starting to work with any new patients who are presently hospitalized, who have been hospitalized in the very recent past, or who are very likely to need to be hospitalized in the coming few years, because of a too-intense proclivity toward overt psychosis or suicide. My practice is conducted in such a way as to make it infeasible for me to see patients in hospitals. Further, I have managed thus far not to work with patients who require phenothiazines or other psychotropic medication—strange, odd, crazy or criminally negligent as this may seem to many of my colleagues. Whatever one's individual abilities and limitations, it seems to me that it is only insofar as one can develop a mode of practice within which one can live and work with essential comfort and confidence, that one now has a strong base from which, and within which, to analyze the so-needful and so-demanding schizophrenic patient.

References

Arlow, J. A. (1969), Unconscious fantasy and disturbances of conscious experience. *Psychoanal. Quart.*, 38:1-27.

Baker, G. L. (1970), Environmental pollution and mental health. (Unpublished.)

Bellak, L. (1974), The concept of psychoses as a result and in the context of the long-term treatment modalities. In: *Long-Term Treatment of Psychotic States*, ed. C. Chiland, with P. Bequart. New York: Human Sciences Press, 1977, pp. 47-62.

Benedek, T. (1959), Parenthood as a developmental phase: A contribution to the libido theory. *J. Amer. Psychoanal. Assn.*, 7:389-417.

Berman, L. E. A. (1972), The role of amphetamine in a case of hysteria. *J. Amer. Psychoanal. Assn.*, 20:325-340.

Bion, W. R. (1959), Attacks on linking. *Internat. J. Psycho-Anal.*, 40:308-315.

Bradbury, R. (1950), *The Martian Chronicles*. New York: Bantam, 1967.

Brand, M. (1968), *Savage Sleep*. New York: Crown.

Breuer, J. (1893-1895), Theoretical. In: Studies on hysteria, by J. Breuer & S. Freud. *Standard Edition*, 2:185-251. London: Hogarth Press, 1955.

Burnham, D. L., Gladstone, A. I., & Gibson, R. W. (1969), *Schizophrenia and the Need-Fear Dilemma*. New York: International Universities Press.

Busch, F., & McKnight, J. (1973), Parental attitudes and the development of the primary transitional object. *Child Psychiat. & Human Devel.*, 4:12-20.

Bychowski, G. (1952), *Psychotherapy of Psychosis*. New York: Grune & Stratton.

Carson, R. (1962), *Silent Spring*. New York: Fawcett World Library.

Cohen, M. B. (1952), Countertransference and anxiety. *Psychiatry*, 15:231-243.

Coleman, M. L. (1956), Externalization of the toxic introject: A treatment technique for borderline cases. *Psychoanal. Rev.*, 43:235-242.

——— & Nelson, B. (1957), Paradigmatic psychotherapy in borderline treatment. *Psychoanalysis*, 5(3):28-44.

Coppolillo, H. P. (1967), Maturational aspects of the transitional phenomenon. *Internat. J. Psycho-Anal.*, 48:237-246.

Cotton, S., ed. (1970), *Earth Day: The Beginning. A Guide for Survival*, compiled & edited by the National Staff of Environmental Action. New York: Arno Press & Bantam Books.

Cousins, N. (1970), Needed: A new dream. *Saturday Rev.*, June 20, p. 18.

Curtis, R., & Hogan, E. (1970), *Perils of the Peaceful Atom: The Myth of Safe Nuclear Power Plants*. New York: Ballantine Books.

Deutsch, H. (1942), Some forms of emotional disturbance and their relationship to schizophrenia. *Psychoanal. Quart.*, 11:301-321.

Duhl, L. J. (1951), The effect of baby bottle feedings on a schizophrenic patient. *Bull. Menninger Clinic*, 15:21-25.

Ehrlich, P. R. (1968), *The Population Bomb*. New York: Ballantine Books.

Ekstein, R. (1965), Puppet play of a psychotic adolescent girl in the psychotherapeutic process. *The Psychoanalytic Study of the Child*, 20:441-480. New York: International Universities Press.

Elkisch, P. (1957), The psychological significance of the mirror. *J. Amer. Psychoanal. Assn.*, 5:235-244.

Erikson, E. H. (1950), *Childhood and Society*. New York: Norton.

—— (1956), The problem of ego identity. *J. Amer. Psychoanal. Assn.*, 4:56-121.

—— (1958), *Young Man Luther*. New York: Norton.

—— (1959), *Identity and the Life Cycle* [*Psychological Issues*, Monogr. 1]. New York: International Universities Press.

Fairbairn, W. R. D. (1952), *An Object-Relations Theory of the Personality*. New York: Basic Books, 1954.

Farber, L. H. (1961), Faces of envy. In: *The Ways of the Will—Essays toward a Psychology and Psychopathology of Will*. New York: Basic Books, 1966.

Freud, S. (1917), Mourning and melancholia. *Standard Edition*, 14:243-258. London: Hogarth Press, 1957.

—— (1922), Some neurotic mechanisms in jealousy, paranoia and homosexuality. *Standard Edition*, 18:223-232. London: Hogarth Press, 1955.

—— (1923), The ego and the id. *Standard Edition*, 19:12-66. London: Hogarth Press, 1961.

—— (1940), Splitting of the ego in the process of defence. *Standard Edition*, 23:275-278. London: Hogarth Press, 1964.

Friedman, R. J., Gunderson, J. G., & Feinsilver, D. R. (1973), The psychotherapy of schizophrenia: An NIMH program. *Amer. J. Psychiat.*, 130:674-681.

Fromm, E. (1941), *Escape from Freedom*. New York & Toronto: Farrar & Rinehart.

—— (1955), *The Sane Society*. New York & Toronto: Rinehart.

Gibson, R. W. (1966), The ego defect in schizophrenia. In: *Psychoneurosis and Schizophrenia*, ed. G. L. Usdin. Philadelphia: Lippincott, pp. 88-97.

Giovacchini, P. (1969), Aggression: Adaptive and disruptive aspects. *Bull. Phila. Assn. Psychoanal.*, 19:76-86.

Goldstein, M. (1970), Premorbid adjustment, paranoid status, and patterns of response to a phenothiazine in acute schizophrenia. *Schizophrenia Bull.*, No. 3.

Greenacre, P. (1953), Certain relationships between fetishism and faulty development of the body image. *The Psychoanalytic Study of the Child*, 8:79-98. New York: International Universities Press.

Greenson, R. R. (1958), On screen defenses, screen hunger, and screen identity. In: *Explorations in Psychoanalysis*. New York: International Universities Press, 1978, pp. 111-132.

———— (1965), The working alliance and the transference neurosis. In: *Explorations in Psychoanalysis*. New York: International Universities Press, 1978, pp. 199-224.

———— (1967), *The Technique and Practice of Psychoanalysis*, Vol. I. New York: International Universities Press.

———— & Wexler, M. (1969), The nontransference relationship in the psychoanalytic situation. In: *Explorations in Psychoanalysis*. New York: International Universities Press, 1978, pp. 359-386.

Grinker, R. R., Sr., Werble, B., & Drye, R. C. (1968), *The Borderline Syndrome: A Behavioral Study of Ego-Functions*. New York: Basic Books.

Groddeck, G. (1923), *The Book of the It*. London: Vision Press, 1950.

Gunderson, J. G., & Mosher, L. R., eds. (1975), *Psychotherapy of Schizophrenia*. New York: Jason Aronson.

Guntrip, H. (1961), *Personality Structure and Human Interaction: The Developing Synthesis of Psychodynamic Theory*. New York: International Universities Press.

———— (1969), *Schizoid Phenomena, Object Relations and the Self*. New York: International Universities Press.

Hartmann, H. (1939), *Ego Psychology and the Problem of Adaptation*. New York: International Universities Press, 1958.

Heimann, P. (1962), Notes on the anal stage. *Internat. J. Psycho-Anal.*, 43:406-414.

Herner, T. (1965), Significance of the body image in schizophrenic thinking. *Amer. J. Psychiat.*, 19:455-466.

Hill, L. B. (1955), *Psychotherapeutic Intervention in Schizophrenia*. Chicago: University of Chicago Press.

Hinsie, L. E., & Campbell, R. J. (1970), *Psychiatric Dictionary*, 4th ed. New York: Oxford University Press.

Holzman, P. S. (1975), Problems of psychoanalytic theories. In:

Psychotherapy of Schizophrenia, ed. J. G. Gunderson & L. R. Mosher. New York: Jason Aronson, pp. 209-222.

Horton, P. C. (1973), The mystical experience as a suicide preventive. *Amer. J. Psychiat.*, 130:294-296.

Jacobson, E. (1964), *The Self and the Object World*. New York: International Universities Press.

Jones, E. (1953), *The Life and Work of Sigmund Freud*, Vol. 1. New York: Basic Books.

Kafka, J. S. (1969), The body as transitional object: A psychoanalytic study of a self-mutilating patient. *Brit. J. Med. Psychol.*, 42:207-212.

Kayton, L. (1975), Clinical features of improved schizophrenics. In: *Psychotherapy of Schizophrenia*, ed. J. G. Gunderson & L. R. Mosher. New York: Jason Aronson, pp. 361-395.

Kernberg, O. F. (1972), Treatment of borderline patients. In: *Tactics and Techniques of Psychoanalytic Therapy*, ed. P. L. Giovacchini. New York: Science House, pp. 254-290.

Khan, M. M. R. (1960), Regression and integration in the analytic setting. A clinical essay on the transference and counter-transference aspects of these phenomena. In: *The Privacy of the Self: Papers on Psychoanalytic Theory and Technique*. New York: International Universities Press, 1974, pp. 136-167.

———— (1963), The concept of cumulative trauma. In: *The Privacy of the Self: Papers on Psychoanalytic Theory and Technique*. New York: International Universities Press, 1974, pp. 42-58.

———— (1964), Ego distortion, cumulative trauma, and the role of reconstruction in the analytic situation. In: *The Privacy of the Self: Papers on Psychoanalytic Theory and Technique*. New York: International Universities Press, 1974, pp. 59-68.

———— (1969), On symbiotic omnipotence. In: *The Privacy of the Self: Papers on Psychoanalytic Theory and Technique*. New York: International Universities Press, 1974, pp. 82-92.

———— (1974), *The Privacy of the Self: Papers on Psychoanalytic Theory and Technique*. New York: International Universities Press.

Klein, M. (1933), The early development of conscience in the child. In: *Contributions to Psycho-Analysis, 1921-1945*. London: Hogarth Press, 1948, pp. 267-277.

———— (1946), Notes on some schizoid mechanisms. *Internat. J. Psycho-Anal.*, 27:99-110.

————, Heimann, P., & Money-Kyrle, R. E., eds. (1955), *New Directions in Psychoanalysis*. New York: Basic Books.

Knight, R. P. (1953a), Borderline states. In: *Drives, Affects, Behavior*, ed. R. Loewenstein. New York: International Universities Press, pp. 203-215.

—— (1953b), Management and psychotherapy of the borderline schizophrenic patient. In: *Psychoanalytic Psychiatry and Psychology*, ed. R. P. Knight. New York: International Universities Press, 1954, pp. 110-122.

Lens, S. (1970), *The Military-Industrial Complex*. Philadelphia: Pilgrim Press.

Lewin, B. D. (1958), *Dreams and the Uses of Regression*. New York: International Universities Press.

Lichtenstein, H. (1961), Identity and sexuality: A study of their interrelationship in man. *J. Amer. Psychoanal. Assn.*, 9:179-260.

—— (1963), The dilemma of human identity: Notes on self-transformation, self-objectivation, and metamorphosis. *J. Amer. Psychoanal. Assn.*, 11:173-223.

—— (1964), The role of narcissism in the emergence and maintenance of a primary identity. *Internat. J. Psycho-Anal.*, 45:49-56.

Little, M. (1960), On basic unity. *Internat. J. Psycho-Anal.*, 41:377-384.

—— (1966), Transference in borderline states. *Internat. J. Psycho-Anal.*, 47:476-485.

Mahler, M. S., in collaboration with Furer, M. (1968), *On Human Symbiosis and the Vicissitudes of Individuation. Vol. I. Infantile Psychosis*. New York: International Universities Press.

Malin, A., & Grotstein, J. (1966), Projective identification in the therapeutic process. *Internat. J. Psycho-Anal.*, 47:26-31.

Martin, P. A. (1970), The end of "our" world. *Psychiat. Dig.*, June, pp. 10-13.

Marx, W. (1967), *The Frail Ocean*. New York: Ballantine Books.

McDonald, M. (1970), Transitional tunes and musical development. *The Psychoanalytic Study of the Child*, 25:503-520. New York: International Universities Press.

Milner, M. (1952), Aspects of symbolism in comprehension of the not-self. *Internat. J. Psycho-Anal.*, 33:181-195.

—— (1957), *On Not Being Able to Paint*. New York: International Universities Press, 1967.

—— (1969), *The Hands of the Living God: An Account of a Psycho-Analytic Treatment*. New York: International Universities Press.

Modell, A. H. (1963), Primitive object relationships and the predisposition to schizophrenia. *Internat. J. Psycho-Anal.*, 44:282-292.

—— (1968), *Object Love and Reality: An Introduction to a Psychoanalytic Theory of Object Relations*. New York: International Universities Press.

—— (1970), The transitional object and the creative act. *Psychoanal. Quart.*, 39:240-250.

Nelson, M. C. (1962), Effect of paradigmatic techniques on the psychic economy of borderline patients. *Psychiatry*, 25:119-134.

——, Nelson, B., Sherman, M. H., & Strean, H. S., eds. (1968), *Roles and*

Paradigms in Psychotherapy. New York: Grune & Stratton.

Olinick, S. L., Poland, W. S., Grigg, K. A., & Granatir, W. L. (1972), The psychoanalytic work ego: Process and interpretation. Presented at meeting of the Washington Psychoanalytic Society, Washington, D.C., March 17.

Pao, P-N. (1969), Pathological jealousy. *Psychoanal. Quart.*, 38:616-638.

Rangell, L. (1952), The analysis of a doll phobia. *Internat. J. Psycho-Anal.*, 33:43-53.

Reston, J. (1970), Editorial. *The New York Times*, Sun., May 24.

Rogers, C. R. (1942), *Counseling and Psychotherapy*. Cambridge, Mass.: Riverside Press.

Rosenfeld, H. A. (1947), Analysis of a schizophrenic state with depersonalization. In: *Psychotic States: A Psychoanalytical Approach*. New York: International Universities Press, 1965, pp. 13-33.

—— (1952a), Notes on the psycho-analysis of the superego conflict in an acute schizophrenic patient. In: *Psychotic States: A Psychoanalytical Approach*. New York: International Universities Press, 1965, pp. 63-103.

—— (1952b), Transference-phenomena and transference-analysis in an acute catatonic schizophrenic patient. In: *Psychotic States: A Psychoanalytical Approach*. New York: International Universities Press, 1965, pp. 104-116.

—— (1962), The superego and the ego-ideal. In: *Psychotic States: A Psychoanalytical Approach*. New York: International Universities Press, 1965, pp. 144-154.

—— (1965), *Psychotic States: A Psychoanalytical Approach*. New York: International Universities Press.

Schafer, R. (1968), *Aspects of Internalization*. New York: International Universities Press.

Searles, H. F. (1949), (I) Two suggested revisions of the concept of transference and (II) Comments regarding the usefulness of emotions arising in the analyst during the analytic hour. To be published in *Internat. J. Psychoanal. Psychotherapy*.

—— (1951), Data concerning certain manifestations of incorporation. In: *Collected Papers on Schizophrenia and Related Subjects*. New York: International Universities Press, 1965, pp. 39-69.

—— (1955), Dependency processes in the psychotherapy of schizophrenia. In: *Collected Papers on Schizophrenia and Related Subjects*. New York: International Universities Press, 1965, pp. 114-156.

—— (1958a), Discussion of "Learning Theories and the Analytic Process," by G. Piers and M. W. Piers. Presented at combined meeting of the Washington Psychoanalytic Society and Washington Psychiatric Society, Washington, D.C., Oct. 24.

—— (1958b), The schizophrenic's vulnerability to the therapist's unconscious processes. In: *Collected Papers on Schizophrenia and Related Subjects*. New York: International Universities Press, 1965, pp. 192-215.

—— (1959a), The effort to drive the other person crazy—an element in the aetiology and psychotherapy of schizophrenia. In: *Collected Papers on Schizophrenia and Related Subjects*. New York: International Universities Press, 1965, pp. 254-283.

—— (1959b), Integration and differentiation in schizophrenia. In: *Collected Papers on Schizophrenia and Related Subjects*. New York: International Universities Press, 1965, pp. 304-316.

—— (1959c), Integration and differentiation in schizophrenia: An overall view. In: *Collected Papers on Schizophrenia and Related Subjects*. New York: International Universities Press, 1965, pp. 317-348.

—— (1960), *The Nonhuman Environment in Normal Development and in Schizophrenia*. New York: International Universities Press.

—— (1961a), The evolution of the mother transference in psychotherapy with the schizophrenic patient. In: *Collected Papers on Schizophrenia and Related Subjects*. New York: International Universities Press, 1965, pp. 349-380.

—— (1961b), Schizophrenic communication. In: *Collected Papers on Schizophrenia and Related Subjects*. New York: International Universities Press, 1965, pp. 381-428.

—— (1961c), Sexual processes in schizophrenia. In: *Collected Papers on Schizophrenia and Related Subjects*. New York: International Universities Press, 1965, pp. 429-442.

—— (1961d), Schizophrenia and the inevitability of death. In: *Collected Papers on Schizophrenia and Related Subjects*. New York: International Universities Press, 1965, pp. 487-520.

—— (1961e), Phases of patient-therapist interaction in the psychotherapy of chronic schizophrenia. In: *Collected Papers on Schizophrenia and Related Subjects*. New York: International Universities Press, 1965, pp. 521-559.

—— (1962a), The differentiation between concrete and metaphorical thinking in the recovering schizophrenic patient. In: *Collected Papers on Schizophrenia and Related Subjects*. New York: International Universities Press, 1965, pp. 560-583.

—— (1962b), Scorn, disillusionment and adoration in the psychotherapy of schizophrenia. In: *Collected Papers on Schizophrenia and Related Subjects*. New York: International Universities Press, 1965, pp. 605-625.

—— (1963a), The place of neutral therapist-responses in psychotherapy with the schizophrenic patient. In: *Collected Papers on Schizophrenia and Related Subjects*. New York: International Universities Press, 1965, pp. 626-653.

—— (1963b), Transference psychosis in the psychotherapy of chronic schizophrenia. In: *Collected Papers on Schizophrenia and Related Subjects.* New York: International Universities Press, 1965, pp. 654-716.

—— (1963c), The intensive psychotherapy of schizophrenia. Presented at V.A. Hospital, Lexington, Ky., Nov.

—— (1965a), *Collected Papers on Schizophrenia and Related Subjects.* New York: International Universities Press.

—— (1965b), Review of Edith Jacobson's *The Self and the Object World.* *This Volume*, Chap. 3.

—— (1965c), The sense of identity as a perceptual organ. Presented as part of the Scientific Day Program at the Sheppard and Enoch Pratt Hospital, Towson, Md., May 29.

—— (1966), Feelings of guilt in the psychoanalyst. *This Volume*, Chap. 2.

—— (1966-1967), Concerning the development of an identity. *This Volume*, Chap. 4.

—— (1967a), The schizophrenic individual's experience of his world. *This Volume*, Chap. 1.

—— (1967b), The "dedicated physician" in psychotherapy and psychoanalysis. *This Volume,* Chap. 5.

—— (1968-1969), Reviews of *Roles and Paradigms in Psychotherapy* by M. C. Nelson et al. *Psychoanal. Rev.*, 55:697-700.

—— (1969), A case of borderline thought disorder. *This Volume*, Chap. 7.

—— (1970), Autism and the phase of transition to therapeutic symbiosis. *This Volume*, Chap. 9.

—— (1971), Pathologic symbiosis and autism. *This Volume*, Chap. 8.

—— (1972a), The function of the patient's realistic perceptions of the analyst in delusional transference. *This Volume*, Chap. 12.

—— (1972b), Intensive psychotherapy of chronic schizophrenia. *This Volume*, Chap. 14.

—— (1973a), Concerning therapeutic symbiosis: The patient as symbiotic therapist, the phase of ambivalent symbiosis and the role of jealousy in the fragmented ego. *This Volume*, Chap. 10.

—— (1973b), The patient as therapist to his analyst. *This Volume.* Chap. 19.

—— (1973c), Psychoanalytic therapy with schizophrenic patients in a private-practice context. *This Volume*, Chap. 24.

—— (1974), The development of mature hope in the patient-therapist relationship. *This Volume,* Chap. 21.

—— (1976), Transitional phenomena and therapeutic symbiosis. *This Volume*, Chap. 22.

Segal, H. (1964), *Introduction to the Work of Melanie Klein.* New York: Basic Books, 1973.

Singer, E. (1971), The patient aids the analyst: Some clinical and theoretical observations. In: *In the Name of Life—Essays in Honor of Erich Fromm*, ed. B. Landis & E. S. Tauber. New York: Holt, Rinehart & Winston, pp. 56-68.

Spitz, R. A. (1965), *The First Year of Life*. New York: International Universities Press.

Stevenson, O. (1954), The first treasured possession: A study of the part played by specially loved objects and toys in the lives of certain children. *The Psychoanalytic Study of the Child*, 9:199-217. New York: International Universities Press.

Stierlin, H. (1959), The adaptation to the "stronger" person's reality: Some aspects of the symbiotic relationship of the schizophrenic. *Psychiatry*, 22:143-152.

——— (1975), Some therapeutic implications of a transactional theory of schizophrenia. In: *Psychotherapy of Schizophrenia*, ed. J. G. Gunderson & L. R. Mosher. New York: Jason Aronson, pp. 229-240.

Storr, A. (1968), *Human Aggression*. New York: Atheneum.

Sullivan, H. S. (1940), *Conceptions of Modern Psychiatry: The First William Alanson White Memorial Lectures*. New York: Norton, 1953.

Szasz, T. (1965), *The Ethics of Psychoanalysis*. New York: Basic Books.

Thoreau, H. D. (1854), *Walden*. New York: Modern Library, 1950.

Tolpin, M. (1971), On the beginnings of a cohesive self: An application of the concept of transmuting internalization to the study of the transitional object and signal anxiety. *The Psychoanalytic Study of the Child*, 26:316-352. New York: Quadrangle.

Volkan, V. D. (1972), The linking objects of pathological mourners. *Arch. Gen. Psychiat.*, 27:215-221.

——— (1973), Transitional fantasies in the analysis of a narcissistic personality. *J. Amer. Psychoanal. Assn.*, 21:351-376.

——— (1976), *Primitive Internalized Object Relations*. New York: International Universities Press.

——— & Kavanaugh, J. G. (1973), The cat people. Presented at meeting of the American Psychoanalytic Association, New York City, Dec. 15.

Wangh, M. (1962), The "evocation of a proxy": A psychological maneuver, its use as a defense, its purposes and genesis. *The Psychoanalytic Study of the Child*, 17:451-469. New York: International Universities Press.

Wexler, M. (1951), The structural problem in schizophrenia: The role of the internal object. In: *Psychotherapy with Schizophrenics*, ed. E. B. Brody & F. C. Redlich. New York: International Universities Press, 1952, pp. 179-201.

Whitaker, C. A., & Malone, T. P. (1953), *The Roots of Psychotherapy*. New York: Blakiston.

Winnicott, D. W. (1941), The observation of infants in a set situation. In:

Collected Papers. New York: Basic Books, 1958, pp. 52-69.

———— (1947), Hate in the countertransference. In: *Collected Papers*. New York: Basic Books, 1958, pp. 194-203.

———— (1953), Transitional objects and transitional phenomena—a study of the first *not-me* possession. In: *Collected Papers*. New York: Basic Books, 1958, pp. 229-242.

———— (1958), *Collected Papers: Through Paediatrics to Psychoanalysis*. New York: Basic Books.

———— (1971), *Therapeutic Consultations in Child Psychiatry*. New York: Basic Books.

Wolfe, T. (1969), *The Notebooks of Thomas Wolfe*. Raleigh: University of North Carolina Press. (Quote reprinted in Newsweek, Feb. 23, 1970, pp. 102-103.)

Wurster, C. F., Jr. (1967), DDT reduces photosynthesis by marine phytoplankton. *Science,* 159:1474-1475.

Zetzel, E. R. (1956), Current concepts of transference. *Internat. J. Psycho-Anal.,* 37:369-376.

———— (1965), The theory of therapy in relation to a developmental model of the psychic apparatus. *Internat. J. Psycho-Anal.,* 46:39-52.

Index